P9-APK-698

EDUCATION OF THE GIFTED
AND TALENTED

EDUCATION OF THE GIFTED AND TALENTED

THIRD EDITION

GARY A. DAVIS

University of Wisconsin

SYLVIA B. RIMM

*Case Western Reserve University School of Medicine
and The MetroHealth Center*

ALLYN AND BACON
Boston   London   Toronto   Sydney   Tokyo   Singapore

Series Editor: Ray Short
Editorial Assistant: Christine Shaw
Cover Administrator: Linda Dickinson
Manufacturing Buyer: Louise Richardson
Editorial-Production Service: Walsh Associates
Cover Designer: Suzanne Harbison

Copyright © 1994, 1989, 1985 by Allyn and Bacon
A Division of Simon & Schuster, Inc.
160 Gould Street
Needham Heights, MA 02194

All rights reserved. No part of the material protected by this copyright notice may be reproduced or utilized in any form or by any means, electronic or mechanical, including photocopying, recording, or by any information storage and retrieval system without written permission from the copyright owner.

Library of Congress Cataloging-in-Publication Data

Davis, Gary A., 1938–
    Education of the gifted and talented / Gary A. Davis, Sylvia B. Rimm. — 3rd ed.
        p.   cm.
    Includes bibliographical references and index.
    ISBN 0-205-14806-9
    1. Gifted children—Education—United States.   I. Rimm, Sylvia B., 1935–   .   II. Title.
LC3993.9.D38   1993
371.95'0973—dc20   93-28084
                                                                                                    CIP

Printed in the United States of America

10 9 8 7 6 5 4 3   98 97 96

To our families

Cathy, Kirsten, Ingrid, and Sonja
Buck, Ilonna, David, Eric, and Sara

CONTENTS

To provide programs designed to help meet the psychological, social, educational, and career needs of gifted and talented students.

To assist students in becoming individuals who are able to take self-initiated action . . . and who are capable of intelligent choice, independent learning, and problem solving.

To develop problem solving abilities and creative thinking skills; develop research skills; strengthen individual interests; develop independent study skills; strengthen communication skills; receive intellectual stimulation from contact with other highly motivated students; and expand their learning activities to include resouces available in the entire community.

To maximize learning and individual development and to minimize boredom, confusion, and frustration.

To enable them to realize their contributions to self and society.

These are the goals of educational programs for gifted and talented students, and these are the purposes of this book. Gifted and talented students have special needs and special problems; they also have special, sometimes immense, talent to lend to society. We owe it to them to help cultivate their abilities; we owe it to society to help prepare tomorrow's leaders and professional talent. Gifted and talented students are a tremendous natural resource, one that cannot be squandered.

In the mid 1970s, interest in accommodating the educational needs of gifted and talented children began its climb to higher levels and with greater public awareness than ever before. Federal statements, definitions, funds, and professional staff were created. States passed legislation that formalized the existence and needs of gifted children and often provided funds for directors, teachers, and programs. Cities and districts hired program directors and teacher-coordinators who have designed and implemented identification, acceleration, and enrichment plans. In those schools and classrooms where help from the outside did not appear, many enthusiastic teachers planned challenging and worthwhile projects and activities for the gifted children in their classes.

While the ball was still rolling, around 1990 or slightly before, the gifted movement began its step backward and it remains to be seen how large a step it is. We are cautiously optimistic the damage will not be extensive. As we will see in Chapter 1, a reborn commitment to equity in education—in the form of the de-tracking movement—is leading some school districts to trash their gifted programs along with their tracking plans. While the concepts of de-tracking (to promote equity) and providing for the gifted (to promote excellence) are not mutually exclusive, too many zealous educators perceive gifted programs as a type of tracking, and are pitching the baby with the bathwater.

Another few inches of the backward step is the growing cooperative learning style of teaching. Cooperative learning does provide academic and social benefits for most children, but usually not for gifted ones. Gifted students need accelerated academic work, independent projects that develop creativity and thinking skills, and grouping with gifted peers. They should not be required to work at a too-slow pace, or serve as teachers to others in the group.

One more visible factor that is taking its toll of gifted programs is simply the economy and squeezed school budgets. When the going gets tough, gifted programs—perceived by some as luxuries for "students who don't need help"—often are the first to go.

This book may not change the minds of critics who feel that special services for the gifted are unfair, undemocratic, or elitist. The list of virtues at the beginning of this preface, plus the argument that a true democracy includes full individual opportunity, may not make a dent in their well-intentioned defenses. However, this book can help minimize the mistakes that plague so many programs for gifted students, mistakes that sometimes destroy the program itself. Mistakes are made at every step, from selecting program goals and student participants to evaluating program success. There are many issues to consider, and many alternatives to choose from. This book should help the reader make better, more informed decisions. There are few absolutely right answers for G/T program plans, since their "rightness" depends upon the specific student needs and the particular educational circumstances. However, there are many absolutely wrong answers and methods. This book should help the reader decide which is which.

This text was prepared as an introduction to the exciting field of gifted education. It is suitable for college undergraduate and graduate readers, for in-service teachers in elementary or secondary schools, for school psychologists, counselors, and administrators, and for parents of those bright but often bored and ignored gifted children and adolescents. The text provides an introduction—sometimes an in-depth one—to virtually all aspects of program planning and development, from (a) formalizing a statement of philosophy, rationale, goals, and objectives, to (b) identifying students, (c) outlining theory-based acceleration and enrichment activities, and (d) evaluating the ongoing or completed program. Often, specific rating forms and questionnaires for identification or evaluation are presented as models that may inspire the creation of specific, program-relevant instruments. Also, lists of philosophy and goal statements, enrichment strategies, acceleration plans, strategies for teaching creative and critical thinking, and other central matters are described. Curriculum models that direct program planning and models that guide program evaluation are reviewed. In most cases, an underlying theory, or at least a good rationale, accompanies the strategies and suggestions.

Importantly, the book does not ignore the special identification and programming needs of *female* gifted students or *culturally different, economically disadvantaged, handicapped,* or *underachieving* gifted students. Many existing programs do not adequately accommodate the needs and problems of these children.

Changes to this third edition of *Education of the Gifted and Talented* include both updating and new material. For example, the press of de-tracking and cooperative learning inspired us to add these topics up front in Chapter 1. New approaches to identifying disadvantaged and culturally different gifted also have been added. The most notable change for this edition is our new chapter on counseling. It is intended to help you understand the social, emotional, and educational/career needs and problems of gifted students. The chapter also outlines specific counseling-related roles for teachers, parents, counselors, and even school administrators. You likely will be surprised by some of the unique counseling needs of gifted students. And the greater their gift, the greater the counseling urgency.

The authors wish to thank secretary Joanne Riedl for her efficient and ever-helpful contributions, Allyn and Bacon editor Ray Short for his experienced and amiable super-vision of the project, and many families with gifted children who have supplied real-life examples. Finally, we are grateful to our families for their encouragement, support, and real-life experiences that helped enrich our text.

GARY A. DAVIS

SYLVIA B. RIMM

CHAPTER 1

GIFTED EDUCATION
MATCHING INSTRUCTION WITH NEEDS

The mismatch between gifted youth and the curriculum they are forced to study most of the time is nothing short of an American tragedy. The human waste in terms of both student and faculty time is inestimable, and this waste can be found in both rich schools and poor, and even in schools that have well established programs for the gifted.

Joseph Renzulli (1991a, pp. 75–76)

Tens of thousands of gifted and talented children and adolescents are sitting in their classrooms—their abilities unrecognized, their needs unmet. Some are bored, patiently waiting for peers to learn skills and concepts that they had mastered two years earlier. Some find school intolerable, feigning illness or creating other excuses to avoid the trivia. Some feel pressured to hide their keen talents and skills from uninterested and unsympathetic peers. Some give up on school entirely, dropping out as soon as they are legally able.

Other gifted students tolerate school but satisfy their intellectual, creative, or artistic needs outside of the formal system. The lucky ones have parents who will sponsor their dance or music lessons, chemistry kits and telescopes, art supplies, frequent trips to the library, and home computers. The less fortunate ones make do as best they can, silently paying a price for a predicament they may not understand, and that others choose to ignore. That price is lost academic growth, lost creative potential, and sometimes lost enthusiasm for educational success and eventual professional achievement.

Some educators—and many parents of non-gifted students—are not swayed by the proposition that unrecognized and unsupported talent is wasted talent. A common reaction is, "Those kids will make it on their own," or "Give the extra help to kids who really need it!" The argument is that providing special services for highly able or talented students is "elitist"—giving to the "haves" and ignoring the "have-nots"—and therefore unfair and undemocratic.

Our "love-hate" relationship with gifted education has been noted by J. J. Gallagher (1991), Colangelo and Davis (1991), and others. We admire and applaud the individual who rises from a humble background to high educational and career success. At the same time, as a nation we are committed to equality. In his book *Anti-Intellectualism in American Life*, Richard Hofstadter (1963) noted that Americans and others typically admire those who excel at sports, dance, music, or art. However, the label *intellectually gifted* elicits hostility because it threatens the self-esteem of both youth and adults.

The educational pendulum swings back and forth between strong concern for *excellence* and a zeal for *equity*; that is, for helping bright and creative students develop their capabilities and realize their potential contributions to society, or for helping below-average and troubled students reach minimum academic standards. While interest in the gifted has mushroomed worldwide since the mid 1970s, at the time of this writing the pendulum is swinging forcefully back to *equity*. Programs for the gifted are being cut because they are not "politically correct."

Particularly, the anti-tracking/anti-ability grouping movement and the companion dilemma of cooperative learning are inflicting damage on G/T programs and gifted children themselves. Gifted education leader Joseph Renzulli (1992) expressed his perception of this "quiet crisis" by stating that for many people "the word *gifted* has become the worst [type of] ethnic, gender slur word."

Of course, America and the world need both equity *and* excellence. Many students need special help. The rights of slower learners, students with physical or psychological disabilities, and students with language and cultural differences are vehemently defended, and they should be. However, a good argument can be made that gifted students have rights too, and that these rights are often ignored. Just as with other exceptional students, students with gifts and talents also deserve an education commensurate with their capabilities. It is unfair to them to ignore, or worse, to prevent the development of their special skills and abilities and to depress their educational aspirations and eventual career achievements. Our democratic system promises each person—regardless of racial, cultural, or economic background and regardless of sex or handicapping condition—the opportunity to develop as an individual as far as that person's talents and motivation will permit. This guarantee seems to promise intrinsically that opportunities and training will be provided to help gifted and talented students realize their innate potential.

To those who argue that gifted students will "make it on their own," sensible replies are that (a) they should not be held back and required to succeed in spite of a frustrating educational system, and (b) some do not make it on their own. Nyquist (1973), for example, reported that a full 19 percent of high school dropouts in New York State would be classed as "gifted." Almost invariably, gifted

dropouts are underachievers, talented students who are unguided, uncounseled, and unchallenged (Rimm, 1986b; Whitmore, 1980). The widely cited *A Nation at Risk* report by the National Commission on Excellence in Education (1983) reported that ". . . over half the population of gifted students do not match their tested ability with comparable achievement in school."

It is not only the gifted students themselves who benefit from specific programs that recognize and cultivate their talents. Teachers involved with gifted students learn to stimulate creative, artistic, and scientific thinking, and they learn to help students understand themselves, develop good self-concepts, and value educational and career accomplishments. In short, teachers of the gifted become better teachers, and their skills benefit "regular" students as well. Society also reaps a profit. Realistically, it is only today's gifted and talented students who will become tomorrow's political leaders, medical researchers, artists, writers, innovative engineers, and business entrepreneurs. Indeed, it is difficult to propose that this essential talent be left to fend for itself—if it can—instead of being valued, identified, and cultivated. Tomorrow's promise is in today's schools, and it must not be ignored.

To continue our introduction, the next section presents an overview of the history of gifted education, including the 1990s history-in-the-making events of the National Research Center on the Gifted and Talented, directed by Joseph Renzulli, and the growing anti-tracking and cooperative learning movements. We then turn to definitions of *gifted* and *talented*, which both clarify characteristics of gifted students and guide the selection process.

HISTORY OF GIFTEDNESS AND GIFTED EDUCATION

Giftedness over the Centuries

A capsule survey of the history of efforts to cultivate the abilities of gifted and talented children around the world might include the following.

In ancient Sparta, military skills were so exclusively valued that all boys beginning at age seven received schooling and training in the arts of combat and warfare. Giftedness was defined in terms of fighting skills and leadership. The process of selecting candidates for military education took place at birth—babies with physical defects or who were otherwise of questionable value were flung off a cliff (Meyer, 1965).

In Athens, upper-class free Greeks sent their boys (not girls) to private schools that taught reading, writing, arithmetic, history, literature, the arts, and physical fitness (Warmington, 1961). Higher education also was restricted to the upper crust. Sophists (professional teachers) were hired to teach young men mathematics, logic, rhetoric, politics, grammar, general culture, and "disputation." Apparently, only Plato's Academy charged no fees and selected both young men and women based on intelligence and physical stamina, not social position.

Across the Adriatic Sea, Roman education emphasized architecture, engineering, law, and administration. With more liberal attitudes, both boys and girls attended first level (elementary) schools and some girls attended second level (grammar) schools, but higher education was not permitted for females. According to Good (1960), Rome valued mother and family, and some gifted women emerged who greatly affected Roman society, for example, Cornelius, Roman matron and famous mother of statesmen Gaius and Tiberius Gracchus.

The Renaissance period in Europe (1300–1700) produced remarkable art, architecture, and literature. Strong and wealthy governments rewarded their creatively gifted with wealth and honor. Such aesthetically able persons as Michelangelo, da Vinci, Boccacio, Bernini, and Dante were sought out and supported well.

Moving back a thousand years, early China, beginning with the Tang Dynasty in A.D. 618, placed high value on gifted children and youth. For example, child prodigies were sent to the imperial court where their gifts were recognized and cultivated.

Said Tsuin-Chen (1961), China historically anticipated four principles of modern G/T education. First, they embraced a multiple-talent concept of giftedness. They valued literary ability, leadership, imagination, and originality, and such intellectual and perceptual abilities as reading speed, memory capacity, reasoning, and perceptual sensitivity. A second interesting notion was their recognition of (a) apparently precocious youth who grow up to be average adults, (b) seemingly average youth whose gifts emerge later, and (c) true child prodigies whose gifts and talents are apparent throughout their lives. Third, the early Chinese recognized that abilities of even the most gifted children would not fully develop without special training. Support was considered especially important because of the belief that these children were weak and unhealthy and would not live long. Finally, a fourth notion, attributed to Confucius about 500 B.C., was his nail-on-the-head belief that while education should be available to children of all social classes, they should be educated differently according to their abilities.

In Japan, during the Tokugawa Society period (1604–1868), schools of each clan tracked children of Japanese Samurai differently than children of commoners (Anderson, 1975). Children of Samurai nobility received training in Confucian classics, martial arts, history, composition, calligraphy, moral values, and etiquette. Poor village children were taught to value loyalty, obedience, humility, and diligence. However, a few individual scholars established private academies for the intellectually gifted, including children of both Samurai and commoners.

Giftedness in America

In early America, concern for the education of gifted and talented children was not great. Some gifted youth were accommodated in the sense that attending secondary school and college was based both on academic achievement and the ability to pay the fees (Newland, 1976).

With compulsory attendance laws, schooling

became available to all, but special services for gifted children were sparse. As a few bright spots:[1]

In 1870, St. Louis initiated tracking; some students were allowed to accelerate through the first eight grades in fewer than eight years.

In 1884, Woburn, Massachusetts, created the "Double Tillage Plan," a form of grade-skipping in which bright children attended the first semester of first grade, then switched directly into the second semester of second grade.

In 1886, schools in Elizabeth, New Jersey, began a multiple-tracking system that permitted gifted learners to progress at a faster pace.

In 1891, Cambridge, Massachusetts, schools developed a "double-track" plan; also, special tutors taught students capable of even more highly accelerated work.

Around 1900, some "rapid progress" classes appeared that telescoped three years of school work into two.

In 1901, Worcester, Massachusetts, opened the first special school for gifted children.

In 1916, "opportunity classes" (special classes) were created for gifted children in Los Angeles and Cincinnati.

By about 1920, approximately two-thirds of all larger cities had created some type of program for gifted students; for example, special classes were begun in 1919 in Urbana, Illinois, and in 1922 in Manhattan and Cleveland.

In the 1920s and into the 1930s, interest in gifted education dwindled apparently for two reasons. Worcester (Getzels, 1977, pp. 263–264) referred to the 1920s as "the age of the common man" and "the age of mediocrity," a time when "the idea was to have everybody just as near alike as they could be ... administrators' ideal was to bring everyone to the standard, with no interest in carrying anybody beyond the standard." The focus was on *equity*. The second reason was the great depression, whose devastation reduced most people's concerns to those of survival. Providing

[1]Sources: Greenlaw and McIntosh (1988); Heck (1953); Abraham (1976); Witty (1967, 1971).

special opportunities for gifted children was low on the totem pole.

CONTEMPORARY HISTORY OF GIFTED EDUCATION

Recent history underlying today's strong interest in gifted education begins with abbreviated stories of the contributions of Francis Galton, Alfred Binet, Lewis Terman, and Leta Hollingworth, followed by the impact of Russia's Sputnik, a 1990s look at the gifted movement in America and worldwide, the National Research Center on the Gifted and Talented, the anti-grouping educational reform movement, and the cooperative learning dilemma.

Hereditary Genius: Sir Francis Galton

The English scientist Sir Francis Galton (1822–1911), a younger cousin of Charles Darwin, is credited with the earliest significant research and writing devoted to intelligence (or genius) and intelligence testing. Galton believed that intelligence was related to the keenness of one's senses; for example, vision, audition, smell, and touch. His efforts to measure intelligence therefore involved such tests as those of visual and auditory acuity, tactile sensitivity, and reaction time. Highly impressed by cousin Charles's *Origin of the Species*, Galton reasoned that evolution would favor persons with keen senses—persons who could more easily detect food sources or sense approaching danger. Therefore, he concluded that one's sensory ability—that is, intelligence—is due to natural selection and heredity. The hereditary basis of intelligence seemed to be confirmed by his observations—reported in his most famous book *Hereditary Genius* (Galton, 1869)—that distinguished persons seemed to come from succeeding generations of distinguished families. Galton initially overlooked the fact that members of distinguished, aristocratic families also inherit a superior environment, wealth, privilege, and opportunity—incidentals that make it much easier to become distinguished.

Galton's emphasis on the high heritability of intelligence is today shared by some psychologists. Gage and Berliner (1988), for example, drawing upon Jensen's (1969) twin studies, estimate that intelligence is 75 to 80 percent inherited and 20 percent due to environment. Other psychologists and educators argue that environment and learning play a much larger role.

Roots of Modern Intelligence Tests: Alfred Binet

Modern intelligence tests have their roots in France in the 1890s. Alfred Binet, aided by T. Simon, was hired by government officials in Paris to devise a test to identify which (dull) children would not benefit from regular classes and therefore would be placed in special classes to receive special training. Someone had perceptively noticed that teachers' judgments of student ability were biased by such traits as docility, neatness, and social skills. Some children were placed in schools for the retarded because they were too quiet, too aggressive, or had problems with speech, hearing, or vision. A direct test of intelligence was badly needed.

Binet tried a number of tests that failed. It seemed that normal students and dull students were not particularly different in (a) hand-squeezing strength, (b) hand speed in moving 50 cm (almost 20 inches), (c) the amount of pressure on the forehead that causes pain, (d) detecting differences in hand-held weights, or (e) reaction time to sounds or in naming colors. When he measured the ability to pay attention, memory, judgment, reasoning, and comprehension, he began to obtain results. The tests would separate children judged by teachers to differ in intelligence (Binet and Simon, 1905a, 1905b).

One of Binet's significant contributions was the notion of *mental age*—the concept that children grow in intelligence, and that any given child may be at the proper stage intellectually for his or her years, or else measurably ahead or behind. A related notion is that at any given age level, chil-

dren who learn the most do so partly because of greater intelligence.

In 1890, noted American psychologist James McKeen Cattell had called for the development of tests that would measure mental ability (Stanley, 1978a); his request was at least partly responsible for the immediate favorable reception to Binet's tests in America. In 1910 Goddard described the use of Binet's methods to measure the intelligence of 400 "feebleminded" New Jersey children, and in 1911 summarized his evaluation of two thousand normal children. The transition from using the Binet tests with below-average children to employing them with normal and above-average children thus was complete and successful.

Lewis Terman: The Stanford-Binet Test, His Gifted Children Studies

Stanford psychologist Lewis Madison Terman made two historically significant contributions to gifted education that have earned him the title of father of the gifted education movement. First, Terman supervised the modification and Americanization of the Binet-Simon tests, producing in 1916 the forerunner of all American intelligence tests, the *Stanford-Binet Intelligence Scale*.

Terman's second contribution was his identification and longitudinal study of 1,528 gifted children, published in the five-volume *Genetic Studies of Genius* series (Cox, 1926; Terman, 1925; Terman, Burks, and Jensen, 1930; Terman and Oden, 1947, 1959). In 1922 Terman and his colleagues identified 1,000 children with Stanford-Binet IQ scores above 135 (most were above 140), the upper one percent. By 1928 he added another 528. Of the 1,528, 856 were boys, 672 were girls. The average age was twelve years. All gifted and most comparison children were from major California cities: Los Angeles, San Francisco, Oakland, Berkeley, and Alameda. They had been initially identified by teachers as highly intelligent. Tests, questionnaires, and interviews in ten major contacts (field studies or mailings, in 1922, 1927–28, 1936, 1939–40, 1945, 1950, 1955, 1960,

1972, and early 1990s) traced their physical, psychological, social, and professional development for nearly three-quarters of a century. The earliest research involved parents, teachers, medical records, and even anthropometric (head) measurements. The grave seems the only escape from Terman's project.[2]

Regarding his subject sample, in comparison with the populations of the California urban centers at the time, there were twice as many children of Jewish descent as would be expected; fewer children of African-American or Hispanic parents. Chinese children were not sampled at all because they attended special Asian schools at the time. Note also that the effects of heredity versus environment were hopelessly tangled in Terman's subjects. Parents of these bright children generally were better educated and had higher-status occupations, and so the children grew up in advantaged circumstances.

Terman's high IQ children—called "Termites" in gifted education circles—were superior in virtually every quality examined. As we will elaborate in Chapter 2, they not only were better students, they were psychologically, socially, and even physically healthier than the average. With scientific data to back him, Terman stressed that the myth of brilliant students being weak, unattractive, or emotionally unstable was simply not true as a predominant trend.

Some other noteworthy conclusions related to the Terman studies are these:

• While in elementary and secondary school, those who were allowed to accelerate according to their intellectual potential were more successful. Those not permitted to accelerate developed poor work habits that sometimes wrecked college careers.
• Differences between the most and least successful gifted men indicated that family values and parents' education were major factors. For

example, 50 percent of the parents of Terman's "most productive" group were college graduates, but only 15 percent of the parents of the "least productive" group had college degrees.
• On the downside, and with benefit of hindsight, restricting the identification of "genius" or "giftedness" to high IQ scores is severely limiting; artistic and creative genius and genius in a single area were ignored.
• As another negative, Terman's conclusions regarding the mental and social health of his bright children swayed educators for many decades to ignore the sometimes desperate counseling needs of gifted children (Chapter 17).

Leta Hollingworth: "Nurturant Mother" of Gifted Education

According to Stanley (1978), Galton was the grandfather of the gifted-child movement, Binet the midwife, Terman the father, and Columbia University's Leta Hollingworth the nurturant mother. Her pioneering efforts began in 1916, when she encountered an 8-year-old boy who tested 187 IQ on the new Stanford-Binet scale. Said Hollingworth (1942, p. xii), "I perceived the clear and flawless working of his mind against a contrasting background of thousands of dull and foolish minds. It was an unforgettable observation." Indeed, the observation changed the direction of her career and life (Delisle, 1992).

Hollingworth's efforts supporting gifted children and gifted education in the New York area included initiating programs for the gifted in New York City schools, searching for other high-ability children, and in 1937 working extensively at Speyer School, P.S. 500, with 50 children who scored between IQ 130 and 200 on the Stanford-Binet. Hollingworth believed that gifted children are the "original thinkers" of their generation, and therefore require instruction to help them develop attitudes and drives related to productive habits and leadership (Delisle, 1992). A sample of Hollingworth's enrichment experiences for the children included teaching them French, nutrition,

---

[2]Although Terman died in 1956, the work was continued by others, for example, Anne H. Barbee, Melinda Oden, Pauline S. Sears, and Robert R. Sears.

dramatics, music, and chess, as well as having them write biographies based on library research at Columbia University.

Hollingworth made early contributions to counseling the gifted, or as she put it, to their "emotional education." Unlike Terman's overemphasis on the mental health of bright children, Hollingworth (1942) underscored that highly intelligent children also are highly *vulnerable*. Social and emotional problems emerge because intellectual development outstrips the child's age and physical development. For example, the child's advanced vocabulary, interests, and preferences for games with complicated rules will alienate average children. Hollingworth sought to help gifted children understand that less talented students could be friends and, in many circumstances, even mentors.

In the classroom, said Hollingworth (1942, p. 299), children above 140 IQ waste about half their time; children above 170 IQ spend most of their time in many kinds of "bizarre and wasteful" activities. Further, many adults do not understand precocity, observed Hollingworth. They may tease a child about his or her knowledge, or a teacher may prevent a child from exploring advanced resources. The combination of adult ignorance with childhood knowledge causes problems for the precocious child (Delisle, 1992). A common difficulty, noted Hollingworth, is that many gifted children become apathetic in schools that ignore their intellectual needs, and may develop negative attitudes toward authority figures.

Hollingworth's experiences with gifted children are summarized in two books, *Gifted Children: Their Nature and Nurture* (Hollingworth, 1926) and *Children Above 180 IQ Stanford-Binet: Origin and Development* (Hollingworth, 1942). One noteworthy 1931 quote is: "It is the business of education to consider all forms of giftedness in pupils in reference to how unusual individuals may be trained for their own welfare and that of society at large" (Passow, 1981).

Hollingworth was an early advocate for women's rights; she died in 1939.

Sputnik: The Russians Are Gaining! The Russians Are Gaining!

Our last significant historical event to predate the 1970s resurgence of interest in gifted education is the launching in 1957 of the Russian satellite Sputnik. To many, the launch of Sputnik was a glaring and shocking technological defeat—Russia's scientific minds had outperformed ours (Tannenbaum, 1979). Suddenly, reports criticizing American education and, particularly, its ignoring of gifted children became very popular. For example, a 1950 Educational Policies Commission had noted that mentally superior children were being neglected, which would produce losses in the arts, sciences, and professions. In a book entitled *Educational Wastelands*, Bestor (1953) charged that "know-nothing educationists" had created schools that provided "meager intellectual nourishment or inspiration," particularly for bored gifted students.

Following the 1957 launch, more reports compared the quality and quantity of American versus Russian education, and especially the numbers of American versus Russian children being trained in defense-related professions. America lost hands down. A report by the First Official U.S. Education Mission to the USSR (1959), entitled *Soviet Commitment to Education*, claimed that the typical Russian high school graduate had completed ten years of math, five years of physics, four years of chemistry, one year of astronomy, five years of biology, and five years of a foreign language.

Tannenbaum (1979) referred to the aftermath of Sputnik as a "total talent mobilization." Academic coursework was telescoped (condensed) for bright students. College courses were offered in high school; foreign languages were taught in elementary schools. Public and private funds were earmarked for training in science and technology. Acceleration and ability grouping were used, and efforts were made to identify gifted and talented minority students. New math and science curricula were developed, most notably the School Mathematics Study Group (SMSG) math, Physical Science Study Committee (PSSC) physics, and Biological Science Curriculum Study (BSCS) biology. In high school there was a new awareness of and concern for high scholastic standards and career mindedness. The bright and talented students were expected to take the tough courses, to ". . . fulfill their potential, and submit their developed abilities for service to the nation" (Tannenbaum, 1979).

While Sputnik itself was a great success, the keen interest in educating gifted and talented students fizzled in about five years. The awareness and concern was rekindled in the mid 1970s, however, and while struggling in some states and districts—and moving backward in others due to the anti-tracking movement—gifted education is here to stay. In many cities—for example, Chicago—it appears to be thriving (R. M. Gallagher, 1991).

Gifted Education in the 1990s

By 1990, the U.S. government and all 50 states had enacted legislation and many states allocated funds. Many teachers and administrators nationwide and across Canada had become more and more committed to gifted education. Most large school systems and many small ones had initiated programs and services for gifted children. Researchers, teachers, materials writers, and others continue to write articles, books, tests, and new materials for teaching computing, math, art, science, communication skills, learning-how-to-learn skills, values, leadership, and creativity and other thinking skills. Counseling has become increasingly recognized as an essential program component. Enthusiasm among many educators—and certainly among parents of the gifted—remains high.

The gifted movement also has become worldwide, with programs developed, for example, in England, Scotland, Russia, Bulgaria, Poland, mainland China, Taiwan, Japan, Hong Kong, the Philippines, Guam, Israel, Egypt, South Africa, Saudi Arabia, Iraq, India, Mexico, Dominican Republic, Brazil, Columbia, Indonesia, Micronesia, and Aus-

tralia (e.g., Sisk, 1990). Because tomorrow's world leaders and professionals are today's gifted children, Passow (1989) recommended creating a global curriculum to increase awareness of and responsibility for world problems. The curriculum would emphasize, for example, cross-cultural understanding and peace, and problems of nuclear proliferation, hunger, and Third World population pressures. Quoting Dean Rusk: "The rest of the world will be in our living rooms for the rest of our lives" (Passow, 1989, p. 26).

NATIONAL RESEARCH CENTER ON THE GIFTED AND TALENTED

Joseph Renzulli's contributions to gifted education are recognized nationally and internationally, and appear in many chapters of this book. Renzulli's most recent major brainchild is his *National Research Center on the Gifted and Talented* (NRC/GT), based at the University of Connecticut (Renzulli, 1991a, 1991b, 1992; Gubbins, 1991).[3] The purpose of NRC/GT is to conduct "consumer-oriented" research related to key problems and practices pertaining to educating gifted and talented students. The research aims at the realities of schools, classrooms, and teachers, and is intended to influence educational practices and policies (Renzulli, 1991b).

In addition to the University of Connecticut, the NRC/GT is a collaborative effort that includes:

- The University of Georgia, University of Virginia, and Yale University, which are conducting large-scale research projects.
- 54 state and territorial departments of education.
- Over 260 public and private schools that represent many ethnic, socioeconomic, and demographic differences. These cooperate in research and in making training videos and guidebooks, and will serve as model sites for visitations.

[3]NRC/GT is funded by the Jacob K. Javits Gifted and Talented Students Education Act of 1988, Office of Educational Research and Improvement, U.S. Department of Education.

- Over 200 content area consultants, with expertise in such areas as special populations, identification, program development, personal and social development, policy development, and program evaluation.
- "Stakeholders" representing professional organizations, parent groups, government agencies, businesses, state and local boards of education, state and local legislators, and others.

The five aims of NRC/GT are to:

1. Identify fair identification procedures and effective programming practices.

2. Describe financial, administrative, policy, and staff training activities that will make these practices a reality in schools serving students from various ethnic, cultural, non-English-speaking, socioeconomic, handicapped, and geographic groups.

3. Disseminate information about these practices to educators, policymakers, and parents.

4. Implement effective practices across all grade levels, which requires integrating the practices into state and district policies, regulations, and resources, and into school reform and restructuring activities.

5. Explore the implications of good practices for the gifted with the future of gifted education, the future of education in general, and the future interaction of gifted education with regular education (Renzulli, 1991a).

Reflecting its applied bent, NRC/GT identified its initial research projects via a mailing to 19,000 persons in gifted education asking: What do you want to know? Some initial research projects aim at clarifying the following pivotal problems and topics:

- *Studying classroom practices used with gifted and talented and regular students.* What are the most successful classroom practices?
- *Evaluating the effects of different programming arrangements on student learning outcomes.* Are we making a difference?

- *Giftedness in special populations.* What identification, programming, and counseling problems are unique to various groups?
- *Investigating instruments and practices used to identify gifted students.*
- *Identifying and programming for artistically gifted students.*
- *Studying ways to evaluate programs for the gifted.*
- *Evaluating the impact of different staff development techniques on the implementation of curricular modifications.*
- *Applying a theory-based approach* (School-wide Enrichment Model, Chapter 7) *to identification, teaching, and program evaluation.*
- *Studying methods for and effects of compacting, the elimination of mastered material.*
- *Studying standards for teacher certification in gifted education.*

Some classroom practices currently being studied include independent projects, creative writing on self-selected topics, teaching thinking skills, encouraging discovery, and using classroom questions that encourage reasoning and logical thinking (Gubbins, 1991).

As sample research results, the Classroom Practices Study (Renzulli, 1992; Brown, Emmons, and Zhang, 1992; Archambault and Hallmark, 1992; Westberg, Dobyns, and Salvin, 1992) surveyed 7,000 teachers. Overall, concluded Archambault and Hallmark (1992), it's a "very disturbing picture . . . teachers make only minor modifications in regular classrooms to meet the needs of gifted and talented students." Specifically, among various teacher groups (e.g., public or private school), 42 to 62 percent had no training whatever in teaching gifted students. Most schools (54 percent public, 64 percent private) do not have policies permitting acceleration. Forty-eight to 60 percent of the teachers reported that, in their classes, gifted students were *not* identified. Small surprise that when asked to compare specific teaching practices (e.g., ability grouping, sending to higher grade, questioning for thinking, providing challenges and choices, curricular modifications, enrichment centers) for gifted versus regular students, there were "very, very small" differences (Archambault and Hallmark, 1992). There were essentially no opportunities to work in other locations, work on advanced projects, work in enrichment centers, engage in self-directed learning, work with advanced curriculum, or work with other gifted students.

The work of the NRC/GT seems on target and promising indeed.

ABILITY GROUPING AND GIFTED EDUCATION

A sweeping reform movement is underway to eliminate ability grouping, with bad consequences for gifted children. The movement includes abolishing not only accelerated classes, but sometimes special classes for the gifted and gifted programs themselves. Reis (Reis *et al.*, 1992) referred to the trend as a "national hysteria." Renzulli (1991a) noted that "bright kids learn nothing new until January" with heterogeneous grouping.

The most common target of critics is *between-class grouping*, also called *tracking*, *XYZ grouping*, or *homogeneous grouping*, in which, for example, low, average, and high ability students are placed in three different classes at each grade. Two other common forms of ability grouping are *cross-grade grouping* and *within-class grouping*. Cross-grade grouping, or the *Joplin Plan*, means placing students for part of their day in the next higher grade, usually for reading, math, or science (Kulik, 1991, 1992; Schatz, 1990).

Within-class grouping includes separating students in each class for small-group instruction, for example, based on reading or math ability. Within-class grouping also includes cooperative learning, in which two to four students interact to master material or produce a group answer to a problem; skill groups, in which small groups work on specific (e.g., math or reading) skills; groups created to complete projects of various types; and peer teaching (Schatz, 1990).

Leading the de-tracking attack is Jeanie Oakes, author of *Keeping Track* (Oakes, 1985). Oakes (1991a, 1991b; Goodlad and Oakes, 1988) argues three core points. First, she claims that tracking is *ineffective*—students learn less and they lose motivation and self-esteem. Second, she alleges that the practice is *discriminatory* and racist because too many minority children are in slow tracks. Tracking thus promotes reduced contact between the races, a type of segregation. Third, she asserts that tracking is *unfair in principle*; it is simply wrong to deny access to deeper academic content and opportunities based on ability. It is not surprising that the American public finds such arguments compelling (Kulik, 1991), and the de-tracking, de-grouping movement is steaming ahead.

Oakes (1991a, 1991b) pointed out that decisions regarding tracking involve deep political and technical issues such as the purposes of schooling; democracy and unequal opportunities; conceptions of ability and individual differences; assessment methods; relations between schools and their constituents; curricular and instructional methods, including new ways to meet special needs; restructuring teachers' lives; and implications of de-tracking for gifted and special education students and their parents. "And," said Oakes (1991b), "everything is connected to everything else."

Gifted education and gifted students are in deep trouble without grouping practices, which is why the de-grouping movement is threatening gifted education (e.g., Feldhusen, 1991a; Kulik, 1992; Kulik and Kulik, 1991; Renzulli, 1992; Renzulli and Reis, 1991a; Rogers, 1991). Various G/T program designs place capable students in part-time or full-time *special classes* for enriched or accelerated work; in weekly or more frequent *pullout* or *resource room* groups for independent projects or other skill-development activities; in small *cluster groups* in one classroom at each grade for advanced learning activities and projects; in *talent*, *interest*, or *project* groups (Schatz, 1990); in higher grades for part of the day (*cross-grade grouping*); or in *school-within-a-school* plans, in which gifted students attend academic classes with other gifted students, non-academic classes with regular students.

What does research say about ability grouping? Kulik (1991, 1992; Kulik and Kulik, 1991) conducted meta-analyses on 51 controlled studies of between-class grouping.[4] Results of meta-analyses are reported in *effect size*, which is the difference between two groups in standard deviation units. Effect sizes may be interpreted as follows (Kulik, 1992):

.10 to .35 = small difference
.35 to .70 = moderate difference
Above .70 = large difference

For practical purposes, effect sizes larger than about .30 indicate a practically significant difference between an experimental condition (e.g., ability grouping) versus its control (e.g., heterogeneous classes)—approximately three months additional achievement on a grade-equivalent score scale (Rogers, 1991).

While research results are somewhat mixed, the Kuliks' conclusions favor grouping gifted kids, if not all kids. First of all, Kulik (1991) reminds us of the highly successful effects of grouping mathematically talented adolescents for acceleration in summer or college programs; such students make phenomenal gains in math achievement (e.g., Stanley, 1991). Kulik (1992) reported that students in lower and middle level tracks learn the same amount as equivalent pupils do in mixed classes. However, "Students in the top classes in XYZ programs outperform equivalent pupils from mixed classes" (p. vii). Also, the Kuliks found a worthwhile achievement advantage with two types of grouping likely to be used in gifted programs. With part-time *cross-grade grouping*, the overall achievement advantage of homogeneously grouped versus heterogeneous classes was reflected in an effect size of about .30. Achievement

was higher for low, medium, and high ability students, with effect sizes of .29, .35, and .40, respectively. *Within-class grouping* (to teach arithmetic) produced an overall achievement advantage effect size of about .35; low, medium, and especially high ability students benefitted, with effect sizes of .20, .15, and .40, respectively. *An important conclusion of the Kuliks is that the achievement of low-ability students has not been harmed by homogeneous grouping.*

Analyzing 13 research syntheses, including those of the Kuliks, Rogers (1991) reached the same conclusions: "While . . . tracking for regular instruction makes no discernible difference in the academic achievement of average and low ability students, it does produce substantial academic gains for gifted students enrolled in full-time special programs." She also noted that grouping for enrichment, either within the class or in a resource room (pullout program), produces substantial gains in academic achievement, creativity, and other thinking skills. Especially, grouping for accelerating curriculum produces substantial academic gains for gifted students, for example, in telescoping, early college admission, and nongraded classroom plans.

Rogers noted that the higher achievement of gifted students likely is due to a combination of higher ability, interested teachers, and "the willingness of gifted students to learn while in a classroom with other interested, high ability learners." Table 1.1 summarizes effect sizes, across the 13 syntheses, for various grouping practices currently used with gifted students. The data strongly support the practice of grouping gifted students.

But what about self-esteem? According to "stigma theory" grouping should cause slow-track students to label themselves "dummies" and lower their self-expectations (e.g., Oakes, 1985). Perhaps so; but self-concepts also are shaped by successes and failures that occur when interacting with others of higher or lower ability. In mixed-ability classes less able students observe others learning faster and see themselves as the last to understand. Such day-after-day comparisons can devastate self-concepts

---

[4]Meta-analysis, according to Kulik (1991), involves the four steps of (1) locating as many research studies as possible, (2) coding the specific features of each study, (3) reporting overall differences in *effect sizes*, and (4) describing significant relations between specific features and study outcomes.

TABLE 1.1   Effect Sizes for Acceleration and Enrichment Options Used in Gifted Programs

Option	Effect Size
Options in which Grouping is Central	
Pullout Programs (Enrichment; Curriculum Extension)	.65
Ability Grouped Enriched Classes	.33
Cross-grade Grouping (Reading, Math)	.45
Nongraded Classes	.38
Regrouping for Specific Instruction (Reading, Math)	.34
Advanced Placement Programs	.29
Cluster Grouping (within regular class)	.62
Special Classes for Gifted	.33
Cooperative Learning (three methods)	0, .38, .30
More Individualized Options; Grouping is Less Central	
Early Entrance to School	.36
Subject Acceleration	.49
Curriculum Compacting (Compression)	.45
Grade Skipping	.78
Concurrent Enrollment (e.g., junior and senior high school)	.36
Credit by Examination	.75
Grade Telescoping (e.g., 4 years of high school into 3)	.56
Mentorships	.42

Adapted from Rogers, 1992

and devitalize children, even more than the effect of labeling (Feldhusen, 1989a; Kulik, 1991). Many teachers are aware of the blossoming effect that occurs for some average- or low-ability children when the gifted leave for pullout enrichment activities or are removed altogether for special classes (Feldhusen, 1989b). Said one student, "When Bill (the gifted one) was in class, it was like the sun shining on a bright, clear day. But, when he went out to work with other gifted kids, it was like when the sun goes over the horizon. The rest of us were like the moon and the stars—that's when we finally got a chance to shine" (Fiedler-Brand, Lange, and Winebrenner, 1990, p. 6).

Kulik (1991, 1992) discovered that the self-concepts of low- and medium-ability students tend to be *higher* when ability grouped than in heterogeneous classes. However, high-ability students, when grouped (and competing) with others of high ability seem to be "taken down a peg;" their self-concepts are slightly lower—perhaps an appropriate dose of humility.

Rogers' (1991) and Kulik's (1992) conclusions regarding the de-tracking movement take the form of guidelines that are combined in Inset 1.1.

In his book *Perils of Reform*, Hunt (1991) used the anti-ability grouping movement as an example of how good-intentioned educational reforms can produce retrograde movement for some students, in this case, gifted ones. Indeed, many overzealous administrators are interpreting the de-grouping movement to include abolishing *all* ability-related grouping and opportunities. It is a return to a lock-step "one size fits all" curriculum (Schatz, 1990).

INSET 1.1 _____

Guidelines About Grouping the Gifted

Based on reviews of research syntheses, Rogers (1992) and Kulik (1992) summarized their conclusions relating to ability grouping in these guidelines.

- *Schools should resist calls for the wholesale elimination of ability grouping* (Kulik; Rogers). Some grouping programs help students a great deal. Programs for gifted students are beneficial. Also, slow, average, and bright students benefit from grouping programs that adjust the curriculum to aptitude levels of the groups, specifically, cross-grade grouping and within-class grouping.
- *Benefits are slight from programs that group children by ability, but prescribe common curricular experiences for all ability groups* (Kulik). Schools should not expect student achievement to change dramatically by either eliminating or initiating such programs.
- *Students who are academically or intellectually gifted should spend the majority of their school day with others of similar ability and interests* (Rogers). Such grouping (e.g., in special classes, special schools) has produced marked academic achievement gains as well as improved attitudes.
- *When full-time gifted programs are not available, gifted students might be offered cluster-grouping or cross-grade instructional grouping according to their individual proficiencies in school subjects* (Rogers).
- *Gifted students, individually or in groups, should be offered acceleration-based options* (Kulik; Rogers). Highly talented youngsters profit greatly from work in programs of accelerated work.
- *Mixed-ability cooperative learning plans should be used sparingly for gifted students* (Rogers). Cooperative learning might be used with the gifted for developing social skills. Research thus far indicates that—for gifted students—cooperative learning seems to produce fewer academic benefits than grouping plans.

Proponents of gifted education are having fits, and gifted children are suffering. See Inset 1.2.

COOPERATIVE LEARNING

Cooperative learning is students working together and helping each other learn, almost always in groups of two to four. Typically, groups are composed of a mixture of ability levels; for example, a four-student group might include two average students, a mainstreamed student with a learning disability or retardation, and a fast-learning student. Cooperative learning has proven remarkably effective, leading some experts to recommended it as the *primary* instructional method for teaching reading, writing, and math (Slavin, Madden, and

Stevens, 1990). The difficulty is that gifted students:

- Often prefer not to work in cooperative groups, because they know they can learn faster alone. For example, a study of preferred learning styles with 169 gifted high school students showed that both boys and girls preferred individualistic learning styles over cooperative styles *for all subjects* (Li and Adamson, 1992).
- Often must assume the role of tutor ("You know it, now teach them").
- May get stuck doing most of the work for their group.
- Miss opportunities for accelerated or enriched work that matches their abilities, for example, with other gifted students.

INSET 1.2 _____

A Bicycle Ride: Why We Need Grouping

Rimm (1992c) assembled her thoughts on ability grouping by comparing the issue to bike riding with her husband and youngest daughter—both of whom needed a faster pace and longer ride to obtain a suitable fitness experience. Thinking analogically about children of varying abilities in the same classroom, she imagined not three but 23 bike riders, and posed the following questions. As you read, think first about your answer to the biking question, then think of the answer as though you were a student in a classroom:

1. Was the main purpose of our biking social or physical fitness? (While social fitness is important, the primary purpose of school is not social but educational fitness.)
2. Would it have been possible for us to all meet our social and physical fitness goals with the same activity? (We cannot meet all students social and educational fitness needs with the same activities; they can be better met with grouping for some parts of the curriculum, and not grouping for others.)
3. How would my husband and daughter have felt if I asked them to slow their pace for me, or spend most of their time teaching me to bike better? (Students who need more challenge may resent teachers and other students who slow their learning process; they feel bored in class and tend to feel superior to other kids if they spend their time teaching instead of learning.)
4. How would I feel about myself if the more able bikers were to spend most of their time teaching me or slowing down to wait for me? (Slower students hesitate to ask questions or to volunteer and discuss if they feel they are slowing other students. Believing they are slowing down others is not good for self-esteem.)
5. Would the better bikers enjoy biking with persons of similar skills, strength, and endurance? (Very capable students enjoy learning with intellectual peers and often miss the stimulation when peers are unavailable.)
6. How could I feel good about my physical fitness activity even though I was slowest? (All children experience satisfaction in learning if they feel they are making progress; setting and reaching personal goals is important for children at all levels.)
7. How would I feel if an outsider insisted that I keep up with the faster bikers? (Children feel pressured if they are rushed beyond their capacity.)
8. How would I feel if others did not see the value of my physical fitness activity for me? (Children who are not viewed as achieving by parents and teachers do not feel good about themselves; all students should experience a sense of accomplishment and "worth-whileness" of effort.)
9. How would I feel if my fitness and strength improved, but I was forced to continue to ride at my same speed and distance? (It is important to show children paths for movement between groups, particularly upward mobility through effort.)

A bike ride provides physical fitness only when all riders are encouraged to exercise to their abilities.

Let's look briefly at some dynamics, claims, and methods of cooperative learning.

Dynamics.   Two core features are *group goals* and *individual accountability*. While specific cooperative learning methods vary, most assignments and procedures are structured so that individual students can achieve their goals (master the material, earn a good score or grade) only if teammates also reach their goals—individual recognition is based on group success (Johnson and Johnson, 1987, 1989, 1990a; Johnson, Johnson, and Holubec, 1988; Slavin, 1990b, 1990c, 1991b). In most cases, the teacher creates the groups, sets the problem, and explains the strategy that students will use to work together on the learning assignment or problem.

Cooperative learning is considered a humanistic, pro-social form of instruction (Slavin, 1991b). Students work face-to-face with each other, with mutual goals and a division of labor (Johnson and Johnson, 1990a). Because each member must contribute, students get to know and trust each other. They learn to communicate accurately and clearly, respect each other's opinions, support each other, ask probing questions, check for understanding, and resolve conflicts constructively, for example, criticizing ideas without criticizing people. Many of these skills must be taught, usually by teacher modeling (Johnson and Johnson, 1990b).

Cooperation and competition.   Johnson and Johnson (1989) argue that the *cooperative structure* is the essential feature of cooperative learning—students working together to achieve a common goal. While Slavin also argues the merits of learning through cooperation (e.g., Slavin, 1991b), he claims that *intergroup competition* provides the motivation for successful cooperative learning (1990c; Slavin, Madden, and Stevens, 1990).

The issue of whether cooperation or competition should be fostered in students actually has been a lively one. In the Li and Adamson (1992) study cited earlier, high school boys (but not girls) preferred a competitive learning style over a cooperative format. Speaking to the problem of underachievement, Rimm (1991, p. 1) contended "that the priority achievement lesson children require is learning how to function effectively in competition." She noted that competition is a successful motivating element in, for example, Future Problem Solving, Odyssey of the Mind, Math Olympiad, Academic Decathlon, as well as in music and athletic programs. Experience with both successes and failures is essential for life adjustment, said Rimm.

The opposite view is expressed, for example, by Rimmerman (1991), who argues that failure in school competition can be emotionally devastating to children, and that cooperative social skills—knowing how to "get along"—are more necessary for success in life. He conceded, with tongue in cheek, that group competition is indeed very powerful—because "it creates double and triple the amount of losers in less time."

Benefits of cooperative learning.   The claims for cooperative learning, if only half correct, justify its flourishing popularity—with all but gifted students.[5]

Achievement is said to run higher for all students, regardless of age, subject, or learning task (Augustine, Gruber, and Hanson, 1990; Kelly, 1991; Johnson and Johnson, 1987). Slavin, Madden, and Stevens (1990) claim substantial achievement gains for high-ability students as well.

Higher *motivation* stems from mutual encouragement for achievement; students are more responsible for their own learning (e.g., Hannigan, 1990).

Cognitive growth and thinking skills are stimulated by the discussions, conflicting points of view, creative thinking, and "sorting sense from nonsense" (Johnson and Johnson, 1987; Slavin, 1987b). Because children think and talk about what they are learning, they construct knowledge of the world around them (Hannigan, 1990; Johnson and Johnson, 1987).

Social and interpersonal skills improve; and stu-

[5]For overviews by Slavin, Johnson and Johnson, Sharan and Sharan, and many others, see the entire December, 1989/January, 1990 issue of *Education Leadership*.

dents learn to work together, explain ideas clearly, manage conflict, and accept each other regardless of race, sex, ability, or disability (Johnson and Johnson, 1990b; Kelly, 1991; Slavin, 1990b).

The *classroom climate* and *school attitudes* are said to improve (Sharan and Sharan, 1990, 1992; Johnson and Johnson, 1990a); *classroom management* is less of a problem (Hannigan, 1990).

Self-confidence and *self-esteem* improve because students discover they can contribute good ideas that will be well-received (Hannigan, 1990). Mainstreamed children have shown dramatic improvements in social skills, psychological health, and achievement (Augustine, Gruber, and Hanson, 1990).

Small wonder there is excitement about cooperative learning among teachers and other educators.

Cooperative learning methods.   There are many cooperative learning strategies ranging from simple to complex. Most may be used with students of any age. With *Think-Pair-Share*, students sit it pairs and the teacher poses a question. Students first *think* individually of a response, then *pair* with their partner to reach agreement, then *share* their answer with the class.

In *Learning Together* (Johnson and Johnson, 1990a), the teacher presents a lesson, then students in groups work on a single worksheet. Group scores and group grades are based on members' quiz scores. There is no direct competition between groups or individuals.

With *Student Team Learning*, a team of four students splits up, each member going to a different "expert's table" that contains, for example, Spanish vocabulary definitions. They return, teach the others, then split up again to go to "competition tables" to be tested and earn points for a team score. Individual grades are based on later tests composed of the same questions given at the competition tables.[6]

[6]See, for example, Johnson and Johnson (1987, 1989, 1990a), Robinson (1991), Sharan and Sharan (1990, 1992), and Slavin (1990b) for descriptions of many more cooperative learning methods.

Comment.   The current social and educational focus is more strongly upon equity than excellence. In fact, all students deserve an optimal education. While cooperative learning serves most children well, it is indeed distressing to educators and parents of gifted children. The argument that cooperative learning also benefits the gifted (e.g., Augustine, Gruber, and Hanson, 1990; Slavin, 1990a, 1991a) seems not to convince those who believe that other educational opportunities—for example, accelerated academic work, self-selected independent projects, group work with other gifted students—would supply a more appropriate education, one that matches the needs and talents of gifted students (e.g., Mills and Durden, 1992; Renzulli, 1992).

DEFINITIONS OF GIFTEDNESS

Defining *gifted* and *talented* is both an important and a complicated matter. First, the particular definition adopted by a school district will guide the selection process, and thus determine who is selected for the special services and training of a gifted program. Second, there is danger that one's definition and consequent identification methods will discriminate against such special populations as poor, minority, handicapped, underachieving, and even female students. Third, one's definition of gifts and talents also is tied to programming practices; opportunities should be available for different specified types of gifts and talents. Fourth, the labeling effect of defining a student as "gifted" can have both positive and adverse effects, for example, raising self-esteem and self-expectations on the one hand, but sometimes alienating peers and siblings on the other.

There is no one definition of "gifted," "talented," or "giftedness" that is universally accepted. Common usage of the terms even by experts is ambiguous and inconsistent. For example, it is acceptable to use the terms interchangeably, as when we describe the same person as either a "gifted artist" or a "talented artist." Some dictionaries list *talent* as one meaning of *gift*, and vice versa. For convenience, your authors and others use the single word *gifted*, or *giftedness*, to abbreviate *gifted and talented*.

Some writers and the general public apparently see *talent* and *giftedness* on a continuum, with giftedness at the upper end (Cox, 1986; Perrone and Pulvino, 1979). Noted Cox, we speak of talented musicians, writers, and scientists and the few who are truly gifted, but no one reverses this usage.

Related to this continuum definition, every program will include students who barely meet the established criteria, along with one or two others who are extraordinarily brilliant or astonishingly talented in a particular area. No accepted label distinguishes between these two visible groups, although "extremely gifted" or "low-incidence gifted" are used, along with the tongue-in-cheek "severely gifted" or "profoundly gifted" (e.g., Milgram, 1989).

June Cox (Cox, Daniel, and Boston, 1985) avoids the term *gifted*, preferring *able learners*. Renzulli (1986, 1991b; Treffinger and Renzulli, 1986) prefers the phrase "gifted behaviors," which can be developed in certain students at certain times and in certain circumstances. They argue that the title of "gifted"—and by exclusion, "not gifted"—should not be bestowed on children as a result of the identification process. Renzulli's conception may alter the next federal definition of *gifted*.

All of the following definitions seek to delineate what is meant by "gifted and talented." However, some definitions are primarily *operational*, that is, designed to guide the selection process. In this category, especially, are Stankowski's categories of definitions and the authoritative U.S. Office (Department) of Education definition. Other definitions focus more on *clarifying* characteristics of gifted and talented persons, although these definitions also can guide selection. In this later category are Renzulli's three-ring definition; the Cohn and Gagné emphasis on general intellectual gifts versus specific talents or performances; Taylor's Multiple-Talent Totem Poles; and Gardner's seven intelligences.

Five Categories of Definitions: Stankowski

Stankowski (1978) outlined five categories of definitions of "gifts" and "talents." All but the first category have been (and are) used to guide the identification process.

First, *after-the-fact* definitions emphasize prominence in one of the professions as the criterion of giftedness. The "gifted" thus are those who have shown consistently outstanding achievements in a valuable sphere of human activity.

Second, *IQ* definitions set a point on the IQ scale, and persons scoring above that point are classed as "gifted." Terman's Stanford-Binet cutoff of 135 is a classic example. The practice remains popular despite its glaring shortcomings of (1) ignoring creative and artistic gifts, (2) ignoring gifts in particular areas, (3) discriminating against culturally different and low socioeconomic level students, even in cases where some subtests show extreme highs, and (4) branding students who score one IQ point below the cutoff as "not gifted," perhaps despite high creativity or high motivation to participate in the program. According to the Richardson Study (Wilkie, 1985), 82 percent of the school districts responding to their survey reported using IQ scores in identification, although not necessarily exclusively.

Third, *percentage* definitions set a fixed proportion of the school (or district) as "gifted." The particular percentage may be based on intelligence test scores, overall grade-point averages, or sometimes just grades in particular areas, especially math and science. The percentage figure may be a generous 15 to 20 percent or a more restrictive 1 to 5 percent.

A particularly irksome—but frequently heard—comment is that "five percent of our children are gifted!" Nature has not made the selection problem so easy. The fact is, any gift or talent is distributed according to a normal, bell-shaped curve. A specific percentage cutoff point is purely a matter of choice, usually based on available space, facilities, personnel, or the superstition that "five percent of our children are gifted."

Fourth, *talent* definitions focus on students who are outstanding in art, music, math, science, or other specific aesthetic or academic area.

Fifth, *creativity* definitions stress the significance of superior creative abilities as a main criterion of giftedness. Curiously, while all G/T programs have implicit or explicit goals of increasing creative growth and cultivating persons who will make creative contributions to society, Torrance (1984) reported that some states do not list creativity tests as acceptable selection criteria, or else specify that creativity tests are *not* acceptable as criteria.

The 1972, 1978, and 1988 Federal Definitions of Gifted and Talented

Any discussion of definitions of *gifted* and *talented* must include the original U.S. Office of Education definition of gifted and talented (Marland, 1972).[7]

> Gifted and talented children are those identified by professionally qualified persons who by virtue of outstanding abilities are capable of high performance. These are children who require differentiated educational programs and services beyond those normally provided by the regular school program in order to realize their contribution to self and society.

Children capable of high performance include those with demonstrated achievement and/or potential in any of the following areas:

1. General intellectual ability
2. Specific academic aptitude
3. Creative or productive thinking
4. Leadership ability
5. Visual and performing arts
6. Psychomotor ability

The appeal of the federal definition is that it recognizes not only high general intelligence, but gifts in specific academic areas and in the arts. It further calls attention to creative, leadership, and

[7]The Office of Education is now the Department of Education.

psychomotor gifts and talents. As we will see in Chapter 4, many specific identification strategies are based on the categories of the federal definition. It recognizes that gifted and talented students require "differentiated educational programs and services beyond those normally provided," thus justifying the development of gifted programs. It recognizes the two fundamental aims of gifted programs: to help individual gifted and talented students develop their high potential, and to provide society with educated professionals who are creative leaders and problem solvers. By including "demonstrated achievement and/or potential ability" it takes into consideration the underachieving student who may not be demonstrating giftedness in school.

In 1978 the U.S. Congress revised Marland's definition to read:

> (The gifted and talented are) ". . . children and, whenever applicable, youth who are identified at the pre-school, elementary, or secondary level as possessing demonstrated or potential abilities that give evidence of high performance capability in areas such as intellectual, creative, specific academic or leadership ability or in the performing and visual arts, and who by reason thereof require services or activities not ordinarily provided by the school." (U.S. Congress, Educational Amendment of 1978 [P.L. 95–561, IX (A)])

And in 1988 an even shorter version reads:

> The term "gifted and talented students" means children and youth who give evidence of high performance capability in areas such as *Intellectual*, *creative*, *artistic*, or *leadership* capacity, or in *specific academic fields*, and who require services or activities not ordinarily provided by the school in order to fully develop such capabilities (P.L. 100–297, Sec. 4103. Definitions).

The main difference between the 1972 version and the two later statements is that psychomotor ability was excluded. The reason for this change is that artistic psychomotor ability talents (for example, dancing, mime) could be included under performing arts, and athletically gifted students typically are well-provided for outside of G/T programs. In fact, athletic programs may be seen as almost ideal gifted programs: Special teachers (coaches) are hired; expensive equipment and space are provided; training is partly individualized; students meet with others like themselves, who encourage and reward each other for doing their best; and students even travel to other schools to meet and compete with other talented individuals and teams. Not much was lost by dropping "psychomotor ability" from Congress's definition.

Because of its official status, most states and individual school districts accept this federal definition in their formal legislation and in written program plans (e.g., Cassidy and Hossler, 1992). However, some blithely base actual identification upon intellectual criteria alone—such as IQ or achievement scores, grades, or teacher nominations for academic excellence—and ignore creative and artistic children and children who are outstanding in just one or two academic areas.

Renzulli's Three-Ring Model

Based upon descriptions of creatively productive persons, primarily adults, who have made valuable contributions to society, Renzulli (1986; also Renzulli and Reis, 1991b) argues that

> Gifted behavior ... reflects an interaction among three basic clusters of human traits— these clusters being above average (but not necessarily high) general and/or specific *ability*, high levels of *task commitment* (motivation), and high levels of *creativity*. Gifted and talented children are those possessing or capable of developing this composite set of traits and applying them to any potentially valuable area of human performance (Figure 1.1).

The combination of the three are "brought to bear" on general and specific performance areas, resulting in gifted behaviors.

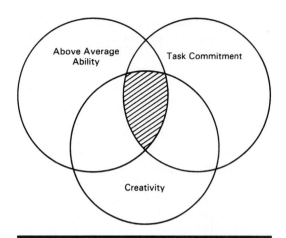

FIGURE 1.1.   Renzulli's three-ring model. Reprinted by permission of the author.

Some gifted program developers mistakenly have taken the well-known three-ring model as a recommendation to select for their programs *only* those children who are high in all three characteristics. As we will see in Chapter 4 on identification, Renzulli outlines a reasonable identification plan that is not tied strictly to the three parts (rings) of his conception of giftedness; for example, it includes selecting students with unusual interests or talents, as well as using nominations by parents and previous teachers based on idiosyncratic criteria.

General Giftedness vs. Specific Talents

Some educators use the word *gifted* to describe the highly intelligent, "intellectually gifted" person and the word *talented* to refer to persons with superior skills and abilities—"talents"—in just one or a few areas, for example, art, math, science, language, or social areas. There are several variations on this "general gifts" vs. "specific talents" theme.

Cohn's (1981) model differentiates three main domains of "giftedness" each of which is subdivided into categories of "talents." *Intellectual* giftedness subdivides into quantitative, verbal, spatial, and "other specific talent dimensions." *Artistic* giftedness divides into talent in the fine arts, performing arts, and "other specific talent dimensions." *Social* giftedness breaks down into leadership talent, empathic/altruistic talent, and (you guessed it) "other specific talent dimensions."

In another variation of general gifts vs. specific talents, F. Gagné (1985, 1991) built upon Cohn's model and Renzulli's (1978, 1986; Renzulli and Reis, 1991b) three-ring definition of giftedness. Gagné concluded that "gifts" vs. "talents" should reflect the psychological distinction between *ability* vs. *performance*. That is, a gifted person is one who is distinctly above average in intellectual, creative, socioemotional, sensorimotor, and other general *ability* domains, each of which may be subdivided into specific abilities (Figure 1.2). Talent refers to distinctly above average *performance* in fields of activities (e.g., math, music, astronomy, sculpture), the activities being "talents." Said Gagné, interests, personality traits, and environment are catalysts that orient a person toward a particular talent. Motivation, in conjunction with ability, contributes to the intensity of expression

of the talent. One implication of Gagné's ability-performance distinction is that an underachiever is classed as gifted, but not talented; he or she has the ability (gifts), but not the performances (talents).

Taylor's Multiple-Talent Totem Poles

Calvin Taylor's (1978, 1986, 1988) *multiple-talent totem pole* concept does not define "gifts and talents." Rather, it raises our awareness that the majority of students will possess special skills or talents of some type. Taylor's (1978) original six talents (academic, creative, planning, communicating, forecasting, decision-making) were expanded into the nine talents in Figure 1.3. The second through sixth talents (productive thinking, communicating, forecasting, decision-making, planning) were called "thinking talents" that contribute to creativity and problem solving. The final three (implementing, human relations, discerning opportunities) are essential for getting ideas into action.

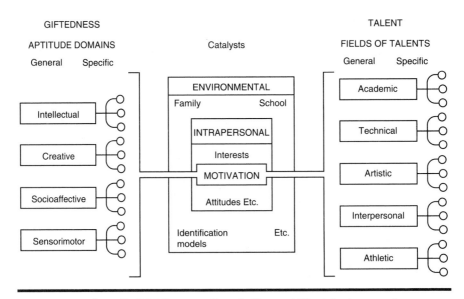

FIGURE 1.2. Gagné's (1991) conception of gifts as ability, talents as performances.

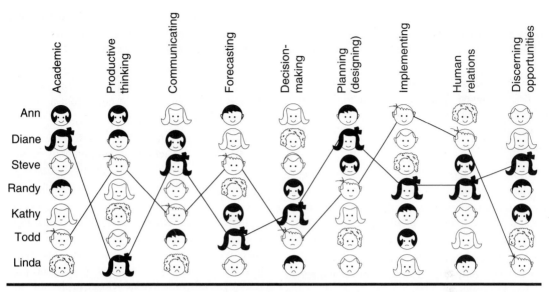

FIGURE 1.3.   Taylor's multiple-talent totem poles, extended version. Copyright © 1984, Calvin W. Taylor. Reprinted by permission.

The multiple-talent totem pole concept complicates the question: Who should be selected to participate in the G/T program? Looking at Figure 1.2, if we use traditional academic ability (IQ, achievement) for identifying gifted students, Ann—who is at the top of the academic and productive thinking totem poles—is the natural choice. However, if we look at communicating (speaking, writing), Kathy is the most talented. For forecasting and planning (organizing, designing) talents, Randy heads the top of the totem pole.

How do we define gifted and talented? Who should be selected to participate in a gifted education program? Different children would be chosen depending upon which talent is emphasized. Said Taylor (1986, p. 317), "Everyone has both strengths and weaknesses all the way across the totem poles" Further, "The more talents that students have activated in schooling, the more chance that the students will find one or more talents in which they are above average or even highly talented" (p. 320).

As a caution, if a G/T program tried to accommodate the unique strengths and talents of all or even most children, it actually would be an enrichment program for everyone, and would qualify only as a watered-down gifted program. Perhaps Taylor's broad definition of giftedness may be best viewed as an appropriate way to perceive, understand, and teach all children.

Gardner's Seven Intelligences

Since 1983 when his book *Frames of Mind* was published, Howard Gardner's (1983; Ramos-Ford and Gardner, 1991) seven-part conception of intelligence has increasingly attracted the attention of gifted educators. Most agree with Gardner that there is more to intelligence than a single IQ score. In his *theory of multiple intelligences*, Gardner describes seven ". . . separate and somewhat independent intellectual domains" (Ramos-Ford and Gardner, 1991). Gardner based his theory partly on evidence from persons suffering brain injury (e.g., a stroke), which indicated that brain damage often disrupts functioning in one domain, but not the others.

Many educators see Gardner's seven intelligences as seven types of intellectual gifts. Any one person may be gifted in one or several areas, but not in the others. As a brief overview, the seven intelligences are:

1. *Linguistic* (verbal) intelligence, which includes verbal comprehension, syntax, semantics, and written and oral expression. A novelist or lawyer would require linguistic intelligence.

2. *Logical-mathematical* intelligence, which includes, for example, inductive and deductive reasoning and computing, as required by a mathematician or physicist.

Note that linguistic and logical-mathematical intelligence are two fundamental competencies measured by traditional intelligence tests and are most valued in school settings (Ramos-Ford and Gardner, 1991).

3. *Spatial* intelligence, the capacity to represent and manipulate three-dimensional configurations, as needed by an architect, engineer, interior decorator, sculptor, or chess player.

4. *Musical* intelligence, which includes such abilities as pitch discrimination; sensitivity to rhythm, texture, and timbre; the ability to hear and perform themes in music; and in its most integrated form, music composition.

5. *Bodily-kinesthetic* intelligence, the ability to use all or part of one's body to perform a task or fashion a product. It would be present to a high degree in a dancer, athlete, or mime.

6. *Interpersonal intelligence*, which is the ability to understand the actions and motivations of others and to act sensibly and productively based on that knowledge. Counselors, teachers, politicians, and evangelists need this ability.

7. Finally, *intrapersonal intelligence* refers to a person's understanding of self, that is, one's own cognitive strengths and weaknesses, thinking styles, feelings, emotions—and intelligences. Further, it includes the ability use that knowledge in planning and carrying out activities. As one of Ramos-Ford and Gardner's (1991) examples, a child exemplifying high intrapersonal intelligence might remark, "Drawing is my favorite activity, even though I don't draw as well as I want to" (p. 58).

Implications for identifying and teaching gifted students are not mysterious: Gifted educators might look for strengths in each area as evidence of giftedness, and plan activities to help develop the abilities. Lazear (1991) outlined many activities to strengthen each type of intelligence (Table 1.2) As a final comment on the definition challenge,

TABLE 1.2 Ways to Strengthen Multiple Intelligences

Type of Intelligence	Teaching Suggestion
Linguistic	General Learning and Vocabulary
Logical-Mathematical	Inductive, Deductive, Scientific Reasoning
Spatial	Forming and Manipulating Mental Images, Spatial Relationships Exercises
Musical	Raising Awareness of Sounds, Tone Qualities, Musical Structures
Bodily-Kinesthetic	Movement Control Exercises
Interpersonal	Working in Groups, Raising Awareness of Nonverbal Communication
Intrapersonal	Raising Awareness of Feelings, Metacognition (Thinking about Thinking)

Adapted from Lazear (1991).

we repeat that (1) there is no one final and agreed-upon definition of "gifted" and "talented," (2) the specific definition that a program accepts will influence the identification instruments and procedures, and (3) for any given program those instruments and decision criteria will actually define who is gifted and talented, that is, who receives the special training and who does not.

SUMMARY

Despite increased public awareness of gifted education, many gifted students remain ignored in school. Critics claim that gifted programs are elitist.

We admire gifted people, but we also are committed to equality—a love-hate relationship. The public alternates between an interest in excellence and the desire for equity. The de-tracking movement stresses equity, at the expense of gifted students.

Gifted students, like students with disabilities, deserve an education consistent with their needs and abilities. Society benefits from helping gifted students become professionals.

Ancient Sparta defined giftedness in military terms. Athenian boys attended private schools and were taught by sophists. In Rome, boys and girls attended first-level schools, but higher education was for boys only.

Renaissance Europe rewarded its gifted artists, architects, and writers with wealth and honor.

China's seventh-century Tang dynasty brought child prodigies to the imperial court. They accepted a multiple-talent conception of giftedness, recognized that talents must be nurtured, and believed children should be educated according to their abilities.

Into the late 1800s, Japan provided high level education only for Samurai children. A few private academies accepted gifted children regardless of birth.

In early America, plantation children attended private schools; northern children needed ability and wealth to attend secondary school and college. From about 1870 to the depression years, some schools, especially in large cities, initiated tracking, grade-skipping, telescoping, and special classes.

Sir Francis Galton produced the first significant research and writing on intelligence. He believed that intelligence was related to keen senses, sharpened by natural selection, and so his "intelligence tests" evaluated sensory acuity and reaction time. His book *Hereditary Genius* argued for an hereditary basis of intelligence.

Alfred Binet in Paris developed the first successful intelligence test. He created the concept of mental age, the notion that a child may be intellectually ahead or behind his/her chronological age.

Lewis M. Terman Americanized the Binet tests, creating in 1916 the Stanford-Binet Intelligence Scale. In the 1920s, he identified over 1,500 high-intelligence children, who have been tracked and studied into the 1990s. Contradicting then-popular conceptions, the "Termites" were psychologically, socially, and physically healthier than average persons. He noted that acceleration is valuable, and that family values are crucial to adult success.

Leta Hollingworth recognized that gifted students waste time in regular classes. Over several decades prior to 1939, she developed G/T curriculum and counseling programs in the New York City area and authored two books on gifted children.

The launching of Sputnik in 1957 triggered an American effort to improve education, particularly in science and for gifted students. Enthusiasm faded after about five years.

In the mid 1970s, a new and continuing national and worldwide gifted education movement began, one that includes federal and state legislation, special funds, and high commitment by many educators.

Renzulli's National Research Center on the Gifted and Talented is a nationwide "consumer-oriented" effort related to key problems and practices, for example, identification, programming, and special populations. One study concluded that little is being done for gifted students in most classrooms.

The anti-tracking movement assumes that ability grouping practices are ineffective, unfair, and discriminatory. Not only fast-track classes but some gifted programs are being abandoned. Research indicates that achievement of slow- and middle-track students is no different in heterogeneous classes compared with ability-grouped classes; part-time cross-grade grouping and within-class grouping raise achievement for all students; self-esteem of low-ability students is lower in heterogeneous classes; and gifted students benefit tremendously from grouping with gifted peers for advanced work.

For the majority of students, cooperative learning produces improvements in achievement, motivation, cognitive growth, and social and communication skills. However, it prevents gifted students from engaging in more beneficial educational experiences.

Defining *gifted* and *talented* is important because one's definition influences the selection of students for G/T programs, and may prevent poor, minority, handicapped, underachieving, and female gifted students form participating.

There is no universally accepted definition of gifted and talented. The terms may be used interchangeably. Some see talent and gifted on a continuum, with gifted at upper end. Extraordinary students have been labeled "low-incidence" gifted or "severely" or "profoundly" gifted.

Cox avoids the term *gifted*, preferring *able learners*. Renzulli prefers the phrase *gifted behaviors*.

Some definitions are primarily operational, influencing the selection process. Others primarily clarify the nature of gifts and talents.

Stankowski's five categories include after-the-fact, IQ, percentage, talent, and creativity definitions.

The 1972 U.S.O.E. definition is cited in many state and district G/T plans. A multi-talent definition, it includes the six categories of (1) general intellectual ability, (2) specific academic aptitude, (3) creativity, (4) leadership, (5) visual and performing art ability, and (6) psychomotor skills. The statement recognizes the need for differentiated educational programs and cites the two basic goals of gifted education: helping capable students realize their potential and providing society with high-level talent. The 1978 and 1988 revisions excluded psychomotor skills.

Renzulli's three-ring model emphasizes above-average ability, high task commitment (motivation), and high creativity, which are characteristics of creatively productive adults.

Cohn's model differentiated three domains of general gifts (intellectual, artistic, social), each of which subdivide into specific talents.

Gagné argued that gifts should refer to abilities and talents to performances, implying that underachievers have gifts, but not talents.

Taylor's multiple-talent totem pole model raises the possibility that most students possess special gifts and talents, if we look carefully enough.

Gardner's seven intelligences include linguistic, logical-mathematical, spatial, musical, bodily-kinesthetic, interpersonal, and intrapersonal. His multiple-intelligence theory helps raise awareness that intelligence is more than a single IQ number.

CHAPTER 2

CHARACTERISTICS OF GIFTED STUDENTS

In order for a child to become truly gifted, five factors have to interweave most elegantly: (1) superior general intellect, (2) distinctive special aptitudes, (3) a supportive array of nonintellective traits, (4) a challenging and facilitative environment, and (5) the smile of good fortune at crucial periods of life.
Abraham J. Tannenbaum (1991, p. 29)

Gifted children differ from each other not only in size, shape, and color, but in cognitive and language abilities, interests, learning styles, motivation and energy levels, personalities, mental health and self-concepts, habits and behavior, background and experience, and any other mental, physical, or experiential characteristic that one cares to look for. They differ also in their patterns of educational needs.

Most of the descriptions that follow are "usual" characteristics, traits that have appeared and reappeared in studies of gifted children and adults. All traits will not and cannot apply to each and every gifted and talented child. For example, students who are extremely intellectually gifted often are more emotionally sensitive and have greater social problems that less gifted or average students (e.g., Dauber and Benbow, 1990; Piechowski, 1991).

This chapter will look at characteristics of Terman's gifted children mentioned in Chapter 1; Herbert Walberg's summary of characteristics of historically eminent men and high school students who have won art or science awards; and then turn to other mental and personal traits of intellectually and creatively gifted youth. Finally, we will examine lines of research by Benjamin Bloom and

David Feldman that outline the environmental and hereditary origins of extreme high talent and precocity, followed by a note on preferred characteristics of teachers of the gifted. Characteristics of gifted and talented minority, female, economically disadvantaged, underachieving students, and students with disabilities will be reviewed in later chapters.

THE TERMAN STUDIES

Our review of characteristics of gifted children must begin with Terman's 1,528 high-IQ children. One of the most frequently cited findings of the Terman studies was the fact that these students not only were better scholars, they were better adjusted psychologically and socially, and were even healthier than the average person. Now just a few decades before, Cesare Lombroso (1895), naming specific famous persons, claimed that "signs of degeneration in men of genius" included stuttering, short stature, general emaciation, sickly color, rickets (leading to club-footedness, lameness, or a hunched back), baldness, amnesia/forgetfulness, sterility, and that awful symptom of brain degeneration—left-handedness. Lombroso's proclamation was well known and widely accepted, no doubt because it made a lot of average people feel better about being average. Terman's scientific data trashed the myth that brilliant students are predominantly weak, unattractive, and emotionally unstable. They not only were well-adjusted in childhood, but in adulthood reported greater personal adjustment, emotional stability, self-esteem, professional success, and personal contentment (Terman and Oden, 1947, 1959; Sears, 1979). They showed a below-average incidence of suicide and mental illness.

Terman and Oden (1947) summarized the main characteristics of the gifted children as follows:

The average member of our group is a slightly better physical specimen than the average child . . .

For the fields of subject matter covered in our tests, the superiority of gifted over unselected children was greater in reading, language usage, arithmetical reasoning, science, literature and the arts. In arithmetical computation, spelling and factual information about history and civics, the superiority of the gifted was somewhat less marked . . .

The interests of gifted children are many-sided and spontaneous, they learn to read easily and read more and better books than the average child. At the same time, they make numerous collections, cultivate many kinds of hobbies, and acquire far more knowledge of plays and games than the average child . . .

As compared with unselected children, they are less inclined to boast or to overstate their knowledge; they are more trustworthy when under temptation to cheat; their character preferences and social attitudes are more wholesome, and they score higher in a test of emotional stability . . .

The deviation of the gifted subjects from the generality is in the upward direction for nearly all traits. There is no law of compensation whereby the intellectual superiority of the gifted tends to be offset by inferiorities along nonintellectual lines.

As a few health-related details, compared with other children, Terman's students weighed more at birth, learned to walk a month earlier, and learned to talk three and one-half months earlier. At the outset of the study in 1922 they were taller, heavier, and healthier—with better breathing capacity, superior nutritional status, fewer headaches, and less general weakness. A recent study of 842 adolescents who participated in a summer residential G/T program at Duke University confirmed that the general health of gifted students continues to be better than average (Goldstein, Stocking, and Sawyer, 1992). However, in both studies the relationship between giftedness and health is muddied by a third related factor of socioeconomic level.

Regarding character traits, Terman's girls generally achieved higher scores than boys in trustworthiness, emotional stability, and good social attitudes. However, the gifted boys were equally honest.

The superior mental and physical characteristics continued into adulthood. Said Terman (1954, p. 227), "So far, no one has developed post-adolescent stupidity!" Compared largely with U.S. Census data, as adults the gifted persons showed superior general health, a lower mortality rate, and a below-average incidence of criminal behavior, personality disorders, insanity, alcoholism, and divorce. Particularly, they were strong in emotional and social adjustment and in their desire to achieve. Success, said Terman, ". . . was associated with well-balanced temperament and with freedom from excessive frustration."

While high IQ was common to all, Terman's gifted persons differed among themselves in many ways; they were a heterogeneous group. One important difference was adult productivity. When they were children, the most productive adults had been rated by parents and teachers as higher in self-confidence, leadership, sensitivity to approval, perseverance, desire to excel, and "force of character." They rated themselves as higher in persistence, goal-directedness, and self-confidence.

As a caution, the descriptions of Terman's gifted children present them as near-perfect children. However, while they were uniformly intelligent, there was a serious bias in their selection. The 1,528 children were identified from a larger group of children who first were nominated by their teachers as "gifted." We know that teachers have higher expectations for and will identify as "gifted" those children who are pleasant, well-behaved, prompt, conforming, high-achieving, attractive, neat, and popular, and who wear expensive clothes and speak standard English (e.g., Good and Weinstein, 1986; Keneal, 1991; LeTendre, 1991). Perhaps it is not surprising that Terman could describe his students' physical and mental health in such glowing language. Generally, his conclusions would not necessarily apply, for example, to students who are artistically or creatively gifted, who are bright underachievers, or who are intelligent but rebellious.

It is significant that two Nobel Prize winners, Luis Alvarez and William B. Shockley, were excluded from the Terman study because their IQ scores were not sufficiently high (Hermann and Stanley, 1983).

WALBERG'S STUDIES OF HISTORICALLY EMINENT MEN AND HIGH SCHOOL ARTISTS AND SCIENTISTS

Walberg (1982, 1988; Walberg *et al.*, 1981; Walberg and Herbig, 1991) reviewed childhood traits of over 200 eminent men from artistic, scientific, religious, and political domains born between the 14th and 20th centuries. The following traits that were common to virtually all of these gifted persons:

- Versatility
- Concentration
- Perseverance
- Superior communication skills

- At least moderately high intelligence

In addition, the majority were rated as:

- Ethical
- Sensitive
- Optimistic
- Magnetic and popular

In childhood they were exposed to stimulating family, educational, and cultural conditions. About 80 percent were successful in school and liked it. About 90 percent were given considerable autonomy in their school years, although 70 percent also were guided by more clear parental expectations. Many showed outstanding early accomplishments.

Despite commonalities, Walberg and his colleagues found traits that were considerably different for different groups. For example, statesmen (e.g, Ben Franklin) were persuasive, popular, and economic-minded; religious leaders (e.g., Martin Luther) were scholarly, ethical, and sensitive; generals (e.g., Simon Bolivar) were tall and motivated by external incentives; historians and essayists (e.g., Jean Jacques Rousseau) were persevering, intelligent, and tended to have an absent father; poets and dramatists (e.g., Johann Wolfgang von Goethe) were neurotic, only children, and also fatherless; and scientists (e.g., Isaac Newton) were single-minded, opportunistic, and often had an absent mother.

Turning to Walberg's study of 771 high school students, he identified three groups: (1) students who won competitive awards in science, (2) students who won awards in the arts, and (3) average classmates. The scientist and artist groups showed a number of traits in common. According to self-reports, students in both groups:

- Visited libraries for nonschool reading; had greater numbers of books at home; enjoyed professional-technical books; found books more interesting that people.
- Had early strong interests in mechanical and scientific objects as well as the arts.

- Were more interested in work with fine detail.
- Were more persistent in carrying things through; reported they had "less time to relax."
- Liked school, studied hard, and completed their work faster than classmates.
- Felt more creative, imaginative, curious, and expressive than others; found satisfaction in expressing ideas in creative ways; believed it is important to be creative.
- *Selected creativity, rather than wealth and power, as the "best characteristic to develop in life."*
- Indicated they were brighter and quicker to understand than their friends.
- Attached greater importance to money and expected to earn higher salaries than the average; expected to earn graduate degrees.

The gifted scientists and artists differed in many respects. The scientists were more concerned with things and ideas rather than people and feelings; they avoided emotional closeness. For example, the science award winners reported more difficulty making friends after changing schools, and they did not date much. The scientists also were more persistent; they tended to complete work regardless of problems or distractions. They were more "bookish" and less involved in school activities. While the scientists valued their intelligence more highly than creativity, the artists valued their creativity more highly. The scientists made more detailed plans regarding their future education, and were more concerned about future job security. The artists leaned toward "letting fate take its course."

Walberg's two lines of research sketch important traits of intelligent and creatively productive eminent persons and contemporary youth. He was not the first, however, to study personal, family, and environmental traits of eminent persons. See Inset 2.1.

TRAITS OF INTELLECTUALLY GIFTED CHILDREN

Let's examine more closely what it means to be "intellectually gifted."

Precocious Language and Thought

The overriding trait—indeed, *the* definition—of very bright students is that they are developmentally advanced in language and thought. Their intelligence test performance matches that of older children. Their mental development, or *mental age* as Binet named it, simply outstrips both their chronological age and their physical development.

Piaget (Piaget and Inhelder, 1969) tells us that children will verbalize only what they can deal with conceptually. Therefore, the accelerated improvement in speech and language reflect not only a quickly growing vocabulary and knowledge base, but rapidly improving abstract thinking ability, including the abilities to think spatially, form complex concepts, solve problems, think metacognitively (think about thinking), understand others' reactions to them, and make or see relationships among disparate ideas (e.g., Benbow and Minor, 1990; Delisle, 1992; Moss, 1990; Van Tassel-Baska, 1988c).

Early Reading, Advanced Comprehension

Some gifted preschoolers not only talk and conceptualize at an advanced level, they may learn to read at age 4 or even 3 (e.g., Jackson, 1988). Some children teach themselves, and at a runaway pace. They might demand that mother or father point to each word in a book as the parent reads to the child; or the child may persistently ask, for example in a grocery store, "What does that say?" Other gifted preschoolers learn to read in a more traditional way, with mother, father, or the nursery-school teacher teaching the child to recognize letters, relate letters to sounds, recognize and pronounce words, and associate words with meanings. Whether they learn spontaneously or are taught by family members, what is most dramatic is the ease and swiftness with which they learn. Not all gifted children learn to read early or quickly—for example, Albert Einstein did not learn until he was 8—but many do.

The advanced language ability of the intellectually gifted child includes a superior comprehen-

Studies of Eminent Personalities: Cox and the Goertzels

Catherine Cox (1926), a colleague of Lewis Terman, took an approach to understanding traits of gifted persons that was quite the reverse of her famous cohort. Instead of beginning with bright children and tracking their accomplishments, she began by identifying 282 eminent persons, and then examined their biographical and personal records in order to reach conclusions regarding their intellectual and personal traits. The findings related to intelligence are most enlightening. Cox estimated their IQ scores to range from 100 to 200, with an average of 159. However, many estimated IQs were rather modest: Thirteen IQ scores fell between 100 and 110, 30 between 110 and 120, and 30 between 120 and 130. Extraordinary innate brilliance helped, but was not essential. Cox concluded that individuals who achieve eminence are likely to (1) be born of intelligent parents and raised in advantaged circumstances, (2) show precocious childhood traits and behavior that indicate unusually superior intelligence, and significantly (3) be ". . . characterized not only by high intellectual traits, but also by persistence of motive and effort, confidence in their abilities, and great strength and force of character."

In two studies, the Goertzels (Goertzel and Goertzel, 1962; Goertzel, Goertzel, and Goertzel, 1978) reviewed the family background and personal lives of some 700 adults who had achieved eminence via highly creative achievements that made a strong impact on society. A composite picture, based on recurrent traits and behavior, runs as follows:

The eminent man or woman is likely to be the firstborn or only child in a middle-class fam-

ily. . . . In these families there are rows of books on shelves, and parental expectations are high for all children . . .

Children who become eminent love learning but dislike school and school teachers who try to confine them to a curriculum not designed for individual needs. They respond well to being tutored or to being left alone, and they like to go to special schools such as those that train actors, dancers, musicians, and artists . . .

. . . they are more self-directed, less motivated in wanting to please than are their peers or siblings. They need and manage to find periods of isolation when they have freedom to think, to read, to write, to experiment, to paint, to play an instrument, or to explore the countryside. Sometimes this freedom can be obtained only by real or feigned illnesses; a sympathetic parent may respond to the child's need to have long free periods of concentrated effort . . .

They treasure their uniqueness and find it hard to be conforming, in dress, behavior, and other ways . . . (Goertzel, Goertzel, and Goertzel, 1978, pp. 336–38).

The Goertzel and Goertzel (1962) study revealed two consistent family characteristics across all talent areas. First, the parents of all 400 creative persons were highly energetic and goal-directed. (Although one mother was described as "somewhat lazy," her extremely high-energy husband was said to have more than compensated for her lacking.) Second, almost all of the families displayed an intense and intrinsic love for learning and achievement that was not simply attached to materialistic goals.

---

sion skill. Therefore, the intellectually gifted child usually acquires a large working vocabulary and a large store of information about many topics. The child may grasp complex and abstract concepts and relationships that normally are learned at an older age.

According to Bryant (1989) and Smith (1991), characteristics of children who read at an early age include: eagerness to learn; ability to work independently; advanced knowledge, thinking ability, and problem solving ability; inquisitiveness and questioning; competitiveness; perfectionism; good memory; long attention span; good judgment; ability to produce original ideas and products; and not surprisingly, a large vocabulary.

Logical Thinking

Compared with the average child, the thinking processes of the gifted child are quick and logical, two traits that can disturb impatient parents and teachers. Combined with a natural curiosity and an urge to learn, the precocious child can be forever asking questions, wanting to know, and wanting to know "Why?" The bear-trap logic may not accept an abrupt "Because!" or any other incomplete or illogical response. In light of their swift and logical thinking, it is no surprise that questioning ability, a good understanding of cause-and-effect relationships, convergent problem solving, persistence (Cox, 1926; Walberg *et al.*, 1981), and insight (Davidson, 1986; Davidson and Sternberg, 1984) are frequently cited as traits of gifted children.

Early Writing, Math, Music, Art

The intellectually gifted child also may begin writing at a precocious age. This talent will result from some combination of teaching by parents, older siblings, or preschool teachers, added to the child's strong drive and mental readiness to imitate and learn. For many gifted children, advanced mathematical, musical, and artistic abilities also appear early, paralleling the verbal and conceptual skills.

The mathematically precocious child may be counting by fives and tens and adding and subtracting two-digit numbers by kindergarten. If you ask the child how he or she arrived at an answer, the child may explain with surprisingly good reasoning his or her own special way of deducing or calculating a mathematical solution. For example, one such second-grade child concluded that "There certainly must be numbers below zero because temperatures can go below zero."

Incidentally, it is not unusual for the child's

slower-developing motor ability to stand in the way of some accomplishments. For example, while some young gifted children may be able to manipulate complex calculations and ideas in their heads, or even read at a fifth-grade level, they may not be able to write numbers or letters or illustrate their ideas because of immature eye-hand coordination.

Motivation, Persistence, Advanced Interests

One of the single most recurrent traits of productive gifted students and eminent adults is high motivation and persistence (e.g., Bryant, 1989; Dunn and Griggs, 1985; Franks and Dolan, 1982; Renzulli and Reis, 1991b; Walberg and Herbig, 1991). One main reason that some of Terman's students became successful and some did not was differences in their levels of motivation, due in large part to family values (Terman and Oden, 1959). Albert (1975) stressed that a crucial trait of the geniuses he studied—eminent scientists, musicians, artists, and psychologists—was the compulsion to be productive, the ability to work hard. Even with gifted nursery-school to second-grade children, Burk (1980) found that persistence was related to both achievement and personal adjustment.

Galton (1869) himself, in his book *Hereditary Genius*, noted that natural ability included both "... qualities of intellect and disposition, which urge and qualify a man to perform acts that lead to reputation. I do not mean capacity without zeal, nor zeal without capacity, nor even a combination of both of them, without an adequate power of doing a great deal of very laborious work."

The high motivation and urge to learn found in many gifted children, combined with their curiosity and their advanced comprehension and logical abilities, frequently lead to surprisingly advanced interests. The nature and complexity of topics and projects tackled by enthusiastic gifted children seems unlimited. One group of gifted elementary students in Manitowish Waters, Wisconsin, conducted an environmental impact study that led the

State Highway Department to move a section of a proposed freeway.

AFFECTIVE CHARACTERISTICS

Social Skills, Personal Adjustment, Self-Concepts

We noted earlier that, on average, Terman's students generally were well-adjusted both personally and socially. They were more emotionally stable and less neurotic than his unselected children. With a noteworthy qualification, Terman's contemporary Leta Hollingworth (1942) mentioned that moderately gifted students (IQ scores between 120 and 145) do indeed adjust well socially, but students above this level cannot relate well to agemates. They are too different. She recommended that counseling, or "emotional education," be part of the gifted program.

As a general rule, gifted students are as well or better adjusted than regular students, and have better self-concepts (e.g., Chapman and McAlpine, 1988; Dauber and Benbow, 1990; Feldhusen, 1989; Janos *et al.*, 1988; Grossberg and Cornell, 1988; Olszewski-Kubilius, Kulieke, and Krasney, 1988). Milgram and Milgram (1976a) noted that "Intellectual giftedness is an asset in coping with life's challenges and is associated with . . . favorable social and personal adjustment."

However, research on self-concepts of gifted children and adolescents has produced contradictory results, complicated by age differences, gender differences, level of giftedness, or which "self" the researcher is looking at ("academic self" or "social self"). For example, Colangelo and Kelly (1983) compared scores on the *Tennessee Self-Concept Scale* of gifted students, regular students, and students with learning problems in grades 7, 8, and 9. For the overall scale, gifted students scored significantly higher than regular students, who in turn scored higher than students with learning problems. However, on closer examination the gifted students scored significantly higher only on the *academic self* subscale; on the

social self subscale the gifted students scored about the same as the other students.

Regarding the effects of gender, Kelly and Colangelo (1984) found that gifted adolescent boys had better overall self-concepts than non-gifted boys, but there were no differences in self-concepts between gifted and nongifted adolescent girls. With upper elementary students (grades 4, 5, and 6) Loeb and Jay (1987) found the reverse: Gifted girls had a more positive self-concept and higher internal locus of control than nongifted girls. Their high classroom success was congruent with ". . . a positive sense of self and feelings of control over their life space." However, there were no differences between gifted and nongifted boys in self-concept or locus of control. Explained Loeb and Jay, the intellectual orientation of gifted upper elementary boys is disturbingly inconsistent with their ideal male image of aggressiveness, self-reliance, and individualism, leading naturally to lowered self-esteem. They suggested defeminizing the elementary school with more male teachers, more tolerance for independent thought and behavior, more traditionally masculine subjects (for example, mechanics, outer space), and a new definition of the "masculine ideal" that includes academic striving and excellence (Loeb and Jay, 1987).

In high school there seems to be a reversal of attitudes, with high school norms supporting a masculine achievement style, thus producing a positive self-image. The high school female, however, may experience conflict over her role as a gifted, aggressive achiever versus her emerging identity as a woman, and her self-concept suffers (Loeb and Jay, 1987; Rodenstein, Pfleger, and Colangelo, 1977).

One affective problem peculiar to extremely bright students is their emotional excitability and high sensitivity, which we will describe more fully in Chapter 17. For example, due to high energy they tend to talk rapidly and compulsively, and may become workaholics. They have sprightly imaginations and sensual experiences that are "more alive." Their emotional reactions are more intensely joyful, but also more fearful and depressed. They develop steadfast values, with strong concerns for right and wrong (Piechowski, 1991).

As with any other population, some gifted and talented students—partly because of their gifts—will have upsetting social problems and some will be anxious and depressed (e.g., Gallucci, 1988). The general tendency for healthy adjustment must not blind educators to frequent turbulent problems and strong needs for counseling (Chapter 17).

Independence, Self-Confidence, Internal Control

An important set of personality characteristics of the gifted child relates to his or her typically high level of self-confidence and independence. Such as attitude is a natural outgrowth of years of favorable comparisons with less able peers; of glowing feedback and evaluations from parents, teachers, peers, and siblings; and from the child's clear history of success in school.

The concept of high *internal control* describes the confident children or adolescents who feel responsible for their successes and failures and who feel in control of their destinies (Milgram and Milgram, 1976a; Tidwell, 1980). The child with high internal control is likely to use errors and failures constructively; he or she learns from mistakes. Importantly, the internally controlled child usually attributes failure to lack of effort, not lack of ability, and so a failure is a momentary setback that motivates the student to "try harder next time." In contrast, the externally controlled child is more likely to attribute success or failure to luck, chance, easy or difficult tasks, generous or unfair teachers, lack of sleep, a sick cat, and so on. The "external" child also is less likely to try harder after failure—since he or she does not accept responsibility for the outcome in the first place.

Their generally higher levels of internal control and personal responsibility often lead gifted students to set high goals for themselves. When these goals are not met, the natural outcome is disappointment, frustration, and feelings of incompetence, ineptness, or stupidity. Parents and teachers are frequently mystified by displays of frustration and self-criticism by students who are obviously extraordinarily capable and talented. The frustration occurs not because the students are comparing their own performances with those of others, but with their own high expectations and perfectionism.[1]

Learning Styles

In view of the high motivation, persistence, self-confidence, independence, and high internal control of many gifted students, it is not surprising to discover that their preferred learning styles match these characteristics. In a summary statement, Griggs and Dunn (1984; see also Dunn, Bruno, and Gardiner, 1984; Dunn and Dunn, 1987; Dunn and Griggs, 1985, 1988) concluded that, compared with nongifted students, gifted students tend to be independent self-motivated learners more than teacher-motivated. They need and enjoy learning tasks that are unstructured and flexible, rather than the highly structured tasks needed by less able students. They prefer active participant approaches to learning, rather than spectator approaches; and they have "well-integrated perceptual strengths," meaning that they can learn through varied sensory channels, including auditory, visual, tactile, and kinesthetic. Further, they generally are more responsible, prefer a quiet learning environment, and they prefer to learn alone or with "true peers"—other gifted students—rather than with regular students (Dunn and Griggs, 1985).

Ricca (1984) compared differences between gifted and regular upper-elementary students in preferred learning conditions and activities as measured by the Dunn, Dunn, and Price (1981) *Learning Styles Inventory* and the Renzulli and Smith (1978b) *Learning Styles Inventory* (see below). For both gifted and regular students, the first choice in learning activities was teaching games

---

[1]The problem of perfectionism will be discussed in Chapter 17.

and the last choice was drill and recitation. No surprise here. Between these extremes, the gifted students preferred independent study more than did the regular students, while the regular students preferred peer teaching and lecture more than did the gifted. Gifted students also preferred tactile learning, instead of visual learning, and high mobility—they wanted to get into a topic actively and physically. Further, said Ricca, preferences for flexibility and independence reflect the strong needs of gifted students for opportunities for self-determination and self-selection of learning experiences.

Griggs and Dunn (1984) and Griggs (1984) make two important points. First, within the gifted group there are large individual differences in preferred learning conditions and activities, and educators should be aware of each youngster's preferred style. Second, there are significant improvements in academic achievement, school attitudes, and behavior when students' learning styles preferences are accommodated.

The two apparently most well-developed and widely used instruments for assessing learning styles are the Dunn, Dunn, and Price (1981; Dunn and Dunn, 1978, 1987) *Learning Styles Inventory* (LSI) and the Renzulli and Smith (1978b) *Learning Styles Inventory* (also LSI). The Dunn, Dunn, and Price LSI assesses learning preferences in these areas: *environmental* (light, sound, temperature, design), *emotional* (motivation, persistence, responsibility, need for structure or options), *sociological* (self, peer, team, adult, varied), *physical* (time of day, need for intake, mobility, etc.), and *psychological* (global/analytical, left/right, impulsive/reflective). The Renzulli and Smith LSI evaluates, in the order of gifted students' choices found by Ricca (1984), preferences for: teaching games, independent study, programmed instruction, projects, simulation, peer teaching, discussion, lecture, and drill and recitation.

Superior Humor

The superior sense of humor of most gifted children would seem to follow quite naturally from their abilities to think quickly and see relationships, and from their general confidence and social adeptness. The humor will appear in art, creative writing, and other areas as well as in social interaction.

High Moral Thinking and Empathy

As with language ability, moral development also is tied to intellectual development (Diessner, 1983). As a general trend, gifted students are more sensitive to values and moral issues and they intuitively understand why certain behavior is "good" and other behavior is "bad." Piaget and Inhelder (1969) explain that developmentally advanced children are less egocentric; that is, they are able to view a situation from another person's point of view. Therefore, gifted students are more likely to acknowledge the rights of others and to be sensitive to the feelings and expectations of others. Bright students are less likely to steal from peers or to be abusive, and they are more likely to be fair and to empathize and sympathize with the feelings and problems of others.

Gifted children and youth are likely to develop, refine, and internalize a system of values and a keen sense of fair play and justice at a relatively early age. This internalized value system leads to consistency in behavior and attitudes (Perrone, Karshner, and Male, 1979). The child not only is likely to be more fair, empathetic, and honest, he or she will evaluate others according to the same standards. It follows that gifted students are less likely to show behavior problems in school (e.g., Ludwig and Cullinan, 1984).

Gifted students, especially the brightest ones, may develop an interest in social issues, particularly those in which his or her sense of reason and justice seems to be violated. Teachers or parents may find themselves embroiled in serious discussions with gifted children about why adults litter streets and highways with beer cans and burger wrappers, why politicians cut benefits and programs for the elderly and poor, and why parents voted against enlarging the crowded school building. Hollingworth (1942, p. 281) described a 6-year-old boy of 187 IQ who "wept bitterly after reading how the North taxed the South after the Civil War."

Hollingworth also described one not-so-moral tendency. She noted that most of her very bright students engaged in "benign chicanery." That is, the children used their intelligence to get their own way with less intelligent peers or to avoid disagreeable academic or other tasks. Because such talent could be helpful in the adult world, Hollingworth helped them to be aware of when they were taking advantage of their ability (Delisle, 1992).

Be cautioned: Despite their high mental ability and high capacity for moral thought, "benign chicanery" may progress to delinquency and crime, where the talents of bright and clever students are quickly rewarded (money, status) by an antisocial peer group (e.g., Parker, 1979).

CHARACTERISTICS OF THE CREATIVELY GIFTED

Creativity and Intelligence: The Threshold Concept

The student who is highly intelligent may or may not be creatively gifted as well. The relationship between creativity and intelligence is a long-standing issue. On one hand, creativity and intelligence are recognized as separate capabilities. For example, landmark research by Getzels and Jackson (1962) and Wallach and Kogan (1965) contrasted highly intelligent versus highly creative students, confirming that the two traits are indeed *not* the same. Of interest to teachers, Getzels and Jackson reported that highly creative and highly intelligent students did equally well in course work—but teachers preferred the highly intelligent students!

Our review of personality characteristics of the creatively gifted should convince you that they differ dramatically from the intellectually gifted.

On the other hand, there is good evidence that creativity and intelligence are related. For example,

Walberg's (e.g., Walberg and Herbig, 1991) review of eminent men led him to conclude that "There is no doubt that IQ and [creative] eminence are linked." Regarding his study of creative high school artists and scientists who won competitive awards, he remarked that "They indicated they were brighter than their friends and quicker to understand."

The increasingly accepted resolution to this apparent inconsistency—creativity *is not* versus *is* related to intelligence—lies in the *threshold* concept: A base level of intelligence is essential for creative productivity; above that *threshold*, however, there is virtually no relationship between measured intelligence and creativity (MacKinnon, 1978). For example, Walberg (Walberg and Herbig, 1991) agreed that outstanding performance requires a base level of moderately superior intelligence, but that "The brightest . . . are not necessarily the best," and that higher levels of intelligence are less important than other psychological traits and conditions. Particularly, as we will see, creative persons must be independent and confident, motivated and energetic, and dare to make changes, challenge traditions, make waves, bend rules, and sometimes fail in the process.

One important implication of distinguishing between intellectual and creative giftedness is that if students are selected for a gifted program based upon scores in the top 1 to 5 percent in intelligence, the large majority of creative students will be missed. Another implication is that when asked to identify "gifted" students, as we noted earlier in this chapter, many teachers will quickly nominate the well-behaved, conforming, neat, and dutiful "teacher pleasers," rather than less conforming students who are highly creative and more unconventional. Also, in many classes (for example, math or science in the middle school), the special talents of the creatively gifted may not be required. Creative students therefore will be less visible, and less likely to be nominated as "gifted" than intellectually gifted students who more quickly grasp complex concepts.

Ultimately, the achievements and contributions to society of many highly creative students will surpass those of brighter, conforming grade-getters (e.g., Renzulli, 1986; Renzulli and Reis, 1991b).

Personality Traits

There is a recurrent group of personality traits that appear again and again in studies of the creative personality (e.g., Barron, 1969, 1978, 1988; Mac-Kinnon, 1962, 1975, 1978; Perkins, 1988; Simonton, 1988; Sternberg, 1988; Tardif and Sternberg, 1988; Torrance, 1981a, 1984, 1987, 1988; Walberg and Herbig, 1991). Of course, not all of the following characteristics will apply to all creative people. There simply are too many forms of creativity and creative people to make such a generalization. Most of the traits are not surprising; they square well with our intuitive understanding of a creative person.

Creativity consciousness. Creative people—at least from adolescence onward when the word "creative" becomes meaningful—are consciously aware of their creativeness. They are in the habit of doing things creatively and they like being creative. If asked, they will modestly admit that, yes indeed, they probably are more creative than the average person.

Confidence, risk-taking. The creative person also is high in self-confidence and independence and is more willing to take a creative risk. These are essential traits. The innovative person must dare to differ, make changes, stand out, challenge traditions, make waves, bend rules—and make mistakes and fail. The importance of risk-taking and its built-in likelihood of failure are reflected in a statement by Thomas J. Watson, founder and president of IBM: "The way to succeed is to double your failure rate." Interestingly, Treffinger (1983) contended that creative people may not be great risk-takers. He argued that their innovative plans and zany products are so carefully organized and thought out, with possible problems, implica-tions, and contingency plans already taken into account, that the chances of failure are much smaller than they appear to be.

High energy, adventurousness. Creative people typically have a very high energy level—a certain enthusiastic zest and a habit of spontaneous action. The creative person often becomes totally immersed in his or her ideas and creations, literally unable to rest until the work is complete. Amabile (1986) called it a "labor of love;" Torrance (1987, 1988) used the even stronger phrase "blazing drive."

Curiosity. The creative person has strong curiosity, a childlike sense of wonder and intrigue. He or she may have a history of taking things apart to see how they work or exploring attics, libraries, or museums, or a generally strong urge to understand the world about him or her. The curiosity frequently produces wide interests and unusual hobbies and collections.

Humor, playfulness. As in the description of the intellectually gifted, an especially frequent trait of creative students is a good sense of humor. Humor is first cousin to the ability to take a fresh, childlike, and playful approach to problems. Many discoveries, inventions, and artistic creations are the result of "fooling around" with ideas and playing with possibilities, unconstrained by well-learned habits, traditions, and conformity pressures. Both Carl Rogers and Sigmund Freud agreed that regression to a more childlike, fanciful, playful state of mind is an important feature of creative thinkers. A favorite quote is that "The creative adult is essentially a perpetual child, the tragedy is that most of us grow up" (Fabun, 1968).

Idealism and reflectiveness. More serious traits of idealism and reflectiveness also are common. The creative person, more than the average, may ponder his role and goals in life. Their idealism and individuality may surface in antiestablishment cynicism or in dropping out of high school or college.

Alone time.   Related to reflectiveness is the common need for some privacy and alone time. The urge to create demands some time for thinking, for reflection, for solving problems, for creating.

Artistic and aesthetic interests.   Creative students usually will rate themselves high in being artistic—whether they can draw or not—and will be more conscious of artistic considerations. A considerable interest in art galleries, plays, concerts, and theatre is common.

Attraction to the novel, complex, and mysterious. Another creative trait is the characteristic preference for complexity and attraction to the mysterious. For example, Barron (1969, 1978) found that creative individuals, similar to good artists, preferred drawings on the *Barron-Welsh Art Scale* (Welsh and Barron, 1963) that are smudgy, complex, asymmetrical, and imbalanced. Noted Martindale (1975), "Confronted with novelty, whether in design, music, or ideas, creative people get excited and involved while less creative people turn suspicious or even hostile."

There also is an interesting tendency for the creative person to be a strong believer in such mysterious matters as spirits, extrasensory perception, mental telepathy, precognition, flying saucers, and other psychic and mystical happenings (Davis, Peterson, and Farley, 1973).

Tolerance for ambiguity.   By its nature, creative problem solving involves considerable ambiguity (e.g., Sternberg, 1988; MacKinnon, 1978). Ideas are incomplete and ambiguous, relevant facts are missing, rules are unclear, and "correct" procedures are unavailable. Whether writing a novel, creating a work of art, or solving an engineering problem, the ideas will evolve from the original insight through a series of modifications, approximations, and improvements—which requires coping with uncertainty and ambiguity (Davis, 1992a). Said Sternberg (1988, p. 143), "To be creative, one must be willing and able to tolerate at least some ambiguity in order fully to manifest one's creativity."

Reflectiveness versus impulsiveness.   The authors' own research suggests that the characteristic of impulsiveness versus reflectiveness (Kagan, 1965) shows an interesting developmental change. Creative elementary school children tend to be more reflective in their thinking; they are more careful and meticulous in their work and decisions. However, somewhere in adolescence there frequently is a transformation to impulsiveness—the confident and adventurous spontaneity of the creative adult appears.

Perceptiveness and intuitiveness.   Creative people tend to be more perceptive, to see relationships, to make "mental leaps." Tardif and Sternberg (1988) described this trait as an "aesthetic ability" that comes into play in defining and solving problems.

Other traits and some negative traits.   Torrance (1981b) itemized additional traits that might help the teacher or parent recognize and understand creative students:

Likes to work by himself/herself
Is a "What if?" person
Sees relationships
Is full of ideas
Imaginative, enjoys pretending
High verbal, conversational fluency
Flexibility of ideas and thoughts
Persistent, persevering, unwilling to give up
Constructs, builds, rebuilds
Copes with several ideas at once
Irritated and bored by the routine and obvious
Goes beyond assigned tasks
Experiments with familiar objects to see if they will become something other than what they were intended to be
Enjoys telling about his/her discoveries or inventions
Finds ways of doing things differently from standard procedures

Is not afraid to try something new

Does not mind consequences of appearing different

So far, the creative personality looks pretty good. However, creative children, adolescents, and adults may show some habits and dispositions that will upset normal parents, teachers, or administrators, and other students and colleagues as well. Torrance (1962, 1981b) and Smith (1966) suggested the items below as not-uncommon characteristics of creative students. Most of these "negative traits" are related to creative students' confidence, independence, curiosity, interest in novelty, humor, and persistence. Some traits are likely to cause personal or social adjustment problems.

Indifference to common conventions and courtesies

Stubbornness

Resistance to domination

Arguments that the rest of the parade is out of step

Nonparticipation in class activities

Uncooperativeness

Capriciousness

Cynicism

Low interest in details

Sloppiness and disorganization with unimportant matters

Tendency to question laws, rules, authority in general

Egocentrism

Temperamental

Demanding

Emotional

Withdrawn

Overactive physically or mentally

Forgetfulness, absentmindedness, mind wanders

Sometimes uncommunicative

Watches windows

Won't join scouts

When stubborn Sammy or independent Elissa shows some of these upsetting characteristics, the teacher or parent might consider the possibility that the symptoms are part of a larger picture of original, energetic creativeness that may need rechanneling into constructive outlets.

True creativity is the product not only of personality traits that predispose a person to think creatively, but a constellation of creative abilities as well. Important creative abilities and ideas for strengthening them will be described in Chapters 10 and 11.

Biographical Characteristics

Biographical traits may be of two sorts: subtle and not-so-subtle. Not-so-subtle factors are simply the student's history of creative activities. Creative students and adults will have a background of creative accomplishments, such as having built things, hobbies and collections, art and handicraft projects, writing, composing, theatrical performances, scientific inventions, and so on. Such biographical facts are not highly surprising; however, they are very useful in identifying creative students.

Other biographical trends are more subtle. Schaefer (1969) discovered that creative high school students were more likely to have friends younger or older than themselves rather than the same age, and they were less interested in sports. They had lived in more than one state, and had traveled outside the US. High school girls who were good at creative writing were more likely to own a cat.

Schaefer, confirmed in studies reviewed by Somers and Yawkey (1984), also found that creative students more often had an imaginary childhood playmate. Said Somers and Yawkey, imaginary companions contribute to creativity by developing originality and elaboration and by fostering sensitivity in relationships.

According to Davis (1992a, 1993), two biographical traits are especially accurate as predictors of creativeness: having had an imaginary playmate and/or participation in theatre activities.

ORIGINS OF HIGH TALENT AND EXTREME PRECOCITY

Heredity and environment, working together in some favorable combination, are obvious explanations for the origin of high talent. But this kind of glib answer, though accurate, tells us little. Recently, two scholars sketched in some detail just how heredity and environment, especially the latter, guide the development of extremely high levels of gifts and talents.

Parental Support and Intense Individualized Instruction: Bloom

Benjamin Bloom (1985; Bloom and Sosniak, 1981) examined the home environment and the early training of exceptional, accomplished pianists, sculptors, swimmers, tennis players, mathematicians, and research neurologists whose talents roughly represented artistic, motoric, and cognitive skill areas. Bloom discovered that the home environments and the gifted persons' parents were almost entirely responsible for nurturing the children's early interests and developing their skills to extraordinary levels.

Almost always, one or both parents had a strong interest in the particular talent and were themselves above average in the skill. In every case the parents strongly supported the children, encouraging and rewarding their interests, talents, and efforts. Importantly, the talented parent or parents served as role models, exemplifying the personality and lifestyle of the highly talented person. In essence, the children could not resist exploring and participating in the particular talent area; it was expected and accepted as proper.

Initially, parents themselves provided the necessary training and supervision of practice. However, at some point each child switched to a professional instructor. In many cases parent support was so strong that the family would uproot and move to another location to be closer to an outstanding teacher or better facilities. Often, the single outstanding student would be the central concern of the devoted instructor. During this time the student's dedication to the talent area would grow very strong—which explains his or her willingness to spend approximately fifteen hours per week in lessons and practice.

Importantly, these students who eventually achieved extremely high levels of proficiency learned to handle failures constructively. That is, failures were learning experiences used to pinpoint problems to be solved and new skills to be mastered. In contrast, according to Bloom, among "talent dropouts" failures led to feelings of inadequacy and quitting.

Bloom contrasted the development of talent with traditional educational philosophy and methods. The four-point comparison is instructive. First, in the early years of home instruction, talent development is informal, exploratory, and similar to play; the school setting is traditionally serious, formal, and on a set schedule. Second (and most important), with talent development instruction is totally individualized, with praise and rewards based completely on individualized objectives and standards. School learning, of course, is group oriented, usually with a minimum of individualized attention, and rewards, at least to some extent, are based on group achievements. Third, the purpose of school is to provide all students with a broad basic education. Students are expected to do well in all areas and overly strong specialization is not encouraged. In talent development, the student and his or her teacher are fully mobilized toward moving the learner to higher and higher levels of accomplishment in just one specialized area. Fourth, for many students school learning is seen as devoid of meaning, something "to be suffered through." On the other hand, the purposes and meaning in talent development are quite clear, which inspires the necessary dedication and hard work.

Precocity, Available Knowledge, and Coincidence: Feldman

David Feldman (1986a; 1986b; Feldman and Goldsmith, 1986; Morelock and Feldman, 1991) reviewed the precocious talents and early achievements of such rare individuals as chess player Bobby Fisher, who became a grand master by age 15, and Wolfgang Amadeus Mozart, who composed mature works by age 10. Feldman also has been studying a group of six prodigies since 1975—two chess players, a young mathematician, a musician-composer, a writer, and an "omnibus prodigy who showed prodigious achievement in a number of areas, but who eventually began to focus on music composition and performance . . . [and whose] . . . IQ exceeded the measurement capabilities of available instruments" (Morelock and Feldman, 1991, pp. 353, 354). All six were performing in their chosen field at the level of an adult professional before the age of 10.

Feldman attributed such amazing youthful accomplishment to a coincidence of *individual, environmental,* and *historical* forces, which he dubbed the *Co-Incidence Theory* (Morelock and Feldman, 1991). The *individual* component of this co-incidence is the rare prodigies themselves, whom Feldman described as highly intelligent, developmentally advanced, and remarkably "pre-organized." A biological propensity toward giftedness in a certain area is needed, as is family support. Physical, social, and emotional development factors, such as manual dexterity and peer influence, determine a prodigy's receptiveness to, for example, violin playing or math.

Environmental factors include the existence of a highly evolved field of knowledge that can be taught to the precocious child. Sophisticated literatures and instruction are available in math, chess, and music, as are child-size violins. *Historical* factors, such as the value society attaches to a domain, affect opportunities for learning. In past years, for example, Russia was more likely to support a gifted chess player than was the United States.

Feldman noted that Bobby Fisher taught himself to play a fair game of chess by age 6, and from that time on he read hundreds of chess books. As with Bloom's talented people, he received intense formal instruction. Mozart too, while clearly a gifted and precocious child, grew up in a home where music was composed, played, continuously discussed, and valued. Mozart thus received considerable personal instruction, based on an existing body of knowledge, plus extensive exposure to the values and lifestyles of musicians.

Based on biographies of prodigies and observations of his six precocious persons, Morelock and Feldman (1991) itemized conclusions regarding the prodigies and their teachers, most of which duplicate Bloom's main results:

- The children possessed extraordinary native ability.
- The children were born into families that recognized, valued, and fostered that ability.
- The children received instruction from master teachers who possessed superior knowledge of a domain and its history, and who imparted that knowledge in ways that engaged interested and sustained commitment.
- The children showed strong inner-directedness and a passionate commitment to their field; they derived a strong sense of joy from their achievements.

Morelock and Feldman (1991) described another type of genius that teachers of the gifted will never encounter—*idiot savants,* persons with severe retardation who demonstrate mind-boggling gifts in limited areas (Inset 2.2).

CHARACTERISTICS OF TEACHERS OF THE GIFTED

Before we leave the topic of characteristics, Inset 2.3 summarizes personal characteristics and teaching habits that make for a good teacher of the gifted.

SUMMARY

Identifying characteristics of gifted students is important because it helps teachers and parents recognize and understand gifted children. Even though all children differ in physical, intellectual, affective, and behavioral traits, some characteristics of gifted and talented students recur frequently in the research literature.

INSET 2.2 _____

The Strange Case of Idiot Savants

Idiot savants present a fascinating, baffling, and seemingly impossible phenomena. These are persons with severe mental disabilities (retardation, autism, or schizophrenia) who display spectacular islands of ability in narrow areas. Savant brilliance occurs in art and mechanical ability, but the highest levels are almost always found in mathematics ("lightning calculating"), music (consistently piano), and memory (Morelock and Feldman, 1991; see also Feldman, 1986; Treffert, 1989).

The term *idiot savant* was coined in 1887 by J. Langdon Down of London. However, they are neither "idiots" nor "savants." While *idiocy* used to be defined as IQ scores between 0 and 20, idiot savants typically score between 40 and 70 (Treffert, 1989). Further, *savant* is the French word for "person of learning"—hardly the correct description of these unique people. The phenomena is six times more common in males than females; it can be congenital or acquired by a normal person after an accident; and the skills can appear and disappear in sudden and unexplained ways (Treffert, 1989).

While idiot savants have an immediate and intuitive access to the underlying structural rules of a domain, they are restricted by those rules—they are not flexible and creative. For example, musical performances are said to be imitative, shallow, and lacking in subtlety and emotional expressiveness.

George and Charles were identical twin "calendar calculators." At the age of nine they could answer questions like "On what day of the week was your third birthday?" or "In the year 31,275, on what day of the week will June 6th fall?" Given a date, these twins could name the day of the week over a span of 80,000 years, 40,000 forward or 40,000 backward. They swapped 20-digit prime numbers for amusement; they could easily factor the number 111; and they could remember up to 30 digits. Incredibly, they could neither add nor count to 30; their tested IQ scores were between 40 and 50.*

Leslie Lemke was blind almost from birth, palsied, and mentally handicapped. At age 5½ he could repeat verbatim a whole day's conversation while impersonating each speaker's voice. He is most famous for his musical precocity; in fact, he gives concerts. He was introduced to the piano at the age of seven, and began playing by ear. By age eight he also played the ukelele, the concertina, the xylophone, the accordion, and the bongo drums, and at age nine the chord organ. He required help in dressing and feeding himself, however.

The "miracle" of Leslie began at age 14, when at 3:00 in the morning his parents heard him playing Tchaikovsky's Piano Concerto No. 1, the theme song in a movie they had seen earlier and which Leslie had heard only once (Treffert, 1989). After hearing a 45-minute opera once, Leslie can transpose the music to the piano and sing the entire score in its original foreign language. He seems never to forget his music; his repertoire includes thousands of pieces.

Perhaps the most credible explanation of idiot savants is that of Treffert (1989), who suggested simply that injury to the left hemisphere of the brain (language and analytic thought) produces compensatory growth in the right hemisphere (music and spatial/mathematical abilities). Further, injury to the cerebral cortex causes memory functions to shift to more primitive brain areas, causing memory to become habitual, emotionless, and involuntary—essentially a conditioned reflex. Treffert concedes, however, that such extreme alterations in brain function cannot explain the savants' seemingly intuitive access to the structural rules of domains such as mathematics or music.

*For further information on George and Charles and other fascinating cases, see D. J. Hamblin's *Life Magazine* article, March 18, 1966, pp. 106–108.

INSET 2.3 _____

Preferred Characteristics of Teachers of the Gifted

The following desirable characteristics of teachers who work with gifted and talented students have been collated from several sources (e.g., Lindsy, 1980). Note that some of these intuitively sensible traits are personal/social characteristics, others are teaching and work habits—and virtually all would be noble traits of every effective teacher. Teachers of the gifted should:

- Be able to conceptualize, develop, and carry out programs for the gifted that are flexible, meaningful, and adaptable to individual needs.
- Create a warm, safe, accepting, and democratic (not autocratic) environment.
- Respect personal self-images and reinforce positive ones.
- Respect individuality and personal integrity.
- Respect creativity and imagination.
- Have skill in leading young people to successful accomplishments.
- Guide rather than coerce.
- Focus on process as well as product.
- Be innovative and experimental rather than conforming.
- Seek new solutions through continued learning.
- Be able to work closely with other members of the gifted staff.
- Be able to communicate to others the needs of gifted children.
- Be knowledgeable about a wide range of topics.
- Establish a comfortable working relationship with students, parents, and other professionals.
- Be at ease in new and unknown settings.
- Have control over one's personal life.
- Be able to convince a variety of people about the appropriateness of the program.
- It is highly desirable for teachers of the gifted to be gifted persons themselves.

Terman's gifted children were better adjusted as children and adults. Compared with other children, they were better achievers and learned more easily, had more hobbies, read more books, were more trustworthy, healthier, and even better "physical specimens." The traits continued into adulthood. The most productive of the group were rated as high in confidence, leadership, goal-directedness, and desire to excel. The selection of Terman's group was biased due to the initial nomination by teachers prior to testing.

Walberg's study of eminent persons indicated that virtually all possessed versatility, perseverance, superior communication skills, high ethics, personal magnetism, a stimulating early environment, and at least moderately high intelligence.

His high school art and science award winners showed confidence, early interests in art and science, much non-school reading, persistence, and a liking for school. Unlike his artists, Walberg's scientists valued intelligence more than creativity.

Bright children are developmentally advanced in language and thought. Early, rapidly improving speech reflects a growing conceptual ability and knowledge base. They may learn to read early, sometimes teaching themselves. Comprehension, retention, vocabulary, stored information, and logical abilities are also usually superior.

Writing, math, music, and artistic abilities appear early.

Motivation and persistence are common, and are important for later adult success. Gifted students' high motivation and curiosity lead to advanced interests.

Gifted students frequently show superior affective characteristics, such as lower anxiety and depression and better self-concepts. However, some G/T children will suffer from social inadequacies, anxieties, and depression. Students with IQ scores above 145 may have special difficulty relating to peers, said Hollingworth. Very bright students also be highly excitable and sensitive.

Research on gender differences in self-concepts has produced inconsistent results. Self-concepts of elementary age boys may be improved by "defeminizing" the elementary school.

The gifted student's history of success usually leads to high self-confidence, independence, and feelings of internal control. However, high self-expectations can lead to frustration.

Gifted students tend to have an independent, self-motivated learning style. They usually prefer unstructured and participant learning activities. Two popular inventories for assessing learning styles are the Dunn, Dunn, and Price LSI and the Renzulli and Smith LSI.

Intellectually gifted students intuitively comprehend values and moral issues and are less egocentric, thus able to empathize with the rights, feelings, and problems of others. They are usually more honest and trustworthy, although some may be delinquent. Values and a sense of fairness and justice develop early, leading to consistency in attitudes and behavior and an interest in social issues.

Creativity and intelligence are different traits. They are moderately correlated, but above a threshold IQ score of about 120 the correlation disappears. If students are selected for G/T programs based on IQ scores, most creative students will be missed. Teachers often select "teacher pleasers" for gifted programs. Highly creative students, who may be less visible than highly intelligent students, may ultimately make greater contributions to society.

The creative personality includes high self-confidence, independence, risk taking, high energy, adventurousness, creativity consciousness, playful-

ness and humor, idealism, attraction to the complex and mysterious, tolerance for ambiguity, need for alone time, and artistic and aesthetic interests.

Creative elementary school children tend to be reflective; creative adults lean toward impulsiveness.

Torrance suggested that creative students prefer working alone, see relationships, go beyond assigned tasks, and are imaginative, flexible, highly verbal, persistent, and irritated by the routine and obvious.

Some negative traits of some creative children are stubbornness, uncooperativeness, egocentrism, discourteousness, indifference to conventions, and resistance to teacher domination.

A background of creative activities is an unsurprising biographical characteristic. Less expected ones include having younger or older friends, having an imaginary playmate, and much traveling.

Studying gifted pianists, swimmers, mathematicians, and others, Bloom concluded that home and parental influences were critical to high levels of talent development. Parents supported the child and modeled the appropriate personality, values, and lifestyle. All instruction was individualized. Student (and teacher) motivation and dedication ran high. Rather than quitting, students benefited from failures. Compared with traditional schooling, talent development is informal, individualized, specialized, and more meaningful (Bloom).

Feldman reviewed the training and personal lives of such prodigies as Bobby Fisher and Mozart, along with six contemporary prodigies. His co-incidence theory stressed the combination of individual, environmental, and historical factors. In agreement with Bloom, Felman stressed the importance of a strongly supportive family, excellent instruction, and a passionate commitment by the prodigy.

Teachers of the gifted ideally should possess such personal and teaching characteristics as the ability to develop flexible programs, respect for individuality and creativity, innovativeness, giftedness, and others.

CHAPTER 3

PROGRAM PLANNING

We must create an openness to fly, to be challenged, to grow for . . .
gifted and talented children.
John F. Feldhusen (1992, p. 49)

There are many issues and considerations in planning a sound program for gifted and talented students, one that is successful in providing an education consistent with gifted students' needs, yet which does not alienate needed supporters. This chapter will look first at four global areas, which may be recast as why, who, what, where, when, and how questions. The main body of the chapter will examine fifteen areas of program planning. A brief section on scope and sequence will look at aligning actual classroom activities with broader, program-level goals. We then turn to not-uncommon attitudes and views of school board members and "other teachers," with suggestions for improving negative attitudes. A final section surveys common criticisms, issues, and problems that arise in many programs—and indeed are virtually built into the design of some programs—along with suggestions for solutions.

MAIN COMPONENTS OF PROGRAM PLANNING

Based in part on Treffinger's (1981, 1986a, 1986b) *Individualized Programming Planning Model*, the following are four core components of any G/T program. Program planners must attend to these components—in either a knowledgeable and systematic way or else a haphazard, hit-or-miss fashion.

1. Program philosophy and goals. Key questions:
   What is our attitude toward gifted children?
   Why are we doing this?
   What do we wish to accomplish?
2. Definition and identification. Key questions:
   What do we mean by "gifted and talented?"
   Which categories of gifts and talents will this program serve?
   How will we select gifted students?
3. Instruction—grouping, acceleration, and enrichment. Key questions:
   What are students' needs?
   How can we best meet those needs?
   How can we implement our instructional plans?
4. Evaluation and modification. Key questions:
   Was the program successful? How do we know?
   What did we do right?
   What did we do wrong?
   What changes shall we make?

WHY, WHO, WHAT, WHERE, WHEN, HOW QUESTIONS

As an embellishment on the above components, one can view program planning as a set of questions:

Why are we doing this? Can we prepare a defensible statement of philosophy on gifted and talented? A rationale for our general and specific goals and objectives?

Who will the program be for? Which grades? Which students? How will "gifted and talented" be defined? How will the students be identified?

Who will direct and coordinate the program? Who will serve on the school G/T committee?

What will we do? What are our goals and objectives? What sorts of grouping, acceleration, and enrichment opportunities should we provide? Which will produce the best results? Which will be the most cost-effective?

Where will we do all of this? In the regular classrooms? Special classes? A district resource room? A special school? A "school-within-a-school"? In the community?

When can the training take place? When the students finish regular assignments? On Wednesday afternoon? All day every day? After school? Saturdays? Summers?

How and *when* will we implement the plan? When can the plan begin? Can we formulate timelines for completing the planning? For beginning the identification procedures? For initiating the instructional program?

How will we evaluate gains in students' knowledge and skills? How will we evaluate the effectiveness of each program component? Each instructional activity? See Inset 3.1.

PROGRAM PLANNING: FIFTEEN AREAS

This section will describe fifteen problem areas in program planning that relate to the four main components and to the "why, who, what, where, when, and how" questions. The fifteen areas are not sequential in the one-at-a-time sense. Many will be dealt with simultaneously in planning a G/T program. Some areas are major ones, dealing, for example, with whether there will be a program at all and, if so, the directions the program will take and the students who will be served. Other problem areas are lesser managerial or administrative matters necessary for smooth program operation. As an overview, the problem areas are listed in Table 3.1.

1. Needs Assessment

A *needs assessment* aims at determining the discrepancy between the current status of gifted education in the school or district and the desired status. All fifty states have passed legislation formally defining "giftedness" in their state (Cassidy and Johnson, 1986; Cassidy and Hossler, 1992); they also have allocated funds for gifted programs and/or mandated that special services be provided. Therefore, for many schools and districts the former question of "*Is* there a need for a program?" has become "*What* are the needs of the gifted and talented students in the school (or district)?"

There are three excellent sources of information regarding school and district needs for a G/T program and specific student needs: *parents* of gifted and talented students, gifted *students* themselves, and *teachers* and *administrators* who have become "gifted conscious." First, many parents of gifted students have been frustrated by and vocal about the lack of specific services for their children. The authors regularly receive phone calls and letters from exasperated parents who register these types of complaints: "My third-grade daughter has a Stanford-Binet IQ of 145, but the teacher says she can't help because the superintendent is opposed to special programs for the 'haves,' and current rules do not even permit skipping a grade." "My son obviously is gifted and does wonderful and creative things at home, but in school he has become bored and lazy, and I am afraid his talent and enthusiasm are going to waste."

Second, many upper elementary and older gifted students can explain their strong special interests. Their curiosity and high energy levels also may be visible. Would they like to learn advanced computer programming? Would they like a special Saturday science or drama class? Would they be able to handle math or social studies at higher grade levels? Would they like to spend time with a professional artist, executive, or medical researcher? Would they be interested in a three-week summer education program at State University? You bet they would.

A Few Considerations in Planning a Gifted Program: Treffinger

Gifted education leader Donald Treffinger (1982b, 1986a) itemized a number of thought-provoking problems and issues related to planning a gifted program, many of which appear below. In conjunction with each problem is one or more idea-stimulating questions in the form of an IWWMW statement—"In what ways might we . . . ?"

1. Gifted and talented students are present *now* in our school buildings. Pleading that we can't take action without special funds is like "waiting for Santa Claus." While extra support can be helpful, we must find ways to begin without it.

*IWWMW initiate action for gifted programming with our own existing resources?

2. While administrators must provide the support ("clout") for gifted education, someone must also be responsible for the day-to-day tasks of program implementation, management, and monitoring.

*IWWMW provide time and support for trained staff members to carry out daily responsibilities for gifted programming?

3. Individualized professional development, involving more than "listening to speeches on in-service day," is essential within the building.

*IWWMW identify and respond to individual staff members' professional development interests and needs?

4. The role of "teacher" should involve more than direct services to students all day long, every day.

*IWWMW provide opportunities for staff members to conduct professional activities not involving direct contact with students?

*IWWMW provide our staff with more planning time and improve their planning skills?

*IWWMW provide opportunities for staff members to confer about students' characteristics and needs?

5. Gifted programming that is blended effectively with the total school program does not "just happen." It must develop deliberately and gradually.

*IWWMW formulate a specific plan for effective growth and change in our programming over a three- to five-year period?

6. Students and their accomplishments are the best "salespersons" for gifted programming.

*IWWMW make our community and our educational policymakers aware of the activities and accomplishments of our students?

7. Parents are not (necessarily) adversaries, and they often have talents to share, as well as valuable, unique data to share with us.

*IWWMW incorporate parents' input and assistance into our gifted programming efforts?

*IWWMW build upon the resources of existing parent organizations (e.g., PTA)?

8. You must expect obstacles and objections to come from the least likely issues and the most unexpected sources.

*IWWMW anticipate difficult issues, obstacles, and criticisms, and prepare to deal with them?

*IWWMW involve our critics in helping us solve problems that are of mutual concern?

*IWWMW insure that our plans will lead to action?

9. Test scores should not be used as "badges" or as "bludgeons." We should not stamp IQ scores proudly upon the student's forehead, nor allow small differences to be overblown in importance.

*IWWMW use test data intelligently, to provide a basis for instructional planning?

10. The gifted program should not merely be "fun and games," nor should it consist merely of things that should occur for many students in all classrooms.

*IWWMW provide appropriate services in the regular classroom?

*IWWMW define the unique contributions and justifications for gifted programming?

TABLE 3.1   Overview of Fifteen Areas in
Program Planning

1. Needs Assessment
2. Preliminary Personal and Staff Education
3. Philosophy, Rationale, Goals, Objectives, and a Written Program Plan
4. Types of Gifts and Talents to be Provided for and Estimated Enrollment
5. Identification Methods and Specific Criteria
6. Specific Provisions for Identifying Female, Underachieving, Handicapped, Culturally Different, and Economically Disadvantaged Gifted Students
7. Staff Responsibilities and Assignments
8. Arranging Support Services
9. Acceleration and Enrichment Plans
10. Organizational and Administrative Design
11. Transportation Needs
12. Community Resources: Professionals and Organizations
13. In-Service Workshops, Training, and Visits
14. Budgetary Needs and Allocations
15. Program Evaluation

Third, another confirmation of the need for G/T programming may come from teachers and administrators who attend conferences or take courses that address the needs and problems of gifted children. With their newly found awareness, they may take an enthusiastic leadership role in helping document district needs and initiating gifted programs.

The need for a G/T program and specific student needs may be documented formally or informally, briefly or extensively depending on the size and formality of the school district and the type and source of the available information or evidence. If a school board or district administration prefers a formal and objective documentation of needs, a needs-assessment questionnaire may be distributed to parents, teachers, and perhaps students. Such a questionnaire should include two main components: (1) perceptions of what needs to be provided in the community, and (2) opinions regarding the extent to which current school programs are meeting these needs. The questionnaire

will quantify the desire for differentiated educational services, the preferred directions for the services, and the extent of community support. One example of a needs-assessment questionnaire appears in Table 3.2.

Gifted children and parents of gifted children are minorities in the community, so one cannot expect landslide majority support for such programs. Therefore, the criteria for deciding that programs are needed should only be "sufficient" support, not necessarily strong majority support.

After a need for special services is confirmed (formally or informally), a committee of teachers, administrators, and parents can meet to discuss possible directions for gifted programs. The fifteen problem areas may provide topics for discussion. Eventually, a formal steering committee will be organized, usually appointed (on request) by a district administrator or school principal, to make concrete plans with a definite timetable. In the elementary school, the steering committee might be composed of a district coordinator; teachers from the lower, middle, and upper grades; administrators at the school and district levels; one or two school board members; the school librarian; a school psychologist or counselor; and parents. It may also be helpful to have some gifted high school students represented; they may be able to provide important insights into the kinds of challenges which, in their experience, have been effective, ineffective, or absent.

If a program already exists, and improvement is the goal, a needs assessment will consider such matters as: What are the gaps in the current program? Given "what is," "what might be?" and "where should we be?" in regard to process and product outcomes? (Van Tassel-Baska, 1988b). Do our classroom teaching units, activities, and resources align with our district-wide planned objectives? If not, what can be adjusted?

2. Preliminary Personal and Staff Education

The goal of building a gifted education program cannot wait for several teachers and administra-

TABLE 3.2 Needs-Assessment Questionnaire

Please rate the statements below in two ways. The first rating relates to the strength of a particular program as you see it in the school. The second rating refers to the way in which you think the program should be. Program need will be determined by subtracting Rating 1 from Rating 2. Programs that are presently weak but are determined to be important preferences will be set as first priorities.

Rate 1 if you STRONGLY DISAGREE with the statement.
Rate 2 if you DISAGREE SOMEWHAT with the statement.
Rate 3 if you are UNDECIDED.
Rate 4 if you AGREE SOMEWHAT with the statement.
Rate 5 if you STRONGLY AGREE with the statement.

	NOW	*FUTURE*
1. In general, the needs of gifted children in the school district are being met.	1 2 3 4 5	1 2 3 4 5
2. The attitude of most teachers toward the gifted child is positive and helpful.	1 2 3 4 5	1 2 3 4 5
3. The program provides individualization of curriculum for gifted children.	1 2 3 4 5	1 2 3 4 5
4. Special enrichment opportunities are provided for gifted children.	1 2 3 4 5	1 2 3 4 5
5. Classes that teach creative and critical thinking are available.	1 2 3 4 5	1 2 3 4 5
6. The school has appropriate guidelines for determining early entrance to kindergarten.	1 2 3 4 5	1 2 3 4 5
7. The school has appropriate guidelines for determining subject or grade skipping.	1 2 3 4 5	1 2 3 4 5
8. The school provides for the needs of the underachieving gifted child.	1 2 3 4 5	1 2 3 4 5
9. The special social-emotional needs of gifted children are being addressed.	1 2 3 4 5	1 2 3 4 5
10. The special needs of the highly creative child are being met.	1 2 3 4 5	1 2 3 4 5
11. The school provides for the needs of gifted and talented girls.	1 2 3 4 5	1 2 3 4 5
12. The school provides for the needs of gifted and talented minority children.	1 2 3 4 5	1 2 3 4 5
13. The school includes parents in the planning and guiding of gifted and talented children.	1 2 3 4 5	1 2 3 4 5
14. Teacher-education opportunities in the area of gifted and talented are provided for the teaching staff.	1 2 3 4 5	1 2 3 4 5
15. The administration supports education of the gifted and talented.	1 2 3 4 5	1 2 3 4 5

tors to take one or two college courses in gifted education. Teachers must educate themselves and each other in the essential basics—preferably before they all make some uninformed assumptions and mistakes.

Part of a preliminary education will include becoming acquainted with the present status of gifted education in your school, district, city, and even state. One might ask such questions as:

1. What is being done at the present time?

2. What kinds of G/T services are needed?

3. Do other schools in the area have programs? What exactly are they doing?

4. What do school board members and the district superintendent think about special programs for the gifted?

5. Do existing district policies allow students to enter kindergarten early? Skip a grade? What screening procedures are in effect? What are the criteria?

6. Can high school students take college courses in person or by correspondence?

7. Is there a written district policy? A district G/T coordinator? A state G/T director?

8. What exactly does the state legislation on educating gifted children say?

9. Are other teachers interested and supportive? Are they just being agreeable, or are some willing to assume responsibility for the work?

10. Are parents or parent groups becoming restless about their ignored children?

Some of these questions can be answered with a few phone calls. Others will require lengthier exploration and thought.

People seriously interested in gifted education must acquaint themselves with any written district policies or position statements. They should read any state legislation and state plan on behalf of the gifted. The *state legislation* will at the very least (1) define gifted and talented, (2) endorse the concept of differentiated educational experiences, and usually (3) allocate funds for developing and maintaining programs. (Eventually, one can ask the State G/T Director how to apply for the funds.) A *state plan*, which is formally accepted by the superintendent or the state board of education rather than the state legislature, will also define gifted and talented and endorse providing G/T services and programs. The state plan may further itemize specific objectives related to program development, and will usually itemize training services and resources that may be used to meet those objectives.

Many state and local educational organizations sponsor one- or two-day conferences and workshops usually led by one or more experienced leaders in gifted education or related areas. For one- or two-hour workshops, chances are good that a nearby college or state education office can suggest speakers to address specific topics in gifted education.

National and state conferences are immensely informative, for example, those sponsored by the National Association for Gifted Children, the Council for Exceptional Children, the National/State Leadership Training Institute for Gifted/Talented, and by state parent groups and state educational associations. Speakers at national and state conferences will describe the workings of their programs, the pros and cons of their own identification, acceleration, and enrichment strategies, and how they coped with some of the same problems the reader will face. Several journals and magazines are also devoted to the education of gifted, talented, and creative students, especially the *Gifted Child Quarterly, Gifted Child Today, Roeper Review, Journal for the Education of the Gifted, Advanced Development Journal, Journal of Creative Behavior,* and *Creativity Research Journal.*

A highly enlightening staff activity is visiting schools with successful programs. By speaking directly with involved teachers one will get an inside look at how plans are implemented and how problems are dealt with. One will also gain valuable insight into what works and what does not, tips that will help avoid common pitfalls.

3. Philosophy, Rationale, Goals, Objectives, and a Written Program Plan

A brief statement of philosophy and goals is essential because everyone (parents, teachers, administrators, the local school board) will want to know exactly what the program entails and why. The Richardson Foundation study (Cox and Daniel, 1985) discovered, as a general trend, that districts with substantial programs tended to have a written philosophy and goal statement, along with a special G/T supervisory staff and a special budget. The written philosophy and rationale should include the reasons for the program—a position statement explaining why the program is necessary—plus general and, if desired, specific program objectives. An excellent guide for preparing a statement of philosophy is Kaplan's (1974) *Providing Programs for the Gifted and Talented*, which supplies examples of rationale statements and program goals. Two other fine sources of ideas are the Fall 1979 issue of the *Gifted Child Quarterly* and Joyce Juntune's (1981) book *Successful Programs for the Gifted and Talented*, both of which include summaries of many gifted programs around the country. Most of the descriptions present a brief program philosophy and list general and specific program goals. Also, a state plan, if one exists, will undoubtedly include a statement of philosophy and objectives that could be modified to fit a specific program.

A sample of the possible contents of a philosophy and goals statement appears in Appendix 3.1 at the end of this chapter. Take the time to read it now. A one-page philosophy statement for a small Wisconsin city appears in Inset 3.2.

If a statement of philosophy and goals is expanded, it can serve as a written plan for a program. A written program plan should present sufficient detail to answer any question that anyone could possibly ask about a proposed program. The written plan is often built around:

1. A definition of gifts and talents. For example, the federal definition is often used.

2. Philosophy and goals. This section explains

INSET 3.2

A Philosophy of Gifted and Talented Education

The Watertown, Wisconsin, Public School System is committed to an education program that recognizes individual student differences. Embodied in this commitment is a responsibility to talented and gifted students to help them maximize their high potential.

Gifted children differ from others in learning ability: they learn faster, have wider interests, remember more, and think with greater depth about what they learn. An education program can be designed that will more adequately meet the needs of the gifted student.

A program for gifted students should provide a comprehensively planned curriculum that utilizes within-discipline and/or cross-disciplinary studies. These studies should allow for both vertical (acceleration) and horizontal (breadth and depth in a topic) movement that is educationally relevant. The program should stress higher-level thinking skills such as inquiring skills, problem solving, and creative thinking. In addition, development of self-direction, risk-taking, curiosity, imagination, and interpersonal relations should be emphasized. The program framework will allow for individual projects and peer-group interaction.

The long-range goals of this program are self-actualization for the gifted person and the development of a sense of responsibility to self, school, and society.

(Watertown, Wisconsin, School District, 1980. Reprinted by permission.)

---

why a program is necessary. Itemizing the cognitive and affective goals can be brief and general or tedious and specific.

3. Screening and identification methods. This section describes the information used (test scores, grades, teacher nominations, teacher ratings, self-nominations, and so on), and how the various sources of information will be combined in making selection decisions. The identification section should also comment on provisions for identifying culturally different, economically disadvantaged, underachieving, and handicapped gifted students. Selection information will be scrutinized by any state or federal funding agency reading your plan.

4. Instructional programming strategies. This section outlines the curriculum model (if any) on which the program is built. Also included are the specific grouping, acceleration, and enrichment plans, along with the necessary organizational changes; subject areas of concentration and planned activities; the use of community resources; and so on.

5. Program evaluation and modification. This section outlines specific evaluation plans, both of the *formative* type, which provide continuous feedback regarding the ongoing methods and activities, and the final *summative*, did-we-succeed type at the end of the unit, the semester, or most likely, the year.

Specific sections of the written plan may deal with any of the fifteen points described in Table 3.1 and in this chapter. Three good sources of ideas for your written plan are Kaplan (1974), Sato, Birnbaum, and LoCicero (1974), and Van Tassel-Baska (1988a).

4. Types of Gifts and Talents to Provide for and Estimated Enrollment

The topics of *types of gifts and talents* and *definitions of giftedness* are intimately related, and both belong in any statement of philosophy or written plan. The problem of specifying types of gifts and talents to be accommodated is also intimately related to the identification problem—defining who will be "in" the program—and it relates closely to the proposed program plans. Some relevant questions and considerations are: Will the program serve only bright, intellectually gifted students? Or will a multidimensional definition of gifts and talents be used, providing special opportunities to students with specific academic talents, scientific talents, creative talents, communication (speaking, writing) talents, artistic and musical talents, and others?

As for the size of your gifted population, Stanley's (e.g., 1979, 1991a) original *Studies of Mathematically Precocious Youth* program catered to students in the top one percent in math ability. In contrast, Renzulli's (Renzulli and Reis, 1985a, 1991b) increasingly popular *Schoolwide Enrichment Model* identifies 15 to 20 percent of the school population for a *talent pool*. These students individually revolve in and out of a resource room to work on special projects. A common size for a single "pullout" or other special class is about 12 to 15 students.

If grade-skipping, taking advanced classes, or some other acceleration strategy is to be part of the plan, then fixing a number of "in" students is not as sensible as setting criteria that can qualify *any number* of students for the acceleration. For example, standardized achievement test scores, probably already on file, are one good basis for decision making. But here is a warning: Due to random score variability, a single cutoff score should never be rigidly used to exclude students who are close to a magical cutoff number. Selection should be flexible and include subjective judgments as well as test scores.

5. Identification Methods and Specific Criteria

Issues and methods related to identifying gifted and talented students are at least sufficiently complex to merit a chapter of their own—a highly condensed chapter at that (Chapter 4). For now, we will simply mention (or repeat) a few basic considerations.

1. Identification methods must be consistent with one's definition of gifted and talented students. It is common for a stated plan to endorse the federal multiple-talent definition, but then use IQ scores for the selection procedure. The identification methods define exactly who is "gifted and talented" for any given program.

2. Identification methods must be coordinated with the type of program(s) one plans to implement. For example, intelligence test scores, reading and math abilities, and teacher nominations might be appropriate for selecting students for grade-skipping. Math ability would be critical for participation in an accelerated math program. If a program accommodates many types of gifts and talents, a variety of ability, achievement, creativity, and interest information will be appropriate, again, including both test scores and subjective evidence.

3. Identification methods must be defensible to the community. Parents will ask why one child was selected for a program while another (theirs) was not. Selection decisions must be clearly justifiable. Some identification methods are intelligence tests, standardized achievement tests (particularly reading and math), creativity tests and inventories; inventories assessing interests, hobbies, special needs, and past special opportunities; teacher ratings of various characteristics (for example, academic talent, abstract thinking, creativity, motivation, leadership, organizing ability, visual or performing art talents); peer ratings of various characteristics, parent ratings and inventories, and self ratings; and work samples and products (for example, in art, music, or science). An advantage of the talent pool approach, mentioned above, is that larger numbers of students can be included, selection and admission to the program are flexible, and complaints about exclusiveness and elitism are reduced. More will be said about the Schoolwide Enrichment Model later in this chapter, and especially in Chapter 7.

6. Specific Provisions for Identifying Female, Underachieving, Handicapped, Culturally Different, and Economically Disadvantaged Gifted Students

We mentioned earlier that not only males and females must be fairly represented, but also economically disadvantaged, minority, and handicapped gifted students. The problem is not that these students have no gifts and talents; it is that educators many times do not look to these populations for G/T students (e.g. Frazier, 1989).

Gifted underachievers may be even less visible than gifted minority, economically disadvantaged, or handicapped students. For underachieving students, their lost talent development is a personal crisis for them and a lost natural resource for humankind. More than one underachieving gifted student has become motivated toward higher educational and career achievement by the specific attention of teachers in gifted programs and, in some cases, by individual and family therapy (Rimm, 1984, 1986b).

7. Staff Responsibilities and Assignments

There is a large difference between the passive acceptance or even hearty endorsement of a new gifted program versus the willingness to roll up one's sleeves and do the work. It is an essential preliminary problem to decide just who will assume responsibility for what and when.

It is not unusual to include some accountability checks, for example, by setting deadlines for obtaining certain information, preparing reports, purchasing tests or materials, conferring with administrators, and so forth. Scheduled weekly or biweekly meetings have the effect of establishing accountability—getting things done.

8. Arranging Support Services

A successful program for gifted and talented students will involve experts and professionals beyond the immediate teaching staff. The school psychologist, counselors, the district or state coordinator, and outside consultants will all play important roles.

Very few school psychologists have taken any formal coursework whatever in gifted education. If a school psychologist does have expertise in the gifted area, he or she can be helpful with all aspects of program planning and implementation.

If the school psychologist is not an expert in gifted education (some are, some are not), his or her main contribution will probably be the administration and interpretation of tests. Individual intelligence tests, mainly the Stanford-Binet and the WISC-III, require a trained administrator. The psychologist might also administer and interpret interest or personality inventories such as the *Edwards Interest Inventory* or the *Kuder Preference Record* to help secondary students better understand themselves, their possible career directions, and the educational preparation necessary for various career alternatives. The school psychologist might supervise the administration of group achievement or group intelligence tests. In addition, many school psychologists are able to work with underachieving gifted students and their parents, or with gifted students with different problems. It is advisable to encourage your school psychologist to educate himself or herself in the area of giftedness by attending conferences, reading relevant books and journals, and so on.

School counselors also may or may not have expertise in gifted education. If not, the elementary school counselor will be involved in helping students cope with academic difficulties and with personal problems. The counselor can also help educate parents of gifted children regarding the child's particular talents, academic strengths and weaknesses, and personal difficulties. Importantly, the counselor can help specify the parents' role in developing the capabilities of their gifted children. For example, the counselor can recommend participation in the school's gifted program (many parents are surprisingly reluctant) and can recommend valuable summer programs such as science, art, music, language, or computer camps and workshops. As with the school psychologist, it is important that counselors learn about the special needs of gifted children. Without such additional background, they may make shortsighted and inappropriate recommendations, for example, by stressing social adjustment and conformity instead of achievement and uniqueness.

In both the junior and senior high schools, counselors serve an invaluable function in fostering self-understanding with gifted and talented students. The educational and career counseling services of the secondary-level counselor should help steer the gifted adolescent into an education program that is challenging and suitable to the student's college and career needs. Again, a special knowledge of personal and career needs of gifted students is mandatory for guiding them appropriately. Chapter 17 of this book is devoted entirely to understanding and counseling gifted students.

Planning a gifted program frequently involves a series of consultants, for example, state or district coordinators, university instructors with relevant experience or knowledge, professional G/T consultants or workshop leaders, or experienced teacher-coordinators from other locations. These consultants can present workshops for the entire school staff, perhaps dealing with methods of identification, alternative instructional models and strategies, program evaluation methods, problems of gifted girls, or other topics. Particularly, some might describe in colorful detail the workings and problems of their own successful program.

You may also work with consultants on a one-to-one basis, outlining strategies for:

Obtaining funds

Preparing written statements

Selecting goals and objectives

Designing relevant acceleration and enrichment activities

Installing a particular program model, such as the Schoolwide Enrichment Model

Selecting or creating nomination forms, rating forms, or questionnaires for identification

Insuring proper representation of different student groups

Designing program evaluation procedures

Selecting or creating instruments for program evaluation

Promoting good public relations

9. Acceleration and Enrichment Plans

Issues, details, and recommendations regarding acceleration (for example, grade-skipping, advanced classes) and enrichment (for example, resource room or Saturday programs) are elaborated in

Chapters 5, 6, and 7. For now, we will simply emphasize that specific instructional plans must be designed to produce sensible, defensible, and valuable educational benefits. While this recommendation may sound obvious and trivial, as Renzulli and his colleagues (e.g., Renzulli, 1984; Renzulli and Smith, 1978a; Renzulli and Reis, 1985b, 1991b) have repeated, far too many programs entertain the children with fun-and-games time fillers and interest-getters, with little attention to worthwhile, theory-based goals. For inspiration regarding valuable goals and activities, you may review the philosophy and goals ideas in Appendix 3.1 and the Curriculum for the Gifted material in Table 5.1 at the beginning of Chapter 5. Aligning specific classroom activities with higher-level program goals—scope and sequence concerns—will be re-emphasized later in this chapter. For now, some examples of high-level goals that guide specific acceleration and enrichment plans are:

High achievement; advanced academic skills and content

Complex, abstract, theoretical thinking

Creative, critical, evaluative thinking; other thinking skills

Scientific research skills

Library research skills

Communication (speaking, writing) skills, including creative writing

Career-related content

College preparatory content

Self-awareness, affective, and humanistic principles

Each of the curriculum models outlined in Chapter 7 is based on these and other potentially valuable instructional outcomes. One or more of the models often serves as the basis for planning specific acceleration and enrichment activities.

10. Organizational and Administrative Design

Most G/T plans require some administrative reshuffling of the school organization and budget to staff the program; provide the necessary time, space, and facilities; and coordinate the G/T activities with the rest of the school schedule. If the program is district-wide or city-wide, the planning will take place partly, not entirely, at these higher levels. In addition, any program for gifted and talented students will require considerable record-keeping by those directly involved—the teacher or teacher-coordinator, although secretaries can carry some of the burden.

For example, acceleration plans as straightforward as grade-skipping or taking college or correspondence courses will require that new types of records be created and maintained, and that student progress be monitored. Also, clear arrangements will have to be made with the local college. University registration staff have been known to become disagreeable when an unexpected troop of grinning 15-year-olds march in to register. A more complicated acceleration plan such as telescoping (for example, condensing three years of math or science into two) will require not only a teacher, a classroom, and a time slot, but complete coordination with the rest of the school course offerings and organization, along with creating and keeping records of student participation and success.

Enrichment plans also require attention to organizational and administrative matters. A Wednesday pullout program will require at the very least a teacher-coordinator and a resource room, plus such miscellaneous supplies and equipment as resource books, workbooks, chemistry and biology supplies, calculators, microcomputers, typewriters, art supplies, perhaps a 35-mm camera, a videocamera, and so forth. Other enrichment plans, such as Saturday classes, extra classes, field trips, and mentoring programs, also will require attention to organizational, administrative, and managerial matters of staff, space, scheduling, transportation, materials, and record keeping.

If a plan is district-wide or city-wide, particularly when special schools for the gifted and talented are created or Saturday or summer programs are planned, the organizational and administrative planning is clearly more involved. It is not unusual for metropolitan areas to have several full-time G/T personnel in the central office to help plan and manage city-wide programs. However, regardless of the size and type of program, a local school staff member must be designated as having administrative responsibility for the G/T program in that school. A designated responsible person—at whose desk the buck stops—is essential.

11. Transportation Needs

Transportation plans may be simple and relatively minor, but they cannot be ignored. Transportation problems and costs must be considered for students who attend special schools, take college courses, or travel to schools with special resource-room programs. Transportation must also be considered for field trips, mentoring programs, after-school projects and clubs, summer programs, and Saturday programs.

12. Community Resources: Professionals and Organizations

Community resources, namely professional people and organizations, will be invaluable in at least three types of instructional plans and programs for the gifted: mentoring plans, enrichment-oriented field trips, and career education. Therefore, in planning a program at either the elementary or secondary level, potentially valuable community resources should be reviewed and itemized.

Mentoring plans involve the placing of gifted students with a community professional for usually a few hours each week. The professional could be in any area of the arts, science, or business. There can be no substitute for the values, attitudes, skills, job requirements, and knowledge of daily routines and lifestyles acquired by gifted students in such a personal educational experience.

While mentoring plans are used almost entirely at the secondary level, using community resources for field trips and career education is useful with any age group. Some possibilities for field trips are art galleries and museums; university art, sci-

ence, and engineering facilities; police and government facilities; manufacturing plants, and so forth. Engineering and computer departments enjoy showing off their latest robots.

Do not forget that all students—not just the gifted—profit from field trips in increased knowledge, better school attitudes, and perhaps raised aspirations.

Capitalizing on community resources for career education also can involve inviting professionals to make presentations to the class—to all students. If a field trip or class presentation is not relevant to the needs of all students, small groups or even individuals can visit with a professional and receive a guided tour of his or her organization. To ensure an educational benefit, the concrete plans for such a trip must include specific questions to be answered. Follow-up activities can include discussions and/or the preparation of written or oral reports on the experience.

13. In-Service Workshops, Training, and Visits

We mentioned earlier (Item 8) that consultants such as state or district coordinators, university staff, professional workshop leaders, or experienced teachers of the gifted can provide workshops for the entire school staff or guidance for individual G/T teachers and coordinators. Let's elaborate on the importance and role of workshops, continued training, and visits to other programs.

Initially, workshops should be at an *awareness* level. Introductory exposures should (1) attempt to improve attitudes of teachers who believe that gifted children do not require special services, and (2) heighten the interest and commitment of all teachers and staff. Some good awareness topics are characteristics and needs of gifted students, general approaches—programs and strategies—designed to meet these needs, and how G/T activities are related to other aspects of the curriculum.

Next in order should be in-service training dealing with the *identification* of gifted children and the teacher's role in this process. A good understanding of selection tests, criteria, and weighting procedures—and the role of subjective judgment—may prevent some special problems later. For example, teachers should understand why Johnny, a highly creative "B" student, should be included in the program even if his tested IQ is not over 125.

The choice of other topics will vary according to the direction of the G/T program. If acceleration strategies are planned, teachers must understand both the reasons behind these strategies and the specific procedures for conducting the acceleration. If an enrichment resource program is used, all teachers should understand the curriculum of that program and how they can help their own students' participation. They also must help resolve a traditional dilemma: the extent to which their students will be expected to make up missed work while in the resource room.

Some additional important inservice topics are:

• Identifying and teaching poor, minority, economically disadvantaged, and underachieving gifted students.
• Program goals and objectives, and coordinating classroom activities to meet these goals.
• Program models and prototypes.
• Role expectations of school staff.
• Instructional strategies and teaching skills in specific content areas and with particular age groups.
• Understanding and teaching creative students.
• Helping students understand and cope successfully with competition.
• Strategies, materials, and programs for teaching creativity and thinking skills to gifted students and all students.
• Counseling needs of gifted children and adolescents.
• Understanding and coping with perfectionism in students.
• Evaluating the gifted program and making changes and modifications.
• The de-tracking, anti-ability grouping movement and the critical need to group gifted students.
• Cooperative learning and gifted students.
• Parent-school relationships.

Inservice training also can deal with handling time conflicts, scheduling and organizing activities, and assisting less-experienced teachers (Roberts and Roberts, 1986).

Weiss and Gallagher (1986) suggested that in-service training dealing with curriculum for the gifted should emphasize that a variety of learning activities and strategies should be used to reach program goals. Further, the content of the in-service training must be directly applicable to the teachers' situations and should involve demonstration and practice with new techniques.

From a survey, Tomlinson (1986), found that teachers were most interested in obtaining information concerning methods and techniques for use with gifted students at their particular grade level and/or in their subject area. Further, teachers strongly preferred group participation and hands-on experience—working through types of activities that could be used immediately with their gifted students—rather than "lecture only" approaches.

An excellent source of inspiration for planning or improving a G/T program is visiting other successful programs. It is best to visit several types of programs. These may include special schools for gifted and talented students along with schools with resource-room or pullout programs, special classes, Saturday programs, mentoring plans, telescoping plans, or whatever else you might be considering for your own school. Do not be surprised if the visits help you decide what *not* to do. You can speak with teachers regarding such matters as:

What they are doing and how they are doing it.
Who the target students are and how they were identified.
What the students are specifically supposed to get out of the program (goals and objectives).
Their perceptions (and evidence) of the success of their program.
The difficulties they experienced and how they were resolved.
The sorts of resistance they encountered from other teachers, parents, or the community.

You also might speak with the gifted and talented students in various types of programs. How do they like school? Do they like the program? What are their problems? How could the program be improved?

14. Budgetary Needs and Allocations

Many programs operate on a shoestring, using part of the regular school budget to purchase special workbooks, calculators, art supplies, or other inexpensive items. It can be done. However, to plan a proper program one should consider expenses related to some or all of the following:

A full-time or part-time teacher/coordinator—
or several, in a larger district
Physical facilities
Texts and workbooks
Special equipment and supplies
Transportation costs
Tests and inventories
Secretarial services
Office supplies
Duplicating expenses
Consultant and in-service training expenses
Travel to visit other programs
Travel to state and national conferences
Services of psychologists and counselors
Evaluation expenses (a consultant; purchasing
or constructing tests, rating scales, or questionnaires)

Budgetary matters must be considered at the time you are planning the various identification strategies, instructional program alternatives, and needed evaluation data. From the outset, one should be concerned with cost-benefit matters. Some programs clearly cost more than others, and priorities may have to be modified in light of the available dollars. However, with creative cost-cutting, many goals can be achieved relatively economically, without a large loss in interest value or educational benefit.

Finally, a search for federal, state, or private funding surely will be worthwhile. Even though funding may be scarce for "a program for gifted and talented students," requesting funds for a specific category of persons or subject matter—such as handicapped or minority gifted, computer literacy, math and science, or arts and humanities—can improve one's chances for an award or grant. Local service organizations, medical and health organizations, or local businesses or industries may be willing to provide small amounts of designated funding. Usually, a newspaper story or other publicity can be arranged to reward such contributions. Note too that chances for a financial commitment by the school district will be improved if administrators recognize that funds from other sources also are forthcoming.

15. Program Evaluation

The evaluation of gifted programs is an important and complex topic that will be discussed in Chapter 18. For now, the reader should keep in mind that good evaluation information has a direct bearing on (1) the survival and continuation of the program, (2) the continuation or improvement of budgetary allocations, and (3) the modification and improvement of the program. Evaluation is indeed important, and should be part of the program planning from the beginning. *Every* aspect of the program—the staff, the materials, the identification procedures, the acceleration and enrichment activities, and each and every goal and objective—can be evaluated regarding its effectiveness in contributing to program success.

Evaluation is of two types—first, a *formative*, ongoing process aimed at continuous modification and improvement of the program; second, a *summative*, final assessment of the overall success of the program. Both are necessary. Evaluation can be aimed at determining how well students' needs and goals were met; evaluation also is sometimes directed at assessing how well the program plan was carried out.

THE VIEW FROM THE SCHOOL BOARD

The main function of the district school board is to set policy governing school administration and programs. Because board members are either elected directly by the community or appointed by elected officials, they are accountable to the public. Whether or not school board members support providing educational services for the gifted therefore may be a political question (for example, "What will my constituency think?") as well as an educational issue. The scope of a gifted program—the number of grades and categories of gifted children served, the diversity of program alternatives and activities, the types of support services—will be affected by the support and funding by school board members.

Programs for gifted and talented students, by definition, are directed at a minority of children and adolescents. Therefore, teachers and parents must convince board members that even though gifted children are a minority, their educational needs are genuine and they must be served as part of a comprehensive educational program. How can educators and parents encourage board members to maintain a quality gifted program in a school district? The following are some suggestions for fostering support:

Keep board members educated and aware. Before board members voted for that gifted program, parents probably attended meetings and, in a positive way, showed interest in gifted education. When the G/T program is in place, that communication process must continue. Teachers or coordinators may make yearly presentations on program progress. If an oral presentation is not feasible, a short written report is helpful. Brevity is critical, since board members often are overwhelmed with reports.

Keep board members involved. One or two board members should be included on each district or school G/T steering committee. Board members can be invited to in-service meetings, parent meetings, or student performances and shows. They also may be invited to speak at local or state parent meetings or other educational meetings.

Help board members to be accountable. For board members to justify continued support and

funding for gifted programs, they absolutely must be assured that the program is achieving its objectives. Educators therefore must keep board members informed of the effectiveness and accomplishments of the G/T program.

There also may be pressure on board members to jump on the de-tracking bandwagon and, in the process, eliminate grouping opportunities for gifted students and the gifted program itself. They must be reminded that the issues are separate—that tracking plans can be changed (if necessary) without trashing G/T programs, and that the very real academic, social, and personal needs of the gifted require grouping.

Encourage boards to have a written policy. Board policy is a formalization of philosophy and should be incorporated into a formal policy manual. The written policy becomes the basis by which the school administration and teaching staff can justify decisions favorable to gifted education. An example of a written school board policy is shown in Inset 3.3.

Be patient, but not too patient. Board members need time to gather support and plan resources for a comprehensive gifted program. Furthermore, they logically must view the gifted program in relation to the total needs of the district. At the same time, however, parents and educators must not permit board members to forget or indefinitely postpone the needs of gifted children, regardless of the stresses of educational problems and too-small budgets.

Remember that all board members should be encouraged to support gifted education. On any school board there always will be a variety of viewpoints on gifted education. Some members will be active supporters, and it may be tempting to believe that they alone can keep programs going. It is necessary, however, to also focus one's attention on those less willing potential supporters, those who require further convincing. Note their doubts and questions and make a special effort to personally give them the information they need to convince them that gifted education truly is legitimate,

A Sample School Board Policy

The Board of Education and professional staff members are dedicated to developing a comprehensive program for the identification and education of the gifted and talented child. Empathy and understanding are of paramount importance for all personnel having contact with such a child, and are basic to achievement of the district goals.

The gifted and talented child is an individual who, by virtue of outstanding abilities, is capable of high performance. This child possesses demonstrated or potential intellectual or specific academic abilities, leadership capabilities, creativity, or talent in the performing or visual arts. This child may need educational services beyond those being provided by the regular school program in order to realize his/her potential.

To provide a comprehensive program for the gifted and talented child, the Board recognizes that:

1. Early identification of the gifted and talented child is necessary to maximize the opportunities for the child's own self-realization. This shall be accomplished through the application of several criteria.

2. The educational program should provide for continuity and overlap among the elementary, junior high, and high school levels. The program should specify long-range goals for the district, with major emphasis on differentiated curriculum and programming.

3. The objectives of the educational program shall be to meet the gifted and talented child's needs, whether they be intellectual, social, physical, or emotional.

4. Active parental involvement is viewed as an integral and crucial ingredient of a quality gifted and talented program. Every effort should be made to foster parental involvement in all aspects of their child's educational program.

5. Qualified instructional and administrative personnel with appropriate knowledge, training, and experience are required to implement an effective program of education for the gifted and talented.

6. The achievement of a quality gifted and talented educational program demands the presence of a competent ancillary support staff, particularly for the early identification of the gifted or talented child.

7. The administration of the gifted and talented program shall provide leadership and coordination in developing and maintaining a comprehensive district K–12 program.

8. The placement and progress of the gifted or talented child will be continually evaluated and documented, with periodic progress reports issued to the parents of the child.

---

important, and a widespread national, even international movement. Even if they cannot be converted into strong supporters, the strength of their opposition might at least be reduced.

Help board members be answerable to their public. Board members will be asked by constituents why they support gifted education. They will also be given reasons why they should *not*

help gifted students. In raising their awareness of the needs of the gifted, give board members the information they will require to justify to their constituents the existence and funding of special programs for the gifted. The issues they will need to debate may not always seem reasonable, but they nonetheless must be prepared with answers. Some issues to which board members often must respond are included in Inset 3.4.

INSET 3.4 _____

Some Questions School Board Members Must Answer

1. *Isn't gifted education elitist?*

RESPONSE: Gifted education only provides appropriate education for children who need a special challenge. These children come from all neighborhoods and economic backgrounds. Children from poor families often need G/T education the most because their families frequently cannot afford enrichment opportunities for them. Also, difficult financial circumstances and backgrounds sometimes prevent parents from having higher expectations for their children. If we are to keep our country a place where people can achieve regardless of their economic background, gifted education can help us. It provides a special challenge to all very bright and talented children, regardless of their cultural or economic background.

2. *We have special programs for the low-ability child and the high-ability child—but what about the average child?*

RESPONSE: Most educational programs are geared to the needs of the average child. In a real sense, most money is now spent on the average child. We agree that the average child should never be short-changed in the educational process, but neither should the gifted child.

3. *Aren't all children really gifted, so don't we need to provide for all their gifts?*

RESPONSE: In a sense, yes, all children certainly do have special gifts and talents. Some may play basketball well; some sew well; others have marvelous personal charm. The purpose of a gifted program is to provide for students' academic and creative needs not met by the regular educational program. For example, a star basketball player already has the team; the sewer has an opportunity to do excellent work in home economics courses. However, the young creative writer or poet rarely has a writing class to challenge and focus his/her skill; nor is the mathematics whiz provided with advanced or accelerated math. These students may be bored, and their talents are not challenged or strengthened. When we find special gifts and talents, we must provide opportunities to develop them.

4. *Why should we spend more money for kids who will make it anyway?*

RESPONSE: While many gifted kids will "make it anyway," it is nonetheless unfair to hold them back and make them succeed in spite of the system. More importantly, many gifted children do not "make it anyway." Their lost talent is both a personal tragedy for them and a loss to society. Studies of high school dropouts have found that between 9 and 20 percent are in the gifted IQ range—certainly many more than one would expect based on their ability, and certainly a waste.

Schools often turn off gifted children because they do not provide appropriate challenges. Further, when children become bored they sometimes use their creative energy and their giftedness in inappropriate, antisocial, and even destructive ways. They need special help and guidance.

5. *Can we afford to pay for more special education?*

RESPONSE: Gifted programs can be very inexpensive, compared to all other kinds of special education. Also, we save money in the long run by investing small amounts to help make school more meaningful. This small investment helps insure us against larger problems that can be more costly—for example, bored, apathetic, or even antisocial students, to say nothing of lost talent development.

6. *What do the rest of the kids get out of it?*

RESPONSE: Teachers who become involved in gifted education learn to stimulate creative development, to use questions effectively, to foster good self-concepts and humanistic attitudes, to individualize instruction, and other valuable concepts and skills. Much of this can be—and is—applied in the regular classroom. They become better teachers, and this benefits other children as well.

Also, when there are gifted programs in a school, it becomes apparent to all that excellence is rewarded and valued. When excellence is valued more children become motivated to achieve, and we sometimes discover giftedness where we might not have expected to find it. For example, if there has been peer pressure not to achieve, some students will hide their abilities and talents. Gifted programs encourage these children to achieve, too. So while providing for the special needs of gifted children, we also encourage hard work and excellence in our schools for all children.

Support school board members who support gifted education.   When school board members visibly endorse a program, they need to know there is a public "out there" supporting them. Be vocal in expressing your appreciation to board members who assist with the education you believe in. You can also help them in their campaigns, both formally and informally (for example, by telling your friends what a fine job you believe they are doing). Keeping supporters of gifted education in office will help them to provide appropriate educational opportunities in your community.

PERSPECTIVES OF OTHER TEACHERS

Not all teachers agree that gifted students truly need special services. In fact, some are downright antagonistic. However, with time and exposure some indifferent teachers come to understand the issues and concerns and will become more receptive to gifted programming. Others will never change, and progifted teachers simply have to work around them.

What are their concerns? Some will have the same reservations expressed to school board members (see Inset 3.4); others will express different problems. For example:

Some teachers will object to their brightest students leaving their classes; they will miss the contributions these students make.

Some will argue that they already are challenging the gifted children in their classrooms (sometimes they are, more often they are not; Archambault and Hallmark, 1992)

Some will complain that the gifted program requires additional work, and they already are overworked.

Some believe that the gifted child is somehow "getting out of" required work, and will individually penalize those children by requiring makeup work or even "busy work."

If they teach a section of gifted students, some teachers will penalize them by grading on a normal curve, ignoring the fact that the students were preselected. A few might delight in awarding gifted children *C*'s and *D*'s to somehow prove the students are *not* gifted.

Some may quote Jeannie Oakes (1985) regarding questionable benefits of ability grouping, citing damaging effects on the self-concepts of slow-track students. Others may quote *The Hurried Child* (Elkind, 1981), a book that describes harm caused by pushing children beyond a natural developmental pace.

Some negative teachers may subtly attempt to sabotage the gifted program.

There is no secret psychological strategy to elicit the cooperation and support of every teacher. One should, however, be ready for antigifted attacks and not take them personally. In remaining positive there is a better chance of gaining converts and allies. For example, you can listen to their arguments and try to explain the unmet needs of gifted children. Negative teachers can be encouraged to take a course in gifted education or to attend a conference with you. Lend them this book. Make the assumption that they *do* care about *all* children and that with a better understanding of the issue they may develop a sincere concern for gifted children as a mistreated minority.

Fortunately, in most school districts there will be more allies than enemies. There will be many teachers who enthusiastically support the program and contribute time and ideas. There will be many who enjoy the new challenge of gifted education and the excitement of seeing new enthusiasm in energetic and talented children. Without these supporters, being a teacher of the gifted would be lonely indeed.

SCOPE AND SEQUENCE IN GIFTED PROGRAMS

Scope and sequence refers to the relationship—or alignment—of broad program goals and objectives to actual classroom experiences. Van Tassel-Baska (1988a, 1988b, 1988c) emphasized that learning activities for the gifted in one area and at one grade level affect all other areas and levels. Therefore, curriculum planning and development should have a long-term focus, encompassing grades K through 12. Curriculum for the gifted should include (1) adapting current curriculum to the needs of the gifted, (2) adapting other appropriate curriculum for gifted students (e.g., *Junior Great Books*), and (3) developing new curriculum.

A common tendency is to develop curriculum at the unit level, rather than a broader school or district level. For example, at the district's urging an individual teacher may develop a special curriculum unit designed for a particular age group of gifted students. On one hand, developing individual classroom units is both worthy and necessary. On the other, such units often turn out to be idiosyncratic, interpretable and teachable only by the person who developed them, not related to units created by other teachers, and out of sync with the broader goals of a district-wide, long-term program (Van Tassel-Baska, 1988b). A common result for gifted children is wearisome repetition in a later grade.

In designing a district-wide plan, Van Tassel-Baska (1988b) recommended considering these questions pertaining to *scope*:

• How important are certain skills and concepts for gifted learners?
• How broadly should various skills and concepts be presented?
• What is critical new content to which gifted learners should be exposed?
• How much time will be needed to engage in various topics at an appropriate level of depth?
• Is the teaching staff capable of delivering the nature and extent of the proposed curriculum?

Program developers might consider these questions pertaining to *sequence*:

• At what stages are the gifted learners ready for certain curriculum experiences?
• What developmental transitions must be considered in planning a curriculum sequence?

• What is the desired cumulative effect of gifted students' engagement in specified curriculum experiences?
• How can learning experiences be organized at sufficiently abstract levels to accommodate fully the capacities of gifted learners?
• What contents, processes, and products should appear in the comprehensive curriculum plan at different points in the schooling process (i.e., over 13 years)?

Such questions aid the design of a comprehensive program plan, and the *alignment* of program-level goals and objectives with specific exemplary classroom materials, resources, activities, and teaching units.

THE DEATH OF GIFTED PROGRAMS

We noted in Chapter 1 that many have interpreted the detracking movement as a call to exterminate programs for the gifted, which almost invariably require grouping. Other concerns also have led to the demise of gifted programs.

Mosley (1982) discussed problem areas that he cast as "Suggestions to Ensure the Brevity of Your Gifted Program."

1. Make sure that the program always is "fun." Entertaining students is a high priority.

2. Talk about the program continuously; other teachers love to hear about your innovative program, your challenging students, and your field trips. Try also to tell parents of average children about the marvelous qualities of gifted students.

3. Try to interrupt the regular school day as much as possible, and on a regular basis. Other teachers enjoy this.

4. Emphasize that you are a "loner" and that your program is "different." You must separate yourself from the rest of the school system.

5. Avoid reading literature in the gifted education area. Because each program is different, you will learn nothing from the experiences of others.

6. Be sure to ignore professional adults in the community. They have little to offer.

7. Avoid using parents in the program. They sometimes are demanding and will only confuse matters.

8. If the program is challenged, it is easiest to concede that the program is of borderline relevance. If a response is necessary, try to use jargon and clichés, such as "high taxonomic levels," "Marland's U.S.O.E. definition," and "Renzulli's Schoolwide Enrichment Model."

9. Try to get widespread publicity for expensive activities such as field trips, so everyone will know that the program is adequately funded.

Mosley (1982) and Hickey (1990) identified common problems that alienate other teachers, perhaps administrators, and certainly parents of average and troubled learners:

• Making the program look like a fun-and-games waste of time.
• Leading other teachers to believe that your students are motivated, easy to teach, and receive marvelous opportunities unavailable to regular students—while they are struggling with slow learners, at-risk students, and perhaps students with disabilities.
• Leading parents to believe that upper-crust children are receiving opportunities that their children cannot have.
• Program participants behaving arrogantly.
• Students not in the program having poor self-concepts.
• Disrupting class routines by pulling out gifted kids, for example, forcing regular teachers to deal with whether or not critical skills were missed.
• Losing gifted students' contributions to class. As we noted earlier, many teachers like gifted students in their classes; they serve as "good student" models, and are available to help other students.
• Separating the G/T teacher and gifted students from the rest of the school program and providing them with expensive equipment, materials, and field trips, thus making charges of elitism easy to defend.

• Creating problems of content coverage repetition, for example, in the next grades.
• G/T teachers not communicating with regular teachers about the program.
• Regular classroom teachers not being adequately trained; they are unaware of needs, resources, and curriculum appropriate for educating gifted students and have difficulty generating assignments.

The dilemma is that many G/T programs are guilty of many of these charges; some problems are built-in to the program design.

In an article entitled "Life and Death of a Gifted Program: Lessons Not Yet Learned," Starko (1990) described a G/T program that existed from 1958 to 1969—spawned in part by Sputnik—which included both acceleration and enrichment components. It was abandoned for many of the same reasons for which programs are folding up today.

As background, students were selected if they scored 125 IQ (Stanford-Binet), had good school attitudes, were emotionally and socially mature, and were high achievers in *all* subjects. Teachers had no training in teaching the gifted: "[the principal] just whirled into the room and said, 'We're going to have a special class next year. Want to teach it? We think you're creative,' and whirled right out again." Program objectives were honorable, and essentially the same as those formulated in the 1990s: (1) To prevent underachievement by very capable children; (2) to stimulate interest by providing opportunities to learn at one's own rate; (3) to prevent disciplinary problems resulting from boredom; and (4) to provide challenging and deep learning experiences commensurate with the capabilities of the children.

The acceleration classes telescoped the basic skills of first, second, and third grade into two years. However, they differed from other classes not only in pace, but in "'lots of projects, fairs, displays, lots of writing—more poetry than any group since,' writing stories, poems, ballads, and a particular emphasis and enjoyment in science that seems a far cry from the *Dick and Jane* workbooks and coloring dittos faced by other classes" (p. 35).

The enrichment classes also worked at a rapid pace ("Man, we moved!" "We accelerated more than we should have . . . parents really wanted acceleration.") In addition, enrichment teachers focused on developing creativity, with greater spontaneity in class activities ("An idea came up and we could run with it!") and individual research and problem solving ("Kids would lead, do the searching, go to the library," p. 35).

A program evaluation showed that the accelerated and enriched students achieved equally well, but the enrichment students seemed superior in depth of understanding, creativity, and written expression. Questionnaires from teachers *not* in the program uncovered the following problems. As you read the criticisms, consider whether they could apply to G/T programs in the 1990s.

• Students not selected were resentful.
• Too much reliance on IQ scores in selection.
• An "intellectual class structure" (snobbishness) appeared.
• There was too much pressure on students; levels of competition were unhealthy.

The accelerated classes were abandoned in 1965; enrichment classes for grades 4 to 6 continued. In 1967 these parent and teacher criticisms and concerns about the enrichment program surfaced:

• Students were isolated, segregated from others; there was limited interaction with regular students.
• There was too much pressure and stress.
• Snobbishness existed.
• Junior and senior high school students seem successful without having participated in a special elementary program.
• Community composition shifted to more blue collar workers, resulting in less parent pressure for a gifted program. Teachers believed that the school focus should shift to less capable students.
• Identification was too restrictive.
• A teacher survey indicated that "many teachers

believed that the needs of capable students could be met in heterogeneous classes through individualization, technology (e.g., tape recorders), and team teaching" (p. 36).

• Students acquired (unhealthy) levels of perfectionism (Chapter 17).
• Students "leveled off" after they were in the program; some no longer seemed superior.
• Lower-ability students were deprived of opportunities to develop leadership.
• The program appeared to be a reward for polite, cooperative, high-achieving children with good attitudes; it was a status symbol.
• There were concerns that all parents would want the best teachers for their children.
• There were concerns that these activities would be good for all children.

Concluded Starko, "As long as the best education happens in the gifted and talented program and less than the best education happens in regular classrooms, gifted education is destined to be a viewed as a prize, a status symbol, a plum. Programs viewed in that way are, so to speak, ripe for the picking" (p. 38).

Starko did report positive comments on the program. As with many of the criticisms, these also are valid in today's G/T programs.

• Good preparation for later academics.
• Elimination of boredom.
• Opportunities to follow interests.
• Sense of community among gifted students.
• Good effects on social and emotional maturity.
• Good academic stimulation.
• Great special opportunities (e.g., Learning French, making up silly operas on the playground).

There are solutions to the difficulties itemized by Mosley (1982), Hickey (1990), and Starko (1990). A first principle, which has been articulated by Treffinger (e.g., 1986a) and others, is to blend or integrate the gifted program into the regular school program in ways that allow *all* children to benefit—and which help the gifted program and "gifted" students become less conspicuous.

Feldhusen (1992), for example, observed that we typically identify, label, and honor the "gifted few"—then are embarrassed when we must refer to others as "nongifted." His solution to the labeling problem is a plan he calls *Talent Identification and Development* (TIDE). The plan includes *diagnostic selection*, which is identifying students who are most likely to profit from the high-level, fast-paced, and enriched curriculum that a school plans to offer. The opportunities can include, for example, honors and elective classes, acceleration opportunities such as higher-level classes and early high school and college admission, Saturday and summer programs (e.g., Feldhusen, 1991b), and specialized clubs and organizations. Schools thus can offer special services for talented youth in, for example, math, chemistry, biology, art, or photography, yet avoid problems associated with the word "gifted" and "the bestowal of gifted status."

Another way to integrate the gifted program with the regular school program is to adopt Renzulli's Schoolwide Enrichment Model (to be elaborated in Chapter 7). Briefly, enrichment activities, which in most programs are restricted to gifted students, are brought into the regular classroom for all students, sometimes by the G/T coordinator and sometimes by the regular teacher. These include creativity, thinking skills, research skills, self-concept development, and others. To open the program to more students—and simultaneously reduce elitism charges—a comparatively large subset of the school population, about 15 to 20 percent, is identified for a *talent pool*. Talent pool students are encouraged to develop independent projects that they can pursue in a resource room with the G/T coordinator. Opportunities for such independent projects, in fact, are available to *all* students who show sufficient motivation and creativity. The gifted program is thus blended into the regular program; participation is not restrictive; and program activities are worthwhile ones that develop analytical, creative, and other thinking skills, as well as skills in areas of high student interest. Importantly, gifted students have oppor-

tunities to meet with others like themselves for social and intellectual support.

SUMMARY

Four main components of a gifted education program are (1) program philosophy and goals, (2) definition and identification, (3) instruction (grouping, acceleration, enrichment), and (4) evaluation and modification.

One can view program planning as a series of who, what, where, when, how, and why questions.

Fifteen problem areas in program planning are summarized as follows.

1. A needs assessment aims at determining the discrepancy between the current and the desired state of G/T education in the district. Key question: What are the needs of the gifted and talented students? Because gifted students are a minority, only "sufficient" (not majority) support should be needed to establish a clear need for G/T services. A steering committee for planning a program may consist of teachers, parents, administrators, school board members, and perhaps the librarian, school psychologist, counselor, and gifted high school students.

2. Preliminary personal and staff education, such as determining the present status of gifted education in the area and an acquaintance with state legislation and state plans, is necessary for informed planning.

3. A written statement of philosophy and rationale should explain the reasons for, and the goals and objectives of, a program. An expanded statement can serve as a written program plan.

4. Types of gifts and talents to be accommodated must be specified, a matter related to one's definition of giftedness. Regarding numbers, while some programs are highly restrictive (e.g., SMPY), the talent pool approach accepts many students.

5. Identification methods and criteria must be consistent with one's definition of giftedness and coordinated with the type of program being planned. The methods must be defensible, yet both objective and subjective.

6. Identification methods must include plans for locating gifted female, culturally different, economically disadvantaged, underachieving, and handicapped students.

7. Staff responsibilities and accountability checks (such as monthly meetings or reports) must be planned.

8. Support staff and services will include school psychologists and counselors, district and perhaps state coordinators, and consultants. Counseling services are essential. Consultants can give workshops or work individually with staff.

9. Program plans should include both acceleration and enrichment alternatives. There are many specifics to select from. They should aim at defensible goals and objectives, namely, the development of high-level skills and knowledge.

10. Any plan will require attention to the organizational and administrative design, including space allocations, record keeping, modifications to the budget, and much more. Much planning usually is at the district level.

11. Transportation needs cannot be ignored.

12. Community professionals and organizations can supply enriching field trips for all students or for small groups of G/T students, mentorships, and career education—for example, class presentations.

13. In-service workshops begin with general "awareness" information and proceed to the identification of the gifted or talented child and then other matters. Workshop content should be directly applicable (e.g., methods, techniques), perhaps including hands-on activities. Visits to several types of programs are valuable.

14. Budgetary needs and cost-effectiveness must be considered from the outset. Some programs operate on almost nothing; others pay for teacher-coordinators plus plenty of materials and equip-

ment. Federal, state, or private funds often can be obtained.

15. Program evaluation is important for survival and expansion. Every component of the program can be evaluated. Formative evaluations are continuous ones aimed at modification and improvement. Summative evaluations at the end of the year evaluate overall success.

School board members must be convinced that G/T students have important unmet needs. Suggestions for fostering support include keeping board members educated and involved, helping them be accountable, and changing the attitudes of nonsupportive members.

For various reasons, many teachers may not support a G/T program in a given school. One should attempt to alter their attitudes in a more positive and helpful direction.

Considerations of scope and sequence refer to aligning actual classroom units and activities with higher-level program goals and objectives—preferably across the entire K-12 spectrum. Van Tassel-Baska recommended that scope considerations include the value of certain skills, the depth in which they should be taught, and time allotments for various topics. Sequence considerations included coordinating curriculum (contents, processes, products) with developmental stages, and considering the desired cumulative effects of the curriculum experiences.

Some reasons for the death of gifted programs include, in addition to the de-tracking movement: "fun-and-games" activities; teachers and parents believing (rightfully) that other students are deprived of high-quality opportunities; separating G/T teachers and students from the rest of the school program; no training for G/T teachers; resentfulness of students not selected; snobbishness; restrictive identification methods (particularly, over-reliance on IQ scores); high pressure on students in the program; and the program appearing to be a reward for high achievement and cooperation.

One solution is Renzulli's talent pool approach

(Schoolwide Enrichment Model), which blends the G/T program with the rest of the school, includes many students, provides many enrichment activities to all students, and provides worthwhile learning activities for gifted students.

APPENDIX 3.1 IDEAS FOR STATEMENTS OF PHILOSOPHY, RATIONALE, AND OBJECTIVES

To provide gifted and talented students with an educational environment that will provide the greatest possible development of their abilities, thus enabling them to realize their contributions to self and society.

"The gifted and talented represent a group of students whose learning style and thinking dimensions demand experiences which are outside the educational mainstream . . . (we need) an education commensurate with each child's ability to learn" (Kaplan, 1974).

To provide programs designed to help meet the psychological, social, educational, and career needs of gifted and talented students.

To assist students in becoming individuals who are able to take self-initiated action and accept responsibility for that action, and who are capable of intelligent choice, independent learning, and problem solving.

(Our program will include) ". . . administrative procedures and instructional strategies which afford intellectual acquisition, thinking practice, and self-understanding" (Kaplan, 1974).

To meet the special needs of minority gifted children.

To develop a functional procedure for identifying gifted and talented students in the school in order that they may express and develop their gifts or talents.

To provide a program that will stimulate individual interests and develop individual abilities in academic and/or talent areas.

To provide the superior learner with new and highly challenging learning experiences that are not ordinarily included in the regular classroom curriculum.

At the conclusion of their elementary school experience, students will demonstrate competency in basic skills at least equal to that of other elementary schools in the district, even though they are exposed to numerous areas of instruction not commonly found in traditional elementary school programs.

To provide opportunities that will develop self-awareness, personal strengths, and social responsibilities beyond those in the regular school program.

To provide gifted children with the opportunity to explore personal interests through independent study and community involvement.

To foster high-level thinking and self-development processes, resulting in a more complete, productive individual who is challenged by the school environment.

To provide a learning atmosphere that will enable the gifted child to develop his/her potential and exceptional abilities, particularly in the areas of decision making, planning, performing, reasoning, creating, and communicating.

To provide experiences that develop the higher operations of analyzing, synthesizing, divergent production, and evaluation.

To provide activities and experiences that will stimulate critical thinking, comprehension, competency, and creativity.

To enable those students desiring to do so to prepare for advanced placement.

To prescribe particular curricula to meet individual needs.

To encourage cross-discipline exploration.

To include strong components of basic skills, career awareness, sex-equity, and multiethnic experiences.

To develop an ability to transfer information to humanistic goals.

To develop intrinsic motivation.

To provide experiences that guide a student toward independence.

To provide gifted and talented students with a positive self-concept.

To foster awareness of self and others.

Many parents and other community leaders will be involved in the learning process.

To develop problem-solving abilities and creative thinking skills; develop research skills; strengthen individual interests; develop independent study skills; exercise communication skills in the humanities (visual, oral, and written); receive intellectual stimulation from contact with other highly motivated students; expand their learning activities to include resources available in the entire community area.

"The goal of any program for the gifted should be to provide meaningful experiences in the most efficient and effective way in order to maximize learning and individual development and to minimize boredom, confusion, and frustration" (Fox, 1979).

CHAPTER 4

IDENTIFYING GIFTED AND TALENTED STUDENTS

Rather than developing identification procedures and programs that are elitist and exclusive, programs for the gifted should reflect American pluralism.

E. Susanne Richert (1991, p. 93)

There probably are as many different strategies and policies for identifying gifted and talented students as there are programs. And in the words of Feldhusen, Hoover, and Sayler (1990), "The ideal identification system has not been developed." Logically, if the many types of abilities, gifts, and talents are combined with the many possible measures of each—student tests, grades, and questionnaires; teacher, parent, and peer questionnaires, ratings and nominations; plus evaluations of products, performances, and perhaps motivation—the number of permutations and combinations will boggle even a gifted mind.

For example, some programs will base identification entirely upon intelligence test scores, either admitting all students who score above a certain cutoff, or else selecting the top 3 to 5 percent regardless of the particular scores. According to Cassidy and Johnson (1986), one state defines giftedness as the "top 3 percent" in intellectual ability; another as scoring two standard deviations above the mean (top 2.28 percent) in intellectual development; a third state allows for artistic and other forms of giftedness, but absolutely requires that "Persons shall be assigned to a program for the gifted when they have an IQ score of 130 or higher." According to Burns, Mathews, and Mason (1990), to qualify for placement in a Louisiana

public school gifted program, preschool children must score three standard deviations above the mean (IQ = 145), or two and one-half standard deviations above the mean *and* score in the 98–99th percentile in reading *and* math capabilities; children in grades 1 to 3 must score two and one-half standard deviations above the mean to qualify (IQ = 138); children in grades 4 to 12 must score two standard deviations above the mean to qualify (IQ = 130). Such restrictions intrinsically demand IQ identification criteria.

In the various *Talent Search* programs, college-based summer courses for gifted junior high school students (e.g., Cohn, 1983a, 1991; Benbow, 1991; see Chapter 5), *Scholastic Aptitude Test-Mathematics* (SAT-M) and *Scholastic Aptitude Test-Verbal* (SAT-V) scores, which measure mathematical and verbal reasoning, respectively, and sometimes *American College Testing Program* (ACT) scores, are virtually the sole admission criteria.

Other programs take a multidimensional approach. As a common but minor modification of the strict IQ criterion, teachers may review IQ scores, achievement scores, and grades to nominate students for a G/T program. Such nominations tend to be closely related to student grades (Richert, 1985, 1991). More serious multidimensional approaches will identify students who seem high in any one of a number of criteria, particularly the five components of the U.S. Department of Education definition: general intellectual ability, specific academic talent, creativity, leadership, or talent in the visual or performing arts. Cassidy and Hossler (1992) reported that most states have adopted definitions of giftedness—which are supposed to guide identification—that are consistent with the federal statement.

As we will see later in this chapter, the *Kranz Talent Identification Instrument* (KTII; Kranz, 1981, 1991) assesses 10 categories of gifts and talents, including most on the Department of Education list. The *Baldwin Identification Matrix* (Baldwin, 1977, 1984) evaluates 11 or 12 talents, also including most of the Department of Education talents. Unlike the "either/or" Department of Education and KTII approaches, in which a student may be selected for G/T services if gifted in any area, ratings on the total Baldwin Matrix subtests are added to produce a single total score, which makes ranking students rather easy.

A survey of 1172 school districts by the Richardson Foundation (Wilkie, 1985) showed teacher nomination to be the most common means of identification (91 percent), followed by achievement tests (90 percent), intelligence tests (89 percent), and grades (50 percent). Self-nomination and parent nominations each were used by 6 percent of the school districts.

While identification procedures and policies are mixed, to say the least, gifted educators do agree the problem is central. A recent poll of 29 experts rated *identification* as priority number 1 among a list of 12 issues (selection and training of teachers, and curriculum selection were other high priorities; Cramer, 1991).

Overview

This chapter will first review some issues that complicate the significant—and often delicate—matter of selecting participants for a G/T program. An awareness of these issues should help the program developer design procedures that are as rea-

sonable, fair, accurate, defensible (for example, to parents), and appropriate to the program goals as possible. We then will turn to descriptions of specific identification strategies and instruments. For each, its unique advantages and difficulties will be noted, along with suggestions for proper use and interpretation.

THOUGHTS AND ISSUES IN IDENTIFICATION

Pros and Cons of Formal Identification Methods

In her article "The Case Against Formal Identification," Davidson (1986) expressed strong frustration with all formal testing, rating, and nomination procedures, including the use of point systems and cutoffs. Said Davidson, such procedures do not allow students actually to demonstrate their abilities in areas in which they are interested and talented (see Inset 4.1). Regarding IQ scores, Davidson noted that a student with a tested IQ of 110 may show greater giftedness in the sense of originality and thought-provoking ideas and answers than a student with a tested IQ of 140—who naturally will be selected for the program. Even creativity tests do not measure every aspect of a child's creativeness, noted Davidson, and peer, parent, and teacher nominations often are biased in favor of popular, English-speaking, middle-class students.

Davidson's three-step solution, designed to not exclude truly gifted children, included, first, setting a liberal selection quota of about 15 to 20 percent of the school, in accord with Renzulli's talent pool philosophy (Renzulli and Reis, 1985a, 1991b). Second, and apparently despite her reservations about testing, students who score in the 90th percentile or above on intelligence, achievement, or creativity tests (according to local norms) have clear needs and should automatically be placed in the program. Third, and most importantly, Davidson recommended the increased use of *informal* parent and teacher nominations, based

INSET 4.1 _____

The Case Against Formal Identification

The following is a condensation of a spoof by Karen Davidson (1986) that illustrates how formal testing and identification measures could inadvertently exclude truly gifted students from programs for the gifted and talented.

John loved to run and he was very good at it. He always ran the four miles down country roads from school to home. In early September John's school began a formal identification process to select students for the cross-country team.

With the peer nomination procedure, few of his fellow students had ever seen him run, and so he was nominated just once and received one point. Teachers nominated the students with the flashy jogging pants—the ones who looked like runners. One teacher saw John chase a dog and thought he was fast, and nominated him—one more point. With parent nominations, John's dad thought cross-country teams were silly, but John got two points because his dad knew he was fast.

On the *California Standardized Test of Running Skills*, a written test, John scored at the 56th percentile because he did not know such terms as "hitting the wall" and "pacing yourself." Other students had taken running lessons and scored above the 90th percentile. John earned one point.

A test of running ability partly evaluated knowledge of famous runners and muscles used in running. When John finally had a chance to run, the teacher evaluated only his form and style. He earned two more points.

John's total score in the identification procedure was seven points. With a cutoff of 15, he wasn't even close.

The moral of the story is that: "Many students who would profit from enrichment and from differentiated programs are not identified; formal identification procedures do not allow them to demonstrate their abilities in the areas in which they are most interested and able" (Davidson, 1986).

---

on observations of creativity, critical thinking, problem solving, or motivation.

Top 3 to 5 Percent or a Liberal Talent Pool Approach

The traditional method for selecting students for participation in a G/T program is this: Each fall, a school screening committee reviews data from many sources for each potential candidate, for example, ability and achievement scores and nominations. The top 3 to 5 percent are selected and labeled "gifted"—and the identification process is ended for the year.

More and more, districts and individual schools are adopting Renzulli's *talent pool* strategy, part of the *Schoolwide Enrichment Model* (Renzulli and Reis, 1985a, 1991b; see Chapter 7). Currently, it is the most popular programming model in the United States, Canada—and the world (Renzulli, 1987), and for good reason. With the talent pool approach, a generous, open and flexible 15 to 20 percent of the school population is identified according to ". . . general ability or any and all performance areas that might be considered high priorities in a given school's programming effort" (Renzulli, 1986, p. 76). In professional communities with large numbers of high ability students, the talent pool may consist of 25 percent or, in extraordinary neighborhoods, even 100 percent of the student body (Renzulli, 1987). From the talent pool, some students—high in motivation and creativity—self-select an intensive research, literary, artistic, or other creative project. A detailed recommendation for identifying talent pool candidates by using many criteria will be presented later in this chapter.

The main identification-related attractions of the talent pool approach are that, most importantly, (a) more students receive the *opportunities*, *resources*, and *encouragement* provided in special programs—the door remains open to many children whose gifts and talents simply are not measured by tests nor easily recognized by teachers. As Renzulli (e.g., 1986, 1987) has stressed repeatedly, society's most creative contributors are not always found in the "top 3 to 5 percent." In addition, with the talent pool solution (b) teachers remain concerned with identifying students for independent projects throughout the school year, not just in September; (c) charges of elitism are reduced; and (d) the difficult problem of deciding "who is and is not admissible" becomes a non-problem. When in doubt, admit.

Disadvantaged, Minority, Handicapped, and Female Students

The identification of gifted and talented minority, economically disadvantaged, and culturally different students is an especially sensitive problem. Too often administrators claim they have "none of those children in our school." Teachers, too, are guilty of this oversight. LeRose (1977), for example, reported, "Martin Jenkins, who has conducted more studies of high IQ African-American children than anyone else, has commented on how frequently children with IQs above 150 have not been spotted as outstanding by their teachers."

Culturally different learners do tend to score, on the average, about one standard deviation (15 points) lower than middle-class students on stan-

dardized intelligence tests. We repeat, "on the average." Many minority children will score extremely high in both verbal and nonverbal measures of intelligence. Nonetheless, if IQ testing is part of the selection battery, there is frequently a built-in bias against minority and economically disadvantaged children (Baldwin, 1975, 1991; Skuy *et al.*, 1990). And if your school population includes minority and culturally different students (for example, African-American, Hispanic, Native American, Native Hawaiian, Vietnamese, immigrant), it simply will not be acceptable to produce an all-white list of children of middle-class professional parents.

Issues related to minority and culturally different students will be explored in more detail in Chapter 13, along with suggestions for identification and programming. For now, we will emphasize that a multidimensional approach to identification is essential for identifying gifted and talented minority students—a procedure that looks beyond IQ scores. The quota system is one frequently used solution to the problem of ensuring racial, gender, geographical, or economic balance in G/T programs (Gallagher, 1991b; LeRose, 1978; Smith, LeRose, and Clasen, 1991). For example, if a school contains 30 percent African-American children, then the G/T program would contain 30 percent African-American children.

Often we overlook gifted students among the ranks of physically or psychologically disabled (for example, learning disabled) students. Do not be shocked when ten-year-old Joe Smith, whose dyslexia prevents him from reading or writing normally, is nominated as an intellectually or artistically gifted child. Albert Einstein, Thomas Edison, Nelson Rockefeller, Picasso, and other "slow learners" have had the same problems.

Regarding girls, we should be aware in our identification activities that if math scores, science grades, or computer expertise are criteria, girls can be discriminated against. Girls also may be more conforming, less aggressive, and less success-oriented than boys, which can influence nominations.

Biases in Ratings and Nominations

As noted earlier, there is a natural and understandable tendency for teachers to favor students who are cooperative, smiling, and anxious to please, who do their work well, neatly, and on time, and who absolutely never talk back. While "teacher pleasers" are a pleasure to work with, they may or may not be the most gifted and talented students in the class. However, they have a high likelihood of being perceived by teachers as "gifted," and of being nominated for participation in special programs. If teachers rate students on specific qualities such as academic talent, leadership, motivation, or sometimes even creativity, teacher pleasers again are likely to be selected. The extremely bright or the creative, curious, and questioning students, who may be stubborn, rule-breaking, egotistical, or otherwise high in nuisance value, may not be the teachers' favorites, but they sometimes are the most gifted.

Test Reliability and Validity

Reliability refers to the accuracy or consistency of a test, inventory, rating scale, or other selection procedure—the degree to which a person is likely to receive the same score or rating if he or she is assessed again, perhaps at another time. *Validity* is the degree to which a test or inventory actually measures what it is supposed to measure. Does the motivation, creativity, or leadership test truly measure these traits or abilities? Does the "total giftedness" score truly identify gifted students? Evidence for reliability and validity normally appears in manuals accompanying published tests and inventories.

When considering tests, questionnaires, rating scales, and nomination procedures for identifying gifted and talented students, one always must consider both the reliability and the validity of the test or procedure. No test, rating scale, questionnaire, or nomination procedure will have perfect reliability or perfect validity, and the usefulness of the instrument or procedure is tied very closely to its degree of reliability and validity. Sometimes, "face validity"—the degree to which a test simply looks like it should measure what it is intended to measure—will be the only information one has to go on.

Political Problems in Identification

In the real world of schools, identification of giftedness is surrounded by political and personal problems that go beyond reliability and validity. Teachers and administrators must be prepared for some controversies that surround identification. The criticisms one can expect will include everything from "Why isn't my child in the program?" to "Don't you dare identify my child as gifted," and anything in between. School board members may complain that teachers' children appear to be favored; teachers may note that offspring of administrators and board members are being selected. Some will call the selection process discriminatory and elitist; others will say it favors disadvantaged children.

NATIONAL REPORT ON IDENTIFICATION

In 1982, Susanne Richert, James Alvino, and Rebecca McDonnel completed the *National Report on Identification: Assessment and Recommendations for Comprehensive Identification of Gifted and Talented Youth*, a study commissioned by the U.S. Department of Education (Richert, 1985, 1991). The study focused on such issues as definitions adopted, principles of identification, identification instruments and procedures, and practices that screen out gifted students. The following are some capsule conclusions pertinent to identifying gifted students.

As for appropriate definitions, using the multidimensional U.S. Department of Education definition (Chapter 1) was endorsed because it ". . . attempts to be comprehensive in order to be applicable in many settings . . . (and) it has the legitimacy of national law behind it" (Richert, 1985).

Some principles that should underlie identification are:

1. *Advocacy.* Identification should be designed in the best interests of all students.

2. *Defensibility.* Procedures should be based on the best available research and recommendations.

3. *Equity.* Procedures should guarantee that no one is overlooked (e.g., disadvantaged children).

4. *Pluralism.* The broadest defensible definition of giftedness should be adopted.

5. *Comprehensiveness.* As many gifted learners as possible should be identified and served.

Some common but questionable practices include:

1. Despite the common adoption of the broad U.S. Department of Education definition, identification instruments tend to limit selection to academically achieving gifted students.

2. Local districts tend to seek and find white, middle-class academic achievers. Minority groups such as African-Americans, Hispanics, and Native Americans are under-represented by 30 to 70 percent.

3. Identification instruments sometimes are used to identify categories of giftedness for which they were not designed. For example, achievement and intelligence tests are used interchangeably, thus confusing the categories of specific academic ability and general intellectual ability. They also are used inappropriately to identify creative and leadership talent.

4. Diagnostic tests, designed for placement within a subject area, are inappropriately used for initial screening.

5. Multiple criteria often are combined in statistically unsound ways, producing a quantitative score that obscures important indicators of high potential.

6. Despite evidence that academic performance is not highly predictive of adult giftedness, most identification procedures are limited to achievement tests, intelligence tests, grades, and teacher recommendations.

Based on these principles and problems, some recommendations were:

1. Because giftedness has many dimensions—abilities, personality factors, and environment—measures that go beyond academic achievement must be used to find students whose abilities are not indicated by tests and school performance. Both informal and formal data must be used validly.

2. Subjective procedures such as rating scales, checklists, and nominations are a legitimate part of the identification process, especially in the early nomination stage. Rating scale and checklist items should include "negative" and unexpected characteristics indicated by research.

3. Nominations by teachers, parents, peers, and students themselves are useful if the content of the nominations is clearly related to the program options and plans.

4. Data from multiple measures, such as formal tests and informal checklists, should not be combined because their purposes and results are different.

IDENTIFICATION METHODS

Intelligence Tests

Virtually every G/T program is interested in intellectual giftedness. The bottom-line instruments for confirming suspected high intelligence are individual intelligence tests, particularly the *Wechsler Intelligence Scales for Children* and the *Stanford-Binet Intelligence Scale.* Every school psychologist is qualified to administer and interpret either of these.

Stanford-Binet Intelligence Scale.   The newest, 1986 *Stanford-Binet Intelligence Scale-Fourth Edition* is not recommended for gifted children, despite its advantage of producing four "standard age scores" (think of them as IQ scores) in the areas of *verbal reasoning*, *quantitative reasoning*, *visual/abstract reasoning*, and *short-term memory*, along with its composite standard age (IQ) score. One problem is that the upper limit of the Fourth Edition is lower (about IQ 164) than the previous edition, Form LM; extraordinary intellectual talent (e.g., IQ 180) will be missed. Form LM produces one IQ score that may be in the ozone: For elementary children there is virtually no ceiling.

A closely related yet more important complication is that the Fourth Edition produces IQ scores for gifted children that run about 13.5 points lower than Form LM, according to developers Thorndike, Hagen, and Satler (1986). Kluever and Green (1990) found one child with a Form LM IQ of 160, but a Fourth Edition IQ of 110(!); two others showed Form LM IQ scores of 144 and 160, but Fourth Edition IQs of 112 and 121, respectively.[1] It's difficult to be gifted when tested with the Stanford-Binet, Fourth Edition.

While administering the Stanford-Binet, the examiner will record relevant behavior during the test—for example, attention, activity level, self-confidence, persistence, reactions to a challenge, anxiety, coping with failure, and others.

Wechsler Intelligence Scale for Children.   Many school psychologists have used the *Wechsler Intelligence Scale for Children-Revised* (WISC-R), designed for children age 6 to 16, which produces a *Verbal* IQ score and a *Performance* (nonverbal) IQ scores, along with the combined *Full-Scale* IQ score. Therefore, a student with spatial or mechanical gifts can be identified, not just the verbally gifted. In one study, Hollinger and Kosek (1986) found that a full 35 percent of their sample of gifted students (N = 26, age 6 to 15) produced significantly discrepant *Verbal* vs. *Performance* IQ scores—they were much more outstanding in one area than the other. Further, 85 percent of the gifted students showed individual subtest scores that deviated significantly from their own average *Verbal* or *Performance* score. Examination of subtest patterns provide insights into individual

students' cognitive functioning, noted Hollinger and Kosek.

The WISC-III appeared in 1991. Changes were comparatively minor: more sample items for students, materials in color instead of black and white, and minority children appeared in the testing materials. As before, the *Verbal* and *Performance* IQ scores combine into a *Full-Scale* IQ, and all three produce IQ scores with a mean of 100 and a standard deviation of 15. Like previous editions, the WISC-III was standardized with samples of white, African-American, Hispanic, Puerto Rican, American Indian, and Asian students represented in about the same proportions as they appear in the American population. Similar to the Stanford-Binet, a school psychologist can use the WISC-III testing situation to diagnose such traits and behaviors as reactions to stress, coping with failure, the use of defense mechanisms, the child's approach to intellectual tasks, and persistence.

The WISC tests show two problems. First, the highest possible score on the Wechsler tests is 155. Second, the renorming of the WISC-III in 1991 generally shifted IQ scores down about five points. However, at the high end of the distribution, where gifted children score, WISC-III scores run about 8 or 9 points lower than WISC-R scores. Therefore, while WISC-III IQ scores cannot be fairly compared to WISC-R scores for any students, the differential is even more pronounced for gifted students. As with the Stanford-Binet, Fourth Edition, it is more difficult to be gifted when tested with the WISC-III. Finally, the ceiling on both the Stanford-Binet, Fourth Edition, and the WISC-III suggests that producers of new individual intelligence tests are not concerned with differentiating among highly gifted children.

Ben

Second-grader Ben complained to his parents of a lack of challenge at school. The teacher reported that Ben was careless in his work and needed to pay attention to detail. Ben's parents reported their concern to the school and also brought him to Rimm's Family Achievement

[1] Similar results were found by Tyler-Wood and Carri (1991).

Clinic for an evaluation. Unaware that the school psychologist had recently tested Ben with the WISC-R, the Clinic gave Ben the WISC-III and the Peabody Individual Achievement Test-Revised, *Ben's full-scale WISC-III IQ score was 128, yet his achievement test scores were 99+ percentile for all achievement subtests. A conversation with the school psychologist revealed that Ben's WISC-R score was 139; a full 11 points higher than his WISC-III score. In light of the high WISC-R score, Ben was placed in a self-contained classroom for gifted students. The lower WISC-III IQ score would not have allowed Ben special programming.*

Generally, intelligence tests scores may be used to bring curriculum more in line with gifted students' abilities. Tests with low ceilings or depressed individual scores may underestimate a child's acceleration needs. The Stanford-Binet, LM, despite being outdated, is the only test that discriminates well for highly gifted children.

Group Intelligence Tests.   IQ scores from group intelligence tests are useful for identifying gifted students because they continue to be administered routinely in many school systems, and so scores may be in the office file. Some of the better-known group intelligence tests are the *Cognitive Abilities Test*, the *SRA Primary Mental Abilities Tests*, the *Henmon-Nelson Test of Mental Ability*, the *Otis-Lennon Mental Ability Test*, and the *Kuhlman-Anderson Intelligence Tests*. However, despite their comparatively low cost and convenient group administration, consider these shortcomings: Group tests tend to be less reliable and less valid than individual tests. Also, children who are not motivated will produce lower IQ scores than their informally observed ability would indicate. Group tests are mainly verbal and are highly correlated with actual school achievement; therefore, they are biased against children who are nonverbally gifted (or who speak a subcultural

dialect). Because most group tests were designed to discriminate in the midsection of the bell curve, they tend to be unreliable at high IQ levels; a few chance errors may substantially lower a bright student's IQ score. Speed is an important factor in group tests, since all are timed. This is not true of individual intelligence tests.

In view of these problems, one well may question the value of group intelligence tests. However, children who score high on these tests virtually always will be capable and certainly should be included in a G/T program.

The SAT-M and the SAT-V, and to a lesser extent the *American College Testing Program* ACT tests, are used to identify high-level mathematical and verbal reasoning talent among seventh-graders for the *Study of Mathematically Precocious Youth* (SMPY) and *Talent Search* programs (e.g., Benbow, 1991; Cohn, 1991; Stanley, 1991a; see Chapter 5). The SAT and ACT typically are taken by college-bound high school seniors, but arrangements obviously can be made for younger students to take the tests.[2]

Based on research with adolescents who scored above 700 on the SAT-M or above 630 on the SAT-V—the 1 in 10,000 range—Benbow and Minor (1990) concluded that mathematically talented and verbally talented students represent two distinctly different forms of intellectual giftedness. Mathematically precocious students scored high on nonverbal reasoning, spatial ability, and memory tests; verbally precocious students scored higher on verbal and general knowledge types of tests.

Chapter 1 reviewed Gardner's multiple-intelligence theory, which suggested not two but seven types of intelligence: linguistic, logical-mathematical, spatial, musical, bodily-kinesthetic, interpersonal, and intrapersonal intelligence (Gardner,

[2]For example, by contacting the testing companies, College Board in Princeton, New Jersey, or American College Testing program in Iowa City, or by contacting Talent Search program directors at Johns Hopkins University, Northwestern University, Duke University, Arizona State University, or the University of Denver.

1983; Ramos-Ford and Gardner, 1991).[3] An implication is that an informed or "intelligence-fair" search for intellectual giftedness should look beyond even mathematical and verbal kinds of intelligence, and therefore beyond standard types intelligence tests, for example, to observational and qualitative types of assessment (e.g., art portfolios, music activities, peer interactions, and athletic skill; Ramos-Ford and Gardner, 1991).

A big plus for intelligence tests, group or individual, is that they may identify underachieving students: students whose grades and classroom performance give no hint of the students' true—and unused—potential. In the negative column, a continuing problem is that if undue weight is given to intelligence test scores, students with other legitimate gifts and talents will be missed—particularly creative students, but also students with gifts in one special academic or aesthetic area, such as art, music, computers, mathematics, or even dinosaurs.

Achievement Tests

Specific academic talent is an important category of giftedness. An excellent indicator of academic talent is standardized achievement tests, such as the *Iowa Tests of Basic Skills*, the *Stanford Achievement Tests*, the *Metropolitan Achievement Tests*, the *SRA Achievement Series*, the *California Test of Basic Skills*, and the *Sequential Tests of Educational Progress* (STEP). Other good indicators of specific academic talent are teacher-made achievement tests and school grades.

Standardized tests produce scores based upon national norms (for example, grade-equivalent, percentile, or stanine scores). Consider this advantage. A teacher in an upper-middle-class neighborhood may be accustomed to very bright students who learn quickly. He or she may not realize that, compared with national norms, there are many talented and high-potential students in the class who

[3]See Chapter 1 for brief definitions.

should be participating in the district's G/T program. On the other hand, a teacher accustomed to working with slow learners may believe that a particular student is unusually able when, relative to a national comparison, the student is just slightly above average.

Two important problems should be considered relative to standardized achievement test scores. The first concerns the *grade-equivalent* score. "Grade-equivalent" refers to the average score earned by children at a particular grade level on a particular test—not to the grade level at which a specific gifted child can function well in the classroom. Experienced teachers, administrators, and psychologists, as well as parents, make the faulty assumption that if a gifted fourth-grade child performs at the eight-grade level on, say, a math achievement test, he or she could be moved into an eighth-grade classroom and perform successfully. Not so. While certainly a good math student, this child probably lacks many skills of the average eighth grader. The score is misleading and should only be used as an indication that the child needs special challenge. Further diagnostic testing would be used to determine the child's specific mathematics skills and other skill levels.

The second problem relates to the *low ceiling* score of typical achievement tests. For very able children, most achievement tests are not sufficiently difficult to measure their high ability, knowledge, and skill levels. A considerable number of students will score above the 95th percentile or at the ceiling grade-equivalent level; they "top out." It sometimes is incorrectly assumed that all of these children are equally talented and need a similar skill development program. In fact, after diagnostic testing with more difficult tests, a wide range of skill levels will be found among these children. (Of course, an obvious solution is to give high-potential children higher-level achievement tests in the first place.) One example of this problem comes from Stanley's (1979, 1991a) SMPY program in which seventh and eighth graders who are selected to take the SAT-M must have performed above the 95th percentile on a group achievement test. The SAT-M scores for this group of "similar" children will vary between 200 and 800 on this more difficult test.

Teacher Nominations

Teacher nominations may be very informal ("Say, we're starting a new gifted program, be thinking about one or two kids you want in it!") or quite formal, involving rating forms or checklists that will be objectively scored. Teacher nomination definitely is one of the most common identification methods, yet it can be troublesome. We already noted a tendency for some teachers to favor well-dressed, cooperative, nonhandicapped, English-speaking "teacher pleasers" who do work neatly, on time, and with no smarting off. Bright underachievers might be overlooked, along with bright disruptive students and unconventional creative ones.

With elementary students, Rimm and Davis (1976) found an interrater reliability coefficient of only .18 for teacher ratings of creativity, indicating that those teachers perceived creativeness quite differently. Some reliability and validity difficulties can be overcome by better acquainting teachers with characteristics of gifted students and by training them to rate and identify G/T candidates. We also recommend that teachers get to know students well before nominating them.

One form designed by Renzulli to help structure the nomination of students for Schoolwide Enrichment Model programs appears in Appendix 4.1 at the end of this chapter. Many more are available in Martinson (1974), Clasen and Robinson (1979), and Renzulli and Reis (1985a). The *Kranz Talent Identification Instrument* (Kranz, 1981), also a structured teacher nomination strategy, and Renzulli's *Scales for Rating Behavioral Characteristics of Superior Students* (SRBCSS; Appendix 4.5) are discussed later. Teachers, schools, or school districts also may develop their own teacher nomination forms that help synthesize, for example, ability scores, reading and math scores, grades, parent or peer nominations, creativity, motivation, leadership, or other abilities and skills pertinent to the particular G/T program.

Creativity Tests

In some classes and with some creativity-conscious teachers, it may be easily apparent which students are highly creative and which are not. Creativity tests can be used to confirm a teacher's suspicions about the creativeness of one or more students. The tests also may be used to identify creative students whose unique talents are not visible in many classrooms.

It is important to emphasize that creativity tests are not perfect. Especially, scores from a single creativity test might be quite misleading in the sense that a student who, in fact, does extraordinarily creative work in an art or science area could produce a strictly average creativity score. Validity coefficients of published creativity tests (the correlation of test scores with another criterion of creativity, such as teacher ratings or ratings of creative products) typically range from about .25 to .40, which is moderately low. Creativity is a complex ability that can take innumerable forms. It is impossible to measure creativity exactly (e.g., Davis, 1989, 1993). The authors have repeatedly emphasized that data from creativity tests—including their own—must be combined with other information to make valid decisions regarding creativeness (Rimm and Davis, 1976). Using two criteria of creativeness is recommended (Davis, 1975, 1989b, 1993). For example, a student who scores high on a creativity test and is rated as "highly creative" by a teacher is virtually certain to be a *bona fide* creative person.

Teachers who have the opportunity to observe creative ideas and products may be asked to rate students' creativeness. For example, art teachers or teachers who supervise original science projects, creative writing, or drama activities are in a good position to identify creative talent.

As for creativity tests themselves, there are two main categories: divergent thinking tests and inventories that assess personality and biographical traits (Davis, 1989b, 1993). Divergent thinking tests require students to think of all the ideas they can for open-ended problems, such as listing unusual uses for a newspaper or brick, imagining consequences of an unlikely event ("What would happen if people had an eye in the back of their head?"), or asking as many questions as possible about an object or event. Such tests are scored at least for ideational fluency (the number of ideas produced) and originality (uniqueness of the ideas). The *Torrance Tests of Creative Thinking* (Torrance, 1966) are the most widely used divergent-thinking tests (see Inset 4.2). They include verbal and nonverbal (figural) subtests, and are scored for *fluency*, *flexibility* (number of different categories of ideas or approaches to the problem), *originality*, and, with the figural tests, *elaboration* (number of additional details and embellishments). Torrance and Ball (1984) developed a "streamlined" scoring procedure for the figural tests which produces 18 measures of creative characteristics and is said to expedite scoring. Other divergent thinking batteries are the Guilford (1967, 1977) tests, the *Monitor Test of Creative Potential* (Hoepfner and Hemenway, 1973), Williams's (1980) *Exercise in Divergent Thinking*, which is part of his *Creativity Assessment Packet* (CAP), the Wallach and Kogan (1965) tests, the Getzels and Jackson (1962) tests, and for preschool children Torrance's (1982) *Thinking Creatively in Action and Movement*. See Davis (1992a) for descriptions of published creativity tests.

In view of their extensive development and evaluation, and the standard administration and scoring procedures, the Torrance tests are the recommended divergent thinking battery. If money is a problem, the Wallach and Kogan tests and the Getzels and Jackson tests apparently may be used without charge. In the negative column, the administration and scoring of any divergent thinking test are very time-consuming.

As for inventories that assess personality and biographical information, the authors—without bias or prejudice—recommend their own *PRIDE*,

GIFT, GIFFI I, and *GIFFI II* instruments (Rimm and Davis, 1983). There is a stereotype of personality traits and biographical characteristics that appears again and again in studies of creative people of all ages (for example, curiosity, humor, risk taking, and a history of creative activities; see Chapter 2).

PRIDE (*Preschool and Primary Interest Descriptor*; Rimm, 1982) is a preschool/kindergarten inventory that parents fill out. *GIFT* (*Group Inventory for Finding [Creative] Talent*) consists of yes-no items in lower-, middle-, and upper-elementary school forms. *GIFFI I* and *II* (*Group Inventory for Finding Interests*) are in a rating scale form designed for junior and senior high school students, respectively.

These tests have been validated in seven different countries and with many student populations, including minority, learning disabled, and gifted. The tests produce subscale scores (for example, confidence, imagination, many interests) that can be used to help understand and guide gifted children.

Two instruments for assessing creative personality traits were designed by Williams (1980). First, his *Exercise in Divergent Feeling*, from his CAP battery, asks students in grades 3 through 12 ". . . how curious, imaginative, complex and risky they believe they are." Second, the *Williams Scale*, also a CAP test, consists of rating-scale items used by a parent or teacher to evaluate student creative abilities and traits. Schaefer's (1971) *Creativity Attitude Survey*, designed for grades 4–6, measures many of the same traits evaluated by GIFT and the GIFFIs.

Two creativity tests resembling divergent thinking tests are *Sounds and Images* and *Onomatopoeia and Images*, both part of Torrance, Khatena, and Cunnington's (1973) *Thinking Creatively with Sounds and Words*. *Sounds and Images* requires students to describe mental images suggested by each of four abstract sounds. *Onomatopoeia and Images* is similar except that ten image-stimulating onomatopoetic words (for example, zoom, fizzy, moan) are used instead of ab-

INSET 4.2 _____

Torrance Tests of Creative Thinking

The *Torrance Tests of Creative Thinking* (Torrance, 1966) measure creative abilities of *fluency* (number of ideas), *flexibility* (number of different types or categories of ideas), *originality* (uniqueness), and *elaboration* (number of embellishments). Exercises similar to Torrance's subtests are presented below. Spend a few minutes on each one. Are you fluent? Flexible? Original? Are you high in elaboration?

Directions: Make a meaningful picture out of each of the nonsense forms below. Try to be original. Give each one a name.

Directions: List as many unusual uses as you can for discarded rubber tires.

Reprinted by permission of Scholastic Testing Service, Inc.

stract sounds. Both tests produce a total originality score.

Parent Nominations

No one knows children and adolescents better than their own parents. For example, only the parents will know a child spoke in sentences at age two, taught him- or herself to read at age four, and drew the solar system, composed melodies, produced creative art, and asked about reasons for the Middle East strife at age five. Unfortunately, parent nominations are not used as much as they should be. Martinson (1974) recommended that in a child's early school years, parents may be asked to provide information regarding advanced knowledge and abilities. A one-page form may simply state that the teacher is interested in planning "appropriate" educational experiences for the child, and would the parent please provide information pertaining to:

1. The child's special interests and hobbies
2. Recent books he or she has enjoyed or read
3. Special interests other than reading
4. Unusual accomplishments, past or present
5. Special talents
6. Special opportunities the child has had
7. Preferred activities when alone
8. Relationships with others
9. Special problems and/or needs

Another nomination rating form, developed by Tongue and Sperling (1976), appears in Appendix 4.2. This form evaluates precocious cognitive development (items 1–5, 9, 20), creativity (items 6, 8, 10–13), leadership (item 14), motor coordination (item 16), energy and persistence (items 7, 15, 19), and other characteristics of gifted and creative children. Using descriptions of gifted and talented students presented in Chapter 2, a teacher or G/T coordinator could tailor-make an even more suitable parent nomination inventory.

As a few cautions, some parents may not know their children well and do not follow all of the adventures and creations of their gifted child. Others, particularly nonintellectually oriented ones, may not understand their own child's precocity, gifts, or talents. Some parents overestimate their child's abilities, while others underestimate them.

Peer Nominations

Peers are very good at nominating gifted and talented classmates, which accounts for their use by about 25 percent of gifted programs (Cox, Daniel, and Boston, 1985). They may be especially helpful in identifying minority, culturally different, disadvantaged, handicapped, and rural gifted students (Banbury and Wellington, 1989; Cox and Daniel, 1983a; Spicker, Southern, and Davis, 1987). Children have a special relationship with their peers; they know who's who. For several years they have watched Miguel and Kirsten finish their math first, read the best, and answer the most confusing questions correctly. They know about Miguel's and Kirsten's wealth of information, their spelling prowess, their original ideas, and their scientific and artistic projects in and out of school.

Peer nomination forms are not difficult to construct. One example appears in Appendix 4.3. Such forms almost always ask class members to name peers with special characteristics. A first consideration is therefore the *characteristic(s)* you wish selected; that is, the purpose of the nomination(s) (Banbury and Wellington, 1989). One guide is the Department of Education categories of general intellectual ability, specific academic ability, creativity, talent in the visual and performing arts, and leadership. A peer nomination form called "Let's make believe" (Jenkins, 1979; see also Gagne, 1989) asks children to imagine they are stranded on a deserted island, and name which classmate is the best *organizer* (leader, gets others to do things), *fixer* (improves or makes things better), *artist* (makes pretty things or makes up good stories), *inventor* (invents, discovers), *judge* (helps settle arguments), or *entertainer* (acts, tells jokes, sings).

A second consideration is *grade level*. Some research has suggested that children below fourth grade (i.e., K through 3) may have difficulty evaluating peers' attributes and abilities (Banbury and Wellington, 1989; Granzin and Granzin, 1969; Johnson, 1986). For example, to many lower elementary children *smart* means *fast* (Rimm, 1991b), and peers who skip parts of the assignment or otherwise do fast-but-poor work earn peer recognition as "smart." Of course, the wording of peer-identification items must be age appropriate.

A third consideration is *style*—questions can be *direct*, *disguised*, or take a *game* format. Apparently, all three work equally well—perhaps because they are not that different. For example, with a *direct* approach, the teacher or printed nomination form can ask:

Who is the smartest kid in class?
Who is best at math?
Who is the best reader?
Who has the best memory?
Who always finishes his/her work first?
Who has the most unusual ideas?
Who tells great stories?
Who could invent the most games with a box of stuff?

The "Let's Make Believe," stranded-on-a-deserted-island approach mentioned above is an example of a *disguised* format. A variation asks children to imagine that a spaceship with friendly aliens has landed and they are visiting class:

Who will probably ask the aliens the most unusual questions?
Who will probably remember the most details about the aliens' visit?

Even without a colorful story scenario, disguised questions can ask, for example, "If the class were trying to reconstruct the events of the first day of school, who would probably remember the most details?" or "If there were a costume party next week, who would you expect to come with the most unusual disguise?"

The *game* mode described by Banbury and Wellington (1989) took the form of a "Guess Who?" game. Following a brief description of a characteristic, students would name someone who fits: "I am thinking of one member of this class who has a great memory. Who do you think it is?" "I am thinking of one of your classmates who always comes up with unusual ideas. Who do you think it might be?"

As a fourth format, Davidson (1986) suggested that students above the lowest primary grades may nominate each other with a form that simply says:

I believe _____ should be placed in the gifted program because I have observed the following behaviors: _____.

Said Davidson, "This type of nomination eliminates the possibility that a student may be excluded simply because some unique abilities may not be included on a standardized nomination form."

One danger is that children tend to nominate friends. As in the example in Appendix 4.3, instructions to "Pick someone who you think is the best choice and not just your friends" will help. Students also should understand that they can nominate the same person as often as they wish, and that their nominations will be strictly confidential. Banbury and Wellington (1989) recommended waiting nine to twelve weeks after the beginning of school to ask for peer nominations to insure that students are familiar with each other's names and abilities.

Finally, a peer nomination form can serve simultaneously as a *self*-nomination, if students are encouraged to nominate themselves if they believe they are the best choice.

Self-Nominations

Some students have strong artistic, creative, scientific, or other interests and talents, and they want to participate in a special program—but nobody asks them. Teachers may be unaware of the talent, creativity, and high motivation. A self-nomination form used in Charlottesville, Virginia, simply asks students to "Check the area(s) in which you think you have special abilities or talents, and tell why you think you have special abilities or talents in these areas." The ten areas were general intellectual ability, math, science, social studies, language arts, reading, art, music, drama, dance, creativity, and leadership, areas based upon the Department of Education definition. Self-nomination is especially recommended at the junior and senior high school levels, where peer pressures may cause youths to mask their special talents. Renzulli (1987) stated that in high school self-nomination is the *only* identification strategy he uses or recommends.

Product Evaluations

A good index of academic, artistic, creative, or scientific talent is simply the quality of work the student has done or is doing. Art teachers are in a unique position to evaluate artistic talent and creativity. Other teachers also may have an opportunity to evaluate the quality of students' poetry, science projects, electronic or computer projects, dramatic talent, photography, unusual hobbies, and so on. Such information—"face valid" reflections of gifts and talents—should be very useful in the overall identification process.

Usually, product evaluations are quite informal; the product may obviously reflect high creativity, science ability, writing skill, analysis or synthesis talent, and so on. However, if a more structured and objective product rating form is desired, Appendix 4.4 presents a form developed and used by the State of Michigan Education Department. It is helpful to use more than one rater, since teacher variation (inter-rater reliability) in judgments of creative products needs to be considered.

Rating Scales

We already have seen several rating scales in conjunction with teacher-, parent-, peer-, and self-nomination procedures and product evaluations. Renzulli (1983) developed a set of ten rating scale instruments, used by teachers, entitled *Scales for*

Rating Behavioral Characteristics of Superior Students (SRBCSS). The four most widely used scales evaluate intellectual ability (learning), creativity, motivation, and leadership and are reproduced in Appendix 4.5. Others assess artistic, musical, dramatic, and planning characteristics, communication-precision, and communication-expressiveness.

Rimm's (1986a) *Achievement Identification Measure* (AIM), filled out by parents, consists of 77 rating-scale items designed to identify underachievement. It is, in essence, a measure of student academic motivation. The *Group Achievement Identification Measure* (GAIM; Rimm, 1987a) is virtually identical except that it is administered directly to students. A third instrument, *Achievement Identification Measure-Teacher Observation* (AIM-TO; Rimm, 1988), is used by teachers to measure the same construct. All three instruments produce subscale scores of *Competition* (for example, "My child enjoys competition, win or lose"), *Responsibility* (for example, "My child seems to ask for more teacher help than most children"), *Self-Control* (for example, "My child is well behaved in school"), *Achievement Communication* (for example, "The father in the family thinks good grades are important"), and *Respect* (for example, "My child usually obeys his mother").

Kranz Talent Identification Instrument

The *Krant Talent Identification Instrument* (KTII; Kranz, 1981, 1991) is an update of Kranz's successful *Multidimensional Screening Device* (MDSD). The KTII involves training teachers to rate all children in their classes on ten different talent dimensions, some of which are rather unusual. A frequent outcome—if not the main purpose—of the training is to raise teacher's awareness of the multidimensionality of their students. As Fiedler (1982) said, "It forces teachers to walk all the way around the kids and look at them from different perspectives."

Significantly, and uniquely, the KTII specifically aims at identifying gifted and talented children from among students who are underachievers, minority members, poor, or whose parents are immigrants or blue-collar workers who are not education oriented.

The KTII procedure involves three main steps: (1) in-service training of the teachers, (2) the rating of every student, and (3) the final selections by a separate screening committee, based upon the ratings and other student data. "Other student data" usually will include information from the *KTII Peer Nomination Forms*, the *KTII Parent Questionnaire*, and the *KTII Pupil Questionnaire*, an interest inventory. The ten KTII talents are:

1. Visual arts talent
2. Performing arts talent
3. Creative talent
4. One-sided talent
5. Academic talent
6. Leadership and organizing talent
7. Psychomotor talent
8. Spatial and abstract thinking talent
9. Underachievement talent
10. Hidden talent

The KTII videotape and the KTII manual explain each of the talents and how they are recognized. The manual also suggests specific classroom activities and exercises that enable a teacher to observe and evaluate each type of talent.

Most of the talents need not be defined here; in fact, they almost duplicate the categories of the U.S. Department of Education definition. However, (4) "one-sided talent," (9) "underachievement talent," and (10) "hidden talent" require a brief comment. One-sided talent refers to the energetic student who has maintained a long-term involvement with—and is an expert on—one particular hobby or interest. It might be photography, red-tailed hawks, the Beatles, or in Kranz's favorite example, salamanders. No matter what the topic of the class lesson or discussion—math, history, geography, spelling, social studies, or weather—the Salamander Kid can twist it into something relevant to salamanders.

Underachievement talent is not, as the name seems to suggest, a highly polished excellence in performing below one's ability. It simply refers to underachieving, the combination of high ability with low academic performance.

The most interesting of the Kranz talents is hidden talent, which comes in many forms. Primarily, it is the unusual ability to cope with school problems despite significant home difficulties. The hidden talent student may show ". . . fantastic oral ability, poetry-writing talent, or dramatic storytelling ability; the ability to think in two languages (English at school, native language at home); music and art talent; or an unusual depth of understanding" (Kranz, 1981).

Kranz recommends some specific rating methods that might well be applied to any student-rating procedures. (1) She recommends "rating vertically," that is, rating each student in the class on one particular talent before proceeding to the next talent. (2) With the KTII, a 7-point scale is used. With the exception of academic talent (talent 5), Kranz recommends awarding only one 7 for each of the talents for each class, although there many be many 6's, 5's, 4's, and so on. (3) Rate students after January, when you know them. (4) Do not rate them in subject matter areas; the ten scales are intended to be content-free. Grades and achievement tests scores will provide plenty of information on specific academic talents.

As for the screening committee itself, Kranz recommends a group consisting of the principal, librarian, art teacher, music teacher, and G/T teacher. The screening committee gathers information about every child, including the ten KTII ratings, parent and peer nominations, the student interest questionnaire, and any other academic, ability, or creativity information. The screening committee, not individual teachers, will make the final decision.

Baldwin Identification Matrix

The *Baldwin Identification Matrix* (Baldwin, 1977, 1978, 1984, 1991a) summarizes scores and ratings on a variety of criteria. As shown in Table 4.1, standardized intelligence and achievement test data are used for rating intelligence, reading, and math (Items 1.1–1.4). The Renzulli (1983) *Scales for Rating Behavioral Characteristics of Superior Stu-* *dents* (Appendix 4.5) are used for evaluating *learning, motivation, creativity*, and *leadership* (Items 1.5, 2.1, 5.1, 6.1). The Matrix entries are added to produce a single total score, allowing students to be easily ranked. Simplicity in decision making is the

TABLE 4.1   Sample form for *Baldwin Identification Matrix*

Area	Assessment Items	M*	S*	5	4	3	2	1	b-na	No*	RS*	Area Score (RS/N)
						Ratings						
Cognitive	1.1 General IQ Binet	44.1	150			3						
	1.2 Stanford Reading	11.1	7			3						
	1.3 Math	11.1	8		4							
	1.4 Reading	11.2	91		4							
	1.5 Renz-Learning	22.2	28		4							
	Total Cognitive			0	12	6	0	0	0	5	18	3.6
Psychosocial	2.1 Renz-Leadership	22.4	29					1				
	2.2 Supplemental	33.5	4		4							
	2.3 Peer Nomination	33.5	3			3						
	2.4											
	2.5											
	Total Psychosocial			0	4	3	0	1	0	3	8	2.7
Creative Prods	3.1 Art Products	33.6	7			3						
	3.2 Musical Performance	33.6	8		4							
	3.3 Supplemental	33.5	4		4							
	3.4											
	3.5											
	Total Creative Products			0	8	3	0	0	0	3	11	3.7
Psychomotor	4.1 School Assessment	33.5	4		4							
	4.2 Supplemental	33.5	5	5								
	4.3											
	4.4											
	4.5											
	Total Psychomotor			5	4	0	0	0	0	2	9	4.5
Motivation	5.1 Renz Motivation	22.1	29			3						
	5.2 Supplemental	33.5	3			3						
	5.3											
	5.4											
	5.5											
	Total Motivation			0	0	6	0	0	0	2	6	3
Creative Prcss	6.1 Renz Creativity	22.3	29			3						
	6.2 TTC Creativity	11.2	85%		4							
	6.3											
	6.4											
	6.5											
	Total Creative Process			0	4	3	0	0	0	2	7	3.5
	Matrix Totals		Maximum Points for this Matrix									30
			Student Total									21

Copyright © 1984 Trillium Press, Inc.

M* — Mode of Score Code
S* — Score
No* — Number of Items
RS* — Raw Score

Reprinted by permission of the author and Trillium Press.

main advantage of such a point system. A cutoff score may be set and any student producing a total score above that cutoff is selected, or else the top 3 or 5 percent may be chosen. In addition to the handy total score, the Baldwin Matrix also provides a profile of strengths and weaknesses for each student.

The main disadvantage of the Baldwin Matrix, and most other identification systems based on total points, is that students who are gifted or talented according to only a few criteria (for example, in a particular area) are very likely to produce mediocre total scores, and therefore will be quickly excluded despite obvious qualifications and needs. Feldhusen, Asher, and Hoover (1984) noted that a better use of the Baldwin Matrix would be to match student gifts to program goals. For example, a combination of the ratings in reading, writing, language arts, and verbal intelligence could be used to select students for a special program emphasizing the development of writing talent. Flexibility in use is recommended.

IDENTIFYING GIFTED PRESCHOOLERS

According to developmentalists, the first five years of a child's life have a tremendous impact on intellectual development and capability for future learning (e.g., Bloom, 1964; White, 1975; see also Burns, Mathews, and Mason, 1990). An obvious implication is that preschool programs are valuable for *all* children.

Burns, Mathews, and Mason (1990) described a three-step solution to the challenge of identifying intellectually gifted preschoolers in Louisiana, a state that offers publicly funded preschool gifted programs. Similar plans could be used by any individual or district seeking to develop and promote programs for gifted preschoolers.

The first phase aimed at informing parents and preschool teachers about characteristics of preschool giftedness and the availability of the public programs. This was accomplished by a blitz of feature articles in newspapers and local magazines, TV interviews on morning talk shows and evening news shows, speaking engagements at

parent and church organizations, and in-services at preschools.

Phase two was a general screening, accomplished by a *Gifted Preschool Screening Packet* that included a parent questionnaire, a teacher questionnaire (if the child was in a preschool), along with a brochure and application form. The questionnaires asked parents or teachers to rate the child on 45 different behaviors—some of which were and some of which were *not* characteristic of gifted preschoolers—and to "describe additional exceptional behaviors displayed by the child."

The third phase was an individualized screening, first with the *Hess School Readiness Scale* (Hess, 1975), a test similar to the Stanford-Binet. If the child survived this hurdle (IQ = 120 or higher), the Stanford-Binet itself plus tests of math and reading were given.[4]

While few school systems offer public preschool programs for the gifted, the Burns, Mathews, and Mason (1990) guides can help solve the sticky problem of selecting highly intellectually gifted 3- to 5-year-old children.

IDENTIFYING GIFTED SECONDARY STUDENTS

As gifted children move into middle and high school, their talents become increasingly differentiated. The problem is not knowing "whether" they are gifted, but "how are they gifted?" and "what are the areas of talent?" Feldhusen, Hoover, and Sayler (1990) developed identification procedures and rating scales designed specifically to identify gifted and talented youth in middle and high school. The *Purdue Academic Rating Scales* (PARS) and *Purdue Vocational Rating Scales* (PVRS) allow teachers to assess specific information suitable for secondary program selection and

---

[4]As mentioned in the second paragraph of this chapter, Louisiana's criterion for placement in a public preschool gifted program is an IQ score that is three standard deviations above the mean, *or* two and one-half standard deviations plus scores in the 98–99th percentile in reading *and* math.

placement, in contrast with more general scales useful at the elementary level, such as Renzulli's SRBCSS.

As general identification recommendations, Feldhusen, Hoover, and Sayler advised, for example, (1) using their scales in conjunction with other information (e.g., ability scores, direct observation, student self-assessment, information from parents); (2) training teachers in the interpretation of the scales in relation to student behavior; (3) obtaining ratings of students by several teachers; and (4) watching out for the *halo effect*—the tendency to bias ratings in line with overall attitudes toward the student.

There are five academic scales (PARS: math, science, English, social studies, and foreign languages) and four vocational scales (PVRS: agriculture, business and office, home economics, and trade and industrial). All scales contain fifteen 5-point rating-scale items. Space does not permit total reproduction of the scales. Some sample items appear in Table 4.2.

RECOMMENDATIONS FROM THE NATIONAL REPORT ON IDENTIFICATION

The *National Report on Identification* (Richert, 1985, 1991; Richert, Alvino, and McDonnel, 1982), mentioned earlier, included an alphabetized list of over 60 tests, rating scales, checklists, and inventories (Table 4.3). The table includes (1) categories of giftedness assessed by each instrument, (2) appropriateness for advantaged and disadvantaged children, (3) suitable age range, and (4) appropriate stage for their use (i.e., for nominating/identifying gifted students, assessing their abilities, or evaluating their skill development).

TALENT POOL IDENTIFICATION PLAN: RENZULLI

With the talent pool approach, the intent is to be inclusive, to "cast a wide net" that will catch many kinds of gifts and talents. When in doubt about a student, admit flexibly. Renzulli and Reis (1991b)

outlined a plan that addresses these identification goals. It is basically a five-step procedure with the last two steps designed as "safety valves" to pick up students missed in the first three steps.

Step 1. Test Score Nominations. About half of the talent pool can be selected via standardized intelligence and/or achievement tests. Students who score above the 92nd percentile are admitted without further evaluation. Said Renzulli and Reis, "This approach guarantees that traditionally bright youngsters will automatically be selected" (p. 116).

Step 2. Teacher Nominations. Teachers are advised of students who are admitted via Step 1 (test scores) in order to avoid needless concern and paperwork. In Step 2 teachers nominate students who display other worthy characteristics—particularly, high creativity, high motivation, unusual interests or talents, or special areas of superior performance or potential. Teacher nominations are treated on an equal basis with test score nominations. In the case of teachers who are overnominators, the teachers are asked to rank order their recommendations which then are reviewed by a schoolwide screening committee.

Step 3. Alternate Pathways. Alternate pathways to the talent pool include many of the identification options described in this chapter: self-nominations, parent nominations, peer nominations, creativity test results, "and virtually any other procedure that might lead to initial consideration by a screening committee" (p. 116). Admission is not automatic in Step 3, but depends upon the decision of the screening committee, which interviews students, teachers, and parents, and examines all previous school records. Sometimes admission is on a trial basis.

Step 4. Special Nominations (Safety Valve No. 1). To avoid biases of current teachers, the list of all students nominated is circulated to all teachers in the school and in previous schools if the student

TABLE 4.2   Sample Items from the Purdue Academic Rating Scales and the Purdue Vocational Rating Scales

From Purdue Academic Rating Scales

Mathematics
1. Generalizes mathematical relationships, relates concepts in various applications.
2. Learns math concepts and processes faster than other students.

Science
1. Has science hobbies, is a collector, likes gadgets.
2. Understands scientific method, able to formulate hypotheses and conduct experiments carefully.

English
1. Motivated to write even when writing is not assigned; writes stories, poems, or plays; keeps a journal or diary.
2. Has a good sense of humor; uses and understands satire, puns, and second meanings.

Social Studies
1. Reads widely on social issues from a variety of books, magazines, or newspapers.
2. Skilled in analyzing topics, finding the underlying problem, questioning, investigating.

Foreign Language
1. Learns new vocabulary words and grammatical concepts rapidly.
2. Shows curiosity and inquisitiveness when introduced to new grammatical or cultural concepts.

From Purdue Vocational Rating Scales

Agriculture
1. Exhibits leadership in shop activities/organizations.
2. Comes up with good, high-level ideas for projects or for agricultural problems.

Business and Office
1. Shows creativity in solving problems or designing reports.
2. Is viewed by other students as showing talent in business and office classes.

Home Economics
1. Learns and applies new skills, techniques, or methods rapidly and easily.
2. Is enthusiastic in all or most class activities.

Trade and Industrial
1. Shows good manual skills in use of tools and equipment.
2. Seems to have a lot of ideas.

TABLE 4.3   Alphabetical listing of instruments and recommendations for use

Column groups: **CATEGORY** (General Intellectual, Specific Academic, Creativity, Leadership, Visual and Performing Arts) · **POPULATION** (Advantaged, Disadvantaged, Early Childhood, Grades 4-8, High School to Adult) · **AGE** (K-12) · **ID STAGE** (Nomination, Assessment, Evaluation)

INSTRUMENT	General Intellectual	Specific Academic	Creativity	Leadership	Visual and Performing Arts	Advantaged	Disadvantaged	Early Childhood	Grades 4-8	High School to Adult	K-12	Nomination	Assessment	Evaluation
A.S.S.E.T.S.	+	+	+		+	+		+	+			+	+	
Barron-Welsh Art Scale					+	+		+	+	+	+	+		
Biographical Inventory-Form U		+	+	+	+	+			+	+			+	
California Achievement Tests		+				+				+	+	+		
California Psychological Inventory						+		+	+				+	
Cartoon Conservation Scales	+						+	+	+			+	+	
Lattell Culture Fair Intelligence Series	+						+	+	+			+		
CIRCUS	+	+				+	+	+				+	+	
Cognitive Abilities Test	+					+		+	+	+		+	+	
Columbia Mental Maturity Scale	+					+	+	+	+			+		
Comprehensive Tests of Basic Skills		+				+				+	+	+		
Cornell Critical Thinking Tests						+				+			+	+
Creativity Assessment Packet			+			+		+	+	+		+		
Creativity Tests for Children			+			+		+	+			+		
Design Judgement Test				+	+			+	+			+		
Differential Aptitude Tests	+	+				+		+	+			+	+	+
Early School Personality Questionnaire						+	+		+				+	
Gifted and Talented Screening Form	+	+	+	+	+	+		+	+	+		+		
Goodenough-Harris Drawing Test	+					+	+	+	+	+		+		
Group Inventory for Finding Creative Talent (G.I.F.T.)			+			+		+	+			+	+	
Group Inventory for Finding Interests (G.I.F.F.I.)			+			+				+		+	+	
Guilford-Holley L Inventory						+				+			+	
GuilFord-Zimmerman Aptitude Survey	+					+				+			+	
Henmon-Nelson Tests of Mental Ability	+	+				+					+	+	+	
High School Personality Questionnaire						+		+	+				+	
Horn Art Aptitude Inventory				+	+	+			+			+		
Iowa Tests of Basic Skills		+				+		+	+	+		+	+	
Kaufman — ABC	+	+				+	+		+			+	+	
Khatena-Torrance Creative Perception Inventory			+			+		+	+			+	+	
Lorge-Thorndike Intelligence Tests	+					+		+	+	+		+		
Maier Art Judgement Tests				+	+			+	+			+		
Metropolitan Achievement Tests		+				+						+	+	
Multi-Dimensional Screening Device	+	+	+	+	+	+						+		
Musical Aptitude Profile				+	+	+		+	+	+		+	+	
Otis-Lennon Mental Ability Test	+					+						+	+	

(continued)

TABLE 4.3   (Continued)

INSTRUMENT	General Intellectual	Specific Academic	Creativity	Leadership	Visual and Performing Arts	Advantaged	Disadvantaged	Early Childhood	High School to Adult	Grades 4-8	K-12	Nomination	Assessment	Evaluation
												CATEGORY / POPULATION / AGE / ID STAGE		
Peabody Individual Achievement Test		+				+					+	+		
Pennsylvania Assessment of Creative Tendency			+			+		+	+			+		
Piers-Harris Children's Self-Concept Scale						+		+	+			+		
Preschool Talent Checklist	+	+	+	+	+	+	+	+				+		
Primary Measure of Music Audiation					+	+	+	+				+		
Progressive Matrices — Advanced	+					+			+			+		
Progressive Matrices — Standard	+					+						+		
Remote Associates Test			+			+			+			+	+	
Ross Test of Higher Cognitive Processes	+					+		+				+	+	
Scales for Rating Behavioral Characteristics of Superior Students	+		+	+	+	+	+			+		+		
Seashore Measure of Musical Talents					+	+	+		+	+		+		
The Self-Concept and Motivation Inventory (SCAMIN)					+	+	+	+	+			+		
Sequential Tests of Educational Progress (STEP)		+				+		+	+			+	+	
Short Form Test of Academic Aptitude	+	+				+		+	+			+		
Slosson Intelligence Test	+					+		+	+			+		
SOI Gifted Screening Form		+	+		+	+	+	+	+			+	+	
SOI Learning Abilities Test		+	+		+	+	+	+	+			+	+	
SRA Achievement Series		+				+				+	+	+		
Stallings' Environmentally Based Screen	+						+	+				+		
Stanford Achievement Test		+				+		+	+			+	+	
Stanford-Binet Intelligence Scale	+					+		+	+	+		+		
System of Multicultural Pluralistic Assessment (SOMPA)	+						+	+				+		
Tennessee Self-Concept Scale						+			+	+		+		
Test of Creative Potential			+			+		+	+			+	+	
Tests of Achievement and Proficiency		+				+						+	+	
Torrance Test of Creative Thinking — Verbal			+			+			+					
Torrance Test of Creative Thinking			+			+			+	+	+			
Torrance Test of Creative Thinking — Figural										+	+	+		
Vane Kindergarten Test	+	+				+						+	+	
Watson-Glaser Critical Thinking Appraisal	+					+		+	+			+	+	
Wechsler Intelligence Scale for Children Revised (WISC-R)	+					+		+	+	+		+		
Weschler Preschool and Primary Scale of Intelligence	+					+		+				+		

Reprinted by permission of Dr. E. Susanne Richert, Education Information and Resource Center, Sewell, NJ, and *Roeper Review*.

has transferred. The purpose is to allow previous-year teachers to nominate students who are not on the list. The procedure also allows resource teachers to make recommendations based on their enrichment experiences in the regular classroom, for example, students who seem unusually creative or to have unusual strengths in a special area.

Step 5. *Action Information Nominations (Safety Valve No. 2).* Teachers are oriented to spot students who have an usually high interest in regular curriculum topics or who might stand out in classroom enrichment experiences. Part of the Schoolwide Enrichment Model includes *Action Information Messages*, which usually are used to describe talent pool students who are extremely interested or excited about a topic, area of study, or idea and wish to pursue it as an independent project. Action Information also may be used to nominate non-talent pool students for projects, and thus for inclusion in the talent pool. Such nominations are reviewed by the screening committee.

COMMENT

The identification procedure clearly is a crucial part of any G/T program. The procedures themselves operationally define who is "gifted" (or has the potential for gifted behavior) and by exclusion who is "not gifted." While intellectual giftedness—reflected in high grades and high IQ scores—is an important, even central consideration, gifts and talents extend beyond high intelligence. Most programs are moving toward multiple selection criteria and flexible procedures that use both objective test scores and subjective evaluations and nominations. The U.S. Department of Education definition, Taylor's Totem Poles, Renzulli's rating scales, and the *Kranz Talent Identification Instrument* all emphasize the multidimensionality of gifts and talents.

Nonetheless, seemingly irrational procedures persist. For example, a program may publicly accept the five-part U.S. Department of Education Definition then brazenly use only IQ scores or science grades to identify participants. Another program might use grades and IQ scores—intellectual criteria—for selection, then involve children in theater, literature, and art activities. A major sin is enforcing a rigid IQ cutoff score—a student with an IQ of 130 is "gifted," but one (who may be more creative and energetic) with an IQ of 129 is "not gifted" and is excluded from the program. And the rumor that "5 percent of our children are gifted" (not 6 percent, not 20 percent) persists and guides selection policy (Culross, 1989; Steele, 1991).

Selection should be flexible, reasonable, and show a true concern for children. Many program coordinators are viewing identification as a year-round process rather than a once-in-September activity. A low test score or a teacher-child conflict should not eliminate an obviously gifted child from a challenging program that he or she needs. Clasen and Clasen (1989) recommended that selection methods involving teachers should be "teacher-friendly"—clear, understandable, and require little time; and that valuable data can be obtained unobtrusively, for example, by using vocabulary test data from teacher's files and anecdotes from other teachers about collections, cartooning, clowning, or the like.

Finally, we feel compelled to reiterate some of the advantages of a liberal identification policy, namely, the talent pool approach of Renzulli's Schoolwide Enrichment Model (Renzulli and Reis, 1985a, 1991b): More students have an opportunity to participate; identification is flexible and multidimensional; identification for independent work continues all year; motivated students self-select for independent work; uninterested, unsuccessful students do not waste resource room time and facilities; charges of elitism are reduced or eliminated; the need for painful, hard-and-fast decisions (for example, based on cutoff scores or a 3–5 percent criterion) is eliminated; and silly situations in which, due to altered identification criteria, last year's gifted student is "not gifted this year" are eliminated. There is much to be said for such a plan.

SUMMARY

There are many strategies for identifying gifted and talented students for programs. While some programs stress only intelligence (aptitude) scores, a multidimensional assessment is recommended.

Davidson argued against formal identification systems involving tests, ratings, and nominations, including point systems and cutoff scores. Davidson recommended a liberal 15 to 20 percent quota; automatic selection of students with high IQ, achievement, or creativity scores; and especially the increased use of informal parent and teacher nominations based on observations.

Another issue concerns the annual selection of 3 to 5 percent versus a more flexible and generous 15 to 20 percent talent pool approach.

Multidimensional criteria and a quota system will insure representation of disadvantaged and minority students. Gifted handicapped students must not be overlooked. Girls may be discriminated against if math, science, and computer skills are weighted heavily.

Teachers may favor "teacher pleasers," ignoring more gifted students with less agreeable habits.

Reliability refers to the accuracy of a test (or other instrument or procedure) or the test-retest consistency. Validity is the degree to which the instrument measures what it is supposed to measure. One must consider the reliability and validity of any instrument or selection procedure.

The 1982 *National Report on Identification* endorsed the U.S. Department of Education multidimensional definition of giftedness. It recommended that identification procedures be equitable, based on research, designed in the best interests of all students, based on a broad definition of giftedness, and designed to identify as many gifted learners as possible. The report identified such questionable practices as limiting selection to high-achieving students, overlooking minority students, using instruments inappropriately, and combining criteria inappropriately. The report recommended using both formal tests and informal rating and nomination procedures, and not combining the data (i.e., into a total score).

The Stanford-Binet Form LM, which produces a single IQ score, is preferred over the newer Fourth Edition, which has a lower ceiling.

The *WISC-R* and *WISC-III* produces Verbal, Performance, and Full-Scale IQ scores.

Group intelligence tests are useful, but suffer from lower reliability and validity, lower ceilings, and high verbal content.

The SAT-M and SAT-V, and occasionally the ACT, are used to identify bright seventh-graders for SMPY and Talent Search programs.

Math talent and verbal talent seem to represent two distinct forms of intellectual giftedness. Gardner's influential multiple-intelligence theory argues for seven intelligences.

Any intelligence (aptitude) test will help identify underachieving students. Undue weight on intelligence scores will exclude students with other gifts.

Achievement tests are good indicators of specific academic talent. However, they tend to have relatively low ceilings and therefore will not discriminate among gifted students who "top out." Grade equivalent scores do not mean that the student belongs in the grade indicated by the score.

Teacher nominations are widely used, yet among the least reliable and valid. However, teachers can be trained. Teachers also may use structured nomination and rating forms.

Creativity tests may identify creative talent that is otherwise not visible. Because of its complexity, validity coefficients for creativity tests are not high. Using two criteria of creativeness is recommended in order to accurately identify creatively gifted students.

Two main categories of creativity tests are divergent thinking tests, such as the Torrance tests, and personality/biographical inventories, such as PRIDE, GIFT, GIFFI I and II, Williams' *Exercise in Divergent Feeling* and the *Williams Scale*, and Schaefer's *Creativity Attitude Survey*.

Parents can provide valuable and valid information for identification. However, they may be unaware of their child's gifts, or else exaggerate or underestimate their child's abilities.

Peer nominations are valuable, and may be especially helpful in identifying minority, handicapped, and rural gifted students. Three considerations are the characteristic you wish evaluated, students' grade level, and the style of the nomination questions (direct, disguised, or game).

Self-nominations are highly recommended, especially at the high school level.

Product evaluations may be informal or use structured evaluation forms.

Renzulli's most widely used rating scales allow a teacher to rate intellectual ability, creativity, motivation, and leadership.

Rimm's AIM and GAIM may be used to identify underachievement patterns.

Kranz's KTII evaluates ten talents, excluding specific academic talent. The procedure emphasizes training teachers to evaluate accurately. The KTII is designed to evaluate gifts and talents among underachieving, minority, poor, immigrant, and blue-collar children, as well as others. Most notable are her "one-sided" and "hidden" talent categories.

The *Baldwin Identification Matrix* summarizes scores and ratings on a variety of criteria, combining them into a single total score. This procedure risks overlooking students with strength in just one or a few categories.

A three-step model for identifying intellectually gifted preschoolers included raising parents and preschool teachers' awareness, a screening in the form of parent and teacher questionnaires, and individual intelligence testing.

The *National Report on Identification* includes a list of sixty instruments, with specifications for each test of the categories of giftedness assessed, appropriateness for advantaged and disadvantaged children, suitable age range, and appropriate stage in the G/T program for use.

Renzulli's talent pool identification plan includes five steps of (1) test score nominations (to identify 50 percent of the talent pool), (2) teacher nominations, (3) alternate pathways (e.g., self, parent, or peer nominations, creativity tests, etc.), and two "safety valves" of (4) special nominations by previous and other teachers, and (5) action information nominations.

Identification should be flexible, reasonable, and fair. Multidimensional criteria are necessary. Unreasonable practices include adopting the multidimensional Department of Education definition, then using only intellectual criteria; not matching selection procedures (e.g., IQ) with program content (e.g., art); rigid IQ cutoff scores; and assuming that exactly 5 percent of the student population is "gifted." The talent pool approach solves many problems.

APPENDIX 4.1 TEACHER NOMINATION FORM

1. Student _____ Teacher _____
2. Date of Referral _____ School _____
3. Grade _____ Date of Birth _____
4. Average Grades for Current School Year

   Language Arts _____

   Social Studies _____

   Arithmetic _____

   Science _____

5. Parent Nomination (Check if appropriate): _____
6. SRBCSS Scale Total _____ 1. _____ 2. _____ 3. _____ 4. _____
7. Why do you think this student should be included in the Talent Pool? (You may wish to list examples of ideas, projects, creative endeavors, etc.)

   _____

   _____

   _____

   _____

   _____

INTERESTS

Please indicate the areas of interest that the student has displayed in your class this year. If you've noticed other specific topics (interest in dinosaurs, computers, etc.), please note this in the column entitled "Other."

	HIGH	AVERAGE	LOW		HIGH	AVERAGE	LOW
Fine Arts/Crafts				Music			
Science				Drama			
Creative Writing				Mathematics			
Social Studies				Language Arts			
Psychomotor				Other			

CURRICULAR STRENGTH AREAS

Please indicate the curricular areas in which the student has demonstrated proficiency and could possibly be considered for curriculum compacting.

   Language Arts _____   Mathematics _____

   Science _____   Social Science _____

Reprinted by permission of J.S. Renzulli.

APPENDIX 4.2 SAMPLE PARENT NOMINATION FORM AT THE EARLY CHILDHOOD LEVEL

Name of Student _____ Age _____

Address _____ School_____ Grade ___

Parent's Name _____

Instructions: In relationship to the typical child in your neighborhood, please circle a number for each item which best describes your child: 5—has this trait to a high degree; 4—has this trait more than the typical child; 3—compares with the typical child; 2—has this trait less than the typical child; 1—lacks this trait.

1.	Has advanced vocabulary, expresses himself or herself well	5 4 3 2 1
2.	Thinks quickly	5 4 3 2 1
3.	Recalls facts easily	5 4 3 2 1
4.	Wants to know how things work	5 4 3 2 1
5.	Is reading (before he/she started kindergarten)	5 4 3 2 1
6.	Puts unrelated ideas together in new and different ways	5 4 3 2 1
7.	Becomes bored easily	5 4 3 2 1
8.	Asks reasons why — questions almost everything	5 4 3 2 1
9.	Likes "grown-up" things and to be with older people	5 4 3 2 1
10.	Has a great deal of curiosity	5 4 3 2 1
11.	Is adventurous	5 4 3 2 1
12.	Has a good sense of humor	5 4 3 2 1
13.	Is impulsive, acts before he/she thinks	5 4 3 2 1
14.	Tends to dominate others if given the chance	5 4 3 2 1
15.	Is persistent, sticks to a task	5 4 3 2 1
16.	Has good physical coordination and body control	5 4 3 2 1
17.	Is independent and self-sufficient in looking after himself/herself	5 4 3 2 1
18.	Is aware of his/her surroundings and what is going on around him/her	5 4 3 2 1
19.	Has a long attention span	5 4 3 2 1
20.	Wanted to do things for himself/herself early — example: dressing and feeding himself/herself	5 4 3 2 1

Developed by the Staff of the Gifted and Talented Section, Division of Exceptional Children, North Carolina Department of Public Instruction. This instrument is part of an identification model developed by Cornelia Tongue and Charmian Sperling, 1976. Reprinted by permission.

APPENDIX 4.3 WHO KNOWS WHO'S WHO? PEER NOMINATION FORM

The Milwaukee Public School System created a structured peer nomination form which seems to ask: Who has a lot of information (1)? Who does school work quickly and easily (2)? Who is creative (3 and 5)? Who is a leader (4)?

Directions to Teacher

Read the following statements to your class:

1. "Each of you has been asked to assist in an information gathering survey for the Milwaukee Public Schools."
2. "Please take out a sheet of paper and a pencil."
3. "Number your paper from 1 to 5."
4. "Please answer each question that I will read with the *complete* name of one student in our class."
5. "Pick someone whom you think is the best choice and not just your friends."
6. "You can pick the same person for more than one question if you think that person is your best choice."

Questions

1. If a person from outer space wanted someone in your class to tell him about different things on earth, who do you think could tell the most?
2. What student in class can complete his or her work and still have time to take part in other activities?
3. Who says things in class that are most original, things that you never thought of before?
4. If kids didn't have to go to school, what student in your class could talk you into going?
5. Who do you think might invent or make something that no one ever made before? (This is the person you might ask to help you write a poem or play, or help you make something for a school science fair.)

APPENDIX 4.4 INSTRUMENT FOR RATING THE EXCELLENCE OF PROJECTS SUBMITTED BY STUDENTS

---

1. Briefly describe the product.

2. To what extent does the product represent an in-depth or superior handling of the subject?

5	4	3	2	1
To a great extent		Somewhat		To a limited extent

3. To what extent is this product of a "quality-level" beyond what one might expect of a student of this age?

5	4	3	2	1
To a great extent		Somewhat		To a limited extent

4. To what extent does the product indicate close attention to detail?

5	4	3	2	1
To a great extent		Somewhat		To a limited extent

5. To what extent is the central idea/ conception of the product beyond what a student of this age might undertake?

5	4	3	2	1
To a great extent		Somewhat		To a limited extent

6. To what extent is the product of overall excellence?

5	4	3	2	1
To a great extent		Somewhat		To a limited extent

7. List some of the criteria you used in evaluating the excellence of this product.

APPENDIX 4.5 SCALES FOR RATING BEHAVIORAL CHARACTERISTICS OF SUPERIOR STUDENTS

Name_____   Date_____

School_____   Grade_____ Age_____
                                                          Yrs.   Mos.
Teacher or person completing this form_____

How long have you known this child?   _____months

DIRECTIONS: These scales are designed to obtain teacher estimates of a
student's characteristics in the areas of learning, motivation, creativity, and leadership. The items are derived from the research literature dealing with characteristics of gifted and creative persons.
It should be pointed out that a considerable amount of individual differences can be found within this population; therefore, the profiles
are likely to vary a great deal. Each item in the scales should be
considered separately and should reflect the degree to which you have
observed the presence or absence of each characteristic. Since the
four dimensions of the instrument represent relatively different sets
of behaviors, the scores obtained from the separate scales should not
be summed to yield a total score. Please read the statements carefully
and place an X in the appropriate place according to the following
scale of values.

    1. If you have <u>seldom</u> or <u>never</u> observed this characteristic
    2. If you have observed this characteristic <u>occasionally</u>
    3. If you have observed this characteristic to a <u>considerable</u>
       degree
    4. If you have observed this characteristic <u>almost all of the</u>
       <u>time</u>

Space has been provided following each item for your comments.

SCORING: **Separate scores for each of the four dimensions may be**
obtained as follows:

    <u>Add</u> the total number of X's in each column to obtain the
    "Column Total."
    <u>Multiply</u> the Column Total by the "Weight" for each column to
    obtain the "Weighted Column Total."
    <u>Sum</u> the Weighted Column Totals across to obtain the "Score"
    for each dimension of the scale.
    <u>Enter</u> the Scores below.

          Learning Characteristics   _____
      Motivational Characteristics   _____
        Creativity Characteristics   _____
       Leadership Characteristics   _____

Reprinted by permission.

APPENDIX 4.5 (Continued)

PART I: LEARNING CHARACTERISTICS

	1*	2	3	4
1. Has unusually advanced vocabulary for age or grade level; uses terms in a meaningful way; has verbal behavior characterized by "richness" of expression, elaboration, and fluency.				
2. Possesses a large storehouse of information about a variety of topics (beyond the usual interests of youngsters his or her age).				
3. Has quick mastery and recall of factual information.				
4. Has rapid insight into cause-effect relationships; tries to discover the how and why of things; asks many provocative questions (as distinct from information or factual questions); wants to know what makes things (or people) "tick."				
5. Has a ready grasp of underlying principles and can quickly make valid generalizations about events, people, or things; looks for similarities and differences in events, people, and things.				
6. Is a keen and alert observer; usually "sees more" or "gets more" out of a story, film, etc., than others.				
7. Reads a great deal on his or her own; usually prefers adult-level books; does not avoid difficult material; may show a preference for biography, autobiography, encyclopedias, and atlases.				
8. Tries to understand complicated material by separating it into its respective parts; reasons things out for himself or herself; sees logical and common sense answers.				
Column Total				
Weight	1	2	3	4
Weighted Column Total				
TOTAL				

———————————————
* 1—Seldom or never
  2—Occasionally
  3—Considerably
  4—Almost always

APPENDIX 4.5 (Continued)

PART II: MOTIVATIONAL CHARACTERISTICS

	1	2	3	4

1. Becomes absorbed and truly involved in certain topics or problems; is persistent in seeking task completion. (It is sometimes difficult to get him or her to move on to another topic.)

2. Is easily bored with routine tasks.

3. Needs little external motivation to follow through in work that initially excites him or her.

4. Strives toward perfection; is self-critical; is not easily satisfied with his or her own speed or products.

5. Prefers to work independently; requires little direction from teachers.

6. Is interested in many "adult" problems such as religion, politics, sex, race — more than usual for age level.

7. Often is self-assertive (sometimes even aggressive); stubborn in his or her beliefs.

8. Likes to organize and bring structure to things, people, and situations.

9. Is quite concerned with right and wrong, good and bad; often evaluates and passes judgment on events, people, and things.

Column Total

Weight	1	2	3	4

Weighted Column Total

TOTAL

APPENDIX 4.5 (Continued)

PART III: CREATIVITY CHARACTERISTICS

	1	2	3	4

1. Displays a great deal of curiosity about many things; is constantly asking questions about anything and everything.

2. Generates a large number of ideas or solutions to problems and questions; often offers unusual ("way out"), unique, clever responses.

3. Is uninhibited in expressing opinion; is sometimes radical and spirited in disagreement; is tenacious.

4. Is a high risk taker; is adventurous and speculative.

5. Displays a good deal of intellectual playfulness; fantasizes; imagines ("I wonder what would happen if ..."); manipulates ideas (i.e., changes, elaborates upon them); is often concerned with adapting, improving, and modifying institutions, objects, and systems.

6. Displays a keen sense of humor and sees humor in situations that may not appear to be humorous to others.

7. Is unusually aware of his or her impulses and more open to the irrational in himself or herself (freer expression of feminine interest for boys, greater than usual amount of independence for girls); shows emotional sensitivity.

8. Is sensitive to beauty; attends to aesthetic characteristics of things.

9. Is nonconforming; accepts disorder; is not interested in details; is individualistic; does not fear being different.

10. Criticizes constructively; is unwilling to accept authoritarian pronouncements without critical examination.

	1	2	3	4
Column Total				
Weight	1	2	3	4
Weighted Column Total				
TOTAL				

APPENDIX 4.5 (Continued)

PART IV: LEADERSHIP CHARACTERISTICS

	1	2	3	4
1. Carries responsibility well; can be counted on to do what he or she has promised and usually does it well.				
2. Is self-confident with children his or her own age as well as adults; seems comfortable when asked to show his or her work to the class.				
3. Seems to be well-liked by classmates.				
4. Is cooperative with teacher and classmates; tends to avoid bickering and is generally easy to get along with.				
5. Can express himself or herself well; has good verbal facility and is usually well understood.				
6. Adapts readily to new situations; is flexible in thought and action and does not seem disturbed when the normal routine is changed.				
7. Seems to enjoy being around other people; is sociable and prefers not to be alone.				
8. Tends to dominate others when they are around; generally directs the activity in which he or she is involved.				
9. Participates in most social activities connected with the school; can be counted on to be there if anyone is.				
10. Excels in athletic activities; is well-coordinated and enjoys all sorts of athletic games.				
Column Total				
Weight	1	2	3	4
Weighted Column Total				
TOTAL				

CHAPTER 5

ACCELERATION

*The pacing of educational programs must be responsive to the capacities
and knowledge of individual children.*
Camilla P. Benbow (1991, p. 157)

This and many of the following chapters describe strategies and models that guide programming decisions, teaching strategies, and curriculum content. In order to provide a framework for "what to do with gifted and talented kids," Table 5.1 summarizes suggestions for program content based upon student needs. These were integrated from lists prepared by Feldhusen (1986), Feldhusen, Hansen, and Kennedy (1989), Ganapole (1989), Kaplan (1974), the National/State Leadership Training Institute for Gifted and Talented, Sato and Johnson (1978), Smith (1990), and Davis and Rimm (1985). Read through Table 5.1 before proceeding. You likely will refer back to this table as you read the following chapters.

There are many types of programs and services designed to fit the needs summarized in Table 5.1, while at the same time accommodating the level of interest, commitment, and resources of the particular school or district. Programs may differ in (1) the categories of students served, (2) the general curriculum model(s) followed, (3) specific enrichment curricula content and program goals, (4) acceleration plans, (5) grouping and organizational arrangements, (6) instructional or delivery strategy used, (7) community professionals and resources involved, and (8) program level (national, state, district, school, or classroom; Fox, 1979).

Overview

We will divide programming into four topics. This chapter will summarize characteristics, advantages,

disadvantages, and recommendations related to a number of *acceleration* strategies. Chapter 6 will focus on *enrichment* and *grouping* options. Chapter 7 will summarize several main *curriculum models*. The topics are interrelated in the sense that grouping is for the purpose of enrichment or acceleration; enrichment and acceleration invariably include elements of the other; and program models prescribe the kinds of learning activities and grouping needed for enrichment and/or acceleration opportunities. Together, these four topics help clarify what can be done in successful programs and provide ideas for how to do it.

ACCELERATION VERSUS ENRICHMENT

One issue pertains to the definitions of and relationships between *acceleration* and *enrichment*, a matter that some see as a passionate controversy. For example, acceleration advocate Julian Stanley (1978b) argued that ". . . most of the supplemental educational procedures called 'enrichment' and given overly glamorous titles are, even at best, potentially dangerous if not accompanied or followed by acceleration . . . in subject matter and/or grade." Stanley and Benbow (1986) referred to most kinds of enrichment as "busywork and irrelevant." In his address to the Sixth World Conference on Gifted and Talented in Hamburg, Germany, Stanley (1985; see also Stanley, 1989) began his speech with ". . . educational nonacceleration is an international tragedy." At a 1981 "Great Debate," Van

TABLE 5.1   Curriculum for the Gifted

1. Maximum achievement in basic skills
   A. Learning activities at an appropriate level and pace
   B. Advanced pace/placement of content or skills; extension of depth or breadth of the content
   C. Based on student needs and readiness, not grade-level appropriateness
   D. Oral communication skills; sharing ideas verbally and in depth
   E. Study skills
   F. Report writing, outlining
2. Content beyond the prescribed curriculum
   A. Extends or replaces traditional curriculum; not just "more work"
   B. Content related to broad-based issues, themes, and problems
   C. Resources beyond the designated grade-level—materials, equipment, information (not just books)
   D. Learning that is interrelated with other areas; not "separate entity learning"
3. Exposure to a variety of fields of study
   A. Opportunity for in-depth study of major ideas, problems, and themes from multiple disciplines
   B. New disciplines; interrelatedness of disciplines; connections of major ideas and concepts within and between disciplines
   C. Various occupations—the arts, professions
   D. Access to and stimulation of reading
4. Student-selected content
   A. Based on student interests and needs
   B. In-depth learning of a self-selected topic within an area of study
   C. Freedom to select from a wide range of materials and resources
   D. Opportunity to pursue areas of inquiry as far as personal interest dictates
5. High content complexity
   A. Working with abstract ideas and theories that require reflective, evaluative, critical, and creative thinking
   B. Working with concepts and generalizations, not just names, dates, facts, and figures
   C. Applying learning, not just parroting it
   D. Developing products that challenge existing ideas and produce "new" ideas
   E. Developing products that use new techniques, materials, and forms
   F. Exposure to varied ideas, topics, issues, and skills at rates appropriate to individual capabilities
6. Experience in creative thinking and problem solving (see Chapters 10 and 11)
   A. Opportunities for creative expression and creative products
   B. Creative writing that stresses free flow of ideas and developing values
   C. Involvement in art and drama; literature enrichment
   D. Learning creative attitudes and awarenesses
   E. Responding to open-ended problems and tasks
   F. Understanding creative people, processes, techniques
   G. Strengthening fluency, flexibility, originality, visualization, analogical thinking, and other creative abilities
   H. Discovery and inquiry skills
   I. Learning to seek problems (problem finding)

    J. Learning to define problems

    K. Freedom to solve problems in diverse ways

    L. Reconceptualizing existing knowledge; generating new knowledge

    M. Futuristic thinking

    N. Learning things as they should be or could be, not only as they are

7. Development of thinking skills (see Chapter 12)
   A. Independent, self-directed study skills
   B. Library skills
   C. Research/scientific skills and methods
   D. Bloom's higher-level skills: application, analysis, synthesis, evaluation
   E. Critical thinking, in the sense of evaluating biases, credibility, logic, consistency; critical reading and listening skills
   F. Decision making, planning, organizing
   G. Developing expert processing strategies—skills and techniques of a professional in a given field

8. Affective development
   A. Developing self-awareness and self-understanding; accepting one's capabilities, interests, and needs
   B. Recognizing and using one's abilities
   C. Appreciating likenesses and differences between oneself and others
   D. Relating intellectually, artistically, and effectively with other gifted, talented, creative students
   E. Moral, ethical thinking; humanitarian attitudes

9. Development of motivation
   A. Independent thinking and work
   B. Becoming self-directed, disciplined in learning
   C. Achievement motivation; internal locus of control; high-level educational and career aspirations

Tassel-Baska (1981b; "For Acceleration") argued that ". . . acceleration implies no more than allowing students to move at a rate with which they are comfortable and can excel, rather than holding them back to conform to a 'speed limit' set by the average learner. As for enrichment," she continued, "the term has no meaning for the gifted unless it is inextricably linked to good acceleration practices. . . ."

Speaking for the opposition, Frost (1981; "For Enrichment") pointed out that enrichment ". . . implies a supplementation of the depth, breadth, or intensity of content and process as appropriate to the students' abilities and needs . . . [and is the prevailing practice because] . . . of the diversity in meeting student needs."

Defining Acceleration and Enrichment

On the surface, the distinction between acceleration and enrichment seems simple enough. Acceleration implies moving faster through academic content, which typically includes offering standard curriculum to students at a younger-than-usual age or lower-than-usual grade level. Enrichment refers to richer and more varied educational experiences, a curriculum that is modified to provide greater depth and breadth than is generally provided (Schiever and Maker, 1991). Both acceleration and enrichment accommodate the high abilities and individual needs of gifted students, and both lead to greater knowledge and skills and the development of creativity and other thinking skills.

Looking closely, the terms *acceleration* and *enrichment* are in fact used in overlapping and ambiguous ways. For example, is a special math, science, computer, or foreign language class in the elementary school considered "enrichment" or "acceleration?" What about a similar course taught in high school?

We will use a rule-of-thumb definition (suggested by Fox, 1979) that permits a reasonably clear distinction between acceleration plans versus enrichment plans: Any strategy that results in advanced placement or credit may be titled *acceleration*; strategies that supplement or go beyond standard grade-level work but do not result in advanced placement or credit (that is, anything else) may be called *enrichment*. Thus the special foreign language, math, or science material taught in elementary school, and the special high school drama or photography class that does not result in advanced credit or standing, would be enrichment. However, if a junior or senior high school course or curriculum plan leads to advanced standing (for example, in math or languages), early high school graduation, or advanced standing in college, it is acceleration. Any type of early admission to kindergarten or college, skipping a grade, or condensing (telescoping) three years of junior high school algebra into two years also is acceleration.

Karen Rogers (1990), who has studied the topic of acceleration closely, proposed a definition that is quite close to ours. According to Rogers, *acceleration* is "any program adaptation that (1) shortens the time a student remains in a grade-progressive educational setting; and/or (2) advances the level of curriculum attained in a given time or age." Her slightly broader definition includes *mentorships* and *curriculum compacting* (e.g., speeding through a lesson or skipping a spelling test), which we will discuss in Chapters 6 and 7, respectively. In common usage, teachers and others often refer to virtually any variety of advanced subject-matter or curriculum compacting as "acceleration," whether or not students earn advanced placement or credit.

Any well-rounded, coherent and long-range gifted and talented program will provide both enrichment and acceleration opportunities. Gifted students should be permitted to work at their own rapid pace, accelerating through and out of primary and secondary schools. They also should have opportunities for greater variety in content, greater depth, and the development of affective, creative, scientific, and other high-level skills, that is, enrichment. In addition, they should receive educational and career counseling to help them understand themselves and make their best educational decisions (Chapter 17).

EARLY ADMISSION TO KINDERGARTEN OR FIRST GRADE

Early admission to either kindergarten or first grade is an acceleration strategy that accommodates gifted children's high energy, enthusiasm, curiosity, imagination, and their intellectual needs to investigate, observe, and examine (Feldhusen, 1992). Unfortunately, teachers, principals, and school psychologists express these kinds of concerns regarding any form of elementary school acceleration: Accelerated children will not socialize well with older children, will have fewer friends, will not be happy, and will miss important social interactions; they will be deprived of necessary childhood experiences; they will be involved in fewer extracurricular activities; acceleration will make excessive academic demands, cause stress, and lead to problems of early burnout, rebelliousness, and/or emotional maladjustment; accelerated children will not do well because of increased academic competition; they will miss leadership experiences and not develop leadership skills; they will become conceited and arrogant (Cornell *et al.*, 1991; Southern, Jones, and Fiscus, 1989).

Despite these worries, early admission to kindergarten or first grade and other acceleration strategies are well-supported by research (e.g., Birch, 1954; Cornell *et al.*, 1991; Feldhusen, 1992; Feldhusen, Proctor, and Black, 1986; Hobson, 1948; Proctor, Feldhusen, and Black 1988). The vast majority of early-entering precocious children—who are carefully selected for readiness—

adjust at least as well as nonaccelerated gifted control children. Further, their achievement not only is equal to that of others in their grade, it typically is superior (Feldhusen, 1992; Proctor, Black and Feldhusen, 1986; see Inset 5.1).

Teachers' negative experiences usually stem from accelerated children who were too immature to function well in their classes. The problem sometimes is that these children were not carefully screened.

One difficulty is related to the finding that highly gifted children often have more social difficulties than other gifted children (e.g., Hollingworth, 1942). However, it is these children who have the greatest need for early admission to kindergarten. Kindergarten and first-grade teachers should allow time for adjustment. Also, highly verbal gifted children may be unaccustomed to sharing adult attention, and may thus appear troublesome and immature whether or not they are

---

INSET 5.1 _____

Benefits of Acceleration: Academic, Psychological, and Social

Karen Rogers (1990) evaluated academic, psychological, and social effects of acceleration at elementary and secondary levels with a "best evidence synthesis" (meta-analysis) of the results of 314 studies that evaluated these 12 procedures:

Early entrance	Grade skipping
Non-graded classes	Curriculum compacting
Grade telescoping	Concurrent enrollment (e.g., in high
Subject acceleration	school and college)
Mentorships	Advanced Placement (AP) courses
Credit by examination	Early admission to college
Combinations of two options	

Two blanket conclusions were that "No form of acceleration led to decreases in any area of performance—academic, social, or emotional" and "There appear to be generally positive academic effects for most forms of acceleration."

Her criterion of a "practically significant" academic benefit was an achievement advantage of accelerated students of at least one-third year over non-accelerated control students. All acceleration strategies produced a significant academic benefit, except concurrent enrollment, AP courses (nearly significant), and combinations of two options. Further, significant academic benefits occurred at all four grade levels, primary (grades K-2), intermediate (3–6), junior high (7–9), and senior high (10–12).

None of the accelerative options damaged either socialization or psychological adjustment. In fact, grade skipping and credit by examination *aided* social relations as well as academic achievement; and concurrent enrollment and mentorships *aided* psychological adjustment in the form of improved self-concepts.

Rogers recommended these acceleration options as the most beneficial at different age levels:

Elementary children: Early entrance, grade-skipping, non-graded classes, and curriculum compacting.

Junior high students: Grade-skipping, grade telescoping, concurrent enrollment, subject acceleration, and curriculum compacting.

Senior high students: Concurrent enrollment, subject acceleration, AP classes, mentorships, credit by examination, and early admission to college.

entered early (Rimm, 1990b). Here is a recent example:

Robert

Robert, an only child, was highly gifted and very verbal. His parents took the advice of the school to hold him back for a year because of his young age and their perception that Robert was immature. Robert waited a year and entered as one of the oldest in his class.

Robert brought two backpacks into school for each show and tell. He had learned so much and wanted to share so much. When he was not called on as frequently as he would have liked, class clowning and disruption followed. Lack of challenge continued to be a problem, although with therapeutic help for Robert, his parents, and teachers, Robert's behavior problems disappeared. He was subject accelerated in reading in first grade, but Robert knew he was also ahead in math. The school was not eager to move him ahead because of his earlier behavior problems. Finally, Robert was allowed to skip fourth grade; he was placed with age mates. There will be more need for challenge, but it is obvious to his parents and teachers that this is a better fit for Robert. He likely will need further subject or grade acceleration.

If Robert had entered school as youngest in his class, his behavior problems likely would have been blamed on his young age. It took time before the problems were correctly associated with his lack of challenge.

How can a school district resolve the differences between the results of multiple research projects and the typical teaching staff impressions? An early admission policy that gives careful consideration to the following variables is likely to select gifted children who will be successful despite their younger age.

Intellectual Precocity. An individual intelligence test score of 130 or more is recommended for early admission (Feldhusen, 1992).

Eye-hand Coordination. Tests of eye-hand coordination should suggest at least average perceptual-motor skill, since problems in this area may put unnecessary stress on the early entrant who must participate in cutting, pasting, drawing, writing, and so on.

Reading Readiness. Reading is the skill most critical to early school success. Test scores should show clear readiness to read. Many gifted children are able to read prior to school entrance. Feldhusen (1992) recommended that for early admission to first grade, the child should demonstrate both reading comprehension and arithmetic reasoning at or above the level of second semester of first grade.

Social and Emotional Maturity. The child should not have serious adjustment problems. Ideally, the child would have adapted readily to preschool experiences, adapted to other group activities, and/or have friends in the grade he/she wishes to enter (Feldhusen, 1992). Observations by a psychologists can be helpful in determining school social adjustment.

Observations of immaturity may be misleading and biased by the often-held assumption that small children and young children are automatically immature. Here are two examples:

Timmy

Based on her observations of his immaturity, Timmy's nursery school teacher recommended that he wait an extra year before entering kindergarten as a young kindergartener. Timmy was already reading beyond first-grade level and doing math beyond second-grade level. The school psychologist tested and found him to be in the very superior range of ability.

Timmy's parents asked what the symptoms of his immaturity were. His small size was given as one indicator, and his inability to sit still during story time was another.

At the recommendation of the psychologist, Timmy's dad asked him to work hard at sitting still during story hour each day and to report his progress to him each day. After two weeks, Timmy's parents called the teacher who commented on Timmy's jump in maturity.

Both of Timmy's parents are short and both have high energy. One specific change in behavior made a difference in the teacher's perception of Timmy's maturity. He is now in fourth grade and has made excellent adjustment, although he continues to require further academic challenge. He also continues to be short for his age and will undoubtedly never become a professional basketball player.

David

David was tested for early entrance to kindergarten. Academic and intelligence testing showed him to be beyond readiness for first grade. The teacher observed him as shy and somewhat of a loner and thus recommended he not be entered early. Despite the teacher's recommendations, David entered kindergarten.

All teachers have indicated excellent adjustment for David. They also usually comment on his quiet personality. In fifth grade at the time of this writing, David searches for challenge and loves learning. He expresses himself well and has a few good friends. An extra year of nursery school likely would not have changed his quiet personality.

Health.   A child who has a history of good health is more likely to attend school regularly and concentrate on classwork. Frequent health problems combined with a young age may put too much stress on even a very gifted child.

Gender.   Although each child must be considered individually, males do mature later than females and physical maturity is an important consideration. For this reason, it is not unusual or necessarily unfair for girls to be favored for early entrance.

School of Entrance.   The average IQ in some schools may be 120 or 125, while in others the average may be 100 or less. Thus an early-entering child's intellectual ability should be considered relative to the school population. If the school has many very bright children, its regular fare is likely to provide adequate challenge. The gifted child therefore may do just as well by waiting to enter with same-age children.

The Receiving Teacher.   Ideally, the child's teacher should favor early admission and be willing to help the child adjust; the child does not need a pessimistic or hostile teacher (Feldhusen, 1992). However, the child should not be held back because of the teacher's initial attitudes. Most teachers change their attitude if children truly show readiness.

Family Values.   The child who is permitted to enter school early needs the support of a family that values education and academic achievement. For example, if success in team sports is an important family goal, there is a high risk of stress for the undersized accelerated boy. Hobson (1948) found that 550 early admitted youth compared favorably to nonaccelerates in general high school extracurricular activities; however, in a ten-year review of underage gifted boys he found only two who were outstanding in contact sports.

In sum, early entrance to kindergarten or first grade is definitely recommended for gifted children who are carefully screened according to the above criteria. If parents are considering early kindergarten admission for their precocious child, teachers and principals might recommend that they enroll the child in a quality nursery school. The nursery school will be helpful in providing parents and educators an opportunity to observe the child's social and cognitive adjustment in a school setting. The experience also will foster further skill development and will acquaint the child with some social and academic classroom routines. Finally, note that admitting a child early to kindergarten or first grade is not a rigid, unchangeable decision. In fact, noted Feldhusen (1992, p. 47), "All cases of early admission should be on a trial basis." While Feldhusen recommends a trial period of 6 weeks, Rimm (1992b) found that some children required as much as a semester for a completely smooth adjustment. All students she recommended for early entrance, based on careful screening, adjusted successfully.

GRADE-SKIPPING

Grade-skipping is the traditional method of accelerating precocious elementary school students. It requires no special materials or facilities, no G/T coordinator, not even a G/T program. In fact, it is extraordinarily cost-effective in moving the gifted or talented child through and out of the school system ahead of schedule. Grade-skipping may be initiated by parents who are aware that their child is one or two years ahead of the rest of the class and is bored with school and impatient with his or her peers, or by a teacher who makes the same observation. Grade-skipping or "double promotion" usually takes place in the lowest elementary grades, but sometimes in advanced grades. Some gifted children skip two or three grades (occasionally more) and enter college at age 15 or 16. Some parents become frustrated and agitated if their district does not permit grade-skipping; many districts do not.

There are at least two major concerns regarding grade-skipping. The first is the problem of missing critical basis skills. Many teachers feel that if a child is not taught an important math or reading skill, he or she will be at a great disadvantage in later grades. They frequently predict that the child (1) will not be able to maintain good grades, (2) will see him- or herself as less capable, and therefore (3) will lose school motivation. It is true that some skills are absolutely critical to the learning of later skills, and their absence could place stress on the student. However, many gifted students have acquired knowledge and skills far ahead of their grade levels, learned either independently or from an interested parent or older sibling. That is, the "missing skills" may not be missing at all. As a precaution, a series of diagnostic tests for the grade to be skipped can identify missing skills, and the motivated gifted child typically can learn these quickly, either working independently or with the help of interested adults.

The second concern, social adjustment to peers, is even more common. The concern here comes mainly from parents and teachers familiar with a gifted child who skipped a grade and experienced social problems or maladjustment. Once again we find a conflict between research conclusions and what many teachers, administrators, and parents claim. The current research-based consensus is that in most cases gifted students are quite comfortable with their *intellectual* peers—older students—and suffer no noticeable maladjustment or neuroses (for example, Brody and Benbow, 1987; Daurio, 1979; Feldhusen, 1992; Feldhusen, Proctor, and Black, 1986; Gregory and March, 1985; Kulik and Kulik, 1984; Rimm, 1991a, 1992b; Southern and Jones, 1992; Stanley, 1991a; Van Tassel-Baska, 1986).

Among Terman's gifted children, those who had been accelerated one or two years made *better* adjustments than those who were not (Terman and Oden, 1947). Based on a survey of former high-ability high school students, some of whom had skipped one or more high school grades or entered college early, Brody and Benbow (1987) found that accelerated students did as well or better than the others in all areas of achievement, had higher career aspirations, and attended more select colleges. There were no differences in social or emotional adjustment. Said Brody and Benbow, "This study did not reveal any harmful effects as a result of acceleration."

Van Tassel-Baska (1986) based these conclusions on all forms of academic acceleration. Accelerated gifted students:

- Improve in motivation, confidence, and scholarship.
- Do not develop habits of mental laziness.
- Complete their professional training earlier.
- Reduce the cost of their college education.

Reservations about grade-skipping may be based on some faulty assumptions and interpretations, for example:

1. Many persons look back to their adolescence as being a difficult time for social adjustment; persons who have been accelerated may incorrectly blame these problems on their acceleration. Persons who were not accelerated might blame their problems on other factors.

2. Research has confirmed that gifted children, on average, are better adjusted socially and emotionally than typical students. However, children with very high intelligence have special problems relating to others because of their differentness (e.g., Delisle, 1992; Hollingworth, 1942; Piechowski, 1991; see Chapter 17). Because these children are the ones most likely to be skipping grades, their social problems, actually related to their extremely high intelligence, may mistakenly be blamed on acceleration.

3. When outsiders observe a school child who is noticeably smaller or younger than average, based on appearance alone they may infer that the child certainly must be having social problems, even though testimony from the child him- or herself does not indicate any special problems.

To reduce the risk of problems related to grade-skipping we recommend the following guidelines, some of which duplicate the above recommendations for early admission to kindergarten or first grade:

1. A child should have an IQ score of 130 or higher. Feldhusen (1992; Feldhusen, Proctor, and Black, 1986) recommended that a level of mental development one standard deviation above the mean for the grade to be entered also would indicate the intellectual readiness to skip a grade.[1]

2. Regardless of ability, for elementary students only one grade should be skipped at a time. After the child has had several years for adjustment, there may be reason to consider skipping another

---

[1]One standard deviation above the mean would put the child at the 84th percentile; that is, the child would score higher in intelligence than 84 percent of the children in the grade in which the child is to be placed.

grade. Older students, say age 14 or upward, who are socially and emotionally mature have successfully moved directly from *junior* high school to college (Gregory and March, 1985; Stanley and McGill, 1986).

3. Skill gaps should be diagnosed so that the child can be assisted in acquiring any missing basic skills.

4. A supportive teacher, counselor, and/or group of gifted peers should be available to help the child with social problems related to grade-skipping.

5. Parent value systems need to be considered. Especially, if families place more emphasis on athletics than academics, grade-skipping may put considerable pressure on the student who may not be big enough to compete in some sports.

6. An appraisal of the child's present intellectual and social adjustment should be considered in the decision making. If the child is not showing good social adjustment in the present grade, grade-skipping cannot be assumed to improve that adjustment. Also, continued poor adjustment in the higher grade should not necessarily be attributed to the grade-skipping. Grade-skipping is not a cure-all, and a given child may require further guidance regardless of the grade-skipping decision.

7. Every grade-skipping decision needs to be made separately. Physical maturity, height, general emotional stability, motivation, and ability to handle challenge all should be part of the decision making. Centrally important is the gifted child's need for intellectual stimulation.

8. Feldhusen (1992; Feldhusen, Proctor, and Black, 1986) recommends that, as with early admission to kindergarten or first grade, all cases of grade-skipping be arranged on a trial basis of about six weeks. Rimm (1992b), based on her experience as a psychologist, recommends that a semester be allowed for adjustment. Although some children adjust within a few weeks, others take longer. The child should be made aware that if the advancement does not go well, he or she may request to be returned to the original grade. Counseling services should be available. Further, the child should not be made to feel he or she is a "failure" if the grade-skipping does not succeed.

Teachers and parents too often conclude that it is simply easier to avoid making a decision that favors grade-skipping. Administratively, and in view of general inertia, they are of course correct. However, teachers and parents should recognize that keeping a highly precocious child in an unstimulating environment is also making a decision—one that communicates to the gifted child that he or she is not expected to perform up to his or her capability, and that social life is more important than academic challenge. That decision can be more intellectually and even socially harmful to the gifted child than the decision to skip grades. Boredom, restlessness, frustration, underachievement, and disruptiveness can be replaced by enhanced motivation, improved self-concepts, and improved study habits and productivity (e.g., Benbow, 1992, 1993; Benbow, Argo, and Glass, 1992; Feldhusen, 1992; Karnes and Chauvin, 1982a, 1982b; Rimm and Lovance, 1992a, 1992b; Van Tassel-Baska, 1986).

As examples of the effectiveness of elementary school acceleration, Gross (1992) described five extremely precocious students (IQs = 160 to 200) who, because of carefully planned and monitored grade-skipping and radical subject-matter skipping, "are more stimulated intellectually, enjoy closer and more productive social relationships, and display healthier levels of social self-esteem than do equally gifted children who have been retained with age peers of average ability." Rimm and Lovance (1992a, 1992b) used grade-skipping and subject-skipping to prevent or reverse underachievement in 14 high IQ children, all of whom had been brought by parents to Rimm's Underachievement Clinic. Note the irony: The children were doing poor work—and therefore would hardly be teachers' choices for acceleration—yet the grade- and subject-skipping provided the academic challenge needed to stimulate interest and achievement consistent with their high ability. Later interviews confirmed that all parents and

(initially reluctant) administrators agreed that acceleration was the right move.

SUBJECT-SKIPPING

Grade-skipping is sometimes called *full acceleration*, and subject-skipping therefore is *partial acceleration*. Subject-skipping involves taking classes or studying particular subjects with students in higher grades. It is especially appropriate in sequential types of subject matters, particularly reading, math, and languages, but possible in other subjects as well. Subject-skipping therefore is for the student with special skills and talents primarily in a single area. The acceleration may begin in the elementary school and continue through high school.

Subject-skipping has important advantages and only one major disadvantage. On the positive side, it permits the child to be intellectually challenged in a specific area of strength while he or she continues to develop appropriate grade-level skills in other areas. It also permits the child to remain with peers to whom he or she already may be socially adjusted. Subject-skipping also may be used experimentally to determine if grade-skipping would later be appropriate. Thus if the child is accelerated in his or her strongest subject, the teacher can observe the academic and social adjustment of the child in the new setting and make a more confident decision about full acceleration.

Rimm (1992a, 1992b) found that students who were first subject-skipped and later grade-skipped felt relief at no longer having to explain their participation in two different grade levels.

The disadvantage of subject-skipping is the problem of continuity. Too often a particular school or teacher may be willing to accelerate a student in a single subject, such as math, but makes no overall organizational plan for continuous progress. Therefore, the child who masters three years of math in just one may suddenly discover that he or she must repeat two of them. Such repetition is likely to be more boring and damaging than moving the child through the material more slowly in the first place. However, if continuous accelerated coursework can be planned for the child, subject acceleration is an ideal approach for children with high abilities in specific areas.

EARLY ADMISSION TO JUNIOR OR SENIOR HIGH SCHOOL

This particular acceleration alternative seems not to be popular. However, for some students, the best grade to be skipped is the one just before junior or senior high school, that is, grade five or six, or grade eight or nine (Brody and Stanley, 1991). From an academic perspective, the student may be ready and anxious for advanced work in the specialized and departmentalized junior or senior high school. Socially, it may be an opportune time to accelerate, since new friendships inevitably develop when students from several elementary or junior high schools meet for the first time in the new school setting.

CREDIT BY EXAMINATION

In the junior or senior high school, one cost-free mechanism for justifiable subject-skipping is credit by examination. For example, if a talented mathematics or language student feels he or she already has acquired the content of a semester course, perhaps through home study or foreign travel, the student should be allowed to "test out" of the course and, if mastery is demonstrated, receive academic credit. In addition to preventing repetition and boredom, allowing credit by examination will encourage gifted students to accept challenges, set goals, and work toward them.

As a precaution in using this option, the student should be provided with an outline of the material to be included in the test. This gives the student a fair opportunity to appraise his or her own skills and to concentrate study on those not yet mastered. Failure experienced on tests due to lack of adequate preparation, or else miscommunication about the test content, is likely to be an unpleasant experience for both the student and the school staff.

College credit, which permits advanced placement when the student enters college, may be earned through examination, as in the *Advanced Placement* (AP) program described below or in the *College Level Examination Program* (CLEP; see, e.g., Karnes and Chauvin, 1982a; Zimmerman and Brody, 1986). Unlike the AP program, CLEP does not offer courses, just examinations. CLEP examinations for college credit are available in 30 subject areas, for example, math, English (composition and literature), business, computer science, nursing, education, psychology, and foreign languages. The exams are 90-minute multiple-choice tests, although optional essay exams are available if colleges require them. Students taking only language exams can earn 6 or 12 college credits; students taking other CLEP exams can earn 3 or 6 college credits. The exams may be taken by anyone (e.g., junior or senior high school students); the cost in early 1993 was $38 per test. Before registering, one should check to determine if the college of one's choice will accept CLEP credits, because not all do.[2]

COLLEGE COURSES IN HIGH SCHOOL

Regarding academic acceleration in high school generally, Robinson and Noble (1992b, p. 20–21; see also Robinson and Noble, 1992a) made this perceptive comment: "For the young person whose intellectual development is markedly above average, the pace of ordinary secondary school classes can be deadly, 'like going through every day in a slow motion movie,' according to one student. . . . folklore to the contrary, the senior year is often the hardest to endure." A solution available to many bright and motivated secondary students is taking college-level courses while in high school.

For example, with a *dual enrollment* program a student may be excused from high school for part of the day to take one or more courses on the college campus. The earned college credits may be used at the particular college when he or she actually is admitted; alternatively, the credits normally

[2]For additional information, write to College Board, Box 1842, Princeton, NJ 08541, or phone (609) 951-1026. Schools may use 1-800-257-9558 to request information.

can be transferred to another college of the student's choice. Importantly, the courses also should be credited toward high school graduation requirements so that the student is not burdened—punished—with double the amount of coursework.

Another desirable option, the *Advance Placement* (AP) program, like CLEP, is sponsored by College Board. The AP program consists of college-level courses and examinations for high school students (see, e.g., Brody, Assouline, and Stanley, 1990; Brody and Stanley, 1991; Zimmerman and Brody, 1986). The courses may take the form of an honors class or a strong regular class, either of which would be taught by an instructor who follows an AP course description ($8.00). Students in middle school, high school, or college or anyone else may prepare individually, perhaps with a tutor, and then take the tests. The tests are given only at high schools.

The AP program offers courses and exams in several dozen areas, for example, English literature and composition, foreign languages (including Latin), chemistry, economics, music theory, calculus, psychology, history (U.S., European, art), computer science, government and politics, and biology. The cost of exams was $67 in early 1993; they are given over a two-week period in May of each year. The examination for each course includes a 90-minute multiple-choice test plus a 90-minute essay test. Over 1,300 colleges accept AP credits. Courses require a full year to complete, although a few are broken into two one-semester segments with separate exams (e.g., Micro-Economic Theory, Macro-Economic Theory; both exams for $67).

Colleges that accept AP credits (not all do) differ regarding the maximum number of credits that can be used. However, consider this arithmetic: A semester of college work (five courses, 15 credits) could be earned for $335 (5 X $67), which compares with college tuition/boarding/spending money that *begins* at about $2,500 per semester.[3]

[3]For additional information, write to College Board, Princeton, NJ 08541, or phone (609) 771-7300.

Generally, the factor most critical to the success of permitting—indeed, encouraging—high school students to accept the challenge of earning college credits in high school is administrative flexibility.

CORRESPONDENCE COURSES

Every major university offers correspondence courses at least at the college freshman and sophomore levels. Correspondence courses thus present valuable opportunities, particularly for the talented student who lives in a rural area or a small city or town. Correspondence courses carry full college credit. They are written by professors and are supervised by college professors, instructors, or qualified graduate students. Courses are available in a variety of areas, for example, college math, algebra, statistics, introductory psychology, educational psychology, sociology, economics, anthropology, astronomy, history, foreign languages, and others. The University of Wisconsin, Madison, offers a correspondence course in gifted education, using this text. Correspondence courses may be taken in the summer, as a form of independent study, or as a form of enrichment in conjunction with a regular high school program. Typically, courses requiring student-teacher interaction or laboratories are not taught by mail—for example, biology, physics, or chemistry.

A considerable amount of self-motivation and independence is needed to complete a correspondence course successfully. Students are more likely to be successful if several of them take the same course, thus permitting mutual support, stimulation, and assistance. It also is helpful if a high school faculty member can serve as an advisor for the students in case they need help understanding or interpreting the material or solving practice problems.

TELESCOPED PROGRAMS

Telescoping means, for example, collapsing three academic years' work into two, or four years of high school into three. In the junior high school, if enough talented young mathematicians are available, a normal three-year math and algebra sequence might be taught at an accelerated pace in two years. It is less common, but the same telescoping can be used with other subjects, for example, by condensing three years of junior high school science into two years.

In high school, telescoping four years' work into three is almost entirely a counseling problem, assuming that district policies will permit such acceleration. The energetic and capable student, with the assistance of his or her counselor, simply cuts down on the "study hall" classes and schedules four years of high school requirements into a more compact and busier three. If three years is unrealistic, a three-and-a-half year program still would permit a capable student to begin college a semester early.

Planning telescoped programs can be complicated. Schools generally prefer that students design their plan before beginning even their freshman year. However, not many 13-year-olds can predict whether or not telescoping their high school education is a good tactic. Until students have had a year or two of experience in high school, they may not be ready to make a decision that trades more work for early graduation. A counselor who specializes in giftedness may be able to guide a student flexibly, helping him or her to make a decision after acquiring experience in high school.

EARLY ADMISSION TO COLLEGE

Many gifted and talented high school and some junior high school students are permitted to enter college early on a full-time basis (Brody, Assouline, and Stanley, 1990; Brody and Stanley, 1991; Cornell, Callahan, and Lloyd, 1991a, 1991b; Gregory and March, 1985; Karnes and Chauvin, 1982a, 1982b; Stanley and Benbow, 1983, 1986). In some cases high school requirements are met early, as in telescoping plans. In other cases high school requirements are flexibly waived and a qualified student simply enters college full-time without meeting all of the usual graduation requirements. With the latter plan, in view of college entrance requirements one must be sure that the particular college admissions office is agreeable to such short-cutting before plans reach an advanced stage. Some college admissions offices are not wildly enthusiastic about early entrants. Other colleges, for example, Johns Hopkins, California State University at Los Angeles, University of Wisconsin-Madison, and the University of Washington, welcome qualified senior and even junior high school youth as full-time students.

As an example, after a successful pilot study the California State University at Los Angeles (CSULA) in 1983 installed a permanent Early Entrance Program—a full-time college program for junior and senior high school-aged students (Gregory, 1984; Gregory and March, 1985). Students must be at least 14 years old. They also must produce scores on the *Washington Pre-College Test* or the *Scholastic Aptitude Test* (SAT) above the 80th percentile on either the verbal or math section and above the 50th percentile on the other. Students initially attend CSULA part-time, while continuing their junior or senior high school classes. Thus if the program is unsuitable, little is lost and usually some college credits are banked for future use. Students who do register full-time seem to realize social and emotional benefits as well as intellectual ones (Gregory and March, 1985). The program works well.

Early admission to college, with or without graduation from high school, is an excellent way for a mature gifted student to accelerate his or her education. Unfortunately, although the authors feel that school policies should support such initiative, many high school teachers and administrators discourage early graduation and early college admission. Also, high school students who consider this approach may feel pressure to remain in high school in the form of missing opportunities for scholarships and honors and, of course, missing the social and extracurricular activities. The early college entrant should be prepared to trade some of these opportunities for the challenge of college work. If the student or his or her parents have doubts about early full-time college work, the CSULA strategy of first enrolling part-time while still in secondary school will make the decision much easier.

Caution is indeed required in selecting students for early college admission. Cornell, Callahan, and Lloyd (1991b) emphasized that large individual differences exist in the ability of young people to adjust to college life, and that early admission is inappropriate for some. In their study of 44 female students age 13 to 17 who participated in a residential (live-in) college program, over half suffered from periods of depression; a few showed suicidal tendencies; and 13 left the program for reasons related to stress. They emphasized the importance of socioemotional maturity, good self-concepts, and the ability to relate well to adults, which can lead to *excellent* adjustment and healthy personality growth in early college admissions programs (Cornell, Callahan, and Loyd, 1991a). They suggested also that programs in which students *commute* to college may be less stressful than residential, live-in programs.

In an unpublished report, Stanley emphasized these advantages of entering college at a younger-than-average age. Highly able youths can get more academic stimulation and breadth at a good college than during their last year or two in high school. Remaining in high school, in fact, can have detrimental social and emotional consequences if such students are eager to move ahead. There is greater opportunity to interact with expert professionals. By saving one or two years of schooling, there is more time and flexibility for planning educational and other aspects of life. One also is able to enter a profession at an earlier age, allowing extra years of youthful vigorous work. Graduate and professional schools are impressed by students who graduate from college, especially an outstanding one, at a younger-than-average age. Finally, moving ahead according to one's best ability is exhilarating, motivating, and builds realistic self-confidence.

One accelerated student expressed her feelings about early entrance this way: "When I felt surrounded by highly intelligent students and somewhat inadequate, I would remind myself that I was young for my grade and wasn't doing poorly considering my age." She was pleased that she had entered early and continued on to a doctoral program in psychology. And even there her young age was a comfort to her in her challenging program.

After reviewing successes and some failures of mathematically precocious college entrants, Stanley and McGill (1986) recommended that early entrants should score higher on the SAT than usual college freshman—at least 625 on the SAT-V and 675 on the SAT-M.

RESIDENTIAL HIGH SCHOOLS

A relatively new opportunity for gifted students is special residential (live-in) high schools, such as the North Carolina School of Science and Mathematics, the Louisiana School for Math, Science, and the Arts, the Illinois Mathematics and Science Academy (Gallagher *et al.*, 1991; Marshall, 1988), the Texas Academy of Mathematics and Science, the Mississippi School for Math and Science, and the South Carolina Governor's School for Science and Mathematics (Eilber, 1987; Gallagher *et al.*, 1991; Kolloff, 1991; Stanley, 1987). These schools are based on the assumption that regular high schools simply cannot offer the number of advanced courses or a sufficiently diverse curriculum to provide for gifted students who, for example, master all the math courses the school has to offer within one or two years (Kolloff, 1991). Special residential programs thus are appropriate for students who are capable of mastering content much more rapidly than others, and are able to engage in complex processes at high levels of abstraction (Kolloff, 1991). Stanley (1987) recommended that any state with 300 National Merit semifinalists each year should consider creating a special residential high school for these and other highly capable secondary students.

Thus far, all residential high schools, except the Illinois program, are located on college campuses, which provide the needed dormitories, cafeterias, and recreational facilities, to say nothing of cultural opportunities and academic resources. As indicated by their names, current residential high schools highlight math and science. For some, AP courses in calculus, physics, chemistry, computer science, and biology form the foundation of the curriculum, enabling students to enter college with one or more years of credit in several areas.

The academic and social benefits of residential high schools seem self-evident. Nonetheless, as with any acceleration plan, criticisms have been quick. Some persons complain of a "brain drain"— the best students leave the regular high school. Others worry about the young scholars leaving home two or three years before they normally would leave for college; that contact with college students might be problematic; or that such schools will foster attitudes of superiority and arrogance.

To counter some of these issues, residential school calendars include long weekends at home, as well as opportunities for outside activities. Staff are alert to signs of stress, depression, or homesickness; they watch for symptoms of adjustment problems such as missing classes, not completing assignments, excessive socializing, or social withdrawal. Residential high schools limit interaction between high school and college students by housing them separately and segregating the two groups for social and, usually, academic activities (Kolloff, 1991). Problems of arrogance are countered by requiring community service and some responsibilities for maintaining their school—a broom and mop can be humbling.

A particularly difficult issue is student body composition. Schools are asked to ensure racial, ethnic, gender, geographic, and socioeconomic balance. Most residential schools are indeed committed to a diversified student body, and use flexible admissions procedures that consider geographic and other variables. Stanley (1987) maintained, however, that minimal ability levels should be established, and that these levels not be modified to accommodate outside pressures.

INTERNATIONAL BACCALAUREATE PROGRAMS

Like residential high schools, *International Baccalaureate (IB) Programs* are highly selective, provide excellent acceleration opportunities, but are scarce. They typically are designed as two-year (junior-senior) high school programs that emphasize foreign languages and international concerns, beyond regular high school requirements (Cox and Daniel, 1991). Participants earn college credit for their IB work.

Students are selected by a committee of teachers, counselors, and administrators who evaluate "academic performance, attendance, conduct, extracurricular activities, motivation, and a written statement from the applicant" (Cox and Daniel, 1991, p. 158). Academically, IB programs draw students from the 90th percentile and above.

As an example of an IB curriculum, the International Baccalaureate Program in Houston requires:

A first language (English), which includes a study of world literature from at least two languages, translated into English.

A second language, which can be Latin.

Study of Man, which is one selection from history, geography, economics, philosophy, psychology, social anthropology, or business studies.

Experimental Sciences, which includes selections from biology, chemistry, physics, physical science, and scientific studies.

Mathematics

One selection from art, music, or another (third) language.

A course entitled *Theory of Knowledge*, which is a study of human learning that requires reflection on, for example, individual differences in knowledge and attitudes.

Participation in a creative or aesthetic area such as music, art, dance, drama, or creative writing.

A social service activity, a component entitled *Education for Compassion.*

As a graduation requirement, IB students prepare an extended essay based on independent research.

To prepare students for the high school IB program, some Houston middle schools offer "Pre-IB" courses, which include foreign languages and courses that are "enriched across the board" (Cox and Daniel, 1991).

What is the reception to Houston's IB program? At middle and high school levels, "Parents are eager and the classes are overfull" (p. 166).

STUDY OF MATHEMATICALLY PRECOCIOUS YOUTH AND TALENT SEARCH

The best-known example of accelerating bright secondary students into college-level work is the highly successful *Talent Search* programs, which began at Johns Hopkins University in 1971 as Julian Stanley's *Study of Mathematically Precocious Youth* (SMPY; Richardson and Benbow, 1990; Stanley, 1979, 1988, 1991a; Stanley and Benbow, 1986; see also Benbow, 1986, 1991; Benbow and Stanley, 1983).

The purpose of SMPY has been to locate primarily seventh-grade students with extraordinarily high mathematics talent "and help them find the special, supplemental, accelerative opportunities they sorely need in order to move ahead faster and better in mathematics and related subjects such as physics and computer science" (Stanley, 1991a, p. 36). In an annual mathematics talent search, seventh-grade students are selected on the basis of *Scholastic Aptitude Test-Mathematics* (SAT-M) scores. Students who score 500 or higher, which would be the 51st percentile for male college-bound high school seniors, are considered mathematically precocious. Seventh- and eighth-grade students with such scores reason better mathematically than 99 percent of their agemates. Students take summer mathematics classes, usually taught by a college professor at Johns Hopkins. According to Stanley (1982), by working 5 to 6 hours per day, these students in three weeks can master one to two years of high school algebra and geometry. Said Stanley, many of them learn more effectively in three weeks than in a full academic year—they are working, not sleeping. By eighth grade, they are ready for calculus.

High school SMPY participants are encouraged to pursue any of a "smorgasbord" of acceleration options: (1) They may attend college part-time, earning credit for advanced placement; (2) they may earn college credit by examination in the Advanced Placement program; (3) they may skip a grade, particularly the one at the end of junior high school; (4) they may complete two or more years of mathematics in one year; (5) they may enter college early, either by early high school graduation or ". . . simply by leaving high school before completing the last grade(s) . . ." (Stanley, 1979). In every case, these students receive individual counseling regarding the educational alternatives that might be appropriate for them to pursue.

A few selected and unbiased testimonials by Stanley (1979) may be of interest: "The boredom and frustration of even the average-scoring (SMPY) contestants when incarcerated in a year-long algebra class is difficult to appreciate. Often, highly able youths themselves are not aware of the extent of their slowdown, because it has been their lot from kindergarten onward. . . . Often, they take off like rockets intellectually when allowed to do so. . . . It is clear that a large reservoir of virtually untapped mathematical reasoning ability exists all around the region. . . ."

SMPY expanded in many ways. In 1979 Stanley created the Johns Hopkins Center for Academically Talented Youth (CTY), which conducted talent searches using not only the SAT-M, but SAT-Verbal and SAT-Total scores as well. *Talent Search* programs based on the SMPY model, and which use mainly SAT-M and SAT-V scores for selection, have been created at Arizona State University, California State University at

Sacramento, University of Denver, Duke University, Northwestern University, and Iowa State University.[4,5] As with the Johns Hopkins SMPY and CTY programs, the primary Talent Search activity is accelerated summer course work opportunities, supplemented with counseling regarding educational opportunities. Many Talent Search summer programs offer AP courses, which carry college credit. Seventh-grade students in all 48 contiguous states can apply to participate in their regional Talent Search summer program.[6]

There are several other SMPY-related developments. Since 1980 a continuing activity at SMPY at Johns Hopkins has been a national search for rare math whizzes who score above 700 on the SAT-M, which is about one in 10,000 (Stanley, 1988, 1991a). These students, labeled the "700–800 on SAT-M Before Age 13 Group," are both studied and helped educationally. For example, "SMPY sends members of the group materials, especially including a long quarterly newsletter, suggesting how they can proceed faster and better in mathematics and related subjects. Also, from time to time SMPY obtains scholarships for pre-college summer experiences" (Stanley, 1988, p. 208). As of 1991, CTY assumed responsibility for locating the seventh-graders with SAT-M scores over 700, and began looking also for youngsters in a "630–800 on SAT-V Before Age 13 Group," also a 1 in 10,000 occurrence.

In 1986 SMPY itself had split into two branches, with the second branch established at Iowa State University by Stanley's former colleague Camilla Benbow (Benbow, 1991). Benbow directs a sum-

mer residential Talent Search program. She also has initiated a long-range Terman-like study of 3,000 intellectually talented students, largely to evaluate the impact of educational facilitation on their development. Benbow and Arjmand (1990), for example, reported that acceleration of SMPY students, both male and female, produced no detrimental social or emotional effects, and may have improved social and emotional adjustment. After a 10-year period, Swiatek and Benbow (1992) found that SMPY participants attended more prestigious colleges, and female participants were more likely to attend graduate school.

Sanford Cohn's (1983a, 1983b, 1991) *Project for the Study of Academic Precocity* at Arizona State University, which draws students from western states and Canadian provinces, is a good example of a Talent Search program. This summer program offers about 14 "rigorous academically oriented classes" (Cohn, 1983b), including three computer science courses (Fortran, Pascal, microcomputers, all AP), geology (AP), speech and debate, advanced language and composition (AP), expository writing, vocabulary development, Latin, Latin and Greek, calculus (AP), "fast mathematics," survey of social sciences, chemistry (AP), economics, mythology, and laboratory science. Admission to each class is based on SAT scores plus a fee. For example, Computer Science-Fortran requires an SAT-M score of 450 and a combined SAT-M and SAT-V of 850, along with registration fees and books.

In addition, PSAP has offered classes for 8- to 11-year-olds in math, writing, Spanish, science, and classics. Counseling workshops cover educational planning, communication skills, study skills, and career exploration (Cohn, 1983a, 1983b).

Stanley and Benbow (1983) itemized a few benefits of SMPY participation, which presumably would apply to Talent Search as well as other forms of academic acceleration:

1. Increased zest for learning and life, reduced boredom in school, and better school attitudes.

---

[4]In recent years Talent Search efforts also have begun at the University of California at Berkeley and the University of Wisconsin, Eau Claire.

[5]Talent Search programs recently have begun using *American College Testing* (ACT) scores for selection decisions, as well as SAT scores (Benbow, 1992).

[6]For information on the SAT, write to Educational Testing Service, Princeton, NJ 08541, and ask for a copy of *Taking the SAT*. A student or parent should contact his/her regional Talent Search institution to obtain information about the program and application procedures.

2. Enhanced feelings of self-worth and accomplishment.

3. Reduced egotism and arrogance, due to the humbling effects of working for the first time with intellectual peers.

4. Far better educational preparation and thus improved qualifications for the most selective colleges.

5. Early college and graduate school admission.

6. Better graduate school and fellowship opportunities, due to better preparation, acquaintance with professors, and research skills.

SUMMARY

Table 5.1 is a guide for planning G/T program content, summarized in the categories of basic skills, content beyond the prescribed curriculum, exposure to a variety of fields, student-selected content, high content complexity, creative thinking and problem solving, thinking skills, affective development, and motivation.

G/T programs vary in students served, acceleration, grouping, and enrichment plans, resources involved, program level, and other dimensions.

Acceleration is defined as programming that results in advanced placement or credit; *enrichment* essentially is anything else. Both accommodate the high abilities and needs of gifted students. Educators have debated the merits of each. However, both are required in any well-rounded program.

With early admission to kindergarten or first grade, students are most likely to succeed if they are carefully screened. They should be intellectually precocious (recommended IQ = 130+), at least average in motor coordination, and possess adequate reading readiness, social/emotional maturity, and good health. Girls often are more mature. If a particular school already caters to very bright students, early admission may be unnecessary. The receiving teacher should have positive attitudes regarding early admission. Family values should emphasize academic achievement. Early admission can be on a trial basis.

Grade-skipping can improve motivation and scholarship, social relations, and self-esteem. Grade-skipping and subject-skipping also have successfully reversed some students' patterns of underachievement. The problem of missing some essential basic skills can be solved via diagnostic tests and remedial work, if necessary. Research shows that social adjustment is usually not a problem. Acceleration is sometimes blamed for normal adolescent personal or social problems. Maladjustment due to extremely high IQ also is sometimes blamed on grade-skipping. Grade-skipping may be most successful if the student shows an IQ score of 130+, if one grade is skipped at a time, if support from a teacher, counselor, or gifted peer is available, and if intellectual and social adjustment is considered in the decision.

Subject-skipping permits the child to remain with agemates while being challenged in a particular area of strength. Continuity with later grades probably is the only shortcoming, and one which can be provided for.

Early admission to junior or senior high school is a socially opportune time to skip a grade.

Credit by examination encourages G/T students to accept challenges and saves repetition and boredom. College credit by examination may be earned in the CLEP and AP programs, which are highly cost effective.

In a dual enrollment program, students take college courses while still in high school. Credits from college courses taken in high school should count toward high school graduation. In AP program, students take college courses in an honors class, a fast regular class, or as independent study. With or without taking the AP courses, students may earn college credit by scoring sufficiently high in the May AP examinations.

Correspondence courses require considerable self-direction. It is therefore desirable for a group of students to take the same course and for a high school teacher or counselor to monitor progress and perhaps assist.

Telescoping involves condensing a two- or three-year course, or high school program, into fewer years.

Early college admission, or early high school graduation, is recommended, despite the problem of forfeiting honors or scholarships that require attendance for the full four years. Many good students are socially and academically ready. Selection based on socio-emotional maturity and good self-concept is important.

Residential high schools cater to high math and science talent; AP courses with college credit sometimes are offered. Critics express concern about a "brain drain," as well as adverse effects of leaving home early and negative influences of college students. Student body composition is an issue.

The International Baccalaureate Program focuses on languages and international concerns.

Stanley's SMPY program at Johns Hopkins University uses the SAT-M to identify high-level math talent among primarily seventh grade students. Students take summer math classes and are encouraged to pursue other acceleration options.

CTY expanded the SMPY concept to include students who score high on either the SAT-M or the SAT-V. Other Talent Search programs, such as Cohn's PSAP, also use SAT-M and SAT-V to select primarily seventh-grade students for summer programs.

SMPY, and now CTY, search for extraordinary students who before age 13 score above 700 on the SAT-M or above 630 on the SAT-V in order to study and assist them. Benbow at Iowa State University is conducting a longitudinal study of 3,000 SMPY students.

Benefits of SMPY and Talent Search participation include improved zest for learning, better feelings of self-worth, better educational preparation, early entrance into college and a profession, and better graduate and professional school opportunities.

College Board Offices

New York Office:
888 Seventh Ave.
New York, NY 10019
(212) 582-6210

Middle States Regional Office:
Suite 1418
1700 Market St.
Philadelphia, PA 19103
(215) 567-6555

Midwestern Regional Office:
1 American Plaza
Evanston, IL 60201
(312) 866-1700

New England Regional Office:
470 Totten Pond Rd.
Waltham, MA 02154
(617) 890-9150

Southern Regional Office:
Suite 200
17 Executive Park Dr., NE
Atlanta, GA 30329
(404) 636-9465

Southwestern Regional Office:
Suite 922
211 E. Seventh St.
Austin, TX 78701
(512) 472-0231

Denver Office:
Suite 23
2142 South High St.
Denver, CO 80210
(303) 777-4434

Western Regional Office:
800 Welch Rd.
Palo Alto, CA 94304
(415) 321-5211

CHAPTER 6

ENRICHMENT AND GROUPING

Providing special services for the gifted and talented almost inevitably requires some special grouping. Grouping the gifted for all or part of the school day accommodates achievement and readiness levels and can serve other purposes as well.

John Feldhusen (1989a, p. 9)

We noted at the outset of Chapter 5 that acceleration and enrichment activities usually require grouping gifted children. This chapter will review enrichment activities and grouping plans at elementary and secondary levels.

Two preliminary thoughts are these. First, a common criticism of enrichment activities in G/T programs appears in the question "Wouldn't that be good for all children?" Of course, the answer often must be "yes." Keep your antennae up for enrichment that is good for *all* students (e.g., creativity and thinking skills training, values training, college and career information, field trips to art galleries or scientific laboratories) versus experiences that seem strictly appropriate for bright and talented students (e.g., independent work on complex projects, Talent Search, summer College for Kids, or other accelerated learning opportunities). Treffinger (1992), in the context of emphasizing that teaching the "brightest and the best" must be tied to excellent education for all, made the tongue-in-cheek comment "If you are gifted, you can think, if not, you just do schoolwork."

ENRICHMENT

All enrichment activities for gifted youth should be planned with "higher order" objectives in mind. One list of objectives, collated from many thought-ful sources, was presented in Table 5.1 on page 104. As a reminder, the objectives were listed in the categories of:

- Maximum achievement in basic skills, based on needs, not age
- Content and resources beyond the prescribed curriculum
- Exposure to a variety of fields of study
- Student-selected content, including in-depth studies
- High content complexity—theories, generalizations, applications
- Creative thinking and problem solving
- Higher-level thinking skills, critical thinking, library and research skills
- Affective development, including self-understanding and ethical development
- Development of academic motivation, self-direction, and high career aspirations

Enrichment strategies essentially are delivery methods for achieving *process* and *content* goals. Process goals include developing such skills—or processes—as creative thinking and problem solving, critical thinking, scientific thinking, and interrelating various subjects and concepts. The content is the subject matter, projects, and activities within which the processes are developed.

Enrichment strategies we will review briefly include (1) independent study and independent projects, (2) learning centers, (3) field trips, (4) Saturday programs, (5) summer programs, (6) mentors and mentorships, (7) Future Problem Solving, (8) Odyssey of the Mind, (9) Junior Great Books, (10) Academic Decathlon, (11) Mock Court, and (12) other competitions and aesthetic involvements.

INDEPENDENT STUDY, RESEARCH, AND ART PROJECTS

Independent study, research, and art projects take place within many of the enrichment and grouping strategies described in this chapter, and in many of the acceleration options and program models described in Chapters 5 and 7. For bright and energetic students, the possibilities for independent study and independent projects are without limit. Students may work on library research, scientific research, art, drama, journalism, photography, and so on. They may work alone, in pairs, or in small groups.

Library Research Projects

A library research project must be based on strong student interest and should be student-selected. If students have difficulty selecting a topic, a brainstorming approach is one way to identify interesting possibilities. It may be best to pose a specific problem or challenge, although the nature of the initial problem may change as the project develops. For example, some questions might be "Why and how were pyramids built?" "What are the relationships between Greek and Roman gods?" "What is the evidence for Indian migration from Asia?"

In addition to the library, this type of research also might involve trips to a natural history museum, art gallery, or research laboratory, or visits with or phone calls to relevant university faculty or other community (or national) experts. Students in one Wisconsin gifted program telephoned the National Aeronautics and Space Administration in Cape Canaveral to obtain answers to questions about space and rockets.

With any independent project, it is important that a *product* be produced and that the product or performance be presented to an appropriate *audience*, either students in the class or outside groups (Renzulli and Reis, 1991b). A library research project could produce more than a neatly typed report: It might include a student-made video or narrated slide show; a demonstration of some activity or skill (for example, sand painting, musket loading); a tabletop demonstration (rolling 30-ton stone blocks, dinosaur models); a TV news report on the progress of the battle at Bunker Hill; a miniplay about mythological or historical characters or events; a newspaper column describing recent activities in the Spanish Inquisition; an ESP test for the class; and so on.

Most of the time the gifted student's class—G/T or otherwise—will serve as a suitable audience. However, unusually bright students may need to prepare two reports, one simple enough for peers (or the teacher) to understand and a second full-blown one to be shared with an expert. The following case study reflects this problem.

Eric prepared a complex discussion of space travel for his sixth-grade class. His research, organization, and scientific terminology were of his usual high quality. However, his classmates greeted his enthusiastic report with boredom and teasing because of the incomprehensibility of the material. Although Eric easily could have prepared a much simpler report, it would not have allowed him an honest demonstration of what he had learned and figured out. Two reports would have prevented the difficulty.

Scientific Research Projects

Possibilities for scientific research are innumerable, but actual studies will of course be limited by available equipment and resources. A few phone calls, however, could determine if, say, a physics lab in the local college might be available to supervised junior high school students.

Many elementary and junior high schools organize science fairs in which each student in the science classes creates a small scientific demonstration. Ribbons are awarded to the most elaborate, well-done, or technically competent projects, usually a "first," "second," or "third" type of rating so that virtually all participants can earn a ribbon for their efforts. Projects by G/T students usually are outstanding, and their effort and ingenuity are reinforced with "first" ribbons and usually peer admiration.

With any type of research project, the teacher's main role is "the guide on the side." With elementary or secondary students, the teacher-coordinator directs the budding scientist to appropriate library or human resources for background information, helps the student clarify the problem and plan the research, aids in locating equipment and other resources and tools, and gives advice and assistance when needed.

One group of gifted elementary students prepared a museum exhibit on Drug and Alcohol Abuse for the Children's Museum in Indianapolis (Waters and Bostwick, 1989). Accompanying the Waters and Bostwick article is a list of children's museums in 37 states, probably all of which would exhibit a suitable and high quality science-related project. Outstanding high school science projects should be entered in the National Westinghouse competition, which awards over $150,000 in scholarships to 40 winners, Honorable Mention to 300 students, and prestige to everyone who enters.[1]

Art, Drama, Creative Writing, and Other Independent Projects

In addition to library and scientific research projects, individual art or handicraft projects may include drawing, painting, sculpture, silk-screen, lettering, printing, batik, pottery, ceramics, photography, weaving, or other media.[2] Students in-

terested in theater and drama can research how plays are written and then write, direct, produce, and perform in their own. Pigott (1990) described how the East Manhattan School for Bright and Gifted Children used drama to integrate literature, social studies, and history. All students, from nursery school age 2½ through sixth-grade, take part in Shakespeare plays or historical events (for example, a one-boy Truman speech and Neil Armstrong's flight to the moon). A nine-year-old girl safely insisted on being the *sixth* wife of Henry VIII—the only one not executed or banished. Gangi (1990) used creative dramatics to teach thinking skills such as creativity, analysis, synthesis, and evaluation.[3]

Students talented in creative writing—and perhaps others—can be coached in writing for publication. S. J. Davis and Johns (1989) recommended that a creative writing program can be based on the 10 steps in Table 6.1. Magazines that publish student writing appear at the end of this chapter (Appendix 6.1).

Invent America is a program that provides an outlet for (what else) inventions. One elementary student entered a toilet seat sprayed with luminous paint—his "Glow In The Dark Toilet Seat" now resides in the Smithsonian Institution. Another student invented a method for disposing of doggie doo-doo based on a chemical breakdown process.

A student newspaper is an especially good independent project for a small group of students. Creating a newspaper involves interviewing people and writing stories, taking photographs, planning and designing the paper, and arranging for its printing. Students in one Wisconsin elementary school interviewed and photographed elderly people in a retirement home. They learned first-hand about local and state history and about such hobbies and skills as quilting, candlemaking, tatting, and blacksmithing. Of no small importance, their appreciation and respect for the elderly increased dramatically.

---

[1]For information on the Westinghouse Talent Search, contact Science Talent Search, 1719 N Street, NW, Washington, DC 20036 (phone 202-785-2255).

[2]The entire January/February, 1990, issue of *Gifted Child Today* is devoted to art and drama programs and activities for the gifted.

[3]Creative dramatics ideas and activities are explained in Chapter 9.

TABLE 6.1 Ten Steps in Writing for Publication

1. *Study the market* by examining the content and style of articles in a half-dozen or so magazines. Send for authors' guidelines.
2. *Brainstorm ideas* for potential articles, for example, in the categories of interests, experiences, hobbies, or pet peeves.
3. *Write* rough drafts on two or three of the ideas.
4. *Select one rough draft* that appears most promising.
5. *Prioritize the magazines* and review the qualities of articles published in the top choice.
6. *Revise the manuscript* with the intended magazine in mind; edit carefully for grammar and punctuation.
7. *Use peer reviewers* to evaluate clarity, word choice, and grammar.
8. *Prepare the manuscript for submission* according to the magazines guidelines.
9. *Send the first article* to the first magazine, then begin work on a second article.
10. *Keep articles in circulation;* if the first article is rejected, send it to a second magazine, perhaps after revision. Submit the second article and begin a third.

Adapted from S.J. Davis and Johns, 1989, by permission of the first author and *Gifted Child Today.*

LEARNING CENTERS

Commercial learning centers can be purchased; teachers also construct learning centers. These are tabletop workstations for individual or group work. Hazel Feldhusen (1981, 1986) described the use of learning centers with mainstreamed gifted students. For example, she stocked a *library center* with commercial reading-skill materials and educational games; it contained a rocker and typewriter for creative writing. A *math center* included math kits, math games, and a calculator (and calculator activities). A microcomputer in the math center presented logic games, math challenges, spelling lessons, and "fun" computer games. Her *art center* presented a new art project each week. The *science center* was supplied with two to five science activities, and included a record player, tape player, and filmstrip viewer.

Feldhusen's school library houses a comprehensive *Learning Resource Center* that contains tapes and activities in math and language arts, all aimed at developing thinking skills.

Learning centers also can teach foreign languages; geography, history, and other social studies topics; handicrafts; and music appreciation. Students—gifted and others—may self-select centers and activities, or teachers and students together may plan interesting and valuable learning center goals. Learning centers may be located in the regular classroom, the building instructional materials center, or the district G/T resource room.[4]

The teacher should be certain that learning center time is well spent; that is, learning center activities should meet some of the goals and purposes of enrichment itemized in Table 5.1. Be warned that learning centers also can offer time for unsupervised fooling around.

FIELD TRIPS

Field trips can be used as an exploratory activity, aimed at acquainting students with cultural or scientific areas or with career possibilities. Field trips can also be a source of information for students' independent projects. An entire class or a small group of interested students might visit a natural history museum, manufacturing plant, art gallery, planetarium, local Greek restaurant, and so on. Some carefully written requests might earn a tour of a major newspaper company, a research laboratory, or perhaps seats at a symphony rehearsal.

Field trips are most beneficial if students have specific problems to solve, questions to answer, or post-tour projects or presentations to prepare. Streaking to the gift shop and cafeteria to buy

---

[4]"Learning center" sometimes is used to mean "resource center," an entire room in a school or district set aside for pullout types of learning experiences.

postcards and potato chips is not the main intent of the trip.

Friedman and Master (1980) emphasized that in planning a successful field trip one must evaluate the materials and exhibits and the ability of the guide/educator to communicate effectively with the group. An outline of the program/tour should be planned in advance by the teacher and guide/educator. During the tour the guide should not just "lecture at" students; rather, students should be allowed to touch, respond, and question. During the tour, teacher and guide should work together to stimulate learning, with both partners commenting, contributing, and remaining open to spontaneous twists in the children's interests. Students should be encouraged to discuss and evaluate during the program.

So far, the reader might correctly conclude that field trips are no different for gifted students than for typical students. Indeed, all students, regardless of ability, should have enrichment opportunities, including visits to places of artistic, historic, and scientific interest. However, if the gifted child's field trip is part of a differentiated curriculum, the preparation for the trip, the tasks of the visit, and the resulting reports or projects should be tied to knowledge goals and thinking skill development.

SATURDAY PROGRAMS

Saturday programs present a delightful benefit: They permit gifted students to meet and work with each other away from the stresses and problems of daily school requirements. Saturday programs virtually always take the form of noncredit miniclasses taught by volunteer teachers, college faculty, graduate students, or community experts—often parents of the gifted children.

One model Saturday program is John Feldhusen's (1991b; Feldhusen and Ruckman, 1988; Feldhusen and Wyman, 1980) *Super Saturday* plan sponsored by Purdue University. Feldhusen (1991b; Feldhusen, Enersen, and Sayler, 1992) noted that Saturday (and summer) programs for the gifted present opportunities for students to:

- Interact with supportive yet challenging peers.
- Learn new material at a faster pace.
- Receive instruction at more complex skill and conceptual levels.
- Work with instructors who model high level professional behavior and aspirations.
- Be exposed to topics and disciplines not ordinarily taught in regular school programs.
- Become involved in in-depth creative investigations, with opportunities to explore, inquire, investigate, and identify problems.
- Clarify and confirm their special talents and abilities.

Super Saturday serves children "from age 2½ through high school" (Feldhusen, 1991b, p. 198). Each semester about 40 classes lasting nine Saturdays are offered in science, math, computers, literature, composition, foreign languages, and, for preschoolers, special enrichment areas (see examples in Table 6.2).

Parents provide transportation and pay minimal registration fees and materials charges. Teachers are university faculty and students, public school teachers, and others in the community. They must be good teachers and show energy, enthusiasm, and an interest in teaching gifted kids.

Any one of several criteria are used in selection. Achievement scores above the 90th percentile; IQ scores above 120; or parent or teacher nominations that indicate strong talent or ability. Said Feldhusen (1991b, p. 198), "No child is denied an opportunity to try a semester in the program if a parent or teacher argues the case for the child's talent." The program is designed to be inclusive rather than exclusive. However, high school students enrolling for college credit classes must rank in the top 10 percent in GPA and be recommended by a school official.

As a different model, the Gifted Child Society (1990) of Glen Rock, New Jersey, offers about 50 *one-hour* Saturday morning workshops for children from age 2 (movement, music, songs, rhythm instruments, imagination) through seventh grade. Their goal is to "challenge the learning needs and

TABLE 6.2   Examples of Courses Offered in the Purdue University Super Saturday Program

---

For Kindergarten and Lower Elementary
Students
    Creative Thinking
    Mime
    Exploring Space
For Intermediate Elementary Students
    Art
    French
    Probability and Statistics
For Upper Elementary Students
    TV Production
    Computers
    Native American Culture
For Junior and Senior High School Students
    Economics
    Electrical Engineering
    Computers
For College Credit
    Psychology
    French
    English Composition
    Political Science

---

styles of gifted children . . . [and stimulate] . . . higher levels of thinking, creativity, problem solving, and leadership. An interdisciplinary approach is used and, where practical, courses are future oriented" (p. 2). Offerings include computer LOGO, oceanography, cartooning, metal and clay design, magic, rocketry, astronomy, drama, and "Blood and Guts Biology"—for first and second graders.

SUMMER PROGRAMS

Most cities offer summer programs that are open to all students. Obviously, these may be capitalized upon by the teacher, parent, or counselor seeking enrichment opportunities for energetic and able children. In addition, many school districts and state education departments fund the planning and teaching of summer courses and workshops designed specifically for their gifted and talented children.[5]

Individual teachers or parents also can organize and/or teach summer classes for the gifted. Dermatologist and parent John Tkach (1987) described a heavy-duty physics course that he planned and taught to science-oriented children. Another of his creative efforts was a summer course covering astronomy, geology, paleontology, and evolution, including a camping trip to a dinosaur dig, tapes of Carl Sagan's *Cosmos* TV shows, and a personal letter from Sagan (Tkach, 1986).

Governors' School Programs

The Governor's School concept is a fast-growing form of state-supported summer residential school for gifted teenagers. In 1991 a National Conference of Governors' Schools held in White Sulphur Springs, West Virginia, focused presentations on (1) math, science, and technology, (2) arts and entertainment, and (3) humanities and social studies, which reflects the curriculum content of most Governors' Schools.[6] Currently, at least 32 states support about 43 Governors' schools, almost exclusively serving high-school students (Iowa accommodates 12- to 14-year-olds as well, and Maryland dips down to the fourth grade; Hallowell, 1991). Selection is based on nominations by individual schools, public and private; virtually all schools take steps to ensure a balanced representation (e.g., geographic, racial) of students in their state. Hallowell reported that specific selection criteria included grade point averages (92 percent of schools responding to his questionnaire), aptitude

---

[5]State-by-state lists of U.S. summer gifted programs, prepared by Schenck and Schenck, appear in the March/April, 1990 and 1991 issues of *Gifted Child Today*.

[6]The May/June, 1991, issue of *Gifted Child Today* focused on Governors' Schools, with descriptions of programs in Mississippi, Kentucky, Pennsylvania, Tennessee, Virginia, and the state of Washington. Programs in North Carolina, Florida, New Jersey, and Wyoming, as well as a female governor's school in North Carolina, are described in the July/August, 1991, issue.

test scores (56 percent), achievement tests (44 percent), and intelligence tests (24 percent). Importantly, according to Hallowell, 24 of the 43 schools do not charge students for tuition, room, or board; of the 19 programs requiring students to pay some costs, 14 provided financial aid. Students must transport themselves to the school, and arrive with some spending money.

Enthusiasm of educators and students runs high. For example, Wolfe, Mondschein, and Eicher (1991) reported that "Students who attend the Virginia Governor's School . . . return to their home schools with different outlooks toward learning." Cross, Hernandez, and Coleman (1991) reported that students' likelihood of attending college increased, and that Governors' Schools establish climates in which students feel free to go outside their areas of expertise and possibly fail—risk-taking necessary for their full development. Said one of their students, "For the first time in my life I can really be me. I can talk about opera or heavy metal music, and no one will think I'm weird."

College for Kids

Many colleges and universities offer summer programs for gifted, talented, and creative children and adolescents (see Juntune, 1986, for programs in your area). Especially noteworthy are the national Talent Search programs described in Chapter 5. In view of the restrictiveness of Talent Search, admission to which is based on high SAT scores, it is fortunate that other college-based programs offer more lenient entrance requirements and usually lower costs.

The reader may wish to explore model programs developed at Purdue University (see, e.g., Feldhusen, 1991b; Feldhusen and Clinkenbeard, 1982; Feldhusen, Rebhorn, and Saylor, 1988). The *COMET* program (Feldhusen, Enersen, and Sayler, 1992) is a residential program for fourth-, fifth-, and sixth-grade children that offers a one-week immersion in a single content area, for example, chemistry, microbiology, math, aerodynamics, language arts, sociology, anthropology, Spanish, pre-algebra,

or creative writing. The STAR program is for gifted seventh- and eighth-grade students capable of taking highly accelerated courses in math, science, and humanities. The *Purdue Academic Leadership Seminars* (PALS) are for ninth- and tenth-grade students selected on the basis of both leadership and achievement, as recommended by teachers and counselors. PALS participants also are offered courses in math, science, and humanities. The *Purdue College Credit Program* is for ninth-through twelfth-grade students who are selected via recommendations from their schools. These students have the opportunity to earn college credit in such university courses as psychology, English composition, history, the solar system, and computers. By way of evaluation, Feldhusen noted that ". . . the students made incredible academic gains" in both content mastery and school attitudes (Van Tassel-Baska, 1983).

Many other *College for Kids* plans are similar to the Purdue program in offering high-level summer enrichment for gifted and talented students, almost always in the form of mini-courses. For example, at the University of Wisconsin-Parkside (Kenosha, Wisconsin) a three-week College for Kids plan was initiated in 1979 for children in kindergarten through fourth grade (Robinson, 1981). The purposes of this plan were to provide quality enrichment experiences for gifted students and to train elementary teachers to be more effective with gifted children in their regular classrooms.

Interestingly, course topics were selected by the students themselves. The parent/teacher committee held a brainstorming session with kindergarten to fourth-grade G/T children at one school. The problem: "What courses would be best for a summer enrichment program?" After narrowing an extensive list, and meeting a strict qualification of not conflicting with the regular curriculum, nine winners one year were oceanography, chemistry, astronomy, entomology, drama, photography, animation/cartooning, art, and ancient life. On the registration form, children and parents indicated their first, second, and third choices for courses. Children were assigned to two courses, with a strong effort to put everyone into his or her first choice.

Most children became involved in independent or small-group projects resulting in "real" products. For example, the Ancient Life class placed a time capsule in a new building; the Drama class produced, directed, and performed a play for parents and guests; and the Cartooning/Animation class produced two comic books and a 20-minute animated film.

In 1980, the University of Wisconsin-Madison, began offering an immensely successful three-week program for gifted elementary school children also titled *College for Kids* (CfK). Unlike most such programs, minicourses constitute just a piece of the plan. Core goals include assisting students in developing good self-concepts through discussion and interaction with gifted peers; acquainting them with university life and activities via tours, visitations, and demonstrations; and helping them observe, learn, and practice processes of creative problem solving and related thinking skills.

A complete roll-call of staff and students includes a faculty program director, a half-time program assistant employed for the calendar year, an instructor for a four-week graduate seminar taught in conjunction with CfK, 250 children in grades 4 and 5 who are identified by area school districts as "gifted," 27 elementary school teachers (many of whom are working toward their M.S. degrees in gifted education in the Department of Educational Psychology), and about 35 university graduate students and faculty who offer 50 one-week workshops and a half-dozen large-group "extravaganzas."

Following the morning seminar, each teacher interacts with his or her "family," a group of 10 to 12 children, both before and after their two-hour workshop or extravaganza. They discuss their experiences and practice relevant processes and skills. For example, they brainstorm solutions to problems; they apply other creative thinking techniques; and they learn to evaluate by discussing "What was good (and bad) about today's workshop or extravaganza?" They discuss such issues

as the pros and cons of being gifted, and the value of higher education.

The main agenda for the first week is the first of two five-day workshops, two hours per day, in such art and science areas as chemistry, veterinary science, TV production, photography, and university history. The second week presents a series of extravaganzas, for example, chemistry and physics demonstrations and lectures on astronomy and anthropology. The third week focuses on another workshop. Throughout the three weeks the teacher-leaders arrange visits to such attractions as the geology museum, veterinary school, anthropology exhibits, the historical society, a campus nuclear reactor, and the agricultural campus.

While the University of Wisconsin-Madison College for Kids plan is difficult to organize and administrate, it works very well, based upon evaluations and feedback from students, teachers, university faculty, and parents.[7]

Partly because the Madison campus College for Kids program accommodates fourth- and fifth-grade elementary students, two additional University of Wisconsin summer programs were created for middle school students and lower elementary children. *Middle School College for Kids* offers two-week minicourses to self-selected sixth- to eighth-graders, for example, entitled *Polygons and Crystals; Mathmagic; Chess, Logic, and Problem Solving; BIOlogy, BIOchemistry, BIOreactors, BIOtechnology; Chemistry and Materials Science*; and *Family Tree—Humans and Primates*.

Badger Brain Games is for high-ability children in grades K through 3, selected by teacher nominations. The program directs children's natural enthusiasm for games to the learning of thinking skills. Taught by area teachers, Badger Brain Games uses hundreds of off-the-shelf games (e.g., *Clue, Mastermind*, checkers) to teach thinking skills. Curriculum guides relate specific games to the development of specific thinking skills, and suggest additional teaching-learning activities. As

---

[7]The July/August, 1992 issue of *Gifted Child Today* contains articles describing several university-based summer programs.

with College for Kids, part of the goal is teacher training. After teachers learn to use the Brain Games curriculum for enrichment, they are encouraged to integrate the ideas and games into their regular classrooms.

Music, Art, Language, and Computer Camps

Many colleges and universities offer summer clinics, institutes, retreats, or camps in music, art, and drama, and many now offer computer camps as well. Some sponsor foreign language camps where students eat, sleep, swim, canoe, and communicate in Spanish, French, German, or Russian. An especially good example is the *International Language Village* sponsored by Concordia College in Moorhead, Minnesota.

Although virtually none of these camps and institutes identify themselves as "programs for the gifted," students are attracted to the camp because of their talent and high interest in an area. They are expected to invest many hours of dedicated effort in acquiring specialized knowledge and skills. The students also receive stimulation and support from other students who are equally enthusiastic and talented in the same ability. For students with few peers who share their special talents, the camps are refreshing ways to meet like-minded and like-talented friends.

As a final reminder, summer programs need not be highly involved and sophisticated. We noted above that a single person, parent or teacher, can organize and teach a minicourse. A group of energetic parents or educators can arrange for classes to be taught and instructors to teach them, identification methods and criteria (if any), plus publicity and registration details.

MENTORS AND MENTORSHIPS

The concept of mentoring is hardly new. In ancient Greece Mentor himself tutored Telemachus, son of Odysseus. Socrates was mentor to Plato, Plato to Aristotle, and Aristotle to Alexander the Great (Cox and Daniel, 1983b). Currently, the use

of mentors for gifted students is a rapidly growing trend (e.g., Clasen and Hansen, 1987; Lupkowski, Assouline, and Vestal, 1992; Milam and Schwartz, 1992; Prillaman and Richardson, 1989; Reilly, 1992).

Typically, a mentorship includes an extended relationship between a community professional and a single high school student over a period of months. However, Ellingson, Haeger, and Feldhusen (1986) described a successful mentor program for students as young as fourth grade who meet with their mentors (for example, an engineer, doctor, judge, history professor, or radio broadcaster) in groups of six. Stanley, Lupkowski, and Assouline (1990) described the use of mentors for teaching mathematically precocious middle and high school students, and in one case an eight-year-old boy. They recommended that mentors meet with their charges once per week for two or three hours and make the work interesting and stimulating.

In the typical mentorship program, the high school student is called a *protégé, intern, apprentice, mentee,* or *assistant.* The student visits the mentor at the job site on a scheduled basis to learn first-hand the activities, responsibilities, problems, and lifestyle associated with the particular business, art, or profession. Students normally receive high school credit for the mentorship experience. In some cases a formal work-study plan is developed in which the student is paid for working while learning.

Prillaman and Richardson (1989) described a unique program at William and Mary College in which college students serve as mentors for gifted students after school and weekends for 12 weeks. Area students identified as *gifted* in grades eight through eleven select an area of interest to explore (e.g., marine science, geology, photography, French culture, and archaeology); college student mentors are recruited based on their expertise in that area. The program is a unique effort that links the college, public schools, parents, and children.

Edlind and Haensly (1985) summarized the main benefits of mentorships as (1) aiding career planning, (2) increasing knowledge, skills, and talents far beyond book learning, (3) establishing contacts with influential and knowledgeable persons, (4) building self-esteem and confidence, (5) developing personal ethics and sets of standards, (6) enhancing creativity, and (7) establishing a valuable and deep long-term friendship.

Noted Cox and Daniel (1983b), "Mentorship presumes a commitment on the part of the student and mentor and has as its goal the shaping of the student's life outlook." As more dramatically described by DeMott (1981), one goal of a successful mentorship is to facilitate ". . . that extraordinary inner experience in which the human creature is suddenly seized with the realization—inexplicable, incontestable—that this is what I want. This is how life could be lived!"

Describing mentors as ". . . devoted men and women lighting intellectual sparks and setting the passion for learning aflame" (Epstein, 1981), Mattson (1983) itemized characteristics of good mentors that are intended to help a teacher or steering committee assemble a mentor pool. While the list admittedly is idealistic, it can serve as a guide that will sensitize the teacher or committee to good "spark lighters" when they appear. The ideal mentor should possess expertise in his or her specialized field, of course. The mentor also should be high in personal integrity and have a strong interest in teaching young people. He or she should possess enthusiasm and optimism, and an "anticipation of tomorrow." Also important are tact, flexibility, and humor, all of which contribute to a desirable "acceptance of foolishness and errors." Tolerance and patience contribute to a safe and experimentally oriented environment. Also valuable are agility, creativity, and the ability to bring the protégé to higher levels of thinking and problem solving. Good mentors should provide opportunities for students to use their gifts and abilities, to use their imaginations, and to see their own possibilities. Others have listed these desirable characteristics of mentors: They should be knowledgeable and enthusiastic; able to communicate with students and share their methodology and inquiry skills; able to motivate; able to plan, organize, and direct activities; willing to locate unique opportunities for mentee exploration; and willing to devote time to the entire project (Reis and Burns, 1987; Prillaman and Richardson, 1989).

In planning a mentorship program, Cox and Daniel (1983b) detailed many helpful guidelines. Some of the more salient recommendations were:

1. Elicit the support of the district superintendent, the school board, and community leaders.

2. Specify the purpose of each mentorship and the role of the student.

3. Develop a clear, defensible academic credit policy. If high school credit is given, the work experience should relate directly to the course for which the credit is received.

4. Prepare written criteria for student selection based upon multiple indices, not just one.

5. Try to achieve the best mentor/student match possible. Mentors should be creative producers who will not treat the students as "go-fers."

6. Orientation seminars should be planned to acquaint students with the professional and business environments in which they will work.

7. Students should be prepared for the mentorship with related course work prior to the experience.

8. Students should be helped to develop individual goals.

9. The program must meet the academic needs of students. Students should be assigned required reading; they also should keep journals in which they analyze their activities and experiences.

FUTURE PROBLEM SOLVING

The popular *Future Problem Solving* (FPS) program is an enrichment activity that can take place in a pullout, resource center, special class, or Saturday program, or with gifted students who are mainstreamed or clustered in the regular classroom. If your FPS team is good, it will travel to a state Future Problem Solving bowl or even to the International FPS Conference. FPS was begun in 1975 by E. Paul Torrance at the University of Georgia (Crabbe, 1991; Torrance and Torrance, 1978; Torrance, Williams, Torrance, and Horng, 1978). It grew into a statewide Georgia plan, then a national and even international program.

According to FPS director Anne Crabbe (1982) the objectives of the program are to help gifted children:

1. Become more aware of the future in order to deal with it actively, with feelings of optimism and the attitude that they can effect changes.

2. Become more creative; learning to go beyond the logical and obvious.

3. Develop and increase communication skills, including speaking and writing persuasively, clearly, and accurately.

4. Develop such teamwork skills as listening, respecting, understanding, and compromising.

5. Learn to use a problem-solving model and integrate it into their daily lives.

6. Develop research skills, learning how to gather information, where to go, and who to contact.

The year-long program begins with the registration of each four-student team in one of three grade divisions, *Juniors* (grades 4–6), *Intermediates* (7–9), and *Seniors* (10–12). The teams are sent three practice problems which they solve using the following seven-step model, based on the Creative Problem Solving (CPS) model (e.g., Parnes, 1981; see Chapter 9). As described by Crabbe (1991), the teams:

1. Research the general topic.

2. Brainstorm problems related to a specific ("fuzzy") situation.

3. Select an important underlying problem from the brainstormed problems.

4. Brainstorm solutions to the underlying problem.

5. Develop five criteria by which to judge the ideas.

6. Use the criteria to evaluate the ten most promising solutions to select the "best" solution.

7. Describe the best solution.

A typical problem in FPS begins with a one-page scenario that is read by the four-person team. The problem is accompanied by about twenty recent magazine and newspaper articles pertaining to the issues presented. As an example, the CANUSA problem describes a city on the Canada/USA border designed for the "traditional" family (father, nonworking mother, and 2.5 children). Thirty years later, CANUSA has a population of 65,000, only 2 percent of whom are in traditional families. Using the reading materials provided and other resources students research problems of divorced families, single-parent families, retired persons, families in which mother and father both work, and couples with and without children. The general goal, of course, is to redesign the city, its schools, parks, work arrangements, etc., to meet the needs of the entire community.

Students generate at least twenty problems that may exist or arise in CANUSA. From these, students select what they agree is the best underlying problem and brainstorm possible solutions for it. They create an evaluation matrix, with the most appropriate ideas listed vertically on the left side and criteria cross the top, which permits an objective evaluation of ideas. After the single best solution is identified, it is rewritten in essay form—the solution is carefully presented, and the outcomes and consequences of the solution are elaborated and explained.

Other future-oriented problems, "which are selected annually by a vote of thousands of students and teachers in the program" (Crabbe, 1991, p. 2) have included shrinking tropical forests, poverty, terrorism, garbage disposal, the arms race, school dropouts, crime, drug abuse, child abuse, depletion of the ozone layer, labor shortages, acid rain, and medical advances. Topics for the 1991–92 program were space exploration, the legal epidemic, ethics in sport, use of land, and advertising.

As each problem is completed, it is sent for scoring to the state FPS organization. The first two problems are practice problems. Based on the quality of the third problem, top teams are invited to participate in the state FPS competition. For the state competition, the teams are given a topic in advance which they research. At the competition site, each team is given the problem scenario, then sequestered in a room for two hours to prepare its problem statements and solutions according to the seven steps. The three winning teams in the state competition, one per division, are sent to the International FPS Conference.

In addition to the regular three FPS divisions, another component is the Primary Division for grades K-3. These children are introduced to the problem solving process in a purely non-competitive atmosphere. There are no rules regarding team size—a teacher or coach can engage an entire class. They also solve three practice problems, which are evaluated and feedback provided.

The intrinsic nature of the FPS activities requires teamwork and cooperation—listening, respecting, understanding, and compromising (Crabbe, 1982).

Torrance and Torrance (1978) reported student testimonials on the benefits of FPS. For example, a fifth-grade girl reported, "I learned to cooperate, to share ideas, to produce creative and clever ideas, to be excited, to learn, and to work." The March/April issue of *Gifted Child Today* presents numerous articles on successful FPS programs, including one describing the Primary division (Chapman, 1991) and one that summarizes the use of FPS to motivate underachievers (Rimm and Olenchak, 1991). Information about FPS is available from Ann Crabbe, Box 98, 115 West Main Street, Aberdeen, NC 28315.

ODYSSEY OF THE MIND

Like Future Problem Solving, *Odyssey of the Mind* (OM; formerly Olympics of the Mind) is a national and international program. Also like FPS,

it is an excellent vehicle for teaching creative thinking and problem solving, along with self-confidence, a good self-image, social and communication skills, and more.

The key assumption of its founders, Ted Gourley and Sam Micklus, is that the mind can be trained and strengthened through exercise with mental games just as the body is trained with physical exercise (Gourley, 1981). OM thus was designed to combine "the excitement of athletic competition with fun-filled mental gymnastics for youngsters" (OM Association, 1983).

There are five age classifications: Division I includes grades K through 5, Division II is grades 6–8, Division III is grades 9–12, and Division IV is college students (!). In addition, children in a Primary Level (K-2) division participate in a noncompetitive creative skit. Teams in Divisions I through IV include seven members; in formal competition only five can be "on the playing field." A school district registers with the OM Association for a fee of about $90; each team typically registers with their state OM office for about another $45. The teacher/coach will want to purchase the books *Problems, Problems, Problems* (Micklus and Gourley, 1982) and *OMAha!* (Micklus, 1986), which supply dozens of short-term practice problems and hints for scoring well with long-term problems, and the *Odyssey of the Mind Program Handbook* (Micklus, 1985), which details competition guidelines, rules, and procedures. Other books and videotapes (e.g., *World Finals Videotape*; *Coaches' Training Videotape*) also are offered by the OM Association, Box 27, Glassboro, NJ 08028.

The OM Association provides each team with detailed directions for preparing *long-term* problems that will require months to plan and implement prior to the regional competitions. For example, for 1992–1993 the five long-term problems were:

Pit Stop (Divisions II, III, IV). The team's problem is to design, build, and drive a vehicle powered by one or two mechanical jacks. It must travel a course, make pit stops, and at some point travel in reverse. "Its physical features will change and it will make part of its journey in 'full glory'" (OM Association, 1992).

Dinosaurs (Divisions I, II, III). The team must create and present a story about dinosaurs that will include team-made dinosaurs, one of more of which will "perform technical tasks." Teams also will discover a new dinosaur called a *creivo-saurus*. The performance will have a theme that ties together the various required aspects.

Classics—The Old Man and the Sea Analogy (Divisions I, II, III, IV). The problem is to create and present a performance based on Hemingway's *The Old Man and the Sea*. The performance will include a parody or analogy of the team's interpretation of the story and a conclusion.

Which End is Up? (Divisions I, II, III). The team's problem is to design and build a balsa wood structure to balance and support as much weight as possible. One end, the top or bottom, must fit entirely over a $6'' \times 6'' \times 1''$ block. The other end must fit entirely within a $4'' \times 4'' \times 1''$ space.

Folk Tales (Divisions I, II). The team must create a performance that includes a team-originated folk tale, one or more team-originated legendary or mythical characters, and two or more quotes from a given list. One or two of the characters will be portrayed as the originators of the quotes.

Li'l Gourmet (Primary Level, Grades K-2). This noncompetitive event offers children the opportunity to create and perform a skit about a well-balanced meal. The skit will include costumes and feature an original, team-created song.

In all problems, points are awarded for *style*— the creative presentation of the problem, which may include music, costumes, and mime.

In addition to the long-term problems, students also solve *short-term* "spontaneous" problems both in practice and on the day of competition. For example, students might be asked to improvise with a ping pong ball ("It's a clown's nose!" "It's an egg from a plastic bird!"). Teams are awarded one point for each common idea and three points for each creative idea. They learn to give creative ideas.

JUNIOR GREAT BOOKS

Another popular enrichment program is *Junior Great Books*, currently used in G/T programs in all 50 states and many foreign countries. In a two-day workshop, the Junior Great Books Foundation trains teachers to ask questions requiring interpretation of carefully selected literature. A guiding philosophy is that ". . . if you think you know the answer to a question, don't ask the question" (Will, 1986). Shared inquiry is the goal.

The books themselves consist of traditional and modern literature, selected for each grade level from second grade through high school. Second, third, and fourth grade children read folk tales and fairy tales. Grades four through nine cover children's classics and modern short stories. High school students read short selections from great works of philosophy, political science, economics, and fiction. All readings have proved to be comprehendible, rich enough in ideas for sustained discussion of the interpretive questions, and enjoyable to read and discuss. Teachers engage students in in-depth discussions of their reading in 12 sessions per selection.

Strengthening reading skills (e.g., vocabulary), listening skills, and reading-related thinking skills of interpretation and inquiry are some of the benefits (Nichols, 1992). Most good literature also gives readers greater self-awareness, with insights into psychological and social problems, issues, and philosophies.

For further information, contact the Junior Great Books Foundation, 40 East Huron, Chicago, IL 60611.

ACADEMIC DECATHLON

Academic Decathlon is a challenging high school program that includes regional, state, and national competitions. Each team is composed of two "A," two "B," and two "C" students in grades 11 or 12. Each school competes in one of three categories based on school size. They compete in conversation skills, essay writing, formal speech, economics, language and literature, fine arts, mathematics, physical science, social studies, and a Super Quiz. The Super Quiz topic is provided in advance; in 1988 it was "The History of Flight from Daedalus to Kitty Hawk to Voyager."

For further information, contact Academic Decathlon, c/o World Book, Merchandise Mart, Chicago, IL 60654.

MOCK COURT

Mock Court (or mock trial tournament) is a plan for very talented high school students, most often those interested in a law or political career. There usually are local, regional, state, and national competitions, with the higher-level competitions held in district federal courthouses and presided over by real federal judges. Guided by a school coach, students might deal with a trial based, for example, on a drinking and driving violation. In four phases involving participation in two trials, each participant prepares an argument for the defense, a rebuttal of the prosecutor's presentation, a presentation as the prosecutor, and a rebuttal of the case for the defense. Winners of state competitions travel to Lincoln, Nebraska, for the All State Invitational Mock Trial Tournament each May. For information, contact Mock Trial, Center for Law-Related Education, Drake University, Des Moines, IA 50311.

OTHER ACADEMIC COMPETITIONS

Andrea Williams (1986; see also Williams, 1980) described a number of academic game bowls for students in grades 1 through 12 that can be organized for district- or state-level participation. Each school can enter one or more teams, and both team and individual performances are rewarded with ribbons, certificates, and trophies. The events allow students to solve problems, apply ideas, and make intuitive leaps; strengthen written and oral communication skills; and strengthen creativity, analysis, evaluation, and leadership abilities. In addition, many participants show improved cross-

sex and cross-race cooperation, better school attitudes, better coping skills, and in some big city schools, reduced absenteeism and dropping out.

The academic events themselves may be locally designed, based upon selected academic areas, content and process goals and objectives, and the target population (grade levels or interest groups). Alternatively, the competitions may be tied to national competitions, for example, Future Problem Solving, Odyssey of the Mind, National Academic Games (Box 214, Newhall, CA 91322), National Forensics League (671 E. Fond du Lac Street, Ripon, WI 54971), Computer Convention (Ronald Baillie, 3307 E. Hardies Road, Gibsonia, PA 15044), International Mathematical Olympiad (see Dauber, 1988), and Land of Adwin, which includes an all-day congress, Creative Problem Solving, Calcu-Solve (using calculators), and Creative Convention (Andrea Williams, 2007 Maple Leaf, Collinsville, IL 62234).

GROUPING OPTIONS: BRINGING GIFTED STUDENTS TOGETHER

We have noted the benefits of grouping gifted students, part-time if not full-time, many times in this text. Learning activities can be enriched and accelerated—to fit student capabilities and learning needs, develop creativity and thinking skills, reduce boredom and frustration, and combat underachievement habits by inviting gifted students to work and think for a change. Equally important is the opportunity to interact with others like themselves for social and academic support.

In this section we will summarize briefly grouping options in three categories:

1. Full-time homogeneous classes
   Magnet schools
   Special schools for the gifted
   Private schools
   School-within-a-school plans
   Special classes in the elementary school
2. Full-time heterogeneous classes
   Combined grades in a regular class

Cluster groups of gifted students placed with regular students

Mainstreaming in the regular class

3. Part-time or temporary groups

Pullout programs

Resource-room plans

Special classes

Activity clubs

Honors programs

Full-Time Homogeneous Grouping

The main benefit of full-time grouping of gifted students is illustrated in this anecdote recounted by Elizabeth Connor (1991) in her description of EAGLE School, Connor's private school for the gifted:

Six-year-old Maurit announced to her family at the dinner table that she had just been selected to participate in "Wonderful Wednesdays," her public school's pullout enrichment program. Once a week she could participate in special activities in the gifted/talented resource room instead of doing her regular classwork. Maurit's older sister, Orelia, a student at EAGLE School, . . . greeted the news with delight:

"Oh, Maurit, that means you're gifted. Now you can come to EAGLE SCHOOL!"

Maurit pondered this idea for moment, then replied, "No, I don't think so. If you go to EAGLE, you have to be gifted all the time. I'm just gifted on Wednesdays."

Magnet Schools.   Many large cities have adopted magnet high school plans to accommodate the needs not only of gifted and talented students, but regular students seeking special training for a trade or career. A clear purpose is to make high school relevant to realistic student goals, particularly for potential dropouts who view school as prison rather than a path to economic and social success. Note that gifted students, as well as low-ability students, too often become frustrated and

drop out. All magnet schools offer specialized training in, say, the arts, math and science, business, or trade skills. A school also may be designated as a "superior abilities school." Students are bused in from all corners of the city or district to attend the high school that suits their educational and career interests. In some cases, they are placed in career-related part-time jobs so they may earn money and gain valuable experience while attending school. Such programs are indeed relevant, and they do meet students' needs. They also are known to reduce the dropout rate.

Special Schools for the Gifted.   Special schools for the gifted typically are a medium- to big-city alternative. An entire elementary or secondary school may be designated for gifted and talented youngsters (e.g., Toll, 1991). In all cases the curriculum will include both traditional academic content—based upon district guidelines and requirements—plus special enriched and accelerated training in whatever academic, artistic, scientific, or personal development areas the district and school choose to emphasize.

One example of a special elementary school is the Golda Meir School in Milwaukee. Students are selected from the entire district based upon the federal definition (general ability, specific academic aptitude, creativity, leadership, or visual or performing art talent), as reflected in test scores, grades, and teacher, parent, and peer nominations (Pfeil, 1978). A quota system is used to balance the school composition for sex, race, and representation from all school districts in the Milwaukee system. Because this is an elementary school, subject matter acceleration is limited so that students will not be advanced beyond grade level in particular subjects when they enter the regular junior high school.

Enrichment opportunities, however, are diverse and exciting. They include foreign language training; piano, violin, viola, and general music lessons; drama lessons from members of the Milwaukee Repertory Company; the creation of a school newspaper, aided by Milwaukee Journal reporters; field trips to Milwaukee's civic, financial, and cultural centers (between about 12 and 30 trips per student per year); "MACS Packs" (math-arts-crafts-science) which offer daily student projects; and "Lunch Bunch" involvement in games, films, reading, or just visiting. There is a Classics Club which reads above-grade level books, an Advanced Science Club, a school chorus, a Student Senate, and sometimes an infant-care class featuring a real infant—typically a student's younger brother or sister. Enthusiasm of staff and students runs extremely high. This model plan continually hosts many visitors.

Private Schools. Achievement tends to run higher in private schools than in public schools (Coleman, 1981). Therefore, private schools can be a good alternative for an accelerated education.

Some private schools cater especially to gifted and talented students (see e.g., Connor, 1991; Hollingworth, 1991; Howard and Block, 1991; Kelble, 1991). In Hillsborough, California, for example, the Nueva Learning Center is designed ". . . to provide high potential students (age 4–12 years) with opportunities for developing living skills, attitudes, and knowledge which are rarely available to them through normal learning channels . . . to stimulate curiosity, encourage participation, and generate interest" (Juntune, 1981). There is training in six *R*'s (reading, writing, arithmetic, rights, respect, and responsibility), piano, ballet, math, science, and more unusual topics such as organic gardening, aviation, karate, and cross-country skiing. Responsibility, awareness, and confidence are prime goals.

In Madison, Wisconsin, the EAGLE School filled a strong demand for private schooling for gifted children. Serving grades K through 8, small classes of about 11 children "allow students to be explorers, scientists, mathematical puzzlers, or people in history who have solved problems" (Connor, 1991, p. 16). The curricula—presented by 10 or 11 different specialists per week—include art, drama, music, gym, typing/word pro-cessing, computers, French or Spanish, science, math, language arts, social studies, and electives such as fencing, chorus, math games, robotics, or the popular art studio.[8]

School-within-a-School. Similar to special classes for G/T students (next section), an entire school may be organized around a school-within-a-school concept (e.g., Toll, 1991; Witham, 1991). Here, gifted and talented students from around the district attend a particular school that also accommodates regular students. For part of the day, G/T students attend special classes taught by special teachers. They mix with the rest of the students for nonacademic subjects (for example, physical education, study hall, manual arts, home economics) and for sports and social events.

Special Classes. There is a growing interest in full-time classes for gifted and talented children—because part-time programs provide only a part-time solution. According to one poll (Gallagher *et al.*, 1983), the frequency of full-time special classes in gifted programs (23 percent) is just second in popularity behind pullout plans (41 percent). An elementary school using self-contained G/T classes typically will have just one or two, most often in grades 3 through 6 (Feldhusen and Sayler, 1990; Witham, 1991). Feldhusen and Saylor recommend that students in special G/T classes have opportunities to interact with other students, for example, in art, music, physical education, and playground activities—a strategy resembling school-within-a-school plans.

Special classes for gifted and talented students may take several forms. First, at the elementary level all gifted students within a particular grade level, age, or age range, may be assigned to a special class. In addition to covering prescribed grade-level objectives—and usually extending beyond them—a variety of enrichment, personal

---

[8]See Juntune (1981) for descriptions of goals and curricula of private schools that serve gifted students.

development, and skill development experiences are planned. In a survey of teachers, administrators, and G/T program coordinators, 98 percent felt that special classes were "academically advantageous" to gifted students, 84 percent agreed that motivation ran higher, and 85 percent rated the special classes as good for the social-emotional development of gifted students (Feldhusen and Sayler, 1991).

In the negative column, students may resist being separated physically and psychologically from regular students. Further, it is not unusual for other students to resent their special status and to make them feel socially uncomfortable, for example, by calling them names or by silent ostracism. Another danger, especially at the secondary level, is that teachers of special—and more difficult—classes may grade on a normal curve, thus giving "B's" and "C's" to students who could easily earn "A's" in other courses. It is not unusual for grade-conscious students to avoid "special classes" to protect their grades.

In high school there already is a variety of college preparatory classes to challenge the abilities of gifted and talented students, for example, in chemistry, physics, calculus, art, journalism, and drama. Special classes beyond these also may be created, for example, courses in college algebra, organic chemistry, advanced physics, advanced botany, creative writing, photography, or whatever else students need and the school budget will allow. If some of these can be taught in accord with Advanced Placement program guidelines they may lead to college credit, as described in Chapter 5.

Kolloff and Feldhusen (1986) described high school seminars in Indiana and Illinois designed for gifted students. The goals included exploring abstract and complex ideas and engaging students in reflective, critical, and creative thinking, for example, related to social problems. An interdisciplinary and team-taught curriculum requires students, for example, to interrelate math, science, social studies, and English. Guest speakers, student presentations, and small group work are included.

Full-time Heterogeneous Grouping

Multi-age Classrooms.   Frequently, a school will combine grades—say, a group of fourth-graders with a group of fifth-graders. Sometimes this arrangement is an administrative convenience—the school has too many fourth and fifth graders to fit them into existing classes, but not enough to justify *two* additional classes. Therefore, "good" fourth-grade students usually are selected who might benefit from learning and interacting with children who are one chronological year older. Combining grades is a minimal form of acceleration, and is effective only if the younger students are not required to repeat similar learning experiences the following year.

Cluster Groups.   The phrase "cluster grouping" sometimes is used to mean putting gifted students in special or accelerated classes. The "proper" use of cluster grouping means putting a selected group of about 5 to 10 students together in one regular class, along with 15 or 20 other students.

A cluster group of G/T students in a regular class engages in a variety of enrichment activities either individually or in small groups. For example, they might "contract" for independent learning activities such as a library research report, an independent research project, or the mastery of an advanced math, computer, science, or language-learning assignment. Alternatively, groups of students sharing similar interests and abilities might work on a particular problem or project for a mutually agreed-upon period of time. The teacher, who normally has received some in-service training or taken coursework in gifted education, also might involve the students in exercises and activities aimed at strengthening creative and research skills or other types of high-level thinking abilities.

Kaplan (1974) itemized "necessities" and "checkpoints" in planning a cluster group G/T program:

1. Developing criteria for selecting students.
2. Defining the qualifications of, and the selection process for, the teachers.

3. Clarifying the teachers' responsibilities and activities.
4. Planning the differentiated experiences for the cluster of gifted students.
5. Planning for support services and special resources, for example, counselors and computers.

The teacher will organize individual and small-group meetings, help students plan contracts and projects, perhaps organize field trips and other educational experiences. Kaplan recommended that, with cluster grouping, the gifted students should have opportunities to share their unique learning experiences with the total class, which reduces their isolation. The staff must be certain that the special activities and experiences stimulate—not penalize—students in the gifted cluster. For example, if "special learning experiences" amount to piling on more work, the students may prefer *not* to be gifted.

As an example of a cluster group plan, Project LIFT of Marion, Massachusetts, places groups of five fourth-, fifth-, and sixth-grade G/T students in selected regular classes (Juntune, 1981). The goal of the program is to develop higher-level thinking skills as defined in Bloom's taxonomy: application, analysis, synthesis, and evaluation. Teachers *compact* the regular curriculum by not requiring students to study material they know and by accelerating them through material they do not know. The compacting provides time for enrichment activities, including training in creative and critical thinking and the development of research skills via independent research projects.

Mainstreaming.   Many teachers in regular classrooms use their own ingenuity to provide differentiated and enriched learning experiences to eager, fast-learning, and creative students. For example, earlier in this chapter we described Hazel Feldhusen's (1981, 1986) creative use of learning centers in her regular classroom. Sometimes, "mainstreaming" the gifted is a default program when the school or district has no formal G/T program.

D. R. Clasen (1982) itemized a number of alternatives available to the individual teacher in schools ". . . where there is minimum involvement in programming for the gifted. . . ." Specifically:

1. A student may be individually accelerated, perhaps by reading or working ahead or through the use of advanced or supplementary texts and workbooks.
2. The curriculum may otherwise be modified to permit greater depth, more complexity, or higher levels of abstraction.
3. Enrichment activities may be planned that build on or challenge the student's special skills and abilities, for example, in creative writing, photography, or computer programming.
4. Academic and perhaps career advising may be appropriate, for example, helping students understand their special capabilities and the training necessary for them to realize their full potential.

Looking specifically at helping bright math students in the regular classroom, Tucker (1982) recommended the use of (1) puzzles; (2) mental arithmetic games; (3) projects and applications—for example, computing vacation expenses or plotting data and making inferences; (4) enrichment units, which include strengthening already learned skills and learning new material; and (5) reading, particularly about mathematicians.

To offer two notes on mainstreaming: First, some teachers—in concert with counselors, parents, and students themselves—use *Individualized Education Programs* (IEPs) to structure the independent work of mainstreamed gifted students (just as IEPs are used to plan the education for retarded, learning disabled, or handicapped students; see Inset 6.1).

Second, Treffinger (1982b) itemized 60 suggestions suggestions for teaching gifted students in the regular classroom. Some notable examples are:

Use pretests or mastery tests to permit students to "test out" of material they already know.

Use individualized learning packets, programmed learning, learning modules, learning centers, and minicourses, particularly in the basics.

INSET 6.1 _____

Using Individualized Education Programs (IEPs) with Gifted and Talented Students

The reader probably is aware that Public Law 94-142, the "mainstreaming law," mandated the use of an _Individualized Education Program_ (IEP) for each student classified as having a handicap. IEPs also serve that other variety of exceptional student, the gifted and talented, particularly when they too are mainstreamed in the regular classroom. For students with handicaps, IEPs are prepared jointly ". . . by a qualified school official, by the child's teacher and parents or guardian, and if possible by the child himself. . . ." Consultants such as a psychologist, reading specialist, speech pathologist, social worker, guidance counselor, curriculum specialist, or doctor are also involved in the planning. Similar personnel can help plan IEPs for G/T students.

The IEP serves as a guide for managing the testing, placement, instruction, and procedural safeguards that each handicapped student needs (National Advisory Committee on the Handicapped, 1976). For gifted students, the IEP will include:

1. Present levels of performance, as determined by intelligence tests, achievement tests, rating scales, and informal observations and reports by teachers, parents, school psychologists, or others.

2. Annual goals, which include short-term instructional goals. These goals will dictate most of the instructional methods, learning activities, and individual projects for each student required under item 3.

3. Specific educational services to be provided, based on the needs of the individual student. These will include special teaching strategies, special equipment, individual projects and assignments, field trips, and others.

4. The extent to which the student will participate in the regular program versus special G/T classes and activities.

5. A projected date for initiation and the anticipated duration of the services.

6. Evaluation procedures and appropriate objective criteria, which may result in a review and revision of the IEP.

7. A schedule for determining whether the objectives are being achieved.

Allow uninterrupted time every day for individual or small-group projects.

Incorporate creative thinking into subject areas.

Help students to learn the meaning of such higher-level thinking processes as _analysis_, _synthesis_, and _evaluation_, and to plan independent projects around these processes.

Bring in guest speakers to describe their careers or unusual hobbies.

Use cross-age and peer tutoring.

Help students to understand their own strengths, interests, learning styles, and preferences, and to become sensitive to those of others.

Explore many points of view about contemporary topics and allow opportunity to analyze and evaluate evidence and conflicting ideas and opinions.

Help set personal and academic goals.

As a final caution, do not permit a mainstreaming program to become camouflage for offering no program at all. If gifted and talented children are not truly involved in differentiated curriculum within their regular classrooms, one cannot say that the school is providing for their needs.

Part-Time and Temporary Grouping

Pullout Programs.   The old standby in programming for gifted and talented students is the *pullout* program. With minor variations, elementary students are pulled out of their regular classes two to three hours per week to participate in special enrichment activities, guided usually by a district G/T teacher/coordinator. Often, one G/T coordinator serves an entire district by conducting a pullout class in a different school each afternoon. The meeting place usually is called a *resource room* because it provides special reading material and equipment resources. As with other special classes and cluster grouping, pullout activities focus on acquiring knowledge and skills and involving students in learning activities that strengthen creativity and thinking skills, communication skills, and self-concept development and values clarification.

It is ironic that this most popular programming design also is the most severely criticized (e.g., Cox, Daniel, and Boston, 1985; Toll, 1991; Witham, 1991). We have mentioned that it is a part-time solution to the full-time "problem" of being gifted. Also, it is relatively expensive, largely because of the G/T coordinator's salary. Further, friction develops when teachers are saddled with the dilemma of permitting students to miss regular classwork, or requiring them to make up missed work—thus punishing them for their G/T participation. Many programs assume that G/T kids can afford to miss some regular content, and the students are not held responsible for missed work.

Another problem is that selecting some students for special privileges can damage student social relationships; students may not be comfortable being visibly separated from classmates and classified as special or different. Still another classic criticism is that pullout curricula frequently include too much "fun and games" and too little theory-based training (Renzulli and Reis, 1985a, 1991b).

More positively, the pullout program is a popular and often successful means of bringing G/T students together for social and intellectual support, and for the special differentiated and enriched training they deserve. When it has a well-planned, challenging, and integrated curriculum, this program can offer gifted children good opportunities for developing high-level skills. In a review of research on pullout programs, Vaughn, Feldhusen, and Asher (1991) concluded that these programs typically have a positive effect on achievement, creativity, and thinking skills.

Resource Programs and Resource Rooms.   As with *cluster groups*, the phrases "resource program" and "resource room" are used rather freely. Because pullout students are sent to a resource room, pullout programs are sometimes called *resource programs* or *resource-room programs*. A part-time special class for gifted students (discussed later) might also be held in a resource room and similarly earn the label *resource program*.

The present meaning of *resource program* is a district-wide pullout or magnet-type plan in which students with special needs are transported to specially equipped and taught resource rooms or enrichment centers for one or two sessions per week (see Inset 6.2).

In Ankeny, Iowa, the *Ankeny Gifted and Talented Education* (AGATE) program uses city buses to transport K-9 students to a junior high school equipped with AV equipment, books, magazines, a science lab, a language corner, games, plants, a piano, and miscellaneous materials for independent projects. The enrichment curriculum has included such activities as astronomy, including building a telescope; rocketry, with student-made—and launched—rockets; film animation; journalism, resulting in a newspaper; foreign languages; American Sign Language; art; literature; theatre; photography; oceanography; and more (Juntune, 1981). Students alternate mornings and afternoons, and days of the week, to avoid missing the same activities in the same classes.

INSET 6.2 _____

Resource Room Resources

Cecile Frey (1980) itemized materials she has found to be "absolutely essential" to the decent operation of an elementary school resource room:

A good unabridged dictionary

A copy of *Roget's Thesaurus*

Bartlett's Familiar Quotations

A biographical dictionary (Webster)

A complete atlas

In the "nice but not essential" category she recommended:

The People's Almanac

Isaac Asimov's *Biographical Encyclopedia of Science and Technology*

Mathematics Illustrated Dictionary

Any decent grammar book

The Encyclopedia of Ignorance

As for a set of encyclopedias, Frey said, "I must answer that question with a resounding 'No!'" The reason: Students rely too heavily on them and, anyway, they are (1) expensive and (2) available in the school library. However, if funds are available, and only for limited use, she recommends *The World Book* and the *Encyclopedia Britannica's Micropedia and Macropedia*.

The resource room also should subscribe to:

Art and Man

Literary Cavalcade

Time or *Newsweek*

Science Digest

National Geographic World

New York Times

Part-time Special Classes.   Special classes (discussed under "Full-Time Homogeneous Grouping") may also be offered as part-time or temporary options. For example, in *Project Horizon* (Seattle, Washington) elementary school G/T students are placed in specialized self-contained classes for 50–70 percent of the school day. Their differentiated experiences include independent projects, accelerated subjects, and small-group enrichment activities, all of which aim at developing creative and other high-level thinking skills.

The Wheaton-Warrenville (Illinois) district Talented and Gifted Program includes magnet-type, district-wide special classes for junior and senior high school G/T students. For example, a junior high school offers bused-in students an accelerated math class. One high school offers a specially designed Key Seminar and another a

Humanities class; both classes are cross-subject, and both focus on developing high-level thinking skills.

Honors programs often consist of one or more part-time special classes.

Special Interest Groups and Clubs. Most secondary schools have these, although they are rare in the elementary school. G/T-conscious teachers at any level can assume the leadership necessary for organizing these enriching activities for interested students. There are drama clubs, German clubs, French clubs, computer clubs, chess clubs, math clubs, and others. The teacher-leader can organize meetings, competitions, research projects, field trips, and meetings with community experts, and can provide career information and guidance. One also can organize mini-courses, taught either by teachers or community experts, dealing with special interest areas such as music writing, computer programming, jewelry making, aviation or any other academic, career, or hobby topic. Clubs and courses may meet before or after school or on Saturdays. Activities may include work with equipment not normally available; for example, a high school laboratory might be borrowed for an elementary school physics group.

SUMMARY

Many enrichment activities are good for all students, not just the "gifted."

Worthwhile enrichment should be guided by the types of objectives in Table 5.1.

Enrichment strategies are delivery methods for achieving process and content goals.

Independent projects can involve library research, scientific research, art, drama, creative writing, or others. Projects might be displayed in museums, published, or entered in the Westinghouse or Invent America competitions.

Commercial or teacher-made learning centers can teach languages, science, math, computers, social studies, creative writing, music appreciation, and others.

Field trips are good experiences for regular and gifted students. The teacher and the guide/educator should preplan any tour.

Feldhusen's Super Saturday is a model Saturday enrichment program.

Regular summer programs may be capitalized upon. Many school districts offer special courses and workshops for the gifted.

Governors' Schools are a widespread type of summer program for gifted secondary students. Many universities sponsor College for Kids summer programs, consisting largely of minicourses.

Music, art, language, and computer camps are valuable summer programs that teach high-level content and thinking skills. Peer support in such programs is valuable.

Mentor programs usually involve extended on-the-job, one-to-one interaction with a community professional. Students learn professional activities, problems, and lifestyles of mentors. Ideal mentors are interested in teaching and high in integrity, enthusiasm, humor, creativity, and the ability to stimulate high-level thinking.

Future Problem Solving helps children become future-oriented and strengthens creativity, problem solving, communication and teamwork skills. FPS follows a seven-step creative problem solving model.

Odyssey of the Mind includes long-term problems, worked on over the school year, and short-term problems. OM is designed to strengthen creative problem solving and confidence.

Junior Great Books acquaints students with classic literature and strengthens reading, interpretation, and discussion skills.

Academic Decathlon is a national high school program involving competitions in essay writing, speech, economics, language and literature, art, math, science, social studies, and others.

Mock Court, also a high school plan, requires gifted students to prepare defense and prosecution presentations and rebuttals.

Other academic game bowls and competitions may be organized for district- or state-level competition. The competitions strengthen communication skills, leadership, creativity, analysis, and other thinking skills, and improve attitudes and coping skills.

In the category of full-time homogeneous grouping, magnet high schools draw students to the particular school that accommodates their needs and educational/career interests. Special schools, elementary or secondary, are devoted solely to programs that accelerate and enrich the education of gifted students.

Private schools usually produce higher average achievement than public schools; some private schools are designed for gifted and talented students.

With the school-within-a-school plan gifted students attend special classes for part of the day and mix with regular students for other, usually less academic classes. Special classes for G/T students may be created in the elementary school or the junior or senior high school.

Full-time heterogeneous options include multi-age classrooms, allowing bright younger students to learn with students in the next higher grade.

Cluster grouping involves placing a group of five to ten gifted students in the same regular class for special assignments. Curriculum may be compacted to allow time for enrichment activities.

Mainstreaming is planning special learning experiences and projects in the regular classroom, for example, with learning centers or special assignments and projects. IEPs may be used to individualize instruction for mainstreamed gifted students.

Treffinger itemized suggestions for providing for gifted students in the regular class, for example, permitting students to "test out" of material they know; using learning centers, minicourses, and independent projects; and helping students understand their own strengths, interests, and learning styles.

Part-time and temporary grouping options include these: Pullout programs, the most common elementary level G/T plan, involve sending gifted students to a resource room for one or two afternoons per week. It is criticized for being a "part-time solution." Other problems include dealing with missed work and damage to social relations.

A resource program is a district-wide pullout plan in which students travel to a resource room once or twice per week for special learning activities and projects.

Special classes may be used on a part-time as well as full-time basis. For example, elementary students may attend special classes for part of the day; secondary students may be bused to a district-wide special class in, say, accelerated math or humanities. Honors programs use part-time special classes.

Special interest groups and clubs are a good outlet for students whose enthusiasm and ability exceed the regularly offered coursework.

APPENDIX 6.1

Magazines that Publish Student Work

Child Life
Box 567
1100 Waterway Blvd.
Indianapolis, IN 46206

Children's Album
Box 6086
Concord, CA 94524

Children's Digest
Box 567
1100 Waterway Blvd.
Indianapolis, IN 46206

Creative Kids
GCT Inc.
Box 6448
Mobile, AL 36660

Flip Magazine
Art Center
265 Emmett Stteet
Battle Creek, MI 49017

Highlights for Children
803 Church Street
Honesdale, PA 18431

Kid City
1 Lincoln Plaza
New York, NY 10023

Listen
"Graffity"
6830 Laurel Street, NW
Washington, DC 20012

McGuffy Writer
400-A McGuffy Hall
Miami University
Oxford, OH 45056

Odyssey
Kalmback Publishing Company
1027 North 7th Street
Milwaukee, WI 53223

Prism
1040 Bayview Drive
Suite 223
Fort Lauderdale, FL 33304

Scholastic Scope
Student Writing
730 Broadway
New York, NY 10003

Spinoff: Gifted Children Monthly
Box 115
Sewell, NJ 08080

Stone Soup
Box 83
Santa Cruz, CA 95063

Wombat
365 Ashton Drive
Athens, GA 30606

Young Authors' Magazine
Theraplan, Inc.
3015 Woodsdale Blvd.
Lincoln, NE 68502

CHAPTER 7

CURRICULUM MODELS

Research tells us that gifted behaviors can be developed in a far broader spectrum of the school population than the small percentage of students who are usually identified by high scores on intelligence or achievement tests.

Joseph Renzulli and Sally Reis (1985b, p. 3)

Curriculum models help provide a theoretical framework within which specific enrichment activities may be planned. This chapter will briefly summarize eleven curriculum models, all of which have provided justifiable bases for planning differentiated experiences for G/T students. In most cases—but not all—the models and their prescriptions are quite consistent and complementary, permitting a teacher-coordinator to draw ideas from two or more curriculum models simultaneously. Some models, such as the *Schoolwide Enrichment Model* (Renzulli and Reis, 1985a, 1991b), the *Pyramid Model* (Cox, Daniel, and Boston, 1985; Ondo and Session, 1989), and the *Autonomous Learner Model* (Betts, 1985, 1991), provide extensive details regarding program philosophy, recommended selection procedures, curriculum content, and specifics of carrying out the entire plan. In the case of the Schoolwide Enrichment Model, the details fill a 522-page book (Renzulli and Reis, 1985a). Other models make general and specific recommendations, and leave it to the teacher-coordinator to fill in many of the particulars. These are the eleven models:

1. Enrichment Triad Model (Renzulli, 1977; Renzulli and Reis, 1991b)

2. Schoolwide Enrichment Model (Renzulli and Reis, 1985a, 1986, 1991b)

3. Multiple Menu Model (Renzulli, 1988)

4. Pyramid Project (Cox, Daniel, and Boston, 1985)

5. Purdue Three-Stage Enrichment Model (Feldhusen and Kolloff, 1986)

6. Guilford/Meeker Structure of Intellect Model (Guilford, 1967, 1977, 1988; Meeker, 1969; Meeker and Meeker, 1986)

7. Treffinger's (1975) model for increasing self-directedness

8. Autonomous Learner Model (Betts, 1985, 1991)

9. Williams' (1970, 1982, 1986) Cognitive-Affective Interaction Model for developing thinking and feeling processes

10. Multiple-Talent Totem Pole Model (Schlichter and Palmer, 1993; Taylor, 1986, 1988)

11. Diagonal Curriculum Model (Kranz, 1993)

ENRICHMENT TRIAD MODEL

The *Enrichment Triad Model*, originated by Renzulli (1977; see also Renzulli and Reis, 1985a, 1986, 1991b; Reis and Renzulli, 1986) is the best known and most widely used model for guiding "what to do" for gifted students. The plan has been implemented almost entirely with elementary students, but can be used effectively with secondary students as well.

The Triad Model in the Elementary School

As an overview (Figure 7.1), the three more-or-less sequential but qualitatively different steps include: Type I enrichment, general exploratory activities designed to acquaint the student with a variety of topics and interest areas; Type II enrichment, group training activities dealing with the development of cognitive and affective processes—for example, creativity and research skills; and Type III enrichment, the investigation of real problems ". . . that are similar in nature to those pursued by authentic researchers or artists in particular fields" (Renzulli, 1977). Importantly,

Type I and II activities are valuable for—and should be used with—all students. Indeed, Olenchak and Renzulli (1989) discovered that student attitudes toward learning and school improved measurably due to exposure to Types I and II enrichment. Type III activities are felt to require the special creativity, ability, and energy of students with gifted potential.

Type I Enrichment

The three main purposes of Type I enrichment, general exploratory activities, are to (1) expose students to topics that are not a normal part of the school's curriculum, (2) make general enrichment activities available to all interested students, and (3) invite highly motivated students to find and

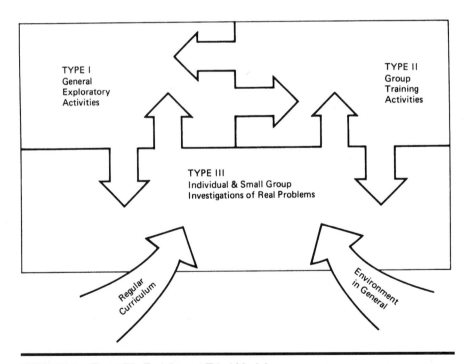

FIGURE 7.1. Renzulli's Enrichment Triad Model.
From J.S. Renzulli, *The Enrichment Triad Model: A Guide for Developing Defensible Programs for the Gifted And Talented.* Mansfield Center, Conn.: Creative Learning Press, 1977. Reprinted by permission.

pursue a later Type III independent project (Reis and Burns, 1987). Gifted students should understand that they are to explore these interest areas purposefully, with a view toward identifying ideas for further study. Some students already will have longstanding interests or hobbies which are well suited for Type III projects (photography, drama, calligraphy, and so on). In these cases, Type I activities serve mainly to expose students to new areas.

Resource centers should be well stocked with books, magazines, and other media dealing with a large number of topics. Appendix 7.1 at the end of this chapter, based on ideas from Renzulli (1977) and Reis and Burns (1987), lists well over 200 possibilities, some of which are categories (for example, languages, history). Topics typically are selected jointly by teachers and students and may be studied in groups or individually.

Another good exploratory activity is field experiences in which gifted and talented students meet dynamic people involved in creative and problem-solving endeavors—artists, actors, engineers, museum and art gallery curators, TV show directors, business leaders, restaurant owners, and so on. This type of field trip goes beyond just visiting an art gallery or planetarium or taking a guided tour through the Schlitz Brewery. The purpose is not to "look at"—Renzulli's "museum experience"—but to *become involved with* professionals and their activities.

The design of profitable Type I exploratory activities will require effort and ingenuity.

Type II Enrichment

The purpose of Type II enrichment—group training activities—is to promote the development of a broad range of thinking and feeling processes (Renzulli and Reis, 1991b). While these skills, abilities, attitudes, and strategies should be developed in *all* students, ". . . an escalation of process development should be a primary goal of programs that serve gifted and talented students" (Renzulli and Reis, 1985a). Type II enrichment also includes process skills directly related to gifted students' independent projects, for example, techniques for writing a script for a play, silk screening or lost-wax casting, or using scientific equipment. Renzulli and Reis (1985a, 1991b) especially recommended developing general and specific skills in these four categories:

1. Creative thinking, problem solving, critical thinking, decision making, and affective processes such as sensing, appreciating, and valuing.

2. Learning-how-to-learn skills, such as listening, observing, note taking, outlining, interviewing and surveying, classifying, analyzing and organizing data, drawing conclusions, and others.

3. Using advanced-level reference and resource materials, such as reader's guides, directories, abstracts, and information retrieval systems.

4. Written, oral, and visual communication skills that will maximize the impact of students' products upon appropriate audiences.

Which of these process skills will help gifted students with their Type III projects? Which would be good for all students?

Additional affective concerns, which will be elaborated in Chapter 8, include helping students form good self-concepts and feelings of high self-worth; helping them develop constructive social and interpersonal values; increasing their awareness of others' perceptions, points of view, problems, and handicaps; and increasing their educational and career motivation, in part by helping them understand that they can control their destinies.

Incidentally, many programs for the gifted focus exclusively on the Type II kinds of process activities—creativity, thinking skills, affective development, and others. In their article entitled "Developing Defensible Programs for the Gifted and Talented," Renzulli and Smith (1978a) warn that too strong an emphasis on process activities definitely is not defensible, which brings us to Type III enrichment.

Type III Enrichment

With Type III enrichment activities, the gifted young person becomes an actual researcher investigating a real problem, or an artist formulating and creating an original product. Students should act as *producers* of knowledge and art, not merely consumers of information. For example, for a research project they should not be asked to consult encyclopedias, textbooks, or other already summarized sources and then write a report. Rather, they should use raw data as their main information source, from which they draw their own conclusions.

The student should play an active part in formulating the problem, designing the research or artistic methods, and planning the final product. The teacher, as the "guide on the side," helps with clarifying the problem, designing the project, locating materials and equipment, and recommending information sources or community experts. Ten steps for Type III projects, as presented to Talent Pool students, are summarized in Table 7.1.

Outlets for Creations

It is important for students to have audiences for their Type III products. Grown-up artists, scientists, and other professionals do not keep their work to themselves. Indeed, a good part of their motivation and satisfaction derives from at least a limited amount of publicity and public awareness of their accomplishments (Renzulli, Reis, and Smith, 1981). Gifted students also are product-oriented; they wish to hold up their accomplishments and perhaps inform or influence a particular audience.

Local organizations such as historical societies or science or dramatic groups might be suitable audiences. Displays of work sometimes can be set up in children's museums, shopping centers, hospital foyers, the school district office building, the state capitol—or at least the school hallway. Children's magazines publish children's writing and research reports. If children's art shows and science fairs are not available, an energetic G/T teacher-coordinator might think about creating some. Local newspapers like a human-interest

TABLE 7.1   Ten Steps for Type III Enrichment Projects

1. Find out what your interests really are.
2. Learn more about your interest, and find some questions you want to learn more about.
3. Develop a time line and a plan (with your teacher).
4. Use multiple resources to learn more about your topic.
5. Decide (with your teacher) which question(s) should be researched.
6. Decide what process (Type II) skills you will need to learn (e.g., interviewing, recording data).
7. Work. And keep a log that outlines what you accomplish each week and your ideas.
8. Brainstorm different ideas for your final product (story, article, book, play, demonstration, slide show, video, slide-tape show, etc.).
9. Do your best work: "Working hard on something that you love is great."
10. Evaluate what you have done (with Student Product Assessment Form).

Adapted from Renzulli and Reis, 1985a, by permission of Creative Learning Press.

story, and good publicity will not hurt any G/T program. Appreciative audiences for dramatic productions and puppet plays, and perhaps other kinds of products, can be found in children's hospitals and retirement homes. You can invite the press to these also. Of course, as we noted in Chapter 6, the student's own class is a ready audience, for example, for a video production, a weaving or pyramid-building demonstration, or a report on school and community attitudes about year-round schooling.

SECONDARY TRIAD MODEL

The newer *Secondary Triad Model* (Reis and Renzulli, 1986) includes the same three types of enrichment as the original model. However, it requires a high school reorganization in the form of creating *talent pool* classes within each discipline.[1] The recommended selection of students for these classes follows the *Talent Pool Identification Plan* presented in Chapter 4, which is based on ability, achievement, and creativity test scores, as well as peer, parent, teacher, and self nominations—or, in the high school model, a strong interest in conducting a Type III project in a subject area such as English, math, or art. Talent pool members receive a thorough orientation to the Triad model and descriptions of talent pool classes in each area, either in an assembly program for the talent pool or individually.

The self-contained special classes in each discipline teach a regular curriculum that is compacted—accelerated—to permit time for Types I and II enrichment activities and, for energetic and creative volunteers, Type III independent projects. Type I enrichment includes exposing students to a broadened range of knowledge in the particular subject area, which helps them select Type III projects. Type II enrichment, as in the elementary school Triad model, includes creativity, problem solving, self-directed and independent study skills, research and reference skills, and other thinking and affective skills, as well as skills related to the specific subject area.

Type III projects will be of high quality, perhaps requiring consulting services of outside professionals. Regarding audiences, projects might be, for example, published in professional journals or presented to appropriate local groups. Such audiences motivate high quality work because they "add a dimension of reality and relevance" (Reis and Renzulli, 1986, p. 283).

SCHOOLWIDE ENRICHMENT MODEL

We hope the reader appreciates the challenge of summarizing a thoughtfully prepared, comparatively fat book containing four billion details (Renzulli and Reis, 1985a), or even the 30-page (two column, small print) summary in Renzulli and Reis (1991b), in the next few pages.

The *Schoolwide Enrichment Model* (SEM) is an adaptation of the earlier *Revolving Door Model* (RDIM; Renzulli, Reis, and Smith, 1981), with the new name emphasizing the literally "schoolwide" focus of the program. Like the RDIM, the SEM is based on the Enrichment Triad Model. One reviewer, displaying uncanny perceptiveness and foresight, said this of the Revolving Door Model, "The RDIM [now SEM] probably will be recognized as one of the most significant and revolutionary contributions to gifted education to date" (Davis, 1981b). Presently, the SEM is the single most popular programming model, and for good reasons.

The first high-appeal feature is Renzulli's *talent pool* approach to identification and selection. As we noted in Chapter 4, the usual strategy is to identify about 5 percent of the school's population in the fall; after which teachers stop worrying about who is "gifted" until fall of the next year. The names of students who are "in" are etched in granite; they begin participating in wonderful accelerated and enriched learning activities, most often in a pullout format; and parents of excluded students, and sometimes the excluded students themselves, complain of unfairness and elitism.

With the SEM, about 15 to 20 percent of the students are selected for the talent pool. Although schools may select students however they wish, Renzulli and Reis (1985a) recommend the procedure described in Chapter 4 and, briefly, in the previous section. The selection process is intended to *include* students, not *exclude* them; when in doubt, admit. Further, students not initially selected who strongly wish to conduct an independent project probably will be allowed to do so, and will automatically become part of the talent pool. Identification thus continues year round, the program serves more students, and the SEM generally avoids charges of elitism and unfairness.

The second high-appeal feature is the "schoolwide" one. We already noted that Enrich-

---

[1]The *talent pool* concept has appeared several times in this text. In Reis and Renzulli's (1986, p. 274) summary definition, "it is easiest to think of them as the top 15 to 20 percent of the general population in either general ability or in one or more specific areas of ability in the major categories of school achievement (i.e., math, science, language arts, etc.)."

ment Types I and II are good for all students. *In the SEM concrete plans are made to incorporate Types I and II enrichment in every class.* Sometimes this "general enrichment" is presented only to subgroups of students, depending upon difficulty level of the material, the size of the group that can be accommodated, or student interests.

An abbreviated orientation for all students (from Renzulli and Reis, 1985a) appears in Inset 7.1. This orientation contains an explanation of the three-ring model, the Enrichment Triad Model, and their participation in Types I and II enrichment. Note the invitations to all students to develop an interest in pursuing a Type III project. The orientation would be presented by the SEM resource teacher.

Talent Pool students request permission to pursue a Type III investigation by filling out a Light Bulb—an Action Information Message—which the regular teacher forwards to the resource teacher (Figure 7.2). If the project is approved, the student works with the resource teacher to plan and carry out the project, which may require a few days, weeks, or months. About 50 to 60 percent of talent pool students muster the creativity and motivation to pursue at least one Type III project each year.

Talent Pool students receive several types of enrichment and related services. Of course, they receive the same *general enrichment* experienced by other students; they also receive Type II enrichment related to skills needed for their particular project, as described earlier. In addition, Talent Pool students are helped to identify interests—perhaps using Renzulli's *Interest-a-Lyzer*—that might lead to a Type III project. The instrument helps students identify interests in arts and crafts, science, creative writing, the legal/political area, mathematics, management, history, athletic and outdoor activities, performing arts, business, consumer action, or ecology.

Another important component is *curriculum compacting*. The regular teacher assists Talent Pool students in compacting learning activities both to provide a more challenging curriculum and to "buy time" for the Talent Pool enrichment

activities and Type III projects. Curriculum typically is compacted in basic skills areas, particularly math, but also language arts, science, and social studies (Reis *et al.*, 1992). Areas of strength can be identified in students' records, standardized test scores, classwork, or teacher observations (Renzulli and Reis, 1991b). One compacting strategy is using pretests or end-of-unit tests to evaluate whether students already know the material. Another strategy is to accelerate the pace of instruction in an efficient and economical matter. In one study with high ability elementary students, Reis *et al.* (1992) reported no lowering of achievement whatever when content and instruction were reduced (compacted) a full 40 or 50 percent; in fact, science achievement *increased* with compacting. Further, students' school attitudes improved, and both students and teachers liked compacting.

The book *Schoolwide Enrichment Model* (Renzulli and Reis, 1985a) presents plenty of step-by-step explanations, examples, plans for organizing Type II activities in the regular classroom, Type I and Type II activity forms, materials specification forms, checklists for preparing Type III fairs, lists of outlets for Type III projects, descriptions and responsibilities of the Schoolwide Enrichment Team, teacher training activities (for example, a simulation of dealing with questions that newspaper reporters typically ask about programs for the gifted and talented), and more. There are forms for nearly everything—nomination forms, management plans, Light Bulbs, class survey sheets, parent questionnaire, student questionnaires, teacher questionnaires, letters to inform parents of their child's participation, student (and parent) product evaluation forms, and so on. Some of the forms serve as staff accountability checks, motivating everyone to do his or her job.

Finally, to reduce worries about not getting SEM "exactly right," Renzulli (1984) advised "I would like to emphasize that there is no such thing as a 'pure' Triad/RDIM [SEM] program. Each school district must examine its own philosophy, resources, and administrative structure and then adopt or adapt those parts of RDIM [SEM] that

INSET 7.1 _____

Schoolwide Enrichment Model: Orientation for All Students

Good morning, my name is _____, and I'm here to explain our enrichment program to you today. Have any of you seen this poster on my door (show poster or slide of Enrichment Triad Model)? Well, this is a picture of the model that we use for our enrichment program. Do any of you know what *enrichment* means? . . . Good, now let's talk about the Enrichment Triad Model.

Three different types of activities are a part of this model. Type I activities bring all of you in touch with topics, ideas, and areas of study you may never have heard about before. . . . You might learn about architecture, anthropology, art history, or other topics. Type I's are for *all* of you. . . . It may be a film or a speech, slide show, a display in your classroom, or even a beautiful poster. . . . Now, if any of you get very excited about a Type I, you should tell you classroom teacher. Remember that and we'll talk about why later.

The second part of the Triad Model is Type II activities. Type II involves skills that will help you become better at research, problem solving, writing, and even thinking. For example, you may learn how to complete an independent project, how to work on your own, or how to have lots of ideas. (If available, show slides or posters about creativity or critical thinking.) All of you will have some classroom involvement in Type II, but some of you will be involved in extra Type II training.

Let's talk about why! How many of you have ever seen this before? (Show poster or slide of three-ring model). This is our definition of what we call *gifted behavior*. Every single one of us is capable or able to show gifted behaviors in some areas in our lives. Some people do but some people do not! One of the things we hope our enrichment program will do is show and teach young people how to develop or learn to display gifted behaviors. How many of you are good at running? How many of you can draw well? How many of you can sing well? How many of you are good at daydreaming? Well, all of us have different talents. One part of this program will be to help you find your talent area! But some people in this room already have shown what they are good at doing. Some people in this room finish their school work early and are very good at subjects like reading, science, or math. Do you know who they might be? . . . These students will be coming to work on Type II in a resource room (with me or with _____) once or twice a week. . . . We call those students members of the Talent Pool. (Mention separate art or music Talent Pools, if they are to be established).

Being in the Talent Pool means that students will do some other Type II work at a time that your teacher believes they can leave your class. . . . Any of you may be able to become involved in the Talent Pool by doing excellent work, but remember—you are all going to be involved in Type I and Type II activities in your classroom anyway!

Now, being in the Talent Pool doesn't mean that someone is gifted! (Point to three-ring sign.) We believe that gifted behavior happens when someone has above average ability and *also works very hard*. That is what task commitment is all about! We also believe that gifted behavior happens when someone takes his or her creativity and works hard to be creative in the area where he or she has an above average ability. How many of you know what creativity is? (Show three-ring sign again.) This is where gifted behavior occurs and this is what the third part of the Enrichment Triad Model is all about. (Show Triad Model again.) Type III Enrichment is only for students who are willing to

(continued)

work very hard in an area in which they are interested. (Show examples of Type III enrichment products.) Type III's involve a lot of work. Some people work for many months and sometimes even a year or more to finish their Type III's.

Any of you can decide to try to do a Type III investigation. You should have some kind of question that you want to answer, some type of problem that you want to solve, or a very strong interest in some area like local history or creative writing or architecture. If you want to try a Type III, either your classroom teacher or I can help you. The first thing you should do is tell your teacher you have an idea and complete this Light Bulb (show slide or poster of an Action Information Message). Remember, a Type III starts to happen when you get your three rings together (hold up three-ring sign)! Now are there any questions?

Remember, *any* of you can fill out a light bulb to become involved in a Type III. . . . Any questions? (Review Types I, II, and III Enrichment.)

Abbreviated from Renzulli and Reis (1985a), by permission of Creative Learning Press.

take into account the unique differences that exist in each local school and district."

MULTIPLE MENU MODEL

Unlike the type of learning experiences in the Enrichment Triad Model and Schoolwide Enrichment Model, Renzulli's (1988) *Multiple Menu Model* focuses on ways to teach content knowledge in efficient and interesting ways. Said Renzulli, the model is a set of planning guides designed to help curriculum developers ". . . identify appropriate content or skills . . . examine various instructional sequences and activity options . . . (and) prepare a blueprint for fitting together the pieces that will allow content and process to work together in a harmonious and effective fashion."

The five planning "menus" are designed to provide guidance for designing curriculum that is consistent with the goals of gifted education.

Knowledge Menu. The knowledge menu received the most attention in Renzulli's (1988) description. Rather than choices, this menu recommends a desirable sequence for teaching knowledge in a particular area.

The menu includes four subcategories or steps:

First, *location, definition, and organization* introduces the learner to ". . . the general nature of a field, the various subdivisions of knowledge within that field, and the specific mission and characteristics of any given subdivision . . . (and) . . . helps the learner see the big picture." Using a branching diagram that visually illustrates the organization of a field of study, the curriculum developer would address the purposes of a field; subareas of concentration; kinds of questions asked in subareas; sources of data; basic reference books and professional journals; major data bases; major events, persons, places, and beliefs; and insiders' humor, trivia, scandals, etc.

Second are *basic principles and functional concepts*. Basic principles are the generally agreed upon truths in an area (for example, the earth orbits the sun every 365¼ days). The functional concepts largely serve as the vocabulary of a field as found in a glossary.

Third, *knowledge about specifics* refers to important facts, conventions, trends, classifications, criteria, principles and generalizations, and theories and structures that comprise a field. About 95 percent of the information in a field

TO: _____ Talent Pool Class Teacher

_____ Program Coordinator

_____ Other

ACTION INFORMATION MESSAGE

MEMO

FROM: _____ Student (print name)

_____ Teacher (print name)

_____ Other

General Curriculum Area: _____

_____

Idea for Investigation or Study: _____

_____

_____

In the space below, provide a brief description of evidence of high levels of task commitment or creativity on the part of a student or small group of students. Indicate any ideas you may have for advanced level follow-up activities, suggested resources or ways to focus the interest into a first-hand investigative experience.

Date Received _____

Date of Interview _____

Mentor Located _____ Yes _____ No

Name of person who will be responsible for facilitating this Type III

Copyright © 1981 Creative Learning Press, Inc. • P.O. Box 320 • Mansfield Center, CT 06250
ALL RIGHTS RESERVED

FIGURE 7.2. Action Information Message.

will be in this "warehouse of information," according to Renzulli.

Fourth, *knowledge about methodology* refers to standard investigative procedures in an area, namely, how to identify problems, state hypotheses, identify data sources, locate or construct data-gathering instruments, summarize and analyze data, draw conclusions, and report findings.

Instructional Objectives/Student Activities Menu. The first of four subsections of the instructional objectives/student activities menu, *assimilation and retention*, refers to information input processes: listening, observing, touching, reading, manipulating, note-taking, etc. The second section of the menu, *information analysis*, suggests ". . . ways information can be processed in order to achieve greater levels of understanding," for example, classifying, ordering, gathering data, interpreting, exploring alternatives, and concluding and explaining. The third section, *information synthesis and application*, deals with the output or products of the thinking processes, for example, writing, speaking, constructing, or performing. Finally, the fourth subsection, *evaluation*, concerns review and judgment of information according to personal values or conventional standards.

Instructional Strategies Menu. The instructional strategies menu itemizes teaching and learning options familiar to all teachers: drill and recitation, lecture, discussion, peer tutoring, learning center activity, simulation and role playing, learning games, and others.

Instructional Sequence Menu. The instructional sequence menu deals with the organization and sequence of events that help maximize the outcomes of planned learning activities. Based on Gagné's (1974) conditions of learning model, this fixed-sequence menu includes gaining attention, informing students of objectives, relating the topic to previously learned material, presenting the material (with either passive or participative student roles), assessing performance and providing feedback, and providing opportunities for transfer and application.

Artistic Modification Menu. Finally, Renzulli recommends that teachers ". . . make their own creative contribution" to the lesson to increase interest and excitement. The artistic modification menu suggests sharing personal knowledge, experiences, beliefs, insiders' information, interpretations, controversies, biases or ". . . additional ways teachers might personalize the material."

Many of the components of the multiple menu model are standard good teaching practices (Davis and Thomas, 1989). However, as Renzulli states, it does ". . . direct us to consider a broad range of options, and to interrelate the many factors that must be considered when attempting to achieve balance and comprehensiveness in curriculum development." For teachers of the gifted, the Multiple Menu Model provides an organizational framework for the creative development of special curriculum in areas that are not typically covered in ordinary school programming.

PYRAMID PROJECT

The *Pyramid Project* grew from many of the conclusions and recommendations of the Richardson Study, a survey of existing G/T programs (Cox, Daniel, and Boston, 1985; Cox and Daniel, 1988; Feldman, 1985; Ondo and Session, 1989). Some pertinent conclusions were: Many current programs for the gifted make no provision for the brightest and most creative youngsters; rigid cutoff scores unreasonably exclude many able learners; many programs are fragmented and discontinuous; and the popular pullout plan is a (you guessed it) ". . . part-time solution to a full-time problem" and is problematic and divisive, for example, causing students to miss work they need, or to make up work they do not need (Feldman, 1985).

Said Cox, the goal of the Pyramid Project is to provide appropriate instruction for all capable students of all ages, from above-average to the highly

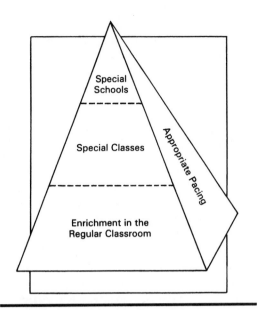

FIGURE 7.3.   The Pyramid Concept.

Reprinted from *Educating Able Learners: Programs and Promising Practices* by June Cox, Neil Daniel, and Bruce O. Boston, copyright © 1985. Reprinted by permission of J. Cox, Gifted Students Institute, and the University of Texas Press.

gifted, in all subjects every day (Feldman, 1985). About one-fourth of all students in Cox's pioneering greater Forth Worth, Texas, Pyramid Project are defined as "able learners."

As represented in the broad base of the Pyramid Model (Figure 7.3), the largest number of able learners receive advanced material in the regular classroom, for example, using learning centers, flexible grouping (e.g., for math and language arts), cluster grouping, individualized instructional methods, cross-grade grouping, curriculum compacting, and resource room enrichment and projects. Cox argued that classroom teachers can do the job of enrichment if they get training, support, and guidance. She recommends Renzulli's Enrichment Triad Model as a good curriculum guide.

Moving to the midsection of the pyramid, a smaller group of more superior students are placed in full-time special classes. Also, students can participate in dual enrollment—elementary students can enroll concurrently in middle school for their strongest subjects, middle school students can enroll in high school, and high school students may take college courses.

At the top of the pyramid, a still smaller number of students with even more specialized needs are served by special (magnet) schools. At the high school level, these schools focus on math, science, languages, or an International Baccalaureate program.

However, even in Cox's own Pyramid Project special schools for students at the top of the pyramid are only a big-city option, that is, they apparently exist just in Forth Worth. Smaller school districts accommodate student needs at the elementary level in the regular classroom using options noted above, as well as special classes. Secondary schools in these smaller districts use special (advanced) classes, for example, in math, science, English/language arts, history/social studies, and fine arts; honors courses; AP courses; and concurrent enrollment arranged with a local junior college.

The concept of *flexible pacing* runs from the base to the peak of the pyramid—the plan requires teachers to recognize that all students do not learn at the same rate. Said Ondo and Session (1989, p. 47), "Basic to the pyramid concept . . . is the conviction that students should move ahead as they master content, concepts, and skills. Schools accelerate the educational process for bright students either by moving students to higher grade levels in their areas of accomplishment or by bringing the advanced material down to students." Ondo and Session noted that flexible pacing primarily takes these forms in the Pyramid Model: early entrance policies, advanced level courses, dual enrollment, compacted courses, grade skipping, and credit by examination.

The Pyramid plan requires longitudinal and interdisciplinary planning by committees of teachers and administrators; continuous staff development; support services, such as special clerical help and resource teachers; a manageable record-keeping system that allows teachers to monitor individual student progress; and cooperation among parents, administrators, and teachers.

PURDUE THREE-STAGE ENRICHMENT MODEL

The *Purdue Three-Stage Enrichment Model* (Feldhusen and Kolloff, 1981, 1986; Kolloff and Feldhusen, 1984) centers upon three levels of skill development. While fostering creativity clearly is central, the training also aims at strengthening many types of thinking skills, convergent problem solving, research skills, and independent learning.

Stage 1 focuses upon the development of basic *Divergent and Convergent Thinking Abilities*, sometimes referred to as *process thinking skills* (Feldhusen and Kolloff, 1986). Instructional activities include relatively short-term, teacher-led exercises and workbook activities mainly in creative thinking, but also other thinking skills in verbal and nonverbal areas. Content and basic skills in science, math, and language arts also can be included in Stage 1 in conjunction with teaching creative and other thinking skill processes. Creativity workbooks by Stanish (e.g., 1977) and thinking skills workbooks by Harnadek (e.g., 1976), Black and Black (e.g., 1986, 1987, 1988) may be used in Stage 1.[2]

Some creativity exercises are, for example, listing unusual uses for trash bags, thinking of improvements for a bicycle, predicting outcomes of unlikely events (What would happen if there were no television or no McDonald's?), or ". . . designing a vehicle of the future using anything you might find in a junkyard" (Kolloff and Feldhusen, 1981). Such exercises are assumed to develop such creative abilities as ideational fluency, originality, flexibility, and elaboration. Thinking skills exercises (e.g., classifying, comparing, analogical

thinking) might stretch logic, critical thinking, analysis, synthesis, evaluation, decision-making, and others.

Stage 2, called *Development of Creative Problem Solving Abilities*, focuses on more complex and practical strategies and systems. Included are creative thinking techniques (e.g., brainstorming and the *synectics* methods; see Chapter 10); the Creative Problem Solving (CPS) model; Future Problem Solving, which is based on the CPS model; Odyssey of the Mind; and other problem solving applications and experiences.

Stage 3 activities aim at the *Development of Independent Study Skills*. Said Feldhusen and Kolloff (1981), "Stage 3 projects should involve gifted youngsters in challenging efforts to define and clarify a problem, ambitious data gathering from books and other resources, interpretation of findings, and the development of creative ways of communicating results." Some examples of Stage 3 projects are writing haiku, short stories, or plays (which are produced), investigating alternate waste disposal systems (which one group presented to the Lafayette City Council), and researching backgrounds of community leaders (which one group presented on local radio).

The Purdue Three-Stage Model might be implemented in a pullout plan, using the first few weeks for Stage 1, followed by Stage 2 activities through weeks 12 or 16, and Stage 3 independent study and projects thereafter.

GUILFORD/MEEKER STRUCTURE OF INTELLECT MODEL

Many people are acquainted with Guilford's original 1967 model of intelligence that includes 120 cells created from the combinations of *contents, products*, and *operations* (see Figure 7.4). For the record, his 1977 model extended the cube to 150 cells by replacing "figural" with *visual* and *auditory*; in 1988 the number of cells grew to 180 by dividing "memory" into *memory recording* (short-term) and *memory retention* (long-term). Joy Paul Guilford, who never used his first name,

---

[2]Creativity workbooks by Stanish and others are described in Chapter 10; thinking skills programs and workbooks appear in Chapter 11.

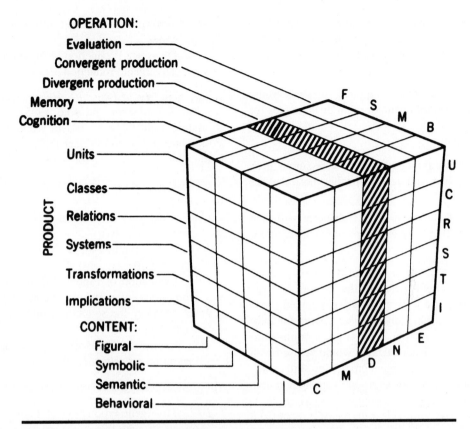

FIGURE 7.4.   The Guilford (1967) Structure of Intellect Model.
From J.P. Guilford, *The Nature of Human Intelligence* (New York: McGraw-Hill, 1967). Reprinted with permission.

invested over three decades creating tests to measure those 180 abilities.

As an example, the darkened slab of the model in Figure 7.4 includes the operations of *divergent production*. Somewhere in that slab will be a cell identified as the "divergent production (operation) of symbolic (content) units (product)," or just *DSU*. Some tests of DSU—or *Word Fluency*—ask the examinee to list words with the first and last letters specified (for example, R_____M); list words that include one, two, or three specified letters; or list words that rhyme with a specified word (for example, *roam*).

Because the main thrust of this section is on the Meekers' (Meeker, 1969; Meeker and Meeker,

1986) use of just 90 cells of Guilford's 1967 model, we will trouble the reader only with Guilford's original model. Meeker and Meeker's (1986) 90 SOI abilities—considered 90 different kinds of intelligence—are comprised of all combinations of Guilford's five *operations* and six *products*, but just three *contents* (figural, symbolic, semantic).

According to Meeker and Meeker (1986, p. 202), "SOI tests have been used in gifted programs in two ways, as a means of identifying gifted students and as a basis for designing individual courses of training within the gifted program." That is, some SOI tests are used for identification by examining students' profiles of scores. The training component amounts largely to a diagnostic-prescriptive approach to evaluating and strengthening SOI abilities that the Meekers believe are especially important. In four steps:

1. Identify the abilities required for the learning of reading or arithmetic or math or requisites for any given job.

2. Test for those abilities.

3. Teach any abilities that are low, maintain those that are gifted, and develop further those that are average.

4. Compare the level of performance with and without SOI training to document the difference it can make.

The Meekers have devised materials to exercise and strengthen each of the 90 abilities. The materials come in two forms, *mini-lesson plans* for group teaching, and *self-help plans* for individualized instruction. As examples, brainstorming and other ideational tasks would be used with students weak in divergent production skills; critical thinking activities are used to strengthen both cognition and evaluation operations. After teachers become comfortable with the SOI model and the recommended tasks, they will be able to select other instructional materials that provide training beyond the exercises in the SOI *Sourcebooks*.

The SOI tests, each of which actually consists of a subset of tests, include the *Gifted Screening Test, Atypical Gifted Screening Test, Test of Learning Abilities, Process and Diagnostic Test, Reasoning Readiness Test*, and *Personal Productivity Assessment*.

The SOI *Gifted Screening Test* includes these 10 subtests:

CFU, Cognition of Figural Units
CMU, Cognition of Semantic Units
CMR, Cognition of Semantic Relations
CMS, Cognition of Semantic Systems
MSU, Memory of Symbolic Units
MSS, Memory of Symbolic Systems
NST, Convergent Production of Symbolic Transformations

NSI, Convergent Production of Symbolic Implications
DFU, Divergent Production of Figural Units
DMU, Divergent Production of Semantic Units

The SOI *Test of Learning Abilities* (SOI-LA Test; Meeker, Meeker, and Roid, 1985) measures 26 abilities said to be central to reading, math, writing, creativity, and critical thinking. For example, abilities necessary for *reading* include:

CFU, Cognition of Figural Units (visual closure)
CFC, Cognition of Figural Classes (visual conceptualization)
EFU, Evaluation of Figural Units (visual discrimination)
EFC, Evaluation of Figural Classes (judging similarities and matching of concepts)
MSU, Memory for Semantic Units (visual attending)
MSS, Memory for Symbolic Units (visual concentration for sequencing)

Abilities necessary for *creativity* include:

DFU, Divergent Production of Figural Units (creativity with things; figural-spatial)
DSR, Divergent Production of Symbolic Relations (creativity with math facts)
DMU, Divergent Production of Semantic Units (creativity with words and ideas; verbal)

The Meekers' SOI approach presents a different perspective on the conceptualization and identification of gifted and talented students, both majority and minority. Meeker (1978) argued that Anglo children, even before they enter school, have the cognitive abilities necessary for learning—for example, those itemized earlier. However, minority children from non-English-speaking, low-education, low-income families often do not. Therefore, with identification based upon intelligence tests, minority children often are excluded from participation in gifted programs. Within the multifaceted SOI theory, however, Meeker finds that non-Anglos—Native American, Hispanic

American, and African-American students—score higher on different SOI abilities than Anglo children. Selection for program participation may be based upon these high, measured abilities. Hengen (1983), for example, used the SOI-LA test to identify gifted native Indians in Regina, Canada. As a group, they scored higher than others on tests of figural-spatial ability. Further, he taught critical thinking with these students by using figural tasks almost exclusively. For further information, contact the SOI Institute, Vida, Oregon.

TREFFINGER'S MODEL FOR INCREASING SELF-DIRECTEDNESS

For the most part, throughout children's educational lives they are told what, when, how, and where to learn. Further, their learning almost always is evaluated by others. They cannot be expected suddenly to become efficient, self-initiated, and self-directed learners with little or no experience or training. Even though gifted children typically are more independent and self-directed than others, many still require help in developing the skills and attitudes necessary for independent study or research.

Donald Treffinger (1975, 1978; Treffinger and Barton, 1988; see also Treffinger, 1986b) developed a seemingly logical four-step plan for teaching increasing degrees of independent, self-initiated learning. (1) In the initial teacher-directed step (*command style*), the teacher prescribes the activities for the entire class or for individual students. The working time, location, end product, and evaluation criteria also are teacher determined. (2) In the first self-directed step (*task style*), the teacher creates learning activities or project alternatives (for example, learning centers) from which students make a selection. (3) In the second self-directed step (*peer-partner style*), students assume a more active role, participating in decisions about their learning activities, goals, and evaluation. The teacher ". . . involves the pupils in creating choices and options concerning what will be learned" (Treffinger, 1975). For example, the teacher discusses with the class topics or projects for

individual or group work. (4) Finally, in the *self-directed style* students are able to create the choices, make the selection, and carry out the activity—in a self-selected location over a self-selected period of time. The students also evaluate their own progress. Of course, the teacher is available to assist.

Students naturally differ in their abilities and experience in directing their own work. Therefore, the teacher must determine the level of self-directedness for which a student is ready. Treffinger (1975) provides checklists designed to help identify the level of help a given student requires. For example, a student would be ready for the fourth stage of self-directedness activity if (1) the student can evaluate progress mainly without teacher advice, and (2) the student can identify strengths and weaknesses in his or her own work or products using the same criteria others would use.

As some general recommendations for fostering self-directedness, Treffinger (1978) suggested:

1. Do not smother self-direction by doing things for children that they can do (or can learn to do) for themselves.

2. Develop an attitude of openness and support for self-directed learning.

3. Emphasize the interrelatedness and continuity of knowledge to help students synthesize and relate various topics and problems.

4. Provide training in problem solving and skills of inquiry and independent research; that is, help students learn to diagnose needs, develop a plan, locate resources, carry out appropriate activities, and evaluate and present the results.

5. Treat difficult situations at school or home as opportunities for independent problem solving, not as problems requiring the unilateral wisdom of an adult.

AUTONOMOUS LEARNER MODEL: BETTS

While Treffinger's model outlines four steps for increasing self-directedness, George Betts' (1985, 1991) *Autonomous Learner Model* (ALM) is a total programming guide (Figure 7.5). In the elementary school the model would be incorporated into a pullout or similar plan, with students meeting two days per week for about 2½ hours. In junior or senior high school the ALM would be installed as an elective course.

According to Betts, the ALM was designed to help students develop more positive self-concepts, comprehend their own giftedness, develop social skills, increase their knowledge in a variety of subject areas, develop their thinking, decision-making and problem-solving skills, demonstrate responsibility for their own learning in and out of school, and ultimately become responsible, creative, independent learners. Such goals square very well with purposes of G/T programs.

Space will not permit a complete explanation of the details of Betts's model; the interested reader should see Betts (1985, 1991) and Betts and Knapp (1981). As an overview, the *Autonomous Learner Model* divides into the five major dimensions summarized in Figure 7.5: Orientation, Individual Development, Enrichment Activities, Seminars, and In-Depth Study.

Orientation. The *orientation* dimension aims at acquainting students, teachers, administrators, and parents with central concepts in gifted education (for example, the nature of giftedness and creativity) and the specifics of the *Autonomous Learner Model* (for example, program goals, opportunities, expectations). Students learn about themselves and what the program has to offer.

Group building and self-understanding exercises give students an opportunity to learn more about each other and themselves and about group processes. A sample exercise is "starve your vulture," best used in an overnight retreat. A "vulture" lives on two types of food—self put-downs and put-downs by others. As your vulture (who lives in your stomach) gets fat on these put-downs, your self-esteem is reduced. After the details of vultures and put-downs are reviewed, students participate in a "Starve Your Vulture" campaign, with signs and stories about the vulture. Statistics are kept on how frequently students feed or starve their own vulture.

Individual Development. The *individual development* dimension of the ALM focuses more clearly on developing skills, concepts, and attitudes that promote lifelong independent, autonomous learning. As shown in Figure 7.5, four basic concerns are learning skills (for example, thinking skills and research skills), personal understanding (for example, of strengths and weaknesses), interpersonal skills (for example, communication and leadership skills), and career involvement (exploration).

Enrichment Activities. Betts's third dimension of *enrichment* activities focuses on "student-based content," that is, students decide what they want to study. Students already may have preferred topics, or "passion areas," that they wish to pursue. They also study "related passion areas" plus unrelated areas. Students may explore an area and make a presentation about it to the group; they may conduct a research-type investigation; they may par-

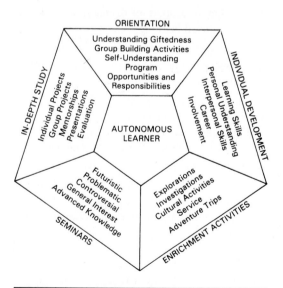

FIGURE 7.5. Autonomous Learner Model (Betts, 1985).

Reprinted by permission of the author and Autonomous Learning Publications.

ticipate in cultural activities, such as visiting a museum, play, concert, speech, or art display; they may perform a service, such as working with the elderly or collecting food or money for shut-ins; or they may plan an "adventure trip," such as studying the geology and archaeology of the Grand Canyon or the cultural aspects of San Francisco.

Seminars.   The *seminar* dimension is designed to give each person in a small group of three to five students the opportunity to research a topic, present it in a seminar format to the rest of the group and perhaps others, and evaluate their seminar according to criteria selected by the group. Students learn to proceed through three steps of presenting general information to the audience to promote understanding of the topic; facilitating discussion of the topic to involve the audience in thinking; and bringing the discussion and activities to a close.

In-depth Study.   Finally, in the fifth ALM dimension of *in-depth study* students pursue areas of interest in long-term individual or small-group studies. These activities resemble Renzulli Type III projects, and students decide what will be learned, what help will be necessary, what the final product will be, how it will be presented, and how the entire learning process will be evaluated.

Overall, the *Autonomous Learner Model* is a very reasonable programming guide that has been installed in many school districts in the United States and Canada.

WILLIAMS' MODEL FOR DEVELOPING THINKING AND FEELING PROCESSES

Frank Williams (1970, 1982, 1986) developed a curriculum model that originally was intended to help teachers enrich educational programs for all students. While not designed specifically for G/T students, it is often used in gifted programs.

The Williams model, summarized in Figure 7.6, is based on three dimensions that may be described as *content, strategy*, and *process* (Will-

FIGURE 7.6.   The Williams Model.

From F. Williams, *Classroom Ideas for Encouraging Thinking and Feeling.* (Buffalo, NY: D.O.K. Publishers, Inc.).

iams, 1979). Dimension 1 is *Curriculum (Subject Matter Content)*, with the six levels of art, music, science, social studies, arithmetic, and language. Dimension 2 is *Teacher Behavior (Strategies or Modes of Teaching)* and includes 18 activities and skills (defined in Table 7.2) that teachers may use to teach skills in any of the 6 content areas.

Dimension 3—containing the "thinking and feeling processes" for which Williams is fa-

mous—is called *Pupil Behaviors*. Its eight levels include the four *Cognitive (Intellective)* processes of fluency, flexibility, originality, and elaboration, plus the four *Affective (Feeling)* processes of curiosity (willingness), risk taking (courage), complexity (challenge), and imagination (intuition). The "D Formula" in Figure 7.6 indicates that curriculum content (D1) interacts with teaching strategies (D2) to produce the pupil behaviors (D3).

TABLE 7.2   Williams' Teaching Strategies

Paradoxes	Self-contradictory statements or observations
Attributes	Inherent properties, traits or characteristics
Analogies	Similarities or situations of likeness
Discrepancies	Unknown elements or missing links
Provocative Questions	Inquiries bringing forth exploration or discovery
Examples of Change	Exploring the dynamics of things by alterations, modifications or substitutions
Examples of Habit	Sensing rigidity and habit-bound thinking
Organized Random Search	Organized structure randomly leading to a production
Skills of Search	Skills of historical, descriptive, or experimental search
Study Creative People-Process	Analyze traits and study processes of eminent people
Evaluate Situations	Setting criteria, deciding, critical thinking
Creative Reading Skill	Idea generation through reading
Creative Listening Skill	Idea generation through listening
Creative Writing Skill	Self expression through writing
Visualization Skill	Expressing ideas in visual form
Tolerance for Ambiguity	Tolerating open-ended situations without forcing closure
Intuitive Expression	Sensing inward hunches and expressing emotional feelings
Adjustment to Development	Developing from rather than adjusting to experiences or situations

Frank Williams, "Williams' Strategies to Orchestrate Renzulli's Triad," *G/C/T* (Sept.-Oct. 1979), 2–6, 10. Reprinted by permission.

Now with 6 subject matters, 18 teaching activities, and 8 thinking and feeling processes, there are a total of 864 (6 × 18 × 8) combinations of classroom activities. Williams (1970, 1982) outlines hundreds of activities and tasks designed (1) for a specific subject matter, (2) using one of the teaching methods, and (3) intended to strengthen one of the thinking or feeling skills. Some of the learning activities are considered appropriate for several cells in the Figure 7.6 model.

MULTIPLE-TALENT TOTEM POLE MODEL

In Chapter 1 we reviewed Taylor's (1978, 1986) *Multiple-Talent Totem Poles* (Figure 1.3) as an approach to defining giftedness, one which argues that if you look at enough talents, almost everyone will be at least above average (if not outstanding) in something. Some have created curriculum for the gifted by designing activities and exercises aimed at strengthening many of Taylor's talent areas (e.g., Eberle, 1974).

Schlichter's (1986a, 1986b, 1987; Schlichter and Palmer, 1993) *Talents Unlimited* is a staff development model for training teachers to recognize and nurture student potential in the six talents described earlier by Taylor (1978). The training involves four major categories of activities:

1. Input sessions on multiple talent theory and 22 specific thinking skill components.

2. Modeling and demonstration of Talents instruction.

3. Classroom practice teaching sessions.

4. One-to-one and small-group planning sessions.

As examples of how teachers are coached in concepts and strategies for teaching the talents: *Productive thinking* is strengthened by having students generate many, different, and unusual ideas and add details. *Decision making* involves having students outline, weigh, make final judgments, and defend a decision on the many alternatives to a problem. *Planning* involves designing the means to implement an idea, identifying needed resources, planning the steps, pinpointing possible problems, and making improvements to the plan. *Forecasting* involves having students make predictions about possible causes and/or effects of various phenomena. Teaching *communication* focuses on using and interpreting verbal and nonverbal forms of communication to express ideas, feelings, and needs. *Academics* talent is strengthened via acquiring information and concepts to form a good knowledge base in a given topic.

According to Schlichter (1986b), students themselves should be taught the model to help them "become actively involved in efforts to improve their thinking skills" (p. 362). The *Talent Train* (Figure 7.7) is used—by adding car after car to the Academics engine—to explain the Talents

FIGURE 7.7.   The Talent Train, for introducing elementary students to the Talents Unlimited model.

Reprinted by permission of Carol Schlichter. Original concept by artist Donna H. Goodman.

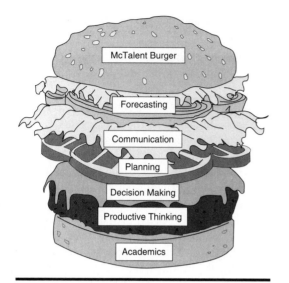

FIGURE 7.8.   The McTalent Burger, for explaining the Talents Unlimited to the Secondary Power model to students in grades 7–12.
Reprinted by permission of Carol Schlichter. Original concept by artist Donna H. Goodman.

Unlimited model to elementary children. The *McTalent Burger* (Figure 7.8) introduces secondary students to the model; the basic Academic bun represents the knowledge base which is enhanced with the other tasty ingredients represented by the five creative and critical thinking talents.

DIAGONAL CURRICULUM MODEL: KRANZ

Enrichment sometimes is called *horizontal* expansion of curriculum, while acceleration is called *vertical* expansion. Kranz (1993) views her *Diagonal Curriculum Model* (DCM) as a combination of the two. Kranz's DCM emphasizes interdisciplinary themes and concepts that cut across preferably three areas. For example, an AIDS theme can integrate together sociological, biomedical, and geographical (e.g., human migration) components. A theme of *balance* ties together mathematics, art, and music. Near Dr. Martin Luther King's birthday, a thematic frame-

work emphasizing *struggle* (perhaps entitled "Dreaming the Impossible, Achieving the Impossible") would include conceptual problems of African-Americans, Native Americans, Mexican-Americans, women, and labor, which can be tied to *obstacles* (which impede but entice) and *art* (which, like dreams, helps make the impossible possible).

According to Kranz, themes and concepts should focus on significant, broad-based conceptual issues or problems that are neither too extensive nor too trivial; that can be presented at a proper level of depth and complexity; and that can be repeated in more complex forms at higher age levels (spiraling). Sometimes teacher teams are needed to plan the curriculum. For example, a teacher strong in science (biology) might work with another strong in humanities (philosophy and art) to create a unit on social implications of genetics, and which includes poetry (thematic title: "Who am I? What am I?").

Kranz (1993) presents many good ideas for interdisciplinary lessons that cut across math, science, and art.

COMMENT

The thoughtful program planner should consider all of the models in this chapter, along with specific strategies for acceleration, enrichment, grouping, counseling, career education, affective development, the teaching of creativity, critical thinking and other thinking skills, and other possibilities. Select what seems to best meet the needs of the students in your district or school. There can be no single "best" program; aim for the most suitable combination for your particular situation.

SUMMARY

Some of the eleven curriculum models make highly specific procedural recommendations, others make more general suggestions.

In Renzulli's Enrichment Triad model, Type I enrichment (general exploratory activities) exposes students to a variety of topics; Type II (group training activities) focuses on creativity and other thinking skills, learning-to-learn skills, communication skills, and resource and information retrieval skills; Type III is investigations of real problems. Types I and II are deemed appropriate for all students.

The Secondary Triad Model requires talent pool classes, similar to honors classes, in each discipline. Compacting "buys time" for Type III projects in the particular area.

The Schoolwide Enrichment Model is a complete programming guide that includes Types I and II enrichment in the regular classroom for all students. Talent pool students who show creativity and motivation volunteer for Type III projects. Identifying student interests and curriculum compacting are central. A thick book presents a profusion of details.

Renzulli's Multiple Menu Model is a series of five planning guides or "menus" that suggest sequences and alternatives for teaching content efficiently: a knowledge menu, instructional objectives/student activities menu, instructional strategies menu, instructional sequence menu, and an artistic modification menu.

The Pyramid Project is a three-level schooling plan intended to overcome many criticisms of G/T programs, especially the popular pullout plan. Above-average students are mainstreamed in the regular classroom, more able students are placed in full-time special classes, and the most able students attend magnet or residential schools.

Feldhusen's Three-Stage Enrichment Model focuses mainly on fostering creative thinking, but also on research and independent-learning skills and positive self-concepts. Stage 1 develops basic divergent and convergent thinking abilities, as well as basic skills, largely with short-term exercises. Stage 2 involves more complex creative problem solving, partly by teaching creativity techniques and using Future Problem Solving and Odyssey of the Mind. Stage 3 focuses on developing independent study and research skills via independent projects.

The Meekers use 90 of Guilford's (1967) 120 SOI abilities for (1) identifying giftedness and (2) diagnosing and remediating specific learning abilities, particularly those relating to reading, math, writing, creativity, and critical thinking. The SOI approach may to used to identify gifted minority students.

Treffinger outlined four steps in increasing self-directedness. (1) The command style is totally teacher-directed; (2) in the task style students select from among teacher-prepared activities; (3) the peer-partner style includes more student decisions about learning goals, activities, and evaluation; (4) in the self-directed style students create the choices, make the selections, and choose the location and the amount of working time. Some general recommendations for fostering self-directedness included encouraging self-directedness, providing training in problem solving and inquiry, and using home problems as an opportunity for independent problem solving.

Betts's Autonomous Learner Model, a relatively complete programming guide, includes the five main dimensions of orienting students and others to giftedness and to the content and purposes of the program; individual development in areas of learning skills, personal understanding, interpersonal skills, and career development; student-selected enrichment activities; seminars; and individual or small-group in-depth studies.

The Williams model includes classroom activities suggested by many combinations of subject-matter content (6 types), teaching strategies (18 types), and his eight "thinking and feeling" processes.

The Taylor Multiple-Talent Totem Pole Model suggests that learning activities focus upon developing academic ability, creativity, planning/organizing, communicating, forecasting/predicting, and decision making/evaluating. Schlichter's Talents Unlimited program trains teachers to teach totem pole talents.

Kranz's Diagonal Curriculum Model emphasizes an interdisciplinary approach that combines enrichment and acceleration.

APPENDIX 7.1 POSSIBLE TOPICS FOR ENRICHMENT ACTIVITIES

Visual Arts, Performing Arts

Acting
Architecture
Art appreciation
Artists
Ballet
Candle making
Cartooning
Folk art
Dance, choreography
Designing (clothes, toys, machines, etc.)
Folk music
Graphics
Leather craft
Mime, pantomime
Music composition
Musical instruments
Opera
Photography, cameras
Political satire
Print making
Radio shows
Sculpture (clay, metal, wood, etc.)
Silk screening
Television
Theater—dramatic production, acting techniques, dramatic literature, set design, lighting, creative dramatics, improvisational theatre, history of theater, makeup

Antiques
Art history
Art in various cultures
Batik
Calligraphy
Costume design
Folk music
Dance history
Drawing
Film making (animation, drama)
Jewelry making
Macrame
Movie making
Music history
Musicians
Painting
Plays
Pottery, ceramics
Puppet making
Rug hooking
Shakespeare
Slide show making
Soft sculpture
Weaving

Math, Science, Computers

Aeronautics
Anatomy
Animals, animal behavior
Aquarium planning
Botany
Chemistry
Computer repair
Diseases
Electricity, electronics
Engineering
Forestry
Geology

Agriculture
Archaeology
Astronomy
Biology
Brain science
Computer programming
Conservation
Ecology
Energy—solar, geothermal, tidal, wind, etc.
Evolution
Fossils
Genetics

APPENDIX 7.1 (Continued)

Horticulture
Math—algebra, geometry, measurement, math
puzzles, statistics, probability
Metals
Microbiology
Minerology, rocks
Natural resources
Nutrition
Ornithology
Physiology
Prehistoric animals
Robots
Scientists
Space, space travel

Icthyology
Marine biology
Medicine, health
Meteorology
Microscopes
Money management
Nuclear energy
Optics, optometry
Physics
Pollution
Reptiles
Rocketry
Solar power
Veterinary science

Literature, Writing, Communication

Broadcasting
Literature appreciation
Mythology
Play writing
Short story writing
Sports writing
Word processing

Journalism
Mysteries
Poetry writing
Public speaking
Speed reading
Typing

Social Sciences, Culture, Language

African-American history
Alcohol, drug abuse
Anthropology
Archaeology
Children, child development
Contemporary cultures
Current events
Debate
Editorial writing
Etymology
Festivals, holidays
Foreign languages
Geology
Government (U.S., foreign)
History (local, state, U.S., Russian, military, etc.)
Legends, myths
Minority groups
Parapsychology, occult
Philosophy
Political cartoons

Ancient Egypt, Greece, Rome, China
Aztecs, Mayas, Incas
Careers
Civil rights
Crime, criminology, prisons
Death, dying
Divorce
Elections, voting
Famous people
Folklore
Future thinking
Geography, mapping
Handicapped people
Humor
Law, courts
Linguistics
Newspapers
Poetry
Political science
Population problems

APPENDIX 7.1 (Continued)

Prehistoric life
Problems of the elderly
Public opinion surveys
Social problems
Sociology
Women's rights

Presidents
Psychology, mental illness
Religion
Sign language
Travel

Business, Economics

Accounting
Banking
Economics (models, theories)
Insurance
Operating a small business
Transportation, trucking

Advertising
Careers
Finance
Law, lawyers
Stock market

Miscellaneous

Bridge
Careers
Coins, stamps
Creativity
History of football
Interior decorating
Law enforcement
Running
Test taking

Bicycles, bicycling
Chess
College preparation
Gardening
Horses
Karate
Magic
Sailing

CHAPTER 8

AFFECTIVE LEARNING AND LEADERSHIP

A strong drive among the gifted to excel, and succeeding at it, should provide them with better self-concepts. However, . . . the evidence is equivocal.

Abraham J. Tannenbaum (1991, p. 35)

This chapter looks at two important goals of programs for gifted students: affective learning and leadership. The topic of *affective learning* runs through many chapters. We frequently have stressed the importance, for example, of building good self-concepts, healthy social adjustment, high academic and career aspirations, constructive attitudes and values, and self-motivated learning. These topics are important for all gifted students, but take special significance in relation to "at risk" gifted—students who are culturally different, economically disadvantaged (Chapter 12), or underachieving (Chapter 13); students with handicaps (Chapter 15); and sometimes female gifted students (Chapter 14). Chapter 17 on counseling, especially, will focus on understanding and aiding the self-understanding and social and emotional development of gifted students.

Leadership is one of the five U.S. Department of Education categories of giftedness. In recent years several programs and strategies have clarified the nature of "leadership" and specified how leadership traits and skills can be taught to gifted and other students. We will explore some of these.

AFFECTIVE LEARNING

In our early discussion of characteristics of gifted and talented children we noted that, compared with the average, G/T students are better able to understand moral issues and to be honest, truthful, and ethical. If they are moderate-to-high achievers, they are also likely to have good self-concepts, high self-esteem, and reasonably high levels of achievement needs. Nonetheless, just as we try to strengthen the cognitive skills of students who already are cognitively superior, we also can help affectively superior students to better understand themselves and their values, to be more empathic towards others, and generally to acquire high-level values, ethics, achievement needs, and humanistic attitudes.

It also is true that some gifted students do go astray morally and legally, and many drop out of high school and college. They forfeit both their full development and self-actualization and their potential contributions to society.

The following five sections will examine, first, the nature of the self-concept—how it is formed and how its protection can lead to subtle defensive behaviors. We next look briefly at how the classic Kohlberg (1974) stages in moral development can serve as a guide for teaching moral and ethical thinking. The remaining sections review curriculum content and strategies for imparting constructive attitudes, awarenesses, values, and humanistic thinking, and the qualities of a humanistic teacher.

SELF-CONCEPT

Feelings of personal competence and self-esteem are closely tied to experiences of success. For adults, there are many types of success experience that can strengthen feelings of adequacy and self-esteem—for example, job or career success, or success as a parent or church member, as a home decorator or union member, and so on. For children, however, the school setting looms very large: Feedback from schoolwork and the teacher is extremely important in telling each child whether he or she is a capable, competent, and worthwhile person. The following are some dynamics of self-concept development:

1. Developing a healthy self-concept in school is a goal in itself. Moreover, because a student who feels capable and confident will be more motivated and will have higher academic and career aspirations, promoting good self-concepts also is a means of stimulating higher school achievement.

2. There are many facets of the self. A person may perceive an academic self, a social self, an emotional self, and a physical self (Jordon, 1981). Gifted students sometimes have better academic selves than social selves (Ross and Parker, 1980; Winne, Woodlands, and Wong, 1982).

3. The self-concept is organized, relatively stable, and evaluative. The evaluative component (self-esteem) relates to mental health—a person may or may not like his or her self-concept. According to Carl Rogers (1949), mentally healthy people see their actual selves as similar to their ideal selves. Underachieving gifted students and adults have worse self-concepts and lower self-esteem than high achieving gifted persons.

4. The *mirror theory* of self-concept development assumes that the self-concept is created via assessments ("reflections") from others.

5. The *self-accepting* student understands him- or herself and therefore is aware of strengths and weaknesses. This student values him- or herself despite the weaknesses. The *self-rejecting* student considers him- or herself of little worth, and may have other symptoms of maladjustment.

6. Academic failure implies low worth as a person and prevents students from maintaining feelings of competence. Failure after great effort is especially devastating to feelings of competence (Covington and Omelich, 1981).

7. Excuses and rationalizations, constructed to explain why the effort did not succeed, will protect the self-concept.

8. Self-esteem and pride are greatest when the student succeeds at a difficult task; the success is attributed to both high ability and high effort (Covington and Omelich, 1981).

9. Most critically, feelings of self-esteem and self-worth are a highly treasured commodity. *All students are strongly motivated to protect their feelings of self-esteem.*

Most often, the gifted student succeeds. The person's history of success inspires confidence in his or her abilities, a sense of responsibility for his or her actions, and feelings of control over his or her environment. When failure occurs, it typically is attributed to lack of effort, not lack of ability. Failures therefore may be used constructively to evaluate shortcomings and prepare for next time. "The person has temporarily fallen short of a goal, and has not fallen short as a person" (Covington and Beery, 1976).

Many students, however, are motivated not by strong needs to succeed, but by strong needs to avoid failure. And when failure threatens, any of several defense mechanisms may be used to ward off threats to the self-esteem.

One is *deliberate underachieving*: There will be no humiliation or destroyed self-esteem due to poor performance if the student does not really try. If the fear-of-failure student *accidentally* scores high on a test or paper there is a bonus. Doing well without trying is clear evidence of extra-high ability, thus reinforcing the underachievement pattern. In college, defensive underachieving produces the "gentleman's *C*" syndrome. An effortless *C* maintains the illusion of intellectual superiority without testing the scholar's actual abilities.

If failure avoidance becomes combined with a strong need to achieve, the result may be *compulsive high achievement*. Again, with feelings of self-worth tied closely to classroom success, this individual makes more and more self-demands in order to sustain a high level of achievement.

We already noted that excuses can protect the delicate ego of a fear-of-failure student. Failures are attributed to external causes, not internal ones. Such students may blame anything and everything; for example, "The test was unfair," "My friends wouldn't let me study," "My computer trashed my report," or "I wasn't feeling good." Ironically, these students may not accept credit for successes either, because success implies the ability and obligation for continued good work.

The case history of Dan, a real-life underachiever unable to take credit for success, is instructive. Dan had been a consistent *C* student when he came to the author, Rimm, for underachievement counseling. After one quarter, his achievement had improved sufficiently to earn him a place on the honor roll. When the counselor asked Dan how he felt about his achievement, he replied, "I like it, but I guess I was just lucky." He had even thanked his English teacher for "giving" him an *A*. The counselor pointed out to Dan that he had both improved his study habits and increased the time he spent learning. He finally acknowledged, hesitantly, that there probably was some relationship between his new efforts and the improved grades.

One recommended solution to self-defeating, self-perpetuating defense mechanisms is individualized instruction (Covington and Beery, 1976). By engaging fear-of-failure students in independent-learning assignments and projects, success is redefined in terms of meeting and exceeding one's own standards, not publicly competing with others for scarce classroom rewards and recognition. According to Covington and Beery, when students are not forced to compete they will set reachable, realistic goals, and these provide both the best challenge and the best conditions for a satisfying success.

MORAL DEVELOPMENT: THE KOHLBERG MODEL

Based upon research with the same group of 75 boys over a period of twelve years, Lawrence Kohlberg (1976; DeVries and Kohlberg, 1990; Kuhmerker, 1991; Power, Higgins, and Kohlberg, 1989) developed a model of moral thinking that has proven very valuable for (1) understanding sequential stages in moral development and (2) suggesting how to teach for moral thinking.

Kohlberg's six stages of moral development are divided into three main levels, each containing two stages. According to Kohlberg, they are true invariant stages: (1) They occur one at a time; (2) every person proceeds through the stages in the same order; (3) movement is always forward, never backward; and (4) stages are never skipped.

In both stages of the *Preconventional* level (ages 0–9) the orientation is toward the physical consequences of an action, regardless of any higher level notions of "right" or "wrong." Thus in Stage 1 obedience and good behavior are valued because they avoid punishments. This "might makes right" stage is characteristic of preschool children. In Stage 2 "right" action is that which produces rewards and satisfies one's needs or the needs of others—who will reciprocate ("You scratch my back, I'll scratch yours").

In the *Conventional* level (ages 9–15) behavior is heavily influenced by conformity pressures, strict stereotypes, social conventions and expectation, and rules and laws. Thus in Kohlberg's Stage 3 good behavior is that which pleases others or avoids disapproval, producing the "good boy-good girl" orientation. There is much conformity here. In Stage 4 right action is based upon rules and authority, "doing one's duty," and respecting the system. Laws are to be obeyed, not revised, leading to the "law and order" syndrome. Many adults do not rise above Conventional moral thinking.

The highly desirable *Postconventional* level includes the acceptance of universal and personal moral principles (for example, "Do unto others . . .") that are valid apart from authority. In Stage 5 right action is defined by general rights and standards which have been examined and agreed upon. Personal values and opinions present the possibility of rationally changing these rights and standards. For the chosen few, Stage 6 includes self-chosen principles and ethics based upon such universal principles and rights as justice, equality, and respect for individual differences.

Kohlberg found that children and adolescents comprehend all stages up to their own, and understand only one additional stage. Importantly, *they preferred this next stage*. Children move to the next stage when they are confronted with the appealing views of peers who are in this higher stage.

In one study of gifted students ages 9 to 15, Karnes and Brown (1981) found that the tendency to make Postconventional responses was positively correlated with age and with verbal intelligence scores. The authors concluded that gifted students may reach Level III (Postconventional) moral reasoning during their secondary school years, a level attained by only 10 to 15 percent of adults.

In contrast, Tan-Willman and Gutteridge (1981) found that the rate of Postconventional responses of gifted 16- and 17-year-olds was only slightly higher than that of regular students. "They are functioning predominantly at the Conventional level of moral judgment just like their age group in the general population . . . (and) the subjects' ability to reason morally is an area that needs serious and immediate attention."

As for teaching for moral development, Kohlberg suggests that teachers might expose children to concepts just *one step higher* than their current stage, and encourage them to think at this more mature stage. Children also may be given opportunities to think about moral matters by role-playing someone who has been treated rudely or cheated. A related strategy is to discuss moral dilemmas and let children practice making moral decisions that require high-level moral thinking.

High school English teacher Joan Weber (1981) used moral dilemmas from literature to encourage higher-level moral thinking. For example, *Old Man Warner* by Dorothy Canfield describes a 93-year-old obstinate man who, despite family pressure, refuses to move in with relatives or even move closer to town. Weber asks her class, "What should the man do? Why? Would it make a difference if he lived in a big city? If he were physically ill? If he were a woman and not a man?" Literature is a rich source of personal problems and conflicts centering on moral issues and values.

Especially for gifted students, Kohlberg's six stages themselves can be good curriculum content for helping students understand moral thinking. What is "good" and what is "bad" about Preconventional, Conventional, and Postconventional thinking? Should we get "stuck" at the Conventional level? Discussions of universal values, based upon the impact of our behavior upon others (e.g., honesty, kindness, pleasantness, fairness, helpfulness, empathy, dependability, and concern for safety, community welfare, and others' rights) also would be good content.

AN AFFECTIVE, HUMANISTIC CURRICULUM

Gifted students often question values earlier and may be out of step with their agemates. Thus activities and exercises that give them opportunities to share their concerns become an important component of gifted affective education.

Fantini (1981) itemized a number of suggestions for creating an affective, humanistic curriculum for children. For example:

1. Emphasize the desirability of "caring" values and behaviors as they relate to the self, to others, and to nature and the environment. Specifics might relate to clarifying values and ethics and understanding ecology, principles of health and hygiene, and related topics.

2. Students can read about and discuss difficulties of persons with handicaps and the elderly.

3. Students can learn about people, both common and famous, whose behavior demonstrates humanistic, caring values.

4. High school students can become involved in community service programs, working in day-care centers, hospitals, or nursing homes or other centers for the elderly. These assignments may be voluntary or mandated as a graduation requirement. They may receive course credit or recognition on their school records. Elementary school children can make gifts or perform plays for the elderly or the hospitalized; they can participate in recycling efforts, or in drives to collect food or coats for the needy or refugees.

5. Students can participate in many walk-a-thons, swim-a-thons, and so forth, aimed at raising research funds for cancer, multiple sclerosis, AIDS, heart disease, and other charitable causes.

6. Students can review social issues, for example, relating to refugees seeking asylum in America, political prisoners, military actions, migrant workers, and so on, from the perspective of humaneness.

7. Importantly, while the above are good for all children, gifted children can initiate, plan, implement, and evaluate such social action projects, perhaps as Renzulli Type III enrichment.

MATERIALS AND STRATEGIES FOR ENCOURAGING AFFECTIVE GROWTH

Values clarification strategies are effective in helping gifted students explore their beliefs and feelings. Affective education leaders Simon, Howe, and Kirschenbaum (1972, 1978) present no fewer than 79 values clarification strategies. One of the authors' favorites, which can be modified and revised for any student population, centers on a list of attitudes and behaviors (see Table 8.1). The question is asked, "Are you someone who . . . ?" and the student checks yes (A), maybe (B), or no (C)—requiring the student to decide on the spot what he or she *strongly favors*, is *neutral toward*, or is *opposed to*. Discussion follows, of course.

The traits in Table 8.1 list only a few of the hundreds of possibilities. Simon and Massey (1973) suggested that students will have a rousing time brainstorming other lists of behaviors, which could include such items as "Blushes at a compliment," "Talks loudly when nervous," "Cheats on unfair tests," "Gambles on parking tickets," and so on. Adolescents will be intrigued by listing personal traits, and then responding "yes," "maybe," or "no" to the question, "I am looking for someone who is. . . ." Other values clarification strategies include writing letters to newspapers expressing views on issues, or classifying yourself as a Cadillac person or a Ford Escort person and then discussing reasons why.

The *Magic Circle* technique helps children learn ". . . why people are sometimes happy or unhappy, how to feel good about themselves, and how to get along with others" (Lefkowitz, 1975). Seven to twelve children in a circle—few enough to maintain everyone's attention—voluntarily respond to "Today's Topic," such as "I felt good when . . . ," "I felt bad when . . . ," "I made someone else feel good when . . . ," or "Something I can do (or wish I could do) is . . ." The teacher encourages learning and understanding with follow-up questions such as "Who can tell me why Dizzy Jones felt good on the roller coaster?" or "Why was he proud of himself?"

One workbook jammed with exercises for clarifying feelings and teaching values is the *Affective Education Guidebook* (Eberle and Hall, 1975; see also Eberle and Hall, 1979). For example, in their *Mini-Speech* strategy students draw a topic from a sack and prepare a two- to four-minute speech that expresses feelings about the matter. Some topics are:

- I get real angry when . . .
- I think I'm pretty good at . . .
- Compared to most people, I'm different because . . .
- I like people who . . .
- I am embarrassed when . . .
- Getting along with another person is easy if . . .
- My feelings are hurt when . . .

Class discussion follows each mini-speech.

With the *What's It Like?* exercise, students clarify and identify their own feelings, and learn that their behavior can make other people feel good or uncomfortable. Students discuss "What it's like" when:

- People yell at you.
- Someone tells you that you have done something very well.

TABLE 8.1   Are You Someone Who . . . ?

(A = yes, B = maybe, C = no)

A	B	C	Are you someone who:
			1. Likes to break the curve on an exam?
			2. Likes to stay up all night when friends visit?
			3. Will stop the car to look at a sunset?
			4. Puts things off?
			5. Will publicly show affection for another person?
			6. Will do it yourself when you feel something needs doing?
			7. Will order a new dish in a restaurant?
			8. Could accept your own sexual impotence?
			9. Could be satisfied without a college degree?
			10. Could be part of a mercy killing?
			11. Is afraid alone in the dark in a strange place?
			12. Is willing to participate in fund raising?
			13. Eats when you are worried?
			14. Can receive a gift easily?
			15. Would steal apples from an orchard?
			16. Is apt to judge someone by his or her appearance?
			17. Would let your child drink or smoke pot?
			18. Watches television soap operas?
			19. Could kill in self-defense?
			20. Needs to be alone?

From Sidney Simon* and Sara Massey, "Values clarification," *Educational Leadership,* May, 1973. Reprinted with permission of the Association for Supervision and Curriculum Development. Copyright © 1973 by the Association for Supervision and Curriculum Development. All rights reserved.

*For information about current Values Realization materials and a schedule of nationwide training workshops, contact Sidney Simon, Old Mountain Rd., Hadley, MA 01035.

- Somebody doesn't do what they said they would.
- You get a gift you didn't expect to get.

Students and teachers can brainstorm more "What's it like" questions. The class also can reverse the roles, for example:

- "What's it like to yell at people?"
- "What's it like to tell someone they have done something very well?"
- "What's it like to give someone a gift they don't expect?"

In What Ways? asks students to answer the questions "In what ways might I:"

- Show my appreciation to those who are helpful to me?
- Give pleasure to others?
- Show a person that I value her/his friendship?
- Gain the respect and love of all human beings?

The *What Kind of Person Are You* exercise likely was inspired by the "Are you someone who?" strategy of Simon, Howe, and Kirschenbaum (1972, 1978). Students mark the

"Hardly Ever," "Sometimes," or "Always" column in response to the statements "I am the kind of person that:"

- Tells people when they do good.
- Puts out a foot to bother or trip someone.
- Cuts in line at the drinking fountain.
- Picks up something for another person when it is dropped.
- Waves my hand when others are talking.
- Yells at people if they make a bad play.
- Listens and tries to understand what others are saying.
- Makes smart-aleck remarks to others.
- Observes how others feel about something.
- Says "please" and "thank you."
- Likes to gripe.
- Finds fault with others.
- Wears a smile.
- Gives compliments.

Eberle and Hall's (1975) advice to teachers about clarifying feelings and values: "Be happy, feel good, and work proudly—you are doing something for the infinite good of your pupils, yourself, and the larger community" (p. 13).

In his *Good Person Book: Creative Teaching of Values and Moral Thinking*, Davis (1992b) describes seven strategies, with dozens of exercises for each, designed to stimulate creative thinking and at the same time:

1. Raise awareness of affective and behavioral problems.

2. Help students understand why particular values and behaviors are good and others are bad.

3. Help students empathize with people who are victimized by theft, vandalism, rudeness, bad manners, etc.

4. Help students understand that they will feel better about themselves, have more self-respect, and earn the respect of others if they decide to be "good persons."

5. Most importantly, help students clarify their own feelings and identities regarding affective matters, and make personal commitments to positive attitudes and behavior.

With the *brainstorming* approach, students might be asked: "Why is it important to be honest? List all of the ideas you can think of." "What rights do students (teachers, parents, brothers and sisters, store clerks) have? Think of all the ideas you can." "How many reasons can you think of to get as much education as you can?" Or with reverse brainstorming, "What can we do to lose friends or make people not like us?" "How many ways can you think of to show the school custodians that you are a thoughtless and crummy person?"

In *"What would happen if . . . ?"* exercises, students imagine and think about consequences of hurtful behavior. For example, what would happen if everyone were a thief? If the school were vandalized every night? If nobody were friendly to anybody else? If everybody tried to hurt the feelings of everybody else? If nobody paid any attention to their health? If nobody went on to technical school or college? If we all ignored all safety rules? If everyone in the school wasted as many school supplies as they possibly could?

With *analogical thinking* students make imaginative comparisons. For example: "How is a good person like a good pizza?" "How is an honest person like a comfortable old pair of jeans?" "How is trustworthiness like a good movie?" "How are bad friends like Monopoly money?" "How is sharing like Saturday?"

The *empathy* approach requires students to imagine themselves in another role. For example, "Imagine that Nancy's parents gave her a new digital watch for her birthday. The first day she wears it to school it is stolen from her locker. How does Nancy feel? What does Nancy think about after this happens—what ideas go through her head? What will her parents think? How will they feel? What was the thief thinking about when he or she stole the watch? Was the thief thinking of Nancy's feelings? Why not?"

The *visualization* strategy is similar to the empathy approach. Students relax and shut their eyes while the teacher leads them through an episode eliciting empathy and constructive attitudes, values, and feelings. For example:

> Imagine you are a jogger . . . Today you are out jogging around the park . . . You look at the trees . . . tulips and roses . . . Birds are chirping . . . Children are swinging on the swings . . . Then a car filled with young adults passes by, and they toss out a box of empty beer bottles . . . The bottles scatter all over . . . Most of them break . . . Then you notice that lots of other soda cans, beer cans, and burger wrappers have been dumped around the park . . . Soon you see picnickers pack up their ice chest and their blanket . . . They climb into their car and drive away . . . But they left some dirty paper plates, a pork and beans can, some napkins and a potato chip bag . . . Their mess is ugly too . . . You wonder why these thoughtless people make messes that others must clean up . . . You can see that it makes the park ugly . . . that somebody else will have to clean up their garbage . . . Why can't they understand these things? . . .

Follow-up questions elicit thoughts regarding, for example: Are parks prettier or uglier when people throw their trash all over? What kind of people mess up roads and parks with trash? Are they considerate? Intelligent? Do they think about others' rights and feelings? Is it fair to leave messes for others to clean up? Are you the type of person who will mess up parks and streets with your trash?

The *questioning and discussion* approach also elicits awareness and commitment. For example, "Does a good person think about other people's feelings?" "What is wrong with stealing?" "Have you ever had anything vandalized? How did you feel? What did you think of the person who did this to you?" "Is it good to be trustworthy? Why?" "What happens to our valuable friends if we cheat them, lie to them, or treat them rudely?" "What is the opposite of courtesy?" "Which is more important, lots of money or good health? Why?" "Is it all

right to be different? Or does everyone have to be exactly the same?" "Is it important to develop our talents and skills? Why?" "Is it important for others to respect us? How do we earn respect at school? At home? In the community?"

Davis's *problem-solving* approach follows just two steps. The first step is *clarifying* an affective problem, which includes helping students understand how others or themselves are hurt by bad attitudes and behavior. The teacher can ask: Why is the situation bad? Why is it wrong? Who is hurt? When does this happen? Where does it happen? Do we hurt ourselves when we do that? How? How are others in the school, family, or community affected? What would happen if everyone did this?

The second step is *finding solutions* for what can or should be done. The teacher might probe for ideas with:

> What are some examples of correct behavior? What might a helpful, thoughtful person do? What would earn us respect from others?
>
> How can we try to help others who are making mistakes like this? How can we help these people who don't understand how bad they look to others?
>
> How might we help the victims of the bad behavior?

THE HUMANISTIC TEACHER

A teacher who has internalized humanistic values will be better able to communicate these values to students, both in direct teaching and by serving as a good role model. Pine and Boy (1977) listed characteristics of such a humanistic teacher. While the teacher who fully meets all of these criteria may not exist, we can view the traits as ideals toward which we all should work. The self-actualized, humanistic teacher:

1. Thinks well of him- or herself; he or she has a good self-concept.

2. Is honest and genuine; there is no conflict between the real inner person and the role-playing outer person.

3. Likes and accepts others.

4. Is a forward-growing person, continually in the process of "becoming" by learning, exploring, and changing.

5. Lives by humanistic values; is honestly concerned with the welfare of fellow humans and the improvement of human society.

6. Is sensitive and responsive to the needs and feelings of others.

7. Is creative, adventurous, risk-taking, willing to try something new, and secure enough to learn from the inevitable mistakes.

8. Has confidence in his or her feelings, intuition, decisions, and reactions.

9. Is open to the viewpoints of others, to new information and experiences, and to his or her own inner feelings.

10. Exercises control over his or her life and environment; initiates needed changes.

11. Is responsive, vibrant, and spontaneous, and tries to live optimistically and energetically.

If there is one enrichment topic in this text that is "good for all children," it is teaching positive attitudes and values.

LEADERSHIP

There is little disagreement that leadership is important for gifted and talented students, who often are labeled "tomorrow's leaders." Said Richardson and Feldhusen (1986), "Our nation's leadership is not limited to our political offices such as the President, the Congress, governors or representatives.... Any field of human endeavor is represented by its leaders, including the creative areas of art, music and literature ... research, exploration, and technology require creative leadership. Each person is faced with leadership whether it be in church, schools, business, or in the home." It seems sensible that leadership training should supplement the development of other cognitive and affective skills of G/T students.

The following sections review definitions of leadership and then turn to specifics of what is taught when you "teach leadership."

As an overview, first, "definitions" of leadership typically amount to lists of traits, characteristics, and skills of leaders. Second, leadership training in the schools, when it is attempted at all, typically includes some combination of three approaches: (1) Students learn about traits of leaders, leadership styles, group dynamics, and how to be a good leader; (2) students are placed into leadership situations with the intent that on-the-job experience will strengthen leadership characteristics and skills; or (3) students receive training in component leadership skills, such as communication, creative problem solving, critical thinking, decision making, persuasion, and even understanding others' needs.

LEADERSHIP DEFINITIONS: TRAITS, CHARACTERISTICS, AND SKILLS

Different leadership traits and skills naturally are required for different leadership situations. At the same time, however, there are traits and skills that are cross-situational and that seem to characterize all leaders.

One definition of leadership is found in the Renzulli (1983) leadership rating scale, reproduced in Appendix 4.5, on which teachers evaluate student leadership according to the following criteria:

1. Carries responsibility well and can be counted on to do what has been promised.

2. Is self-confident with both agemates and adults; seems comfortable when showing personal work to the class.

3. Is well liked.

4. Is cooperative, avoids bickering, and is generally easy to get along with.

5. Can express him- or herself clearly.

6. Adapts to new situations; is flexible in thought and action and is not disturbed when the normal routine is changed.

7. Enjoys being around other people.

8. Tends to dominate; usually directs activities.

9. Participates in most school social activities; can be counted on to be there.

Plowman (1981) itemized six aspects of leadership in the form of adjectives: *charismatic, intuitive, generative, analytical, evaluative*, and *synergistic*.

Charismatic traits include an almost mystical ability to instill others (partly by example) with a sense of mission, and to energize them to think and act to achieve objectives. *Intuitive* characteristics include the ability to sense what is about to happen via an extrapolation of current events or a keen sensitivity to subtle cues. It includes the ability to sense the needs of individuals and groups and to respond to those needs even before they are expressed. *Generative* refers to creativeness: defining problems in new ways and creating unusual ideas, processes, and courses of action. *Analytic* leadership includes seeing component parts of systems and analyzing their individual contributions. The *evaluative* involves judging the effectiveness or efficiency of activities or programs. The *synergistic* aspects ". . . are those which make the unbelievable happen"—goals are reached in half the expected time, or production is five or ten times what was expected.

Plowman (1981) also reported the results of a 1980 leadership session at the California Association for the Gifted Annual Conference in Los Angeles in which 16 traits of leadership were identified. Each trait was categorized as *cognitive* (C), *affective* (A), or *both* (B):

1. Assertive decision making (B)
2. Altruistic (B)
3. Persuasive/innovator (A)
4. Sensitive to the needs of others (A)
5. Ability to be a facilitator (B)
6. Goal-oriented (C)
7. Strong communication skills (B)
8. Integrity (A)
9. Organizational ability (C)
10. Resourceful (B)
11. Risk-taker (B)
12. Charismatic (A)
13. Competent (knowledgeable) (B)
14. Persistent ("hangs in there") (A)
15. Accepts responsibility (B)
16. Creative (B)

Just two traits were rated as *cognitive* only, indicating both the importance of affective characteristics in leadership and the complexity of the traits. Each of these traits, as with the traits and "aspects" in the previous lists, could be seen as objectives or competencies of leadership curricula. That is, G/T students can be helped to understand these traits and skills, and to acquire them through practice and exercise.

LEADERSHIP TRAINING

Again, recommendations and strategies for leadership training invariably include some combination of teaching students about leadership styles, traits, and group dynamics; putting students into leadership roles; and teaching them component skills of leadership.

Magoon (1980), for example, recommended:

1. *Classroom monitorships*, in which students assume responsibility for regulating the behavior of peers (for example, in lineups), record keeping (roll taking), or other jobs (blackboard or A-V duties). Such activities teach leadership and followership, including the notion that there are menial tasks which must be carried out for the system to function.

2. *Mentorships*, in which gifted and talented students tutor peers or younger students. The mentors learn to communicate in an acceptable and challenging manner.

3. *In-school leadership projects*, identified via brainstorming, such as improving student behavior (for example, in the halls or cafeteria), improving the physical plant (classrooms, restrooms, or temperature or noise levels), or solving problems related to curriculum selection, classroom rules, safety, sanitation, etc.

4. *Community projects*, in which students tackle neighborhood problems or undesirable conditions.

This activity requires the development of communication skills, tact, diplomacy, and patience.

5. *Simulations*, which can involve, for example, establishing "banks" and "stores," making rules, and establishing a legal system for maintaining the rules.

Magoon (1981) also proposed that students be exposed to the "topic and content" of leadership itself. For example, training can include teaching students about leadership and followership, principles of participatory democracy, group processes, and characteristics of leaders, along with developing communication skills. Magoon's strategy is ". . . based, in part, on a leadership program that has been classroom tested with talented and gifted students for over three years with exciting results."

Plowman (1981) recommended strengthening leadership with exercises aimed at developing the component skills of critical thinking, decision making, persuading, planning, and evaluating. More complex objectives included helping students understand others' needs, exploring patterns of individual and group behavior, and showing students ways that changes are made in political, social, economic, and other spheres.

Parker (1983) suggested that leadership could be trained by strengthening the four component skills of *cognition* (especially, research, exploration, and investigative skills), *problem solving* (including creative thinking), *interpersonal communication* (including self-awareness, concern for others, cooperation, and conflict resolution), and *decision making*.

Maker's (1982) suggestions for leadership training include providing practice in leading, helping students understand leadership, and teaching them component skills. She recommended that as the school year progresses, the G/T teacher should allow gifted and talented students to assume progressively more leadership responsibilities. For example, they can teach small groups of students, a task that intrinsically requires leadership, and they can take responsibility for various projects. She noted that a teacher can raise understanding and awareness of leadership via discussions of leadership qualities, focusing partly on

which traits help make leaders successful and why. Also, the teacher can foster discussion skills, public speaking, and group control and group dynamics skills.

Thomson (1989; see also Malcomson and Laurence, 1986) described a unique approach to leadership training that is part of a sixth-grade *College Days for Kids* program at the University of Wisconsin-Stevens Point. One of 25 mini-courses, *Operation Adventure*, is a two-Friday course taught by officers and senior cadets in the university's ROTC program. It focuses on two main characteristics of leadership: problem-solving ability and courage. During the first Friday, students take a brisk walk through a nature preserve. Student teams solve imaginary challenges that require physical movement: How can you get your team out of an enclosure surrounded by an electric force field? How can we create a moving "human trolley" to cross a swamp filled with alligators? How can we cross a poisoned river? The importance of good communication skills quickly becomes evident.

The second Friday presents a true hair-raiser. After proper coaching and safety training, they rappel from a 20-foot tower—each student eagerly making his or her "jumps." Thomson noted that the activity "gives the students opportunity to practice initiative and determination in the face of somewhat frightening circumstances (p. 59)." They also learn followership in the sense that they must trust and rely on their ROTC leaders. The officers and cadets themselves were good models of leadership in showing qualities of professionalism, enthusiasm, and sensitivity to the children's needs. One student evaluated the experience with these words: "It made you believe in yourself."

Leadership Skills Development Program: Karnes and Chauvin

Karnes and Chauvin (1987) developed a two-part Leadership Skills Development Program aimed at developing important traits and skills in upper elementary and secondary students. The first part of the program centers on their *Leadership Skills In-*

ventory (LSI). The LSI evaluates these kinds of seemingly universal leadership traits and skills:

Fundamentals of leadership, including understanding leadership styles and terms.

Written communication, including outlining, speech writing, and report writing.

Speech communication, including defining one's view on an issue, delivering speeches, and giving constructive criticism.

Values clarification, including identifying things that one values, understanding the importance of free choice, and affirming one's choices.

Decision making, including gathering facts, analyzing the consequences of decisions, and reaching logical conclusions.

Group dynamics, including serving as group facilitator, achieving consensus, and achieving compromise.

Problem solving, including identifying problems, revising problem-solving strategies, and accepting unpopular decisions.

Personal development, including self-confidence, sensitivity, and personal grooming.

Planning, including goal setting, developing timelines, and creating evaluation strategies.

The LSI is used in several ways. It provides a profile of leadership abilities and skills for each student and for the group as a whole. It thus serves as a needs assessment instrument and guides the planning of a leadership development program based upon individual and group weaknesses. Because the results are shared with students, they learn about the nature of leadership and leadership skills, and they receive an objective assessment of their own present leadership skills. This record is used as a basis for later comparison and evaluation of progress.

The second part of the training stems from the *Leadership Skills Activities Handbook*. The handbook contains activities designed to strengthen each skill or trait described in every item on the LSI. Most activities are designed to be self-directed, with the teacher serving as a facilitator.

For example, one LSI item reads "I am ambitious and desire success." The coordinated activity in the handbook is leading a discussion on "how the self-confident person views success." The student-leader would pose such (supplied) questions as "Are all leaders success-oriented? How important is this quality to a leader?" Another LSI item is "I can describe my own style of leadership." The corresponding handbook activity asks students to describe how they would solve some fictitious problem situations.

The culminating activity for the entire Leadership Skills Development Program is the "plan for leadership." Said Karnes and Chauvin (1986), "It is a written plan whereby the student is asked to think through all the things learned about leadership and formulate a plan to put these skills into action. The individual is asked to direct activities toward a particular selected goal and formulate objectives, a timeline, and a list of resources. It is through implementation of this plan that leadership will become a reality." The Leadership Skills Development Program has been field tested, apparently with very positive results.

Leadership Education: Richardson and Feldhusen

Richardson and Feldhusen's (1986) book *Leadership Education* was written primarily for secondary students themselves who are participating in leadership education programs. The book presents a balanced mix of theory and principles, characteristics of leadership, guides for becoming an effective leader, plus activities and problems designed to exercise and strengthen leadership traits and skills.

By way of explaining leadership, Richardson and Feldhusen reviewed four definitions or types of leaders. The *personality* approach defines a leader as one who possesses a constellation of personality traits that are attractive to others, for example, confidence, humor, and popularity. Students with these traits often are elected to school leadership positions. Leadership as a form of *persuasion* is based on the ability to "... convince or inspire others to follow their directions, orders, or commands ... to inspire people to action." Leadership as a *power relation* goes to the person with the highest rank, as in democratic government or clan leadership. Finally, a leader can be a self-directed and motivated person who *initiates action and maintains structure* when working toward group goals, as when a private citizen organizes a group to combat drug use or automobile deaths among young people.

To help students understand leadership, Richardson and Feldhusen explain that good leaders are confident and have good self-esteem. They take risks and admit mistakes. They tend to be responsible, empathic, and more assertive and extroverted than average. Good leaders also are good speakers, good listeners, and can give directions, lead discussions, and write well. They have good interpersonal skills, delegate authority, and are prepared to help others. They have good organization and planning skills; can involve group members in a task and clarify the goals and issues. They develop group cohesiveness and an atmosphere of respect, cooperation, and teamwork; refrain from harsh criticism; are fair; make decisions based on majority views; protect rights of individual members; help all members to achieve their personal goals; are good at public relations—keeping the community informed and supportive; and understand parliamentary procedures.

Students learn steps to use in leading discussions, and steps to use in brainstorming and problem solving. The authors also suggest tips for reading body language and nonverbal communication; communicating effectively; making introductions; writing letters; preparing a speech; setting and clarifying individual and group goals; planning meetings; planning work activities for the group; serving as a committee chairperson; and serving as a committee member.

Overall, the book not only provides convincing evidence that leadership can be taught, it carefully explains and provides exercises in the skills needed to improve one's leadership ability.

Leadership Education by Telecommunications

Telephone and television were used to teach leadership traits and skills to gifted middle school students in four rural school districts (University of Wisconsin-Eau Claire, 1992).[1] Table 8.2 presents the discussion guide that all students reviewed and discussed via telephone. Before the telecommunications session began, the students had read several selections pertaining to popularity, giftedness, and leadership. The main objectives of the session were to help the seventh and eighth graders become sensitive to the differences between *leadership* and *popularity*, and to understand the variety of leadership roles within schools and communities. One student spontaneously displayed leadership by asking students in different schools to share addresses so they could continue their friendships by letters and telephone calls.

SUMMARY

The topic of affective learning includes self-concepts, personal and social adjustment, educational and career motivation, values and moral thinking, and others. Strategies for teaching leadership have appeared recently.

High-achieving gifted students usually have good self-concepts, and gifted students usually attain higher levels of moral thinking. The self-concept is closely tied to success experiences, which makes feedback from schoolwork and the teacher extremely important for children. Academic failure implies low self-worth.

Developing good self-concepts is a goal in itself. We have many "selves" (academic, social, emotional, physical). The self-concept is organized, stable, and evaluative. Underachieving G/T students have poor self-concepts. The self-concept may be formed according to "mirrored" reflections from others. Achieving students are confident and use failures constructively.

[1]Written and conducted by Sylvia Rimm.

TABLE 8.2   Leadership—Distance
Learning

1. What different kinds of student leadership exist in your school and community? Let's all list these.

2. What are the characteristics leaders need in any two of these?

3. Are these characteristics the same in both or are there differences?

4. What do all leadership roles seem to have in common?

5. What is the importance of talk in leadership? What is the place of listening?

6. What are some types of leadership in adult communities?

7. What kinds of school leadership are likely to lead toward adult leadership roles?

8. What kinds of school leadership will not be likely to lead to adult leadership?

9. What does the story, *Gifted Kids Have Feelings Too,* have to do with school leadership and lifetime leadership?

10. How do the articles on popularity relate to school leadership and lifetime leadership?

Prepared by Sylvia Rimm for the University of Wisconsin-Eau Claire (1992).

Because self-esteem is highly valued, failure-oriented students will use defense mechanisms, such as deliberate underachieving, compulsive overachieving, or attributing failures to external causes. Individualized learning is one solution to self-defeating defensive behaviors.

Kohlberg's six stages of moral development are true, invariant stages. In the two stages of the Preconventional level, right action avoids punishment and satisfies one's needs or the needs of others (who will reciprocate). In the two stages of the Conventional level, correct behavior is defined by strict social conventions. In the two stages of Postconventional thinking, right action is defined by universal and self-determined principles. Children understand all previous stages and one more, and prefer this next one. Research is mixed re-

garding whether or not gifted adolescents truly do think at the Postconventional level.

Children should be exposed to moral thinking at the next higher level. They should have opportunities to think about moral problems, for example, using moral dilemmas. Kohlberg's stages themselves can be taught.

Fantini emphasized teaching "caring" values; exposing students to problems of the elderly and handicapped, to examples of humanistic thinking, and to social issues; and involving students in community service programs, which G/T students can design and carry out.

Values clarification strategies (Simon and colleagues; Eberle and Hall), including the Magic Circle technique, help students understand and accept positive values.

The *Good Person Book* contains creativity-type exercises designed to help students understand and make commitments to positive values. Seven strategies included brainstorming, "What would happen if . . . ?", analogical thinking, empathy, visualization, questioning and discussion, and problem solving.

The humanistic teacher has a good self-concept, likes others, initiates change, and is honest and genuine, forward-growing, sensitive, creative and adventurous, confident, and open to other viewpoints.

Definitions of leadership usually amount to lists of traits, characteristics, and skills of leaders. Traits that seem common to leaders, regardless of the situation, include high responsibility and confidence, being well-liked, adaptability, tendencies to dominate and direct, plus skills in communication, group dynamics, planning, persuasion, public relations, and others.

Six "aspects" of leadership (Plowman) included being charismatic, intuitive, generative (creative), analytical, evaluative, and synergistic. These and other cognitive and affective traits could be used as objectives and competencies for creating a leadership curriculum.

Leadership training includes some combination of teaching students about leadership styles, traits, and group dynamics; placing students in leadership roles; and teaching students component skills of leadership, such as communication, creative problem solving, planning, decision making, and others.

Magoon described five leadership training activities: classroom monitorships, mentorships, in-school leadership projects, community projects, and simulations.

Maker recommended allowing G/T students progressively more leadership responsibilities as the year progresses.

Operation Adventure focused on two characteristics of leadership. Problem solving was exercised in solving imaginary team challenges; courage was strengthened by rappelling from a tower.

Karnes and Chauvin's Leadership Skills Development Program included (1) using their *Leadership Skills Inventory* to assess leadership traits and skills, and then (2) prescribing leadership activities from their *Leadership Skills Activities Handbook* to strengthen each weak skill. Each student also prepares a written plan for leadership.

Richardson and Feldhusen's high school book *Leadership Education* teaches types and characteristics of leaders; steps to use in leading discussions, brainstorming, and problem solving; and many other specific leadership skills, including goal-setting, communication, and planning skills.

One effort used telephone and television to teach leadership to gifted students in rural school districts. The focus was a discussion of leadership as it relates to popularity and giftedness.

CHAPTER 9

CREATIVITY I

THE CREATIVE PERSON, CREATIVE PROCESS, AND CREATIVE DRAMATICS

When I examined myself, and my methods of thought, I came to the conclusion that the gift of fantasy has meant more to me than my talent for absorbing positive knowledge.
Albert Einstein

There can be no more important topic in the education of gifted and talented children than *creativity*. Indeed, the two interrelated purposes of gifted education are (1) to help these children and adolescents develop their gifts and talents and realize their potential—that is, to help them become more self-actualized, creative individuals; and (2) to better enable them to make creative contributions to society.

Overview

This chapter and Chapter 10 are designed to help the reader better understand creativity and creative students, and to suggest ideas for stimulating creative growth. This chapter will review these three creativity topics: (1) traits and characteristics of creative people and some important creative abilities; (2) the nature of the creative process; and (3) creative dramatics. The important topic of testing for creative potential was discussed in Chapter 4 in conjunction with identification. The relationship of creativity to intelligence was reviewed in Chapter 2. Chapter 10 will focus more specifically on teaching for creative development.

CHARACTERISTICS OF CREATIVE STUDENTS

Chapter 2 summarized recurrent personality, motivational, and biographical characteristics of creative children and adults. To review briefly, creative people are frequently high in self-confidence, independence, risk-taking, energy, enthusiasm, adventurousness, curiosity, playfulness, humor, idealism, and reflectiveness. They tend to have artistic and aesthetic interests, to be attracted to the complex and mysterious, and to need some privacy and alone time. They tend to be more perceptive and "intuitive." Importantly, they are willing to tolerate the ambiguity that accompanies engaging in creative problem solving (e.g., Sternberg, 1988). The majority of these traits originally were uncovered by Frank Barron (1969, 1988) and Donald MacKinnon (1978) in their classic Berkeley studies of creative architects, writers, and mathematicians.

Further, as we also noted earlier, some traits will be troublesome to teachers. Especially, the admirable characteristics of independence and high energy, combined with nonconformity and unconventionality, may lead to stubbornness, resis-

tance to teacher (or parent) domination, uncooperativeness, indifference to accepted conventions,
cynicism, too much assertiveness, sloppiness, low
interest in details, a tendency to question rules and
authority, forgetfulness, overactivity, uncommunicativeness, and the attitude that the rest of the parade is out of step. Note that some of these traits
resemble those of children with attention deficit hyperactivity disorder (e.g., Heward and Orlansky,
1992).

The biographical traits listed earlier included
some unsurprising ones, namely, a background
filled with creative activities and hobbies. Frequent performances in dramatic productions is a
very strong indicator of creativeness, since such
performances necessarily require important creative traits (humor, energy, aesthetic interests and
risk-taking, for example). More subtle biographical characteristics of creativity include a background of traveling, living in more than one state,
preferring friends who are younger and older, having had an imaginary playmate as a child, and a
tendency to believe in psychic phenomena (and a
higher than average likelihood of having psychic
experiences). Naturally, not all characteristics apply to all creative students.

Many of these (positive) traits probably can be
enhanced by a creativity-conscious teacher. Indeed, as we will see in the next chapter, there is
every reason to believe that attitudes and personality traits can be changed to produce a more flexible, creative and self-actualized person.

Torrance (1979; 1981b) itemized other nontest indicators of creativeness in the kinesthetic
and auditory areas:

Shows skillful, manipulative movement in
crayon work, typing, piano playing, cooking, dressmaking, and so on
Shows quick, precise movements in mime, creative dramatics, and role playing
Works at creative movement activities for extended periods of time
Displays total bodily involvement in interpreting a poem, story, or song

Becomes intensely absorbed in creative movement or dance
Interprets songs, poems, or stories through creative movement or dance
Writes, draws, walks, and moves with rhythm
and is generally highly responsive to sound
stimuli
Creates music, songs, etc.
Works perseveringly at music and rhythmic
activities

The characteristics listed here are intended to
help the reader recognize creative children and
adolescents in the classroom. The lists also might
increase one's patience with the obnoxious kid
who shows a few too many of the negative traits.
Perhaps the creative energy, unconventionality,
stubbornness, inquisitiveness, and so forth, require constructive redirection.

Note also that many academically average and
below average students will demonstrate marvelous creative talent, for example, in art, dance, or
any other area in which the student possesses special knowledge and skills.

Is it easy to recognize creative talent? See Inset
9.1.

CREATIVE ABILITIES

There are a great many intellectual abilities that
contribute in one way or another to creative potential. Indeed, it would be difficult to isolate mental
abilities having absolutely nothing to do with creativeness. The list below includes seemingly important creative abilities. Most have appeared
elsewhere in the creativity literature, especially in
Torrance's work (for example, Torrance, 1962,
1979, 1980, 1984, 1988). The first four are the
classic Guilford/Torrance *fluency*, *flexibility*,
originality, and *elaboration* abilities which are
measured by the Guilford (1967) tests and the *Torrance Tests of Creative Thinking* (Torrance,
1966). Some people have mistakenly assumed that
these four are a definitive and exhaustive list of
creative abilities, which is not true at all.

INSET 9.1 _____

Is it Easy to Recognize Creative Talent?

While an awareness of traits of creative people will help us recognize creative students, we are not likely to reach perfection in our identification of creative talent. Consider these creative persons who were *not* recognized by their teachers, professors, or supervisors:

- *Albert Einstein* was four years old before he could speak and seven before he could read; he performed badly in almost all high school courses.
- *Thomas Edison* was told by his teachers that he was too stupid to learn.
- *Werner von Braun* failed ninth-grade algebra.
- *Winston Churchill* was at the bottom of his class in one school, and twice failed the entrance exams to another.
- *Pablo Picasso* could barely read and write by age 10. His father hired a tutor—who gave up and quit.
- *Louis Pasteur* was rated mediocre in chemistry at the Royal College.
- *Charles Darwin* did poorly in the early grades, and failed a university medical course.
- *F. W. Woolworth* worked in a dry goods store when he was 21, but his employers would not let him wait on customers because he "didn't have enough sense."

- *Walt Disney* was fired by a newspaper editor because he had no good ideas.
- *Caruso's* music teacher told him, "You can't sing, you have no voice at all!"
- *Louisa May Alcott* was told by an editor that she could never write anything popular.
- *Charles Dickens, Claude Monet, Isadora Duncan*, and *Mark Twain* never finished grade school.
- *George Gershwin, Will Rogers*, both *Wright brothers*, and newscaster *Peter Jennings* dropped out of high school; *Harrison Ford* (Indiana Jones) and *Leo Tolstoy* flunked out of college.
- *David Suchet*, who portrays Hercule Poirot in the British Agatha Christie TV series, laughingly described how several acting schools would not admit him because he was too short, could not sing, and showed no promise as an actor.
- A 1938 letter found in 1991 said that western movie star *Gene Autry* "needed to improve his acting," that an acting course was "evidently wasted," and that "he needed darker make-up to give him the appearance of virility." Replied the 83-year old Autry, "A lot of that is true."

While amusing, such historical facts raise our awareness of the complexity and subtlety of creative talent.

Fluency. The ability to produce many ideas in response to an open-ended problem or question. The ideas may be verbal or nonverbal (for example, mathematical, musical, and so forth). Other names are "associational fluency" or "ideational fluency."

Flexibility. The ability to take different approaches to a problem, think of ideas in different categories, or view a situation from several perspectives.

Originality. Uniqueness, nonconformity in thought and action.

Elaboration. The important ability to add details to a given idea, which includes developing, embellishing, and implementing the idea.

Sensitivity to problems. The ability to find problems, detect difficulties, detect missing information, and ask good questions (Dillon, 1982).

Problem defining. An important capability that includes the abilities to: (1) identify the "real" problem, (2) isolate the important aspects of a problem, (3) clarify and simplify a problem, (4) identify subproblems, (5) propose alternative problem definitions, and (6) define a problem broadly. Abilities 5 and 6 both open the door to a wider variety of problem solutions.

Visualization. The ability to fantasize and imagine, "see" things in the "mind's eye," and mentally manipulate images and ideas.

Ability to regress. The ability to think like a child, whose mind is less cluttered by habits, traditions, rules, regulations, and the firm knowledge of "how it ought to be done" and "how we've always done it"—strong barriers to creative thinking.

Analogical thinking. The ability to borrow ideas from one context and use them in another context; or the ability to borrow a solution to one problem and transfer it to another problem.

Evaluation. The very important ability to separate relevant from irrelevant considerations; to think critically; to evaluate the "goodness" or appropriateness of an idea, product, or problem solution.

Analysis. The ability to analyze details, analyze a whole into its parts.

Synthesis. The ability to see relationships, to combine parts into a workable, perhaps creative whole.

Transformation. This includes the ability to adopt something to a new use, to "see" new meanings, implications, and applications, or to change one object or idea into another creatively. Guilford (1986) considers transformation to be an extremely important creative ability.

Extend boundaries. The ability to go beyond what is usual, to use objects in new ways.

Intuition. The ability to make "intuitive leaps" or see relationships based upon little, perhaps insufficient information; the ability to "read between the lines."

Predict outcomes. The ability to foresee the results of different solution alternatives and actions.

Resist premature closure. This is another important ability, and one in which many students are deficient. It translates as deferring judgment and not jumping on the first idea that comes along.

Concentration ability. The ability to focus on a problem, free from distraction.

Logical thinking ability. The ability to separate the relevant from the irrelevant, to deduce reasonable conclusions.

Tardif and Sternberg (1988) suggested these information processing traits, which they extracted from various chapters in Sternberg (1988). Creative people:

Use existing knowledge as basis for new ideas
Avoid perceptual sets and entrenched ways of thinking
Build new structures, instead of using existing structures
Use wide categories, see the "forest" instead of "trees"
Are alert to novelty and gaps in knowledge
Find order in chaos
May prefer nonverbal communication
Are flexible and skilled in decision making

If we take a broad view of "creative abilities," many of the thinking skills to be described in Chapter 11 also could be seen as abilities important to creative thinking and problem solving, for example, planning, reasoning, considering all factors, prioritizing, recognizing the essential and nonessential, discovering relationships, making inferences, and projecting consequences. Some creative personality traits could be viewed as "abilities," for example, humor, curiosity, reflectiveness, perceptiveness and intuition, tolerance for ambiguity, spontaneity, and probably others. And remember Guilford's structure of intellect (SOI) model that we reviewed in Chapter 7? His *divergent thinking* abilities overlap with the above lists. For example, *humor* in the SOI model is considered "divergent production of semantic transformations" (DST). Of course, in any scientific, business, artistic, or social field there are innumerable learned skills and abilities that are essential for creative thinking within the particular knowledge area.

THE CREATIVE PROCESS

There are several ways to view the creative process (Davis, 1992a). First, the traditional approach is to describe a sequence of *stages* through which one might proceed in solving a problem creatively. Second, the creative process can be viewed as a *change in perception*—literally "seeing" new idea combinations, new relationships, new meanings, new implications, or new applications that simply were not perceived a moment before. These approaches to the creative process will be briefly summarized subsequently.

A third approach to understanding the creative process is to examine creative thinking *techniques*—strategies used by creative individuals to produce the new idea combinations and relationships that comprise creative ideas and products. This topic is postponed until Chapter 10.

Steps and Stages in the Creative Process

The Wallas Model.   The best-known set of stages in the creative process is the *preparation, incubation, illumination,* and *verification* stages suggested in 1926 by Graham Wallas. The *preparation* stage includes clarifying and defining the problem, gathering relevant information, reviewing available materials, examining solution requirements, and becoming acquainted with any other relevant innuendos or implications, including previous unsuccessful solutions. This stage basically involves clarifying "the mess."

The *incubation* stage may best be viewed as a period of "preconscious," "fringe conscious," "off-conscious," or even "unconscious" activity which takes place while the thinker, perhaps deliberately, is jogging, watching TV, playing golf, eating pizza, walking along a river bank, or even napping. Guilford (1979) suggested that incubation takes place during reflection, a pause in ac-

tion, and that some people are simply more reflective than others. Many creative people keep a pad and pencil on the bedstand or a small notebook ("idea trap") in their pocket in order to jot down spontaneous ideas for incubated problems.

The third, *illumination* stage is the sudden "Eureka, I found it!" or "Aha!" experience. A solution appears, usually suddenly (although it may follow weeks of work and incubation), that seems to match the requirements of the problem.

The final *verification* stage, as the name suggests, involves checking the workability, feasibility, and/or acceptability of the illumination.

The reader may note that these stages resemble steps in the classic scientific method: state the problem, propose hypotheses, plan and conduct the research, then evaluate the results. Note also that the stages are not an invariant sequence. Some stages may be skipped or the thinker may backtrack to an earlier stage. For example, the process of defining and clarifying the problem (preparation) often leads directly to a good, illuminating idea. Or if the verification confirms that an idea will not work or will not be acceptable, the thinker may move back to either the preparation or the incubation stage.

Actually, one of the most important steps in creative thinking was ignored in the Wallas model: implementation. The idea must be developed and elaborated upon, and the solution carried out. Perhaps this step was assumed.

A Two-Stage Model.   The creative process often, if not always, involves two fairly clear steps: A *big idea* stage and an *elaboration* stage (Davis, 1992a). The big idea stage is a period of fantasy in which the creative person is looking for a new, exciting idea or problem solution. After the idea is found, perhaps using a personal creative thinking technique, the elaboration stage includes idea development, elaboration, and implementation. The artist must do preliminary sketches and create the final work; the novelist must put words on the page—and revise and re-revise—to create characters and plot; and the research scientist or business entrepreneur must organize the details and sequentially carry out the work necessary to implement the big idea.

Creative Problem Solving Model.   The *creative problem solving* (CPS) model is an extremely useful set of five stages originated by Alex Osborn (1963) and more recently articulated by Parnes (1981) and by Treffinger and his colleagues (Isaksen and Treffinger, 1985; Treffinger and Firestien, 1989; Treffinger, Isaksen, and Firestien, 1982; see Figure 9.1). The model typically is presented as five steps, but Parnes and Treffinger and colleagues also note a sixth step—the preliminary one, called *mess-finding*, of locating a "challenge, opportunity, need, or problem" (Treffinger and Firestien, 1989, p. 36) to which to apply the model. We will look briefly at the five core steps of *fact finding, problem finding, idea finding, solution finding* (idea evaluation), and *acceptance finding* (idea implementation). The five steps are useful because they guide the creative process— they tell you what to do at each step to eventually produce one or more creative, workable solutions. One noteworthy feature is that each step first involves a divergent-thinking phase, in which lots of ideas (facts, problem definitions, potential solutions, evaluation criteria, implementation ideas) are generated, and then a second convergent phase

in which only the most promising ideas are selected for further exploration.

The first stage, *fact finding*, involves "listing all you know about the problem or challenge" (Parnes, 1981). For example, let's say the problem is thinking of ways to stimulate creativity in an elementary school resource room G/T program. An individual or group first would list all of the facts they could think of relating to training creative thinking and perhaps to the nature of creativity and creative abilities. Parnes recommends the use of who, what, when, where, why, and how questions. That is:

Who is or should be involved?
What is or is not happening?
When does this or should this happen?
Where does or doesn't this occur?
Why does it or doesn't it happen?
How does it or doesn't it occur?

The list of ideas is then convergently narrowed to a smaller number of facts that might be especially productive.

The second stage, *problem finding*, involves listing alternative problem definitions. One principle of creative problem solving is that the definition of a problem will determine the nature of the solutions. It helps to begin each statement with, "In what ways might I (we) . . ." (for example, find

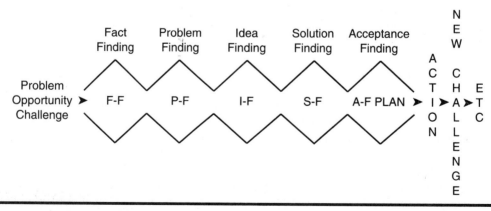

FIGURE 9.1.   The creative problem solving (CPS) model.

lists of strategies, locate someone who knows about training creativity, locate books on the topic, have someone else do it, have the kids themselves solve the problem, and so on).

One or more of the most fruitful definitions is selected for the third stage, *idea finding*. This is the divergent-thinking, brainstorming stage; ideas are freely listed for each of the problem statements accepted in the second stage.

In the fourth stage of *solution finding*, criteria for idea evaluation are listed, for example: Will the strategy strengthen important creative abilities? Will it strengthen good creative attitudes? Will it teach usable creative thinking techniques? Will it cost too much? Will it take too much time? Are the materials available? Will the principal and other teachers accept it? Will the children cooperate? And so on. The list may be reduced to the most relevant criteria.

Sometimes, an *evaluation matrix* is prepared, with possible solutions listed on the vertical axis and the criteria across the top (see Figure 9.2). Each idea is rated according to each criteria (perhaps on a 1 to 5 scale), the ratings are entered in the cells and then totaled to find the "best" idea(s).

Finally, *acceptance finding* (or implementation) amounts to thinking of ". . . ways to get the best ideas into action" (Parnes, 1981).

In his inspiring book *The Magic of Your Mind*, Parnes leads the reader through problem after problem with the goal of making the five steps habitual and automatic. That is, when encountering a problem, challenge, or opportunity, one quickly would review relevant facts, identify various interpretations of the problem, generate solutions, think of criteria and evaluate the ideas, and speculate on how the solution(s) might be implemented and accepted. After 30 years as president of the Creative Education Foundation, and much experience teaching creative problem solving, learning these steps is Parnes's best recommendation for becoming a more creative problem solver and a more effective, self-actualized human being.

In the classroom, the CPS model would be used to guide a creative-thinking session that (1) improves

FIGURE 9.2.   Example of an Evaluation Matrix. Each idea is rated on a 1 (low) to 5 (high) scale according to each criterion. Total scores are then tallied.

students' understanding of the creative process, (2) exposes them to a rousing creative-thinking experience, and (3) solves a problem. With much practice with the steps, students might become habitual creative thinkers, as Parnes intended.

Parnes (1981) noted that "the five steps are a guide rather than a strict formula. Frequently, a change of sequence may be introduced into the process; and it is always advisable to provide plenty of opportunity for incubation." Over one and one-half chocolate sundaes, which Parnes ordered, he told the author (Davis) that people tend to use the five stages too rigidly. On a napkin he scribbled a star-shaped model enclosed in a circle (Figure 9.3), emphasizing that—if it helps the creative process—one may flexibly move directly from any one step to any other.

Treffinger, Isaksen and Firestien (1982) described some convergent techniques that can be used in any of the five CPS steps to aid in finding "good" facts, problem definitions, ideas, evalua-

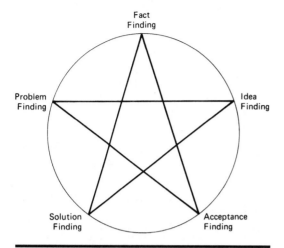

FIGURE 9.3. An alternative conception of the Creative Education Foundation Stages emphasizing that one may flexibly move from any stage to any other.

tion criteria (and solutions), and implementation strategies. Especially interesting are their *hits* and *hot spots*. *Hits* are ideas that strike the problem solver as important break-throughs—directions to be pursued further because they could form the basis for a good solution. Groups of related hits are called *hot spots*. Hot spots are thus ". . . a collection of hits that center around a specific issue or relate to a similar aspect of the problem." The hot spot is given a label that paraphrases the essential meaning of this group of hits. In the convergent part of each CPS step, hits and hot spots are excellent leads for further exploration.

The CPS model may be taught to secondary students and even elementary children, as in the book *CPS for Kids* (Eberle and Stanish, 1985). The *Future Problem Solving* program, summarized in Chapter 6, is based on the CPS model. Osborn originally had reversed steps 1 and 2—*problem finding* preceded *fact finding*. Would this work?

Keating's Four Stages in Socially Relevant Creativity. Keating (1980) emphasized that the act of producing socially relevant creative innova-

tions involves more than just divergent thinking. His four components take ". . . a vaguely temporal sequence." Component 1, *content knowledge*, is based on the assumption that it is virtually impossible to advance beyond the status quo in a field unless one has a thorough working knowledge of the particular discipline or art form. A deep familiarity with the work of one's predecessors in any field is ". . . if not an absolute prerequisite, at least a virtually universal concomitant of creative breakthroughs."

Component 2 is *divergent thinking*, which Keating identified mainly with ideational fluency and flexibility. He considered divergent thinking to be about equal in importance to content knowledge.

Component 3 is *critical analysis*. Noted Keating, it is inaccurate to assume that critical thinking is the antithesis of creative thinking. As colorfully stated by Keating, "Critical analysis has an undeserved reputation as the tough heel on the fragile throat of creativity." Rather, ". . . some judgments must be made so that highly promising ideas may be separated from unpromising ones."

Finally, component 4, *communication skills*, assumes that an idea or artistic conception that exists only in the head of the potential creator is not "creative" in the strict sense. "Something must be made, produced, concretized in some fashion before it has a chance to succeed in contributing to the collective human experience."

An important message in Keating's four components is that enrichment programs for teaching creative thinking should not focus totally on his component 2, divergent thinking exercises. For "real," socially relevant creative contributions, the components of background knowledge and skills, critical thinking, and communication/implementation skills also are essential.

The Creative Process As a Change In Perception

Many creative ideas and problem solutions result from a change in perception—the usually abrupt experience of "seeing" a new idea combination, new relationship, new meaning, new application, or new perspective on a problem. This phenomenon occurs whether the transformation is a simple modification of a cookie recipe (e.g., substituting mint candies for chocolate chips), or a complex discovery in engineering, medicine, or astronomy.

One simple way to illustrate the sudden perceptual change is with visual puzzles. For example, look at Figure 9.4. There is one main, meaningful figure, created in fact from a photograph. After you find this figure, try to locate: (1) a flying pig, (2) an Al Capp *Li'l Abner* character with a snaggle lower tooth, (3) a woman with her hair in a bun reclining on a sofa (she is in white). If you can find these easy (?) ones, you may proceed to (4) the Road Runner (heading left), (5) Harry Belafonte, (6) Popeye, (7) Blackbeard the Pirate, (8) a side profile of Jesus, (9) right next to Jesus a lady in a bouffant hairdo, and (10) E.T. You will find your-

self exclaiming, "Oh! There it is!" or "Now I see it!" The solutions are outlined at the end of this chapter.

We do not understand this sudden perceptual change or mental transformation particularly well. It some simple cases the "Eureka!" seems due simply to viewing (or visualizing) one or two objects or ideas, and then mentally modifying them, combining them, or otherwise creating a new meaning or relationship; or to suddenly seeing a relationship between your problem and a more familiar one. For example, a candy bar mogul, always alert for new products, may receive a sample package of macadamia nuts on an airline flight and instantly "see" a chocolate/macadamia treat. A Silicon Valley computer chip expert, upon checking his wristwatch, may suddenly visualize a baseball game or some other video game incorporated into the wristwatch. A novelist may "see" an intriguing story take shape as the result of a visit to

FIGURE 9.4.   Visual Puzzle.

Reprinted with permission of Charles Scribners Sons, an imprint of Macmillan Publishing Company from *Creative Actionbook* by Sidney J. Parnes, Ruth Noller, and Angelo M. Biondi. Copyright 1976 by Charles Scribners Sons.

Cuba or Iraq or from reading a description of a middle east or central America conflict.

The creative change in perception is arguably a complex, mysterious, and elusive process. Torrance (1980), for example, described the "suprarational" nature of "insight, intuition, and revelation" that happens in an instant. He noted that such phenomena do not fit the rational model of science, and therefore have not been studied scientifically.

The discussion of creative thinking techniques in the next chapter will outline some unconscious creative processes that have been made conscious, knowable, and teachable. Most of these techniques are based on forcing the thinker to "see" new relationships and transformations of ideas.

CREATIVE DRAMATICS

Creative dramatics most definitely is a unique classroom activity. According to Way (1967), it is "the education of the whole person by experience." As with other creativity exercises, creative dramatics stimulates divergent thinking, imagination, and problem solving. It also may strengthen sensory awareness, concentration, control of the physical self, discovery and control of emotions, humor, self-confidence in speaking and performing, empathic and humanistic understanding of others and even critical thinking (e.g., Carelli, 1981; Cresci, 1989; Davis, Helfert, and Shapiro, 1992; McCaslin, 1974; Robbins, 1988; Way, 1967). It also is as fun as it is beneficial. Furthermore, sessions are not difficult to lead: The two main requirements are a good sense of humor and enough energy to crank up a people machine or wade through a peanut butter swamp.

Creative dramatics activities are described in the categories of *warm-ups*, *movement exercises*, *sensory and body awareness exercises*, *pantomime, and playmaking*.

Warmup Exercises

Any creative dramatics session must begin with some simple loosening up exercises, movements that stretch a few muscles but require little or no thinking. Some suggestions are:

Holding Up the Ceiling.   As the leader narrates, the students strain to hold up the ceiling, slowly letting it down (to one knee), then pushing it back up into place.

Biggest Thing, Smallest Thing.   Another easy one is to have everyone stretch his or her body into the "biggest thing" he/she possibly can. No one has any trouble guessing what the second part of the exercise is.

Stretching.   There are many ways to stretch. One strategy is to have students begin with their heads and work down, stretching then relaxing every part of the body. Vice versa, begin with the toes. Either may be done lying down.

Warmup at Different Speeds.   Children run in place in slow motion, then speed up until they are moving very fast. Variations include jumping, skipping, or hopping.

Movement Exercises

Circles.   The group stands in a large circle. Each participant, in turn, thinks of a way to make a circle by using his or her body. It may be a fixed or moving circle, using part or all of the body. All others must make the same circle. Names add to the fun—for example, "This is a halo circle," "This is a shoulder circle," "This is a chicken circle," "This is a Steve Martin circle." Circles will be more original if originality is clearly encouraged.

Mirrors.   Everyone needs a partner. One person becomes a mirror who mimics the movements of the partner. Roles are reversed in about three minutes.

Circus.   Each child becomes a different circus performer or animal. Variations include the leader directing what every one should be, for example, tightrope walkers, trained elephants, lion tamers, jugglers, and so forth.

People Machines. This is everyone's favorite. There are two main strategies. Students can form *groups* of six to twelve persons and take 10 or 15 minutes to design and practice their machine. They are performed one at a time for the others, who try to guess what the machine is. Alternatively, with the *add-on* method an idea for a machine is agreed upon and then one person starts the action. Others add themselves. Sounds—beeps, dings, buzzes, pops, and so on—are recommended. One of the best is an old-fashioned pinball game, which can absorb fifty volunteers.

Obstacles. With chalk, the leader draws a "start" and "finish" line on the floor, about eight feet apart. One at a time, each student makes up an imaginary obstacle that he or she must climb over (past, through, under, around) to get from start to finish. Since only one person participates at a time, it works best with small groups.

Gym Workout. Participants pantomime activities as if they were in an imaginary gym. They run in place, lift weights, roll a medicine ball, climb a rope—all at once or one at a time.

Robot Walk. Each person is a robot with a unique sound and walk. Whenever one robot touches another robot, both stop, sit down, and begin again to rise with a new sound and a new walk.

Balloon Burst. There are two main versions. First, each person is a balloon who is blown up, and up, and up. The balloon can be released and zip around the room, or else blown up until it pops. In the second version the entire group is one balloon that is blown up to the limit, then bursts.

Creative Locomotion. Have children walk like a Crooked Man, the Jolly Green Giant, Raggedy Ann, a robot, and so forth; run like a squirrel, mouse, Miss Muffett frightened by a spider, or the fattest person in the world running for a bus; jump like a kangaroo, popcorn, a jack-in-the-box; or walk through a peanut butter swamp, flypaper, a jungle, tacks, deep sand, or deep Jell-O. The leader and students call out new characters, animals, substances, surfaces, and so on.

Making Letters. Have individuals or two people shape their bodies to become alphabet letters. Others guess the letter. A small group can spell a word.

Imaginary Tug-of-War. Ask for ten volunteers (or pick them, if reluctance prevails). They are divided into two five-person teams. The leader narrates: "This side is struggling hard and seems to be winning. Now the other side is recovering. Look out! The rope broke!" Warn them to listen to the narrator, and be sure they hear the last instruction.

Sensory and Body Awareness

Trust Walk (or Blind Walk). This is an absolute must. Each person has a partner. The member with eyes shut, or blindfolded, is led around the room, under tables and chairs, and allowed to identify objects by touch, smell, or sound. Students walk down the hall, get a drink of water, try to read names or numbers on doors (such as "Boys"), go outside and explore trees, the sun, shade, a flower, and so on. Ask about experiences and discoveries in a follow-up discussion.

Exploring an Orange. Give everyone an orange to examine closely. How does it look, feel, smell, taste? What is unique about your orange? Take the orange apart and examine and discuss the colors, patterns, and textures. Eat the orange.

Listening. Have students sit (or lie) silently, listening first for sounds that are close, then for sounds that are far. Encourage concentration, letting sounds evoke associated images and memories. With all eyes shut, students can describe the sounds with their hands, communicating nonverbally.

Smelling. Small bottles are prepared in advance with such familiar scents as vanilla extract, Vicks Vaporub, peanut butter, used coffee grounds, cinnamon, cloves, rubbing alcohol, lipstick, and so on. In small groups the scents are passed around and students discuss the memories that are stimulated by each smell. The smells also can be imagined, for example, how does the smell of warm apple sauce and cinnamon make you feel?

Touching.   Have students touch many surfaces, concentrating fully on the feel. Use strange objects (for example, a piece of coral) and familiar ones (for example, a piece of paper). A paper sack or box may be used to hide the objects from sight.

Pantomime

Many of the movement and sensory exercises cited thus far also include an element of pantomime (for example, circus, people machines, tug-of-war, creative locomotion). With more "serious" pantomime, students create appropriate positions, physical movements, and even eye movements as they perform in an imaginary environment. With encouragement, students can use their faces, hands, and bodies to express sadness, glee, love, fear, and so on. Pantomime can include relatively simple, short-term involvement, or else lengthier miniplays without lines.

Some pantomime activities include:

Invisible Box.   Six to ten students form a circle. In turn, each person lifts the lid on an invisible box (or trunk), removes something, does something with it, then puts it back in the box and closes the lid. The action may go around the circle two or three times.

Invisible Balls.   An invisible ball is passed from person to person several times around a small circle (or up and down each row in a class). As each person receives the ball, it changes size, shape, weight, smell, and so forth.

Inside-Out.   Children become fish in a tank or zoo animals in cages. Others look in.

Animal Pantomimes.   Each child moves to the center of the circle to pantomime his or her animal. Others guess the animal. For variety, two or three animals can act out a simple plot, for example, a cat sneaking up on a mouse; a bear looking for honey but finding bees; a bull spotting some picnickers; a squirrel and a bluejay both trying to get the same piece of bread; a rabbit and a turtle preparing for a short race. Students can think of more.

Creating an Environment.   This exercise is much like an add-on people machine. Students think of and create an environment, such as a bowling alley, fishermen in a boat, a playground, ballet class, sea fish and animals, gym class, football team warming up, farm animals, an assembly line processing freshly caught salmon, and so on. The class will think of more possibilities.

Miscellaneous Pantomime.   Many brief sketches may teach characterization. With no lines allowed, students pay high attention to movements and expressions. As some examples: a jolly McDonald's counterperson waiting on two or three impatient customers, a fussy person trying on hats or shoes, scared mountain climbers unable to go up or down, three stooges hanging wallpaper or performing heart surgery, a grouchy cab driver in 5 o'clock traffic getting a worried person to the airport, the President of the United States being locked out of the official airplane, and others.

Playmaking

Playmaking involves acting out stories and scenes without a script. To improve the expressiveness of movements and gestures, a sketch may be practiced without lines, that is, in pantomime. With one straightforward strategy, students are given a simple scene (plot), characters are explained, and then students improvise the action.

Way (1967) suggested that mini-plays need not be silly. They can involve, for example, miners working against time to reinforce a mine about to cave in; slow-moving astronauts assembling something on the moon; toyshop toys or museum displays coming alive at the stroke of midnight; Californians experiencing an earthquake; or witches and goblins cooking up a magic brew with improvised important ingredients. Historical episodes, folklore, mythology, fairy tales, nursery rhymes, and animal stories also present possibilities: for example, the Boston Tea Party, Columbus discovering America, Goldilocks and the Three Bears, Cinderella, and others.

A more structured playmaking strategy might run as follows. After a few warmup exercises, the leader tells a story. Then leader and students review the sequence of events—what happened first? Second? The group then discusses characterization, considering physical, emotional, and intellectual qualities (limping, slow, quick-stepping, nervous, angry, happy, excited, calm, conceited, dull-witted, scientific-minded). The play typically is broken down and worked out scene by scene. The group may first act out a scene without dialogue to explore the movements, expressions and general believability of the characters. After improvements, it is replayed with improvised dialogue. A given scene may be replayed many times, with different students trying different roles. As noted above, ideas may be found in historical or mythological material, or in children's books, nursery rhymes, or other stories. Also, brainstorming may be used to generate plots and ideas.

For playmaking with gifted students, Carelli (1981) mentioned that the students may select the theme, assign responsibilities, plan and implement the activities, including researching the particular historical or mythological event, and evaluate both the process and the final product.

To conclude, creative dramatics is a worthwhile activity that may be used at any age level, from the elementary school pullout program to the high school drama class. By giving students a perfectly logical reason to be silly, feelings of self-consciousness and fear of failure are reduced, and confidence is built. Humor, as we noted earlier in this chapter, is a common component of creative-ness, and certainly one encouraged in creative dramatics sessions.

SUMMARY

Creative students tend to be independent, risk-taking, energetic, curious, witty, idealistic, artistic, attracted to the mysterious and complex, and to need alone time.

Negative traits include stubbornness, resistance to domination, uncooperativeness, cynicism, tendencies to question rules, uncommunicativeness, and others.

Torrance suggested a number of characteristics of creativeness in the kinesthetic and auditory areas, for example, skillful movement and talent in dance and music.

In addition to the popular fluency, flexibility, originality, and elaboration, important creative abilities include sensitivity to problems, the ability to define a problem well, the ability to resist premature closure, and visualization, analogical thinking, analysis, synthesis, evaluation, transformation, intuition, concentration, and logical thinking abilities. Some additional information processing abilities include using existing knowledge for new ideas, avoiding perceptual sets, "seeing the forest instead of trees," finding order in chaos, and decision making.

Many thinking skills and personality traits may be considered creative abilities.

The creative process may be viewed, first, as stages in creative problem solving. Wallas's four stages included preparation, incubation, illumination and verification. A two-stage model included a big idea stage followed by an elaboration and development stage.

The creative problem solving model included fact-finding, problem-finding, idea-finding, solution-finding, and acceptance-finding. Treffinger's hits and hot spots aid in convergently selecting the best ideas in each step.

Keating's four components of socially relevant creativity included content knowledge, divergent thinking, critical analysis, and communication skill.

The creative process also may be viewed as a change in perception, seeing new idea combinations, new relationships, new meanings, new implications, and new applications. This sudden change in perception is not well understood, leading to speculation of suprarational thinking.

Creative dramatics seeks to strengthen divergent thinking, imagination, problem solving, and sensory awareness, as well as discovery and control of emotions and the physical self, humor, self-confidence, and empathic understanding. Five categories of activities include warm-ups, movement exercises, sensory and body awareness, pantomime, and playmaking.

Solutions to Visual Puzzle.

Flying Pig

Cow

Popeye

Dog Patch Person

Road Runner

E.T.

Harry Belafonte

Jesus

Lady With Bouffant Hair

Napping Lady

Blackbeard

CHAPTER 10

CREATIVITY II
TEACHING FOR CREATIVE GROWTH

It is unprofitable to think of creativity as a process of emergence out of nowhere. It is rather a transformation of the given into something radically different—not a rabbit produced by magic out of a silk hat, but a silk purse produced by art out of a sow's ear.
Matthew Lipman (1991, p. 202)

CAN CREATIVITY BE TAUGHT?

The authors frequently are asked a key question: Can creativity be taught or are you born with it? The answer is an unequivocal yes and yes. Some people are born with a special combination of creative genius and intelligence which, activated by high motivation and a sense of destiny, leads them to dream their dreams and implement those creations that make the world a better place. The names of da Vinci, Beethoven, Curie, Edison, Einstein, and George Washington Carver come to mind. No amount of creativity training can elevate an average person to such lofty creativeness.

Despite genetic limits, however, it is absolutely true that everyone's personal creativity can be improved. In the case of gifted and talented children, efforts to strengthen their creative abilities—and get them to use the abilities they were born with—can have visibly dramatic effects, for example, as evidenced in the marvelous products and performances in the Future Problem Solving and Odyssey of the Mind programs.

Many teachers already are creativity conscious and integrate creativity exercises into class work perhaps daily. For example, some teachers arrange independent projects in language arts, sci-ence, or art areas. These projects help students develop such creative problem solving attitudes and skills as independence, problem defining, information gathering, idea generating, evaluating, decision-making, and communication, along with valuable technical skills.

Some teachers give divergent thinking exercises, either as a classroom brainstorming activity or in asking students individually to write their ideas. Divergent thinking problems may or may not be tied to the subject matter at hand. For example, teachers might ask students to think of unusual uses for ping pong balls or for the math balance scales; improvements for bicycles or better ways to evacuate the building in case of fire; or clever ways to make the school burglar proof or keep the hallways clean. Some ask "What would happen if . . .?" questions: What would happen if gasoline engines were never invented? If nobody went to school? Many workbooks are filled with divergent thinking and other creativity exercises and activities. Some favorites are *Hearthstone Traveler* (Stanish, 1988), *Mindglow* (Stanish, 1986), *Hippogriff Feathers* (Stanish, 1981), *I Believe in Unicorns* (Stanish, 1979), *Sunflowering* (Stanish, 1977), *Teaching is Listening* (Gordon and Poze, 1972a), *Strange and Familiar* (Gordon and Poze, 1972b), and *Making it Strange* (Gordon, 1974).

Some teachers review biographical information about creative people, for example, the training, life styles, attitudes, and thinking habits of Edison, Einstein, Curie, or Picasso. They might ask students to research the life of a creative person, and even design and create a learning center that explains the person's thinking style, personality, struggles, and accomplishments. On parents' night, students can even dress as famous creative characters and explain "what it's like being me" (Betts, 1985, 1991). The goal of the biographical approach is to help students better understand creativity and creative people, and possibly motivate them to acquire some of the attitudes and technical talents they have learned about.

As we saw in Chapter 9, creative dramatics is another strategy that some teachers use to strengthen imagination, divergent thinking, problem solving, sensory awareness, confidence, humor, and others.

Goals of Creativity Training

The above strategies are common and logical efforts to "teach creativity." However, creativity training might be better structured if we itemize main goals and objectives of such training, and then review ways to achieve each objective. The list is brief and uncomplicated. We will look at:

- Raising creativity consciousness and teaching creative attitudes.
- Improving students' metacognitive understanding of creativity.
- Strengthening creative abilities through exercise.
- Teaching creative thinking techniques.
- Involving students in creative activities.

Our recommendation is that a sensible creativity training effort should include *all* of these objectives and their corresponding activities. By a remarkable coincidence, a sensible order of objectives and their related learning activities exactly matches the order in which these topics are presented.

CREATIVITY CONSCIOUSNESS AND CREATIVE ATTITUDES

Increasing creativity consciousness and creative attitudes is the single most important component of teaching for creative growth. Creative attitudes are taught in every creative thinking course and program, and for good reason. To think creatively a person must be consciously aware of creativity. He or she must value creative thinking, appreciate novel and farfetched ideas, be open-minded and receptive to the zany ideas of others, be mentally set to produce creative ideas, and be willing to take creative risks, make mistakes, and even fail.

Improving creative attitudes and awarenesses probably is 90 percent of the problem of stimulating people of any age to think more creatively (Davis and Bull, 1978). Many students are capable of creative achievements. However, they do not think about creativity or appreciate the importance of creativity for their personal growth—for developing their talents and potential, for coping successfully with their world, and for simply getting more out of life. Students also should become more aware of the importance of creative innovation in the history of civilization, and for solving society's present and future problems. Indeed, without creative innovation and creative people we still would be living in caves during our short and sick lives, and digging roots and clubbing rodents for lunch.

Strengthening Creative Personality Traits.
Creative personality traits are tied closely to creative attitudes and awarenesses. We normally do not speak of "teaching personality traits." However, teachers can reward and encourage the (positive) kinds of traits and behaviors that relate to creative thinking—confidence, independence, enthusiasm, adventurousness, a willingness to take risks and fail, curiosity, playfulness, humor, time alone for thinking, interest in complexity, perceptiveness, and artistic and other aesthetic interests.

Teachers also may take a more direct approach: A creativity program in Ohio known to the authors found measurable growth in creative characteristics simply by teaching them. Students were helped to understand the traits and why they are essential for creativeness.

Creative Atmosphere. Creative attitudes and awareness also are intimately related to the notion of a creative atmosphere, an environment where creativity is encouraged and rewarded. Carl Rogers (1962) called it *psychological safety*, a prerequisite for creative thinking. In brainstorming it is called *deferred judgment*—the noncritical, nonevaluative and receptive atmosphere where fresh and even wild ideas may be safely proposed.

It is an ancient and honored principle of psychology that rewarded behavior will persist and become stronger, while punished or ignored behavior will disappear. A creative atmosphere rewards creative thinking and helps it become habitual.

Blocks to Creativity.   Creative attitudes and predispositions may be aided by raising students' awareness of blocks and barriers to creative thinking, which may be categorized as *perceptual, cultural*, and *emotional* (Davis, 1992a; Simberg, 1964). With *perceptual blocks* we become accustomed to perceiving things in familiar ways, and it simply is difficult to view them in a new and creative way. As an illustration of a perceptual block, given BSAINXLEATNTEARS cross out six letters to find a meaningful word. (See footnote when you give up.[1])

Cultural blocks, as with perceptual blocks, also result from learning and habit. With cultural blocks we have the creativity-squelching effects of traditions, conformity pressures, and social expectations, which along with "fear of being different" will nip creativeness in its proverbial bud.

Conformity pressures and social expectations can take the form of idea-squelchers. The following are some favorites, condensed from a longer list by Warren (1974; Davis, 1992a). You may

wish to think about installing an innovative G/T program as you read these:

> It won't work . . .
> It's not in the budget . . .
> We've never done it before . . .
> We're not ready for it yet . . .
> What will parents think . . .
> We're too small for that . . .
> We have too many projects now . . .
> Somebody would have suggested it before if it were any good . . .
> You'll never sell it to the union . . .
> We can't do it under the regulations . . .
> It's not in the curriculum . . .
> It'll mean more work . . .
> I'll bet some professor suggested that . . .

Such idea squelchers are the products of unreceptive, inflexible, and uncreative attitudes.

It is true, of course, that the human processes of socialization, education, and even healthy peer relations necessarily require a good measure of conformity. *However, children and adults should realize that there is a time for conformity and a time for creativity.*

Emotional blocks are the insecurities and anxieties that interfere with creative thinking. Here we find temporary states, such as job anxieties, school pressures, emotional problems, or health concerns. We also have more permanent emotional blocks, such as a chronic fear of making mistakes or failing, fear of being different, fear of rejection, fear of supervisors, timidity, poor self-concept, and other persistent anxieties.

Some of us need a whack in the side of the head to jostle us out of our uncreative attitudes (see Inset 10.1).

Fortunately, a heightened creativity consciousness and creative attitudes are a natural outgrowth of most types of classroom creativity exercises and activities. As we noted in Chapter 2, the main difference between people who *have* creative abilities and those who *use* their creative potential lies in attitudes, awareness, and related creative personality traits that predispose people to think

---

[1]The solution is BANANA. What did you cross out?

INSET 10.1 _____

A Whack on the Side of the Head

One popular book on stimulating creativity, written for corporate readers, is entitled *A Whack on the Side of the Head* (Von Oech, 1983). The entire book focuses on removing 10 mental blocks. As the book title suggests, it can take a whack on the side of the head to jolt us out of our anti-creative attitudes.

The first mental block, *The Right Answer*, is the well-learned assumption that there is one right answer. Not so. We should look for the second right answer, the third right answer, and more. A later "right answer" probably will be more creative.

Von Oech's second block, *That's Not Logical*, is based the common assumption that logical thinking is better than illogical thinking. However, illogical thinking stimulates the imaginative play and new perspectives that can generate creative ideas.

A third block to creative thinking is *Follow the Rules*. Instead of following the rules, said Von Oech, we should play the revolutionary and challenge rules. He recommended holding "rule-inspecting and rule-discarding" sessions.

Pressure to *Be Practical* is his fourth block. Instead, we should ask creativity stimulating "what if" questions, and encourage "what-iffing" in others.

Avoid Ambiguity is the fifth block. In fact, ambiguity inspires imaginative ideas.

Von Oech's sixth block is *To Err is Wrong*. While a fear of making mistakes inhibits trying new things, creative innovation necessarily requires making errors and even failing. Thomas Watson, founder of IBM, claimed that "The way to succeed is to double your failure rate" (Von Oech, 1983, p. 93).

The seventh block is the notion that *Play is Frivolous*. Countless creative innovations and scientific discoveries have been born by playing with ideas; and childlike thinking, humor, and playing with ideas are common traits of creative people.

Block number eight is *That's Not My Area*. This block is an excuse for not even trying to solve a problem. Many innovations are born by adapting ideas from outside of a field.

Don't Be Foolish, block nine, is another cultural barrier. Said Von Oech, you occasionally should play the fool, and you certainly should be aware of when you or others are putting down a creative "fool."

Finally, the tenth block is the self-squelcher: *I'm Not Creative*. If you seriously believe this, you will be correct.

Do you need an occasional whack on the side of the head?

---

and behavior in creative ways. Sternberg (1990) itemized tips that encourage students to develop creative habits and traits—and to use them (see Inset 10.2).

UNDERSTANDING THE TOPIC OF CREATIVITY

Any creativity training will have more impact and make a more lasting impression if students are helped to understand the topic of creativity. There is a large body of information that contributes to this understanding (see Davis, 1992a, or Dacey, 1989, for an overview). Some main topics that could comprise lessons "about creativity" are:

The importance of creativity to self and society
Characteristics of creative people
The nature of creative ideas as modifications, combinations, and analogical "connections"

INSET 10.2 _____

Tips for Strengthening Creativity

- _Know when to be creative and when to conform._ For example, be creative in artistic and research projects; do not be creative on multiple-choice exams or by violating normal school requirements.
- _Find out what you are best at._ Experiment and explore; take risks and challenge yourself. You might discover new talents.
- _Be motivated from inside yourself, not from the outside._ Work to please yourself; do things that interest you. Seek satisfaction in a job well done.
- _Do not let personal problems stop your thinking and work._ Accept that everyone sometimes has problems, and try to take them in stride. Work can take your mind off problems.
- _Do not take on more—or less—than you can handle._ Find the balance that allows you to do a thorough job, but without accomplishing less than you could.
- _Be persistent._ Do not let frustration, boredom, or fear of failure stop your creative work. Finish what you start—but also know when to quit if you hit a dead end.
- _Make your environment more creative._ Do your parents, teachers, and friends support your creative efforts? Does your room inspire creative thinking? Can you change your environment to make it more creative?

Based on Sternberg (1990), by permission of Free Spirit Publishing.

The nature of the creative process: Stages, changed perceptions, modifying, combining, analogical thinking

Creative abilities

Theories and definitions of creativity

Tests of creativity and the rationale underlying them

Creative thinking techniques

Barriers to creative thinking, including Von Oech's 10 blocks

As we noted above, biographies of well-known creative people provide a useful way to teach students about desirable creative characteristics, attitudes, habits, and lifestyles. The _Torrance Tests of Creative Thinking_ may be used as the basis for a lesson in the meaning of _fluency, flexibility, originality_, and _elaboration_ and their importance in creative thinking.

Students also can learn "principles" of creative thinking, such as:

- Creativity will help you live a more interesting, successful, and enjoyable life.
- Creative people are not rigid; they look at things from different points of view.
- Creative people are aware of pressures to conform—to be like everybody else.
- Creative thinking includes taking risks and making mistakes—and the more creative the idea, the greater the risk of mistakes and failure.
- Creative people play with ideas, consider lots of possibilities, use techniques, think analogically, evaluate their ideas, and get their ideas into action.
- Creative people use their talents, not waste them.

STRENGTHENING CREATIVE ABILITIES

In Chapter 9 we itemized abilities that logically underlie creativity. It is a common and reasonable strategy to try to strengthen creative abilities through practice and exercise, the same way we strengthen skills of reading, math, word processing, solving chemistry problems, and shooting baskets.

We will look again at some of those abilities, noting strategies, exercises, or materials that aim at strengthening each ability. Note that most activities not only exercise creative abilities, they also implicitly raise creativity consciousness and bend attitudes in a creative direction.

Fluency, Flexibility, Originality, Elaboration. Many types of questions and problems will exercise these traditional creative abilities. As we noted earlier, students can do the exercises as a class, perhaps following brainstorming rules, or else individually. One of the most involving methods is to divide students into problem-solving teams. All teams work on the same problem and then report all or the best ideas to the entire class. Students often are surprised at the different problem interpretations, approaches, and ideas from the other groups.

Some useful types of exercises for stimulating fluency, flexibility, originality, and elaboration are as follows.

1. With "What would happen if . . .?" exercises students list consequences for unlikely events. The events may be imaginary or potentially real. What would happen:

If each person had an eye in the back of his or her head?

If we did not have books?

If the British had won the Revolutionary War?

If the only musical instruments were drums?

If there were no gravity in this room?

If people with blond hair were not allowed in hotels or restaurants, and could not vote?

If the earth shifted and your town became the north pole?

If Edison had become a plumber and we had no light bulbs?

If no one ever smiled?

If everyone were a litterbug?

If we had no bricks or wood to build homes?

If we had no automobiles, TV, video games, peanut butter, bicycles, football?

2. Thinking of *product improvements* is another type of open-ended question. Students may be asked to think of improvements for any product or process—pencils, desks, jogging shoes, classrooms, skateboards, pianos, school lunches, soda pop, Cracker Jacks, computers, a bathtub, and so on.

3. Thinking of *unusual uses* for common objects is probably the single oldest creativity test item; it also makes a good exercise. How might we use discarded rubber tires? A coat hanger? Empty plastic gallon milk containers? A wooden stick? A sheet of paper? Leftover and wasted cafeteria food?

4. Posing *problems and paradoxes* is intrinsically interesting and challenging. A problem may require a solution, or a puzzling situation may require a logical explanation. The problem may be realistic or fanciful. For example: How can bicycle thefts be eliminated? How can the lunch menu be improved? What can we buy for parents for Christmas/Hanukkah for ten dollars? How can the school (family) light bill be reduced. How can our health be improved? What can be done for Mr. Smith, a former night watchman who is 55 years old, out of work, with no special skills? How could we remove a stubborn elephant from the living room? How can we keep gremlins from stealing the melons from the melon patch? How can the three bears prevent burglaries?

Here are some examples of problems requiring explanations: The principal suddenly cancels recess. Why? The grass behind billboards in pastures is often lush. Why? Ten paintings were discovered missing from the art gallery, but there was no sign of a break-in. How could they have disappeared?

5. With *design problems*, students can design an ideal school, an airplane for hauling nervous kangaroos, a better lawnmower, more functional clothes, safer ways to travel, a more efficient way to serve lunch in the cafeteria, new sandwiches or other treats for McDonald's, a better mousetrap, and so on.

Looking more specifically at each ability, *fluency* can be exercised by having students list things, for example, that are round, square, sweet, sour, blue, white, made of metal, made of wood, long and slender, short and stubby, smell good, taste bad, or have sharp edges. Some *flexibility* exercises ask students to look at things from different perspectives: How does this room look to a tidy housekeeper? A hungry mouse? An alien from outer space? How does a highway look to a tire? A crow? A lost pilot? *Elaboration* exercises require the learner to build upon a basic idea, for example, developing the dog walking or cat petting machine in detail—measurements, materials, costs—or elaborating and embellishing a short story, drawing, or invention.

Sensitivity to Problems.   Exercises aimed at strengthening problem sensitivity should have the learners find problems, detect difficulties, or detect missing information. Therefore, one type of exercise is having students *ask questions* about an ambiguous situation or even a common object. For example, what questions could you ask about clouds, Mexico, Mickey Mouse, a typewriter, the moon, or the school lunch program. Another type of problem sensitivity exercise would begin with "What don't we know about . . .?" Or "What is wrong with . . . ?"

Problem Defining.   *Problem defining* is a complex ability. Relevant exercises would evolve around:

Identifying the real problem and simplifying and clarifying the problem.

What is the basic problem here? What are we really trying to do? What really needs attention (fixing)?

Isolating important aspects of a problem. What is relevant? Essential? What should we focus on? What can we ignore?

Identifying subproblems. What problems are

related to the main problem? What problems will follow from each solution?

Proposing alternative problem definitions, as in the IWWMW ("In what ways might we . . .?") tactic of the CPS model (see Chapter 9).

Defining the problem more broadly, to open up new solution possibilities.

Visualization and Imagination.   *Visualization* and *imagination* are obviously central creative abilities. Three books filled with imagination stimulation exercises are *Put Your Mother on the Ceiling* (DeMille, 1973), *Scamper* (Eberle, 1971), and *200 Ways of Using Imagery in the Classroom* (Bagley and Hess, 1984). All ask students to relax, shut their eyes, and visualize some colorful narration, for example: "Now put a light bulb in each hand . . . Hold your hands straight out to the side . . . Pretend that your light bulbs are jet engines . . . Run down the street for a take off . . ." (Eberle, 1971).

Another exercise guaranteed to elicit visualization is a creative writing activity suggested by Helman and Larson (1980); "Cut out headlines from a newspaper dealing with unusual stories and have the kids make up the stories." The familiar grocery store rags provide an endless supply of candidate headlines. Some recent winners: "Angry Dad Sells Bratty Kids," "Baby Born Talking Gives Dad Winning Lottery Numbers," "Lightning Bolt Zaps Coffin—And Corpse Comes Back To Life!" "Titanic Survivor Afloat for 65 Years," "Teacher Picks Up Hitchhiking Ghost," and "Woman Weds Two-Headed Man—And Gets Sued for Bigamy!"

Analogical Thinking.   As we will see in the next section, analogical thinking is not just a cognitive ability, it also is the single most common and important creative thinking technique used by creatively productive people (Davis, 1992a; Gordon, 1961). Many exercises for exercising analogical thinking appear in workbooks by Gordon (1974), Gordon and Poze (1972a, 1972b), 1980), and Stanish (1977, 1986, 1988). A teacher or G/T coordinator also can make up his or her own with the format "How is a hamburger like a good day at school?" "What animal is like a bass fiddle? Why?" "What kind of weather (animal, fish, vegetable, car, book, fish, sport, magazine, etc.) is like *you*?" And perhaps "What color is sadness?" or "How can noise be seen?" In the next section we will see the *direct analogy method*, which involves finding ideas by asking how nature has solved particular problems, for example, "How do animals, birds, and plants keep warm in winter?" "What could have given a cave dweller the idea for a spear? What was the connection?"

Analysis, Synthesis, Evaluation. *Analysis, synthesis*, and *evaluation*, of course, are Bloom's (1974) higher-level thinking skills that we will see in Chapter 11. Ideas for exercises are suggested in that chapter.

Resisting Premature Closure. Most children and adults are guilty of grabbing the first idea that presents itself. However, considering lots of ideas and deferring judgment are two of the most basic principles of creative problem solving, principles that students should thoroughly understand. Brainstorming, with heavy emphasis on the rationale behind deferring judgment, should help with this pivotal ability (or attitude).

Other Creativity Exercises

There are many types of creativity and problem solving exercises that may be used to strengthen creative abilities. Some are relatively simple divergent thinking exercises; others ask for more complex aesthetic products or solutions to difficult invention or design problems.

Shallcross (1981) created exercises that could be integrated into specific subject matters. As some examples:

1. Sculpt something using leaves, rocks, paste, and a paper bag (art).

2. List ways to get children to enjoy brushing their teeth (health).

3. Invent a one-step "meal-in-one" (home arts).

4. Plan a mystery or soap opera series using the morphological synthesis approach (language arts; described in next section).

5. Think of new ways to measure time, water, air, or height (math).

6. Have someone strike three notes on a piano. Use them as the basis for a melody (music).

7. Invent stretching exercises for joggers (physical education).

8. Brainstorm ways endangered species might be preserved (science).

9. Brainstorm ways different cultures could learn to understand each other better (social studies).

A recent workbook by Stanish, *Hearthstone Traveler*, includes instruction and exercises for poetry writing (cinquains, diamanté), creative writing, humor, analogical thinking, values, recognizing patterns in nature, idea-finding techniques, the CPS model, idea evaluation, and more. Consider the cinquain writing strategy:

> Select a title word (for example, merry-go-round).
> Brainstorm words associated with the title (for example, wild horses, beasts, children, music, mirrors, ticket to ride).
> Brainstorm a second list of "-ing" words descriptive of the title (for example, smiling, laughing, playing, circling, spinning, galloping, running).
> Brainstorm a third list of feeling words also ending in "-ing" (for example, exciting, wondering, thrilling, mastering, owning the world, riding high).
> Write the title on one line, two associated words on the second line, three "-ing" words on the third line, four feeling "-ing" words on the fourth line, and another word associated with the title on the fifth line.

As evidence that it works, the following was created on the spot by nonpoet Davis:

Merry-go-round
Music, wild horses
Galloping, playing, laughing
Thrilling, wondering, mastering, owning the world
Ticket to ride.

Said Stanish, such cinquain may be used to write about oneself, to capture the essence of a reading assignment or an important person one has studied, or as the conclusion to a unit of study. Try it. Some of Stanish's (1988) other exercises include:

In what ways is our circulatory system like a tree?

Investigate the use of spirals in computer art, Van Gogh paintings, the human face, the horns of animals, floral patterns, religious temples.

If I were a hawk, in what ways might I assert an opinion?

Consider a starfish pattern. What could you create with this design if it had a fragrance (or pockets, wheels, legs, handles, many colors), if it were smaller (larger than a house), if it were in an automobile (aircraft), if it had wings (or a battery, one long arm), if it were made of clear plastic (or styrofoam, rubber), or if it rotated (could be thrown), etc.

Something that few people know about me is . . .

Create a humorous drawing that merges two meanings of a word (for example, horn, school, bark, sock, punch).

What kind of sound would an exclamation point (question mark, dollar sign) make?

Invent a Rube Goldberg machine, with at least five steps, to time your suntan (walk your dog, tickle an armadillo's stomach).

The possibilities for mind-stretching, ability-strengthening exercises are endless, particularly with a little searching and brainstorming by the G/T teacher.

CREATIVE THINKING TECHNIQUES

Personal Techniques

Personal creative thinking techniques are methods that are developed and used, consciously and unconsciously, by every creative person regardless of the subject or content of his or her creations. This topic lies at the core of central questions such as "Where do ideas come from?" and "What is the nature of the internal creative process?" (Davis, 1981a).

Most personal techniques are *analogical* in nature. That is, the innovator based the idea for the creation on a news event, a historical event, or an earlier book, movie, melody, art or architecture style, invention, scientific discovery, business, idea, some other previous innovation, or some phenomenon in nature. Indeed, whenever we hear the phrase "was inspired by . . ." or "was based upon . . . ," we can be sure that a deliberate or accidental analogical technique was used by the particular innovator.

An important point is that every one of the *standard* techniques described in the next section originated as a *personal* creative thinking technique—a method that some creative person used in his or her day-to-day high-level creative thinking. The standard techniques are unconscious methods made conscious, knowable, and teachable.

To present the flavor of personal creative-thinking techniques, let's look at a few examples. In science, Einstein used what he called "mental experiments." In his most noted example, he once imagined himself to be a tiny being riding through space on a ray of light, which led to his general theory of relativity.

In art we find recurrent subjects and styles with every famous painter, reflecting their personal creative thinking techniques. Picasso, for example, is known for his African, harlequin, blue, and pink (rose) periods, during which his paintings were inspired by particular themes. He also deliberately disassembled faces and other pictorial elements and put them back together in more original arrangements. Paul Gauguin painted South Pacific natives in his unique style, time and again. Edgar Degas is noted for his graceful ballerinas. Renoir's trademark is his soft pastel, female subjects and still lifes. Georges Seurat used a "dot" painting style (pointillism), often with water and sailboats as subjects.

Seurat's most famous painting, *Sunday Afternoon on the Isle of La Grande Jatte*, inspired the Broadway musical *Sunday Afternoon in the Park with George*—another example of analogical thinking. Andrew Lloyd Weber's *Cats* was based on T. S. Eliot's *Old Possum's Book of Practical Cats*.

Even the great Leonardo da Vinci reportedly wandered Italian streets, sketchbook in hand, to locate interesting faces for his painting *The Last Supper*. Throughout art history, ideas for paintings have been taken from mythology, the Bible, or historical events.

All of Franz Liszt's *Hungarian Rhapsodies* were drawn from the folk tunes of Hungarian gypsies. Tchaikovsky, too, developed folk tunes into symphonies. Aaron Copland's marvelous *Appalachian Spring* was based on the folk tune *Simple Gifts*. Even the ever-popular *Star Spangled Banner* came from an English drinking song.

Cartoonists continually use a deliberate analogical thinking strategy for finding ideas. For example, during the week of the 1992 presidential election Bill Clinton was portrayed as the straw man from *Wizard of Oz* ("If only I had your trust!"), President George Bush as the Tin Man ("If only I had a plan!"), and Ross Perot as the Cowardly Lion ("If only I hadn't quit!"). After the war with Iraq, Saddam Hussein was portrayed as the Wizard behind the curtain ("I am Saddam the great and powerful!"). See the *Far Side* cartoon.

Columnist-humorist Art Buchwald also uses deliberate analogical thinking—borrowing ideas and concepts from one area and using them to make a humorous political comment in another. In

THE FAR SIDE   **By Gary Larson**

Moses as a kid

The Far Side. Copyright 1988 by Universal Press Syndicate. Reprinted with permission. All rights reserved.

one column he borrowed ideas from TV soap operas and used them to discuss a new "Seamy, Steamy Tale of Power and Greed—The Budget of the United States Government:"

> I couldn't put it down. I kept turning the pages to see what government programs would be cut next. It's more frightening than *Rosemary's Baby.*
>
> You mean it's a thriller?
>
> It's more of a whodunit. Or, specifically, who's doing it to whom. It's about money and power, the struggle for survival, death and taxes and man's fate in a world he never made.
>
> Any sex?
>
> The military chapters are very sexy, particularly the love scenes between the President of

the United States and the new weapons that the Pentagon has seduced him into buying.

You mean the President is in bed with the military-industrial complex?

All through the book! Some of the scenes are so hot that Tip O'Neill has threatened to ban the book in Boston . . .*

Toward the end of the sixteenth century, Holinshed's *Chronicles*, a history book, was published. William Shakespeare used it extensively as a source of ideas for *Macbeth, Henry IV, Henry V, Henry VI, Richard II*, and others. He drew from Plutarch's *Lives* to write *Antony and Cleopatra* and *Coriolanus. Troilus and Cressida* came from various accounts of the story of Troy.

Contemporary writers continue to use identifiable procedures to inspire novels and movies. For example, Truman Capote used a Midwest murder as the inspiration for *In Cold Blood*. The Normandy invasion was the basis of the novel and movie *The Longest Day*; Pearl Harbor was the source of ideas for *Tora, Tora, Tora!* and *From Here to Eternity*. Another movie, *All the President's Men*, was based on Watergate. In an interview, the screenwriter of *High Noon* confessed that the inspiration for his award-winning suspense western came from the intimidation of writers and actors in Hollywood by organized crime in the 1950s. Countless other ideas for movies and novels have been found by looking at Greek and Roman history (*I, Claudius*, for example), Biblical history (*Moses*), American history (*Gone with the Wind*), Egyptian history (*Cleopatra*), and so on.

The successful *Star Wars* series was based partly on an effective personal creative thinking technique used by the creator George Lucas. While writing the script for *Star Wars*, Lucas read books on mythology. Said Lucas in a *Time* magazine interview, "I wanted *Star Wars* to have an epic quality, and so I went back to the epics." Thus we find a young man who must prove his manhood to himself and to his father; who rescues a princess in distress;

*Reprinted by permission of Art Buchwald.

who has an older and wiser mentor (actually two, Ben Kenobi and Yoda); and who battles with a villain, Darth Vader. Some western movies have been built deliberately around the same principles.

Professional comedians also use personal creative-thinking techniques, both for their unique type of humor and for their original delivery. The comedian Don Rickles insults people, using the same insults again and again ("Shut up dummy, you're makin' a fool of yourself!"). Rodney Dangerfield's "I don't get no respect" theme makes him one of the most successful American comedians. He continually puts himself down: "When I was born the doctor told my mother, 'I did everything I could, but he's gonna be okay.'" "I couldn't play hide-and-seek 'cause nobody wanted to find me!" "I remember when I called this girl for a date. She said, 'Sure, come on over, nobody's home.' So I went over an' nobody was home!" "Last week I went to a psychiatrist. He said 'I think you're crazy.' I said I wanted another opinion, so he said 'Okay, I think you're ugly too!'"

The list of creations and innovations produced via personal creative thinking techniques, usually analogical in nature, could be endless.

Developing Personal Creative Thinking Techniques

There are several ways students may be encouraged to develop personal creative thinking techniques. First, students should understand how even extraordinarily creative people have "found" ideas. This demystifies creativity and helps convince students that they also can legitimately build upon existing ideas without feeling "uncreative." After all, if William Shakespeare, Franz Liszt, George Lucas, and Art Buchwald can borrow plots, tunes, and ideas, so can they. Many young writers, artists, and composers are erroneously convinced that their ideas must be 100-percent original and never inspired by an outside source.

Second, some recurrent personal creative thinking techniques may be teachable. For example, some techniques include:

1. Deliberately using analogical and metaphorical thinking. For example, in aesthetic creations students can find ideas by looking at what others have done and where their ideas come from. In many kinds of problems students can learn to ask: What else is like this? What has worked for others? What could I adapt from similar problems or situations? What would professionals do (Davis, 1992a)?

2. Modifying, combining, and improving present ideas.

3. Starting with the goal and working backward to deduce what is required to reach that goal.

4. Beginning with an "ideal" or "perfect" solution—such as having the problem solve itself—and again working backwards to design a creative solution.

5. Asking yourself how the problem will be solved 25, 100, or 200 years from now.

Because personal creative thinking techniques develop (1) in the course of doing creative things or (2) from instruction by people who use and understand such techniques, G/T students should become involved in such inherently creative activities as art, photography, creative writing, acting, journalism, science projects, or other activities requiring creative thinking and problem solving.

Mentorships may be especially good, since they involve many hours of direct, personal work with a creative professional. Field trips lead to exposure to experts, to creative ideas, and to sophisticated elaborations and embellishments of ideas.

Visitors also can teach personal creative thinking techniques. For example, a visiting artist program can help children understand the creative processes of a professional artist or writer. School districts in some states contract with a different visiting artist or writer each school year. In this way children have a close view of, and learning experience with, a variety of artists during their school years. University and industry researchers and other creative professionals also may be invited to share their experiences related to creative discoveries and creative thinking.

STANDARD CREATIVE THINKING TECHNIQUES

There are several well-known methods for producing new ideas and new idea combinations that are taught in most university and professional creativity training courses. The strategies also may be taught to middle and high school students, and to gifted and talented elementary students. One lively workbook, *Imagination Express* (Davis and DiPego, 1973), incorporates standard creative thinking techniques into a fantasy story about a Saturday subway ride from Kansas City to Pittsburgh to Dublin to Tokyo to Santa Monica and back. It also teaches good creative attitudes and awarenesses. The workbook was written for approximately the seventh-grade level, but older students (including teachers) and younger students seem to benefit as well. The techniques of brainstorming, attribute listing, analogical thinking, and some others are taught in the upper elementary/ middle school Apple II Computer disk *Creative Thinking and Problem Solving* (Davis, 1985). Workbooks by Stanish (1981, 1988) also teach creativity techniques, including the CPS model (Chapter 9), in a form comprehendible to young learners.

It is worth repeating that every "standard" creative thinking technique began as a personal technique that some perceptive person identified, explained, and thus made conscious and teachable.

Brainstorming

In the case of brainstorming, it was Alex Osborn, cofounder of the New York advertising agency Batten, Barton, Dursten, and Osborn and founder in 1954 of the Creative Education Foundation, who identified the conditions and listed the rules for brainstorming. The main principle is *deferred judgment*: Idea evaluation is postponed until later. As we mentioned earlier, deferred judgment implicitly creates a receptive, creative atmosphere and teaches good creative attitudes: receptiveness to and appreciation for novel, perhaps farfetched ideas. Osborn (1963) observed that any type of criticism or evaluation interferes with producing imaginative ideas, simply because you cannot do both at once. The purpose of any brainstorming session is to generate a long list of possible problem solutions.

Brainstorming is an effective procedure that may be used in the classroom for (1) teaching brainstorming as an effective creative thinking technique, (2) practicing creative thinking (thus strengthening attitudes and abilities), and/or (3) solving some pressing school problem, such as high absenteeism, messy school grounds, drug problems, traffic problems, bicycle thefts, raising money, selling play tickets, and so on. Osborn's four ground rules are quite simple:

1. Criticism is ruled out. This is deferred judgment, which contributes to the creative atmosphere so essential for lively imaginations.

2. Freewheeling is welcomed. The wilder the idea the better. Seemingly preposterous ideas can lead to imaginative yet workable solutions.

3. Quantity is wanted. This principle reflects the purpose of the session: to produce a long list of ideas, thus increasing the likelihood of finding good problem solutions.

4. Combination and improvement are sought. This lengthens the idea list. Actually, during the session students will spontaneously "hitchhike" on each other's ideas, with one idea inspiring the next.

Variations on brainstorming include *reverse brainstorming*, in which new viewpoints are found by turning the problem around. For example: How can we *increase* vandalism? How can we *increase* the electric bill? How can we *stifle* creativity? How can we *decrease* morale? Reverse brainstorming quickly points out what currently is being done incorrectly, and implicitly suggests solutions. With *Stop-and-Go* brainstorming, short (about 10-minute) periods of brainstorming are interspersed with short periods of evaluation. This helps to keep the group on target by selecting the apparently most profitable directions. In the *Phillips 66* technique small groups of six brainstorm for six minutes,

after which a member of each group reports either the best or all ideas to the larger group.

It is easy to run a classroom brainstorming session. The teacher begins by discussing creativity and creative ideas, which leads to brainstorming as one method that stimulates creative thinking. Rules are discussed, a problem selected—such as "How can we turn the classroom into a foreign planet?" or "How can we raise money?"—and a volunteer scribe lists ideas on the blackboard. The teacher-leader's role is to ask frequently, "Anyone else have an idea?" Or the leader might specifically ask the quieter students if they have ideas they wish to contribute. If a serious problem (for example, messy hallways) is the focus, the leader can give the group 48 hours advance notice of the problem. Gifted and talented students can learn to organize and lead brainstorming sessions.

Idea Evaluation.   Merely listing wild ideas does not represent the complete problem-solving process. Therefore, a brainstorming session may be profitably followed by an idea evaluation session. Idea evaluation would be most important if the class intended to present the school principal (or the mayor) with some blue-ribbon solutions to a real current problem. The group can brainstorm evaluation criteria, such as: Will it work? Can the school afford it? Will the community (parents, principal, mayor) go for it? Is adequate time available? Are materials available? And others. As we saw in the previous chapter, the most relevant criteria would be listed across the top of an *evaluation matrix*, the specific ideas in rows down the left side. Table 10.1 shows one evaluation matrix that was constructed to evaluate ideas brainstormed for the problem "How can we build school spirit?" The total scores are a guide to ideas that students may wish to pursue.

The use of objective criteria when evaluating ideas:

1. Helps evaluate the ideas in a mostly unbiased manner.

2. Helps students learn to evaluate as part of the overall creative problem-solving process.

TABLE 10.1   Example of Evaluation Matrix

IDEAS	CRITERIA						
	Cost	Effect on Teachers	Educa- tional Effects	School Spirit Effect	Effect on Students	Effect on Community	Totals
Buy class sweatshirts	+3	+2	+1	+3	+3	+3	15
Establish school baseball team	−2	+2	0	+2	+2	+2	6
Start interclass competition	0	0	+1	+3	+2	0	6
Get new school building	−3	+3	+2	+3	+3	−2	6
Get rid of "hoods"	−3	0	−3	+1	−3	−3	−11

POSITIVE EFFECTS	NEGATIVE EFFECTS
+3 = Excellent	−1 = Slightly Negative
+2 = Good	−2 = Somewhat Negative
+1 = Fair	−3 = Very Negative
0 = Not Applicable	

3. Teaches an effective evaluation technique, one that is used in the CPS model and Future Problem Solving.

4. Requires students to consider many components and views of the problem.

5. In some cases, helps the group explore its values relative to the problem at hand. What criteria are truly relevant?

6. Prevents idea evaluation from becoming a personal attack on specific children.

7. Helps children understand that thinking of "silly" and "far-fetched" ideas truly can lead to good, practical solutions to problems.

Evaluation sessions may follow the use of any of the creative thinking techniques described in this section.

Attribute Listing

Robert Crawford (1978), designer of *attribute listing*, argued that, "Each time we take a step we do it by changing an attribute or a quality of something, or else by applying that same quality or attribute to some other thing." Attribute listing thus is both a *theory* of the creative process and a practical creative thinking *technique*. Following Crawford's definition, there are two forms of attribute listing: (1) *attribute modifying* and (2) *attribute transferring*. Either strategy may be used individually or in a group.

Attribute Modifying. The problem solver lists main attributes (characteristics, dimensions, parts) of an object or process, then thinks of ways to improve each attribute. For example, a group of students might invent new types of candy bars or breakfast cereals by first writing important attributes (size, shape, flavor, ingredients, color, texture, packaging, nutritional value, name, intended market, and so on) on the blackboard, and then listing specific ideas under each main attribute. Particularly good combinations are picked out of the lists of ideas. Not-so-good ideas—the two-pound "Popeye's Delight" candy bar containing spinach and steroids and created for muscle-builders—will keep enthusiasm high. In university design engineering courses the attribute modifying strategy is called the *substitution method* of design.

If there is any doubt that creative people actually use such a mechanical procedure, Fran Stryker (undated; see also Shallcross, 1981) used attribute listing to generate radio and TV episodes for his *Lone Ranger* series. Stryker used the attributes of *characters, goals, obstacles*, and *outcomes*. In the first column he listed specific ideas for *characters*, broadly defined to include objects and animals. *Goals* included things the character(s) wanted to become, to achieve, or to happen. *Obstacles* could be the law, stupidity, soft-heartedness, or blindness. *Outcomes* could include bargaining, sacrificing one's pride or position, or using one's wits. With this technique, augmented by stacks of western novels, Stryker produced lots of ideas in short order.

A modification of Stryker's strategy was used in the computer disk *Creative Thinking and Problem Solving* (Davis, 1985) to teach children (1) the attribute listing method and (2) what components are needed for writing short stories (characters, settings, important objects, obstacles), and (3) how to create ideas for those components. Generally, the attribute listing technique is simple and it works—whether used for inventing breakfast cereals, writing short story plots, or solving any other problem in which attributes can be identified.

Attribute Transferring.   Here we have a pure case of analogical thinking—transferring ideas from one context to another. We noted above how deliberate analogical thinking is used by creative persons in many aesthetic, scientific, or other areas. As one classroom application, ideas for a creative and memorable parents' night or open house might be found by borrowing ideas from a carnival or circus, Disneyland, E.T., the Wild West, a funeral parlor, McDonald's, or a *Star Wars* or *Frankenstein* movie.

Morphological Synthesis

The *morphological synthesis* technique is a simple extension of the attribute listing procedure (Allen, 1962; Davis, 1973, 1992a). Specific ideas for one attribute or dimension of a problem are listed along one axis of a matrix, ideas for a second attribute are listed along the other axis. Plenty of idea combinations are found in the cells of the matrix. One sixth-grade class invented new sandwich ideas with the morphological synthesis technique (see Figure 10.1). With a third dimension (for example, type of bread) you would have a cube with three-way combinations in each cell. Davis (1992b) used morphological synthesis to generate nearly 900 exercises for teaching values and moral thinking.

The method may be used with a half-dozen or so dimensions by listing ideas in columns. The columns may be cut into strips that can be slid up or down to create hundreds (thousands) of combinations found by reading horizontally.

Idea Checklists

Sometimes, one can find a *checklist* which suggests solutions for your problem. For example, the *Yellow Pages* are often used as a checklist for problems like "Who can fix my TV?" or "Where can I get a haircut?" High school counselors have used the *Yellow Pages* for career counseling ideas. A Sears or gift store catalog may be used to solve a gift-giving problem.

Some idea checklists have been designed especially for creative problem solving (see Davis, 1973). The most popular of these is Alex Osborn's (1963) *73 idea-spurring questions* (Table 10.2). Take a few extra seconds as you read through this list and think of how a mousetrap, a backpack, a can of soda pop, or a poster advertising a school play might be improved by the suggestions on the list. Ideas will be elicited virtually involuntarily.

The checklist technique sometimes is called the *SCAMPER* method: *S*ubstitute, *C*ombine, *A*dopt, *M*odify-*M*agnify-*M*inify, *P*ut to other uses, *E*liminate, *R*everse-*R*earrange (e.g., Stanish, 1988).

A sixth grade Milwaukee class used the morphological synthesis method to generate 121 zany ideas for creative sandwiches. Can you find a tasty combination? A revolting one? If you add a third dimension, with five types of bread, how many total ideas would you have?

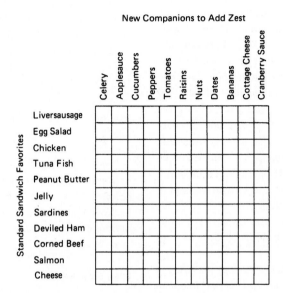

New Companions to Add Zest

	Celery	Applesauce	Cucumbers	Peppers	Tomatoes	Raisins	Nuts	Dates	Bananas	Cottage Cheese	Cranberry Sauce
Liversausage											
Egg Salad											
Chicken											
Tuna Fish											
Peanut Butter											
Jelly											
Sardines											
Deviled Ham											
Corned Beef											
Salmon											
Cheese											

Standard Sandwich Favorites

Ratings of Various Spreads

	Choices				
Flavor	1st	2nd	3rd	4th	5th
Super Goober (Peanut Butter/Cranberry)	17	2	1	0	4
Charlies Aunt (Tuna and Applesauce)	3	16	2	2	1
Irish Eyes are Smiling (Corn Beef and Cottage Cheese)	0	0	16	2	6
Cackleberry Whiz (Hard Boiled Eggs/Cheese Whiz)	1	3	2	14	4
Hawaiian Eye (Cream Cheese and Pineapple)	3	3	3	6	9

FIGURE 10.1. A Morphological Sandwich.

From Creativity is Forever, third ed., by G.A. Davis (Dubuque, IA. Kendall/Hunt). Used with permission.

TABLE 10.2   Osborn's "73 Idea-Spurring Questions"

Put to other uses? New ways to use as is? Other uses if modified?

Adopt? What else is like this? What other idea does this suggest? Does the past offer a parallel? What could I copy? Whom could I emulate?

Modify? New twist? Change meaning, color, motion, sound, odor, form, shape? Other changes?

Magnify? What to add? More time? Greater frequency? Stronger? Higher? Longer? Thicker? Extra value? Plus ingredient? Duplicate? Multiply? Exaggerate?

Minify? What to subtract? Smaller? Condensed? Miniature? Lower? Omit? Streamline? Split up? Understate?

Substitute? Who else instead? What else instead? Other ingredient? Other material? Other process? Other power? Other place? Other approach? Other tone of voice?

Rearrange? Interchange components? Other pattern? Other layout? Other sequence? Transpose cause and effect? Change pace? Change schedule?

Reverse? Transpose positive and negative? How about opposites? Turn it backward? Turn it upside down? Reverse roles? Change shoes? Turn tables? Turn other cheek?

Combine? How about a blend, an alloy, an assortment, an ensemble? Combine units? Combine purposes? Combine appeals? Combine ideas?

Reprinted with permission of Charles Scribners Sons, an imprint of Macmillan Publishing Company from *Applied Imagination* by A.F. Osborn. Copyright © 1963 Charles Scribners Sons.

Synectics Methods

Synectics, taken from the Greek word *synecticos*, means the joining together of apparently unrelated elements. It was his work with creative-thinking groups that led William J. J. Gordon, originator of the synectics methods, to identify strategies that creative people use unconsciously. He made these strategies conscious and teachable in a form for adults (Gordon, 1961; Gordon and Poze, 1980) and for children (Gordon, 1974; Gordon and Poze, 1972a, 1972b; see also Stanish, 1977, 1986, 1988).

Direct Analogy.   With this method the person is asked to think of ways that similar problems are solved in nature by animals, birds, flowers, weeds, bugs, worms, lizards, and so on. For example, ideas for conserving energy could be found by asking how animals keep warm in winter.

In a creativity workshop for the elderly, many expressed concern for their personal safety. With a synectics approach the problem became, "How do animals, plants, birds, etc., protect themselves, and how can these ideas help the elderly?" The list included spray cans of skunk scent, slip-on fangs and claws (mildly poisonous), a compressed air can that screams, an electronic transmitter that secretly "yells" for police assistance, traveling only in groups, camouflage or disguises (for example, wearing a police uniform), and others.

Personal Analogy.   Imagine you are a piece of candy sitting quietly with your candy friends on the shelf of the local drugstore. A little boy walks in, places five cents on the counter and points at you. How do you feel? What are your thoughts? Describe your experiences for the next fifteen minutes. The purpose of such exercises, similar to the "be the thing" exercises in Gordon's *Making It Strange* workbooks, is to give elementary students practice with the *personal analogy* creative thinking technique. With this strategy, new perspectives are found by becoming part of the problem, usually a problem object. What would you be like if you were a highly efficient can opener? A captivating short story? A truly exciting and valuable educational learning experience for children?

Fantasy Analogy. Problem solvers think of fantastic, farfetched, perhaps ideal solutions which can lead to creative yet practical ideas. Gordon sees *fantasy analogy* as a type of Freudian wish fulfillment. For example, one can ask how to make the problem solve itself: How can we make the hallways keep themselves clean? How can we get parents to want to attend open house? How can we get the School Board to want to give us a new instructional materials center? Some years ago design engineers probably asked: How can we get refrigerators to defrost themselves, make their own ice cubes? How can we get ovens to clean themselves? Automobile brakes to adjust themselves? This is fantasy analogy.

Symbolic Analogy. A fourth synectics technique is called *symbolic analogy*; other names are *compressed conflict* or *book titles*. Your dictionary will call it *oxymoron*. The strategy is to think of a two word phrase or "book title" that seems self-contradictory, such as "careful haste" or "gentle toughness." The compressed conflict would be related to a particular problem and would stimulate ideas. For example, the phrase "careful haste" might be used by educators or firefighters to stimulate ideas for quickly and safely evacuating a large school building. "Gentle toughness" might stimulate ideas for designing automobile tires, durable fabrics, or long-distance bicycles.

An exercise from a synectics workbook, *Teaching is Listening*, by Gordon and Poze (1972a), includes a direct analogy and a personal analogy, and illustrates how a symbolic analogy can stimulate ideas:

1. What animal typifies your concept of freedom? (Direct analogy)

2. Put yourself in the place of the animal you have chosen. Be the thing! Describe what makes you feel and act with so much freedom. (Personal analogy)

3. Sum up your description of the animal you chose by listing the "free" and "unfree" parts of your animal life.

Free: _____

Unfree: _____

4. Express each of these parts of your life in a single word. Put together these two words and refine them into a poetic, compressed conflict phrase.

_____   _____

_____   _____

_____   _____

5. Circle the phrase you like best. Write a new essay about freedom. Use any material you may have developed in this exercise.

Does the compressed conflict stimulate ideas for an essay on freedom?

Synectics methods can be used in the classroom either as creativity exercises, or as material for lessons in techniques of creative thinking.

Implementation Charting

Implementation charting helps gifted children see implementation as the realistic next step in creative thinking, following the generation of ideas and the evaluative selection of one or more workable solutions. With implementation charting students prepare a chart specifying both the *persons responsible* for implementing components of the idea(s) and a *completion deadline*. For example, if the best idea for increasing school spirit were to sell school sweatshirts, then an implementation chart such as the one in Table 10.3 might be suitable.

Note also, there is more than one role of *evaluation* in creative problem solving. In the present

TABLE 10.3   Implementation Chart for Selling School Sweatshirts

ACTIVITY	PERSON RESPONSIBLE	TIME FOR IMPLEMENTATION
1. Ask permission for project	Ron	March 10
2. Design sweatshirt	Mary, Ruth	March 15-20
3. Approve design	Student Council	March 22
4. Review possible sweatshirt sellers	Barb, John	March 15–20
5. Make recommendation to Student Council	Student Council	March 22
6. Order sweatshirts	Barb, John	March 24
7. Organize student sales campaign	Tom, Mary & Allan	March 22-31
a. Posters	Bob, Andy	March 25
b. Article in school newspaper	Alice	March 25-31
c. Article in community newspaper	Allan	March 28
8. Actual beginning of sales	Tom, Mary & Allan	April 10
9. Student Sweatshirt Day	Ron, Mary & Ruth	April 12
10. Evaluation of success of project	Original Brainstorming Group	April 20

example, the initial ideas were evaluated in an evaluation matrix (Table 10.1). After the idea(s) are selected and the project implemented, another evaluation must determine if the project was effective and successful and if it should be continued.

INVOLVING STUDENTS IN CREATIVE ACTIVITIES

The most logically sound answer to the question "How can we teach creativity?" is this: Involve students in activities that intrinsically require creative thinking and problem solving. It is virtually assured that creative attitudes, abilities, and skills will be strengthened in the course of this creative involvement. It is no accident that Renzulli's Type III Enrichment from the Triad model and his Schoolwide Enrichment Model (Renzulli and Reis, 1991b; see Chapter 7) focus on developing creativity via individual or small group projects and investigations of real problems. Appendix 7.1 listed several hundred subtopics of art, science, theatre, etc. that would stimulate creative thinking and problem solving. We particularly recommend the *Future Problem Solving* and *Odyssey of the Mind* programs, which were designed to teach creativity through involvement with real problems and projects.

The G/T teacher-coordinator should be continually alert for opportunities to exercise creative thinking and problem solving in content areas. Available opportunities might also be expanded. Are music, science, and art programs adequate? Are students encouraged to become involved in scientific and aesthetic activities? Are community resources and mentors being used to good advantage?

CREATIVE TEACHING AND LEARNING

Torrance (1977) stated that "... people fundamentally prefer to learn in creative ways." These ways include exploring, manipulating, questioning, experimenting, risking, testing, and modifying ideas. Said Torrance, learning creatively takes place during the processes of sensing problems, deficiencies, or gaps in information; formulating hypotheses or guesses about a problem; testing the hypotheses, revising and retesting the hypotheses; and then communicating the results. He explained that problems arouse tension, thus motivating the learner to ask questions, make guesses, and test the adequacy of the guesses, correcting errors and modifying conclusions if necessary.

Some recommendations for creative teaching included the following:

Maintain high teacher enthusiasm.

Accept individual differences, for example, in preferred ways of learning, learning rates, faults, and so forth.

Permit the curriculum to be different for different pupils.

Communicate that the teacher is "for" rather than "against" the child.

Encourage and permit self-initiated projects.

Support students against peer conformity pressures.

Allow or encourage a child to achieve success in an area and in a way possible for him or her.

Respect the potential of low achievers.

Do not be blinded by intelligence test scores; they do not tell the whole story.

Do not let pressure for evaluation get the upper hand.

Encourage divergent ideas; too many "right" ideas are stifling.

Do not be afraid to wander off the teaching schedule and try something different.

Torrance (1981a, 1981c) summarized some signs that creative learning is taking place, which partly represent benefits of creative teaching and learning. These include improved motivation, alertness, curiosity, concentration, and achievement; a charged atmosphere "tingling with excitement;" the combining of activities that cut across curriculum areas, and a continuity of activities, one leading to another; improved communication of ideas and feelings; a "boldness" in ideas, drawings, stories, and so on; improved self-confidence; improved creative growth and creative expression; and importantly, a reduction of unproductive behavior, behavior problems, hostility, vandalism, and apathy, and an increase in enthusiasm about school and learning and improved career aspirations.

Creativity training and creative teaching can indeed make a difference for gifted, normal, and even troubled students.

SUMMARY

Creativity can be increased. Many teachers incorporate creativity training activities into their classrooms.

Goals of creativity training include increasing creativity consciousness and creative attitudes, helping students understand creativity, strengthening creative abilities, teaching creativity techniques, and involving students in creative activities.

Creativity consciousness and creative attitudes includes an awareness of creativity, valuing creativity, a predisposition to think creatively, a willingness to make mistakes, and others. A teacher can reinforce creative personality traits (e.g., confidence, curiosity, risk-taking, playfulness, artistic interests), establish a creative atmosphere, and raise awareness of blocks to creative thinking.

Helping students understand creativity can involve lessons on the importance of creativity, characteristics of creative people, creative abilities, theories of creativity, creativity tests, creativity techniques, blocks and barriers to creativity, and important "principles" of creativity.

Many types of exercises exist for strengthening creative abilities such as fluency, flexibility, originality, sensitivity to problems, problem defining, visualization, analogical thinking, and others. Shallcross suggested some exercises that are tied to specific subject areas. Stanish's workbooks include many kinds of simple and complex (e.g., poetry writing, inventing) exercises.

Personal creativity techniques, usually analogical, are used by every creatively productive person. Examples were cited from science, art, music, political cartooning, political satire, theater, moviemaking, and comedy.

Students may be helped to develop personal creativity techniques by explaining the techniques used by others; teaching such problem-solving strategies as looking for analogically related solutions; working backward from an ideal goal; involvement in creative activities; and instruction from creative professionals who use such techniques.

Standard creative thinking techniques are commonly taught in creativity courses and workshops.

Brainstorming is based on deferred judgment. Variations include reverse brainstorming, stop-and-go brainstorming, and the Phillips 66 procedure.

Students may be taught idea evaluation with an evaluation matrix.

The attribute listing technique takes two forms, modifying important problem attributes and transferring attributes from one situation to another, which is analogical thinking.

Morphological synthesis, an extension of attribute listing, is a matrix approach to generating ideas.

Osborn's "73 idea-spurring questions" is an idea checklist designed for creative problem solving.

Four synectics methods include direct analogy, looking for ways that similar problems have been solved in nature; personal analogy, in which ideas are found by becoming a problem object or process; fantasy analogy, in which the thinker looks for farfetched, perhaps ideal problem solutions; and symbolic analogy, using two-word conflicts to stimulate new perspectives.

Involvement in creative activities such as independent projects, Future Problem Solving, and Odyssey of the Mind is especially important for developing creative skills and abilities.

According to Torrance, creative teaching and learning includes exploring, questioning, experimenting, testing ideas, and other activities. Creative learning includes sensing a problem, formulating hypotheses or guesses, testing, revising and retesting the hypotheses, and communicating the results.

Recommendations for creative teaching included high teacher enthusiasm, the acceptance of individual differences, encouraging self-initiated projects, looking beyond IQ scores, encouraging divergent thinking, and others.

Creative learning can result in improved motivation, achievement, creativity, self-confidence, school attitudes, and others.

CHAPTER 11

TEACHING THINKING SKILLS

Believe all students can think, not just the gifted ones. Let your students know that thinking is a goal. Create the right climate and model it.
James Alvino (1990)

"Teaching for thinking has become a major agenda in schools across this country," wrote Swartz and Perkins (1990, p. xi). Indeed, teaching thinking skills to all students is a core feature of educational reform in the 1990s. And a sure sign of the popularity of a new concept is the appearance of a catchy acronym—"HOTS," higher-order thinking skills.

Teachers in today's schools want to improve all students' ability to compare and classify, analyze and plan, see cause-effect relations, and make good decisions and inferences. We want children to think critically, logically, and evaluatively, for example, about the credibility of messages from salespersons, politicians, and others with strong biases and personal interests (e.g., Lipman, 1991).

Because of gifted students' potential for higher levels of educational and professional development, teaching thinking has a special place in their education.

Three basic approaches to "teaching thinking" run throughout this chapter:

• Strengthening thinking abilities and skills through practice and exercise (*indirect approach*).
• Helping students learn conscious and deliberate strategies for reasoning, problem solving, and critical thinking (*direct approach*).
• Increasing students' understanding of their own and others' thinking (*metacognition*—"thinking about thinking").

We will look at several lists and taxonomies of thinking skills that may guide the development of a thinking skills curriculum. We also will review Bloom's higher taxonomic levels of educational objectives (application, analysis, synthesis, and evaluation), which has been a guide for teaching thinking for several decades. A key part of the chapter is teaching *critical thinking*—a skill that is weak in too many children and adults. Finally, we review some good quality published thinking skills programs and exercise books that can be used, for example, in an elementary pullout program or a secondary school class on thinking, and criteria for selecting materials and activities for thinking skills training.

Issues

By way of introduction, the following issues pertain to teaching thinking skills:

• *Should thinking skills instruction be infused into existing subjects, taught as a separate subject or course, or both*? Integrating thinking skills into the existing curriculum seems most appealing to teachers and administrators. Finding space for yet another subject is indeed troublesome. Language arts and science, for example, are logical places to impart thinking skills because of the natural role of analysis, reasoning, critical thinking, analogical thinking, and others (de Bono, 1983). If possible, we recommend *both* integrating (infusing) thinking skills into existing subjects as well as teaching thinking as a separate topic or even course.

• *What should be the content—the skills—for students of different ages?* We know that young children think concretely, older students more abstractly. Selecting which skills to teach is thus based on students' needs and abilities, along with one's teaching style and the subject matter at hand. Based on a six-year project, Reis (1990a) recommended suggested introducing thinking skills approximately in line with the timetable in Table 11.1. The skills introduced at each level would continue to be reinforced at higher grade levels.

• *How does one best teach thinking?* Alvino (1990) noted that teachers have "too many choices and too little direction." For some, teaching thinking means only a minor modification of their usual teaching patterns, for example, asking more questions that stimulate students to apply, synthesize, analyze, evaluate, or think critically or creatively; along with modeling "good thinking" habits. For

other teachers, creating a "thinking classroom" involves radical changes in teaching and expectations of students. Reis (1990a, p. 46) said not to tackle too much: "Students who are taught fewer thinking skills, but in greater depth, learn them better." She recommended that teachers introduce just a *few* skills, teach them step by step, demonstrate how to use them in a content area or project, and make certain students practice each skill several times during the year.

Thinking skills may be taught either *inductively* (examples first, then the rule or principle), or *directively* (rule first, then examples; Beyer, 1988). See Beyer's recommended lesson plan for teaching thinking skills in Inset 11.1.

• *How does one evaluate the mastery of thinking skills?* Usual achievement tests do not evaluate the mastery of such skills. Some published materials include their own tests. Three standardized tests for measuring thinking skills are the *Cornell Critical Thinking Test*, the *Ross Test of Higher Cognitive Processes*, and the *New Jersey Test of*

TABLE 11.1 Introducing Thinking Skills at Different Grade Levels

Early Elementary Grades (K-2)	*Creative thinking*—brainstorming plus other fluency, flexibility, originality, and elaboration exercises; guided imagery
	Critical and logical thinking—comparing, contrasting, classifying; patterns and figural relationships
Middle Elementary Grades (3–4)	*Creative problem solving and decision making*—creative problem solving (CPS model), future problem solving
	Critical and logical thinking—deductive and syllogistic reasoning; analogical reasoning; also learning-to-learn skills
Upper Elementary and Middle School Grades (5-8)	*Critical and logical thinking*—interpreting, inferring, hypothesizing; analyzing propaganda and bias
	Metacognitive skills—planning, monitoring, evaluating

Based on Reis (1990b).

INSET 11.1 _____

A Thinking Skills Lesson Plan

Barry K. Beyer (1988), author of *Developing a Thinking Skills Program* and *Practical Strategies for the Teaching of Thinking*, recommended a six-step framework for teaching thinking skills. The strategy is designed to move students toward independent use of thinking skills in a variety of media and contexts. As you read the steps, consider the teaching of a thinking skill such as *comparing, recognizing cause-effect relationships*, or *planning*.

1. *Introducing the skill.* To promote a metacognitive awareness of how a skill works, a teacher begins by writing the *name* of the skill on the chalkboard, eliciting *synonyms* and a *definition* from the class (or providing them), and asking for *examples* of where students may have used this skill before, in or out of school.

With an *inductive* (examples then rule) approach, students first practice using the skill and then discuss what they did, reflecting on relevant and irrelevant aspects of the skill. Students try the skill again, and then articulate the basic steps and important rules.

A *directive* (rule then examples) approach may be used with more complex thinking skills, such as *planning*. Following the name, synonyms, definition, and examples (as above), the teacher explains the steps that an expert would use to execute the skill, highlighting principles, criteria, and rules. The teacher demonstrates (models) the skill, pointing out important operational cues. Then the students practice the skill. Finally, they discuss how the skill works and the rules that guide its execution.

2. *Guiding practice in a new skill.* Follow-up lessons begin with another *introduction* that again covers the name, synonyms, definition, and examples as in Step 1. Teacher and students *review* what they know about the skill, its uses, steps, and rules. (Eventually, the introduction and review can be dropped from the guided practice sessions.) Students *apply* the skill to the same type of data as

in the introductory lesson; and again *reflect* on how they executed the skill.

3. *Self-directed application.* This unguided practice step involves putting students into situations where—if they choose—they can use a thinking skill they have learned. Some applications include teacher questions, worksheets that require use of the skill, debates or discussions, writing essays or paragraphs, writing answers to end-of-chapter "Questions for Critical Thinking," or other inquiry or discovery activities.

Beyer (1988, p. 227) noted that "it may take three or more such lessons spaced increasingly apart to get students to the point where they can demonstrate proficiency in using the skill on their own."

4. *Transferring or elaborating a thinking skill.* Because thinking skills do not transfer automatically, teachers must show students how to apply the skill in a variety of subjects and contexts. The teacher reviews what students already know about the skill, then demonstrates the execution of the skill in the new context. Students apply the skill and then discuss what they did.

5. *Guiding practice in the skill in the new context.* To aid generalization, students engage in a mix of guided applications of a skill in the original context as well as in newer contexts: Introduction, review, application, and reflection.

6. *Using the skill autonomously.* Step 6 resembles Step 3, focusing on the use of teacher questions, worksheet questions, discussions and debates, essays, end-of-chapter questions, and other discovery activities. Practice is both in the original context and with new subjects, media, and contexts.

Ideally, students eventually will decide on their own which operations are appropriate and then execute them.

Reasoning Skills. The problem is that such tests may not measure what you have taught—and if the tests show "no improvement" in thinking skills (which you did not teach), your teaching and your gifted program both become suspect.

• *How much of teaching thinking skills actually is teaching "attitudes" or "traits"?* A lot. Some important traits and dispositions seem inseparable from abilities and skills themselves, for example, respect for evidence, a willingness to search for reasons and alternatives, a willingness to withhold or even reverse judgments based on facts, open-mindedness, tolerance for ambiguity, sensitivity to others views (Alvino, 1990; Lipman, 1991), and of course, a creativity consciousness (Davis, 1992a).

INDIRECT TEACHING, DIRECT TEACHING, AND METACOGNITION

Indirect Teaching of Thinking Skills: Strengthening Abilities Through Exercise

Thinking skills may be taught in a comparatively subtle, *indirect* fashion through practice and exercise—the same way we strengthen arithmetic and typing skills. For example, a teacher can strengthen classification skills through instruction and practice with classification problems, including multiple classifications and subclassifications. Similarly, to teach analogical thinking a teacher can use simple exercises of the *dog*: *cat*:: *canine*: ___?___ variety.

In addition to workbook exercises, Costa (1986; Costa and Lowery, 1989) and Swartz and Perkins (1990) recommended that teachers pose problems and ask questions. For example, teachers can ask "Why," "What if," and "How" questions, not just "What" questions. They can have students explore paradoxes, dilemmas, and discrepancies. Teachers also can ask students to compare, classify, evaluate, find similarities and differences, find analogical relationships, induce principles, extrapolate, and so forth. For seatwork, teachers can create their own exercises, perhaps placing them in original thinking skills workbooks. A "Problem Box" permits stu-

dents to suggest problems for the class to work on. Creating a classroom "Think Tank" provides a place where students can spend time working on a favorite interest or project.

Teachers can model pertinent thinking skills by "thinking out loud" while analyzing, evaluating, reasoning, or creating. To encourage creativity, as we saw in Chapter 10, a creative atmosphere is crucial—an atmosphere of openness and receptiveness to original, flexible thinking and to taking risks and making mistakes.

Direct Teaching: Knowing Why, When and How

Many complex thinking skills can be taught *directly* as conscious techniques for reasoning and dealing with problems (Costa and Lowery, 1989). For example, as we will see, critical thinking may be taught by helping students deliberately evaluate biases, qualifications, and ability to observe; to examine whether a statement is an assumption or an opinion; and to evaluate whether particular conclusions necessarily follow. Creative thinking may be taught directly by helping students to understand creative people and creative processes, and by teaching them when and how idea-finding techniques may be used (Davis, 1991, 1992a). *If thinking skills are to be taught, direct teaching is essential.*

One particularly noteworthy program for the direct teaching of complex thinking skills is the *CoRT* (Cognitive Research Trust) *Thinking Program* created by Edward de Bono (1973, 1983, 1985). De Bono's lessons and exercises teach such skills as evaluating, taking other perspectives, planning, prioritizing, and many others as conscious and deliberate thinking strategies. Students are helped to understand each skill and *why*, *when*, and *how* it should be applied. We will look at de Bono's strategies in a later section.

While analogical thinking can be indirectly taught using simple analogy problems, it also may be taught with a direct approach. That is, analogical thinking can be taught as a conscious and deliberate skill. For example, students can be asked to use the language of a rocket launch or a football game to write an essay on "What I did last summer;" borrow ideas from the Cinderella story to create a cartoon about some current news event, as a political cartoonist might; or apply ideas from natural animal defense systems to design a burglary-prevention system for the school.

Later in this chapter we will review several programs for exercising thinking skills and abilities (indirect approach), and for directly teaching more complex thinking strategies.

Metacognition

Metacognition is thinking about thinking, one's own and that of others. As children grow older, metacognitive ability improves as a natural part of their cognitive development. It is their improved metacognitive thinking that enables adolescents to "worry about what others think"—causing wholesale conformity among many students. Regarding thinking skills, to the extent they are able, students should understand their thinking and learning strategies, and they should understand *why*, *when*, and *how* the strategies may be used. As Beyer (1988) noted, metacognitive operations and dispositions direct, control, and drive the use of thinking skills. The de Bono CoRT strategies are good examples of a metacognitive approach to teaching thinking skills. Students come to understand the advantages of using a particular technique, when the technique may be profitably used, and the steps involved in using it.

Other teachable aspects of metacognition include helping students to understand the sources of their own ideas, viewpoints, attitudes, and values, and also where others' ideas and values come from. For example, Barell (1984, 1991a, 1991b) recommended that instead of just intelligently arguing a viewpoint, students try defending the reverse position: What do students think of the proposal for a new swimming pool? What are adult taxpayers without children likely to think? What will teachers and school custodians think?

Instead of just analyzing the theme of a literary work, students try to explain how one goes about analyzing a literary work. A teacher can ask—or students can ask themselves—why they thought of a particular question, and what the question means to them.

Costa (1986) described three components of thinking about thinking that he called *metacognition*, *epistemic cognition*, and *brain functioning*, all three of which suggest worthwhile enrichment content. His "metacognition" referred to students' conscious understanding of problem solving. That is, when solving a problem students should consciously identify what is known and what needs to be known; plan a course of action before they begin; monitor themselves while executing the plan (and consciously back up to adjust the plan as needed); and evaluate their success upon completion. Other aspects of metacognition included classroom discussions of what is going on inside their heads while "thinking," and comparing different students' approaches to problems and decision making.

Costa's epistemic cognition is the study of how knowledge is produced. Here, students might learn about the lives, works, and thinking processes of famous composers, artists, philosophers, and scientists. Discussion would focus on, for example, differences and similarities between artists and scientists, creative processes used by artists, poets, and scientists, and the possible use of scientific inquiry for solving social problems.

Finally, students can learn about brain functions, for example, related to learning and memory, emotions, dreaming, and mental disorders. To these we suggest discussion of thinking styles and personality dimensions such as right-brain versus left-brain thinking processes, reflectiveness versus impulsiveness; global versus analytic (forest versus tress) thinking; being a morning (lark) or a night (owl) person; sensation-seeking (thrill-seeking; "Type T personality;" Farley, 1986); and internal versus external locus of control—which is an especially important thinking style related to achievement and career success. An internal locus of control person feels responsible for successes, failures and his or her destiny; an external locus of control person blames others for failures, attributes success to luck, and generally feels like a sock in the laundromat of life.

Metacognition also can include teaching about individual differences in preferred ways of studying and learning. Some students will prefer visual modes, others auditory, and others tactile. Some prefer lectures, independent study, group work, learning games, high activity, and so forth. Take a vote on preferences and discuss differences in selections. Ask students to share impressions of ways of teaching that make them think.

In the classroom, the indirect, direct, and metacognition approaches to teaching thinking may not be so neatly divided. The teaching of thinking skills often will include a combination of exercising underlying abilities; helping students to consciously analyze problems and plan steps for solving them; and helping them to metacognitively understand the reasons for the steps and for their own thinking and the thinking of others.

TYPES OF THINKING SKILLS

According to Reis (1990b, p. 44), "Teachers need a plan. This plan should consist of a well-thought-out list (taxonomy) of skills, a timetable (scope and sequence) for teaching them, and effective teaching techniques." As one possible list, the thinking skills in Table 11.2 were assembled from various sources. Most of the skills are relatively complex; they also are interrelated. For example, *evaluation* or *deductive reasoning* will involve abilities to compare and contrast, interpret, consider relevance, consider implications, predict outcomes, and so on. Complex processes such as creative thinking, critical thinking, problem solving, and decision making involve a great many subskills and abilities. Table 11.3 presents a related list created by the Association for Supervision and Curriculum Development. Still a third list appears later in this chapter. These lists, along with strategies and perhaps published programs

described later, can help a teacher plan a defensible thinking skills curriculum.

Nobody ever said the topic of "thinking skills" was uncomplicated.

HIGHER ORDER THINKING SKILLS

Bloom's Taxonomy of Educational Objectives

When educators speak of teaching high-level thinking skills the first idea that comes to mind is the top portion of "Bloom's taxonomy," more formally entitled the *Taxonomy of Educational Objectives: Cognitive Domain* (Bloom, 1974; Bloom, Engelhart, Furst, Hill, and Krathwohl, 1956). Bloom's taxonomy has had an international impact on education by drawing attention to the difference between "low-level" academic knowledge, which is commonly taught, and "higher-level" thinking skills—which everyone suddenly seemed to realize were rarely taught. The taxonomy was designed as a guide for the writing of instructional objectives. It therefore helps one plan a thinking skills curriculum, teaching strategies, and learning experiences. Table 11.4 lists the six main levels of the taxonomy, along with examples of learning activities at each level. Note that many of the thinking skills from Tables 11.2 and 11.3 have found their way into one category or another.

The six main levels of the taxonomy describe progressively higher levels of cognitive activity. At the knowledge and comprehension levels students deal with facts, figures, definitions, rules, categories, relationships, and theories. While the *knowledge* and *comprehension* levels naturally are necessary for all students, teachers of gifted students, especially, will want them to *apply* rules, principles, or theories; *analyze* components, relationships, hypotheses, patterns, and causes and effects; *synthesize* parts into creative solutions, plans, theories, generalizations, designs, and compositions; and *evaluate* the accuracy, value, efficiency, or utility of alternative ideas or courses of action.

As a general rule, students normally will progress from learning activities at the knowledge

TABLE 11.2   Thinking Skills

Creativity and Creative Problem Solving (Chapters 10 and 11)

Critical Thinking:	Evaluating bias, credibility, consistency qualifications, recency of information
	Evaluating primary vs. secondary sources, inferences, validity of reasons
	Identifying assumptions, opinions, claims, ambiguities, missing parts of an argument, adequacy of definitions, appropriateness of conclusions
Problem Solving:	Problem clarifying and defining
	Selecting relevant information
	Identifying and evaluating alternatives
	Drawing conclusions and making inferences
Reading:	Finding main ideas
	Justifying interpretations
	Explaining authors' intentions
	Drawing logical inferences, implications, conclusions
	Relating feelings to specific content
Writing:	Stating and defending an idea
	Sequencing appropriate information
	Elaborating
	Communicating clear relationships
	Expressing feelings, values
	Arguing persuasively, logically
	Developing story plots
	Creating mood
Science and Research:	Identifying needed processes and information
	Questioning, formulating hypotheses
	Estimating, guessing
	Observing, measuring
	Applying principles
	Extrapolating, interpolating
	Discovering trends, patterns, cause-effect relationships
	Reading charts, graphs, tables
	Generating graphs from data

(continued)

TABLE 11.2 Continued

	Recognizing mathematical relationships (weight, distance, time)	
Reasoning Skills:	Deductive reasoning	Inductive reasoning
	Analogical reasoning	Verbal reasoning
	Figural/spatial reasoning	Justifying
	Synthesizing, combining	Analyzing assumptions
	Recognizing logical relationships	Elaborating
Classifying Skills:	Comparing, contrasting	Sequencing, ordering
	Part-whole relationships	Overlapping classes
Planning Skills:	Following directions	Planning steps
	Following rules	Prioritizing
	Setting goals and objectives	Considering implications
Evaluating Skills:	Identifying errors	Making decisions
	Asking questions	Making inferences
	Evaluating generalizations	Interpreting
	Recognizing assumptions, beliefs, opinions	Setting criteria
		Verifying
	Recognizing essential and nonessential	Determining relevance and irrelevance
	Making applications to real life situations	Summarizing
	Predicting consequences	

and comprehension levels to activities at higher levels. For example, virtually any independent or small-group research project, from creating a school newspaper or terrarium to photography or physics research, will require the acquisition and comprehension of necessary information, followed by various types of applications, analyses, syntheses, and evaluations. The latter four activities do not always need to occur in a specified order, although a final evaluation usually manages to be last.

Some gifted-oriented educators use the two pyramids in Figure 11.1 to point out the different emphases that should be placed upon different taxonomic levels for regular students and for gifted students. Thus the objectives and instructional focus for regular students might emphasize knowledge and comprehension, with less attention to higher-level skills. Gifted students, who grasp information and relationships more rapidly, should invest more time and effort at the higher levels. The inverted pyramid is misleading in suggesting that evaluation should receive the absolutely largest proportion of emphasis, but you get the idea.

TABLE 11.3   Core Thinking Skills

Focusing Skills (directing attention to selected information)
1. *Defining problems*—clarifying problem situations.
2. *Setting goals*—establishing direction and purpose.

Information gathering skills (acquiring relevant data)
3. *Observing*—using one or more senses to acquire information.
4. *Questioning*—seeking new information by formulating questions.

Remembering Skills (storing and retrieving information)
5. *Encoding*—storing information in long-term memory.
6. *Recalling*—retrieving information from long-term memory.

Organizing Skills (arranging information so it can be used more effectively)
7. *Comparing*—noting similarities and differences between two or more entities.
8. *Classifying*—grouping according to common attributes.
9. *Ordering*—sequencing according to a given criterion.

Analyzing skills (clarifying by identifying and distinguishing among components and attributes)
10. *Identifying attributes and components*—determining characteristics and parts.
11. *Identifying relationships and patterns*—recognizing ways elements are related.

Generating skills (using prior knowledge to add new information)
12. *Inferring*—reasoning beyond available information to fill in gaps.
13. *Predicting*—anticipating or forecasting future events.
14. *Elaborating*—using prior knowledge to add meaning to new information and to link it to existing structures.
15. *Representing*—adding new meaning by changing the form of information.

Integrating skills (connecting and combining information)
16. *Summarizing*—abstracting information efficiently and parsimoniously.
17. *Restructuring*—changing existing knowledge structures to include new information.

Evaluating skills (assessing the reasonableness and quality of ideas)
18. *Establishing criteria*—setting standards for making judgments.
19. *Verifying*—confirming the accuracy of claims
20. *Identifying errors*—recognizing logical fallacies.

Adapted from Association for Supervision and Curriculum Development, 1988, by permission.

An important and common use of Bloom's taxonomy is as a guide for posing questions to students. Certainly, as a means for exercising higher-level thinking abilities, posing classroom questions at the different levels is an obvious and not-too-difficult strategy. Hunkins (1976) wrote a book around questioning at the different levels. Her key verbs for posing knowledge, comprehension, application, analysis, synthesis, and evaluation questions appear in Table 11.5. Take a minute or two and make up a few questions at each level using her key words.

TABLE 11.4 Taxonomy of Educational Objectives: Cognitive Domain

Category	Examples
Knowledge	Defining terminology, symbols Recalling facts, names, examples, rules, categories Recognizing trends, causes, relationships Acquiring principles, procedures, implications, theories
Comprehension	Rephrasing definitions Illustrating meanings Interpreting relationships Drawing conclusions Demonstrating methods Inferring implications Predicting consequences
Application	Applying principles, rules, theories Organizing procedures, conclusions, effects Choosing situations, methods Restructuring processes, generalizations, phenomena
Analysis	Recognizing assumptions, patterns Deducing conclusions, hypotheses, points of view Analyzing relationships, themes, evidence, causes and effects Contrasting ideas, parts, arguments
Synthesis	Producing products, compositions Proposing objectives, means, solutions Designing plans, operations Organizing taxonomies, concepts, schemes, theories Deriving relationships, abstractions, generalizations
Evaluation	Judging accuracy, consistency, reliability Assessing errors, fallacies, predictions, means and ends Considering efficiency, utility, standards Contrasting alternatives, courses of action

From Metfessel, Michael, and Kirsner, "Instrumentation of Bloom's and Krathwohl's Taxonomies for the Writing of Educational Objectives." *Psychology in the Schools* (1969), *6*, 227-310. Reprinted by permission.

Finally, many teachers teach the taxonomy itself to students, acquainting them with different levels of learning, thinking, and skill development. As shown in Inset 11.2, fifth-grader Monica Blanton (1982) understands the taxonomy very well.

Attention to all levels of Bloom's taxonomy, particularly the higher levels of application, analysis, synthesis, and evaluation, will help ensure that G/T activities are not just "busy work" and time fillers.

Thinking Skills: How Would Socrates Teach Them?

Teaching and stimulating thinking by asking questions sometimes is called the *Socratic method*. Paul *et al.* (1989) organized "Socratic questions" that elicit *clarifying, analyzing assumptions, probing reasons and evidence, analyzing viewpoints or perspectives, analyzing implications and conse-*

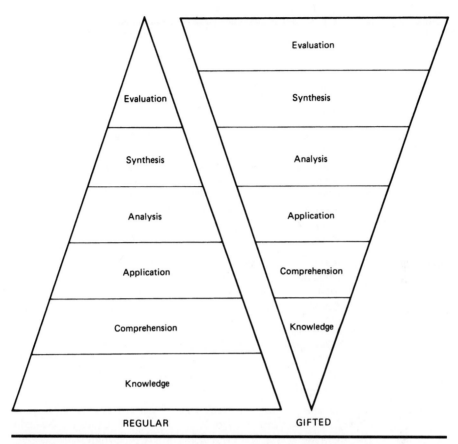

FIGURE 11.1   Based on Bloom's taxonomy, these pyramids illustrate the notion that with gifted students, more time should be invested on higher-level activities and objectives, compared with the reverse for regular students.

quences, and *questioning* (see Table 11.6). Many of the questions focus on critical thinking, which will be clarified in a following section.

Higher-Order Cognitive Processes: Resnick

While "higher-order thinking skills" means Bloom's *application, analysis, synthesis,* and *evaluation* to many, Resnick (1985, p. 10) takes a broader view of this label. She described key features of "higher-order cognitive processes" as follows. Higher order thinking:

1. Is *non-algorithmic*. The path of action is not fully specified in advance.

2. Is *complex*. The total path is not "visible" from any single vantage point.

3. Often yields *multiple solutions*, each with costs and benefits, rather than unique solutions.

4. Involves *nuanced judgment and interpretation*.

5. Involves the *application of multiple criteria*, which sometimes conflict with one another.

6. Often involves *uncertainty*. Not everything is known that bears on the task at hand.

7. Means *self-regulation* of the thinking process. It is not higher-order thinking when someone else calls the plays at every step.

TABLE 11.5   Key Words for Questioning at Bloom's Six Taxonomic Levels

Level	Key Words			
Knowledge	What	Distinguish	Recall	Write
	When	Identify	Reorganize	Which
	Who	List	Show	Indicate
	Define	Name	State	Tell How
Comprehension	Compare	Distinguish	What	
	Conclude	Estimate	Fill in	
	Contrast	Explain	Give an example of	
	Demonstrate	Extend	Hypothesize	
	Differentiate	Extrapolate	Illustrate	
	Predict	Rearrange	Infer	
	Reorder	Rephrase	Relate	
	Which	Inform	Tell in Your Own Words	
Application	Apply	Build	Construct	Demonstrate
	Develop	Plan	Solve	Indicate
	Test	Choose	Show Your Work	Check Out
	Consider	How Would	Tell Us	
Analysis	Analyze	Discriminate	Relate	
	Categorize	Distinguish	Explain	
	Describe	Recognize	What Assumption	
	Classify	Support Your	What Do You	
	Compare	Indicate The		
Synthesis	Write	Suggest	Plan	
	Think of a Way	How	Formulate a Solution	
	Create	Develop	Synthesize	
	Purpose a Plan	Make Up	Derive	
	Put Together	What Conclusion		
	What Would Be	What Major Hypothesis		
Evaluation	What Is	Select		
	Choose	Which Would You Consider		
	Evaluate	Defend		
	Decide	Check		
	Judge	What is Most Appropriate		
	Check the	Indicate		

From Hunkins, 1976. Reprinted by permission of the author and Allyn & Bacon, Inc.

8. Involves *imposing meaning*, finding structure in apparent disorder.

Such skills and learning activities do not fit usual meanings of "minimal competency objectives" of basic skills instruction. Rather, they are likely to be embedded in critical thinking, creative thinking, problem solving, inquiry, and decision making.

CRITICAL THINKING

The phrase "critical thinking" is used rather loosely. It has been taken to mean carping criti-

INSET 11.2 _____

Bloom's Taxonomy Revisited

I like your magazine very much. I read about "Bloom's Taxonomy on Bloom's Taxonomy." I am one of Alice Krueger's fifth grade students at Offerle Middle School.

I'm sending in questions on *Mrs. Frisby and the Rats of NIMH* to put in *G/C/T*. I would appreciate it if you did.

Yours truly,
Monica Blanton

Mrs. Frisby and the Rats of NIMH

Knowledge—Name Mrs. Frisby's four children in order of age.

Comprehension—Restate Mrs. Frisby's first talk with Brutus the time in the rosebush.

Application—Illustrate Mrs. Frisby flying on Jeremy's back going over the river.

Analysis—Break down Mrs. Frisby's big problem and see how many little problems you can find.

Synthesis—Write a new ending to the story pretending Timothy had died.

Evaluation—Pick three animals of those six that were mentioned in the story. Try to find a new name you think would be better than the one in the book. Tell why you think your names would be better.

Source: *G/C/T* (Sept.–Oct. 1982), 22. Reprinted by permission.

cism ("Whatta piece a' garbage that is!"), wholesale skepticism, thoughtful contemplation, analytic thinking (including the analysis of propaganda), reflective (not compulsive) thinking, problem solving, Bloom's evaluation level of thinking, all of Bloom's higher-level thinking skills, all important ("critical") thinking skills, careful thinking, clear thinking, logical thinking (especially!), independent thinking, along with the abilities to recognize biases, assumptions, inconsistencies, opinions, etc.

The present discussion is based upon two main definitions: critical thinking as *evaluating* and as *problem solving*.

Critical Thinking as Evaluating

Swartz and Perkins (1990, p. 37) define critical thinking as "critical examination and evalua-

tion—actual and potential—of beliefs and courses of action." As their first example:

Columbus discovered America in 1492, it's said. How do we know? What are the grounds for believing that? If historical documents are involved, what evidence is there that they are sound?

Said Swartz and Perkins, in critical thinking we:

• Aim at critical judgment about what to accept as reasonable.

• Use standards that themselves are the results of critical reflection in making these judgments.

• Employ various organized strategies of reasoning and arguments in determining and applying these standards.

• Seek and gather reliable information to use as evidence or reasons in supporting these judgments.

TABLE 11.6   A Taxonomy of Socratic Questions

Questions of Clarification

- What do you mean by _____?
- What is your main point?
- Could you give me an example?
- Could you explain that further?
- How does _____ relate to _____?
- Could you put that another way?
- What do you think is the main issue here?
- How does this relate to our discussion (problem, issue)?
- Jane, would summarize what Richard has said? . . . Richard, is that what you meant?

Questions that Probe Assumptions

- What are you (they) assuming?
- What could we assume instead?
- All of your reasoning depends on the idea that _____. Why have you based your reasoning on _____ rather than _____?
- You seem to be assuming _____. How would you justify taking this for granted?
- Is it always the case? Why do you think the assumption holds here?

Questions that Probe Reasons and Evidence

- How do you know?
- Why do you think that is true?
- Could you explain your reasons to us?
- Are those reasons adequate?
- Do you have any (good) evidence for that?
- Is there reason to doubt that evidence?
- Who is in a position to know if that is the case?
- What would convince you otherwise?
- How could we go about finding out whether that is true?
- What other information do we need to know?

Questions about Viewpoints or Perspectives

- Why have you chosen this perspective rather than that perspective?
- Could anyone else see this another way? Why? What would influence them?
- What would someone who disagrees say?
- How could you answer the objection that _____ would make?
- What is an alternative?
- How are Roxanne's and Ken's ideas alike?

Questions that Probe Implications and Consequences

- What are you implying by that?
- When you say _____, are you implying _____?
- If that happened, what else would also happen as a result? Why?
- What effect would that have?
- Would that necessarily happen or only probably happen?
- If this and this are the case, then what else must also be true?

Questions about the Question

- How can we find out?
- How could someone settle this question?
- Is this the same issue as _____?
- How would _____ put the issue?
- What does this question assume?
- Why is this question important?
- Does this question ask us to evaluate something?
- Do we all agree that this is the question?
- To answer this question, what questions would we have to answer first?

Adapted from Paul, *et al.*, 1989, by permission.

A few decades ago Ronald R. Allen and his colleagues (Allen, Kauffeld, and O'Brien, 1968; Allen and Rott, 1969) created workbooks to teach critical thinking in relation to ideas and assumptions implicit in such everyday media as comic strips (for example, the far right *Orphan Annie* and the sexist *Beetle Bailey*), advertising and sales pitches, political messages, movies, and television shows.

Most of Allen's specific critical thinking abilities are worth incorporating into any thinking skills curriculum, for example:

1. The ability to appraise a speaker's testimony ("a statement issued by a source") in terms of the source's ability to observe accurately.

2. The ability to evaluate the particular biases of a source.

3. The ability to appraise the source's qualifications necessary for making an informed statement.

4. The ability to appraise whether the source is consistent with himself or herself and other sources.

5. The ability to appraise whether the source's information is the most recent available.

6. The ability to differentiate between primary—first hand—and secondary sources.

7. The ability to identify arguments based on testimony or based on reasoning.

Other of Allen's principles emphasizing critical thinking and reasoning involve:

Evaluating inferences
Evaluating reasons given for a claim
Checking the reliability and adequacy of information
Following logically valid lines of reasoning
Detecting missing parts of an argument
Discerning the relevance of objections
Recognizing appropriate conclusions

In his Cornell Project on Critical Thinking, Robert Ennis (1962, 1964) compiled a number of aspects of critical thinking that also seem to stress evaluation of sources or statements. Said Ennis, students should learn to judge whether:

1. There is ambiguity or contradiction a line of reasoning.
2. Something is an assumption.
3. A statement is specific enough.
4. A conclusion necessarily follows.
5. An observation statement is reliable.
6. An inductive conclusion is warranted.
7. The (real) problem has been identified.
8. A definition is adequate.
9. A statement by an alleged authority is acceptable.

We will see in a later section that Lipman's (e.g., 1988b, 1991; Lipman, Sharp, and Oscanyan, 1980; Sharp and Reed, 1992) *Philosophy for Children* program also includes critical thinking in the evaluation sense by teaching students to recognize inconsistent and contradictory statements, underlying assumptions, cause-effect relationships, and truth in syllogistic reasoning.

Critical Thinking as Problem Solving

To Budmen (1967), critical thinking is problem solving or an act of inquiry. He emphasized, however, that critical thinking differs from more objective scientific problem solving in that critical thinking involves values, emotions, and judgment. From this perspective, Budmen's message to teachers was that students should learn that there are problems for which there is no single solution—only alternatives and judgments. Said Budmen, "What to consider in arriving at these judgments, how to identify the alternatives and make the choices, is what the process of critical thinking is all about." He outlined four steps that could be taught.

The first step is to identify one's basic assumptions, feelings, beliefs, and values relating to an issue. This was considered ". . . the heart of the process." Second, one examines all sides of an issue. Third, one examines all possible actions and their probable results. "More than anything else, students must understand that all behavior has consequences. . . ." Finally, the process requires a choice among alternatives, a decision.

Budmen stressed that a solution resulting from these steps should be the best one for the particular person. Therefore, problems best suited for the development of critical thinking should be problems without a single right answer.

Dressel and Mayhew (1954) reduced a long list of critical thinking abilities to five central ones, which also follow a problem-solving format:

1. The ability to define a problem, which includes the abilities to break complex elements into simpler, familiar and workable parts, identify central elements, and eliminate extraneous elements.

2. The ability to select pertinent information for the solution of a problem, including the ability to recognize unreliable and biased sources of information, and information that is relevant and irrelevant to the solution of the problem.

3. The ability to recognize stated and unstated assumptions, and unsupported and irrelevant assumptions.

4. The ability to formulate relevant hypotheses, and check the hypotheses against the information and assumptions.

5. The ability to draw valid conclusions and inferences, detect logical inconsistencies, and judge the adequacy of a conclusion as a solution to the problem.

MODELS, PROGRAMS, AND EXERCISES FOR TEACHING THINKING SKILLS

Thinking skills may be taught as a separate course or subject, for example, in an elementary pullout program or part of an honors course in secondary school, or they can be integrated into an existing subject. A separate course could stress creativity, problem solving, critical thinking, logical thinking, analogical thinking, values clarification and moral thinking, as well as other skills listed in Tables 11.2 and 11.3; the skills subsumed under Bloom's higher taxonomic levels (Table 11.4) and the taxonomy itself; thinking skills aimed at coping with personal problems, such as making good decisions (see Nelson-Jones, 1990); and the exercising of specific thinking skills and abilities presented later in Table 11.7. Commercially available materials and programs would be extremely useful for such a course or subject.

The following sections summarize models, strategies and exercises for teaching thinking skills. Space will not allow full descriptions, so interested readers should see the original sources for more complete information. The first two models, the de Bono CoRT approach and Lipman's *Philosophy for Children*, take a direct, conscious, metacognitive approach to skill development. Students fully understand that they are learning about "thinking;" they learn the meaning and purpose of each thinking skill; and they learn why, when, and how the skill should be used.

The remaining programs, including *Project IMPACT*, *Instrumental Enrichment*, Critical Thinking Press and Software workbooks, and *Thinking and Learning*, take a more indirect approach in strengthening simple and complex abilities via practice.

DE BONO CoRT STRATEGIES

The place is Maracaibo, second largest city in Venezuela. There is a meeting of about 20 people (doctors, parents, government officials) to discuss the setting up of a new medical clinic. For three hours the arguments flow back and forth—in the usual fashion.

Suddenly, a 10-year-old boy who has been sitting quietly at the back of the room, because his mother could not leave him alone at home, approaches the table.

He suggests to the group that they "do an AGO (set the objectives), followed by an APC (outline alternatives), and then an FIP (set priorities) and, of course, an OPV (analyze other people's views). In a short while there is a plan of action.

That 10-year-old had participated in the routine thinking skills program that is now mandated by law in all Venezuelan schools (de Bono, 1985).

Edward de Bono (1973, 1983, 1985) created a delightful set of materials for the direct teaching of thinking as a skill. The CoRT (Cognitive Research Trust) program requires little or no special teacher training, is apparently enjoyable for both students and teachers, and focuses ". . . on thinking skills that help a learner to function better in his or her life outside of school, not merely to become more proficient at solving puzzles or playing games" (de Bono, 1983).

The materials were not prepared strictly for gifted children. However, the exercises seem marvelously suited to the talents of gifted children and to the goals of any G/T program.

As one example, the PMI technique is a simple and effective way to teach evaluation. Students learn that ideas, suggestions, proposals, activities, or virtually anything else may be intelligently evaluated by looking at the good points or *pluses* (P), the bad points or *minuses* (M), and points that are neither good nor bad, just *interesting* (I). Students learn the reasons (principles) behind PMI and they practice applying the technique. The principles explain that:

By using the PMI approach one will not hastily reject an idea that initially looks bad.

Vice versa, one will not too quickly adopt a good-looking idea that has serious but overlooked disadvantages.

Some ideas are neither good nor bad, just interesting and relevant and may lead to other ideas.

Without using a PMI, one's emotions may interfere with clear judgments.

With a PMI you pass judgment on an idea after it is explored, not before.

Small groups of fifth-grade G/T students in a College for Kids program directed by the author (Davis) did PMI's on "being gifted." They discovered they were not unique in having social problems at school, and they improved their appreciation for themselves and their high potential.

There are six sets of lessons with 10 lessons in each set, for a total of 60 lessons covering about 50 thinking skills. Many lessons teach complex thinking strategies that require the use of several previously learned skills; for example, *planning* requires subskills of *considering all factors* and *itemizing goals and objectives*. Most lessons are organized into these six sections:

1. *Introduction.* An introduction defines and explains the skill. For example, with the *Consider All Factors* (CAF) skill students learn that whenever they make a decision or choose something there are always many factors to consider. If they leave out some factors, their choice may turn out to be wrong. Further, they can try to see what factors other people have left out of their thinking.

2. *Example.* A sample problem (or statement) is presented and the skill is applied. For instance, in London a law was passed that required all new buildings to provide parking in the basement. They neglected to consider that basement parking would encourage people to drive to work, and so traffic congestion was worse than ever.

3. *Practice.* Four or five practice problems give students first-hand experience using the skill. For example, what factors are involved in choosing a hair style? What factors would you consider if interviewing someone to be a teacher?

4. *Process.* In a class or group discussion, students consider, for example, whether it is easy to leave out important factors; when it is important to consider all factors; what the difference is between a PMI and a CAF; what happens when others leave out important factors; and whether one needs to consider "all" factors or just the important ones.

5. *Principles.* Usually five sensible principles are presented, which amount to reasons for and advantages of using the skill, as illustrated in the PMI technique above. Some principles invariably duplicate information in the introductory explanation, which is fine. With the CAF strategy, five principles were:

> Using a CAF is useful in choosing, planning, or deciding.
>
> It is better to consider all factors first and then select the ones that matter most.
>
> You may have to ask someone else whether you have left out important factors.
>
> If an important factor is left out, an answer that seems right may turn out to be wrong.
>
> A CAF on someone else's thinking may allow you to tell them what they left out.

6. *Project.* These are additional practice problems.

CoRT thinking skills are not tied to any particular subject area. "Thinking" is taught as a subject in its own right, and as a conscious and deliberate metacognitive skill. In fact, said de

Bono (1983), the thinking skills probably would be best taught in a separate class or unit. Many of the impressive CoRT thinking skills are briefly described in Inset 11.3.

PHILOSOPHY FOR CHILDREN: LIPMAN

Matthew Lipman's (1988b, 1991; Lipman, Sharp, and Oscanyan, 1980; Sharp and Reed, 1992) *Philosophy for Children* program is unique in taking the form of stories in a series of upper elementary children's texts (e.g., Lipman, 1980; Lipman and Sharp, 1986; Lipman, Sharp, and Oscanyan, 1977). The program claims significant results in improving reading, interpersonal relations, ethical understanding, reasoning, and critical thinking (Lipman, 1976, 1981; Weinstein and Laufman, 1981). In the stories, fictional children spend much of their time thinking about thinking, with clear explanations of good thinking and bad thinking. The idea, of course, is for the student-readers to identify with the characters and to "think along" with them. Exercises follow the stories, but the main emphasis is upon the story content and the teacher's follow-up discussions.

A few of the 30 thinking skills taught in *Philosophy for Children* are:

Cause-effect relationships. Does this statement necessarily imply a cause-effect relationship: "He threw the stone and broke the window."

Recognizing consistent and contradictory statements or ideas. For example, students can think about whether it is possible to be a true animal lover, yet still eat meat.

Identifying underlying assumptions. What is the assumption underlying a statement such as "I love your hair that way, Peg. What beauty parlor did you go to?"

Learning part-whole and whole-part relationships. Students might be asked to evaluate the truth of "If Mike's face has handsome features, Mike must have a handsome face."

Making generalizations. Students draw generalizations from sets of facts, such as "I get sick when

INSET 11.3 _____

CoRT Thinking Skills: de Bono

Edward de Bono's (1973) CoRT thinking skills are taught in a direct, metacognitive fashion. Children consciously understand the value of each skill and when, why, and how it should be applied. The following are brief descriptions of some of the 50 CoRT thinking skills. Some skills are composed of clusters of simpler skills. The interested reader should see de Bono (1973, 1976, 1983, 1985) for details about these apparently effective and enjoyable lessons.

Thinking of good points (pluses), bad points (minuses), and interesting points of ideas, suggestions, and proposals.

Considering all factors when making choices or decisions.

Thinking of consequences (short-term, medium-term, long-term) of actions.

Thinking of goals and objectives, including seeing other people's objectives.

Planning, which includes skills of considering all factors and itemizing goals and objectives.

Prioritizing, for example, relevant factors, objectives, and consequences.

Thinking of many alternatives, possibilities, and choices, for example, in interpreting causes or in considering alternative actions.

Decision making, which requires considering the factors involved, objectives, priorities, consequences, and possible alternatives.

Seeing other points of view, which exist because other people may consider different factors, see different consequences, or have different objectives or priorities.

Selecting something according to your needs and requirements, that is, according to "best fit."

Organizing by analyzing what needs to be done, what is being done, and what is to be done next. One may need to consider all factors and think of alternatives.

Focusing on different aspects of a situation, that is, knowing when you are analyzing, considering factors, thinking of consequences, etc.

Concluding a thinking project, perhaps with ideas, an answer to a question, a problem solution, an action, or conceding an inability to solve the problem.

Recognizing opinions vs. facts as two types of evidence.

Recognizing evidence that is weak, strong, or key.

Recognizing points of agreement, disagreement, and irrelevant points.

Being right by referring to facts, authority, etc.

Supporting an argument by using value-laden words, such as right, proper, fair, sincere, or ridiculous, dishonest, devious, stupid.

Being wrong in an argument because of exaggerating, making a (e.g., factual) mistake, or by having prejudiced (fixed) ideas.

Challenging existing ways of doing things as a means of stimulating new ideas.

Improving things by identifying faults and thinking of ways to remove them.

Solving problems by thinking about problem requirements.

Recognizing information that is given vs. information that has been omitted, but is needed.

Recognizing contradictory information, which can lead to false conclusions.

Recognizing guesses based on good information ("small guesses," e.g., the sun will rise tomorrow) vs. guesses based on little information ("big guesses," e.g., the final score of a future football game).

Distinguishing between ordinary emotions (e.g., anger, love, fear, sorrow) and those concerned with one's view of oneself (ego-emotions; e.g., pride, power, insecurity).

Understanding that values determine thinking, judgments, choices and actions.

Each of us has things we value highly, and things to which we give a low value.

And more.

I eat raspberries; I get sick when I eat strawberries; I get sick when I eat blackberries."

Analogical thinking. Students practice analogical thinking with problems like "germ is to disease as candle is to (a) wax, (b) wick, (c) white, (d) light.

Syllogistic reasoning. "All dogs are animals; all Lhasa Apsos are dogs." What valid inference can we draw from this?

Reversibility and nonreversibility. "No" statements are reversible: No submarines are kangaroos, and therefore no kangaroos are submarines. However, "all" statements are nonreversible: All model airplanes are toys, but not all toys are model airplanes.

Other thinking skills in the *Philosophy for Children* materials address creativity and understanding descriptions and explanations, universal and particular statements ("all birds are blue" vs. "This bird is blue"), hypotheses, impartiality, consistency, reasons for beliefs, alternatives, and others.

Intelligence expert Robert Sternberg (1984) said of Lipman's materials, "No program I am aware of is more likely to teach durable and transferable thinking skills than *Philosophy for Children.*" However, Sternberg also warned that students in inner-city schools may have trouble identifying with the middle-class story characters and their types of problems. Further, poor readers or students of low-average ability (or below) may have trouble dealing with the program.

PROJECT IMPACT

One impressive thinking skills program is the middle-school level *Project IMPACT (Improve Minimal Proficiencies by Activating Critical Thinking*; Orange County Department of Education, 1981; see Zinner, 1985). In her review of Project Impact, Zinner commented

> The project's merits were tested and the results were remarkable . . . Teachers noticed improvement in students' high-level questioning abilities . . . use of vocabulary, motivation in class, attendance . . . reading and math scores

. . . students enjoy the lessons so much they request them . . . teachers themselves say *IMPACT* has improved their teaching style and renewed their enthusiasm for their career as well . . . it was selected as an Exemplary/Incentive Project and a Model Staff Development Program by the California State Department of Education . . . the U.S. Department of Education ranked it first among 24 funded projects.

In a hierarchical fashion, Project *IMPACT* aims first at strengthening *enabling* skills of observing, comparing, contrasting, grouping, classifying, ordering, sequencing, patterning, and prioritizing. Next are *process* skills of analyzing facts and opinions, relevant and irrelevant information, reliable and unreliable sources, questioning, inferring meaning of statements, cause-effect relationships, generalizations, predictions, assumptions, and points of view, including prejudice. Finally, the program focuses on *operations*, including inductive and deductive reasoning and the evaluation skills of judgment and decision making.

To illustrate, one lesson entitled "Can You Zooley?" focuses on deductive reasoning. The learner studies the arrangement of large and small, round and rectangular, patterned drawings representing zoo animals (see Figure 11.2). A series of questions requires the learner to analyze the illustration and deduce information about the creatures. Try it. If you get stumped, answers appear at the end of the chapter:

1. Which family is visiting the polar bears?
2. Which is the family of spiders?
3. Whose son has Mr. Crocodile just swallowed?
4. Which swimming family has only three sons?
5. Which family has just three daughters?
6. Is the polar bear's cub male or female?
7. Which is a family of snakes?
8. Which is a kangaroo?
9. What will be the surname of the elephant's baby which is soon to be born?
10. What is the zookeeper's name?

The materials are engaging.

Can You Zooley?

Key To Family Names

Gobbie	Squeal	Slizz	Kazoo
Noz	Beeze	Ample	Zuff
Lesger	Swift	Trick	Glup

FIGURE 11.2   "Can You Zooley?" lesson from Project IMPACT.
Reprinted by permission of S. Lee Winocur, Ph.D., Center for the Teaching of Thinking,
Project IMPACT.

INSTRUMENTAL ENRICHMENT: FEUERSTEIN

Reuven Feuerstein spent several teenage years in Nazi concentration camps. He later helped children and adults migrate to Israel, and studied at the University of Geneva and the Sorbonne. In Israel he studied the educational needs of immigrants, many of whom would be classified by intelligence tests as retarded. He designed a program to change the cognitive structure of retarded performers and to transform them into autonomous, independent thinkers, capable of initiating and elaborating ideas (Makler, 1980).

Feuerstein's (1980a, 1980b) *Instrumental Enrichment* program was designed specifically to correct deficiencies in:

Restraining impulsivity
Reducing egocentric thinking and behavior
Recognizing, defining, and solving problems
Considering two or more sources of information at once
Analyzing, making comparisons, categorizing

Planning, testing hypotheses
Recognizing the need for logical evidence
Accurately using time and space dimensions

Instrumental Enrichment is a three-year program that can be accelerated for gifted students. It is designed for students around age 9 and above, those ready for Piagetian formal operational thinking. Teachers cannot obtain the materials unless they complete Instrumental Enrichment training.[1]

There are 13 types of exercises, each of which is said to strengthen a number of underlying abilities. Two examples follow.

Organization of Dots.   Students are presented with amorphous arrays of dots of varying complexity. Their task is to identify and outline specified geometric figures, such as squares, diamonds, and stars, by connecting dots. This exercise is said to strengthen the projection of visual relationships, discrimination of form and size, constancy of form and size across changes in orientation, use of relevant information, discovery strategies, perspective, restraint of impulsivity, labeling, precision and accuracy, planning, determination of starting point, systematic search and comparison to model, and motivation (Feuerstein, 1980a).

Orientation in Space.   A picture is presented containing, for example, a house, a bench, a garden and a tree (Figure 11.3).

To the right is a boy who is facing left, right, front, or back. By filling in a table, the student describes the position of each object in the picture relative to each orientation of the boy. The exercise is said to teach, for example, the ability to use concepts and stable systems of reference (concrete, abstract, and interpersonal) for orientation in space; defining the problem; simultaneous use of several sources of information; systematic work; hypothetical and inferential thought as a basis for logical conclusions; delimitation of alternatives; how to

summarize data using a table; precise and accurate communication of information; and reduced egocentricity.

Comparison exercises strengthen classification abilities and the abilities needed to find similarities and differences between objects, events, and ideas. Verbal and nonverbal syllogisms strengthen formal logic, including the use of sets, subsets, and intersecting sets. Students infer validity, find relationships, discover principles, and choose and process data.

The cognitive functions taught in Instrumental Enrichment fall into three categories of *input* (e.g., organizing information), *elaboration* (e.g., evaluating relevance of information), and *output* (e.g., expressing problem solutions).

Evidence for the effectiveness of the FIE program amounts to observations by teachers' aides and project administrators in Tennessee, Toronto, New York City, and Louisville, who independently agreed that after Intellectual Enrichment training, children:

Used Instrumental Enrichment strategies in other subjects.

Read and followed directions spontaneously.

Improved their accuracy of observation and their inclusion of more relevant detail.

Improved their precision; they began spontaneously correcting their own mistakes.

Increased their social sensitivity, willingness to listen to others, tolerance of others' opinions, and willingness to help others.

Became more willing to defend their opinions on the basis of evidence.

Improved the relevance and completeness of their answers, and their readiness to cope with more difficult problems.

Improved their feelings of success and their self-image.

As for personal endorsements, Nicholas Hobbs (1980) described Feuerstein's book *Instrumental Enrichment* (1980a) as "an intellectual achievement of formidable proportions ... Few single works in psychology equal it in originality, ingenuity, scope, theoretical importance, and potential

---

[1] For information regarding materials and teacher training, contact Frances Link, Curriculum Development Associates, 1211 Connecticut Ave., Washington, DC 20036.

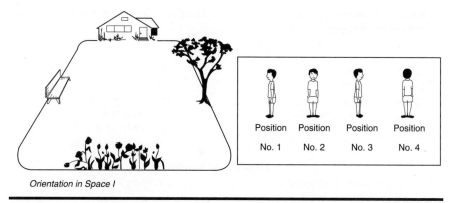

Orientation in Space I

FIGURE 11.3.   Illustration from Orientation in Space problem.
Reproduced by permission of Curriculum Development Associates.

significance." Frances Link (personal communication), an Instrumental Enrichment workshop leader, said "It's fantastic. It changes teachers."

CRITICAL THINKING PRESS AND SOFTWARE WORKBOOKS

One broad-based approach to teaching thinking skills through exercise is found in over a dozen workbooks published by Critical Thinking Press and Software (formerly Midwest Publications). The workbooks by Black and Black (e.g., 1984, 1985, 1986, 1987, 1988) and Harnadek (e.g., 1976, 1977, 1978, 1979) include hundreds of exercises intended to strengthen simple and complex thinking skills. A sample of the kinds of abilities these authors seek to strengthen appears in Table 11.7.

The following are examples of exercises found in the workbooks by Black and Black and Harnadek. A teacher who is aware of these types of exercises and thinking skills will recognize them in language arts and other workbooks, and very likely will be able to create some original ones.

Analogical Thinking.   Analogical reasoning exercises take the classic form *speedometer* : *velocity* :: *thermometer* : _____ (*degree*, *light*, *temperature*) (Black and Black, 1988). With this verbal analogy, the student analyzes the relationship between *speedometer* and *velocity*, then concludes that *thermometer* measures *temperature*. Nonverbal (figural) analogical reasoning can be exercised with geometric figures, as shown in Figure 11.4. Other figural analogy problems require students to draw the one missing figure, or to create a pair of figures that have the same relationship as the given pair (Black and Black, 1984, 1988).

Inductive Thinking.   Inductive thinking abilities are exercised in sequence problems that require students to induce a figural relationship among three (or four) patterns in a sequence, and then draw the next pattern in the series (Harnadek, 1979).

Verbal sequence exercises ask students to line up a sequence of three words (e.g., *believe*, *deliberate*, *read*) in order of size, degree, or, in this case, order of occurrence (Black and Black, 1985).

Deductive Reasoning.   Harnadek (1978) defines deductive reasoning as ". . . a process whereby the thinker reaches a conclusion which is necessitated by the premises." That is, there is one right answer that follows logically from what is given. One type of exercise seeks to teach deductive reasoning with problems that require the logical elimination of alternatives. A matrix is provided which the thinker uses, in conjunction with series of clues, to eliminate untenable possibilities and eventually find the

TABLE 11.7   Some Specific Thinking Skills Taught in Critical Thinking Press and Software Workbooks

Figural Similarities

Matching Shapes	Dividing Shapes into Equal Parts
Combining Shapes	Finding Patterns
Matching Congruent Figures	Matching Similar Figures
Drawing Lines of Symmetry	Matching Volume
Matching Congruent Solids	Recognizing Views of a Solid
Combining Solids	Using Grids to Enlarge Figures

Figural Sequences

Figural Sequence Problems	Rotating Figures Problems
Producing Reflections	Paper Folding
Matching Pattern Pieces	Producing a Pattern

Figural Classifications

Classifying by Shape	Classifying by Pattern
Describing Characteristics	Describing Classes
Matching Classes by Shape	Matching Classes by Pattern
Finding Shape Exceptions	Finding Pattern Exceptions
Multiple Classifications	Overlapping Classes

Figural Analogies

Analogies—Select and Supply Problems
Describing Figural Analogies
Making up Analogies

Verbal Similarities and Differences

Selecting Antonyms	Selecting Synonyms
Denotations	Connotations

Verbal Sequences

Following Directions	Writing Directions
Completing Phrases	Opposites
Similarities	Following Yes-No Rules
True-False Tables	Finding Locations with Maps
Describing Locations	Describing Directions
Deductive Reasoning	Time Sequences
Discriminating Degree of Meaning	

Logical Relationships

Negation	Conjunction ("and") Rules
Disjunction ("or") Rules	Implication ("if-then") Rules
Cause-Effect Words	Intervals of a Day, Year
Schedules	Time Zones

Flowcharting

In Problem Solving	A Sequence
A Cycle	In Planning
In Comparison Shopping	

Verbal Classifications

Parts of a Whole
General to Specific
Explaining Exceptions
Overlapping Classes
Diagramming Classes
Sentences With Classes and Subclasses

Classes and Members
Distinguishing Relationships
Sorting into Word Classes
Branching Diagrams

Verbal Analogies

Antonym/Synonym Analogies
"Kind of" Analogies
"Used to (for)"
Creating Analogies

Association Analogies
"Part of" Analogies
"Degree of" Analogies

---

one correct solution. For example, Angelo, Becky, Conrad, and Doreen are an actor, a bellhop, a comedian, and a trapeze artist; Doreen is not in show business, and Angelo is not the Actor. Using these clues and the matrix in Figure 11.5, match each person's name and occupation.[2]

Similar "mind-bender" exercises require the learner to figure out who is younger or taller than whom, or in Black and Black (1984) the correct order of historical events.

Classifying.   In one sense, classifying is the most basic and important of all learning and thinking

[2]Note that two occupations imply gender.

skills. If we could not classify based on shared characteristics of group members, we would be unable to cope with our complex world.

Black and Black (1984, 1987) and Harnadek (1977) teach classification skills by presenting groups of geometric patterns and asking students to induce the commonality among members. Multiple-classification exercises in Black and Black (1984) teach students that objects simultaneously can be members of several classes, depending upon which characteristics one attends to. For example, in one exercise a black parallelogram can belong to Group "A" because it is a parallelogram and to Group "B" because it is black (Black and Black, 1984).

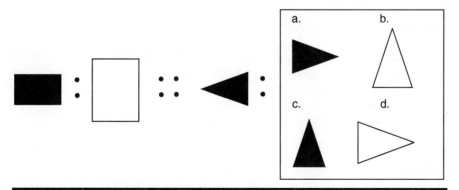

FIGURE 11.4.   Example of figural analogy problem.
From Black and Black, 1984. Reprinted by permission of Critical Thinking Press and Software.

	Actor	Bellhop	Comedian	Trapeze Artist
Angelo				
Becky				
Conrad				
Doreen				

FIGURE 11.5.   Deductive reasoning exercise from Harnadek (1978).
Reprinted by permission of Critical Thinking Press and Software.

Other exercises in Black and Black (1984, 1987) focus on helping students learn the meanings of such classification-related concepts as *includes*, *overlaps*, *is separate from*, and *is included in*.

With verbal classification exercises, students are asked to select which one of five words does not belong—which requires inducing a characteristic that is common to all words except one (e.g., *pencil, chalk, rabbit, crayon, pen*; Harnadek, 1977). Nothing is more frustrating than trying to write with a dull rabbit!

Verbal Relationships.   Many exercises help students learn verbal relationships by using *antonyms, synonyms, similarities*, and *opposites*, sometimes in verbal analogies (e.g., *cease : stop :: proceed : ____?____*. Classification-related exercises, which deal with *includes, overlaps*, etc., and verbal sequence (ordering) exercises also help teach verbal relationships.

Cause and Effect.   Understanding cause-and-effect relationships may be considered a type of inductive thinking—given an effect, one induces cause (Harnadek, 1979). Some of Harnadek's exercises aim at strengthening cause-and-effect

thinking by giving students a short illogical scenario and asking them "Do you think this is right? How come?" or "What do you think?" For example, "Only countries with military forces have wars, therefore we should not have military forces in our country."

Part-Whole Relationships.   Exercises in Black and Black (1984) seek to strengthen students' understanding of part-whole relationships. For example, given four words (*acrobats, animals, clowns, circus*) students identify which word represents the whole and which words are its parts.

Following Directions.   One easily neglected thinking skill is the self-management behavior of following directions. Black and Black (1985) give students practice in attending carefully to directions with exercises such as:

Use a whole sheet of paper. . . . Draw the design step by step, exactly as directed.

a. Draw a line from top to bottom that is one-fourth the page width from the left edge.

b. Divide this vertical line into four equal parts.

c. Divide the right edge into four equal parts.

d. Connect the points one-fourth of the way from the top.

e. Connect the points one-fourth of the way from the bottom.

f. Write "I" in the top right rectangle.

g. Write "DIRECTIONS" in the lower right rectangle.

h. Write "FOLLOWED" in the square.[3]

THINKING AND LEARNING

The *Thinking and Learning* (Wasserman, 1985) materials follow the Black and Black/Harnadek strategy of strengthening thinking skills through "indirect" thinking exercises. In this case, however, all problems and questions are tied to subject areas. Three sets (boxes) of materials include exercises in eight operations: *observing, comparing, classifying, imagining, identifying assumptions, making hypotheses, solving problems*, and *making decisions*. These thinking skills are coordinated with eight subject areas: *language arts, social studies, mathematics, science, music and art, recreation*, "*thinking about tests*," and *computers*.

For example, an exercise in *observing* in *science* shows a photo of a shuttle launch and asks, "Make a careful observation of this photo and then write about what you see. Try to keep your report free of assumptions and judgmental statements." On the back of each card are ideas for *Extending the Activity*, in this case, "What is there about this rocket that enables it to be shot into space? Write your ideas about how this works. How is a rocket different from an airplane in this function? Tell what you think about this."

A *comparing* exercise in *social studies* shows a photo of an artist painting a mural, and a woman pilot sitting in her helicopter. The exercise asks,

"Both of these people are working. Compare their jobs. In what ways are they alike? How are they different?" The extending activity asks, "What kinds of talents does a person need to fly a helicopter? What kinds of talents does a person need to paint murals?"

A *solving problems* exercise in *language arts* shows students at work in an instructional materials center. The problem is, "A new student in your class needs to check out a book on space travel from the library. Write some clear directions for the student. Then, list some other ways you might help the student find the book."

Making decisions in *computers* shows a photo of students of various ages visiting astronauts training in a tank of water. The problem: "You have a chance to go to camp this summer—but you must choose between a computer camp and a space camp. What would you consider in making up your mind? What other facts would you want to know about the camps? Which would you choose? Write your ideas." The extending activity asks, "If you were already a whiz at computers, which camp would you choose? What does this say about you? About how you like to spend your summers? About how you like to learn?"

Making hypotheses in *music and art* presents a picture of a beautiful Asian garden and asks, "Who might have created this garden? What do you think it might have meant to the creator? Write some hypotheses which might give some clues."

An exercise in *imagining* in the area of *thinking about tests* showed a picture of graduation ceremonies, and asked, "Design a report card you think would be helpful. Use your most creative imagination for this activity."

Identifying assumptions in *recreation* were exercised by showing a figure skater and asking, "Marlo is going to join a special class to learn how to figure skate. What assumptions might Marlo be making? Write your ideas about them."

Benefits from the *Thinking and Learning* materials, and the Critical Thinking Press and Software workbooks, will be enhanced if the nature of the skills are (metacognitively) discussed and understood by students.

---

[3]The reader interested in further information about the Black and Black and Harnadek exercises should request a recent catalog from Midwest Publications/Critical Thinking Press and Software, Box 448, Pacific Grove, CA 93950.

OBSTACLES TO EFFECTIVE THINKING

Vail (1990) described a variety of personal, home, and school factors that block students' ability to think. Some comparatively simple problems are being hungry or tired—with similarly simple solutions of switching the time for demanding classroom thinking activities, keeping snacks on hand, and talking to parents about TV watching versus sleep.

Another problem, common to gifted children, is *perfectionism*, which we will elaborate in Chapters 13 and 17. When the curriculum shifts from "How do you spell . . . ?" to "Why do you think . . . ?" the perfectionist student may attempt to parrot an answer from the book or otherwise deliver a teacher-pleasing reply instead of thinking. For students who have gotten by on memorizing and reciting, Vail recommended exercises that reward originality instead of conformity.

Many personal problems can interfere with children's ability to think clearly, for example, a death or divorce in the family (for which they may feel responsible and guilty) or family pressures for correct answers and high grades. In the classroom some obstacles to thinking are a mismatch between the student's learning style (e.g., visual) and the teacher's teaching style (e.g., verbal), and an emotional environment that is stressfully competitive or otherwise potentially humiliating. School and district expectations of high achievement test scores (does the word "accountability" ring a bell?) can damage a teacher's plans for teaching thinking—despite the fact that teaching thinking is more valuable in the long run (Vail, 1990).

On the positive side, noted Vail, feelings of confidence, belonging, and dignity, along with courage, resilience, curiosity, diligence, and humor, will aid the freedom to think and learn.

SELECTING THINKING SKILLS EXERCISES AND MATERIALS

De Bono (1983), Sternberg (1983), and Treffinger, Isaksen and McEwen (1987) itemized criteria for assessing the value and usefulness of thinking skills strategies and programs. A composite of their lists includes:

1. The program should not require extended advanced training. However, appropriate training should be readily available through workshops, seminars or printed resources.

2. A good program should be usable by teachers of varying abilities, not just gifted or highly qualified teachers.

3. The program should be robust enough to "resist damage" as it is passed from trainer to trainer, from trainer to teacher, and finally from teacher to student.

4. The program should use "parallel design," which means that if some parts are taught badly or skipped, what remains will still be usable and valuable.

5. The program should be enjoyable for teachers and children.

6. Materials should be attractive, appropriate to students' interests, and motivating.

7. Important thinking skills should be addressed; objectives should be specified.

8. The program should teach skills that help learners in their lives outside of school.

9. The program should improve metacognitive skills—understanding thinking and thinking skills.

10. Appropriate examples of practical applications of the methods and techniques should be presented.

11. Involvement should be active, not passive; experiential learning and applications are important.

12. There should be opportunities for transfer and generalization of the training.

13. The program should be assessed not only for immediate, direct effects, but also for the transferability and durability of the training.

14. It is desirable for the program to be flexible enough to accommodate individual differences, for example, in age, ability, or preferred working speed.

15. It is desirable to have individual and group activities.

16. It is desirable to be able to relate the skills to curriculum content.

As with all G/T enrichment, the program must be suited to students' needs.

SUMMARY

Issues in teaching thinking skills include whether they should be infused into existing subjects or taught as a separate course or subject, selecting which skills to teach students at different ages, selecting the best way to teach thinking skills, and evaluating mastery of thinking skills. Some thinking skills include attitudes and dispositions.

Thinking skills may be taught indirectly via practice with, for example, classification, analogy, logical reasoning, and many other kinds of problems. Thinking skills also may be taught directly as conscious techniques for reasoning and solving problems.

Metacognition is thinking about thinking. It includes understanding why, when, and how problem-solving strategies should be used, and thinking about one's own thinking, the thinking of others, and sources of ideas. Metacognition can encompass teaching about brain functions, personality and thinking styles, and preferred ways of studying and learning.

Teaching thinking requires a list of skills to be taught. One list included creativity, critical thinking, and problem solving; skills in reading, writing, and science; and reasoning, classifying, and evaluating skills. Another list included the categories of focusing, information gathering, remembering, organizing, analyzing, generating, integrating, and evaluating.

The best known higher-level thinking skills are the application, analysis, synthesis, and evaluation levels of Bloom's taxonomy. The taxonomy guides teacher questioning. Gifted students should spend more time with higher level thinking skills, less at the knowledge and comprehension levels.

Paul *et al.* proposed a taxonomy of Socratic questions in the areas of clarification and examining assumptions, reasons and evidence, viewpoints or perspectives, implications and consequences, and the question or problem itself.

According to Resnick, higher-order cognitive processes include thinking that is not specified in advance (non-algorithmic); it is complex, yields multiple solutions, includes judgment and interpretation, application of multiple criteria, uncertainty, self-regulation of thinking, and imposing meaning.

"Critical thinking" is interpreted in many ways. This section explains critical thinking as evaluating the biases, qualifications, and consistency of speakers, and evaluating assumptions, opinions, ambiguities, whether conclusions follow, and many others. Critical thinking as problem solving includes teaching students to identify assumptions and values, examine different sides of an issue and possible actions, and make decisions (Budmen); or else teaching students to define a problem, select pertinent information, recognize assumptions, formulate hypotheses, and draw conclusions (Dressel and Mayhew).

De Bono's CoRT strategies directly teach thinking as conscious skills that are independent of specific subject areas. About 50 CoRT thinking skills teach evaluating, considering all factors, identifying goals and objectives, projecting consequences, planning, prioritizing, and others.

Lipman's Philosophy for Children program takes the form of children's stories that teach, for example, cause-effect relations, analogical thinking, and critical thinking.

Project IMPACT was designed to strengthen enabling skills (e.g., comparing, classifying), process skills (e.g., analyzing facts, assumptions, cause-effect relationships), and operations (e.g., reasoning, evaluating).

Feuerstein's Instrumental Enrichment program was designed to strengthen a variety of thinking skills and abilities via such exercises as organization of dots and orientation in space.

The Critical Thinking Press and Software

workbooks by Black and Black and Harnadek contain exercises designed to strengthen simple and complex skills such as analogical reasoning, classifying, cause-effect relations, deductive reasoning, and following directions.

The Thinking and Learning materials seek to strengthen thinking skills (e.g., observing, classifying, identifying assumptions, making decisions) within specific subject areas (e.g., language arts, social studies, math, science, music/art, recreation, and computers).

Some obstacles to effective thinking itemized by Vail include being hungry or tired, perfectionism, personal problems, learning style mismatches, and a competitive environment. District emphasis on high achievement test scores can impact on a teacher's plans to teach thinking skills.

Criteria for selecting materials and strategies include, for example, usability by teachers, attractiveness and enjoyability, effectiveness in teaching important transferable skills, a focus on students' metacognitive understanding of thinking and thinking skills, and relatability to school subjects.

Solutions to *Can You Zooley?* Exercise

1. The **Zuff** family. They are the only family group outside of the cages. The polar bears must be **Tricks**.

2. Lesger. They have eight legs.

3. The **Beeze** son, and the crocodiles must be **Gobbies**. This is the only small animal "inside" a different type of large animal. We also learn that rectangles are male.

4. The **Squeal** family. They have fins, and three little sons (rectangles).

5. The **Lesger** family. They have three little circles (females), no rectangles (males).

6. Male. It's a rectangle.

7. The **Slizz** family. They have no legs.

8. The **Swifts**. They seem to have two legs and a big tail, with a little one attached to the front of the mother.

9. Ample. This is the only family with a small animal inside an adult female.

10. Glup. He is the only adult by himself outside of the cages.

CHAPTER 12

CULTURALLY DIVERSE AND LOW SOCIOECONOMIC CHILDREN

THE INVISIBLE GIFTED

Improving our ability to identify and educate gifted students from culturally diverse backgrounds has indeed been of interest and concern to educators for several decades.
Mary M. Frasier (1991b)

The scene is the principal's office in an inner-city elementary school. The principal, an African-American woman, is bright, determined, dedicated, and very professional; she has been carefully selected from among many competitors to lead a daring new approach to educating inner-city youngsters. Many of these children, with learning and social problems, had been written off as "nonlearners" by teachers in other schools. Today, several members of the school board who are interested in the goals and methods of this innovative "fundamental" school program interview the principal. Their questions begin with the who's, why's, and how's of this unique school. She answers that the school is based on certain fundamentals: carefully selected staff, parent involvement, basic skills, mastery learning, firm discipline, and homework.

Then a significant question:

"Ms. Jones, how will you teach your gifted students?" And the response:

"In this school we have no gifted children."

Culturally different and economically disadvantaged African-American, Hispanic, Native American, and white children living in large urban centers, in poor rural areas, and on Indian reserva-

tions rarely are identified or described as gifted or talented. They are grossly underrepresented in programs for the gifted. Their formal educational needs are assumed to be only in basic skills areas; and their adjustment to school and learning almost always involves strict discipline. Their cultural and language differences plus their lack of exposure to mainstream American culture usually combine to obscure from society the gifted children among them. These gifted minority and disadvantaged children typically proceed invisibly through school until they drop out or, with luck, graduate.

In addition to their wholesale exclusion from G/T programs, the families and peers of minority and poor children also typically do not reinforce the development of their intellectual or creative talents. They clearly are in need of strong school support. This chapter will discuss the special needs of these children, factors that contribute to their academic success, identification methods, programming and counseling strategies, and special considerations for rural gifted children.

SPECIAL NEEDS

In 1977 Congresswoman Shirley Chisholm introduced legislation to include funding for gifted and

255

talented minority and culturally different children within the Elementary and Secondary Education Act. She immediately was confronted with the reality of widespread misunderstanding of these students (Chisholm, 1978). She pointed out that her white colleagues did not seem to recognize the existence of *gifted* minority children, and that they assumed that all minority children were in need of academic remediation. Her African-American colleagues, with little apparent support, questioned her sponsorship of programs which ". . . did nothing but promote (discriminatory) IQ testing and money for affluent white children." In her keynote address before the National Forum on Minority and Disadvantaged Gifted and Talented, Chisholm (1978) lamented the failure of our educational institutions to nurture the talents of gifted disadvantaged students. She faulted American education for (1) inadequate methods for recognizing talent among culturally different children and (2) insufficient funding to provide special programs for these children.

The late 1960s and the 1970s saw the introduction of major educational and social programs to improve opportunities for minority, culturally different, and economically disadvantaged children. The Elementary and Secondary Education Act, Head Start programs, educational TV programs for children (Sesame Street, Electric Company), bilingual educational funding, and court-ordered desegregation all contributed to enhancing educational preparation and opportunities. The actual educational and social impact of these investments has been both controversial and difficult to evaluate. However, some statistics were encouraging. For example, the percentage of minority students who dropped out decreased dramatically. According to a 1977 U.S. Department of Commerce report, in the mid-1950s 50 percent of African-American youth and 60 percent of Hispanic youth dropped out of school. By 1977 24 percent of African-American students and 42 percent of Hispanics dropped out. For white students over a similar period of time, drop out rates decreased from 20 percent to 13 percent.

A 1992 report by the U.S. Department of Education indicated that dropout rates for African-American and white students have continued to decline, but Hispanic dropout rates have remained high. From 1972 to 1991, the report showed, dropout rates for African-American students went from 21.3 percent to 13.6 percent; for whites, 12.3 percent to 8.9 percent. The 1991 dropout rate for Hispanic students was 35.3 percent (Watertown, Wisconsin Daily Times, *Sept. 16, 1992*). On a recent visit to a school in North Dakota, it was indicated to author Rimm that the dropout rate for a Native American population in that area runs as high as 50 percent. While these reports indicate some improvements for some minority groups, the statistics remain unacceptable.

A study of 28,000 students in the Public Schools of Montgomery County, Alabama showed a higher percentage of African-American and Hispanic students working below the standard of performance for mathematics at every grade level (Norman, 1988; Figure 12.1). Pool (1990) found that on a test of high-level mathematical proficiency, 7.6 percent of the white students performed at a high enough level to be channeled toward science and engineering. Only 1.2% of Hispanics and 0.3% of African-Americans attained a similar level. For those who are qualified, recruitment is enthusiastic. Major universities and small colleges alike search for minority students talented in the sciences and offer them significant scholarship help. The demand is there, but the supply is lacking.

As we look to gifted minority youth who could direct their talents toward science or mathematics, we would hope to find increasing numbers of Ph.Ds. There are actually *fewer* African-American males earning Ph.Ds in science than 20 years ago (Pool, 1990). Although the numbers for African-American females have increased slightly, that has not compensated for the decrease in males. There has been a slight increase in the number of Hispanic males and females receiving Ph.Ds in the "hard sciences," but they account for only 2 percent of the natural science and engineering doctorates, which

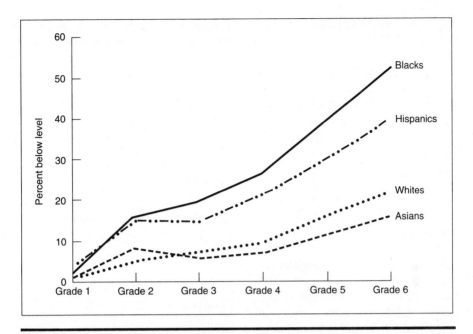

FIGURE 12.1. Falling behind. Percentage of students in Montgomery County schools by racial/ethnic group and grade level who are working below the standard of performace for mathematics at each grade.
From Norman (1988). Reprinted by permission of the American Association for the Advancement of Science.

is low considering Hispanics account for 7 percent of the working-age population.

In educational research the numbers of African-American Ph.Ds decreased from 9.2 percent of all educational research Ph.Ds (691) in 1975 to 7.0 percent (421) in 1986 (Frierson, 1990). Furthermore, half of all African-American faculty members are at predominantly African-American colleges, therefore reducing their effectiveness as mentors to African-American students who attend other universities.

These alarming statistics emphasize the importance of early identification of gifted disadvantaged and minority students and programming for their giftedness. The executive summary from the report *No Gift Wasted* (Alamprese and Erlanger, 1988) warns educators that disadvantaged students are not

yet sufficiently served by elementary and secondary gifted programs. Its main findings follow:

• Minority students are underrepresented in programs designed to serve gifted and talented students. Although minorities make up 30 percent of public school enrollment, they represent less than 20 percent of the students selected for gifted and talented programs;
• Whereas students from low-income backgrounds comprise 20 percent of the student population, they make up only 4 percent of those students who perform at the highest levels on standardized tests (those who score at the 95th percentile or above);
• High school seniors from disadvantaged families (in which the mother did not complete high school) are less than half as likely to have partici-

pated in gifted and talented programs as more advantaged seniors; and

• Disadvantaged students are far less likely to be enrolled in academic programs that can prepare them for college and are about half as likely to take coursework in advanced math and science than more advantaged students. Only 2 percent of high school seniors from poor families take calculus, whereas approximately 7 percent of those from more advantaged backgrounds do.

Estimates of the underrepresentation of minority students in gifted programs vary between 30 and 70 percent (Richert, 1987). Frasier (1990) and Baldwin (1987a, 1987b) have noted that IQ cutoff scores effectively preclude the identification of disadvantaged and culturally diverse gifted students, including many African-American students. McKenzie (1986) found in a study of identification practices that only 3.8 percent of Native Americans, 2.4 percent of African American students, and 1.9 percent of Hispanic students were identified as gifted, compared with 6.8 percent of white students. The study showed that IQ cut-off scores identified 10.1 percent of Asian students as gifted, due likely to the traditional strong emphasis on education among Asian families.

Woliver and Woliver (1991) noted that Asian students are more soft-spoken and less likely to call attention to themselves, thus reducing the liklihood that teachers will identify them as gifted. Therefore, they tend to be identified because of high test scores.

A survey conducted by Patton, Prillaman, and Van Tassel-Baska (1990) summarized the paucity of programs serving disadvantaged gifted learners. Surveys were returned from 52 of the 54 states or state entities surveyed. Three states had no programs that focused on disadvantaged gifted learners. Approximately 30 percent of the states reported "frequent" use of "low socioeconomic status" in identifying gifted students, while 35 percent of the states used the SES variable "a little" or "not at all." Race and ethnicity were not mentioned at all, very little, or a moderate amount in identification by 62 percent of the states. Only 29 percent indicated that a race or ethnicity variable was heavily emphasized. The results of the survey were not encouraging.

Recommendations resulting from the survey included the following:

1. States need to translate their expressed philosophical concerns for culturally diverse and low socioeconomic status learners into their state definitions of giftedness.

2. States need to develop program prototypes for use with atypical gifted learners.

3. States need to collect systematic data on at-risk students in gifted programs.

FACTORS RELATED TO SUCCESS FOR DISADVANTAGED YOUTH

Literature which includes differentiated information on the successes of disadvantaged children can provide insights into appropriate programming to encourage success of these gifted youth.

Werner (1989) provided impressive information in a 30-year study of 201 high-risk children from the Hawaiian island of Kauai. These children had experienced multiple risks, including moderate to severe perinatal stress, chronic poverty, troubled family environments, and parents with fewer than eight grades of education. While two-thirds of these children developed serious problems, one-third grew into adults who "lived well, worked well, and played well." They were successful in accomplishing educational and career goals; 46 of them had completed college. Werner termed these children *resilient* and documented the characteristics in their childhood that appeared to support their success despite their extreme disadvantages.

The critical factor for these resilient children appeared to be their informal support networks. Many mentioned a teacher who had been a role model during periods of family disorganization. Others mentioned a youth leader, a favorite minister, participation in 4H, the school band, a cheerleading team, or the "Y." These important people or activities seemed to help the children develop meaning and a sense of personal control over their lives.

Van Tassel-Baska (1989) used a case study approach to determine the dynamics underlying the success of 15 economically disadvantaged gifted adolescents who had attended public schools in the midwest. She uncovered important home and school variables that can help parents and educators guide disadvantaged youth. Aspirations, expectations, and standards of parents and the extended family were high for these children. Mothers were extremely influential, and for some children grandmothers were critical. Fathers and grandfathers also were cited as important.

School was pleasant and productive for these children. Many were *A* students, and for those who had been accelerated, it had been a positive experience. Involvement in extracurricular activities appeared extremely helpful. Also, the students had many positive relationships with teachers. While they had friends, peer influence did not play a critical role in their educational or career plans.

An important difference between the Werner (1989) and Van Tassel-Baska (1989) studies lies in the role of family versus community. In Werner's research the disadvantaged children all came from dysfunctional families, and the needed support came from school and community sources. In the Van Tassel-Baska study good family relationships seemed critical. One might conclude that the assistance of community members becomes crucial in the absence of role models and high expectations in the disadvantaged child's family.

In reviewing a study by Denny and Arnold of 81 valedictorians, Moses (1991) itemized roadblocks to post-high school achievement of gifted minority students. The group as a whole was very successful. However, the study found that while white middle class students had considerable family support, the eight African-American and Hispanic students struggled with financial issues, family support, and "fitting in" at predominately white colleges. The intellectual self-esteem of women students decreased after they entered college, despite their grades being higher than those of many men. They also often lowered their career expectations. The difficulties that minority gifted students will face in college should undoubtedly be part of their guidance preparation in high school if we wish to increase the likelihood that they will complete college.

IDENTIFICATION

As noted earlier, minority and culturally different gifted children are not easily identified. Indeed, because of cultural bias in test instruments and other identification methods, many typical procedures actually obscure their giftedness—by "proving" these children are *not* gifted. Because actual achievement often is not outstanding, identification must be based upon superior *potential* instead of superior performance. This section will review typical identification methods and evaluate their usefulness for culturally different and economically disadvantaged populations. It also will recommend other identification procedures that in some cases will be more effective.

Intelligence Tests

High intelligence test scores on either group or individual tests are one valid way to identify intellectually gifted minority youngsters. However, an average or even low IQ score may be a poor or misleading indicator of student ability if the child comes from a culturally deprived or culturally different environment.

This issue is exceedingly complex. There are frequent and continuing debates regarding *cultural bias* in mental testing and the dust is far from settled. For example, some argue that the lower average scores of minority groups are simply evidence of discriminatory test bias. From this perspective, intelligence tests ". . . have devastating labeling—and pigeon-holing—effects . . . and they are nothing more than an Anglo yardstick designed to make whites look ingenious and blacks and other minorities stupid" (Hoffman, 1964). For another view, Arthur Jensen (1976; see also Jensen, 1980), known for his "racial differences" hypothesis, argues that intelligence tests ". . . show practically no evidence of differential culture bias . . .," by which he means that the tests do in fact predict school success for both minority and majority cultures.

In an article entitled "The Trouble With IQ Tests," physics professor Zacharias (1977) made a number of specific complaints about intelligence tests: (1) They demand an understanding of the tester's jargon, proper guessing of what the tester wants, and tolerance for boredom; (2) test items often are ambiguous, illogical, meaningless, irrelevant to what the student knows or cares about, time wasting, overprecise or not sufficiently precise, and tricky in appearance even when they contain no tricks; and (3) the tests tend to be frightening, penalizing, damaging to a student's self-image, and misleading for tracking or assigning students to grade levels. Zacharias's opinion is clear enough.

More optimistically, Thorndike and Hagen (1977) argued for the usefulness (prediction ability) of intelligence tests, but further noted that (1) the tests do not determine a person's ability, they simply suggest strengths and weaknesses; (2) they describe how a person is doing at the present time; and (3) we should consider the cultural, personal, and family background in interpreting test scores.

Educators and psychologists—whether liberal or conservative, African-American or white—will agree that culturally different students are more likely than the average student to have a difficult time when taking tests of *verbal ability* (vocabulary, comprehension). These tests, of course, are based upon middle-class English. The problem is that subcultural languages such as African-American English, (Baratz, 1974; Labov, 1974), Hawaiian pidgin, Navajo or other Native American languages are different, and so the person's linguistic structures, categories, and associations are also different. Group intelligence tests depend heavily on language ability and therefore are more likely to be biased than individually administered tests. As we saw in Chapter 4, the WISC-R and WISC-III

separate subtests and IQ scores into *verbal* and *performance* (nonverbal) components, thereby allowing a bright child with deficient English to score high. Several authors have commented on large WISC-R verbal/performance discrepancies of Native American children, due at least in part to language and cultural differences (e.g., Kryaniuk and Das, 1976; Scruggs and Cohn, 1983).

Beyond the language problem, Witty (1978) noted additional sources of cultural bias in testing. For example, minority children may have lower expectations of success, lower test-taking motivation, and higher test-taking anxiety, particularly when the administrator is middle-class white.

A further subtle bias was found by Fuchs and Fuchs (1989), namely, the effects on IQ scores of using examiners familiar to the children. They found no effect on the scores of caucasian students; however, African-American and Hispanic students scored significantly higher when the tests were administered by familiar examiners.

The *System of Multicultural Pluralistic Assessment* (SOMPA) was originally developed to adjust individual IQ test scores for cultural and economic disadvantage in order to avoid mislabeling minority children as mentally retarded (Mercer and Lewis, 1978; Mercer, 1973). However, Matthew *et al.* (1992) found the SOMPA useful in identifying 18 male and 37 female African-American students who would not otherwise have been identified for gifted programming in an urban school in Pennsylvania where the IQ score cutoff for admission to programming was 130. The SOMPA approach appears to be a particularly helpful way to identify students with economic disadvantages in states that use IQ score cutoffs for admission to gifted program.

Helms (1992) pointed out that some African-American cultural issues could negatively affect cognitive ability testing for these students (see Table 12.1). Among other recommendations for cultural equivalence in standardized testing, she suggested the use of separate racial group norms.

In sum, any identification process based on intelligence/aptitude tests will surely underidentify

TABLE 12.1   African Cultural Components in Cognitive Ability Testing: Hypothesized Effects of African-Centered Values and Beliefs

Dimension	General description	Influence on test responses
Spirituality	Greater validity of the power of immaterial forces in everyday life over linear, factual thinking.	It may be difficult to separate relevant aspects of the test stimuli from factors caused by luck or circumstance.
Harmony	The self and one's surroundings are interconnected.	The ambience in which one takes the test may influence one's responses.
Movement	Personal conduct is organized through movement.	Active test-taking strategies may result in better performance than sedentary ones.
Affect	Integration of feelings with thoughts and actions.	Feelings may facilitate or hinder test performance; respondent may find it difficult to "understand" persons in test stimuli who act without feeling.
Communalism	Valuing of one's group(s) more than individuals.	Performance may be influenced when person perceives that it represents the group.
Expressivity	Unique personality is expressed through one's behavioral style.	Test taker may choose the more imaginative response alternative.
Orality	Knowledge may be gained and transmitted orally and aurally.	Test performance may differ when the person is tested orally and aurally.
Social time	Time is measured by socially meaningful events and customs.	The belief that obtaining a "good" answer is more important than finishing on time may lead the test taker to "waste" time.

disadvantaged gifted students, students with underdeveloped potential. A high IQ score, of course, is convincing evidence of high intellectual ability among culturally different and poor children, just as with majority children. However, many gifted minority and economically disadvantaged children will be overlooked if intelligence tests are used as the only or the most important identification instrument. Their use is recommended, but average or low scores should be interpreted with caution, and in consideration of the language, cultural, and family background and the circumstances of testing.

Achievement Tests

Achievement tests typically are administered at regular intervals in virtually every school system, and so achievement information is readily available. However, while standardized achievement tests are highly recommended as an identification tool for most populations, with culturally different students they are plagued by exactly the same problems as intelligence tests. Therefore, while it is critical that achievement scores not be misused because of cultural bias, it certainly is reasonable to use them as one index of gifts and talents for minority children. As with IQ scores, children who produce high scores on achievement tests are showing good evidence of special kinds of giftedness. However, in culturally different populations there are likely to be gifted children who may not score high on these tests despite their giftedness. Achievement tests alone, then, are not a sufficient measure for the identification of gifted minority and poor children.

Because achievement test scores are often used to deny entrance into gifted programming to students with disadvantages, Lynch and Mills (1990) designed a program to improve the achievement of 45 high-potential sixth-grade students in the Pasadena Unified School District. The group included a high proportion of African-Americans and Hispanics as well as socioeconomically disadvantaged students. Their Skills Reinforcement Project (SRP) was sufficiently effective to allow nine of these students into gifted programming without recourse to affirmative action.

Teacher Nominations

In many instances, teacher nominations of giftedness are a highly suspect and invalid identification strategy (see Chapter 4). Nonetheless, it continues to be the most popular identification method used. For minority and poor children, the teacher nomination method creates special hazards. "Teacher pleasers," who are neat and clean, nicely dressed, who speak middle-class English, and who turn in their work neatly done and on time, are likely to be named as "gifted." Other students—poor, African-American, Hispanic, or Native American—are automatically "disadvantaged" by many teachers in the nomination process. Shade (1978) found that African-American gifted achievers, despite their giftedness, receive less praise and attention and more criticism in the classroom than their nongifted African-American counterparts. Clark (1983) observed that there remains the persistent attitude that gifted children are not found in certain populations.

On the other hand, a sensitive and caring teacher who is knowledgeable about characteris-

tics of gifted children may, in fact, be the very best identifier of the culturally different gifted child. Furthermore, such a teacher may be able to guide and inspire a talented child who does not score high on any ability or achievement test. In the hands of a sensitive and aware teacher, the teacher nomination procedure can be a potentially important way to locate economically disadvantaged and culturally different gifted children.

The nomination procedure will be greatly improved by educating teachers regarding characteristics of gifted and talented minority children, some of which are different than usual characteristics of giftedness. For example, Gay (1978) researched common characteristics of gifted children and compared them to parallel characteristics of gifted African-American children. Her list of 11 characteristics stems from twenty years of teaching experience with African-American children and three years of teaching in a program for the gifted and talented (see Table 12.2).

The present authors might repeat an earlier warning in relation to Gay's item 11 in Table 12.2. Gifted African-American children may perform only at an average level in school because of socioeconomic, language, motivational, personal, or cultural handicaps. Therefore, students should be considered potentially gifted if they earn high ratings on many of the first ten characteristics, with or without actual "good" school achievement.

Swenson (1978) constructed a helpful list of characteristics of creativeness in a culturally different and socioeconomically deprived urban school area. Her list came from information generated by 36 teachers and was based on observed original behavior related to classwork, art, and antisocial— yes, *antisocial*—behavior (see Table 12.3). Note that because teachers are accustomed to disciplining children for antisocial behavior they may overlook the creativity exhibited in such behavior (see especially items 2, 9, 18, 23, and 24 in Table 12.3).

Matrix Identification Models

Matrix identification models have been developed to bring together data from a variety of sources

TABLE 12.2 Comparative Characteristics of Giftedness

Concepts from the Literature	Manifestations of Gifted Characteristics in Gifted African-American Children
1. Keen observation	Picks up more quickly on racist attitudes and practices; may feel alienated by school at an early age.
2. Interest and ability in perceiving relationships	Seeks structure and organization in required tasks; may be slow to motivate in some abstract activities.
3. Verbal proficiency, large vocabulary, facility of expression	Many African-American children have large vocabularies inappropriate for the school setting; thinking in African-American English may hinder the facility of expression in standard English.
4. Breadth of information	Difficult to determine many areas of experiential knowledge for African-American children.
5. Questioning, curious, skeptical	Though some ask too many "wrong" questions, some may have been conditioned to suppress questioning behavior.
6. Critical, evaluative, possessing good judgment	Explores (in perception of relationships) better or wiser choices; reads behavioral implications.
7. Creative, inventive, original	Makes up games and activities; expresses original ideas in other ways.
8. Power of concentration, long attention span	May find some have extremely strong conconcentration due to persistent noise in environment; may also express displeasure at having to stop an activity.
9. Independence	Need for less supervision is especially pronounced in African-American gifted.
10. Diversity of interests and abilities	Frequently has artistic, musical, creative writing, psychomotor, or leadership talent in addition to global intellectual ability; may neglect school work due to other interests.
11. Academic facility and strength	Good at basic school tasks; may not show expected achievement due to inferior schooling.

From J.E. Gay, "A Proposed Plan for Identifying Black Gifted Children," *Gifted Child Quarterly*, 1978, *22*, 353-359. Reprinted by permission.

and to specifically include variables that will help identify minority and disadvantaged gifted children. Especially, the *Kranz Talent Identification Instrument* (Kranz, 1981; see Chapter 4) was designed for the identification of culturally diverse, minority, immigrant, and poor gifted children. The *Baldwin Iden-* *tification Matrix* (Baldwin, 1978, 1984, 1991; see Chapter 4) combines objective and subjective criteria and has been reported to be effective for increasing the number of African-American students identified for gifted programs (Dabney, 1983; Long, 1981; McBeath, Blackshear, and Smart, 1981).

TABLE 12.3   Characteristics of Creativity in Culturally Different Students

1. Repeats activities so that he/she can do them differently.
2. Invents imaginative lies.
3. Shows that he/she sees hidden meanings, cause and effect relationships that are not obvious.
4. Writes and illustrates stories without being asked to so as an assignment.
5. Utilizes free time by making up games or making something from paper and material scraps as opposed to more structured activities.
6. Finds many answers to a situational question.
7. Lets his/her imagination "run" when writing a story; sees more possibilities.
8. Finds activities for spare-time work with little or no additional help.
9. Decorates the border of his/her paper when doing an assignment.
10. Doesn't copy other children's ideas in art.
11. Builds and constructs things using unusual materials; uses ordinary materials in different ways.
12. Interrelates his/her experiences and draws on them with ease in discussions.
13. Doesn't let classroom events go unnoticed; questions them.
14. Accomplishes things on his/her own without help.
15. Writes poems and stories in his/her spare time.
16. Asks unusual questions during class discussions.
17. Makes up his/her own ideas when the class does a project together.
18. Suggests to the teacher alternate ways of doing an activity.
19. Is willing to risk friendship to express his/her feelings or thoughts.
20. Enthusiastic about new activities in music and art.
21. Goes beyond what is required in class assignments; makes his/her work "fancier."
22. Comes up with fresh, original comments or an unusual correct answer when there is more than one correct answer.
23. Finds new ways to get attention.
24. Tries original ways to get out of work he/she doesn't want to do.
25. Takes the initiative when he/she wants to know something; reads or asks questions without prompting.

From J.E. Swenson, "Teacher-Assessment of Creative Behavior in Disadvantaged Children, *Gifted Child Quarterly, 22* (1978), 338-43. Reprinted by permission.

Creativity Tests

Creativity tests, both divergent thinking tests and self-descriptive inventories (see Chapter 4), can be very helpful in selecting minority and culturally different children for participation in G/T programs. Specifically, they are useful in identifying highly creative children who are not motivated to achieve and who may not score high on ability or achievement tests. For both kinds of creativity tests, there has been research with minority children that supports their use.

The *Torrance Tests of Creative Thinking* (Figural Form, particularly) have been used in several research projects with minority children. For example, Solomon (1974) found that minority children scored *higher* than other children in some areas of creative thinking in grades 1 and 3. At the fifth-grade level there were no significant differences between scores of minority and other children. Torrance (1971; see also Torrance, 1977) summarized the results of 16 different studies designed to evaluate racial or socioeconomic differences in Torrance Test scores. The results varied, with some favoring the minority children and others favoring majority children, but overall his conclusions supported the notion that there is no racial or socioeconomic bias in open-ended tests of creative thinking.

The *Group Inventory for Finding (Creative) Talent (GIFT)* and the *Group Inventory For Finding Interests (GIFFI;* Davis and Rimm, 1979; Rimm, 1976) are self-report inventories that evaluate personality characteristics, attitudes, interests, and biographical information known to be associated with creativeness. Studies by Rimm and Davis (1976, 1980; Davis and Rimm, 1982) indicated that *GIFT* and *GIFFI* are valid for identifying creative potential in both rural and urban socioeconomically disadvantaged populations, as well as among specific ethnic groups, including African-American, Hispanic, and Native American minority students.

Chambers, Barron, and Sprecher (1980) confirmed that considerable information has been collected to show that some motivational and personality characteristics are indeed related to creativeness. They used this information to help identify gifted Mexican-American elementary students, and concluded that ". . . the abilities and traits necessary for future high-level intellectual/creative contributions appear to be similar for both culturally similar and culturally different persons."

Central to the appropriate use of divergent thinking tests such as the Torrance Tests or personality/biographical inventories is the recognition that (1) scores from a single creativity test should be combined with other information, such as teacher ratings of creativity or scores on a second creativity test, in order to reach a valid decision, and (2) low creativity test scores absolutely must never be used to eliminate children from G/T programs. Creativity tests are not perfect; there simply are too many types of creativity and cre-

ative people. However, creativity tests can identify creatively gifted children, majority and minority, who may not be identified in other ways.

Parent Nominations

As indicated earlier in this text, parents typically know a lot about their children's gifts and talents. For years they may have watched their energetic children create games and stories, invent things, build things, solve problems, create humor, and produce original artwork, writing, musical compositions, mechanical gadgets, and/or scientific products. Parents also will be able to identify specific culturally valued giftedness—for example, caring for siblings and fixing dinner while waiting for Mom to come home from work—better than a person outside of the cultural system. Parents should indeed be given an opportunity to nominate their children for participation in a G/T program.

Peer Nominations

Peers of economically deprived or culturally different gifted children usually do not place a high value on school achievement. However, they are as aware of gifts and talents among their friends and classmates as are other young people. Bernal (1978, 1979), for example, noted that members of a particular ethnic group almost always can identify the "smartest" among their peers.

In order to identify unusual intellectual, creative, or leadership ability, it may be necessary to look beyond the classroom to the out-of-school cliques and crowds. One interesting approach is to meet with students named by peers as out-of-school "leaders." These leaders can explain characteristics of culturally valued giftedness within their own peer culture (Bernal, 1979; Bruch and Curry, 1978), gifts which might qualify the person for the special opportunities of a G/T program. In inner-city areas, for example, creative approaches to self-maintenance or even survival may be reasonable arenas in which to discover giftedness. Culturally valued art and music talent, which is known to peers but not expressed in the classroom, also would be important information for the identification of giftedness. Finally, the "different" or lonely child in a minority culture, even though he or she does not value intellectual pursuit, may be considered suspect for unusual talent. The child may well have special interests and talents, suppressed due to peer pressures, that should be cultivated in a G/T program.

Quota Systems

One reasonable solution to minority representation in G/T programs is the quota system. A fixed percentage of culturally different children are included in a program, based upon the percentage of those students in the school or district. The quota system assumes that the same percentage of minority students are gifted and talented as majority students, and should therefore be included in the program regardless of comparative test scores or grades. As one might guess, this is a much debated assumption. A central issue is the fairness to majority students who are excluded and who, according to objective criteria, appear more qualified.

The effectiveness of the quota system has been borne out by a longitudinal study of minority students identified by the Racine school system using a quota system (Smith, LeRose, and Clasen, 1991). Twelve years later, of the 24 students identified by the quota system for a gifted program, *not one had dropped out*, compared to 45 percent of 67 equally able minority students who were in regular school programs. Admitting minority students to gifted programs can make a dramatic difference.

Additional Identification Plans

Frasier (1991a) summed up the goal of alternative identification models by indicating that we need a paradigm that "accommodates both the children we are missing and the children we are finding." The *Frasier Talent Assessment Profile* (F-TAP) was designed to combine test and nontest criteria

and is based on the following four assumptions (see Figure 12.2):

1. Methods to locate gifted children from diverse cultural backgrounds can be developed without eroding quality and without requiring excessive data collection or excessive expenditures of time.

2. Identification methods should rely on assessing dynamic rather than static displays of gifted behaviors.

3. A profile, rather than cutoff scores or weighting systems, provides the most effective and efficient way to display data for interpretation from test and nontest sources.

4. Results from identification procedures should be used to design programs and develop curricula for gifted students.

Frasier's F-TAP will include aptitude and achievement test data as well as self-report and observational information in *data categories* such as intelligence, specific academic talents, motivation, creativity, and others.

Two programs that effectively use dynamic "activity" approaches to identifying gifted African-American students, rather than "static" test scores, are the Program of Assessment, Diagnosis, and Instruction (PADI; Johnson et al., 1985) and the Potentially Gifted Minority Student project (Alamprese and Erlanger, 1988). These approaches appear to be less culturally biased than others, and thus increase the number of minority students identified (Patton, 1992).

Woods and Achey (1990) increased the percentage of racial/ethnic minority students in their Academically Gifted Project by 181 percent by using a *series* of evaluations. While some students qualified at the first step, based on group aptitude and achievement testing, other students were permitted to proceed through two other steps of group and individual testing. The use of a variety of objective measures was successful in identifying additional gifted minority students for the Academically Gifted Project while following the traditional definition of gifted adopted by North Carolina. Table

The Frasier Talent Assessment Profile (F-TAP)

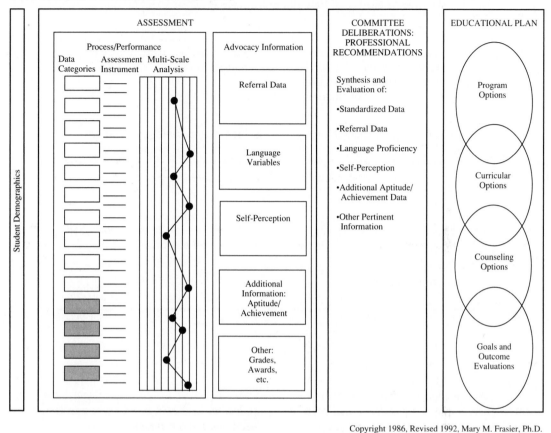

Copyright 1986, Revised 1992, Mary M. Frasier, Ph.D.

FIGURE 12.2. The Frasier Talent Assessment Profile (F-TAP).
Reproduced by permission of Mary M. Frasier.

TABLE 12.4   Differences between Academically Gifted Project Procedures and Traditional Academically Gifted Program Procedures

AG Project Procedures	Traditional Procedures
1. Systematic review of existing test scores for all racial/ethnic group students in grades 2–5 to generate a Target Group (pool) of students to be tested.	1. Parent, school, peer, and self nominations.
2. Informative group meetings with parents of students eligible to participate in the Target Group held prior to initiating the evaluation sequence.	2. Individual conferences held with parents following each group evaluation and, when administered, individual evaluations.
3. Target Group students progress automatically through the evaluation sequence.	3. Students retested only at the request of parents or school-based committee personnel.
4. Two full-time educational diagnosticians assigned specifically to the AG Project.	

From Woods and Achey (1990), by permission of *Roeper Review*.

12.4 compares the AG and traditional methods of identification. The AG Project method differs from the traditional method in that it encourages additional testing for those who would not have qualified in the initial testing.

The Rural and Migrant Gifted Project provides a successful model for identifying gifted Hispanic students (Ortiz and Gonzalez, 1991). It involves the administration of a shortened version of the *Wechsler Intelligence Scale for Children-Revised* (WISC-R) (Ortiz and Gonzalez, 1989) both in English and Spanish. The criteria used for effective selection of gifted Hispanic students were:

1. Information provided by the teacher on the prescreening form.

2. Performance on the WISC-R screening test (students performing in the 85th to 94th percentile are considered *accelerated*, while a score at the 95th percentile or higher is considered *gifted*).

3. Achievement test records (same criteria are applied as in the WISC-R screening test, but in specific academic areas).

4. Motivation and behavior factors.

Creative efforts to identify gifted students with disadvantages are indeed being developed. Hopefully, future research will add to effective identification procedures, which are, of course, the first steps to cultivating giftedness in diverse populations.

PROGRAMMING FOR CULTURALLY DIFFERENT GIFTED STUDENTS

Programming for culturally diverse and socioeconomically disadvantaged gifted and talented children can include any of the curriculum options for acceleration, enrichment, and grouping described in earlier chapters. However, there are important additional components that should be given special consideration: (1) maintaining ethnic identity,

(2) extracurricular cultural enrichment, (3) counseling, (4) parent support groups, (5) development of significant models, and (6) career education. While it may not be possible to include all of these components at the outset, it is desirable to include all of them eventually if minority gifted children are to have an optimal opportunity to develop and use their abilities.

Maintaining Ethnic Identity

The *assimilationist* position holds that upward mobility in the United States requires conformity to the language, culture, and rules of the majority Anglo population. Assimilationists further point out that minority subcultural values prevent or at least discourage integration into the majority community, and thus limit the minority person's educational and socioeconomic opportunities (Banks, 1979). Exum (1983) noted that assimilationist attitudes of African-American families, who wish to succeed and be accepted in the white world, not only may be pro-white but even anti-African-American.

On the other hand, the *cultural pluralist* position emphasizes the importance of pride in one's ethnic identity as an important part of educational and career achievement. Cultural pluralists note the close relationship of ethnic pride to the development of healthy self-concepts, and therefore consider heterogeneity and diversity to be beneficial to both individual and cultural growth.

Ogbu (1992), an anthropologist, emphasized that cultural diversity, as it affects education, continues to be poorly understood and that minority students, whose cultural frames of reference often are oppositional to those of American mainstream culture, face greater difficulties in learning.

Gifted programming by and large gives lip service to a cultural diversity point-of-view. A survey by Van Tassel-Baska, Patton, and Prillaman (1989) suggests that program policies typically do not include accommodations for diversity.

Some practical classroom ideas for teaching students to value diversity by enhancing sensitivity are suggested by Baldwin (1991b):

1. Help students experience what it feels like to be different. Students can use masks and become members of another ethnic group; they should stay "in character" for at least 48 hours. A journal and discussion of emotions can be used.

2. Have students produce resource books on different cultural groups. Include books, film, activities, field trips, and local resource people.

3. Use games that have been developed for the purpose of placing persons in the roles of other ethnic groups.

4. Use other activities such as debates, unfinished stories, and fictional stories such as *Kindred* (Butler, 1988) to develop sensitivity toward different ethnic groups.

One main arena of controversy is found in questions related to bilingual-bicultural education programs for Hispanics, Asians, and Native Americans. Assimilationists oppose such programs, indicating that they slow the process by which the culturally different child is integrated into the mainstream culture. They claim that precious time is wasted in teaching children about their heritage and in their own language. Instead, they maintain that this time should be used for teaching basic skills—in English. However, cultural pluralists argue that the positive self-concepts derived from ethnic pride are extremely important to the minority children's educational and life achievements.

The results of research studies evaluating the effects of bilingual programs on achievement in basic skills have been mixed. The Department of Educational Research and Program Development (1979) in Milwaukee and Rimm (1977) found that children in Hispanic bilingual programs showed better achievement test gains, in both Milwaukee, Wisconsin, and St. Paul, Minnesota, than Hispanic children not in the programs. However, bilingual programs are perceived as deficit programs; thus, giftedness was never perceived as being related. Barkin and Bernal (1991) recommend that gifted bilingual programs be perceived as qualitatively different than regular bilingual programs. They recommend also that bilingual teachers be urged to earn appropriate credentials in the education of the gifted in order to facilitate and encourage gifted Hispanic students.

The cultural pluralist position seems innately reasonable. People cannot totally separate themselves from their cultural backgrounds, and if they view that heritage as somehow negative or derogatory they will see themselves as second-class persons who are restricted in ability, opportunity, or both. In contrast, if a person values his or her ethnic identity, then the pride, confidence, and feelings of acceptance—all of which are basic to constructive mental health—should help motivate the person toward personal growth and achievement.

As a general principle, educators committed to providing programs for the gifted and talented necessarily support the development of diversity. That is, they intrinsically agree that each gifted child is different and therefore requires educational opportunities that fit his or her special strengths and needs. By the same reasoning, it would seem that G/T educators also should value the differences inherent in ethnic cultures, and should recognize the personal growth, mental health, and educational advantages that accompany pride in one's culture.

Banks (1979) proposed an enlightening five-stage framework for understanding ethnicity and for developing ethnic identity and pride.

Stage 1, Ethnic Psychological Captivity. This is a stage of negative self-concepts. Individuals in this stage have internalized the negative stereotypes about their own ethnic group. They show strong out-group identification and strive vigorously to become assimilated.

Stage 2, Ethnic Encapsulation. Interestingly, this stage most often characterizes members of the majority Anglo-American group. In this stage individuals interact only with members of their own ethnic group. Further, they believe their group is superior to other groups. Asian Americans, African-Americans, Hispanics, and Native Americans manage to exhibit ethnic pride without attacking

Anglo-Americans; unfortunately, the reverse has not been true.

Stage 3, Ethnic Identity Clarification. Individuals in this stage have clarified intrapsychic conflicts about who and what they are and have developed positive attitudes toward themselves and their own ethnic group. This self-acceptance is a prerequisite to accepting and responding positively to others.

Stage 4, Biethnicity. Individuals in the biethnic stage possess a positive sense of ethnic identity and pride, but also have the skills needed to participate in another culture as well. While there is double membership in this stage, reference-group orientation—one's primary identity—is with one's own ethnic group. Importantly, there is no reference-group conflict in deciding where one's primary membership and allegiance should be—it is with one's own ethnic group.

Stage 5, Multiethnicity. Banks describes this stage as the idealized goal for all persons in a pluralistic society. Individuals at this stage are able to function within several ethnic sociocultural environments, and they understand and appreciate the variations and differences among the several cultures.

Banks's typology would appear to have direct application to the development of ethnic identity programs, with his Stage 5 as the ultimate goal. Gifted and talented children should not only acquire constructive and unprejudiced attitudes (as all children should), but should learn to function effectively within multiple sociocultural environments.

One might operationalize the Banks model, for example, by identifying the ethnic development stage in which most students in a classroom or G/T program are functioning, and then create an ethnic component designed to help those students move toward higher stages. For secondary and perhaps younger students, the Banks model itself could comprise an eye-opening part of the curriculum, one in which the "highest level of thinking" is in the multiethnic Stage 5.

If a G/T program serves students in a multicultural area, explicit objectives of the program should include the provision of multiethnic experiences and, for minority persons especially, the development of positive ethnic identity.

Kitano (1991) summarizes the differences between assimilationist and pluralist perspectives for gifted programs in Table 12.5. Sources of underachievement, differential differences in purposes of schooling, approaches to identification, instructional processes, and curriculum are included in the table. A review of the points in Table 12.5 could assist gifted educators in determining whether their primary point of view is assimilationist or pluralist.

Extracurricular Cultural Enrichment

The cultural enrichment that comes from attending concerts, theatre, and ballet and visiting exhi-bitions, art galleries, and museums usually is provided by the families of middle-class gifted children. For the socioeconomically deprived child, these experiences typically are nonexistent or else limited to occasional school excursions. Exposure to the arts can be a valuable experience for economically deprived gifted children, as well as a good reinforcement for their participation in the gifted program. Importantly, such exposure would strongly reinforce students' own artistic or scientific efforts and talents.

For maximum benefit, art or science experiences should be tied to other knowledge, skill, or creative components of the G/T program. For example, historical backgrounds of particular artists, composers, or scientists would add knowledge and depth to the experiences. Also, discussions of the antecedents and idea sources of particular

TABLE 12.5   Summary of Assimilationist and Pluralist Perspectives

	Assimilationist	Pluralist
Souce of under-achievement	Within child based on culture and experience; need for intervention aimed at deficits	Within system or within interactions between system and child; need for empowerment of child
Purpose of schooling	Transmission of mainstream values toward maintenance of core culture	Understanding many cultural perspectives toward creation of a society that values diversity
Identification	Standardized assessment	Alternative assessment, nonbiased assessment, multiple measure assessment
Instructional processes	Focus on individual achievement; helping child fit the school	Focus on democratic structures; changing school to fit the child
Curriculum	Problem solving and critical thinking applied to mainstream culture and history	Problem solving and critical thinking applied to culture and history of many groups; building skills to transform society

From Kitano (1991), by permission of the *Journal for the Education of the Gifted.*

products or performances, or comparative evaluations of various works, would further embellish the event. "What would happen if . . . ?" or "In what other ways might we . . . . ?" questions add creative and futuristic thinking to the experiences. Students also can do further research, prepare written or oral reports to the class, or write stories, newspaper columns with photos, or news reports about a person or event, and so on. Finally, as we noted earlier, field trips are most beneficial when students are armed with specific objectives to be met and questions to be answered before they climb onto the bus.

School funding for many enrichment experiences is certain to be limited or even absent. Ideally, travel and admissions monies would be built into the original program budget. If not, local industries, businesses, or civic groups may be encouraged to fund specific trips. For the business owner, such sponsorship has the attraction of combining a small tax-deductible investment with a superb public relations opportunity (news coverage). Note also that, at least in medium to large cities, many museums, galleries, and university facilities are free, reducing expenses to bus fares and the required candy and soda.

Counseling

The support that comes from an intact and secure family structure is less available to many economically disadvantaged or culturally different students. While family problems are not unique to students in these groups, it is true that complicated and temporary marital relationships, alcohol abuse, mobility, and other forms of stress and instability are common. According to one U.S. Census, for example, 36 percent of African-American families are single-parent, female-headed. Health, hygiene, and nutritional values may be minimal. Peer pressure not to achieve is strong. In some difficult circumstances, survival itself takes strong precedence over educational achievement and developing gifts and talents.

Such children need shelters, persons to whom they can go when intellectual, social, developmental, and even safety and survival needs are threatened. This shelter should include an adult, an empathic and professional counselor who understands the local economic and ethnic realities and who cares about the welfare of all children. Exum (1983) recommended that counselors in minority areas should, first, increase their knowledge about the community, for example, by becoming acquainted with population characteristics, availability of resources, availability of public transportation, community leadership styles, and the particular types of problems that frequently come to counselors' attention. Second, Exum noted that the counselor's credibility and trustworthiness will be enhanced if he or she becomes more visible in the community, perhaps by serving on multicultural committees and by patronizing minority businesses. A third recommendation was for counselors to be flexible in scheduling appointments—using evenings and weekends—because so many parents of minority children cannot attend counseling sessions during the regular work day. Generally, said Exum, counselors should seek to build personal relationships with minority families because "parents are much more responsive to counselors whom they believe have a genuine personal interest in their children."

Informal counseling by concerned adults played an extremely important role for the successful disadvantaged youth in the Kauai study (Werner, 1989). Teachers, ministers, and club leaders can be encouraged to support gifted students who may not have the family support and expectations that are important for disadvantaged gifted adolescents (Van Tassel-Baska, 1989).

Harris (1991) emphasized the importance of peer support among gifted new immigrants who came mainly from third world countries. Steinberg, Dornbusch, and Brown (1992) also underscore the critical role of peer culture in achievement. They concluded that the peer group both mediates positive or negative family effects and directly influences attitudes toward achievement. For example, with Asian-American students peer support toward academic excellence can offset negative parenting effects. Unfortunately, among African-American adolescents, the positive influence of parenting is often undermined by a negative peer environment.

Certainly a critical goal of counseling must be to develop a peer support group for academic excellence among gifted youth. Summer enrichment programs can be an effective means of providing peer support for students who are not supported in their intellectual pursuits in their own schools. Cooley, Cornell, and Lee (1991) found that 35 high-ability African-American students were entirely accepted by white peers in a summer enrichment program and also were comparable on measures of self-concept and academic self-esteem.

Parent Support Groups

Although every gifted program should encourage parent education and involvement, parents of socioeconomically deprived and culturally different children have a special and greater need. These parents will become supportive and involved only if (1) they understand their child's gifts and talents and (2) they understand the opportunities available to the gifted in our society. Further, they are more likely to assist their children and contribute to the G/T program if they do not see the program as elitist (for example, for WASPs only) or as threatening. For example, parents may resist a G/T program if they believe the program will psychologically separate them from their children or cause their children to respect them less. It may be frightening to parents with little education to learn that their child is very bright and on a track toward a middle-class education that, they believe, could alienate the child from them.

On the other hand, if the program emphasizes *positive cultural identity*, fears of alienation should be reduced. Parents also will have an avenue for relating to and making contributions to the program. Parent meetings in which the G/T program and activities are explained and the above problems addressed, and in which parents share problems and optimism, will benefit the program and the gifted children involved.

Enhanced parenting skills should be part of parent support group activities. Shade (1978) emphasized that African-American children who do well in school and on achievement tests tend to have parents or guardians who:

1. Maintain a quality of communication that stimulates the child's problem-solving ability, independence, and productivity;

2. Express warmth, interest, affection, and encouragement;

3. Establish close family ties;

4. Maintain structure and order for the child;

5. Establish goals of performance;

6. Use control mechanisms that include moderate amounts of praise and blame, moderate amounts of punishment, and no authoritarian tactics;

7. Give assistance when requested or when the need is perceived.

Shade also concluded that the parent-child interaction is more important to achievement than either family socioeconomic status or family structure.

The *No Gift Wasted* program (Alamprese and Erlanger, 1988) heavily encouraged parent participation. For example, some of its projects required parents to learn about the activity and sign an agreement for their children's participation. The Potentially Gifted Minority Student Project (Alamprese and Erlanger, 1988) took the responsibility of keeping parents informed of their children's progress through telephone calls and written reports. There was always more involvement by parents in elementary school programs; parent participation in high school programs was limited.

Harris' (1991) gifted program, which included new immigrants, stressed the importance of using the parents' own language to communicate the importance of parent involvement.

Development of Significant Models

Significant others are persons who exercise a major influence on the attitudes of individuals. Chapter 13 on underachievement will emphasize the critical role of parents, as significant others, in the modeling of achievement values. Shade (1983) pointed out that for African-American youth, significant others extend beyond the immediate family to include the extended family, the media, and white society. Mother, concluded Shade, is the strongest family influence upon African-American students' school performance. Studies of occupational choice (Pallone, *et al.*, 1973) indicated that African-American high school girls were most influenced by their mothers, while boys were most influenced by persons holding the job to which they aspired. A study of African-American college freshmen by Shade (1978) found that parents ranked last in influence, while peers, teachers, counselors, friends, and siblings ranked at the top. In contrast, earlier studies of African-American college students showed mothers (Gurin and Epps, 1966) or parents (Olsen, 1970) to have the greatest influence.

These studies again emphasize the importance of parent achievement models for academic success. They also point to an important gap: The disadvantaged African-American matriarchal family rarely provides a male achievement model for its adolescent boys. The message supporting education is mainly a female message. As boys move from childhood to adolescence, in order to establish their own sense of masculinity (Hetherington, 1972) they search for male conveyors of achievement and occupational aspirations.

Disadvantaged gifted boys are in almost desperate need of achievement-oriented males to serve as role models for achievement. In the absence of appropriate models, television media (Fedler, 1973; Leifer, *et al.*, 1974) and peer and street culture (Perkins, 1975) strongly influence African-American adolescent male youth. In one study (Bridgeman and Burbach, 1976), a videotape of African-American male youth being rewarded for excellence in school resulted in a significant increase in academic expectations by the African-American male viewers.

The concept of an all African-American male academy has become a resounding answer to the recognized need for positive role models for primary-grade African-American inner city males (Holland, 1991). In addition to providing appropriate role models in teachers and administrators, adult male volunteers from business and industry participate and involve boys in tutoring or learning projects. The first such program was known as Project 2000 because the kindergarteners with whom the program began in the 1988–1989 school year would graduate in the year 2000. The project was adopted by an all-male community service organization, the Washington DC Chapter of Concerned Black Men, Inc.

The model of the all African-American male academy has since been adopted in many urban areas and has been expanded to include all African-American female academies as well. These experimental models are based on the following objectives and principles:

1. Examining the effectiveness of gender specific instructional strategies.

2. Obtaining release time for employees in the public and private sectors to serve as volunteers in classrooms.

3. Investigating ungraded primary grade models.

4. Emphasizing team teaching.

5. Establishing secondary homerooms led by teacher-advisors who will keep the same group of children throughout their junior or senior high school careers, thereby providing them with an adult within the school who can serve as a mentor.

At this time the results appear promising. Providing achievement role models is critical to enhancing giftedness in populations of disadvantaged students, and should be a requirement of every gifted program for these students. Some recommendations are included in Inset 12.1. While this Inset addresses mainly male models, the suggestions also are applicable to providing appropriate female role models.

Accelerated and Enriched Curriculum

Eight effective educational programs described in *No Gift Wasted* (Alamprese and Erlanger, 1988)

INSET 12.1 _____

Curriculum Ideas for Establishing Male Achievement Models

1. Videotapes of achievement-oriented males in various careers (e.g., doctor, lawyer, professor, businessman). Men should tell about childhood experiences that fostered achievement.
2. Videotapes of a panel of minority gifted children (males and females) discussing their problems and successes in achievement. Emphasis may be placed on cultural pride and achievement.
3. Cultural intermediary (Labov and Robbins, 1969)—a young man who is achievement oriented and "streetwise" to meet with and counsel adolescent boys.
4. Speaker series—weekly talks by successful minority community persons (male and female) about their careers and their lifestyles.
5. Lunch seminars for small groups of students with minority community persons to talk about achievement.
6. Parenting classes for fathers only, led by a male counselor or teacher who is also a parent.
7. Parenting classes for single mothers with the specific goal of assisting them in establishing appropriate minority role models.
8. General parenting classes with emphasis on the importance of appropriate role models.
9. Video- and audiotapes of the parenting classes for fathers only, single parents, and general parenting available for loan to parents unable to attend classes.
10. Student interview assignments with achieving adults. The collection of interviews may be assembled into a book for discussion and review.
11. Bibliography of books emphasizing the childhoods of successful minority persons.
12. Visits to college campuses, including meeting with minority college students.
13. Involvement in summer and Saturday college campus enrichment programs.
14. Funding for minority teachers to spend extra personal time with minority adolescents in and out of school enrichment activities (one to one or small groups).
15. Funding for special interest mentor activities with successful adults.

---

used a variety of approaches to enriching and accelerating learning for gifted minority and disadvantaged students in nine inner-city sites. These included specialized high schools, concurrent enrollment in colleges, honors and Advanced Placement classes, and hands-on learning techniques. Three vignettes in Inset 12.2 present the color and flavor of three of the programs.

Some recommendations from *No Gift Wasted* for encouraging participation in high-level math and science programs are these:

• *Offer career awareness activities.* Through career awareness programs, students can learn about occupations related to mathematics and science. Students can visit industries that employ mathematicians and scientists, and they can participate in mentorship programs. Successful mathematics and science professionals and teachers can provide role models for minority and disadvantaged students.

• *Provide specialized curricula and programs.* Curricula that highlight the accomplishments of minority scientists and engineers can stimulate minority students' interests in related professions. Programs can be designed to give students opportunities to enroll in advanced mathematics and science courses at local universities and colleges.

• *Offer counseling and financial assistance.* To help students attend college, guidance can be provided regarding opportunities for financial assistance. Special efforts can be made to obtain contributions from foundations, businesses, and industry to support students' pursuit of higher education.

INSET 12.2 _____

Enrichment and Acceleration for Gifted Minority Students: Three Vignettes

ACCELERATED MATHEMATICS AND SCIENCE

Baltimore Polytechnic Institute
Baltimore, Maryland

Wearing goggles and gloves, one Baltimore Polytechnic Institute student in Baltimore, Maryland works on the drill press to prepare wooden materials for the construction of a miniature balloon-frame house. Nearby, another Poly student lays out sheet metal work using a straight edge, awl, and dividers. In this class, students will cut and form the metal according to the house blueprints—thereby applying the rigorous mathematics and science training they have received at school to the field of architecture.

In another class, a student cuts out a pattern for the split anvil on the bandsaw. Simultaneously, the Hot Metals instructor prepares a mould for casting the anvil. By observing the demonstration and then imitating the teacher, students learn *copes, drags, riddling,* and *gates.* A variety of equipment is available to students here—from milling machines to wood lathes.

Both of these laboratory experiences are required components of the engineering and science classes that Poly students take in the 12th grade. For Poly's 1,600 secondary school students, the curriculum is demanding yet worthwhile. Students soon realize that the highly technical education they receive at Poly will adequately prepare them for the engineering and science professions, or their associated technical fields.

Do Poly's 500 female students object to the grit and grime of these laboratory classes? "Why, no," explain the students. "It just gives us another chance to demonstrate our inherent superiority over the boys."

REAL-WORLD APPLICATIONS IN MATHEMATICS

James A. Garfield High School's Gifted and Talented Program
Los Angeles, California

As 11th grade students enter the lecture hall at James A. Garfield High School in Los Angeles,

sounds of Beethoven's Ninth Symphony fill the room. The students quickly take their seats and open their textbooks to Chapter 10. A short, middle-aged man enters the classroom and talks to a few of the students. After the music stops, the teacher asks, "Are you ready? Are you ready to discuss limits today?" The class sheepishly responds, "Yes." "What? I can't hear you," the teacher says. "Are you ready or not?" "Ready," the class shouts back.

Moments later, the teacher pulls a "toy" from his cabinet—a baseball and mitt appear. He slaps the baseball into the mitt and says to the class, "You know, the way the pitcher throws the ball determines the path the ball will take—am I right?" "Yes," the class responds. "What could this be?" the teacher asks as he simulates a pitcher's actions. "A curve ball," one student remarks. "A fast ball," cries out another. "You know," says the teacher, "the trajectory of the ball is what is called f of x."

Seconds later, on the blackboard, the teacher is busy explaining the concept of limits. After several practice exercises together, the students work individually on homework problems due the next day. The teacher circulates to answer any questions students might have. Finally, with ten minutes remaining in the class period, the teacher distributes a quiz with a picture of the school's mascot in the corner. The class completes the quiz and returns it to the teacher as the bell sounds. Chatter and laughter fill the room. The students have just spent 50 exciting minutes with Jaime Escalante, learning some very difficult mathematics at James A. Garfield High School.

ENRICHMENT THROUGH EXPLORATION

Chicago Public Schools Museum Program
Chicago, Illinois

A young man, equipped with a mask, snorkel, fins, and oxygen tanks, dives into a large glass pool filled with fish and vegetation. As he proceeds to feed the various aquatic creatures, he describes what life is like in this underwater environment. Students, with their brothers and sisters, point to the oversized turtles swimming at the bottom of the pool. Awestruck parents stand and observe the show. The Aquatic Science Program—one of 12 museum programs offered by the Chicago Public Schools Gifted and Talented Program—is sponsoring an open house for students and their families at the Shedd Aquarium. After a brief diving demonstration, students receive awards for completing the program, while a teacher describes their accomplishments.

At the Lincoln Park Zoo several miles away, a zookeeper lifts a chimpanzee from her cage and holds her before a group of 20 juniors and seniors. The zookeeper explains various facets of animal behavior, and responds to questions from the students. Before this presentation, the students learn about primates through a question-and-answer session in the zoo auditorium. The one-year Zoology Program also requires that students design an

exhibit area for a zoo animal and justify their design before the class.

Nine 8th grade students enrolled in the Ecology Program study rain forests at the Chicago Academy of Science. Their teacher distributes a sheet, listing various forms of wildlife that are exhibited throughout the museum. Through a scavenger hunt, students identify the designated plants and animals from lifelike displays on the second floor. In groups of two and three, students help each other find the missing items.

At all three institutions—the Shedd Aquarium, Lincoln Park Zoo, and the Chicago Academy of Science—students engage in hands-on work. Learning is both a joy and a challenge, conclude Chicago's museum programs' participants.

From Alamprese and Erlanger (1988), *No Gift Wasted.* Prepared under contract by COSMOS Corporation, Washington, DC, for the U.S. Department of Education, Office of Planning, Budget and Evaluation.

• *Provide for teacher support of students.* Teachers can assist and encourage students through meetings after school and visits to students' homes. These actions can help address the multiple needs of disadvantaged students, and can provide students with the educational and psychological support they need to succeed academically.

• *Encourage parent participation in school activities.* Parents can be encouraged to become involved in all aspects of their children's educational program. At the elementary level parents can make commitments to assist their children in their academic study. At the middle and high school levels parents can be asked to join parent associations and to support their children's academic development, for example, their participation in academic contests and special events.

Career Education

Career education is an important priority for all students. One problem for disadvantaged gifted students, however, is that "career education" traditionally focuses on occupations and careers that seem suitable or available to the majority of children in a particular school. Thus a curriculum program in a middle-class high school will feature college preparatory coursework and a professional career orientation. A high school in a minority or economically depressed area will focus on blue-collar occupations, with strong offerings in welding, machine shop, auto mechanics, and typing. There is a noticeably reduced awareness and valuing of college training and professional careers, and thus a reduced opportunity for the necessary preparation.

Career education for the gifted child in a lower-SES environment, of course, should stress the professional opportunities available and the necessary educational preparation. However, a realistic career education program also must emphasize the lifestyles, values, ethics, and goals that accompany particular professional careers (Moore, 1979). To compete successfully, the disadvantaged gifted child must acquire the many subtle attitudes and skills that accompany a given profession—attitudes and skills learned at home by children of educated professional parents.

An important—indeed, crucial—component of career education is the involvement of suitable *models*. These are professional persons of similar ethnic backgrounds who have, in fact, emerged from difficult socioeconomic circumstances. They need to share their experiences, their problems, and their strategies for success with gifted young disadvantaged people. Presentations, mentorships, and on-the-job visits are good ways to provide gifted youth with a taste of career and life goals worth working for. The models also can help students understand that within the professional areas there *will* be support; and further, that once high-level positions are attained, both intrinsic and extrinsic rewards will make the educational and economic struggle worthwhile. Professional persons from disadvantaged backgrounds typically are very sensitive to the problems of culturally different and poor gifted youth and are motivated to help.

As an example, the Texas Governor's Honors Program, which follows the theme of Leadership in a Multi-Cultural Society, provides not only in-depth leadership instruction but also instructors and seminar speakers who serve as models and mentors to inspire these gifted students of diverse cultures to look toward college (Sisk, Gilbert, and Gosch, 1991).

An important component of career education should be visits to college campuses and, if possible, actual participation in gifted programs on these campuses. Tennessee State University is one of many universities that is making an effort to attract ethnically diverse students to summer programs to inspire young scientists to consider a biomedical education beyond high school (Adams, 1989). Participation in such programs provides appropriate role models and peer support, an enriched educational opportunity, as well as an opportunity to live and feel more comfortable on a college campus.

As we have seen, career education for gifted minority, economically deprived, and culturally different students usually must be *broader* than typical career education programs. While college-educated parents automatically provide good models and informal information and values to their middle-class children, it is rare for culturally different students to have such models in their immediate families or even neighborhoods. Their parents usually are not aware of the opportunities and obstacles related to a high-level professional education. Therefore, a good career education program for these students will need to provide considerable detailed direction. For example, these young people must learn about colleges and universities that will support both their professional and their ethnic needs. They will require direction in finding scholarships or other funding assistance. They will need to learn how to prepare for entrance examinations and personal interviews. They also must be reassured about the social environment they may encounter.

The extraordinary value of a well-designed career education program for gifted disadvantaged youth is that it may guide very talented persons to become fulfilled and productive individuals, individuals who will make those "valuable contributions to self and society." However, if these gifted youth meet only dead ends and frustration and have no outlet for the development and expression of their talents, society will not only lose their positive professional contributions, but may be taxed (literally) by their negative contributions. Farley (1986) argued that high energy levels can be channeled either into creative and productive outlets or, in the case of many low-SES adolescents, into delinquency and self-destructiveness. Their energy, talents, and frustrations may combine into anti-social behavior—perhaps in a leadership capacity—which constitutes an obviously serious and unnecessary waste of human potential.

GIFTED PROGRAMMING IN RURAL AREAS

Gifted students who live in rural areas may be greatly disadvantaged. Sparse populations, poverty, traditional rural values, small school size, and inadequate school finances all contribute to the paucity of gifted programming. Spicker, Southern, and Davis (1987) noted the following problems in providing gifted education for rural students:

• Resistance to change makes it difficult to initiate new offerings for gifted students. Also, there is much less parental pressure for gifted programs in rural areas.

• A smaller budget precludes expensive program additions, particularly if such additions are perceived as benefiting only a small select number of students.

• Teachers in rural secondary schools have more preparations across several different subjects, making it difficult for them to keep up with newer, specialized content knowledge.

• There typically are fewer counselors, school psychologists, and curriculum specialists to assist the faculty in building adequate programs for the gifted.

• A belief in self-sufficiency and local control makes it less likely that rural districts will seek outside assistance from state agencies or universities to develop programs meet the needs of gifted students.

As one solution, innovative educators can encourage cooperation among small school districts. For example, a consortium of school districts brought Purdue University and seven rural public schools together to provide comprehensive inservice training for their teachers, a resource center, and a broad range of effective programming for gifted and talented students (Ruckman and Feldhusen, 1988).

Witters and Vasa (1981) found the itinerant (traveling) consultant model to be effective in providing services to rural gifted children. Still another solution is for volunteer community persons to take an active role in gifted programs, if school staff are unable to provide suitable programming (Yoder, 1985).

Telecommunications, including electronic bulletin boards (Southern and Spicker, 1989), televised inservices for teachers (Clasen and Clasen, 1989; Lewis, 1989), and "distance learning" using television and telephones (University of Wisconsin-Eau Claire, 1992) are being incorporated effectively to heighten awareness of faculty and provide peer group interaction to overcome the spatial separation of gifted students in rural areas. Technology holds great hope for expansion of opportunities for rural gifted students (Spicker, Southern, and Davis, 1987).

Despite some progress, education for the gifted in small rural schools is in its infancy, and most gifted children in rural schools are not served by appropriate programming (Spicker, Southern, and Davis, 1987).

SUMMARY

Due to cultural and language differences, and lack of family and peer support, culturally and economically disadvantaged students rarely are identified as gifted. Minority students thus are underrepresented in gifted programs.

Dropout rates for minority students have improved in recent years, but remain unacceptably high. Few Hispanic or African-American students show high-level mathematical proficiency; few earn Ph.D degrees.

States need to include concerns for culturally different and low-SES students in their state definitions of giftedness, and develop prototype programs for use with atypical gifted learners.

Studies have shown that support from either the family or others in the community can help gifted disadvantaged students develop their potential.

Low IQ or achievement tests scores may be misused to "prove" the absence of giftedness. Because average or below-average achievement can be common among gifted disadvantaged, identification must be based on potential rather than actual academic performance.

While a high IQ score is valid evidence of giftedness, an average or low score may be misleading. Family, cultural, and language differences and testing circumstances must be considered. IQ cutoff scores will preclude the identification of many gifted disadvantaged students. The SOMPA approach adjusts IQ scores for cultural and economic disadvantage. African-centered values and beliefs can affect ability testing.

While high achievement is good evidence of talent in particular areas, achievement tests scores suffer from the same problems as intelligence test scores.

Teacher nominations may favor members of the majority culture. However, sensitive teachers who understand characteristics of giftedness can be excellent identifiers of gifted and talented minority students. Gay compiled a list of characteristics of gifted African-American children; Swenson itemized characteristics of creativity in culturally different students.

The Kranz Talent Identification Instrument and the Baldwin Identification Matrix are helpful in identifying gifted minority students.

Research indicates that creativity tests such as the Torrance Tests of Creative Thinking and the GIFT and GIFFI inventories are good instruments for identifying creative disadvantaged and minority students. Parent and peer nominations also are good identification strategies.

Quota systems assume that gifts and talents exist in equal proportions in all cultural groups and assure their proportional representation in G/T programs.

The Frasier Talent Assessment Profile combines test and nontest criteria to identify gifted disadvantaged students.

Identification methods based on "activity" rather than static test scores, using a series of evaluations instead of just one, and using a shortened WISC-R administered in Spanish and English have increased minority participation in gifted programs.

Programming options described in earlier chapters may be used with disadvantaged and minority students. However, additional components should be included: (1) maintaining ethnic identity, (2) extracurricular cultural enrichment, (3) counseling, (4) the use of models, and (5) career education.

Cultural pluralism includes maintaining ethnic identity; cultural pride is central to self-esteem and educational and career success. Assimilationism refers to conforming to the majority Anglo system. Differences between the two positions influence many aspects of programming for gifted students.

Banks described five states of ethnic identity. A teacher might identify students' ethnic stages and move them toward higher stages.

Extracurricular enrichment can include knowledge, skill, and creative objectives.

Counseling is important. Exum recommended that counselors learn about the local community, become visible, and be flexible in scheduling appointments. Informal counseling by concerned adults in the community is valuable.

A support group of gifted peers is beneficial; summer enrichment programs create such peer groups.

Parents are more likely to support G/T programs and to become involved if they understand the importance of the program for their child's future, and if they are not threatened by the program or its possible effects on their child. Parent meetings aid in educating parents regarding G/T programs, and allow parents to share problems and optimism.

Disadvantaged gifted children—especially males—need achievement models, as provided in all African-American male and all African-American female academies.

Accelerated and enriched programs can include specialized high schools, concurrent enrollment in colleges, and others. Important components are career awareness activities, specialized programs that highlight minority scientists, counseling and financial assistance for college, teacher support, and parent participation.

Career education must include not only career options and the preparation needed to attain them, but the lifestyles, ethics, and goals that accompany various professions. Visits to colleges are valuable. Models—professional persons from similar disadvantaged backgrounds—are a vital component of career education programs.

Many problems impede the development of gifted programs in rural areas, for example, sparse populations, smaller budgets, and fewer support personnel. Some solutions are cooperation among several small districts, itinerant consultants, volunteer community members, and the use of telecommunications.

CHAPTER 13

UNDERACHIEVEMENT
DIAGNOSIS AND TREATMENT

The presence of unused potential is a tragedy at both the personal and political level of a society.
J. Gallagher, 1991c

The underachieving gifted child represents both society's greatest loss and its greatest potential resource. The child has the potential for high achievement and significant contributions, but is not using that talent in productive ways. Statistics tell us that as many as half of our gifted children do not perform up to their abilities in school (National Commission on Excellence in Education, 1983). Studies of high school dropouts indicate that between 10 and 20 percent of the students who do not graduate are in the gifted range of abilities (Lajoie and Shore, 1981: Nyquist, 1973; Whitmore, 1980).

Richert (1991a) is convinced that even these large figures are underestimates of the amount and degree of underachievement because the figures do not include underachievers who were not identified because IQ scores were the criterion. IQ scores, even of individually tested students, are frequently lowered by the underachieving pattern. It is difficult to measure the exact magnitude of the problem, but it is large.

Because the child's special abilities are recognized, the nonproductiveness often leads to frustration by parents, teachers, and even the child himself or herself. However, if the underachieving pattern can be reversed, the child frequently makes unusual progress in skill acquisition and in positive, productive work. In view of the child's

history of underachievement, the extent of positive change after appropriate intervention usually is quite surprising. Superachievement may indeed be the flip side of the underachievement coin (Rimm, 1991a).

Overview

This chapter will review characteristics, causes, and dynamics of underachievement, along with a strategy for reversing this costly syndrome.

DEFINITION AND IDENTIFICATION OF UNDERACHIEVEMENT

Underachievement is defined as a discrepancy between the child's school performance and some index of his or her actual ability, such as intelligence, achievement, or creativity scores, or observational data. Although many studies use more technical definitions, the discrepancy between potential and actual productivity seems to be part of all definitions (Richert, 1991a).

Test Scores

The chief index of actual ability is test scores. Despite all the faults and problems related to testing, despite test unreliability and measurement error, and despite all the biases that need to be considered related to low test scores, it seems apparent that children cannot score extraordinarily high on tests purely by accident. Test-taking skill alone cannot account for test scores that consistently fall two or more standard deviations above the mean, that is, above the ninety-seventh percentile. Unusually high scores then, whether on intelligence, achievement, or creativity tests, indicate special abilities or skills not apparent in the underachieving child's usual schoolwork.

Intelligence Test Scores

If a child is identified as gifted, even based on intelligence test scores alone, it is important to compare the child's *actual* school performance to the performance that would be *expected* based on those IQ scores. There are several statistical concepts that may be used in this kind of comparison, especially *grade equivalent scores*, *mental age* (MA) *equivalents*, *stanines*, and *percentiles*. For example, a third-grade child of 8 years 6 months may produce intelligence test scores in the ninth stanine (top 4 percent) or a mental age equivalent score of 10 years 2 months, but his or her usual classroom performance might range between the fourth, fifth, and sixth stanines—strictly at grade level. Any of these statistical yardsticks are satisfactory for helping to define underachievement operationally in order to identify children who need help.

However, using *current* test scores alone may underidentify underachievement because scores may be artificially lowered by lack of motivation, tension, negative attitudes toward testing, or many years of not learning in school. Earlier test scores can be important for alerting educators to a child's real potential.

A frequent error in the identification of underachievers is to use a *fixed* number of months of years below grade level as a criterion of underachievement. For example, first-grade children who are six months below their expected achievement level will have far more serious under-

achievement problems than eighth graders performing one full year below the expected level. For the younger children six months may represent being 50 percent behind where they should be; for the eighth-grade children one year represents only 12.5 percent behind where they would be expected to be performing. The main problem related to using a constant number of months is that younger children with underachievement problems are likely to be overlooked because the discrepancy between actual and expected achievement does not appear to be large enough in terms of actual months, even though the problem is quite serious. Because underachievement can be treated more easily when diagnosed early, it is critical to recognize this common identification error (Rimm, 1986b; Whitmore, 1986).

Achievement Test Scores

Many schools do not routinely administer group intelligence tests, but virtually all schools regularly use published (standardized) and/or teacher-made achievement tests. These provide an objective basis for determining the levels of information and skills that a child has mastered. To evaluate underachievement, the teacher can compare actual school performance (for example, the quality of reports, projects, homework, math or reading proficiency, or class participation) with the achievement test scores.

Creativity Test Scores

High scores on divergent-thinking tests such as the *Torrance Tests of Creative Thinking* (Torrance, 1966) or on creative personality inventories such as GIFT and GIFFI (Davis, 1989b; Rimm, 1976; Rimm and Davis, 1980, 1983) strongly suggest that the child has talent in the area of creative and productive thinking. However, high creativity scores do not assure high achievement. On the contrary, some fairly common characteristics of creative students—such as nonconformity, resistance to teacher domination, impulsiveness, and indifference to rules—may cause the creative child serious difficulties in achieving within the classroom structure (Davis, 1992a). Some highly creative students are dramatic underachievers because their personalities and thinking styles are quite at odds with that required for classroom success. Rimm (1987b) found that creative underachieving students often defined their identity in terms of nonconformity. Their concern for thinking and acting differently than others actually prevented them from achieving and making classroom efforts. Other creative students, however, apply their unique talents to classroom assignments and requirements and achieve at the level of students with much higher tested intelligence (Getzels and Jackson, 1962).

Children with high creativity scores but only somewhat above average IQ scores (110–130) have very high potential for making creative contributions (Rimm, 1987c; Renzulli, 1986; Renzulli and Reis, 1985a, 1991b). If students in this category are not being productive in school, they should be identified as gifted underachievers, even though their intelligence and achievement test scores may not be in the "gifted" range.

Observation

Some underachieving gifted children do not perform well on any test due to poor test-taking habits. For example, they may not be motivated to do well. On a group test some students may answer questions randomly. On an individually administered test they may fear making mistakes, so they "play dumb" or avoid answering questions unless they are certain of the correct answer. Teacher and parent observations provide the only basis for identifying these gifted children; there will be little or no objective evidence.

Teachers may note class behaviors, comments, or vocabulary which suggest that the child has much more intellectual, creative, or artistic potential than he or she is exhibiting in school work. Teachers, however, can recognize these behaviors only if they are aware of characteristics of gifted children. Teachers must remain open to the possibility of discovering giftedness in children already labeled

as "average" or even "below average." Many such gifted underachievers are never discovered.

Commonly used certification checklists and rating scales for gifted programs do not include traits of gifted underachievers. Hall's (1983) study of teacher identification procedures found that four gifted children described by the following statements had been considered "below average" students, although their IQ scores were above 130.

> Student A. Makes excuses for not doing assignments, doesn't take an interest in things, passive, dependent.
> Student B. Doesn't get along with others, doesn't do his work, likes to tell jokes.
> Student C. Talks too much, doesn't listen, wastes time.
> Student D. Immature, quiet, withdrawn, short interest span.

Teachers who are aware of characteristics of both underachieving and achieving gifted students can make important observations that will help identify gifted underachievers.

Parents also are in a unique position to observe the talents and capabilities of their own gifted children, even if the children are not high achievers. Note that teachers and principals typically feel uncomfortable and threatened by parents who insist their child is "gifted." Such parents are often described as "pushy." Educators should assure these parents that their perceptions will be given full consideration if they can provide specific evidence of their child's giftedness. If the anecdotal material appears reasonably convincing, further testing may indeed support the parents' observations. If the anecdotal material does not suggest giftedness, the teacher or principal can explain why such behavior does not represent special talent by comparing it to behavior of typical children and highly talented children.

Parent observations that indicate the child makes little effort on assigned homework or study can certainly verify underachieving behavior even when school grades are reasonably good. If gifted students earn good grades effortlessly, the curriculum is not sufficiently challenging, and they are underachieving. Further, they may not be prepared to cope with challenging curriculum and competition when it occurs (Rimm, 1986b)

Underachievement Test Scores

Three tests have been expressly developed for the identification of underachievement syndrome. *Achievement Identification Measure* (*AIM*; Rimm, 1986a) is a parent report inventory used with children in grades 1–12. *Group Achievement Identification Measure* (*GAIM*; Rimm, 1987a) is a self-report inventory for students in grades 5–12. *Achievement Identification Measure-Teacher Observation* (*AIM-TO*, Rimm, 1988) is a teacher observation instrument to be used for students in grades 1–12. These inventories were normed with general student populations and are highly reliable (r = .89, .90, and .97 for AIM, GAIM, and AIM-TO, respectively). All instruments provide a test score which allows one to compare each student to the norm based on characteristics related to high achievement. Subscale scores, described in Table 13.1, provide information on the types of problems the children are exhibiting. The manuals which accompany the tests provide a guide to the interpretation and use of the scores.

AIM, GAIM, and AIM-TO are most useful in identifying children suspected by teachers and parents of being gifted underachievers. The tests also can be used to identify underachieving gifted children already in programs. That is, they can uncover high-risk children with characteristics of underachievement whose superior abilities mask the problems that are likely to appear later if not prevented.

TABLE 13.1   Subscale Scores for *AIM*, *GAIM*, and *AIM-TO*

COMPETITION

High scorers enjoy competition, whether they win or lose. They are good sports and handle victories graciously. They do not give up easily.

RESPONSIBILITY

High scorers are responsible in their home and schoolwork. They tend to be well organized and bring activities to closure. They have good study habits and understand that their efforts are related to their grades.

ACHIEVEMENT COMMUNICATION

Children who score high are receiving clear and consistent messages from parents about the importance of learning and good grades. Their parents have communicated positive feelings about their own school experiences and there is consistency between mother and father messages of achievement.

INDEPENDENCE/DEPENDENCE

High scorers are independent and understand the relationship between effort and outcomes. They are able to share attention at home and in the classroom.

RESPECT/DOMINANCE

High scorers are respectful toward their parents and teachers. They are reasonably well behaved at home and school. They value education. They are not deliberately manipulative.

CHARACTERISTICS OF UNDERACHIEVING GIFTED CHILDREN

Studies of gifted underachievers have identified characteristics that are typical of these children. Joanne Whitmore (1980) summarized some of the most important traits in an identification checklist (Table 13.2). If ten or more of these characteristics are checked, she suggests this would indicate that the child should be further evaluated to determine if the child is indeed a gifted underachiever.

Characteristics of underachievers can be cat-

TABLE 13.2   A Checklist to Identify Gifted Underachievers

Observe and interact with the child over a period of at least two weeks to determine if he or she possesses the following characteristics. If the student exhibits ten or more of the listed traits, including all that are asterisked, individual intelligence testing (Stanford-Binet or WISC-R) is recommended to establish whether he or she is a gifted underachiever.

_____ *poor test performance

_____ *achieving at or below grade-level expectations in one or all of the basic skill areas: reading, language arts, mathematics

_____ *daily work frequently incomplete or poorly done

_____ *superior comprehension and retention of concepts when interested

_____ *vast gap between qualitative level of oral and written work

_____ exceptionally large repertoire of factual knowledge

_____ vitality of imagination, creative

_____ persistent dissatisfaction with work accomplished, even in art

_____ seems to avoid trying new activities to prevent imperfect performance; evidences perfectionism, self-criticism

_____ shows initiative in pursuing self-selected projects at home

_____ *has a wide range of interests and possibly special expertise in an area of investigation and research

_____ *evidences low self-esteem in tendencies to withdraw or be aggressive in the classroom

_____ does not function comfortably or constructively in a group of any size

_____ shows acute sensitivity and perceptions related to self, others, and life in general

_____ tends to set unrealistic self-expectations; goals too high or too low

_____ dislikes practice work or drill for memorization and mastery

_____ easily distracted, unable to focus attention and concentrate efforts on tasks

_____ has an indifferent or negative attitude toward school

_____ resists teacher efforts to motivate or discipline behavior in class

_____ has difficulty in peer relationships; maintains few friendships

---

From Joanne Whitmore, *Giftedness, Conflict, and Underachievement* (Needham Heights, MA: Allyn & Bacon, 1980). Copyright © 1980 by Allyn & Bacon, Inc. Reprinted by permission.

egorized in three different levels in terms of their causes and visible symptoms. The primary characteristic is *low self-esteem*, which appears to be at the root of most underachievement problems. The low self-esteem leads to the secondary characteristics of *academic avoidance* behaviors, which in turn produce the visible tertiary traits of *poor study habits*, *unmastered skills*, and *social* and *discipline problems*. However these causes and effects are often bidirectional. That is, each set of characteristics tends to influence the others, and like the chicken-egg problem, it is difficult to determine which sets serve as the initiators.

Primary Characteristic of Underachievers: Low Self-Esteem

The characteristic found most frequently and consistently among underachieving children is low self-esteem (Fine and Pitts, 1980; Rimm, 1986b; Whitmore, 1980). These students do not believe they are capable of accomplishing what their family or teachers expect of them or what they should expect of themselves. The low self-esteem they feel is, in fact, directly related to these pressures to "be gifted" (Rimm, 1987c; Adderholdt-Elliott, 1989). They may mask their low self-esteem with displays of bravado, rebellion, or with highly protective defense mechanisms (Covington and Beery, 1976; Fine and Pitts, 1980; Rimm, 1986b). For example, they may openly criticize the quality of the school or the talents of individual teachers, or else claim that they "don't care" or "didn't really try" in regard to a mediocre test score or class grade.

Related to their low self-esteem is their sense of low personal control over their own lives (Rimm, 1986b). If they fail at a task, they blame their lack of ability; if they succeed, they may attribute their success to luck. Thus they may accept responsibility for failure, but not for success.

This attribution process in educational achievement has been related to Seligman's (1975) concept of *learned helplessness*. If a child does not see a relationship between efforts and outcomes, he is not likely to make an effort to achieve. This pattern is

characteristic of many gifted underachievers. Weiner (1985) also emphasized that a child's performance will be strongly influenced by whether he or she attributes successes and failures to ability, effort, task difficulty, or luck. Especially, attributing success to *effort* leads to further effort while attributing success to *task ease* or *luck* does not. In their comparison study of elementary gifted underachievers, gifted achievers, and nongifted students, Laffoon, Jenkins-Friedman, and Tollefson (1989) found that gifted underachievers attributed their successes to ability and their failures to bad luck and other external sources more than did the achievers. The authors recommended encouraging persistence and learning from failure as appropriate retraining strategies.

Secondary Characteristics of Underachievers: Avoidance Behavior

Low self-esteem leads the underachiever to nonproductive avoidance behaviors both at school and at home, secondary characteristics of underachievement (Whitmore, 1980). For example, underachievers may avoid making a productive effort by asserting that school is irrelevant and that they see no reason to study material for which there is no use. Students may further assert that when they are really interested in learning, they can do very well. These kinds of avoidance behaviors protect underachievers from admitting their lack of self-confidence, or worse, their feared lack of ability. If they studied, they would risk *confirming* the possible shortcomings to themselves and to important others. If they do not study, they can use the nonstudying as a rationale for the failure, thus protecting their valuable feelings of self-worth (Covington and Beery, 1976). Some familiar examples of defensive excuses appear in Figure 13.1.

Additional defensive avoidance behaviors that operate in a similar fashion to protect underachievers include intense interest or even leadership in out-of-school activities which are less threatening. These successes essentially compensate for academic failures.

FIGURE 13.1. Avoidance behaviors often take the form of defensive excuses.
From Hershey and Crowe, 1989. Reprinted by permission of *Gifted Child Today*.

Extreme rebellion against authority, particularly school authority, provides another route to protect the underachiever. The student seems eager to tell teachers, the principal, the superintendent, even the board of education, exactly how they ought to run the school. Faulting the school helps the underachiever avoid the responsibility of achieving by blaming the system.

Expectations of low grades and perfectionism—though apparent opposites—also serve as defense mechanisms for the underachieving child with low self-esteem. If the underachiever expects low grades, he or she lowers the risk of "failure." Note that low goals are consistent with a poor self-image and low self-confidence.

By contrast, achieving children set realistic goals which are reachable, and failures are used constructively to indicate weaknesses needing attention.

Perfectionism provides a different protection. Since perfection is unachievable, it provides the child with ready excuses for poor performance. For example, students can boast that they set their goals higher than most people, so of course they cannot always succeed. The students thus provide a rationale for failure and do not need to label themselves as incompetent (although they may indeed feel incompetent).

Adderholdt-Elliot (1989) named five characteristics of perfectionistic students that contribute to underachievement: *procrastination*, *fear of failure*, an *all-or-nothing mindset* (even one "B" means failure), *paralyzed perfectionism* (if there is a risk of failure, do nothing), and *workaholism* (which leads to burnout, depression, and a lost balance among school, family, and friends).

Hostettler (1989) described the relationship between perfectionistic habits acquired in elementary school and high school underachievement. He taught a class of tenth-grade *gifted* underachievers whose standardized achievement test scores were above the 85th percentile, yet their mean grade-point average (GPA) was 1.85. Most of them were failing English, French, and/or Algebra. However, high school records showed that in sixth grade the usual GPA of these bright students was 4.0—straight "A"—and typical teacher comments were "perfect student," "marvelous," "wonderful," "doing beautiful work," "impossible to improve," and "set for big things." Two conclusions seemed in order: First, the students' own high grades coupled with superlative feedback led to perfectionistic self-expectations. Second, these students showed a common late onset of underachieving, because perfectionistic students do well when the curriculum is easy enough to permit "perfect" achievement, but become underachievers when work becomes difficult, that is, in secondary school.

Closely related to the issue of perfectionism is the gifted underachiever's inability to function in competition. Students in a clinic setting hardly ever admit this problem when asked; however, when the *Achievement Identification Measure* (AIM; Rimm, 1986a) was factor analyzed to create subscale scores, the main factor included items related to competition, for example, "My child loses his/her temper if he/she fails at something," "My child brags a lot when he/she wins at something" (negatively scored), "My child enjoys competition, win or lose" (negatively scored), and "My child is a good sport whether he/she wins or loses."

Parent observations of underachievers confirm that these children avoid competitive activities in and out of the classroom, *unless they perceive themselves as highly likely to win*. Many young adults who were underachievers as children concede that their early inability to cope with competition was a critical component of their avoidance patterns.

Clinkenbeard (1989) also concluded that competition can have negative effects on the motivation of some gifted students, based on her study of gifted students who chose not to compete. However, her study may have been unique in that it included only highly gifted students in a summer program, who may have viewed the situation as *too* highly competitive or simply as an inappropriate arena for competition. There is ample evidence in all schools of many areas where gifted students

deliberately choose to compete, for example, debate, music, math, and art contests.

Underachievement of gifted students may appear even at the college level if students have not learned to function in competition. The U.S. Department of Education reported that of the top 5% of high school graduates, 40% do not graduate from college (DeLeon, 1989). While the reasons for noncompletion of college may be more than an inability to function in competition, the second author's clinical experience with gifted students who lose confidence in competitive college environments provides evidence for this serious underachievement problem. Here is an example:

Bruce was a National Merit Scholar and valedictorian of his very academic high school. He had received few Bs during his entire educational experience. He was well liked and well adjusted. He loved computers, and became engaged in almost every kind of learning.

Bruce attended the University of Wisconsin-Madison. His freshman year went reasonably well, but in his sophomore year his grades declined. After the first semester of his junior year, his grades were too low for him to be permitted to continue.

Bruce worked at a fast-food restaurant while planning his future. He said he completed a report in his senior year of high school about how he thought the school could improve. It never occurred to him then to ask for more challenge. He had been happy and interested. Bruce said he never realized then how many highly intelligent students there were in the world, nor had he ever had an assignment in high school that he could not easily do. He "hit his first wall" in college and backed away in defeat.

When the counselor asked Bruce about returning to school, he said that, of course, he planned to graduate eventually. When he was further asked if he believed he would be able to graduate, his immediate response was "no."

Achieving students recognize a competitive environment as one in which they may experience success or failure, yet they take the risks in full awareness that they may not be the top (most perfect) scholars.

Two directions of secondary characteristics have been described by Kaufmann (1986) as *aggressive*, *hostile* responses or *withdrawal* responses. Rimm (1988b) found underachievers to exhibit their defenses by *dependency* or *dominance*. Figure 13.2 shows these two directions. Conforming underachievers differ from those in the nonconforming category in their visibility. That is, conforming dependent and dominant stu-

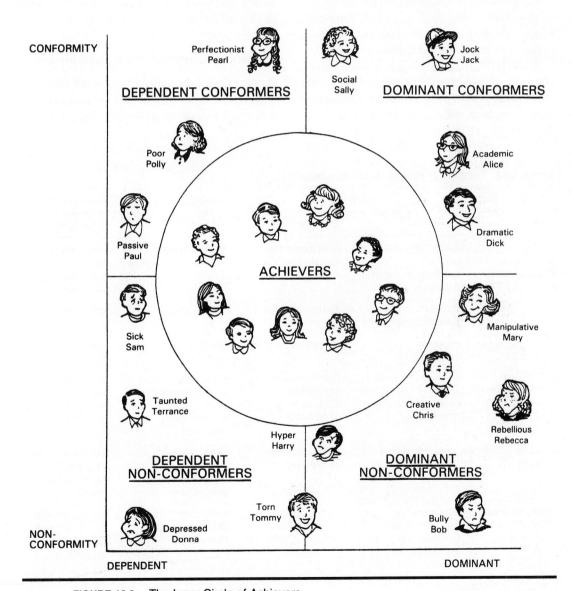

FIGURE 13.2.   The Inner Circle of Achievers.

dents have the characteristics that may lead to greater underachievement problems, but their underachievement is not obvious. Nonconforming dependent and dominant underachievers already are exhibiting serious problems. The prototypical names used in Figure 13.2, Passive Paul, Rebellious Rebecca, etc., are used to emphasize the main characteristics of these underachievers, but any one child typically exhibits a group of these symptoms. Rimm also points out that some underachievers exhibit both dependent and dominant qualities.

Richert (1991a) summarized how others' expectations can influence gifted children not only in the area of achievement (or underachievement), but in values, creativity, self-esteem, social relations, and

"emotional impact" (Table 13.3). Richert's ideal pattern, and one to be encouraged, is to neither fully accept nor reject others' expectations, but *transcend* them with *healthy self-expectations*, which will optimize achievement, independence, creativity, self-acceptance, etc. Note that Kaufman, Rimm, and Richert show considerable agreement in their descriptions and interpretations of behavior of underachieving gifted children.

Tertiary Characteristics of Underachievers

Because underachieving children avoid effort and achievement to protect their precarious self-esteem, tertiary characteristics arise which support the pat-

TABLE 13.3   Patterns of Response to Expectations

Aspects of Potential	Accept		Reject	Transcend
	Conformity	Withdrawal	Rebellion	Maximizing
Ability Achievement Productivity	Successes satisfy others Extrinsically motivated	Safe mediocrity/ Evades pressure to perform	Failure/Rejects external expectations	Satisfies own values Intrinsically motivated
Values	Based on norms Externally dependent	Evades external judgment	Reacts against	Independent
Creativity	Repressed Fear of failure	Repressed/Refuses to take risks	Divergent Negative	Creative Risk taker
Self-Esteem	Insecure/Dependent on others' perceptions External locus of control	Follower/Avoids competition External locus of control	Dependent/ Internalizes negative external judgment External locus of control	Independent Self-accepting Internal locus of control
Social Relations	Roles that lead to rewards/Pleases others	Follower/Avoids competition	Loner or gang leader Isolated or domineering	Withdraws or takes leadership May have few friends
Emotional Impact of Experiences Vulnerability	Reinforces dependence on external rewards and approval for self-esteem	Reinforces feeling of self-dissatisfaction and fear of judgment	Punishment Betrayal Rejection	Potency: Asserts control over own life Compassion

© 1990 E. Susanne Richert

tern of underachievement. These include deficient academic skills (Fine and Pitts, 1980), poor study habits, peer acceptance problems, poor school concentration, and home and school discipline problems. These tertiary indicators of under-achievement seem to be the visible "tip of the ice-berg," characteristics that result mainly from the secondary avoidance behaviors which protect un-derachievers from the primary problem, low self-esteem and the related feelings of low personal control.

Skill deficiencies may cause several kinds of problems. Redding (1990) found that gifted under-achievers did as well as gifted achievers on tasks that required holistic information processing but could not perform as well with detailed or computa-tional tasks requiring precision. Rimm (1991b) similarly found that gifted underachieving elemen-tary children performed well in tasks requiring in-formation, abstract reasoning, and vocabulary, but poorly on tasks that required rapid copying of codes. If writing is difficult, some gifted children will avoid writing assignments in favor of verbal tasks. Further, because many elementary-age chil-dren equate "fast" with "smart," poor writers may worry that their slow writing confirms they are not as "smart" as they or their parents and teachers be-lieve them to be (Rimm, 1991b).

ETIOLOGIES OF UNDERACHIEVEMENT

Children are not born underachievers. Under-achievement is *learned* behavior, and therefore it can be unlearned. Underachievement can be taught by families, by schools, or by cultures. The last, cultural underachievement, its etiology and treat-ment, is discussed in Chapters 12 and 14, focusing on culturally different students and females. The following sections will describe rituals and rein-forcements that maintain patterns of underachiev-ing in the home and school. Recognizing factors that cause, support, and reward underachievers should help the reader understand the dynamics of underachievement and therefore should assist in preventing and reversing the problem.

FAMILY ETIOLOGY

When families of underachieving children are com-pared to families of achievers (Frazier, Passow, and Goldberg, 1958; Zilli, 1971), certain characteristics become apparent. Some of these characteristics are difficult to alter, but some can be easily changed by concerned parents once they are aware of the dy-namics. Among the characteristics resistant to change are general poor family morale and family disruption caused by death or divorce (French, 1959). Among those that can be changed relatively easily are parent overprotection, authoritarianism, excessive permissiveness, and inconsistencies be-tween parents. These frequently result in manipula-tive rituals and parent identification problems that almost always can be recognized.

It is helpful for teachers to be familiar with "problem family" patterns, because an under-standing of these patterns will help the teacher communicate with parents more effectively. Also, family patterns that include manipulations by a child can be extended into the classroom. Thus a sensitivity to underachieving patterns can help the teacher avoid being manipulated.

Identification and Modeling

Terman and Oden's (1947) study of lower-achieving gifted men showed that their most significant characteristic was *non*identification with their fa-ther. Rimm (1984) similarly found that under-achievers frequently did not identify with the same-sexed parent. Interestingly, however, some identified very strongly with a same-sexed par-ent—if that parent appeared from the child's per-spective to also be an underachiever or to be giving the child messages that avoiding school-work is acceptable.

Freud (1949) explained identification with the same-sexed parent as a product of the resolution of the *Oedipal* or *Electra* complexes. During the phallic stage of development (ages 3 to 5), said Freud, the child finds him- or herself romantically attached to the opposite-sexed parent. Recognizing that the parent already has a partner, the child sees the impossibility of the affair and resolves the issue by unconsciously identifying with the same-sexed parent. This identification purportedly causes the child to adopt the behaviors, conscience, and appropriate sex role of that parent. The three-year-old boy walking in Daddy's shoes or the girl imitating Mommy's telephone conversation is said to be evidence of this early identification.

While conceding that it is nice for children to love their parents, contemporary social learning theorists question whether identification truly stems from the unconscious resolution of a sexual conflict. Rather, they describe identification and imitative behavior in terms of *modeling* (Bandura, 1986; Meichenbaum, 1977). Research by Mussen and Rutherford (1963) and Hetherington and Frankie (1967) indicates that the parent model chosen for identification and imitation depends largely on a combination of three variables, *as perceived by the child*: (1) nurturance, (2) power, and (3) similarities between the parent and child.

The *nurturance* variable is very straightforward. The child tends to identify with, and model the behavior of, the parent who is highly nurturant. There may be an especially warm, loving relationship between the parent and a particular child or children in the family. If that parent is an underachiever, or does not stress achievement, the child may adopt similar attitudes.

The way that *power* influences identification, imitation, and underachievement is sometimes direct and at other times more complicated. In the most direct way, if one parent is definitely more powerful from the child's perspective, but does not value education or school achievement, the identifying child is not likely to perform well in school. Teachers need to be aware of this pattern because they may see only the concerned mother of an underachieving boy at parent conferences. However, it may be the *father* with whom the conference should be taking place. It is difficult to motivate a boy who identifies with his father, if the father and the boy view education as "women's work."

Some typical, more complicated power patterns that foster underachievement in children are described by Rimm (1986b) as "Father is an Ogre," "Daddy is a Dummy," "Mother is an Ogre," and "Mother is the Mouse of the House." These power patterns tend to arise because parents unintentionally compete with each other to establish their own child rearing approach as best or to feel like the "good parent." The impact of the rivalry to establish oneself as the better parent is that the opposite parent is given the role of "bad" or "dumb" parent. Rimm (1986b) indicates that awareness by parents of these rituals frequently is sufficient to encourage a change in parenting approaches, and even by itself this awareness may make a major difference for underachieving gifted students.

In the first pattern, "Father is an Ogre," the father is viewed as successful and powerful, the mother as kind and caring. Often, a closer view of the home life shows a father who wears a big "No!" on his forehead. That is, he firmly prohibits many of the activities the children wish to pursue. However, the children learn to bypass his authority by appealing to their kind, sweet mother. Mother either manages to convince Dad to change his initial decision, or surreptitiously permits the children to carry out their desired activities anyway. Children quickly learn the necessary manipulative maneuvers.

The ritual worsens because as the children grow older the father begins to recognize his lack of power over his family, and he becomes more and more authoritarian as he tries to cope with his powerlessness. In response to his increasing authoritarianism, mother feels an increasing need to protect and defend her children. In desperation she invents new approaches to sabotaging her husband's power in the belief that she is doing the best thing for her children. Although girls in this family are likely to be achievement-oriented because they see their mother as powerful and positive, boys will tend to underachieve. They see no effective model in their father, who appears both hostile and powerless. They may fear and resent him, but are not likely to want to emulate him.

"Daddy is a Dummy" is a slightly different but equally disruptive ritual. This syndrome is often discovered in homes where Mother has a college education which includes courses in education and psychology. Dad has no college education or one that did not include psychology. Mother is certain that she knows the "correct" way to bring up the children which, according to her training, should include an important father role. However, whenever Dad attempts to play his parent role, Mother corrects him and explains a better way in which he can play his part. Dad feels uncomfortable and powerless in handling the children and makes every effort to withdraw, sometimes to 70 hours a week at the office. If Mother insists that he come home, the television screen becomes his escape. Sons again tend to be the underachievers in this family since they see their father as either powerless, absent, or as expressing passive-aggressive behavior. These underachieving boys often assume the same passive-aggressive posture in front of the television screen.

In the third parenting pattern, "Mommy is an Ogre," we find a disciplinarian mother and a kind, sweet, but undisciplined father. This results in at least two more poor patterns for identification. (1) If the disciplinarian mother is viewed by the children as fair and strong and supported by "kind father," this provides a weak male image for the sons, but a strong mother figure for female identification. (2) However, if the mother's discipline is overruled by the father, we have potential models for underachievement for both male and female children. The boys may identify with Father because he is viewed as powerful, but he models some characteristics and habits which make for underachievement—ignoring or violating (Mom's) rules, procrastination, and lack of discipline and perseverance. To the girls, Mother may be viewed as insignificant sound and fury, and therefore cannot become the model for an achieving daughter because of the children's perceptions of both her powerlessness and her continuous anger.

"Mother is the Mouse of the House" is the "dummy" ritual that results in rebellious adolescent daughters. It begins with a conspirational alliance between father and daughter, who is often referred to as "daddy's little girl." Mother is not included in the special relationship and is treated as if she were not as intelligent as Dad. The daughter is typically a very good student in elementary school and pleases father, mother, and her teachers. By fourth or fifth grade, although good achievement continues at school, an unexplainable conflict between mother and daughter begins at home. Father takes the role of mediator, or worse yet, rescuer for his daughter who has learned to convince her daddy that she is right and that mother is too controlling and overreacting. This manipulative ritual continues until adolescence when father begins to worry about teenage dangers from which he must protect his daughter. He then takes a firmer discipline position and will no longer give in to his daughter's persuasion. In frustration and surprise at her new ineffectiveness, the daughter may attempt manipulating her mother for support. Mother, impressed by the improved mother-daughter relationship, may then ally herself with her daughter. The manipulations increase and vary between mother-daughter opposed to father and father-daughter opposed to mother. Eventually and usually by high school, the parents identify the manipulations and unite in desperation to control their adolescent who seems to be pushing all limits. The adolescent, who has earlier managed to do exactly what she chose, now feels overcontrolled by her parents and rebels. Her rebellion sparks a series of punishments increasing in severity, which in turn cause more rebellion. The adolescent underachievement becomes only one of the symptoms; other, more severe behaviors, including alcohol and drug abuse, depression, and/or sexual promiscuity, become the acting-out behaviors which capture adult attention. Underachievement is viewed as a minor offense in comparison.

Although these four parenting rituals may appear separately in some families, they sometimes appear simultaneously in the same family. Parents may actually take "good" or "mean" roles differently for each child in the family. They may also change roles between early childhood, later childhood, and adolescence. The crucial issue for underachievement is that if children are exposed to one parent who challenges them and another parent who shelters them, they learn to "take the path of least resistance" and automatically back away from challenge, with the protection and support of the sheltering parent.

In order to prevent a child from developing an underachieving pattern, parents must compromise their points of view to avoid either over-pressuring or overprotecting their children so that an appropriate and positive challenge message is issued by both parents. This permits children to accept challenge and please both parents who have thus set reasonable expectations for them.

In addition to nurturance and power, the third variable that affects identification is the *similarities* the child sees between him- or herself and a parent. This similarity provides a good basis for sex-role identification. High similarity between mother and daughter or between father and son strongly supports same-sex identification when nurturance and power of the parents are equal. However, unusual similarities in appearance, abilities, interests, or personality between boys and mothers or between girls and fathers may lead to cross-sex parent identification. Cross-sex parent identification can contribute strongly to either achievement or underachievement. Achievement motivation may be strengthened by female identification with a powerful and effective father if he is intellectually oriented, but weakened if he is not intellectually oriented. However, only underachievement appears to be fostered by the cross-sex identification of sons with their mothers.

In the relationships which develop after a divorce or in single-parent households, ogre and dummy rituals become more complex and further increase the likelihood of underachievement. It has been predicted that by the year 2000, 61 percent of the children born in 1987 will spend at least part of their childhood in a single-parent home (Kutner, 1991). Although the prognosis for family etiology of underachievement is not optimistic, hopefully further research in new family styles will provide a blueprint for avoiding underachievement in non-traditional families.

Other research has produced findings that relate child-parent identification to achievement and underachievement. For example, Lamb (1976) and Zilli (1971) found that if Father is absent from the home, boys are more likely to be underachievers. Parish and Nunn (1983) discovered that boys and girls whose fathers left home (or died) before the children were 13, tended to be low in internal locus of control, a trait strongly related to achievement. In relation specifically to quantitative abilities, if Father is absent, both boys' and girls' math aptitudes and achievement are more likely to be weak (Carlsmith, 1964). However, girls and boys who identify strongly with father are more likely to have good problem solving, math, and science skills (Helson, 1971; Milton, 1957).

As we will see in Chapter 14, Rodenstein and Glickauf-Hughes (1979) found that a girl's attitude toward a career will be strongly and positively influenced by a successful working mother. However, this holds true only if there is a good family attitude toward Mother's employment and Mother's role conflict is minimal. Almquist and Angrist (1971) similarly emphasized that in order to aspire to a career, young women need good role models who can demonstrate that marriage and a career can be successfully combined.

In summary, the identification literature clearly supports the significance of identification with good parent models as an important family factor in high achievement. The lack of that identification, or the identification with a poor parent model, seems to be related to underachievement. Parents who view their own lives as interesting and successful and who model an equitable and respectful husband-wife relationship provide ideal role models for both male and female children.

Gender Issues in Underachievement

Although gender issues will be described in Chapter 14, it is worthwhile to look at gender differences as they relate specifically to underachievement in this chapter. The patterns found by Kerr (1985), Shaw, and McCuen (1960), Richert (1991a), and Rimm (1986b) appear to be consistent. Gifted boys start their academic underachievement earlier than gifted girls. Rimm finds that 90% of the elementary children who come to her clinic are males. Underachievement in her clinic population increases for girls by the middle and high school years. Among students who begin their underachievement at the college level, more are females. Kerr (1985, 1991) also has documented the career underachievement of females.

One reason for gender differences in the onset of underachievement may lie in educational, family, and peer traditions. Most elementary teachers are female, and mothers have taken primary responsibility for home-school communications. Girls thus receive strong encouragement to achieve from female models. Further, by middle school, peer pressure plays an important part in female underachievement, with peers tying brains and achievement to being a "nerd" (Brown and Steinberg, 1990; Rimm, 1990a). Finally, Table 13.4 sketches some striking differences in videotaped behavior of second-grade boys and girls, and equally striking differences in reactions to that behavior by men and women.

Manipulative Rituals and Counteridentification

The situation in which a parent identifies with his or her child is known as *counteridentification*. The parent who counteridentifies with the child invests him- or herself in the child's activities and empathically shares efforts, successes, and failures. A familiar example of counteridentification is the vociferous father who argues desperately with the referee at the Little League baseball game as if it were he who had been unfairly called "out." Counteridentification is not always bad. Many parents vicariously enjoy seeing their children excel in sports or other talent areas, attend prestigious colleges, or travel, activities which the parents missed in their own youth.

Counteridentification has not been thoroughly explored in research, but it appears to have the potential to influence either high achievement or underachievement. The potential for positive contributions to achievement comes mainly from the parents' sharing of skills and their investment of time and resources. As mentioned in Chapter 2, Bloom (1985; Bloom and Sosniak, 1981) found that the early training of extremely talented youth included coaching by one or both parents who had a strong personal interest in the particular talent field. Bloom emphasized that the parent provided an early and influential model for the child. Based on Bloom's descriptions, it is likely that most of the parents counteridentified with their talented child.

On the negative side, several forms of counteridentification can lead to manipulative rituals by children, supporting underachievement. Two such rituals begin with kind, empathic parents who try to be helpful to their children and try to understand their points of view. In one negative ritual rooted in counteridentification the child manipulates parents into completing his or her homework. This extremely common problem begins innocently enough. The child does not understand an assignment and goes to the parent for an explanation. The counteridentifying parent not only explains the assignment, but in order to prevent the child's "suffering" continues to work with the child. The parent explains the assignment step by step, over and over. The child soon learns that he or she needs only to briefly express confusion and the parent is brought quickly to his or her side for the evening. Together they complete the daily assignments. When father or mother does not cooperate, the child may punish the parent by failing the assignment, thus encouraging the parent to be more helpful with the next homework.

It is not surprising that as time progresses the child finds the assignments more difficult and takes longer and longer to complete the work. Not only has the child found comfortable reinforcement in the form of attention from mother or father, the child loses confidence in his or her ability to achieve independently. Since mother or father

TABLE 13.4   Men's and Women's Reactions to Videotapes of Behavior of Second Grade Boys and Girls

Videotape 1: The Boys

The second-grade boys are physically restless; their idea of what to do involves physical activities; they are continually aware of the hierarchical framework they are in, and they do what they can to mock and resist it; and they show their affection for each other in an oppositional format. They directly disagree with each other, but their disagreement is a natural response to the putdowns and mock assaults that are initiated.

Videotape 2: The Girls

The second-grade girls' conversation in the same situation includes nothing that resembles the ways of talking for the boys. The girls, too, are aware of the authoritarian framework they are in, but they are complying with it rather than defying or mocking it. Far from playfully attacking each other, they support each other by agreeing with and adding to what the other says. Rather than colluding to defy authority, they reassure each other that they are successfully complying. In contrast to the teasing by which each boy implies that the other is doing things wrong, the girls offer assurance they are doing things right.

Typical Female Response to the Videotapes

Women subjects thought Jane and Ellen were sweet little girls. They were touched by the girls' eagerness to fulfill the experimenter's request. The little boys made them nervous. They wished they'd *sit still!* They thought their joking silly, and didn't like their teasing and mock attacks. They felt sorry for poor Kevin, who kept trying to smooth down his hair and was told that another little boy didn't like him.

Typical Male Response to the Videotapes

Men subjects reacted very differently. They thought the boys cute, and they found their energy and glee touching. They were sympathetic to the boys' impulse to poke fun at the situation and defy the experimenter's authority. The girls seemed to them like a pair of "Miss Goody Two-Shoes." Some commented that they didn't trust the girls' behavior; they felt that little children couldn't really enjoy sitting still—they must be on their best behavior to please the experimenter.

Adapted from Tannen (1990).

is now carrying the responsibility for much of the work, the child may no longer believe it is possible to learn the required skills.

An early manifestation of this dependent pattern in the classroom is a child seeking continuous aid from unsuspecting teachers. For example, this is the child who typically waits until instructions have been given twice and then raises his hand and innocently announces, "Ms. Jones, I just don't understand what I'm supposed to do."

This dependent pattern sometimes has it origins in an early teacher recommendation to a parent. For example, in a primary grade a teacher may have suggested that a parent regularly help the child with homework. Teachers should be cautious in making such recommendations, and

CALVIN AND HOBBES

should be explicit in the kinds of help that they suggest so that this help does not lead to overdependence.

This dependent ritual is relatively easy to change if identified early, but very resistant to change in the high school years. By then, there is a sizable gap between the student's developed skills and those necessary to succeed. Furthermore, by this time the youth has little remaining confidence in his or her school-related competence.

The second maladaptive ritual that stems from counteridentification is one in which parents convey *too much power* to their gifted children and the children become dominant or aggressively manipulative. Because the children appear so bright, and because they use adult vocabulary and

adult reasoning, parents find themselves interacting with them almost as adult peers long before the children have attained the wisdom to match their verbalizations (Fine and Pitts, 1980). Parents and sometimes teachers may be awed by the child's adultlike rationalizations for why they need not perform routine school tasks. To their own detriment, these children learn to manipulate their parents and teachers, frequently bypassing skill development because the work is "boring" or "irrelevant." Further, they may claim there is no reason to write material that they can answer orally, and they may depend on their verbal precociousness until writing skills actually become deficient.

Dominant children also may manipulate their parents and teachers into permitting them to avoid assignments in which they are less confident by using their talent area as an excuse. More than one musically or artistically gifted student has managed to avoid "irrelevant" math or science assignments by claiming to need time for his or her special talent (Rimm, 1990b). Furthermore, creatively gifted underachievers often have a history of avoiding tasks they describe as "boring" because they believe they must function creatively *all* the time. While talented students must have extra time to devote to their special interests, these kinds of avoidance habits can become manipulative rituals that deprive them of taking responsibility for learning (Rimm, 1987b).

The teacher who works with dominant students must recognize that the verbally powerful child needs to be carefully led to the conclusion that he or she must learn and study. Opposing this child will lead to a no-win battle, and antagonism is the likely result. Recognizing the power pattern that exists at home can help the teacher guide this child in the classroom. Whitmore (1986) described the necessary relationship as a problem-solving partnership. This alliance minimizes the potential for conflict and an adversary relationship.

We have seen that *intuitive responses* by parents and teachers can reinforce underachievement—make matters worse. For example, with dependent students an intuitive reaction is to do too much (e.g., homework) for them; with abrasive dominant students a natural reaction is to "put them in their place" by overreacting and overpunishing. Less natural, *counterintuitive* measures are more effective. For example, with dependent children adults should insist that the children take small steps forward *independently*, even when they show signs of pressure. For dominant students, attitudes of respect, compromise, working together to solve problems, along with a negotiated and fair agreement regarding school work is a successful strategy for reversing underachievement. Parents and teachers should put such agreements in writing, and hold to them firmly, to avoid again becoming victims of manipulation.

In a comparison of families of gifted under-achievers and families of gifted achievers, Rimm and Lowe (1988) found considerably more dysfunction among families of underachievers. Also noticeably absent from the families of underachievers were the modeling of intrinsic and independent learning, a positive commitment to their careers, and respect for schools and teachers.

That last component of family etiology is worth emphasizing. Erickson and Ellett (1990) point out that American educators, during the last three decades, have been more concerned with students' rights than responsibilities. Perhaps more emphasis at home and in the media on students' personal responsibilities, coupled with a clear message of respect for educators, would be an effective means of encouraging student achievement.

SCHOOL ETIOLOGY

The gifted child often is exposed to the "good year, bad year" syndrome. Archambault and Hallmark (1992; Renzulli, 1992) found that 42 to 62 percent of the 7,000 teachers in their study had absolutely no exposure to methods for teaching the gifted. Teachers without training supply most of the "bad years." However, other teachers—even without training in gifted education—do detect and provide for the special needs of gifted children, creating the "good years." Fortunately, not all "bad years" are devastating. Most gifted children are resilient enough to function well even in a less-than-responsive environment. However, certain personal and classroom conditions seem to create problems for the gifted child and seem to initiate or accelerate underachieving behavior patterns.

School Climate

Whitmore (1980) described classroom environments that appear to cause and support underachievement. The main characteristics she discovered were a lack of respect for the individual child, a strongly competitive climate, emphasis on outside evaluation, inflexibility and rigidity, exaggerated attention to errors and failures, an "all controlling teacher," and an unrewarding curriculum. We will look more closely at the effects of inflexible and competitive classrooms.

Inflexible Classrooms.   The inflexibility and rigidity that demonstrate lack of respect for the individual child provides a strong reinforcement for underachievement by the gifted child. The intellectually gifted child learns faster and integrates information more easily. The creatively gifted child thinks differently and asks frequent questions. The rigid teacher, however, adheres to a schedule that allows little flexibility for those who differ in speed or learning style. The gifted child quickly discovers that rapid completion of assignments usually leads to more assignments. These typically are not more challenging or more exciting, but merely "busywork" to keep the active child occupied.

Initially, the gifted child may be pleased and motivated by the special treatment by the teacher. Eventually, as the child finds the busywork unchallenging and boring, he or she concludes that these additional assignments are punishment for rapid work. To avoid the punishment, the child slows his or her pace and no longer completes assignments before the rest of the class. However, since the student's mind remains active and alert, he or she usually must find other diversions such as daydreaming, troublemaking, or surreptitiously reading an exciting book. In some cases the diversions become powerful reinforcers that distract the child from completing even the regular assignments, which appear dull by comparison. Consider this actual case:

> Robbie, eight years old, was a highly verbal child with an IQ in the very superior range. However, he was two years behind in mathematics and never completed his math assignments. His problem became clear after he was observed in class by the psychologist. On his lap, hidden from the teacher's view, was a book he was reading while the teacher explained the math assignment. The book was shifted to underneath the math book while students were to be doing math written work. Robbie moved further and further behind in mathematics, which was taught too slowly for his quick mind, but he read many exciting books. He was referred to the psychologist as having a "learning problem."

At the 1992 Annual National Rimm Underachievement Institute in Pewaukee, Wisconsin, John Feldhusen, a long-time leader in gifted education, shared his own story of surreptitious reading to avoid his childhood school boredom. Perhaps many adults committed to gifted education recall their own techniques for coping with inflexible and dull classrooms. Can you, the reader, recall your own novel adjustments?

In addition to busywork, other ritual punishments tend to discourage the gifted child from achieving in the rigid, inflexible classroom. For example, if the gifted child responds too frequently in class or asks too many questions, he or she is not called on to speak. However, if the ignored child waves his or her hand too enthusiastically, calls out answers, or talks excitedly to a neighbor, he or she is rewarded with a scolding. The scoldings may serve either to reinforce or punish the child. If the child views them as punishment, he or she stops responding, deciding that such enthusiasm is somehow inappropriate to the school setting. If the child views the scoldings as reinforcing, he or she increases the talking out of turn and the hand waving, which become nuisances to both teachers and peers. Either way, enthusiasm for learning and thinking is diminished.

Competitive Classrooms.   The classroom where comparative evaluation is heavily stressed and where there is extraordinary emphasis on competition is a serious problem for underachievers. The announcement of grades to the class, the comparisons of students' test scores, the surprise expressed by a teacher when a student scores higher or lower than expected, and the continuous ranking of students all foster extreme competition within the classroom. That competition is attached to extrinsic evaluations of performance based on objective criteria that, from the perspective of the child, are viewed as the true measure of his or her competence and worth. Children who are already strong achievers and continue to find themselves at the top of the class may become even more motivated to achieve in very competitive environments. However, even for highly motivated children too much emphasis on extrinsic rewards may detract from the intrinsic rewards of learning and creativity.

It is underachievers, of course, who are most dramatically affected by the severe competition (Covington and Beery, 1976). Underachievers, who do not have a clear sense of their own competence, are informed on a daily basis that they are not measuring up to the standards of excellence of the classroom. These children are given objective evidence of average or below-average abilities. Since competitive achievement is the only source of teacher recognition and rewards in the classroom, and since these children do not believe they are capable of attaining that recognition, they search for other classroom rewards or other evidence of personal worth, or adopt the defensive measures noted earlier in this chapter and in Chapter 8.

A highly competitive environment may be a "good year" or a "bad year" for the achieving gifted child. For the underachieving gifted child it is always a "bad year" because it provides convincing evidence of his or her incompetence. While an overly competitive environment causes problems for many students, learning to function in a gradually more competitive environment is appropriate for students who must adjust to real world competition (Rimm, 1991c; 1992a).

Negative Expectations

Rosenthal and Jacobson's (1968) book *Pygmalion in the Classroom* inspired a landslide of research, most of which strongly supports the notion that a teacher's expectations can have a dramatic impact on children's self-concepts and school achievement (Davis and M.A. Thomas, 1989; Good and Weinstein, 1986; Keneal, 1991; A. Thomas, 1991). The problem is that for children, teachers and school success are the major—if not the only—source of feedback concerning one's ability, competence, and worth (Covington and Beery, 1976). The teacher who sends messages of negative expectations will frequently find exactly what he or she expects: Both regular and gifted students will underachieve. As a perhaps surprising source of negative expectations, Felton and Biggs (1977) concluded that, "remediation, as it is sometimes practiced, may help the student to label herself as *stupid*, and this, in turn, may affect the teacher's attitudinal responses to that individual. This means that underachievement may be caused directly in the classroom and in the 'helping' provided there."

Not all gifted children will respond to the negative attitudes and expectations of a teacher by poor achievement. Some few may see this attitude as a special challenge and make additional efforts to meet that challenge. However, the underachieving gifted child, whose self-concept already is poor, normally will perceive the teacher's expectations of failure as a confirmation of his or her own poor self-evaluation. Another true story:

It was fall conference time for fifth-grade parents. Any teacher can relate to the early confusion of matching the correct parents with students. There were two Amys in Mrs. James' class. One Amy was an excellent and positive student, but the other Amy was quite the opposite.

The second Amy's parents entered the classroom and introduced themselves. Mrs. James, assuming these to be parents of the first Amy, immediately exclaimed glowing praise for their delightful daughter. Amy's parents' faces reflected shock. Their response was, of course, enthusiastic. Mrs. James, immediately realizing that these parents belonged to the other Amy, regrouped quickly. Still on a positive note, she explained that Amy did have a few problems.

The description of Amy's problems never dampened the parents' enthusiasm. They returned home after the conference to tell Amy that this would surely be her best year in school. Amy, too, was delightfully surprised. She agreed that this would surely be a wonderful year.

Amy ended fifth grade with a B *average, in startling contrast to her* D *average of the year before, a very dramatic impact of teacher expectation.*

An Unrewarding Curriculum

Although complaints from the underachieving gifted child that the school curriculum is irrelevant, dull, or unchallenging may only be a defensive avoidance ritual, it is often a real difficulty. Gifted children are particularly vulnerable to the "unrewarding curriculum" problem because of their intellectual and creative needs. Gifted children are often anxious to question, criticize, discuss, and learn beyond the levels that are appropriate for most students in the class. If the students are not challenged by the curriculum, they will find stimulation outside of the curriculum, and school will indeed be viewed as dull and boring. It is not uncommon for gifted underachievers who perform poorly in school to achieve excellence in nonschool-related activities where they create their own rewarding "curriculum." Consider this case:

Ron was described as a poor reader and disinterested in school. In fourth grade he completed assignments rarely, daydreamed, performed his class work sloppily, and in general was considered a below-average student. At home he was immersed in comic books or baseball. He literally read and enjoyed thousands of comic books. As for baseball, he had easily committed to memory baseball statistics of the previous 20 years and talked knowledgeably about batting averages and pitching records that involved mathematics well beyond

what he had learned in school. The same skills he seemed unable to apply in the classroom setting were readily exhibited in his areas of true interest—comic books and baseball. A more rewarding curriculum could have brought together Ron's interests and abilities and expanded both.

Matching Efforts with Outcomes

Whitmore (1986) emphasized that gifted underachievers are not "lazy" or "unmotivated," merely unmotivated for schoolwork. Underachievement syndrome among gifted children may have been caused by complex family and school situations, but it nonetheless is critical to be certain that children understand the relationship between effort and outcomes.

Figure 13.3 (from Rimm, 1987b) illustrates how the appropriate relationship can lead either to achievement or underachievement. Quadrant 1 represents achievement. Children demonstrate appropriate effort. They have learned to work hard. They understand perseverance and have appropriate skills. Intrinsic enjoyment of challenge is part of the process and easy tasks are accomplished quickly in order that they may pursue more challenging activities. Their goals are set appropri-

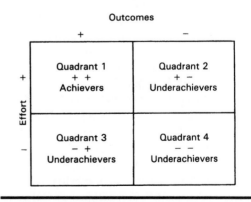

FIGURE 13.3.   Relationship Between Effort and Outcomes

ately high, but not beyond their abilities. They continue to achieve as long as they see the relationship between effort and outcome.

Quadrant 2 leads to underachievement when efforts are appropriate but goals or outcomes are set either too low or too high. In the cases of goals set too low, these children may have internalized a message from parents, society, or their peers that being "smart" is not as important as being well-adjusted or popular. Intellectual accomplishment is less valued than beauty or athletic prowess, and they do not wish to be "geeks" or "nerds."

Examples of goals that are set too low by teachers come from unchallenging cooperative learning environments, where gifted children too frequently play the role of teacher (Rimm, 1992b) or where gifted children must conform to a heterogeneous group. Here's a sample case:

Alex, an extremely gifted young man with somewhat poor social skills, was involved in a cooperative learning group where part of the assigned task was to draw a college campus. Alex could not convince his fellow students to design the campus to show more academics than athletics. Figure 13.4 (top), reflects Alex's description to the therapist of his reasons for frustration. The bottom figure is the drawing he made when he was given the opportunity to work independently.

The Quadrant 2 problem of goals set too high may appear in a highly competitive school environment where, despite the child's excellent intelligence and study skills, good grades are not attainable. If parents set expectations beyond children's abilities (and some do), this too will have the impact of establishing "too high" goals.

Generally, if goals are set too low children will stop making an appropriate effort; they have learned that it is easy to achieve those lower outcomes. If goals are set too high, they give up in desperation because they do not believe that any amount of sustained effort will make a difference in accomplishing these difficult outcomes.

Quadrant 3 leads to underachievement syndrome when achievement outcomes are set at a reasonable level, but the process of making an effort has not been learned appropriately. That is, parents and children value good grades and school performance. Report card grades initially reflect the excellent performance, and children feel positive about school. However, activities are not sufficiently challenging, and the children learn that achievement is easy, that success is readily attainable, and that learning and study should be effortless. Occasionally they may comment on boredom or lack of challenge, but as long as grades continue to be high they exhibit no problem behaviors. Unfortunately, they do not develop the good habits of perseverance, dealing with challenge, or intense study. At some point in their academic development the curriculum material becomes more complex, the student population becomes more competitive, or both. Their goals continue to be appropriately high but they have not learned the processes or efforts required to produce the desired outcomes. Some students will adjust to the additional needed effort. Others will hide behind their threatening feelings. They will worry that they are not as smart as they would like to be and they will invent or discover a whole herd of rituals and excuses that prevent them from making a good effort.

Quadrant 4 represents the most advanced stage of underachievement syndrome. It appears after children described by Quadrants 2 or 3 have not functioned as achievers for a period of time. Quadrant 4 underachievement takes place when children's efforts and skills both show deficiencies for such a long period of time that the children give up on reasonable goal setting. Teachers rarely identify these children as gifted because their intelligence or creativity are no longer exhibited in the classroom. Even parents begin to doubt their children's abilities. In conversation they may refer to the past when, they recall, their children were smart, but at this point they have given up on high-level goals and are willing to settle for their children earning a high school diploma. Quadrant 4 underachievement is most difficult to cure and may require outside therapeutic help.

FIGURE 13.4. Alex's representation of the cooperative learning group's drawing of a college campus (top), and his own version of a campus (bottom).

INSET 13.1 _____

Are Schools Teaching Gifted Children to Underachieve?

Two major changes are taking place in many schools today that are likely to contribute to underachievement by gifted children.

1. By uncritically hopping on the de-tracking bandwagon many schools have abolished _homogenous ability grouping_—and gifted programs along with it. As we saw in Chapter 1, research (e.g., Kulik, 1992) shows clearly that gifted children who are grouped for acceleration and enrichment, compared to gifted students in nonaccelerated and non-enriched classes, outperform the latter substantially—academically, nearly one year on a grade-equivalent scale. Further, if curriculum is too easy, gifted students are not likely to learn perseverance and develop an internal locus of control—the idea that personal effort leads to success (Lafoon, Jenkins-Friedman, and Tallefson, 1989).

2. Some schools emphasize _cooperative learning_ in forms that minimize any competition. To the extent that gifted students do not learn to compete, they will be ill-prepared for the competition they will face in college. They also may suffer decreased self-confidence that comes from a balance of successes and failures. An even greater danger of cooperative learning is that, as in heterogenous grouping, bright students simply are not challenged by assignments geared to the "group."

Because lack of an internal locus of control, poor functioning in competition, and not making a good effort are typical characteristics of underachievers, _schools adopting heterogeneous grouping and cooperative learning may now be teaching underachievement._ Gifted students may interpret the two trends to mean "don't bother to work hard."

The famous quote by Plato says it well: "What is valued in one's country is what will be cultivated." High individual achievement and creativity appear to be less valued in today's quest for equity.

Inset 13.1 suggests that school curriculum which adopts heterogeneous grouping and cooperative learning may, in a _de facto_ way, be teaching underachievement.

THE TREATMENT OF UNDERACHIEVEMENT

As we have seen, the underachieving gifted child continues to underachieve because the home, school, and/or peer group support that underachievement. The student is not motivated to achieve, and there probably are deficiencies in skills necessary for achievement. Working below

one's ability affects both immediate educational success and eventual career achievement; it is an important problem requiring attention.

While it may seem a tall order to reverse a long-standing pattern of underachieving, Rimm's strategies have proven successful in case after case (Rimm, 1986b). She has found that the treatment of underachievement involves the collaboration of school and family in the implementation of six steps of her TRIFOCAL Model (See Figure 13.5):

1. Assessment
2. Communication
3. Changing Expectations

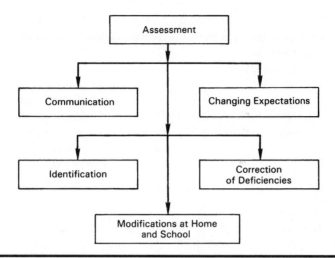

FIGURE 13.5.   TRIFOCAL Model for curing Underachievement Syndrome.

4. Role Model Identification
5. Correction of Deficiencies
6. Modifications of Reinforcements

Most of these concepts have been described in this chapter. It is important to note that to reverse underachieving patterns, all six steps must be implemented approximately simultaneously.

Biographical studies of achievers who indicate they previously had been underachievers show that all six steps usually are included in the change process. These "spontaneous changers" typically initiated their turnabout with Steps 3 or 4, the discovery of a positive model for identification or a change in expectations of important others, for example, a teacher, boyfriend, girlfriend, or spouse. These relationships, which are common in spontaneous underachievement conversion, need to be recognized as important elements in the deliberate treatment of underachievers. Parents and teachers must remain aware of the central role they play in the implementation of the critical six steps, particularly in the areas of setting expectations and finding or becoming a good model. In addition to the use of the TRIFOCAL Model, parents and teachers should

be equipped with "patience, dedication, and support" (Hoffman, Wasson, and Christianson, 1985).

Step 1: Assessment of Skills, Abilities, Reinforcement Contingencies, and Types of Underachievement

The first step in the underachievement reversal process is an assessment that involves the cooperation of the school psychologist, teachers, and parents. The school psychologist should have primary involvement in this process. However, since few school districts allocate time for gifted children within the psychologist's role, it may be necessary for the guidance counselor, G/T coordinator, or classroom teacher to assume some of the responsibility. Ideally, the person should (1) have some background in measurement, (2) be sensitive to various learning and motivational styles and problems, (3) be knowledgeable in behavioral learning theory, and (4) be aware of the special characteristics of gifted and creative children.

The *individual* intelligence test is a highly recommended first assessment instrument. That venerable IQ number has the potential to communicate important expectations related to the child's true abilities. Since the child has not been motivated, it is likely that *group* intelligence test scores have underestimated his or her intellectual potential. It is characteristically difficult to score above 125 on some group intelligence tests, a serious problem for intellectually gifted students. Therefore, the WISC-R or the *Stanford-Binet, L-M*, should be individually administered by a psychologist.

Even with these individually administered tests there are problems for gifted students. As we noted in Chapter 4, the highest possible score on the Wechsler tests is 155, and on the Stanford-Binet, Fourth Edition, 164. Also, IQ scores run lower on the new Stanford-Binet and WISC-III tests. The Stanford-Binet, LM, is the best intelligence test for evaluating gifted children. Further, underachieving gifted children often have uneven skills; thus, several tests may need to be administered in combination to identify strengths and problem areas.

During testing, the examiner should be especially aware of particular task-relevant characteristics of the child: symptoms of tension, attention to the task, perseverance at the task, responses to frustration, problem-solving approaches, defensiveness, and responses to personal encouragement by the examiner. These reflect, in miniature, approaches to educational tasks that the child very likely uses in the classroom and at home.

Intelligence testing should be followed by individual achievement tests to assess strengths and deficits in basic skills, particularly reading and math.

A creativity test or inventory, which can be administered by the teacher or psychologist, also should be part of the assessment. These produce not only a norm-referenced creativity score, but also descriptions of abilities, characteristics, and interests that are relevant to understanding the child's personality, creative potential, and learning style. The GIFT and GIFFI tests include subscale scores such as *Independence*, *Self-confidence*, and *Risk-taking* that provide important insights for understanding underachievement.

GAIM, described earlier in this chapter, can be used for children from Grades 5 through 12, while AIM and AIM-TO can be completed by parents or teachers of all children. The scores provide a description of the extent and type of the child's underachievement. Subscale scores reveal whether the child is mainly dependent or dominant or a mixture of both. Scores also permit insights regarding parent consistency in messages about achievement.

Finally, parent and student interviews also can be very helpful in identifying underachieving patterns unintentionally maintained at home and school. Examples of parent and student interviews, which can be adapted, are available in the *Guidebook to Underachievement Syndrome: Causes and Cures* (Rimm *et al.*, 1989). Ideally both parents should be at the interview. If only one appears, it is important to ask about the other parent's relationship to the child. Overall, the analysis of student abilities and home and school reinforcement contingencies is critical to the second step of the underachievement modification program.

Step 2: Communication

Communication between parents and teachers is an important component of the cure for underachievers. Either a parent or the teacher may initiate the first conference, but the initiator must assure the other person of support, rather than placing blame. If it appears to a teacher that the parents are not interested in or capable of working with him or her, the teacher should select another child advocate in the school, for example, a counselor, gifted coordinator, or resource teacher. Reversing an underachievement pattern without parent assistance is not efficient, but it is possible.

The content of the communication between parents and teachers should include a discussion of assessed abilities and achievements as well as formal and informal evaluations of the child's expressions of dependence or dominance. These are especially important in order that adults at home and at school do not fall into the trap of continuing to reinforce these problem patterns (Rimm, 1991a).

Step 3: Changing the Expectations of Important Others

Parent, teacher, peer, sibling, and self expectations can be difficult to change. As noted above, IQ scores, if higher than anticipated, are very effective in modifying expectations. Anecdotal information also can provide convincing evidence of the child's abilities. For example, a teacher convincing an adolescent or his or her parents of the child's mathematical talent can explain that the child solves problems in an unusually clever way or seems to learn math concepts more quickly than anyone else in the class. A psychologist trying to convince a teacher that a child has unusual talent can describe the unusual vocabulary or problem-solving skills that the child revealed during testing. *Specific* descriptions of unusual strengths are good evidence of giftedness.

Changing self and peer expectations can be done in individual therapy, in group counseling sessions, and in classroom settings. Even a teacher of the gifted, who is not trained as a counselor, can be effective in helping gifted students, underachieving or otherwise, to understand realistic goal-setting, perfectionism, competition, and peer pressure better. A book designed specifically to help gifted students learn about these topics is *Gifted Kids Have Feelings Too* (Rimm, 1990a), which includes stories and poems for and about preadolescents and adolescents. An accompanying discussion and activity book, *Exploring Feelings* (Rimm and Priest, 1990), is for teachers and counselors to use in classrooms or counseling sessions.

It is important to underachieving children that parents and teachers be able to say to them honestly that they believe in their ability to achieve. The expectations of these important others are basic to the personal change in self-expectations that is necessary to reverse from underachievement to high achievement. In their longitudinal research with bright fourth-, fifth-, and sixth-grade underachievers, Jackson, Cleveland, and Mirenda (1975) showed that positive expectations by parents and teachers had a significant long-range effect on achievement in high school. Bloom's (1985) studies of talent development found that parents of research neurologists and mathematicians always expected their children to be very good students.

Since sibling competition frequently is a causal component of underachievement syndrome, changing the expectations of siblings also is important. In the sibling rivalry that often exists, an achieving child may have assigned to a brother or sister the role of "loser," and changing that role may be threatening to the "winner." An individual and personal communication to the "winner" about the expected change is helpful. Parents should provide the assurance that the sibling's status change will not displace the achiever's role. Genetically and environmentally a "whole smart family" is not only possible, but likely. This explanation may deter the achiever from subtly trying to keep the underachiever in his or her underachieving status.

Because it is difficult to change the expectations of persons who know the child, changing the child's school environment sometimes is an effective measure. Changing schools is a drastic step to take unless one is reasonably certain that the change will make a worthwhile difference. If extraordinarily gifted children are stifled by school environments that set only average goals and expectations, the children sometimes will change their entire achievement pattern when put in an environment that expects and values high achievement. However, for most children it is more realistic to try to change relevant expectations within the school.

Step 4: Model Identification

A critical turning point for the underachieving child is the discovery of a *model* for identification. All other treatments for underachievement dim in importance compared with strong identification with an achieving model. As noted above, Bloom's (1985; Bloom and Sosniak, 1981) biographical research with highly talented students showed that parents modeled the values and the lifestyles of successful achievers in the child's talent area. Radin (1976) argued that the best family environment for a gifted boy is provided ". . . when a father is perceived as competent and strong, is pleased with his job, and permits his son to master tasks independently." Since this ideal situation is rarely provided for the gifted underachiever, parents and teachers need to help the student find a good model for identification.

Research on parent identification (e.g., Mussen and Rutherford, 1963) indicates that the selected parent identification figure is nurturant, powerful, and shares common characteristics with the child. These same characteristics can be used to locate an appropriate achieving model for the underachieving gifted child. As a warning, however, an underachieving adolescent sometimes selects a powerful, nurturant model who shares the *underachieving* characteristics of the adolescent. This person then becomes a strong model for underachievement.

Underachieving children should be matched with an achieving person to serve as a model for them. The person selected can serve in a model capacity for more than one child. His or her actual role may be tutor, mentor, companion, teacher, parent, sibling, counselor, psychologist, minister, scout leader, doctor, and so on. However, the model should have as many of the following characteristics as possible:

1. *Nurturance.* The model must care about the child assigned. Many adults are pleased to encourage youth with whom they can counteridentify.

2. *Same sex.* Although identification with an opposite-sexed model is possible, the similarity in gender facilitates identification.

3. *Similarities to child.* These may include religion, race, interests, talents, physical disabilities, physical characteristics, socioeconomic backgrounds, specific problem experiences, or any other characteristics that will create the necessary easy rapport. When the child realizes that the model can be truly understanding, empathic, and sympathetic—because the model has experienced similar

problems—rapport is more easily established and the process of identification is facilitated.

4. *Openness.* A model's willingness to share his or her own real problems in establishing him or herself as an achiever is important for encouraging communication and identification, and for motivating the underachieving child.

5. *Willingness to give time.* Achieving adults frequently have shortages of this most precious commodity. However, it is not possible to be an effective, positive model without providing time. It can be work time, play time, or talk time. Models who work on tasks with their child or play with their child can be most effective. It becomes possible for the child to see first hand such important achievement characteristics as responding to challenge, winning and losing in competition, reasoning styles, leading, communicating and relating to others, and experiencing successes and failures.

6. *Sense of positive accomplishment.* Although the model's life need not be perfect, the model must exhibit to the child the sense that his or her achievements have been personally fulfilling. Achievement involves sacrifice and postponed gratifications. The underachiever must recognize that these costs and postponements are worthwhile.

Research by Emerick (1992) on students who have reversed their underachievement found that they often attributed their reversal to a teacher who was an important inspiration in their lives. A longitudinal study of disadvantaged children in Hawaii (Werner, 1989) showed that teachers, ministers, and other important adults were important as role models for achievement.

The concept of important role models is now being used in hundreds of school programs where community members volunteer to participate in mentorship programs. The concept of all-male and all-female academies for African-American students (Holland, 1991) is intended to provide appropriate role models for underachievers in disadvantaged populations.

Richert (1991a) summarizes role model importance well by the following statement: "The single most awesome influence educators and parents have are as role models."

Step 5: Correcting Skill Deficiencies

The underachieving gifted child almost always has skill deficiencies as a result of inattention in class and poor work and study habits. However, because he or she is gifted, the skill deficiencies can be overcome reasonably rapidly. This is less of a problem for a very young child because the deficiencies are less likely to be extensive.

Tutoring should be goal directed with movement to a higher reading or math group or acceptance into an accelerated class the anticipated aim. It should be of specified duration, for example, weekly for two months until the child takes a proficiency test, rather than ongoing. Ideally, the tutor should be an experienced and objective adult who recognizes the child's underachievement *and* giftedness. Parents or siblings are not appropriate because the personal relationships are likely to cause the child additional pressure and dependency. The correction of skill deficiencies must be conducted carefully so that (1) the independent work of the underachieving child is reinforced by the tutor, (2) manipulation of the tutor by the child is avoided, and (3) the child senses the relationship between effort and the achievement outcomes. Charting progress during tutoring helps visually confirm the rapid progress to both child and tutor.

Step 6: Modification of Reinforcements at Home and School

The analyses in Step 1 will certainly identify some of the manipulative rituals discussed above in the home and school etiology sections. These behaviors need to be modified by setting important long-term goals and some short-term objectives that can ensure immediate small successes for the child both at home and at school. These successful experiences can be reinforced by rewards—anything from gold stars or extra art time to special outings with parents or money.

There are several considerations in determining the rewards to be used. First, they must be meaningful to the child. Money may seem unimportant to a six-year-old, while stars are not particularly motivating to the adolescent. They also must be within the value system and range of possibility for the givers of the rewards. Schools usually do not use money as a reward, and parents may not want to pay (bribe) their children to learn. There are, however, effective rewards within the value system of parents and within the capabilities of teachers to administer—for example, free time. The rewards should not be too large. In fact, they should be as small as possible yet effective enough to motivate behavior. They can be increased in value as necessary; but if one has already used large rewards, small rewards will no longer be effective. It is important always to supply the rewards agreed upon, and to pay them on a regular basis immediately after the activity is successfully completed. Rewards may be based on activities completed, or based on the quality of the activity. Rewards should never be paid for incomplete work or when the work is not attempted.

Modification of reinforcements at school includes much more than reward schedules. For example, acceleration by subject or grade skipping are appropriate reinforcements for some underachievers (Rimm and Lovance, 1992a, 1992b). Participation in Future Problem Solving was found to be effective in reversing underachievement (Olenchak and Rimm, 1991). Encouraging a student's strong interests in the classroom also may facilitate the reversal of underachievement for students (Emerick, 1989).

Modifying reinforcements for homework and study are an important component of reversing underachievement syndrome. However, this modification by itself will not be sufficient. Dozens of other recommendations for home and school changes are described by Rimm (1986b) in her book on underachievement syndrome.

Treatment Beyond Home and School

The preceding recommendations for the treatment of underachievement at home and school are effective with many children and adolescents if the underachievement is not complicated by heavy involvement in drugs, alcohol, crime, or serious depression. However, even the adolescent who shows a long history of "complicated" underachievement also may be able to reverse the underachieving pattern, as well as the drug, crime, or other problems. In addition to the parent and educator working together, this youth is likely to need attention by a psychologist specializing in such problems.

SUMMARY

Underachievement by gifted students is a great loss to them and society. It is defined as a discrepancy between students' high ability and mediocre or poor school performance.

Intelligence, achievement, and creativity scores can be used to help diagnose underachievement. If the gifted student is a poor test-taker, observation by teachers or parents is necessary for determining giftedness. Rimm researched parent and student inventories which identify underachievers and describe patterns of their problem behaviors.

Whitmore prepared a checklist of characteristics of gifted underachievers. The authors describe three levels of characteristics: (1) low self-esteem, which leads to (2) defensive avoidance of threatening academic tasks and (3) deficiencies in skills, study habits, peer acceptance, school concentration, and discipline.

Perfectionistic tendencies may cause underachievement, especially in high school when work gets difficult, due to procrastination, fear of failure, and related avoidance behaviors. Many underachieving gifted students have difficulty functioning in competitive situations, unless they believe they can win.

Avoidance behavior, secondary characteristics, can take the form of aggression or withdrawal (Kaufmann), which is similar to Rimm's identified patterns of dominance or dependence.

Richert noted that others' expectations influence achievement, values, creativity, self-esteem, social relations, and "emotional impact." She recommended transcending others' expectations with healthy self-expectations.

Underachievement is learned and can be unlearned.

Gifted underachievers are less likely to identify with their same-sexed parents, unless the parent also is an underachiever or does not value achievement. Freud explained identification as an unconscious product of resolving Oedipal or Electra complexes. Social learning theorists emphasize the importance of a nurturing relationship, perceived power in the parent, and similarities in child-parent characteristics.

Several parent-power patterns foster inappropriate identification and underachievement. Research shows worse achievement for males in father-absent homes, and worse math and problem-solving skills for both males and females in father-absent homes. Successful career mothers serve as effective models for achieving girls.

In elementary school more boys than girls are underachievers; but due apparently to peer pressure and different behavior patterns (aggressiveness versus conformity), increasing numbers of girls become underachievers in middle and high school and college.

Counteridentification can lead parents to spend time with their children and reinforce the development of academic, artistic, or athletic skills. It can also lead to manipulation by children and to underachievement. If parents complete the child's homework it will encourage excessive dependence. If parents give their highly verbal children too much power, the children may manipulate their environments to avoid effort.

Creative students may dodge academic work by claiming they must to spend time on, for example, their art or music interests.

Counterintuitive responses by parents and

teachers can help reverse underachievement. Dependent children must take small steps independently; dominant children require respect, support, and fair agreements on school work.

Underachievers tend to come from dysfunctional families without good achievement models. An emphasis on responsibility plus respect for teachers and education is recommended.

Teachers who recognize and provide for gifted students create their "good years;" other teachers who cannot, their "bad years." Inflexible teachers, who may pile on extra busywork, encourage underachievement. Attractive diversions also may reward underachieving.

Teachers may ignore or scold the hand-waving, question-asking gifted student, who then stops responding in class.

Competition is devastating to underachievers, whose self-concept is damaged by repeated evidence of incompetence.

Negative expectations by teachers become self-fulfilling prophecies. Remedial work also may label a student as inept.

An unrewarding curriculum prevents the gifted child from fulfilling needs to question, discuss, criticize, and so forth. Challenges may be found outside of school, for example, in hobbies or athletics.

Underachievers must come to understand the relationship between effort and outcomes (goals). Cooperative learning groups can lead to low goal-setting and lack of challenge for gifted students.

The TRIFOCAL model for reversing underachievement requires six steps: (1) assessment of skills, abilities, reinforcement contingencies, and types of underachievement; (2) communication between parents and teachers; (3) changing the expectations of parents, teachers, peers, and siblings; (4) locating an achieving identification model; (5) correcting skill deficiencies; and (6) modifying home and school reinforcements that support underachievement.

Involvement in challenging opportunities such as acceleration or participation in Future Problem Solving can stimulate achievement.

Professional psychological help is needed if underachievement is complicated by drugs, crime, or other serious problems.

CHAPTER 14

THE CULTURAL UNDERACHIEVEMENT OF FEMALES

Although the contributions made by women in the role of wife and mother are not to be denigrated, the realities of a changing world have mandated a different role for women. It is clear from the . . . statistics that many gifted women are adult underachievers.
Sally Reis (1991)

The education of gifted women has been a low priority throughout history, a matter that has led to wholesale female underachievement. Many gifted girls have been, and continue to be, systematically discouraged by peers, family, and sometimes teachers and counselors from using their talent in productive ways. Stockard and Wood (1984) claimed that female underachievement as measured by grades is a myth, since they found in student records of seventh through twelfth graders that females were less likely than males to have English and mathematics grades that were lower than would be predicted by standardized ability tests. However, the underachievement of females is not measured or predicted by early grade and ability comparisons, but by the adult underachievement of highly intelligent women. Reis (1987) pointed out that the underachievement of adult women is indeed a different concept than that which is measured by grades in school and might be better defined as "what a person believes can be attained or accomplished in life." The discrepancy between the giftedness observed in girls' school achievement and their talent development in adulthood has been aptly labeled by Olshen (1987) as the "disappearance of giftedness in girls."

History shows that leading educators and psychologists had played a deliberate role in limiting educational opportunities for females. While many early educators simply ignored the education of females, some were explicit in designing education to maintain women's subservience to men. Smith (1981) quoted one of the most influential educators of the eighteenth century, Jean Jacques Rousseau, regarding his theory for the education of "Sophie," the ideal girl.

> Women's entire education should be planned in relation to men. To please men, to be useful to them, to win their love and respect, to raise them as children, care for them as adults, counsel and console them, make their lives sweet and pleasant. These are women's duties in all ages and these are what they should be taught from childhood on.

Smith also reminds us that Sigmund Freud and Carl Gustav Jung, two illustrious leaders of early psychoanalytic psychology, described what they perceived as inferior female characteristics. Freud noted the main traits of femininity as narcissism, masochism, and passivity. Jung described the mentally healthy female as being more emotional and less rational and logical than an equally mentally healthy male.

G. Stanley Hall (1844–1924), another leading psychologist and educator, reflected Freud's views in recommending that education for women ". . . should aim at nothing but motherhood." Edward L. Thorndike, early in this century, progressed only slightly beyond Hall, suggesting that education is not likely to "harm women's health" and that some women could even be educated toward careers, provided those careers involved nurturing roles (Smith, 1981). All these quaint views both reflected and reinforced prevailing social attitudes.

David Noble (1992) begins his book, *A World Without Women*, with the statement, "that the absence of women from the world of science has been so pervasive historically that it has been taken as a given, something to be overcome, perhaps, and never really explained." Green (1992), a reviewer of the above-mentioned book, questions further: "Why is it that the greater the percentage of women's participation in a given intellectual sphere, the more the general prestige of the sphere declines?" She ponders the reasons for the historical ignoring and underdevelopment of women's intellectual capabilities.

This chapter will review and update some statistics and opinions regarding the present status of gender inequities in the work world and life satisfactions of working versus nonworking women. It also will review arguments and data regarding biological gender differences, along with information regarding the other viewpoint—that observed differences are sociocultural in origin and are maintained by mechanisms that support female underachievement. Suggestions for teaching and counseling gifted females and for reducing gender-role stereotyping, bias, and discrimination also will be itemized. Finally, we will extend the school-home model for modifying general underachievement, described in Chapter 13, to reversing underachievement patterns in gifted girls.

PRESENT STATUS OF WOMEN: WOMEN IN THE WORK FORCE

An analysis of the present status of women in the work force provides the best documentation for the argument that many gifted women are indeed functioning as underachieving adults. They continue to occupy gender-role stereotyped careers and occupations and receive inequitable salaries and responsibilities.

Reis and Callahan (1989) appropriately entitled one paper *Gifted Females: They've Come a Long Way—or Have They?* Recent statistics document women's slow progress toward equality. Nochlin (1988) pointed out that "There have been no supremely great women artists . . . although there have been many interesting and very good ones . . . There are no women equivalents for Michelangelo or Rembrandt, Delacroix or Cezanne, Picasso or Matisse, or even in very recent times, de Kooning or Warhol . . . (pp. 149–150)." Piirto (1991) reminds us that there are few women composers or creative mathematicians or scientists. She cites Brody's (1989) statements regarding the Johns Hopkins Study of Mathematically Precocious Youth (SMPY) that the few women who qualified for the gifted mathematics programs had mothers who held Ph.Ds but did *not* work outside the home. Most of the girls were Asian. The physical sciences continue not to attract gifted females. Only 9% of all Ph.D physical scientists and 4% of all Ph.D engineers are women (National Science Foundation, 1990).

Areas of great progress for women appear to be biology and business. By 1986, the numbers of men and women earning bachelor degrees in the biological sciences showed almost no gender difference, and there was an extraordinary relative increase in the numbers of women majoring in business. The business share of all degrees earned by women changed from 2.8 percent in 1970 to 21.7 percent in 1986 (Turner and Bowen, 1990). However, even this apparent progress is balanced by a downside. In 1990 Stacey showed that in the first year after receiving an MBA, men earn a salary that is 12 percent higher on the average than that of women. In medicine, too, there is improvement, but also a downside. Despite the 34 percent of U.S. medical school graduates who were women in 1989 (Nickerson *et al.*, 1990), Shaller (1990) maintains that there is a "glass ceiling" ef-

By Mike Keefe for USA TODAY, Reprinted by Permission

fect in medicine. Shaller referred to the concept originally described by the *Wall Street Journal* in 1986 in respect to business, which suggested that invisible barriers hinder women from obtaining the highest positions. In business, only 19 of the 4,012 highest positions were occupied by women (Hymowitz and Schellhardt, 1986). In medicine, there were 47 women chairpersons of all clinical departments in U.S. medical schools, and in pediatrics, a field which attracts the largest number of women, there were five chairpersons in a total of 128 U.S. medical school pediatrics departments (Shaller, 1990). Furthermore, in medical school administration for the 1986–87 academic year, only 1.6 percent of all medical school deans, 9.6 percent of associate deans, and 20 percent of all assistant deans were women (Martin, Parker, and Arnold, 1988). As documented by the above cartoon, even Blondie has learned about the glass ceiling effect.

Census Bureau statistics of 1985 reported a dismal picture, with the average annual income of a female college graduate at $20,257, the average male high school dropout getting $19,120, and the male college graduate at $31,487 (*Milwaukee*

Journal, July 22, 1987). Even in the higher paying professions, women earned less than men. In 1986, specific income percentage comparisons of female to male were 77 percent for lawyers, 84 percent for engineers, 78 percent for computer systems analysts, 69 percent for physicians, and 62 percent for financial managers.

The increase in percent of women in science and engineering is dramatic and hopeful (Farnham, 1988). However, the continued underrepresentation of women in most fields of science provides graphic proof of the underachievement of gifted women (see Figure 14.1).

Statistics of the 1990 freshman college class continue to show significant gender differences (see Figure 14.2). Males continue to predominate by a 6 to 1 ratio in expressing an interest in majoring in engineering. Women's interest in engineering has actually declined (Brush, see Figure 14.3). While a similar percentage of males and females indicated an interest in majoring in math, only 30.4 percent of the females, compared to 45.5 percent of the males, rate themselves as above average in mathematics. Considering the higher male self-perception of competitiveness and mental

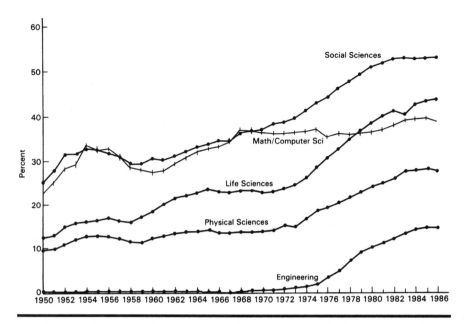

FIGURE 14.1. Percent of Science and Engineering Bachelor's Degrees Earned by Women, 1950–1986.
Reprinted by permission of the Commission on Professionals in Science and Technology

health, one could project that in the highly competitive mathematics-related fields, more males than females are likely to successfully sustain their mathematics-directed careers.

The above figures continue to suggest that education often is less important for upward mobility and high career achievement than gender and that many talented females are indeed underachieving. As Wolleat noted in 1979, "... despite [decades] of formalized guidance services in most high schools, gender remains the best single predictor of who will enter many occupations ..."

The status of women in education further documents female underachievement. Elementary and, to a lesser degree, secondary teaching have long been known as female steretyped professions. In 1980, approximately two-thirds of all K-12 educators were female (Smith, 1981). However, the upper echelon of power in elementary and secondary education is predominantly male and again reflects dramatic achievement inequities for females: Only 15 percent of school principals, and 2 percent of school superintendents are women (Reis and Callahan, 1989). Leadership in teachers' organizations shows similar inequities, with most local, state, and national positions held by men. As a positive note, according to a 1988 government study, beginning in 1983 the number of women earning Ph.D degrees in education has exceeded the number of men.

At the university level, according to a 1988 National Science Foundation report, in science and engineering men are more than twice as likely as women to hold full professor rank (50 percent compared to 21 percent). Further, fewer women than men hold tenure or are in tenure-track positions.

Farnham (1988) identified a relatively recent problem for women in university settings. An increasing number of teaching assistants and postdoctoral students are foreign national males who come from cultural backgrounds that are less accepting of female professionals than is our own culture. Particularly in areas such as engineering, computer science, and physics, these persons may

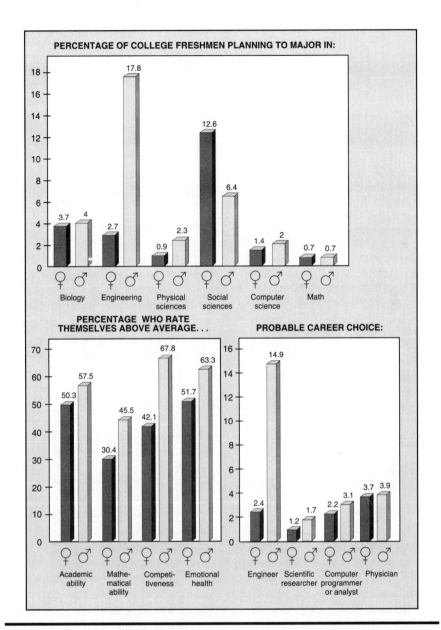

FIGURE 14.2.   A cross-section of the science manpower "pipeline." The latest statistics on 1990's entering college freshmen show that large gender differences persist in the physical and social sciences, as well as in engineering, where males predominate by more than 6 to 1. Males are also much more likely to rank themselves favorably on mathematical ability—as well as on competitiveness and emotional fitness.

Source: "The American Freshman: National Norms for Fall 1990," by the Cooperative Institutional Research Program of the American Council on Education and the Higher Education Research Center, UCLA.

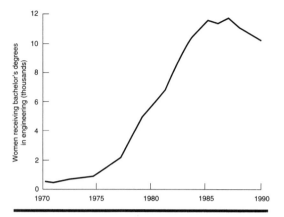

FIGURE 14.3. Decline of women's interest in engineering is particularly striking. Fewer women received bachelor's degrees in engineering in 1990 than in 1984. The proportion of engineering graduates who are women remained about the same throughout the 1980s, fluctuating between 13 and 15 percent. The lack of growth since 1985 is all the more disappointing because there were so few women in engineering to begin with. (Data are from the American Association of Engineering Societies.)

From Brush (1991), reprinted by permission of the *American Scientist.*

subtly discourage females from entering these science programs. If Farnham is correct in her conclusion, the future for women in mathematics appears even more dismal. In 1990, of the 933 doctorates awarded in the United States in mathematics, only 43% went to American citizens, and this is the lowest percentage on record (Browne, 1991).

College administration has been a virtual *no-woman's land.* In 1972 a *Time* magazine article recommended, "If a woman wishes to become a college president, she is advised to become a nun." At the time, just 1 percent of college presidents were women, and virtually all of these were nuns.

On the positive side, as in other traditionally male professions, the number of women entering college administration is increasing (e.g., Reis and Callahan, 1989). For example, at the University of Wisconsin (UW) the Chancellor of the entire UW

system,[1] the President of the UW-Madison campus, and the UW-Madison Dean of Students are women.

Overall, while the trends are in a positive direction, they still document the underachievement of gifted women, particularly in science areas.

LIFE SATISFACTIONS OF WOMEN

In the post-World War II years, even a woman who attended college was expected to achieve life satisfaction vicariously through her husband's career. Her success was tied to his success, along with success in the wife, mother, and home manager role she would play. Qualities of being "good-looking" and "sexy" were part of her definition as a woman. Her primary allegiance was toward her family, while the primary allegiance of her husband was toward his career.

Eminent developmental psychologist Erik Erikson (1959) described the *identity crisis*—deciding who and what you are—as being resolved later for a woman than for a man and as tied directly to marriage, her husband's career, and the birth of their first child. Identity was wrapped in the nurturing role. Adams (1971) suggested that women were caught in a "compassion trap," based on the belief that their most important function was to provide tenderness and compassion.

Note, too, that sociocultural sterotypes allowed a man to receive encouragement and support for his demanding career and professional accomplishments. However, a talented woman did not have a nurturing and supporting "wife" available, nor was anyone particularly anxious to take over home and child-rearing responsibilities for her. The 1988 book *The American Woman* reported that women in paid jobs continue to be responsible for most housework and family care.

This dramatic waste of the talents and contributions of women might be justified if women perceived themselves as fulfilled and happy in their housewife role. Surely, the nurturing of future

[1]At the time of this writing, President Clinton appointed UW Chancellor Donna Shalala Secretary of Health and Human Services.

generations is a critically important contribution to society, as is the support of men who make professional contributions. Research indicates that while some women do find high life satisfaction as homemakers, on the average life satisfaction—including self-esteem and feelings of competence—is greater for working and career women (Birnbaum, 1975). Bernard (1972), for example, found that housewives who derived their identity solely from their role as wife and mother were most likely to suffer the effects of *housewife syndrome*. This syndrome includes a sense of helplessness and hopelessness, depression, and a loss of self-esteem. The years devoted to caring for one's family seem to deprive many women of their sense of autonomy, leaving them with feelings of complete dependence. In counseling women at this stage of their lives, Rimm has found that their confidence may be so low that discussion with other adults about any topic other than child rearing may actually feel terribly threatening. On the other hand, career women usually derive much satisfaction from their work and the recognition they receive (Rodenstein and Glickauf-Hughes, 1979). Nadelson and Eisenberg (1977) reported that husbands of professional women found them to be "more stimulating" people.

A study by Holahan (1981) of life satisfactions of gifted females from Terman's research found that at a mean age of 66, career women expressed greater overall satisfaction with their lives than did homemakers and job holders. There were no significant differences between the latter two groups.

Women returning to college and the work world after devoting five to ten years to full-time wife and child-rearing roles provide rich anecdotal material regarding the dramatic changes in their lives. The following story, shared by a young woman married to a physician, reveals the frustration some of these women feel.

I had worked previous to having had my family and had received recognition and promotions for my accomplishments. When my husband completed medical school and we had our family, I reluctantly gave up my job. There were three children in rapid succession, and although I enjoyed mothering, I became more and more frustrated with my own sense of personal accomplishment. I kept telling my husband that I was anxious to return to college. One day while bathing the baby, I made the decision. I packed my suitcases and set them in the hall. When my husband came home, I simply said, "Either I return to school or I'm leaving." My husband looked strangely at me and said he hadn't realized that I wanted to go back to school, but that I certainly could. I couldn't

MARVIN   **by Tom Armstrong**

Reprinted with special permission of NAS, Inc.

believe his response, because I had been telling him this all year. I guess he didn't really believe me, and I had to do something really dramatic for him to hear what I was saying.

The Home-Career Conflict

Although working outside the home usually provides more self-satisfaction and life satisfaction, gifted women are caught in a very common conflict. The alternative to the *housewife syndrome* is the *working wife* or "Queen Bee" (Staines, Tavris, and Jayaratne, 1974) syndrome, a demanding superwoman role that requires women to meet the obligations of a challenging and worrisome job plus fulfill the traditional responsibilities of cleaning, shopping, cooking, laundry, and child care—and be a loving and supportive wife as well.

Poloma (1972) interviewed 53 couples in which the wives were involved in the male-dominated professions of law, medicine, and college teaching. These woman used one or more of the following four techniques for managing the home-career conflict.

1. *They looked at the* **benefits** *of combining a career and a family, rather than the costs.* As one woman explained, "I am a better mother because I work and can expend my energies on something other than over-mothering my children."

2. *They decided in advance which role came* **first** *in the event of conflicting demands.* In virtually every case, family crises took precedence over career crises. If the baby sitter did not show up or a child got sick, the wife, not the husband, missed work that day.

3. *They* **compartmentalized** *the two roles as much as possible, keeping work and family distinct.* Few of the women brought work home with them, for example, although their husbands often did.

4. *They* **compromised**. The wives controlled the extent of their career commitment to fit the circumstances of their family lives—how the husband's work was going, his income, the ages and number of children, the husband's support (or lack of it), and so on. "When one or more of these factors is out of kilter, the wife makes the necessary adjustment to manage role strain," Poloma found.

Some women felt compelled to make unreasonable concessions. For example, a lawyer would not talk about her practice at home, so that ". . . the children would not think that her work was more important than their father's." Others expected little and asked virtually nothing of the family to help them adjust to the double demands of family and career.

For the professional woman with a family, there is no easy solution to the continuous conflict of her roles. If she is committed to her career, she feels guilty for not fulfilling her nurturing commitment to her family. If she considers family first, she is criticized and feels guilty for not being sufficiently dedicated to her career.

Despite the difficulties of the double-role commitment, Birnbaum's (1975) study provides encouraging statistics for gifted young women who choose to combine *marriage and a career* or choose *careers only*, compared with becoming *housewives only*. Of the three groups, the housewives showed the lowest average self-esteem. Only 14 percent of the housewives, compared to 54 percent of the married professionals and 54 percent of the single professionals, reported "good" to "very good" self-esteem. Seventy-two percent of the housewives, compared with 36 percent of the married professionals and 73 percent of the single professionals, reported "feeling lonely" fairly often. Forty-two percent of the housewives indicated that they missed challenge and creativity, compared to just 4 percent of the married professionals and none of the single professionals. Sixty-one percent of the housewives, 12 percent of the married professionals, and 58 percent of the single professionals viewed themselves as "not very attractive" to men. Interestingly, while 52 percent of the housewives considered themselves happily married, 68 percent of the married professionals rated themselves as happily married. Although the working wife syndrome will pose problems for gifted women, these figures again indicate that it beats out other alternatives in terms of personal life satisfaction.

Rodenstein and Glickauf-Hughes (1979) reported similar statistics with 201 women graduates of the University of Wisconsin, ages 24 to 35. The *single* and the *married* career women rated themselves higher in "work satisfaction" and "recognition for accomplishments" than did the *homemaker* group. Perhaps not surprisingly, while 96 percent of the homemaker and married career women indicated that children were a satisfying aspect of their lives, only 1 percent of the single career women indicated satisfaction in this area. It is noteworthy that 38 percent of the single career women planned to have children at some point in their lives; they were not rigidly locked in to a single, childless career-only lifestyle. They retained their flexibility and kept their options open; they could change their minds and their lifestyle if they wished.

In the area of science, although women are generally published less than men, there is now some documentation that marriage has an enhancing effect on scientific productivity, and parenthood does not adversely affect that productivity (Cole and Zuckerman, 1987). Among eminent female scientists, married women published more than single women and this did not change if married women had children. The most significant factor that increased the rate of publication was marriage to another scientist. This research does not indicate what percentage of these scientist husbands were coauthors of their wives' papers or how many actually worked in the same laboratories. One woman scientist pointed out to the second author that she had observed there was indeed an advantage for women who had career interests similar to those of their husbands. In the competitive world of grant writing, a husband can often include funding for his wife's research and thus save her some time and energy.

The timing of when the "mommy track" begins apparently has a negative effect on women's sci-entific careers (Healy, 1992). A study of 460 former National Science Foundation postdoctoral fellows found that women who began their families during their postdoctoral years did not achieve academic and leadership positions which were as high as those of other women or men. Healy points out, "women in science eventually hit either the 'mommy track' or a 'glass ceiling.'"

The constraints on married women's careers in medicine are quite dramatic (Martin *et al.*, 1988). The divorce rate of women physicians is twice that of males. Among married male physicians, 90% had children, in contrast to 60% to 70% of married female physicians. The women physicians had fewer children and were older when they had them. Child care arrangements of male and female physicians are dramatically different, with half of the wives of male physicians providing full-time child care and another 33% providing a major part of child care. Among women physicians, 75% stated they had major responsibility for household and family care, and husbands were responsible for between 0% and 5% of the child care. Women physicians depended on full-time household help, day care, and relatives for child care.

Perhaps the most telling statistical comparison between male and female physicians was the response to the question which asked if they had changed their career plans or behaviors because of family responsibilities. None of the men had, while 44% of the women had made such changes.

As a final note, the present authors agree that society is the loser when any gifted and talented person, male or female, elects not to become a contributing professional. The authors do not agree on the acceptability of women not having careers. One author (you may guess which) believes that women should be able to choose the wife-mother-homemaker role if they wish, and emphasizes that aesthetic and creative needs may be met in developing high-level homemaking and childcare skills, in artistic and creative hobbies, and in clubs and community work. He points out that none of the research in this section claimed that 100 percent of all housewives were unhappy and unfulfilled. The second author believes that every woman should make a commitment to a career. While parenting may cause that career to be only a part-time one temporarily, a woman without a career, from her point of view, misses too many experiences in life to build a realistic adult identity. A woman without a career may not have the resources to cope with unpredictable life circumstances such as illness or death of her spouse or divorce. The U.S. Department of Labor Census Bureau (1991) reports that only 7 percent of American families have a "stay-at-home" mother.

Both of your authors agree that all young women, and especially high-potential ones, should have both the encouragement and the opportunity to receive training, develop their talents, and become professionals. The door must remain open, and gifted females must have the support of parents, teachers, school counselors, future partners, and society.

SEX DIFFERENCES OR GENDER DIFFERENCES

Reis and Callahan (1989) emphasize the importance of distinguishing between *sex* and *gender* differences; the first relating to the biological, and the latter to the sociocultural. Separating the two provides a basis for determining the extent to which the underachievement of women can be modified. Sex differences are biologically determined and could be viewed as potentially limiting the achievements of gifted women. However, gender differences related to sociocultural norms—stereotypes, bias, and discrimination—can be changed, and the correction of these problems may be seen as freeing women to achieve equally with men.

Biological Differences

Velle (1982) reviewed research on biologically based behavioral differences between the sexes, differences that conceivably could limit achievements of women. Although some of the research was based on animal behavior, some also involved human subjects.

Levels of Physical Activity.   Velle attributes high levels of male physical activity to hormonal influences in the brain during fetal development. He cited research with horses (Schafer, 1974) and monkeys (Goy and Resko, 1972). He also reminds us that castration of male domestic animals invariably produces quieter animals. His only example of actual human gender differences in activity came from research reported by Restak (1979), which showed that hyperkinesis (abnormally high levels of physical activity) is found in boys much more frequently than in girls. The hyperactivity that accompanies about 50 percent of all learning disabilities in school children is known to be largely a boys' problem (e.g., Howard and Orlansky, 1992).

Aggression.   Velle cited various animal studies linking the male hormone testosterone with aggression (for example, Bronson and Desjardins, 1968; Edwards, 1969). He also documented human studies (Conner, Levine, and Wertheim, 1969; Freedman, 1974; Moyer, 1974) which indicated that boys display more aggressive behavior than girls, and suggested that this is related to adolescent competitive behavior. One interesting study (Yalom, Green, and Fisk, 1973) reported the results of giving synthetic estrogen (a female hormone) to pregnant diabetic women. Their sons showed significantly less aggressive behavior at age 16, compared with same-aged boys of normal mothers and of untreated diabetic mothers.

Tomboyism.   *Adrenogenital syndrome* is an abnormal condition in girls characterized by masculinization of external genital organs. It apparently is caused by excessive androgen hormones during fetal development (Enrhardt, 1987; Money, 1987). Girls with this syndrome always have corrective surgery and are raised as girls. However, despite their female socialization, most of them show characteristics usually considered masculine, such as preference for boy playmates, interest in sports and athletics, preference for boys' clothes and toys, preference for a professional career to marriage, higher physical activity levels, and a lack of interest in caring for small children, hence the nickname *tomboyism*. These findings support the reality of biologically determined gender differences which, in tomboyism cases, can override environmental and sociocultural influences.

Cerebral Dominance Differences. In the past three decades, specialization of the left brain hemisphere for speech and verbal abilities and logical and sequential thinking, and the right hemisphere for spatial and other nonverbal abilities, has been continuously researched and written about (e.g., Springer and Deutsch, 1985). Assumptions about abilities related to sex differences based on the more specialized use of one side of the brain or the other are highly controversial and not well supported by any documented research. However, Levy-Agresti and Sperry (1968; see also Benbow and Stanley, 1980, 1981; Kolata, 1983) reported finding stronger right-hemisphere dominance for males, resulting in higher spatial abilities. Buffery and Gray (1972), in clear contradiction, argued that better male bilateral development—equal development of both sides of the brain—is responsible for the apparently superior spatial skills of males.

Levy (Kimura, 1985) theorized that differential brain pattern organizations for the sexes may be due to differences in rates of development both before and after birth, with the left hemisphere developing more quickly in girls and the right hemisphere in boys. The impact of this difference in rate would favor verbal skills in females and spatial skills in males.

If there are hemispheric differences between the sexes, no research makes it clear whether the hemisphere differences cause the differential spatial ability, or whether cultural conditions cause the differential hemispheric development. Camilla Benbow (Benbow and Stanley, 1981), however, even though she would *like* to find an environment difference that has been overlooked, concluded that

the superior verbal skills of girls and the superior math and spatial skills of boys are tied to differential hemispheric functions, and the difference is genetic. She reported one study in which a group of girls were specially taught spatial skills, but even that made little difference in their measured spatial ability.

Durden-Smith and DeSimone (1982) itemized some apparently biological differences between the sexes that, on balance, make females look noticeably superior—physically, psychologically, and socially. Consider these differences:

Men are more likely to be sexual deviates or psychopaths.

Women are stronger in verbal and communication abilities, but suffer more from phobias and depression.

There are more males at both ends of the intellectual spectrum—retardates and geniuses.

More males have heart attacks, since testosterone apparently increases cholesterol and hardening of the arteries.

Girls develop faster.

More males are spontaneously aborted during pregnancy, are born dead, or die in the first month of life.

More males have major birth defects.

Males are born less sturdy.

Boys are four or five times more likely to be *autistic* (being mute or having bizarre speech) or *aphasic* (unable to produce or comprehend speech; aphasia also includes emotional and thinking disorders).

Boys are much more likely to be unable to read (*dyslexia*), unable to do arithmetic (*dyscalculia*), or to have other learning disabilities.

Boys are five times more likely to stutter.

Males commit almost all violent crimes.

Males are more prone to alcoholism.

Males are more prone to schizophrenia.

We also might mention some traditional observations: Boys are more likely to be hyperactive, disruptive, and aggressive in class. Girls have better handwriting and better teeth and, when they get older, they have more hair and they live longer.

Sociocultural Differences

Although gender differences can be described and to some extent even quantified, research cannot delineate the exact extent to which specific differences are cultural versus biological in origin. However, studies of the changing role of women in society provide good documentation that many differences are indeed *not* biologically based.

The pink or blue blanket that identifies gender differences almost at birth is the first step in giving differential direction to the sexes. Next comes the infant's nursery, with pastel colors, lace, frills, and dolls for girls and bright colors, ball heroes, spaceships, and dump trucks for boys. The expectations of *docility* and *conformity* for girls throughout early childhood initiate the gifted girl to her eventual underachieving role in society.

In the process of developing her *Bem Sex-Role Inventory*, Bem (1974) itemized stereotyped characteristics associated with men and women. Interestingly, characteristics considered "masculine" also are typical of successful people, for example: *aggressiveness*, *ambitiousness*, *analytical ability*, *assertiveness*, *competitiveness*, *leadership ability*, *independence*, and *self-reliance*. Characteristics in the "feminine" column included those which might be associated with mothering or, at best, a narrow range of nurturant, female-dominated occupations, for example: *affection*, *cheerfulness*, *compassion*, *gentleness*, *love of children*, *shyness*, *understanding*, and *warmth*.

Bem's gender-role stereotyped traits continued to be reinforced by textbooks, literature, and the media. For example, there are "girls' books," such as *Little Women* and *Little House in the Big Woods*, and "boys' books," which include tales of mystery, adventure, risk-taking, and accomplishment (Sadker, Sadker, and Hicks, 1980). Sternglanz and Serbin (1974) analyzed gender-role stereotypes of ten of the then most popular children's TV shows. They found half to have no female characters at all, while the others had twice as many males as females. Furthermore, females were portrayed as not making or carrying out plans; they were punished if they were too active or aggressive; and they continuously deferred to males. Male characters were highly active, aggressive, and socially dominant, and they made plans and carried them out. The Des Moines Register (December 1, 1987) reported little improvement of female television roles. Twenty percent of TV shows had no females in the cast; among the lead roles on television programs, 36 belonged to males and only 7 to females.

The influence of movies and television on the aggressiveness and morals of children is an important and continuing issue. Research on the influence of television is virtually unanimous in concluding that TV violence influences children's aggressiveness (e.g., Sherman and Dominick, 1986; Singer and Singer, 1986). Closer to the present problem, Pinegree (1978) found that five-minute commercials were effective in influencing children to accept either traditional or nontraditional roles of women.

Can gifted girls overcome the impact of families, schools, and sex-role stereotyped literature and media on their own self-perceptions? Only with high levels of awareness and some deliberate "counterconditioning."

Mathematics Ability

The most prominent and heated argument related to differential abilities regards whether males have superior mathematical abilities (Armstrong, 1980; Benbow, 1986; Benbow and Stanley, 1980, 1981, 1982, 1983b; Coren and Halpern, 1991; National Assessment of Educational Progress, 1975; Pallas and Alexander, 1983; Wiley and Goldstein 1991; see also Stanley, 1992; Stanley and Benbow, 1983). The math difference seems to widen over the years, becoming quite prominent by junior high school (Maccoby and Jacklin, 1974). Giele (1978) and Fennema (1980), in fact, concluded that male and female math abilities are about equal in childhood, but at about age 12 or 13 boys begin to show superiority. However, a longitudinal study by Hall (1980) of 59 gifted students (29 boys and 30 girls) from preschool through grade 12 found no significant gender differences in arithmetic or spatial abilities or SAT-Math scores. She attributed her unique findings to an environmentally specific sample. The students were mainly from a university environment where many of the females' fathers were Ph.Ds, and cross-gender support for education was evident.

A male/female math comparison study in Hawaii of students in grades 4, 6, 8, and 10 found superior achievement for *females* over males (Brandon, *et al.*, 1987). An analysis by ethnic background of these students further indicated that gender differences favoring girls were smaller for Caucasian students than for Japanese-American, Filipino-American and Hawaiian children.

Camilla Benbow and Julian Stanley (1980, 1981, 1982, 1983b)—basing their work on years of SAT-M scores collected for thousands of students in Stanley's *Study of Mathematically Precocious Youth* (SMPY)—concluded that their data support a biological superiority of male math ability, which could be related to male superiority in spatial tasks. They indicated that environmental influences are not likely to so dramatically affect the "extreme absence of extraordinary female talent" among students involved in the SMPY talent search. A November 1983 Associated Press news release, based upon a recently published article in *Science* magazine (Benbow and Stanley, 1983b), noted that in the years 1980, 1981, and 1982 Benbow and Stanley found that the average SAT-Math score for 19,883 gifted seventh-grade boys was 416. For 19,937 gifted girls the average score was a noticeably lower 386. Average SAT-Verbal scores were almost identical, 367 for boys and 365 for girls. Further, boys outnumbered girls by better than 2 to 1 among those scoring above 500; by better than 4 to 1 among those who scored over 600; and by almost 13 to 1 in the group scoring 700 or higher (113 boys, 9 girls). Benbow and Stanley ". . . could not find substantial differences

in attitude, background, or previous mathematical training between boys and girls." See Inset 14.1 for one possible physiological explanation of gender differences in mathematical talent.

Benbow and Arjmand (1990) further reported in the longitudinal Study of Mathematically Precocious Youth that males achieved better in sciences in college, and that the aspirations of females declined significantly during their college years. Noble (1989) concluded that parents encourage gifted girls to get good grades—but not necessarily to channel these grades into careers. Rimm has found in her clinical work that a fear of low grades often prevents girls from risking the competitive and difficult science courses and may be in part responsible for preventing women from taking these more challenging courses.

We noted that a superior male spatial ability has been used to explain their apparently better math ability. The spatial ability-math superiority relationship is not, however, clear cut. In a male/female comparison of 77 gifted boys and 62 gifted girls, Weiner and Robinson (1986) found significantly better mathematics reasoning ability among the boys, but they did not find differences in tests of spatial relations, nor did they find spatial relationship test scores to be predictors of mathematics achievement for either girls or boys.

Analyses of male/female differences in math test scores continue to be reported, and results are mixed. Feingold (1988) reported that there had been a significant decrease in male-female gender differences in arithmetic and figural reasoning in the past 33 years, and Linn and Hyde (1989) also found decreases in gender differences for both mathematics and science. Hyde and Fennema (1990) did a meta-analysis of gender differences in math achievement and aptitude and found that differences that favored males increased with the selectivity of the sample, highly selective samples showing a greater differences favoring males. When Halpern (1989; Coren and Halpern, 1991) looked at the upper levels of mathematics aptitude on the PSAT, SAT, and ACT, he found consistent

INSET 14.1

Does Math Genius Have a Hormonal Basis?

Harvard Medical School neurologist Norman Geshwind proposed that excess testosterone or unusual sensitivity to testosterone during fetal life can alter brain development (Kolata, 1983). Specifically, the right hemisphere of the brain (instead of the usual left) becomes dominant for language abilities, and the person is likely to be left-handed. Further, such individuals—mainly boys, of course—are predisposed to (1) such speech abnormalities as autism, dyslexia, or stuttering, (2) certain kinds of giftedness, particularly artistic, musical, or mathematical, and (3) disorders in the body's immune system. Said Geshwind, "If you get the mechanism adjusted just right you get superior right hemisphere talents, such as artistic, musical, or mathematical talent. But the mechanism is a bit treacherous. If you overdo it, you're going to get into trouble. It's a funny mechanism. At first, it looks like you have to deliberately produce damage to produce giftedness."

According to *Science* magazine writer Gina Kolata, Benbow and Stanley were intrigued by this possible explanation of male superiority in math talent, and promptly contacted their very best students (those who scored above 700 on the SAT-M) to see if they were left-handed or had immune system disorders. "To their surprise and delight, they find that Geshwind's predictions hold up beautifully in their group" (Kolata, 1983). Twenty percent of the mathematically talented students are left-handed, which is more than double the proportion of left-handedness in the general population. A full 60 percent have immune system disorders (allergies, asthma)—which is five times the expected rate.

When Benbow and Stanley contacted students in their list who were less mathematically talented, the students also were less likely to be left-handed or to have immune disorders.

While Geshwind agrees that the data for the precocious students "fit in perfectly, to put it bluntly," he also concedes, "There's been—understandably—an enormous degree of skepticism."

---

discrepancies that favored males for all three tests. In 1986 the *National Assessment of Educational Progress* (Mullis and Jenkins, 1988) found that at age 17 about one-half of the males, compared to only one-third of the females, demonstrated sufficient levels of competence in analyzing scientific procedures and data. Becker and Forsythe (1990) examined 10 years (Grades 3–12) of *Iowa Test of Basic Skills* and *Iowa Test of Educational Development* data and found that at the upper percentiles, males scored significantly better in mathematics (and incidentally, in vocabulary as well).

Friedman (1989) analyzed dozens of studies of math gender differences that were published between 1974 and 1987 and reached these summary conclusions:

• The male advantage in math exists, but is smaller than previously thought.

• The male advantage is larger in secondary school than in elementary school.
• In studies of gifted students the male advantage is larger than in studies of "regular" students.
• The gender difference in math is smaller among minority students.
• Importantly, trends in SAT-Math scores from 1974–75 to 1985–86 show that the gender difference is decreasing over time.

Stanley (1992; see also Linn, 1992) stunned an audience of educators with his report of higher *average* scores for males on the majority of 86 subtests of aptitude and achievement tests, including the *Graduate Record Examination* (GRE), *Scholastic Aptitude Tests* (SAT), the *American College Testing Program* (ACT), and *Advanced Placement* (AP) tests. For example, males scored higher than females on all 17 of the subject area tests of the GRE, with political science, math, chemistry, engineering, and history showing the largest gender differences. There were no differences in Verbal GRE scores, but large differences favoring males in Quantitative GRE scores. On the Law SAT (LSAT), females scored the same as males. Females scored higher than males on the English portion of the ACT, but generally lower on the other tests (Social Studies, Math, Natural Science). Females also scored higher on the French AP test but lower on computer science, physics, chemistry, and calculus. There were no differences on the Spanish and English literature AP subtests.

Stanley found the matter perplexing and unexplainable, particularly since females generally are better students.

Despite the large numbers of analyses of ability test differences, the test score differences apparently do not reflect high school grade differences. Among the 1989 SAT examinees, for example, 54 percent of the females and 46 percent of the males report an *A+* grade-point average, and 58 percent of the females and 42 percent of the males report an *A* grade-point average (Educational Testing Service, 1989a). Furthermore, Kelly-Benjamin (1990) reported that when females are allowed additional time in the SAT they outperform males, indicating they are quite capable of the work, but at a slightly slower average pace.

An absolutely crucial consideration is that no ability is totally and exclusively related to gender. Research reports are based on average test scores involving large numbers of students. There always is near-total overlap in the distributions of male and female ability and achievement test scores.

Regarding the predisposition of very gifted students to left-handedness or immune system disorders (Inset 14.1), Benbow (1986) found slightly more left-handed and ambidextrous students among her brightest adolescents, compared with less-talented students who also were participating in Talent Search (15.1 percent versus 10.2 percent, respectively). However, Wiley and Goldstein (1991; Goldstein, Stocking, and Sawyer, 1992)

found no handedness or allergy-proneness difference at all between extremely precocious students and other Talent Search participants, even when looking at males only.

Culture-Based Explanations of Gender Differences in Math

The counterarguments to a biological explanation of male math superiority assert mainly that any gender differences in mathematics ability are cultural in origin. Some specific arguments are these:

Cultural Stereotypes. During adolescence, when sex differences in math skills begin to become especially prominent, males and females also begin their heterosexual interests. Society encourages boys more often than girls to show superior intellectual ability to attract members of the opposite sex. However, girls, in accord with cultural stereotypes, may believe that boys do not like girls who excel in math, and therefore do not seek to develop mathematical abilities (Fox, 1977). When in 1992 a talking Barbie Doll included in her mechanical conversation the statement "Math is really hard," women protested loudly and Mattel withdrew the stereotyped message ("Barbie's Remarks," 1992; "Mathematicians Talk," 1992).

Kolata (1980) emphasized the impact of cultural influences on attitudes toward math in a summary statement about the Johns Hopkins SMPY research. "Although fewer girls than boys qualify for the accelerated math courses . . . , even fewer girls enroll in them." While females who select math study achieve as well as males, few females choose to study math (Fennema and Sherman, 1978).

Unequal Math Training. Based upon her review of research on mathematics learning, Fennema (1980) argued that conclusions about male superiority often have been based on studies in which the number of previous math courses has not been controlled; that is, males with more math background have been compared to females with less background. However, Fox (1981a; also Benbow and Stanley, 1980, 1981, 1983b) noted that the mathematics talent searches conducted at Johns Hopkins University for the SMPY program were at grades 7 and 8, when males and females had equal math training.

Jacquelynne Parsons (1982) argued that the spatial skills leading to strong math problem solving can be trained, and that gender differences would be removed if the training were at least equal.

Table 14.1 compares high school advanced math and science courses taken by males and females between 1982 and 1987. While there are increases for both males and females, the rates of increase for females unfortunately are not as high as for males (Educational Testing Service, 1989b).

Father Identification. As we saw in Chapter 13, several studies (for example, Sutton-Smith, Rosenberg, and Landy, 1968) reported that early father absence, before age 8 or 9, has a depressing effect on later math scores of both males and females. They hypothesized that children learn a mathematical problem-solving thinking style

from their fathers. Helson (1971) similarly reported that creative women mathematicians and scientists tended to identify with their fathers. As noted previously, Hall (1980) attributed the strong math achievement of the gifted girls in her longitudinal study to support by fathers. Therefore it is possible that learning mathematical thinking and problem solving may take place informally in the family through the process of identification with the father. Since boys are more likely to identify with their fathers than girls, boys logically would acquire superior mathematics abilities.

Different Toys. Still another hypothesis is that gender-role stereotyped toys improve visual-spatial abilities for boys more than for girls. Trains, model airplanes, race cars, trucks, electrical sets, Legos, Tinker Toys, and other construction toys all are more likely to be played with by boys. These toys may enhance spatial skills more than the typical dolls, tea sets, coloring books, jump ropes, and needlecraft supplied to girls.

Teacher and Parent Expectations. Mathematics has been considered a male domain by both students and teachers. Ernest (1976) found in inter-

TABLE 14.1 Percentage of High School Graduates Who Took Selected Mathematics and Science Courses by Sex, 1982 and 1987

Courses	Males	Female	Difference
Trigonometry 1982	12.9	11.3	1.6
Trigonometry 1987	21.9	19.0	1.9
Pre-calculus 1982	6.0	5.5	.5
Pre-calculus 1987	13.6	11.3	1.2
Calculus 1982	5.3	4.2	1.1
Calculus 1987	7.6	4.7	2.9
Chemistry 1982	31.7	30.0	1.7
Chemistry 1987	46.3	44.5	1.8
Physics 1982	18.2	10.0	8.2
Physics 1987	25.3	15.0	15.0

Source: "Nation at Risk Study as Part of the 1987 High School Transcript Study", Tabulations, May 19, 1988, Westat, Inc. for the U.S. Department of Education, National Center for Educational Statistics, Tables 33 and 41.

viewing teachers that 41 percent thought boys were better at math than girls, while none thought girls were better. Since teacher expectations may affect achievement by as much as 20 percent (Brophy, 1982; Good and Weinstein, 1986), a *self-fulfilling prophecy* might easily help perpetuate mathematics as a male domain.

Also rooted in cultural stereotypes and expectations, Brody and Fox (1980) found that parents of gifted boys were more likely to see a career in mathematics for their children than were parents of gifted girls.

Parsons, Adler, and Kaczala (1982) and Dickens (1990) came to similar conclusions. Parent and teacher expectations about children's math abilities had a significant impact on their mathematics achievement. However, Raymond and Benbow (1989) did not find parent encouragement of math different for gifted girls than for gifted boys. They did indicate that the typical gender role stereotyped parent behaviors, with fathers more involved with their gifted children in quantitative areas and mothers more concerned with verbal areas, provide stereotyped role models affecting math preferences.

Further insight into female mathematics and teacher expectations comes from a study by Hallinan and Sorensen (1987) which found that "girls with high aptitude in mathematics are less likely to be assigned to the high-ability group than boys" (p. 71). Such inappropriate grouping is likely to impact on girls taking advanced math and science classes despite their aptitude for these courses.

School Support.   In an analysis of schools that successfully teach math and science to girls, Casserly (1979) found that teachers in those schools were not threatened by mathematically gifted girls, that they used older females to tutor younger girls, and that they began good programs before the sixth grade—before girls come to view math as a male subject. Fox (1974) similarly found that girls were successful in a math program for the gifted when school personnel were enthusiastic and supportive of the girls.

Importance of the Math Differences Hypothesis

Differential skill in mathematics is a critical issue in relation to the professional development of gifted females. Male-dominated fields that convey high status and good financial rewards (for example, medicine, engineering, architecture, pharmacy, computer sciences, and all physical sciences) *require skill in mathematics*. A lack of preparation clearly prevents most females from *ever* entering many challenging and rewarding professions. Said then-President Reagan in his 1983 State of the Union address to Congress, "If a child has not acquired good mathematical training by age 16, he or she will never be able to enter the fields of engineering or science."

DIFFERENCES IN EXPECTATIONS, ACHIEVEMENT ORIENTATION, AND ASPIRATIONS

Differences in mathematical preparation create real barriers to the entrance of females into many male-dominated professions. In addition, family, school, and peer expectations discourage a strong achievement orientation, risk-taking, independence, and self-confidence in girls. These pressures can lead to low aspirations which, in turn, result in underachievement.

Family Expectations and Identification

High educational achievement and high career aspirations begin at home. Both mother role-modeling and father expectations have a compelling influence on the achievement orientation of gifted girls.

In regard to career aspirations, many researchers (for example, Altman and Grossman, 1977; Marini, 1978; Radin, 1974; Sutherland, 1978) concluded that career modeling by mothers motivates females to have higher educational and career aspirations.

Fathers' direct expectations of their daughters also may influence female achievement. Radin and Epstein (1975) found that fathers' short- and long-term academic expectations of their daughters were positively correlated with measures of the girls' intellectual functioning. There may be a chicken-egg problem, however. That is, do higher expectations produce the higher intellectual functioning, or vice versa?

Gender-stereotyped expectations of girls—and all women—by their fathers (Lynn, 1974) and dominating fathers (Heilbrun, 1973; Heilbrun, Harrell, and Gillard, 1967) appear to have a negative effect on girls' achievement.

Research on the comparative importance of the mother versus the father role-model for female achievement is not always consistent, nor are the dynamics uncomplicated. Helson (1971), noted earlier, found that creative women mathematicians tended to be oldest daughters who identified with their fathers. Bardwick (1971) also emphasized the importance of girls' identification with their fathers in order to learn important achievement traits such as independence and self-esteem. Drews and Teahan (1957) and Pierce and Bowman (1960), however, concluded that mother dominance was critical in encouraging girls to become career-oriented achievers. On the other hand, some women have sought careers in a direct response to what they perceived as their mothers' "empty lives"—their mothers served as models of what *not* to do.

A recent study of 60 high-ability females, 42 of whom had left home to participate in an early college entrance program, found a consistent association between self-perceived competence and the quality of communication with parents (Callahan, Cornell, and Loyd, 1990). Better communication with mothers was associated with favorable self-perceptions of both job competence and "romantic appeal." One unusual finding was that girls who enjoyed closer relationships with their fathers had poorer self-conceptions of their athletic ability. Hollingworth's (1926) observation that the most intelligent gifted youth experience more social adjustment problems was supported by a negative relationship between IQ on one hand, and perceived social competence, physical appearances, and athletic ability, on the other.

Incidentally, the influence of the media on parents may also impact on their children. Reports of the Benbow and Stanley (1980) research on gender differences in math reasoning appeared in many popular magazines and newspapers. Jacobs and Eccles (1985) discovered that parents exposed to these research findings changed their math expectations of their daughters. Compared to other mothers, mothers who read about the research appeared to expect *less* of their girls in terms of math success. The effect of the exposure on fathers was to increase the importance of their daughters' taking calculus and higher math. Apparently, although the media coverage seemed to encourage mothers to provide an easy way out for their daughters, it inspired fathers to come to their defense.

In conclusion, despite some special circumstances and exceptions, career-oriented mothers do indeed provide strong role models that, along with positive and supportive father expectations, influence educational and career achievement of gifted girls.

Peer Expectations

From early adolescence, and sometimes before, peer expectations play a strong part in directing achievement. Because high intelligence and an achievement orientation sometimes are considered masculine characteristics, girls risk being considered "unfeminine" if they become too involved in school achievement.

Ruth Duskin Feldman, former Quiz Kid and author of the book *Whatever Happened to the Quiz Kids* (1982), shared an anecdote with Rimm that shows only a small change in peer expectations of gifted females. As a college student, she was asked by a male friend if she would rather be told she was smart or beautiful. Her response at that time was, "Beautiful—I know I'm smart!" A recent sequel to this conversation occurred in her daughter's gifted class. The teacher asked the females in the class if they would rather be beautiful or valedictorian. They all indicated they would prefer the latter. She then asked the males how they would feel about dating the class valedictorian. The boys concluded that dating the valedictorian would be fine—provided she was pretty. If peer pressure to achieve has changed for gifted girls, it has changed mainly from the female perspective. Even bright males continue to rank attractiveness ahead of intelligence.

By college age, parent attitudes toward gifted women's career choices appear less important than peer attitudes (Parsons, Frieze, and Ruble, 1978), especially those of male peers. Trigg and Perlman (1976) found that females were more likely to apply to graduate school in less traditional areas if their male friends encouraged them to do so. Horner's (1972) classic "fear of success" syndrome, in which girls suppress high achievement and success because of their fear of "failing as a female," will be discussed later. As one immediately pertinent finding, Horner found that females who received career encouragement from their male friends were less likely to experience fear of success.

School Expectations

From nursery school onward we find continuous documentation of school biases that deter an achievement orientation for females. Serbin and O'Leary (1975) compared differential treatment of boys and girls in 15 nursery school classes and recorded the following behaviors that they felt would reinforce aggressiveness, confidence, and independence in boys, but not girls. Boys were encouraged to work on their own much more often than girls. Teachers rewarded girls for being dependent by responding more when they were near, but gave similar attention to boys regardless of physical distance. All 15 teachers gave more attention to boys than girls, including more individualized instruction and more tangible and verbal rewards.

When teacher feedback is given to children, Dweck and Bush (1976; Nichols, 1979) found that poor performance often is described as "lack of ability" in girls, while similar poor performance is noted as "not working hard enough" with boys. This difference is important. If poor performance is seen by students (girls) as lack of *ability*, then increased effort will not solve the problem. However, if poor performance is interpreted as lack of *effort*, then the students (boys) will be motivated to work harder to achieve (Weiner, 1985).

Fox (1981b) interestingly noted that the "critical thought and questioning mind" of the young boy is likely to be described as "insolence" or an "argumentative nature" in a girl.

Casserly (1979) reported gender differences in willingness to take Advanced Placement courses. Although girls outnumber boys in traditionally "female" Advanced Placement courses (for example, English, Spanish, and French), girls usually take fewer Advanced Placement courses than boys in math, history, classics, German, and all sciences. In analyzing differences between schools that produce high-achieving girls and those that do not, Casserly identified two disarmingly simple factors: (1) The schools producing high-achieving girls used a tracking program that made Advanced Placement classes a natural sequence, and (2) teachers both actively recruited girls for the Advanced Placement classes and expected them to be high achievers.

School counselors have been found to possess gender stereotypes that work against female achievement. In one survey, Petro and Putman (1979) found that both male and female school counselors agreed that girls are more "... easily excitable in a minor crisis, easily influenced, home-oriented, passive, noncompetitive, indecisive, and easily hurt." Other evidence shows that female counselors often project their own fears of science and math into girls, cautioning them that they may not get good grades if they take difficult math and science courses (Casserly, 1979).

Counselors also suggest to girls, more often than to boys, that they need time for their social lives and/or that they should avoid courses in math and science. Quoting one counselor, "... there are so many fun things going on. I think they'll be busy enough and they [girls] can get into the serious work in college" (Casserly, 1979). The following quote was considered by Casserly to be representative of male counselors: "There are men with Ph.Ds in physics all over the place who can't get jobs. Why should we encourage girls?"

A study by Cooley *et al.* (1984) compared the expectations of male and female teachers for male and female gifted students. Although male teachers are now seeing gifted females in professions that were previously closed to them, male teachers continue to view their female students in a gender-role stereotyped manner. Male teachers saw their gifted female students as more emotional, high strung, and gullible than did female teachers and as less imaginative, less curious, less inventive, less individualistic, and less impulsive than did the female teachers. Both male and female teachers viewed the gifted male students as more competent in critical/logical thinking skills and in creative problem-solving skills than the gifted females.

From preschool to college, then, and despite improvements in recent years, many teachers and counselors by innuendo and by action discourage females from developing their talents equally with males.

Self-Expectations

Female aspirations and achievement orientations surely are changing. This change must include altered self-perceptions and self-expectations. If gifted females are to develop their talents and make their contributions to society they must acquire confidence and strong achievement needs, and they must make plans for a sound education.

Noble (1989), who focuses on problems of gifted females in her clinical practice, reported that gifted females are often unaware of and/or frightened by their own potential. She believes these inappropriate self-expectations are related to concerns about rejection by families, teachers, and peers; growing up in impaired families; and families that underestimate their abilities.

Self-expectations of females may be changing. Karnes and D'Ilio (1989) questioned 49 gifted

boys and 48 gifted girls (Grades 4–6) about their gender-related impressions for a list of 34 leadership positions. Although boys continued to have more traditional gender-role stereotyped biases, females did not. Girls believed that most leadership roles are suitable for either gender.

Research suggests four important factors that seem to be linked to the lower self-expectations and aspirations of females: (1) a lower sense of competence, (2) a tendency to attribute failures to oneself and successes to external factors, (3) lower achievement motivation, and (4) the "fear of success" syndrome mentioned above. These undoubtedly are interrelated, and together decrease the likelihood of gifted women aspiring to challenging professions. Let's look at each of the four.

Low Sense of Competence.   First, studies of the sense of competence among women repeatedly show that, on average, women exhibit lower feelings of competence than do men. For example, Stake (1981) found that females tended to score lower than males in predicting their future ability to perform well in high-level careers. Addison (1981) similarly found that in evaluating their own performance, females tended to underestimate their degree of success while males tended to overestimate it.

In a program in which gifted seventh- and eighth-grade students were given an opportunity for grade acceleration, only 54 percent of the girls chose acceleration, compared with 73 percent of the boys (Fox, 1977). Said Fox, girls were less confident in trying something new and were more fearful of failure. They also experienced more problems of self-esteem—which were unrelated to actual ability—and were more fearful of peer rejection. Hall (1982) similarly reported that girls were less likely than boys to enter college early.

Maccoby and Jacklin's (1974) conclusion that boys are more intensely socialized toward competition and success provides a reasonable explanation for their developing a stronger sense of personal competence.

In a study of the social self-esteem of 260

gifted and talented female adolescents, Hollinger (1985) found that girls who had self-perceptions most similar to male gender-role stereotyped instrumentality had the greatest social self-esteem. In her study of 188 gifted male and 90 gifted female adolescents, Mills (1980) similarly found evidence of intellectual advantage for both sexes among those who showed instrumental or masculine personality characteristics.

Denny (cited in Callahan, 1991) studied self-perceptions of competence of a group of high school valedictorians. At graduation, 23% of the males and 21% of the females rated themselves "far above average." By the end of their sophomore year of college, that percentage decreased one point for males and 17 points for females—only 4% of the females continued to perceive themselves as highly competent.

Attributional Differences. The lower confidence that females exhibit is reflected in studies of causal attributions they make. Studies of both children and adults report a similar gender-related tendency (Deaux, 1976; Frieze, 1975; Post, 1981). Females tend to attribute their successes to hard work or to luck, but their failures to lack of ability. Males tend to follow the reverse attribution process, blaming others, bad luck, or their lack of effort for failures, but crediting their own high abilities for successes.

An extreme form of this attribution difference is found in the *imposter* phenomenon (Clance and Imes, 1978) in which women who have achieved success indicate that they do not believe they are capable of being in their position, and that their inability will somehow be discovered. It is surely an example of extremely low confidence when women who receive recognition for their achievements still are unable to attribute this success to their own ability.

Low Achievement Motivation. Our third factor in female underachievement is low achievement motivation. A basic premise of achievement motivation theory is that persons with strong needs to

achieve will strive to succeed in situations requiring intelligence and leadership (Atkinson, 1974; McClelland, 1976). The need to achieve is a highly consistent personality trait that begins developing as early as the second grade.

Efforts to teach achievement motivation basically encourage the learner to think as achievement-oriented individuals do; that is, to (1) value success and achievement, (2) accept moderate risks, (3) set realistic and achievable goals, and (4) feel confident that he or she can achieve these goals.

We have seen throughout this chapter that cultural stereotypes, biases, and home and school expectations work to reduce female independence and aggressiveness and, consequently, their needs for high-level academic and career achievement. Achievement motivation leaders McClelland (1976) and Atkinson (1974) attribute needs for achievement to learning, rather than heredity, and point to parental influence in childhood as the crucial factor.

As an interesting historical fact, in an 873-page compilation of research into achievement motivation, a single footnote commented on achievement motivation research with women (Atkinson, 1958).

Fear of Success. As early as 1935 Margaret Mead observed that "... the achieving girl [is threatened that she] will never be chosen by a member of the opposite sex." More recent research on women's fear of success (Horner, 1972; Zinberg, 1974) suggests that in mixed gender competition, women are motivated to *avoid* success. Horner hypothesized that aggressiveness traditionally is considered a masculine characteristic. Since competitiveness or being too intellectual is not ladylike, women fear that success in the achievement domain may mean failure as a female.

In Horner's research, 90 female college students were asked to respond to the statement below with "Anne" as the character, while 88 males responded to the same statement with "John" in it:

> After first term finals Anne (John) finds herself (himself) at the top of her (his) medical school class.

The scoring of the stories showed that 90 percent of the males described rosy futures for John—but a full 65 percent of the females predicted an unhappy outcome for Anne. Anne's academic success was described as bringing her social rejection in the form of unpopularity, loneliness, lack of femininity, and low marriageability. Success in competition with males was seen as leading to feelings of anxiety, guilt, despair, and doubt about femininity and normalcy. Based on these sad predictions for bright women, Horner coined the phase *fear of success* and explained that this paradox in women's achievement motivation would cause many women to feel defensive about their achievements if they are successful, and sometimes will prevent them from achieving in the first place.

To be fair, we must note that in the dozens of follow-up studies of women's fear of success, the results have been inconsistent or else have demonstrated qualifying circumstances. For example, both Alper (1974) and Katz (1973) found that fear of success scores are considerably lower when the situation is less threatening. For example, when reference to "medical school" was omitted (Alper) or when it was noted that half of "Anne's" medical school classmates were women (Katz), fear of success scores dropped considerably.

EDUCATING GIFTED FEMALES

Society no doubt will continue to improve in providing a support system in which gifted women may develop their potential equally with men. Schools, however, must take a leadership role in fostering this equal development. In this section the model explored in Chapter 13, dealing with underachievement, will be used to provide some realistic guidelines that can help teachers, counselors, and parents reverse underachievement in females. That model includes the following steps:

1. Assessing skills, abilities, and home and school reinforcement contingencies

2. Improving communication between home and school
3. Changing the expectations of important others
4. Improving model identification
5. Correcting skill deficiencies
6. Modifying reinforcements at home and school

Since cultural underachievement is a more extensive problem than individual underachievement, there will be some additional special problems that educators must consider in programming for underachieving girls.

Assessing Skills, Abilities, and Reinforcement Contingencies

School district administrators, principals, teachers, counselors, and others need, at the minimum, to ask the following questions:

1. Are gender-role stereotyped books, films, and other media avoided in the classroom and library?

2. Are spatially oriented activities, such as mathematics and computer work, introduced early so that both girls and boys begin learning these skills before peer pressures intervene?

3. Are females equally encouraged to participate in competitive activities?

4. Are counselors and teachers being educated in the opportunities for and abilities of females?

5. Are students and their parents being educated regarding the broad range of opportunities for females?

6. Are girls encouraged to take leadership roles in the school?

7. Are gifted girls encouraged to take advanced courses in all curricular areas?

8. Are students exposed to a variety of successful, professional female models?

9. Are opportunities available for assertiveness training for females?

10. Are some all-female group guidance experiences being provided, so that girls may deal with

problems related to femininity, self-confidence, and an achievement orientation?

11. Are efforts being made to erase the stigma of a high achievement orientation for females?

12. Are the rewards for career achievements for females being stressed equally with those for males?

To the extent that answers to these questions reflect nonencouragement of high-level educational and career aspirations for gifted girls, changes should be made.

Communication Between Home and School

Gifted coordinators, guidance counselors, and classroom teachers may all become involved in coordinated efforts to communicate with parents about the achievement, course selection, and career expectations for gifted girls. A series of short letters to the parents of gifted students, including some specific suggestions of ways in which parents can help encourage gender equity and female talent development, may help. One example of such a letter appears in Inset 14.2. Notice that only one topic is addressed in this letter, encouraging girls to take higher-level mathematics and science courses. Other topics for brief letters could include strengthening the girl's career orientation, building confidence, the value of higher education, the role of risk-taking in success, and perhaps even the eventual division of household chores. In each case, it is important to emphasize the rewards available to females who develop their abilities, and to encourage parents to reward girls for accepting special challenges. This is a difficult message to give many parents; they have been socialized in a culture that has fostered underachievement in women, and therefore they themselves usually are guilty of reinforcing gender-role stereotypes.

Changing the Expectations of Important Others

Teachers, parents, and girls themselves must acquire the expectation that females can achieve.

Providing teachers, parents, and gifted students with evidence of female achievement in traditionally male-dominated fields is a most effective method of changing expectations. Internship programs (in which girls work with women executives and other women professionals), career women guest speakers, and field trips to see the accomplishments of talented women all provide living evidence of female accomplishment. Local professional women's organizations, such as American Association of University Women or the local chapter of the National Organization for Women, may be pleased to cooperate with such projects.

Opportunities to hear, see, and work with high-achieving women can be supplemented by reading and research projects that provide students with the opportunity to learn about achieving women and to understand the training and personality characteristics needed for high career achievement. The study of women's achievements in the arts, sciences, and in literature will help gifted girls, their teachers, and their families to recognize the reality of female talent and accomplishment.

Reis and Dobyns (1991) prepared an annotated bibliography of nonfictional books and curricular materials for gifted females which are intended to help girls change their self-expectations. See Appendix 14.1 at the end of this chapter.

Peer expectations are perhaps the most difficult area in which to effect change. One way to encourage peer reinforcement is to provide coeducational group meetings for gifted students, both educational and semisocial. The kind of rapport and mutual support that usually develops in such meetings encourages all gifted students to challenge themselves. Discussion in which students air their concerns (for example, regarding risk-taking or the career-homemaker conflict) help give females the support they will need. Discussions of careers that are appropriate for all gifted students will emphasize the acceptability and desirability of female talent development. The rapport established among gifted peers also can create a more supportive and rewarding social life

INSET 14.2 _____

Challenge Senior High School, Everytown, Wisconsin

Dear Mr. and Mrs. Kirkpatrick:

We would like to recommend that your daughter Sara select Calculus, Advanced Biology, and Advanced Chemistry among her courses in grade 12. Her past performances in mathematics and science suggest that she would benefit from these challenging courses. These courses are complex and do involve more homework than some other selections that she might make. As a result, some high school students, particularly females, are hesitant in selecting them for fear that they may not perform as well as they typically have performed. Mainly these students worry about a negative effect on their grade-point average or about peer pressure that may make high-level science or math courses appear to be more male-related.

We hope that Sara will be encouraged to select these courses because advanced courses in science and math can provide many more career options for her. Challenge Senior High School has taken the following steps to encourage capable girls to select these difficult courses:

1. Course grades are weighted so that a "B" grade in these courses is the equivalent of 4 points or an "A" in easier courses.
2. Courses are taught by both male and female teachers who were selected based on their willingness to provide extra support and help in these challenging courses.
3. Guest lecturers from professional science and mathematics areas will provide information to students on career areas in science and mathematics.
4. Women guest lecturers will share with girls their experiences on how to combine careers and homemaking roles.
5. Students who select these courses will be eligible for Advanced Placement testing and may therefore be able to earn college credits during their senior year in high school.

You or Sara may want to chat with me further about our special program to encourage bright female students to fulfill their intellectual potential. Please don't hesitate to call me to discuss Sara's special concerns. We will also be holding a special meeting for gifted girls and their parents in early March and I hope to meet you at that time.

Sincerely yours,

Margaret Nellon

Margaret Nellon
Guidance Counselor

for gifted girls, which is an important variety of peer reinforcement.

Model Identification

Although there are fewer female models with whom gifted girls may identify—for example, women doctors, lawyers, researchers, or executives—they nonetheless can be located, even in small communities. Such persons provide the aspiring gifted girl with the assurance that it is possible for a woman to achieve a career goal and at the same time enjoy a satisfying marriage if she so chooses.

At extremely high achievement levels, however, the scarcity of female models can lead to doubly strong anxieties related to the conflict of successfully coordinating a marriage with a career requiring long, arduous preparation. The extent of this problem was recently shared by a woman M.D./Ph.D student at Harvard Medical School. She had failed to find even one woman, either at Harvard or in her research field, who had successfully combined marriage with a career in medical research. The recognition that she was investing so much time and energy to prepare for a career-marriage role, with virtually no evidence that success was possible, left her extremely frustrated. She wanted desperately to find a model who could provide encouragement.

Research by Arnold and Denny (1985) found that female high school valedictorians outperformed men in college but did not perform as well in the work world. One of the experiences that was important for women who continued to achieve was close interaction with college faculty and professionals. Kaufmann *et al.* (1986) also verified the importance of mentors for successful females in their study of Presidential Scholars. Having a mentor appeared to equalize the income of women and men. Educators need to help girls locate appropriate role models. The models can share with gifted girls the experiences, rewards, frustrations, and decision-making processes that accompanied

their accomplishments. In view of their own difficult experiences, they are often eager to share insights with gifted young women. Silverman (1991) recommends that teachers or counselors arrange opportunities for girls to shadow women professionals to observe them at work.

Correcting Skill Deficiencies

The skill deficiencies of gifted girls usually are found in math and science. Such deficiencies can be prevented by encouraging high school girls to take the necessary advanced courses, which will permit their eventual entry into desirable college majors and prestigious careers.

One good approach to attracting girls to advanced math classes is to encourage women teachers to teach them. Also, reasonable grading criteria, good teaching, and smaller classes that allow individual attention can make these classes more attractive to all students, and less threatening to gifted girls. Many students, male and female, avoid math classes in fear of lowering their grade-point averages, which can reduce their chances for high school awards and college admission and scholarships. If advanced math course grades are weighted such that an *A* earns 5 points instead of the usual 4, etc., gifted males and females both will be less intimidated by such courses. Some secondary schools have successfully implemented such a grading plan.

Females can be encouraged to receive tutoring in high school mathematics if they find it difficult. Tutoring can facilitate the acquisition of math concepts, increase scores on the SAT-M, and may be important in increasing the academic confidence of females (Olszewski-Kubilius *et al.*, 1990).

We should note that not all areas in which some females are deficient are academic. Teachers and counselors must ensure that gifted girls are helped in developing autonomy, self-esteem, self-confidence, a willingness to compete, leadership, and assertiveness (Addison, 1979; Fox, 1981b; Wolleat, 1979).

Changing Reinforcements at Home and School

This last step is probably the most critical one. Gifted girls are frequently reinforced for being good, perfect, pretty, and well-adjusted. None of these reinforcements helps prepare them for careers ahead. Here are some recommendations for change.

Perfectionism. Take the word *perfect* out of your vocabulary at home and at school. Each time parents and teachers tell girls that they have completed a task "perfectly" or that they are "perfect," they reinforce pressure toward perfectionism. Fathers must be especially careful not to describe their little girls in those extreme terms. Fathers usually believe it to be a compliment that builds confidence, but girls internalize it as an expectation and an impossible pressure.

Social Life. Although making friends can be positive, aloneness and independence are equally valuable. Do not make a child feel uncomfortable in independent activities. Encourage alone time. In her study of the childhoods of eminent women, Kerr (1985) found that they spent an unusual amount of time alone. She cites Gertrude Stein and Eleanor Roosevelt as examples. Most eminent women had a sense of being "different." Overemphasizing the importance of being "well adjusted" has the impact of internalizing a pressure to be popular and to make excessive compromises to please others.

Challenge. The girl who gets all *A*s and pleases everyone is not anxious to take the risk of acceleration or other extra challenge. Explain that you would rather she take the risk of doing harder work even if she is not as successful. Expect her to do more than is required and encourage her to take accelerated courses even if they are difficult. It is better to experience difficulty early and to learn to persevere and struggle than to have eight or ten years of perfect work that is easily accomplished. Pressure for perfection prevents risk taking.

Appearance. Refuse to emphasize appearance. Whether she is pretty or not, from early on do not make a fuss about attractiveness. Reasonable neatness and cleanliness are acceptable values. Early emphasis on beauty and Barbie dolls becomes an internalized pressure to be thin, to wear excessive makeup, and to concentrate on fashion instead of intellectual accomplishment, kindness, creativity, and other important values. This is contrary to the advice given by Marone (1988) in her popular book, *How to Father a Successful Daughter*. She recommends that fathers praise their daughter's appearance. Since praise conveys the praiser's value system, paying too much attention to appearance, and not enough to intellect and creativity, will surely bias the daughter's perception of what's important. If fathers hope that their daughters will become models, fashion queens, or fashion designers, emphasis on appearance is probably appropriate.

Competition. Teach little girls about realistic competition. Do not protect them from failure experiences. Do not just "let them win" at games. Teach them either to laugh at their losses or to analyze them for future learning. Even friendly insults help them to build some resilience to criticism. Do not let them use tears to attract unnecessary protection or shelter.

Careers. As a mother, if you are a career woman do not apologize for your work. Let your daughter know that you and she are better off because you have a career, not only for the money, but for the way you feel about yourself and for the independence you can permit her. If you are an educator, let girls know you are proud of your career so they will not assume that you work only because you must have a salary. Pride in your career will inspire your daughter toward pride in establishing her own career. Meckstroth (1989) suggested that parents encourage their daughters to develop a close relationship with a woman who likes her and is in love with her own life and work.

Male Attitudes.   Perhaps the most difficult reinforcer to change is male attitudes toward females. Convincing gifted boys to appreciate intelligent and assertive females will help prevent the pressures that girls feel about appearing too intelligent. Explaining to males that the best kind of relationships come from mutual respect rather than a perceived need to feel more intelligent than females is a critical key to supporting intelligent thinking and acting in girls. Gifted girls tend to like gifted boys, but the latter often feel threatened in the company

of very bright girls. Also, the deemphasis on appearance or the "pretty girl" message to sons and male students will make for better self-actualization of both females and males.

All-Girl Classes or Schools.   Some evidence suggests that all-girl classes and all-girl schools help some females to take leadership positions and courses they otherwise would avoid (e.g., Riordan, 1990; Tidball, 1973). Tidball (1986) reported that women's colleges produce the largest proportion of women who go on for Ph.D degrees. Sebrechts (1992) pointed out that more women in women's colleges select math and science majors, compared with those in other colleges (Table 14.2). She main-

TABLE 14.2   Percentages of Students Enrolled in Selected Majors by Year at Women's and Coeducational Colleges.

	Women in Women's Colleges	Women in Other Colleges	Men
1971			
Economics	1.2%	.5%	2.9%
Life Sciences	3.8%	2.8%	5.3%
Physical Sciences	1.4%	.8%	3.9%
Mathematics	3.6%	2.5%	3.2%
1976			
Economics	2.1%	.6%	2.3%
Life Sciences	6.4%	4.4%	7.0%
Physical Sciences	1.8%	.9%	3.4%
Mathematics	2.1%	1.5%	1.9%
1981			
Economics	3.2%	1.2%	2.4%
Life Sciences	6.1%	4.0%	5.1%
Physical Sciences	1.9%	1.2%	3.8%
Mathematics	1.6%	1.0%	1.3%
1986			
Economics	4.0%	1.4%	2.9%
Life Sciences	5.4%	3.6%	4.1%
Physical Sciences	1.7%	1.2%	3.2%
Mathematics	2.3%	1.5%	1.8%

Source: National Center for Education Statistics, U.S. Department of Education. From Sebrecht's (1992).

tains that women who are intellectually talented in science and math continue to select women's colleges possibly to avoid sociocultural pressures about women's inability to succeed in these disciplines. Subotnik and Strauss (1990) found that girls in an all-female school performed better in Advanced Placement calculus classes than girls in all-female classes in a mixed-gender school.

SUMMARY

The education of gifted women historically has been largely ignored. Some early influential educators publicly specified a nurturing domestic role for women. The concept of a "disappearance of giftedness in girls" implies that they excel in childhood but frequently underachieve as adults.

In the work force, women continue to be dramatically underrepresented in most traditionally male professions. Salaries also are comparatively poor.

Women are underrepresented in educational administration in elementary and secondary schools, in college teaching, and in college administration. While women's entry into "male careers" is improving, the percentage of women in these fields still is low.

Women's life satisfactions stereotypically have been tied to their husbands' career success plus success as a wife and mother. On the average, working and professional women show higher life satisfaction—greater self-esteem and greater feelings of competence—than full-time housewives.

The main problem is the home-career conflict. While there is no easy solution, some women decide in advance which role comes first (the family), compartmentalize the two roles, and often compromise to fit husband and family needs. In the area of science there is now some documentation that indicates that marriage may have an enhancing effect on scientific productivity, particularly if the woman is married to another scientist.

All gifted women should have the opportunity and encouragement to develop their talents and become professionals.

Research suggests biological gender differences in levels of physical activity and aggression. Some scholars claim stronger right-hemisphere spatial abilities for males. Tomboyism, due to biological masculinization of sex organs, produces girls with many masculine interests and traits.

A list of gender differences in abilities and traits shows that, on the average, females tend to be physically, psychologically, and socially healthier. Sociocultural differences in the treatment of the sexes begin almost at birth. Differences exist in room decorations and toys and stereotyped characteristics, for example, as reflected in Bem's *Sex-Role Inventory*. Textbooks, literature, and the media, especially television, reinforce sex-role stereotypes.

The most heated debate centers on whether males have superior math ability, stemming from allegedly superior spatial abilities. Prominent in the issue are the Benbow and Stanley SAT-M statistics.

Counterarguments propose that the math difference may be due to (1) cultural stereotypes, (2) unequal math training, (3) boys' identification with father, (4) different types of toys, (5) teacher and parent expectations, and (6) lack of school support. The issue is highly important because a lack of mathematical training will close—and is closing—permanently the doors to many high-status and well-paying male-dominated careers.

High educational and career achievements are related to family expectations. Identification with mother, especially a career mother, appears important. Fathers' expectations of their daughters also influence achievement. Gender-role stereotyped family expectations work against girls' achievement. Research shows that creative women mathematicians tend to identify with their fathers. Traits of independence and self-esteem also may be learned from fathers.

Peer attitudes and expectations often depress female achievement. School expectations reward male independence, confidence, and aggressiveness, but reward female conformity. Likewise, female poor performance sometimes is attributed to lack of ability; male poor performance to lack of effort, leading boys to work harder.

Schools that successfully produce high-achieving girls make Advanced Placement classes a natural part of the sequence, and actively recruit girls for the Advanced Placement classes. School counselors sometimes perpetuate cultural stereotypes of male versus female traits, and often counsel girls to avoid math and science. Regarding self-expectations, women tend to have a lower sense of competence and self-esteem, attribute failure to lack of ability, and have lower achievement motivation.

Rimm's six-part model was presented as a guide for dealing with female underachievement.

All-girl classes and all-girl schools seem to foster leadership and the acceptance of academically challenging coursework.

APPENDIX 14.1.

Selected Bibliography of Nonfictional Books and Curricular Materials to Encourage Gifted Females

Sally M. Reis and Sally McClure Dobyns

Publisher	Year	Title	Author	Brief Description
ART				
VSE Publisher 212 South Dexter Denver, CO 80222	1987	History of Women Artists for Children	Epstein, Vivian Sheldon	History of women in art told through brief biographies of 29 women artists of distinction. Includes example of each artist's work. (grades PS–6)
AWARENESS				
Advocacy Press P.O. Box 236 Santa Barbara, CA 93120	1984	Choices: A Teen Woman's Journal for Self-awareness and Personal Planning	Bingham, Mindy; Edmondson, Judy; Stryker, Sandy	A journal designed for adolescent girls. Includes chapters about attitudes of society toward women, economics, values and decision-making, assertiveness, future planning for education, family and work, financial aid for education and exercises for the future. The journal is beautifully illustrated and includes open-ended exercises on budgets and decision-making. In a readable format with cartoons and appropriate quotations. Highly recommended! (grades 8-12)
Avon Books P.O. Box 767 Dresden, TX 38225	1978	Pulling Your Own Strings	Dyer, W.W.	A "how-to" book which focuses on being a decision-maker and action-oriented person. Contains sample dialogues, strategies, and checklists— great for planning activities for bright females.
Bantam Press 666 5th Avenue New York, NY 10103	1987	Free to Be . . . You and Me	Thomas, Marlo; Steinem, Gloria; Pogrebin, Letty Cottin	Collection of stories and songs which are designed to expand children's horizons. Includes: "The Story of X" . . . about stereotypes and expectations: "Atlanta" . . . fairy tale about a princess who is a winner and decides her own future.

Publisher	Year	Title	Author	Brief Description
AWARENESS (Continued)				
National Black Child Development Institute Washington, DC	1987	Beyond the Stereotypes: A Guide to Resources for Black Girls and Young Girls	Moore, E.K.; Vassall, M.A.; and Wilson, J.	This reference book provides lists of books, sound recordings and videos, annotated and classified by age group (3–7, 8–11, 12–15, 16 and up).
Stein and Day Publishers Scarborough House Briarcliff Manor, NY 10510	1983	Beyond Bartlett	Cooper, Jilly and Hartman, Tom	Quotations by and about women.
The Time Inc. Magazine Co. Rockefeller Center New York, NY 10020	1990 (fall)	Women: The Road Ahead *Time:* Special Issue		Topics in this special issue of *Time* include women in politics, inequality around the globe, profiles of 10 extraordinary women, women in the 21st century and the changing family.
BIOGRAPHY Aristoplay P.O. Box 7028 Ann Arbor, MI 48107		Great Women		Three terrific biographical card games to introduce players to outstanding American women—an aspect of America's heritage often missing from our history books. Each game played like rummy. Ages 10 to adult, 2 or more players.
Little, Brown & Co. (Joy St. Books)	1989	Ragtime Tumpie	Schroeder, Alan	Tumpie, a young black girl who will later become famous as the dancer Josephine Baker, longs to find the opportunity to dance amid the poverty and vivacious street life of St. Louis in the early 1900's. (grades K-4)
National Women's Hall of Fame 76 Fall Street, P.O. Box 335 Seneca Falls, NY 13168	1989	Phases and Phrases		Includes biographical information and charcoal illustration of all 42 women in the National Women's Hall of Fame. Among others: Susan B. Anthony Mary Cassatt Margaret Mead Eleanor Roosevelt Elizabeth Cady Stanton Harriet Tubman

APPENDIX 14.1.   (Continued)

Publisher	Year	Title	Author	Brief Description
BIOGRAPHY (Continued)				
Penguin USA 120 Woodbine Street Bergenfield, NJ 07621	1973	They Led the Way: Fourteen American Women. (Original title: Women Themselves)	Johnston, Johanna	Brief biographies of American women were instrumental in American history are presented. (grades 2–6)
CAREERS				
The Equity Institute: Maryland Box 30245 Bethesda, MD 20814		From Here to There: Exploring the Apprentice-to-Journey-Worker Career Ladder with Girls and Boys in Grades 1-9. A Multimedia Approach		This of interest to young gifted girls, not necessarily because they will grow up to work in the trades, but because children are fascinated with details about non-traditional lines of work. Lessons include stories, worksheets, filmstrips, plays, math, games, history, and problem solving.
VSE Publisher 212 South Dexter Denver, CO 80222	1980	The ABC's of What A Girl Can Be	Epstein, Vivian Sheldon	From Architect to Zookeeper—illustrated non-traditional career possibilities for young girls to consider. (grades PS–3)
CURRICULAR MATERIALS				
Feminist Press 311 W. 94th Street New York, NY 10128	1981	Books for Today's Young Readers	Bracken, Jeanne; Wigutoff, Sharon	An annotated bibliography of recommended fiction for ages 10–14.
Feminist Press 311 W. 94th Street New York, NY 10128	1986	Feminist Resources for Schools and Colleges: A Guide to Curricular Materials	Chapman, Anne (Ed.)	An essential resource for school and college teachers who wish to increase their own and their students' knowledge of the new scholarship on women and gender. Entries include books, articles, pamphlets, films, and cassettes, with concise annotations about content, approach, and style. Subject areas covered include American and European history, literature, the social sciences, mathematics, and art.
Learning Publications, Inc. P.O. Box 1326 Holmes Beach, FL 33509	1980	Boys and Girls Together: Non-sexist Activities for Elementary Schools	Cain, Mary Alexander	Activities for establishing sex equity in the classroom using the present curriculum. Uses materials already found in the classroom.

Publisher	Year	Title	Author	Brief Description
CURRICULAR MATERIALS (Continued)				
National Women's Hall of Fame 76 Fall Street P.O. Box 335 Seneca Falls, NY 13168	1986	The Times and Triumphs of American Women	Scott, Elaine (Ed.)	An educational kit featuring women from the past and present: women who have contributed to the development of our country through their outstanding achievements in the arts, athletics, education, government, humanitarianism, and science. Exercises and activities relate directly to the material covered within the book. Some will require additional research. (grades 4-9)
HISTORY Aristoplay P.O. Box 7529 Ann Arbor, MI 48107		Noted Women		A graceful time-line poster highlighting distinguished women from the mid-18th century to the present. Red and black on glossy white paper. 24" x 24".
Feminist Press 311 W. 94th Street New York, NY 10128	1981	Women Have Always Worked: An Historical Overview	Kessler-Harris, A.	An overview of women's work experiences in the United States. Focuses on the tension between women's work inside and outside the home; weaves together material about diverse groups of women— immigrant and black women; wealthy, poor, and middle-class women.
Houghton Mifflin One Beacon Street Boston, MA 02108	1979	Women of America: A History	Berkin, C. and Norton, M.	Traces circumstances of women in America from 1600 and looks at the future of women. Topics include the Protestant and Quaker views of women, Irish working women, Chinese immigrant women in 19th century California, the feminization of academe and the role of women in World War II. Provides extensive suggestions for further reading.

APPENDIX 14.1.   (Continued)

Publisher	Year	Title	Author	Brief Description
HISTORY (Continued) National Women's History Project 7738 Bell Road Windsor, CA 95492-8515		National Women's History Month		Excellent resources for infusing women into the study of history. Books, films, posters.
VSE Publisher 212 South Dexter Denver, CO 80222	1984	History of Women for Children	Epstein, Vivian Sheldon	Designed for children from preschool age through 4th grade, this book balances its message of women's plight through the ages by listing achievements women of all races and creeds have made against great odds. (grades PS-5)
INVENTION William Morrow & Co. Publishers 39 Plymouth Street Fairfield, NJ 07007	1988	Mothers of Invention: From the Bra to the Bomb, Forgotten Women & Their Unforgettable Ideas	Vare, Ethlie Ann and Ptacek, Greg	Women were the co-inventors of everything from penicillin to the bomb. This excellent resource celebrates female inventors.
LITERATURE Houghton-Mifflin One Beacon Street Boston, MA 02108	1976	By Women: An Anthology of Literature	Kirschner, L. and Folsom, M.	Eighty-eight selections, classical to contemporary, representing the creative energies of women. Works of more than seventy writers including: Willa Cather, Emily Dickinson, Isak Dinesen, Sarah Orne Jewett, Doris Lessing, Katherine Mansfield, Edna St. Vincent Millay, Anais Nin, Flannery O'Connor, Katherine Anne Porter, Adrienne Rich, Eudora Welty, Jessamyn West, and Virginia Woolf. Biographical sketch of each writer.
W.W. Norton 500 Fifth Avenue New York, NY 10036	1985	The Norton Anthology of Literature by Women: The Tradition in English	Gilbert, S.M. and Gubar, S.	This landmark collection brings together in a single volume major works by over 150 women authors from all the world's English-speaking countries. Authors include Jane Austen, Ann Bradstreet, Phyllis Wheatley, Sojourner Truth, Shirley Jackson, Toni Morrison, Grace Paley, Maya Angelou, Margaret Atwood, and Alice Walker.

Publisher	Year	Title	Author	Brief Description
MATH				
Eureka Catalog Lawrence Hall of Science University of California Berkeley, CA 94702	1985	Math for Girls and Other Problem Solvers	Downie, Diane; Slesnik, Twila; and Slenmark, Jean Kerr	This book includes curricular ideas and game sheets developed at the Lawrence Hall of Science in a class entitled "Math for Girls." It includes problem solving and other activities geared to make mathematics more interesting and enjoyable for all students at the upper elementary and secondary grade levels.
Gallopade Publishing Group 235 East Ponce de Leon Suite 100 Decatur, GA 30030	1989	Math for Girls: The Book with the Number to Get Girls to Love and Excel in Math!	Marsh, Carole	Stories, puzzles, games, and problems to make math enjoyable. Variety of topics designed to appeal to girls include parties, music, tennis, pizza, and friends. (grades 3-9)
OUT-OF-PRINT-BUT-WORTH-A-TRIP-TO-YOUR-LIBRARY				
Addison-Wesley Publishers South Street Reading, MA 01867	1978	Math Equals: Biographies of Women Mathematicians and Related Activities (out-of-print 1989)	Perl, Teri	The biographies of female mathematicians presented as are their major contributions to the field of mathematics.
Atheneum	1973	Girls Are Equal Too: The Women's Movement for Teens	Carlson, Dale	Grades 6-7
Feminist Press	1982	Everywoman's Guide Colleges and Universities	Howe, Florence, et. al (Eds.)	For young women interested in attending a college or university which has many services, options, and female role models, this is the handbook to consult. It can be used as a check against colleges of interest to see how they rate in opportunities for young women. (If a college checks out unfavorably in 1982, keep in mind that the situation may have improved since this was published.)
Garrard	1971	Susan B. Anthony: Pioneer in Women's Rights	Peterson, Helen S.	Grades 3-6

APPENDIX 14.1.   (Continued)

Publisher	Year	Title	Author	Brief Description
OUT-OF-PRINT-BUT-WORTH-A-TRIP-TO-YOUR-LIBRARY (Continued)				
Lothrop	1967	Petticoat Politics: How American Women Won the Right to Vote	Faber, Doris	Grades 7 and up
McGraw	1971	Single Standard	Harris, Janet	Grades 7 and up
Prentice-Hall, Inc.	1981	Equal Their Chances: Children's Activities for Non-sexist Learning	Shapiro, Kramer, and Hunerberg	
Putnam	1975	Women in Sports Series	Haney, Lynn	Titles included: Chris Evert I Am A Dancer Perfect Balance Show Writer Skater's Profile Ride 'em Cowgirl
Random House	1972	Young and Female: Turning Points in the Lives of Eight American Women	Ross, Pat	Grades 6 and up
T.Y. Crowell	1959	Women Who Led the Way: Eight Pioneers for Equal Rights	Boynick, David	Grades 7 and up
Warne	1963	Women Who Made History	Boter, Mary C.	Grades 7–9
Watts	1972	Women's Rights	Stevenson, Janet	Grades 5–7
	1980	Women of Crisis II— Lives of Work and Dreams	Coles, R. and Dell, J.H.	
		What Can She Be?	Lothrop, Lee and Shephard	Grades 2-5 A series of books each featuring women in a non-traditional career. Careers include: Architect, 1974 Computer Scientist, 1979 Framer, 1976 Film Producer, 1977 Geologist, 1976 Lawyer, 1973 Legislator, 1978 Musician, 1975 Music Librarian, 1975 Newscaster, 1973 Police Officer Veterinarian, 1972

CHAPTER 15

GIFTED CHILDREN WITH HANDICAPS

It appears to be a well-kept secret that a child can be both gifted and handicapped.

Linda Kreger Silverman (1989)

Typically, gifted children with handicaps are recognized for their handicap, not for their gifts and talents. Their special needs stemming from the handicap are provided for by mandated programs in special classes and special schools funded by state and federal governments. Since most handicapping conditions do not preclude or prevent giftedness, it is logical to expect the same percentage of gifted and talented students among students with handicaps as in the general population. However, labeling the child as having a handicap plus attending to the priority needs of the handicapping condition usually obscures the creative, artistic, intellectual, or scientific talents of the child. They are thus much less likely than nonhandicapped gifted children to be identified as gifted and included in school programs that help develop their special talents.

Overview

This chapter will explore the needs and problems of children with handicaps, their identification, and some programming ideas directed toward accommodating their needs.

NEEDS OF GIFTED STUDENTS WITH HANDICAPS

According to the U.S. Department of Education (1990), approximately 9.4 percent of all school-

age children participate in special education programs. During the 1986–1987 school year, 4,421,601 persons between ages 0 and 21 were served under programs for persons with disabilities (U.S. Department of Education, 1988). About 90 percent of students with disabilities are considered mild cases. About two-thirds of all students with disabilities spend at least part of the day in regular classrooms (Heward and Orlansky, 1992). The percentage varies according to the type of disability: According to Gartner and Lipsky (1987), 96 percent of speech-impaired students and 78 percent of students with learning disabilities are in regular classes for part or all of the day; but only 44 percent of behavior disordered and 31 percent of students with retardation are in regular classes.

Public Law 94-142, the "mainstreaming law," defines *individuals with disabilities* as:

> . . . mentally retarded, hard-of-hearing, deaf, speech impaired, visually handicapped, seriously emotionally disturbed, orthopedically impaired or other health impaired children, or children with specific learning disabilities who by reason thereof require special education and related services.

Of these categories, it would seem that only students with mental retardation would preclude most forms of giftedness. If a five percent figure is applied to all but the mentally retarded (about 15 percent of all students with disabilities), 187,918

349

students with handicaps should have been served by gifted programming in the 1986–1987school year. Nonetheless, programs for gifted students with handicaps are rare, even though state and federal funding agencies typically specify that such students must be included in any funded G/T program. At the time Eisenberg and Epstein (1981) initiated their program, they discovered that there were *no* special programs designated for gifted students with handicaps in all of New York City.

Legislation clearly states that children with handicaps must be served. However, Schnur and Stefanich (1979) pointed out that the handicapped gifted child may be omitted from special services (the special education class, a reading teacher, psychological services, Individualized Education Programs) if he or she is functioning reasonably well within the regular classroom. This means that, for example, an intellectually gifted child who performs at grade level, but whose achievement nonetheless is depressed by his or her handicap, would not necessarily be provided with any special services because his or her performance is equivalent to that of average classmates. To the extent that the special services would individualize evaluation and instruction, help the gifted child remediate academic weaknesses, help the child compensate for the handicapping condition, and/or develop individual talents, such special attention is lost.

Bireley (1991) pointed out that children with handicaps who have low incidence disabilities such as hearing or visual impairment are usually taught by specialists who are trained to teach impaired children. Their inexperience with gifted children may cause them to focus more on the impairment, thus making it less likely that they will identify the giftedness.

Several studies have shown that mainstreamed children with handicaps, particularly emotional disturbance, frequently are not accepted by peers in the regular classroom (e.g., Fox, 1979; Gresham and Reschly, 1988; Heward and Orlansky, 1992; Sabornie and Kauffman, 1985). Generally, the greater the severity of the problem, the greater the degree of social rejection. Sometimes, mainstreamed students with handicaps are brutalized by other students, for example, by name-calling or other insults, along with the social exclusion (Zigler and Muenchow, 1979).

Baum and Owen (1988) found gifted students with learning disabilities (LD) to be the most disruptive in class. These students felt less effective in school compared with other gifted students and even with average LD students. A small study by Vespi and Yewchuk (1992) found that gifted LD children had good self-esteem despite their learning difficulties. The children were eager to talk about their *strengths*, and their parents and teachers confirmed their healthy self-concepts. However, the children assumed that learning tasks would be easy for them, and were not prepared for the difficulty of learning activities in an area of disability (e.g., language). Their frustration, tension, and fear of failure led to defensiveness. Bireley (1991) noted that the higher goals of gifted students may be especially frustrating to achieve when the student has a disability.

Maker (1977) suggested that gifted children with handicaps themselves often are willing to accept inferior status because of their handicap, and despite their superior abilities and talents. Eisenberg and Epstein (1981) noted that even though most students with handicaps do indeed have a poor self-image, in the special education room a gifted student with a handicap often is a leader.

The 1986 Amendments to the Education for all Handicapped Children Act,[1] P.L. 99–457, not only extended special educational services to 3- to 5-year-olds, but assisted states in implementing intervention services for handicapped infants and toddlers (Krauss, 1990). For the first time, the service recipient was defined as the *family* in addition to the child, and an *Individualized Family Service Plan* (IFSP) was required. Furthermore, Yell and Espin (1990) believe that the U.S. Congress passed The Handicapped Children's Protection

---

[1]Renamed in 1990 *Individuals with Disabilities Education Act.*

Act of 1986 (HCPA), P.L. 99–372, in response to court rulings which seemed to undercut parents' opportunities to dispute school decisions. This law allows parents injunctive relief when they feel their children are not receiving an appropriate education. Under appropriate circumstances, it may also allow tuition reimbursement for a special school and, in some cases, even reimbursement of attorneys' fees.

Clearly, we are dramatically underserving a segment of the population that has high potential for personal development and achievement and for making high-quality contributions to society. Among outstanding creative individuals who are handicapped, Karnes, Shwedel, and Lewis (1983) listed Ludwig van Beethoven, Thomas Edison, Helen Keller, Vincent van Gogh, and Franklin D. Roosevelt. We might add the names of contemporary musicians George Shearing, José Feliciano, Stevie Wonder, and Ray Charles, all of whom are blind; violinist Itzhak Perlman, crippled by polio; and Hollywood personality Jack Paar, former "Tonight Show" host, who stutters. Unlike most gifted persons with disabilities these people are noted for their gifts and talents, not for their disabilities.

In sum, gifted children with handicaps continue to be ignored, programs for them are lacking, and their problems are compounded by sometimes severe social problems and rock-bottom feelings of self-worth and personal integrity.

IDENTIFICATION

Identifying the gifted handicapped child usually is difficult. A major problem is that their gifts usually remain invisible to teachers and sometimes even parents. Eisenberg and Epstein (1981) described their G/T program for students with handicaps in which forms for nominating gifted and talented students with handicaps were sent to designated New York City schools serving a full 60,000 handicapped students. *Not one student was nominated.*

Another problem is that the handicap itself may obscure the *expression* of the special gifts and talents. For example, blindness, deafness, and some learning disabilities have the effect of slowing development and thus may result in deceptively lower IQ scores. Blind and deaf children, because of their sensory deficits, tend to be more concrete in their thinking, which will hardly help the abstract reasoning necessary for a high IQ score. Children with dyslexia will certainly suffer on verbal components of an intelligence test, although Marx (1982) suggested that these children may have much higher than normal spatial-oriented giftedness. Other handicaps (for example, emotional disturbance or social maladjustments, orthopedic or health impairments, speech or language impairments) also can interfere with obtaining an accurate high score on an intelligence test.

In some cases then, the intelligence test—the most commonly used instrument for identifying gifted children—may add a handicap to the discovery of giftedness among already handicapped children.

A dramatic example of overlooking gifted learning disabled students comes to us from two surveys in Texas (Boodoo *et al.*, 1989). Of the 180 responses by special education centers, 91 percent reported *no* gifted LD children. There were 143 responses from gifted and talented programs, and 77% of these reported no gifted LD children in their programs. Minner (1990) discovered that when teachers were presented with identical vignettes of children, they were less likely to identify for gifted programming those students who were also described as having a learning disability.

An example of a case in which a handicap resulted in dependency and underachievement with the effect of obscuring giftedness is Kevin:

Kevin, a nine-year-old fourth grader, was totally blind. He was a very good looking child and was small for his age. His disability and his young appearance invited adults to "take care of him" and do much more for him than was appropriate. Kevin's initial evaluation indicated his WISC-R verbal IQ score to be 109. It had been recommended that he repeat fourth grade. One year after the initial evaluation and after the dependency patterns were changed and the skills gaps were closed by tutoring, Kevin's IQ score as tested by the same unbiased tester, who had no knowledge of the treatment program, was 141. Kevin appeared to everyone to be a very bright child, but his dependent underachieving behavior related to his blindness had a major impact on the lowering of his ability scores and the initial nonidentification of his giftedness.

The *WISC-R* and the *WISC-III* are the most frequently used intelligence tests and are often used in modified form with children with handicaps. Brown (1984) suggested that other tests, which are specifically designed and normed for children with handicaps, may be more appropriate. Examples of such instruments are the *Nebraska Test of Learning Aptitude* (Hiskey, 1966), used with deaf and hearing-impaired children; the *Arthur Adaptation of the Leiter International Performance Scale* (Arthur, 1950) for the deaf, hearing-impaired, and children with speech or language difficulties; the *Blind Learning Aptitude Test* (Newland, 1969); and *The Pictorial Test of Intelligence* (French, 1964) for children with motor handicaps. Other tests for children with handicapping conditions are described by Bauman and Kropf (1979), Salter and Tozier (1971), and Sullivan and Vernon (1979).

Karnes (1979) reported that identifying gifted children with handicaps through observation was more difficult than with "normal" children and requires a prolonged observation. Providing inservice workshops for teachers of the handicapped, which focus on characteristics of giftedness and the identification of gifted and talented children, should help the teacher identification and nomination process. Teachers who are trained to work with children with handicaps rarely have training in the specific area of giftedness. Eisenberg and Epstein (1981) noted that in their search for gifted children with handicaps, teachers would select conforming students, not the highly active, energetic ones. Concluded Eisenberg and Epstein, teachers definitely needed direction.

In observing possibly gifted children with handicaps, one would, of course, watch for the types of characteristics and behaviors described in Chapter 2, along with an additional interesting one. As Eisenberg and Epstein described their gifted children with disabilities they ". . . understand faster, ask questions, zip through math—and they are terribly disruptive." With "normal" gifted students, disruptiveness is a trait that sometimes appears because the child is bored or frustrated in school. Because frustration and stress can be everyday matters for gifted students with handicaps it is not surprising that *disruptiveness* can be a good indicator of giftedness with these children.

The identification procedure used successfully by Eisenberg and Epstein (1981) included IQ and achievement scores, which conveniently were already on file. They also used the Renzulli (1983) rating scales, not only the frequently used Learning, Motivation, Creativity and Leadership scales, but the less well-known Art, Music, Drama, and Communications scales as well. As noted above, when first approached via a mailing of nomination forms, not one teacher of handicapped students spontaneously nominated a single child for participation in the Eisenberg and Epstein program. However, after looking over the Renzulli rating scales, many began *calling* (not writing) the program coordinator with the same urgent message: "Hey, I think I've got a kid for you!" The rating scales themselves served as quick in-service training for identifying gifted children with handicaps.

Especially good indicators of giftedness from the Renzulli Learning scale were:

2. Possesses a large storehouse of information about a variety of topics (beyond the usual interests of youngsters his/her age).

4. Has rapid insight into cause-effect relationships; tries to discover the how and why of things; asks many provocative questions (as distinct from information or factual questions); wants to know what makes things (or people) "tick."

6. Is a keen and alert observer; usually "sees more" or "gets more" out of a story, film, etc., than others.

Especially good items from the Motivation scale were:

1. Becomes absorbed and truly involved in certain topics or problems; is persistent in seeking task completion. (It is sometimes difficult to get him/her to move on to another topic.)

5. Prefers to work independently; requires little direction from teachers.

Eisenberg and Epstein also found peer nominations and self-nominations to be valuable; more valuable, in fact, than teacher nominations. The peers knew who were bright, creative, and fast-learning. Many students with handicaps *nominated themselves* as gifted or talented, and ". . . nine out of ten were right!" In one case, a student nominated himself for the program, and shortly after had himself *decertified*—examined and taken out of the special education class.

Karnes and Shwedel (1981; Karnes and Johnson, 1991) created a *Talent Screening Checklist* designed especially for identifying gifted preschool youngsters with handicaps. Corresponding to the federal definition, the checklist included the six areas of intellectual ability, specific academic talent, creativity, leadership, visual or performing art talent, and psychomotor ability. The checklist was completed by both a teacher and a parent, and if either rated the child in the top 25 percent the child was moved to the second step of the identification process. This second step involved guided observation of the child in one or more semistructured *Activities for Talent Identification*. For example, a child would pick two other children and teach them to mix paint. Case conferences or a diagnostic evaluation by a psychologist were used if questions about particular children remained. Karnes and Shwedel pointed out that their identification approach minimized the risks of overlooking any truly gifted child with a handicap; further, it did no harm to any participant.

To help in the identification of gifted children with handicaps Maker (1977) recommended that (1) handicapped students should be compared with others who have the same handicap, and (2)

characteristics that enable the child to effectively compensate for his or her handicap should be weighted more heavily. For example, if an orthopedically impaired student cannot write, his compensating verbal and cognitive abilities should receive more weight; if a student cannot speak, his written, artistic, and creative talents should be examined. In addition to these two points, Silverman (1989) added these recommendations: (1) Allow these children into the gifted program at least on a probationary or "guest" basis to see if they are capable of achieving higher level work. (2) Place extra weight on the child's performance in areas unaffected by the disability. (3) Cutoff scores should be dropped 10 points to take into account a depression of scores due to the disability.

As for creativity, the Renzulli Creativity Scale mentioned above apparently is useful. The *PRIDE* (Rimm, 1982), *GIFT* (Rimm, 1976) and *GIFFI* (Davis and Rimm, 1980, 1982) creativity inventories have been specifically validated for use with children with learning disabilities and also should be usable with students with other handicaps.

Identification of Gifted Children with Learning Disabilities

As with other handicaps, gifted children with learning disabilities also may be overlooked by typical G/T program selection procedures. They may function at or below grade level and may exhibit deficits in cognitive ability, including long- or short-term memory problems, visual or auditory processing weaknesses, and/or visual-motor integration problems (Suter and Wolf, 1987). Spatial disabilities also are common. Cognitive areas of giftedness found among many learning disabled children are good problem-solving skills, abstract thinking abilities, and excellent oral communication skills (Daniels, 1983; Hadary, Cohen and Haushalter, 1979; Whitmore, 1980). Behavior problems, poor self-concepts, and dependent behaviors complicate the identification of both the giftedness and the learning disability.

Rimm (1986b) pointed out that sometimes children who are labled as "learning disabled" in school actually are dependent underachievers. Table 15.1 includes characteristics that may help one separate children with learning disabilities from those who are underachieving. Separating the two categories for the purpose of differential treatment is important.

The WISC-R frequently has been used for the identification of children with learning disabilities. The "scatter" or differences between subtest scores (Lutey, 1977) and significant discrepancies between Verbal and Performance scores (Kaufman, 1976a, 1976b, 1979) often are used to identify a learning disability. While the average Verbal-Performance discrepancy is 9.7 IQ points, Schiff, Kaufman, and Kaufman (1981) found an average Verbal-Performance discrepancy of 18.6 points for a gifted learning disabled group. A full 87 percent showed a higher verbal than performance score.

An examination of the case histories of 17,000 children referred to the Temple University Reading Clinic between 1952 and 1979 produced 322 (246 boys, 76 girls) who were both gifted and learning disabled. Large Verbal-Performance discrepancies of 15 points or more were found for half of the gifted sample. *Similarities* (abstract verbal reasoning) and *Comprehension* (common-sense thinking) subtests were highest for these students, while *Digit Span* and *Arithmetic* were lowest. Note that the latter two subtests require considerable concentration and attention, which often are poor in children with learning disabilities (Satler, 1982).

On the affective side, one can easily imagine the confusion caused by such extreme variability in a gifted child's capabilities and school performance. Also, because the learning disability is invisible, even though the child may understand the cause of his or her problems, he or she may feel shame, guilt, and other concerns (Rosner, 1985).

Although the Wechsler Intelligence Scales can be useful tools for discovering learning disabilities, they also can mask disabilities. Silverman (1989) pointed out that "in our zeal to compute averages" of people's abilities, giftedness and handicaps cancel each other out, leaving these children to appear "average."

Fox and Brody (1983), Maker and Udall (1983), and Rosner and Seymour (1983) all have suggested a multidimensional approach to identifying gifted students with learning disabilities. Such an approach might include the WISC-R, achievement tests, an informal reading inventory, teacher and parent reports, creativity tests, and interviews with the child.

Finally, as with the similarly difficult challenge of identifying gifted disadvantaged and minority children, using a *quota system* will ensure that children with handicaps are examined closely for gifts and talents, and that many will be placed in programs for the gifted. The identification of gifted students with handicaps will continue to be difficult. However, a sensitivity to characteristics of giftedness and a willingness to look beyond the too-visible handicap will aid in the discovery of talent.

CRITICAL INGREDIENTS OF PROGRAMS FOR GIFTED CHILDREN WITH HANDICAPS

Programming for gifted children with handicaps may vary in type and content to the same extent as for other gifted children. It can include the same acceleration, enrichment, grouping, and counseling tactics, and with the same view toward developing the child's strengths, promoting high achievement, and enhancing creative and other high-level thinking skills. However, the program also must include some special components based on additional needs related to the handicapping condition.

Instead of categorizing the student first as having a handicap and second as gifted, the G/T program should view the child primarily as a gifted child, but one who may need some special assistance because of his or her handicap. The primary emphasis thus should be on the recognition and facilitation of the child's strengths. A secondary focus is to prevent the disability from becoming a deterrent to the development and expression of the child's talent.

Although different handicaps create different

TABLE 15.1   Ways to Discriminate between Dependence and Disability

Dependence	Disability
1. Child asks for explanations regularly despite differences in subject matter.	Child asks for explanations in particular subjects which are difficult.
2. Child asks for explanation of instructions regardless of style used, either auditory or visual.	Child asks for explanations of instructions only when given in one instruction style, either auditory or visual, but not both.
3. Child's questions are not specific to material but appear to be mainly to gain adult attention.	Child's questions are specific to material and once process is explained child works efficiently.
4. Child is disorganized or slow in assignments but becomes much more efficient when a meaningful reward is presented as motivation.	Child's disorganization or slow pace continues despite motivating rewards.
5. Child works only when an adult is nearby at school and/or at home.	Child works independently once process is clearly explained.
6. Individually administered measures of ability indicate that the child is capable of learning the material. Individual tests improve with tester encouragement and support. Group measures may not indicate good abilities or skills.	Both individual and group measures indicate lack of specific abilities or skills. Tester encouragement has no significant effect on scores.
7. Child exhibits "poor me" body language (tears, helplessness, pouting, copying) regularly when new work is presented. Teacher or adult attention serves to ease the symptoms.	Child exhibits "poor me" body language only with instructions or assignments in specific disability areas and accepts challenges in areas of strength.
8. Parents report whining, complaining, attention-getting temper tantrums, and poor sportsmanship at home.	Although parents may find similar symptoms at home, they tend to be more sporadic than regular, particularly the whining and complaining.
9. Child's "poor me" behavior appears only with one parent and not with the other; only with some teachers and not with others. With some teachers or with the other parent the child functions fairly well independently.	Although the child's "poor me" behaviors may only appear with one parent or with solicitous teachers, performance is not adequate even when behavior is acceptable.
10. Child learns only when given one-to-one instruction but will not learn in groups even when instructional mode is varied.	Although child may learn more quickly in a one-to-one setting he/she will also learn efficiently in a group setting provided the child's disability is taken into consideration when instructions are given.

It is critical to realize that some children who are truly disabled have also become dependent. The key to distinguishing between disability and dependence is the child's response to adult support. If the child performs only with adult support when new material is presented he/she is too dependent, whether or not there is also a disability.

obstacles, there are a core of hindrances that appear to be critical for almost all children with handicaps. It is these that we address as priorities for gifted programs that include children with handicaps.

Coping with Attention Disorders

Attention Deficit-Hyperactivity Disorder (ADHD) and *Attention Deficit Disorder* (ADD) are the new catch-all diagnoses for children, gifted or otherwise (Rimm, in press). These disorders are characterized by difficulty with concentration, distractibility, impulsivity, disorganization, and hyperactivity for the first diagnosis, and all characteristics but the last for the second diagnosis. Table 15.2 lists many characteristics which are used for diagnosing ADHD in children.

While it is tempting to latch on to a "sure cure," and while statistical data reassures parents that stimulant medication is appropriate for some children, it is critical that parents and teachers understand that *all* tests for attention disorders are observational.[2] There are absolutely *no* definitive biological tests for attention deficit disorders. Many people deduce a biological cause—the so called "minimal brain dysfunction"—from observations of children's behavior without any biological evidence whatever.

A great deal of scientific research has been conducted to understand attention disorders. While findings are suggestive of possible neurochemical imbalances, even the best-known specialists admit that "definitive empirical support has been lacking" (Anastopoulos and Barkley, 1991, p. 16). Zametkin (1989) explains that after two decades of an extensive search for biochemical markers for ADHD, findings have been disappointing. He further indicates that it may be a long time before an underlying cause of the disorder is found and recognizes that

interacting biological and psychosocial variables may cause ADHD. Breggin (1991), asserts that "the idea that Ritalin or other stimulants correct biochemical imbalances in the brain of hyperactive children . . . is false on two counts." First, there is no known biochemical imbalance in these children, and second, it generally is accepted that Ritalin has the same calming effect on normal children regardless of diagnosis or behavior (Anastopoulos and Barkley, 1991).

Ritalin is overused and misused (e.g., Safer and Krager, 1988). Incredibly, a teacher of gifted children in Florida reported that *half* of her students were taking Ritalin for ADHD. One teacher of an enthusiastic 10-year-old boy (IQ = 180), known to the first author, recommended that the active child be put on Ritalin. This boy's problem was solved by finding a new teacher and, later, a special school that valued his energetic giftedness. Another gifted child came to the clinic of the second author exhibiting multiple side effects of Ritalin, including tremors and tics, and continuing home and school problems after three years of treatment elsewhere.

Ritalin produces side effects for many children, including loss of appetite (and some growth), tics, insomnia, nausea, stomachaches, headaches, depression or sadness, social withdrawal, flattened emotions, and loss of energy (Breggin, 1991). Ritalin does calm a great many children and even helps them focus attention; it also makes them more docile in the classroom.

Needless to say it would be better if ADHD and ADD children could learn to function well without drugs. Many of the symptoms of attention disorders can be controlled behaviorally, and medication can be avoided for many of these children. A few of them will require both medication and behavioral help in order to work to their abilities in school.

The growing interest in Attention Deficit Disorders has caused a serious problem. There has been an overdiagnosing of the disorder by parents, teachers, and professionals. Ritalin is hailed as a magical cure by many. The problem is especially severe for gifted children. For example, Webb

---

[2]Yes, *stimulant* drugs, primarily Ritalin, are used to calm hyperactive children. One theory (Farley, 1986) is that such drugs raise the child's internal level of mental arousal (stimulation) to a more comfortable level, thus reducing the need for additional external stimulation.

TABLE 15.2   Diagnostic Criteria for Attention Deficit-Hyperactivity Disorder

NOTE: Consider a criterion met only if the behavior is considerably more frequent than that of most people of the same mental age.

A.   A disturbance of at least six months during which at least eight of the following are present:
1. Often fidgets with hands or feet or squirms in seat (in adolescents, may be limited to subjective feelings of restlessness)
2. Has difficulty remaining seated when required to do so
3. Is easily distracted by extraneous stimuli
4. Has difficulty awaiting turn in games or group situations
5. Often blurts out answers to questions before they have been completed
6. Has difficulty following through on instructions from others (not due to oppositional behavior or failure of comprehension), e.g., fails to finish chores
7. Has difficulty sustaining attention to tasks or play activities
8. Often shifts from one uncompleted activity to another
9. Has difficulty playing quietly
10. Often talks excessively
11. Often interrupts or intrudes on others, e.g., butts into other children's games
12. Often does not seem to listen to what is being said to him or her
13. Often loses things necessary for tasks or activities at school or at home (e.g., toys, pencils, books, assignments)
14. Often engages in physically dangerous activities without considering possible consequences (not for the purpose of thrill-seeking), e.g., runs into street without looking

B.   Onset before the age of seven

(1993) reminds us that some of the characteristics used to identify ADHD (Table 15.2) resemble those of high-intensity, high-energy gifted children. Also, characteristics that identify high creativity are similar to some of those listed as indicative of children with ADHD.

The National Association of School Psychologists' (1991; NASP) delegate assembly has taken a strong position on the treatment of Attention Deficit Disorders. Some excerpts follow:

A. NASP believes that attention deficits are not a unitary condition, that they are not reliably diagnosed, and that it is difficult to distinguish attention deficits from the normal range of temperament and fluctuation in attention to which all students are susceptible.

B. NASP believes that effective interventions should be tailored to the unique learning strengths and needs of every student. For children with attention deficits, such interventions will often include the following:

1. Classroom modifications to enhance attending, work production, and social adjustment;

2. Behavior management systems to reduce problems in areas most likely to be affected by attention deficits (e.g., unstructured situations, large group instruction, transitions, etc.);

3. Consultation with families to assist in behavior management in the home setting and to facilitate home-school cooperation and collaboration.

C. NASP believes appropriate treatment may or may *not* include medical intervention. When medication is considered, NASP strongly recommends:

1. That instructional and behavioral interventions be implemented *before* medication trials begin;

2. That behavioral data be collected before and during medication trials to assess baseline conditions and the efficacy of medication; and

3. That communication between school, home, and medical personnel emphasize mutual problem solving and cooperation.

Consistency, appropriate limit-setting, curriculum changes, and emphasis on positive interests and accomplishment are some of the many alternative approaches that can be used for gifted children who are presently being diagnosed with ADHD and ADD (Rimm, 1986b; Rimm, in press b). Very few require medication. While some energetic gifted children are easy to raise, many frustrate their parents and teachers to tears and guilt. There is no easy way out of so great a challenge. While Ritalin may be appropriate for a small percentage of children, overmedicating gifted children in the name of mental health will only prevent the positive direction of their high energy.

REDUCING COMMUNICATION LIMITATIONS

Countless high-achieving college students with handicaps have learned effective and socially acceptable ways to compensate for their handicapping conditions. Blind students use tape recorders, study with sighted friends, and make easy arrangements to take exams orally. Severely visually impaired students will obtain (usually at government expense) head-mounted devices or other machines that magnify the pages of standard college texts. Deaf students will bring an American Sign Language interpreter to class, parking the smiling interpreter squarely next to the on-stage lecturer.

Orthopedically impaired students scoot from building to building in electric wheelchairs; if they cannot write they also will use tape recorders and take exams orally. Dyslexic students pay maximum attention to lectures and illustrations, with little time devoted to frustrating printed words. On one hand, these students are admired for their courage and ingenuity. On the other, as energetic and talented individuals they simply are doing what they must do.

All persons with handicaps must compensate as best they can for their limitations. In school, they must be able to perceive, respond, and express themselves; in short, they must be able to *communicate*. The regular and special education teacher must help ensure that technological aids and special training are available that will permit the gifted child with a handicap not only to function "normally" in the regular class, but to develop his or her superior abilities and gifts. A short list would include wheelchairs, hearing aids, lip reading, sign language, braille training, braille texts, magnifiers, tape recorders, typewriters, artificial limbs and hands, paintbrush and pencil attachments for the head or arm, and microcomputers.

Microcomputers present growing possibilities for extending the communication potential of children with handicaps. For example, children with learning disabilities by reason of poor handwriting skills often do very poorly in written expression until they learn to use a word processing program on a microcomputer. Using a computer for writing assignments has the dual advantages of encouraging both fluent expression and independence. Carnine (1989) pointed out how technology can free teachers from delivering drill instruction and can reduce performance differences between students with and without handicap. He used videodisc, computer simulation, and computer-assisted instruction techniques to help students with handicaps learn earth science, chemistry, health, fractions, reasoning skills, and vocabulary. Gleason, Carnine, and Boriero (in press) compared problem-analyses learning for learning disabled students as taught by an expert teacher to computer-assisted instruction. The pre-post change with the teacher went from 51 percent to 93 percent, and for the computer group it went from 49% to 91%.

Another example of the use of microcomputers is the computerized *Versa Braille*, which permits a child to type English letters and have them translated to braille, or to type braille letters and have them translated to English.[3] *Digispeech* is a computer program which can be used to help learning disabled students recognize their spelling errors and increase their awareness of phrases. It reads back phonetically the stories that children have keyboarded into the computer. Errors become obvious to the children who are listening with headsets.[4]

Technology can be used to help students with handicaps communicate and learn, but teachers must be cautious in assuming that technology has all the answers. Gifted children with handicaps continue to require the emotional support that only people can provide.

In many cases, gifted and talented students with handicaps cannot be identified without aids that allow them to communicate. For example, in Wisconsin teachers in the Arts for the Handicapped Project (O'Connell, 1982) designed several devices that served to free physically handicapped children from some limitations of their disabilities, permitting them to express themselves through art. The strategies allowed talented artists to be identified and they were taught advanced techniques and skills.

Some communication aids, incidentally, may have the initial effect of slowing down responding, learning, and cognitive functioning. However, once the communication skill is mastered, the handicapped child will have a vastly improved potential for in-depth development, achievement, and creative expression.

The gifted child with a disability clearly needs to

[3]*Versa Braille* is available from Telesensory Systems, Inc., 3408 Hillview Ave., P.O. Box 10099, Palo Alto, CA 94304.
[4]*DigiSpeech* is available from Golden Associate, 7621 Murphy Dr., Suite 101, Middleton, WI 53562.

be provided with all possible resources to become a skilled user of substitute means of communication. Without the use of these aids, the expression of talent is impeded and locked within. Leaders of gifted programs not only must help obtain these resources, but must interpret to the community the beneficial effects of the aids and the potential talent that can be uncovered and developed when communication barriers are lifted.

SELF-CONCEPT DEVELOPMENT

We noted earlier that rejection by others, labeling, lowered teacher expectations, and the sense of being different combine to make gifted children with handicaps feel less capable and of less worth than other children. Because a poor self-concept is a primary characteristic of underachievement, dealing with the extremely poor self-images of these children should be a primary underlying goal of a gifted program for students with handicaps.

In addition to feedback from others, the self-concept also is based upon a realistic appraisal of one's own skills and achievements. Therefore, program activities should be directed not only toward helping these children to achieve, but toward helping them to appreciate the worth of their achievements. Nielsen and Mortorff-Albert (1989) found improved self-concepts for gifted students with learning disabilities who were involved in gifted or gifted/learning disability programs compared with gifted students who were involved only in learning disability programs. Appropriate gifted programming can improve their sense of worth.

These achievements can be evaluated according to two sets of standards. The first set of standards would be the same as applied to nonhandicapped persons, which should make it clear to all that these contributions are valuable and even superior to the average. A second set of standards acknowledges the special talent and effort needed to overcome the handicap. If gifted children with handicaps have high expectations placed upon them, and if communication barriers are removed, their academic and creative achievements in the arts, literature, mathematics, science, or social studies can be as excellent as those of anyone else. And it is through the challenge of true high-level achievement that these children can realistically attain the positive self-concept they desperately need for their own personal growth.

Social Skills

Nonhandicapped children use all of their senses and their mobility spontaneously to learn social skills that permit them to be accepted by their peers. Children with handicaps need to learn more concretely and specifically about the social life to which they want and need to belong. This goal is indeed a challenge.

Gifted students with handicaps require social activities with other bright or creative children who have similar handicaps and similar goals and interests so they will not feel alone. Peer support and peer-support groups have been recommended throughout this text as an effective solution to many self-concept and social problems of gifted students. Also, due to lack of experience, gifted handicapped children may require "social coaching" so they do not *guarantee* themselves rejection by, for example, trying to show off, forcing themselves on a group, or withdrawing completely. These are common, self-defeating coping strategies adopted unsuccessfully by many children and adolescents with handicaps who so strongly wish to be "part of the group" (Halverson and Victor, 1976).

The other children in the class, too, probably will require "sensitivity training" and "values clarification" to help them empathize with the handicapped child; that is, to help them understand the problems and feelings of individuals with disabilities so they will *think* before mistreating or excluding them. Encounter-type groups—carefully monitored—which encourage open and honest communication between handicapped and nonhandicapped youth can provide an important avenue for developing social skills and social relationships of handicapped children, while providing

unique sensitivity insights for the nonhandicapped child. Inset 15.1 (Katt, 1988) includes sample activities that the Wyoming, Michigan, gifted and talented program used to increase their students' sensitivity to handicaps.

Classroom Tactics

Several classroom strategies may increase contact and positive feelings between different student groups. For example, mixed learning teams, which require all members to work together, have been successful in improving between-group attitudes and friendships. In Aronson's (Aronson *et al.*, 1975) *jigsaw* method mixed groups of six upper-elementary students are told that in one hour they will have a test to see how well they have learned, for example, about the life of newspaper publisher Joseph Pulitzer. Each of the six is given one paragraph covering a different aspect of Pulitzer's career. To do well, each student must read his or her own paragraph and then explain its contents to the others. Cooperation and interdependence are the only route to success. With mixed-race groups, teachers reported that changes in attitudes and self-concepts—and an improved classroom atmosphere—were very impressive.

Peer tutoring also has the effect of increasing "liking" between different students. Normal gifted students may tutor gifted students with handicaps or the handicapped students may tutor others. The handicapped students also may tutor younger children. Gartner, Kohler, and Reissman (1971) stressed that when anxious, low-esteem, low-achieving students are placed in the important and prestigious role of *teacher*, they learn new skills, feel better about themselves, and their attitudes toward school also improve. In addition, the younger children reap educational benefits, and they learn that persons with handicaps are people too.

Coleman (1992) found gifted children with learning disabilities to be more planful in their use of problem-solving strategies than average learning disabled children. She thus recommended that direct teaching of coping strategies could be help-

INSET 15.1 _____

Activities for Encouraging Awareness of Handicaps

PHYSICAL HANDICAPS

Rent or borrow a wheelchair. Ask nonhandicapped students to do one-hour activities in the wheelchair, including getting a drink from the water fountain, going out to recess, doing an assignment on the blackboard, changing classes, etc.

COMMUNICATIVE DISABILITY

Ask students to assume their speech and language abilities are interrupted. Have them attempt to tell the class something while mute.

VISUAL IMPAIRMENT

Plan a sightless half day by use of blindfold and cane. Alert students to describing how their senses of hearing, touch, and smell can guide them through the day. Students will each need a buddy to guide them through the more difficult adventures such as recess games and equipment. Stop several times to discuss experiences and awareness.

From Katt, 1988.

ful to all learning disabled children. Montague (1991) found considerable differences among gifted students with learning disabilities in mathematical problem solving. She emphasized the importance of teaching effective math problem-solving strategies.

Self-assessment was found to be effective with learning disabled preschool children (Sainato *et al.*, 1990) and with two school-aged gifted learning disabled children (Miller, 1991). The potential for combining self-assessment with the teaching of problem-solving strategies would seem appropriate for gifted learning disabled children.

Encouraging Independent Learning

One-to-one attention is characteristic and often necessary for educational programs for students with handicaps. However, these children sometimes become too dependent upon the individual attention and the continuous positive feedback that supports their learning. Such dependence will limit the motivation and achievement of any child. Therefore, children with handicaps must be encouraged to develop both intrinsic motivation, with learning and success as their own rewards, and the ability to learn independently. Further, they need both independent, self-initiated learning experiences and cooperative small-group activities in which they can serve as leaders and as equal participants.

In selecting methods by which children with handicaps compensate for their handicap, attention to independence is very important. For example, the child who has a writing disability could (1) tell his or her story to a teacher, (2) dictate the story into a tape recorder, or (3) compose the story with a word processor. The first increases dependence; the latter two permit independence. Blind children (1) could have material read to them, (2) they could read the material in braille, or (3) hear it on a tape recorder. Again, the first helps keep the children dependent while the last two aid independence. Dependent help certainly is appropriate occasionally, but too much dependency can permit further crippling for the already handicapped child.

Independent, self-initiated learning, and learning as part of a class group are important for *all* children, especially gifted ones who will be faced with challenging college work and complex professions. We must be innovative in providing independent learning opportunities for gifted children with handicaps just as they are provided for nonhandicapped gifted children.

HIGH-LEVEL, ABSTRACT THINKING SKILLS

We noted earlier that limited sensory input may have the effect of depressing the development of high-level, abstract thinking skills. Compared to persons with unimpaired senses, experiences of sensory handicapped students tend to be interpreted in a more concrete vocabulary. For children with handicaps a weakness in abstract and high-level thinking skills should not be viewed as "lack of ability," but as a deficiency that may require even more attention than with nonhandicapped gifted children.

Even more than for other gifted students, then, the gifted child with a handicap must be exposed to programming methods that foster the development of such skills as *creativity*, *problem solving*, *critical thinking*, *classifying*, *generalizing*, *analysis*, *synthesis*, and *evaluation*. Encouraging such skill development is common in most gifted programs, but is doubly important for the gifted child with a handicap.

An example of the introduction of abstract-thinking skills is provided by a creative problem solving (CPS) program for 16 emotionally handicapped aggressive middle school students who were not identified as gifted (Mathew, 1984). The researcher taught the youths to apply CPS to real problems. The effect of CPS training on these children was increased creativity as measured by the *Torrance Tests of Creative Thinking*. The intervention also reduced aggression significantly.

Baum (1984) described the use of Renzulli's Enrichment Triad Model (Chapter 7) with learning disabled gifted children. Their gifted behavior was exhibited outside of the classroom and was definitely absent within the classroom. Baum emphasized that enrichment activities should be designed to develop strengths and interests and to challenge, not necessarily to provide remediation. Inset 15.2 describes the Triad program that helped them feel more motivated, challenged, and confident. Baum's (1988) success with the Triad model for gifted/learning disabled students was again demonstrated with seven students who met 2½ hours a week over a nine-month period. Gains in self-esteem, learning behavior, and creative productivity were found for six of the seven students. Huntley (1990) also reported a successful gifted learning disabilities program in the Norwich, Connecticut, public schools using the Triad model.

Daniels (1983) itemized the following as curriculum and remediation methods specifically for teaching gifted and talented children with learning disabilities. Note the emphasis on abstract and high-level learning objectives.

Classification
Levels of abstraction
Appreciating relevancy
Labeling
Abstracting
Generalizing
Learning concepts (not "words")
Vocabulary, spelling
Writing, composition
Punctuation, proofreading

Hackney (1986) conducted a summer gifted program for 15 visually impaired students at the Texas School for the Blind. The program included higher-level thinking skills, advanced problem solving, creative writing, mentorships, and most of the same elements included in many gifted programs. Outdoor risk taking, independent learning,

INSET 15.2 _____

Example of Enrichment Triad Model in Action for Learning Disabled Students (from Baum, 1984)

TYPE I—EXPOSURE

The students were taken to see the Lego® Road Show. This is an elaborate display of Lego brick constructions of animals, buildings, and vehicles. These structures, built from thousands of Legos, were designed and built by Lego engineers. The students were overwhelmed by the exhibit and expressed a desire to become more elaborate in their own designs.

TYPE II—TRAINING

We called Lego headquarters (fortunately located in our area) and arranged for consultation with an engineer. He explained to the group how designs evolved; how creative thinking skills, especially flexibility, are needed; and how principles of calculus and physics are part of the building process. Ideas basically come from experimenting with the bricks. Once the concrete structure is completed, the design is drawn. These students were delighted to hear this. So many school assignments reverse this process—"put your plan in writing before you begin."

TYPE III—INVESTIGATION OF A REAL PROBLEM

The Lego executive in charge of marketing asked the students to design original structures for the museum display which the Lego Company was planning. The company agreed to furnish the bricks, offer technical advice, and display the product. Two boys, ages ten and twelve, eagerly accepted the challenge.

The ten-year-old designed and built an 18-wheeler truck, complete with separate tractor and trailer. The trailer was mounted on an appropriate platform and pivoted to facilitate a wide arc of movement. At the end of its two-foot long trailer was a gate that opened and closed by means of a pulley. Concern was shown by the young engineer for streamlined design for maximum function and form.

The twelve-year-old created a motorized amusement park ride. Intersecting aerial arms supported four miniature planes suspended in mid-air that revolved around its three-foot-high base. Twenty-seven revolutions comprised the ride. When asked why there were 27 revolutions, the young designer replied, "Because I set up the gears that way."

Reprinted from "Meeting the needs of learning disabled students" by Susan Baum, *Roeper Review*, 1984, 7 (1), pp. 13–19. Reprinted by permission of the author and *Roeper Review*.

---

and counseling were components that are more unique to gifted handicapped programs. Ironically, this gifted handicapped program endured some of the same criticism which plagues all gifted programming: Some charged that the program was "elitist" and that there was no need to treat gifted blind children differently than other blind children.

PARENTING

Parenting is a critical component of any gifted program. However, parents of gifted children with handicaps must deal with their child's special needs related to the handicap as well as attend to his or her giftedness. Parents of handicapped children often devote resources, time, energy, attention, and patience far beyond that given to a normal child, which can result in advantages or, sometimes, disadvantages for the child. Consider these situations identified by Rimm in her psychology practice:

1. Intensive parental teaching of the child provided on a continuous one-to-one basis increases sensory awareness, knowledge, vocabulary, and skill development. The child will learn a great deal about his or her environment from this abundance of early teaching in the home. This obviously is an advantage.

2. Counteridentification, the parent's deriving of personal feelings of success and failure through the child's accomplishments, may cause a parent to do too much for the child. A too-helpful parent may rob the child of opportunities to learn skills and build independence and self-confidence. In some cases a parent may even deny the existence of the child's handicap (for example, dyslexia, partial hearing loss). In other cases parents may use the child's handicap as an excuse for allowing the child to avoid responsibilities. Of course, the child soon learns to use the same kind of excuse to avoid unpleasant chores, for example, learning math facts. Thwarting independence and skill development is a disadvantage.

3. Manipulation by the child also can be an outcome of counteridentification. Because the parent is so anxious for their united success, the child, perhaps unconsciously, learns that he or she can easily control the parent ("I can't do it! You've got to help me!"). The manipulation skill acquired in the counteridentification process may be extended to teachers and peers. Manipulative attention-getting behaviors may take the form of overly dependent behavior, or a stubborn refusal to put forth effort in anything but the child's most preferred activities. This child and his or her parent will blame the school, the teacher, other children, and the remainder of the child's world for not helping the child to learn, instead of encouraging the child to take responsibility for his or her own learning. Manipulation, dependence, and refusal to work also are disadvantages.

4. Involvement by one parent may be so intense that it precludes the other parent from participating. For example, special skills such as using braille, American Sign Language, or special teaching procedures may need to be learned by a parent. If the second parent (usually father) has not also learned these techniques, he may be omitted from the special relationship and may decide that he is not a very good parent. This is particularly a problem if the child is a boy and the close parent is a mother. The alienation of the father may deprive the boy of an important identification figure and impede his independence and growth. The boy, as he matures, will feel both grateful to his mother for her commitment, but angry and impatient with her for his dependence on her. Neither mother nor son will understand the deterioration of what in childhood was such a strong positive relationship. Excluding one parent from close family relationships will always cause a serious problem.

A parent involvement group always should be part of a gifted program that serves students with handicaps. Such a group can help parents avoid some common problems. The group also can help parents focus on their children's strengths rather than dwell on their handicaps.

The *Retrieval and Acceleration of Promising Young Handicapped and Talented* (RAPYHT) project (Karnes, Shwedel, and Lewis, 1983; Karnes and Johnson 1991) is a program devoted to early education of gifted children with handicaps. It includes an active and effective parent component. Noted Karnes *et al.*, parent involvement helps maintain a consistent philosophy between home and school. In RAPYHT, parents participate in both identification and training. The latter involves parents in helping their children compensate for their handicapping condition and develop in their areas of giftedness. Parents are encouraged to help in the classroom and are given suggested activities to be carried out with their children at home. Large-group meetings, small-group discussion sessions, individual conferences, a newsletter, and a parent library all are part of the family involvement. The professional staff view family members as partners in the program (Karnes, 1984).

Although parents should always be involved in the education of their children, the special stresses and demands of parenting gifted students with handicaps requires an even closer partnership between their formal and informal educators—teachers and parents.

Collaboration

Consultative models which involve collaboration at various levels seem critical to appropriately providing for the needs of the handicapped gifted child (Van Tassel-Baska, 1991). Table 15.3 summarizes the three levels of collaboration advocated for appropriate programming for these children.

SUMMARY

Gifted children with handicaps typically are recognized for their handicaps, not their gifts. There have been few G/T programs designed for the handicapped gifted. Of the many varieties of physically and psychologically handicapping conditions, perhaps only mental retardation precludes most forms of giftedness.

Too often schools fail to accommodate the handicapped gifted. If the gifted child can function

TABLE 15.3   Levels of Collaboration for Addressing the Needs of Handicapped Gifted Learners

Level One	Collaboration as an interactive one-to-one relationship between a student and a significant adult or older student	Personalized treatment of issues, ideas and experiences
Level Two	Collaboration as a team of school-based educators addressing a common problem	1. Use of assessment for direct intervention purposes 2. Development of a tailored curriculum that responds to student's presenting behaviors 3. Evaluation and monitoring effectiveness of the curriculum
Level Three	Collaboration as a linkage to other institutions on mutual issues of concern	1. A broader array of resources for educational intervention 2. A better perspective on student needs may be gained

From "Serving the disabled gifted through educational collaboration," by Joyce Van Tassel-Baska, *Journal for the Education of the Gifted, 14,* 1991, 246–266. Copyright 1991 by The Council for Exceptional Children. Reprinted with permission.

reasonably well, special educational services may be withdrawn. Due largely to social rejection, handicapped students frequently have poor self-concepts.

Identification is difficult. Gifted students with handicaps tend to be unseen by teachers and even parents. Also, the handicap may obscure the expression of gifts and talents. While IQ scores can be extremely useful, they may be depressed by the tendency of sensory-impaired students to think less abstractly. In-service training dealing with characteristics of giftedness and identification methods is important.

Eisenberg and Epstein successfully used IQ and achievement scores, all Renzulli rating scales, peer nominations, and self-nominations for identification. Rimm emphasized the importance of discriminating between learning disabilities and underachievement. Maker and Silverman recommended comparing handicapped students with other similarly handicapped students, and to weight skills used to compensate more heavily. The Renzulli Creativity Scale and the PRIDE, GIFT, and GIFFI inventories might be used for identifying creative giftedness.

G/T programs for gifted children with handicaps can include the same acceleration, enrichment, grouping, and counseling components as other programs. Gifted children with Attention Deficit-Hyperactivity Disorder and Attention Deficit Disorder are especially likely to be put on drugs (Ritalin) because of their high energy and activity levels. Behavioral intervention is a better strategy.

Communication weaknesses must be compensated for via the use of mechanical aids and/or special training.

Developing positive self-concepts should be a main program goal of teaching the gifted with handicaps. Learning to value their own superior achievements and talents should help their self-concepts. Helping other students to appreciate the achievements of gifted students with handicaps also may be valuable. Peer support groups may help gifted students with handicaps develop good self-concepts and social skills.

Other children probably will require sensitivity and values clarification training to help them empathize with the handicapped. Learning teams may help improve attitudes towards students with handicaps.

Despite the necessity of one-to-one instruction for the gifted with handicaps, the teaching of independent learning and learning in small groups also is necessary. Even more than with other gifted students, high-level abstract-thinking skills must be taught.

The great attention parents must pay to their handicapped child may result in superior learning and cognitive development. However, it can also lead to the suppression of self-confidence and independence, learning to manipulate parents, teachers, and peers, and the elimination of one parent from the family relationship.

Parent involvement groups are a critical component of a program for gifted students with handicaps.

CHAPTER 16

PARENTING THE GIFTED CHILD

Parents want for their gifted children the same as all parents want for their children: Opportunities to learn all they are able to learn—no more, but certainly no less.

Gina Ginsberg Riggs (personal communication)

The "good parenting" any child needs is the main requirement for parenting the gifted child. However, there are some special obstacles, risks, errors, challenges, and joys that accompany being the parent of a child with unusual talents. Teachers should be sensitive to these matters in order to help guide parents of gifted children. For example: Contrary to popular belief, all parents everywhere do not believe their children are gifted. Some parents of gifted children will deny their children's special abilities in an attempt to keep them "normal" and "well-adjusted." Other parents, with the opposite attitude, seem to magnify their children's abilities and put excessive pressure on them for high achievement in all areas. This latter problem may include the tacit assumptions that (1) other children necessarily are inferior; and (2) by association, the parents also are superior. Either of these extremes, denying or magnifying giftedness, can cause problems for gifted children.

Overview

This chapter will emphasize some practical approaches to dealing with the special problems of parenting gifted and talented children. Although some concepts found here may apply to parenting all children, they are of special concern to parents—and therefore teachers—of gifted children.

THE "WHO'S IN CHARGE?" PROBLEM

If God had meant gifted children to run their homes, She would have created them bigger (Rimm, 1984).

Children who show unusual verbal and abstract-thinking ability appear to be wise and mature beyond their years, and to a degree they are. These deceptive characteristics may obscure the lack of experience and maturity that is typical of all children. It sometimes happens that devoted parents, intent on providing an ideal climate for their gifted children, fall into the trap of believing that these little beings, by virtue of their extensive vocabularies and impressive speech and logic, are capable very early of making complex decisions and setting their own goals and directions. Their interests and concerns, of course, should be considered, but parents and teachers must not abdicate responsibility for guidance.

Hollingworth (1942), in her pioneering work with gifted children, pointed out how critical it was to reach the "middle ground between arbitrary abolition of all argument and incessant argumentation." Finding that middle ground helps the child to accept the behavioral demands of adults while maintaining reasonable independence (Sebring, 1983). Ginsberg and Harrison (1977) made the following recommendation:

. . . Discipline your gifted child when he needs disciplining. Correct him when he needs correction. Give direction when he needs direction. He should not be granted special privileges nor should unacceptable behavior be tolerated because of his intellectual gifts . . . (p. 7)

Regarding educational guidance, successful gifted achievers will usually agree that throughout their schooling they felt confident that (1) their parents and teachers were concerned and knowledgeable about an appropriate direction for their education, and that (2) following their lead was usually a wise decision.

Empowering children with adult decision-making provides power without wisdom. This can lead to formidable and continuing conflicts between gifted children and their parents as they compete for the power that parents give too early and try to recover too late. The resulting adversary mode may force adolescents to rebel too stubbornly, parents to respond too negatively, and both to lose the positive home atmosphere that is so valuable in educating a gifted child.

Baldwin (1988) described "Cornucopia Kids" as children who were given too much. He indicated that overindulged children acquire an inappropriate sense of power. Whatever the reasons for the overindulgence, it gives the children a sense of control over their parents and the belief that getting what they want is their right. He noted that it sets the stage for problems throughout life in both work and personal relationships. Hollingsworth (1990) constructed a brief informal overindulgence test (Inset 16.1). Parents may wish to check their scores to see if they might be giving too much and risking putting their children "in charge" before they are ready.

PARENTING BY POSITIVE EXPECTATIONS

Parenting by *positive expectations* can be extraordinarily successful in guiding gifted children both in school and out. If high achievement, positive attitudes, and constructive behavior are expected and reinforced by parents, they will become internalized by the child and the need for punishment usually will be negligible. How do some parents guide their children so well without punishment while others seem to need and use it so frequently?

Clear and consistent *messages*, agreed upon by both parents and transmitted to the child, are basic. In Bloom's (1985) study of talent development of concert pianists, sculptors, mathematicians, and neurologists, he found that all had in common some very clear early messages provided by parents.

. . . parents placed great stress on achievement, on success and on doing one's best at all times . . . they were models of the "work ethic" in that they were regarded as hard workers. . . . To excel, to do one's best, to work hard, and to spend one's time constructively were emphasized over and over again (p. 510).

Csikszentmihalyi (described in Adler, 1991) studied 210 high school students who were exceptionally talented in math, science, music, sports, or art. He discovered that the most motivated ones came from families who provided both support and challenge. He compared these students to students from families that provided challenge but not support, support but not challenge, and neither challenge nor support. The students from the supportive and challenging families were more intrinsically interested in learning and were more alert while they were studying.

Parental agreement on such values as (1) the importance of study, learning, and school; (2) respect for individuality; and (3) recognition of the need for reasonable amounts of recreation and fun seem to underly a positive and achievement-oriented atmosphere. Excessive double messages and half-truths related to these matters can cause problems for children. A *double message* is two contradictory messages given by one parent, or else opposite messages sent by two parents. A *half-truth* is a message that is partly true and partly false and therefore is easily misinterpreted by the gifted child. We will look at some common and troublesome parent-to-child messages.

INSET 16.1 _____

Take the Overindulgence Test

Parents should independently and honestly answer the following questions. Put an × in the column that best describes your answer.

	1 little	2 some	3 moderate	4 great amount
1. My child participates in organized activities.				
2. My life is devoted to my child.				
3. I anticipate most of my child's wishes.				
4. I am involved in my child's homework.				
5. My child receives praise for accomplishment.				
6. I select my child's clothes.				
7. I give my child money that is not associated with chores.				

All ×'s in column one get 1 point; in column two, 2 points; in column three, 3 points; and in column four, 4 points. Now total your score. A score of 7–13 may indicate not enough indulgence. A score of 14 to 21 indicates a balanced approach to parenting, while a score of 22 to 28 indicates a tendency to overindulge.

From Hollingsworth (1990). Reprinted by permission of the author and _Gifted Child Today_.

DOUBLE MESSAGES AND HALF-TRUTHS

The "Yes-No" Message

The parent who loses his or her temper with a young child one moment, then apologizes and begs forgiveness immediately after, is giving a confused "yes-no" message to the child. The child does not really understand if the parent approves or disapproves of the behavior. However, the child does learn that the behavior has brought an inordinate amount of valued warmth and attention. Rea-sonably enough, the child may increase the kind of (undesirable) behavior that produces the attention. Punishments are thus punctuated by hugs and affection, and the child, persuaded by a strong basic need for love, may _increase_ the troublesome behavior in a self-perpetuating, self-accelerating negative ritual.

As a variation, confusing yes-no messages also apply to misbehavior for which the child learns to apologize—and for which he or she receives forgiveness and affection. These children learn that virtually any behavior (for example, ignoring chores, misbehavior, or poor schoolwork) is acceptable, as long as it is followed by an apology or an "I'll study and try my best next time." Gifted children who use this strategy can become facile manipulators both at home and at school. For example, after each test for which they fail to study, they will have an excuse and an apology that the teacher frequently believes. The same manipulation ritual learned at home is thus transferred to the classroom. The dynamics of the situation confuse parents, teachers, and the gifted children themselves.

The "That's Good, But Don't Think You're Gifted" Message

This particular message may be transmitted by parents whose primary goal is to raise children who are "well-adjusted." Their expectations include an image of their child becoming a school class officer, an athlete (preferably a star), prom king or queen, and excelling at other forms of leadership and popularity. Their expectations specifically exclude the image of their child being seen as a "nerd" or "egghead," having a too-big vocabulary, having too many intellectual interests, and being socially excluded. In an unreasonable fear that their bright child may become too involved in academics, they will prefer that the child *not* be part of a gifted program. When the child does excel in academic contests or grades, they may respond with, "That's very good, but don't think you're gifted," or "I'm glad you're interested in reading, but you need to be well-rounded. How about the soccer team?"

This child usually begins school as a successful student and quickly finds him- or herself identified as *bright*. If there is a gifted program, the child will be recommended for it. Although the teacher and the school send the child positive messages for his or her accomplishments, the parents' messages are ambiguous. In response, the child may become careless about schoolwork, and friends and playground activities take precedence. Grades and test scores begin to decline, but social leadership improves. Parents may be satisfied for a while—until in a parent-teacher conference the teacher explains that the child is not doing his or her homework and has careless study habits. Worse, he or she seems uninterested in school.

It is now time for a new message, inconsistent with the previous one. Parents now are disappointed with the laziness and poor study habits, and they may begin a withdrawal of privileges based upon grades. Popularity and leadership is suddenly a nonissue. Meanwhile, the child has lost confidence in his or her ability to achieve at a superior level, and the current skills gap may indeed make it difficult to perform well. Sports and friendships have become the highest priority—and these friends do not value brains and achievement.

At this point there no longer is a danger that the child will be labeled "gifted," which, of course, was the parents' initial preference. However, they are not particularly comfortable with the *underachiever* label either. The double messages of "Achievement is fine, but being well-rounded is better" and later "Popularity is fine, but you're not achieving up to your capability" can lead to both irreversible underachievement and a strained parent-child relationship.

The "Let Me Help You Make It Better" Syndrome: Counteridentification

This double message is given by a parent who places a high value on the child's giftedness and also counteridentifies with the child. As we know, in counteridentification the parent sees him- or herself in the child and, perhaps unconsciously, lives through the child's experiences as if they were the parent's own. The child's accomplishments become the parent's victories; the child's losses are the parent's defeats. Parent involvement in the child's projects goes beyond guidance and mutual interest to active participation and, all too often, taking charge of the projects.

Each accomplishment of the child typically is followed by "helpful" parent criticism. This criticism involves more than just small suggestions; it usually changes the child's original idea and remakes it into the parent's project. The completed project may indeed be of adult quality, and in fact wins praise from teachers or wins prizes in contests. The child receives a reputation for excellence, originality, and brilliance. The parents are pleased with the child's performance and deny, even to themselves, their involvement.

Unfortunately, the child acquires feelings of doubt and ambiguity about his or her own abilities. Although delighted with the successful outcomes, the child had difficulty defining his or her own contributions. Moreover, because parental standards are so high, new projects become difficult to start. And once a project is begun, the insecure child's goal becomes perfection and the work is meticulously slow and executed too carefully. Finishing the work thus is difficult because the child feels it will never be good enough.

Goal setting may become "defensive," aimed at protecting against feelings of failure and low ability (Covington and Beery, 1976). The activities the child selects are so easy that he or she cannot fail, or else so difficult that perfectionism and high standards may be used as excuses for not completing them. The child also may manipulate parents into more and more involvement in projects and activities, and because the parents cannot bear to see their child (or themselves) fail, they are pleased with the continuous opportunity to help.

The child may become fearful that the world will discover somehow that he or she is not truly as bright as the schoolwork and IQ and achievement tests indicate. The child also might write off the purported high ability, viewing it as only the ability to get good grades, but not meaning much else in the world.

The double message that counteridentifying parents give their child is that he or she is (1) gifted, but (2) still needs much help in order to perform at an acceptably high level. Such well-meaning parents rob their child of self-confidence, spontaneity, creative thinking, and independent work. Children can only build confidence from competent personal achievement.

This theme has many variations in terms of kinds of achievement (or lack of achievement), type of parental assistance, and the type of defense mechanisms used to cope with the feelings of doubt and ambiguity. However, underlying the observed behavior is a serious *lack of self-confidence*, making the child less resilient during normal failure experiences that are part of competing and achieving. Importantly, observers of this gifted child usually cannot understand the reason for the low confidence, in view of his or her superior talents and abilities.

The "Grades Don't Count—Or Do They?" Double Message

Messages from parents about grades often are inconsistent and confusing. Calling them "double" messages is an understatement because, in any one family, the messages are likely to vary with each parent, for each child, for different subjects, and at different times. For example, Mom might strongly reinforce an *A* on a social studies test, but a week later tell the same child that his or her *C* on the next test is ". . . fine, because it's a hard subject." Furthermore, to add to the child's confusion, still other ambiguous grade messages come from teachers, peers, siblings, and even grandparents.

How can we resolve this dilemma? As parents, we know that grades are the main communicators of achievement from teachers to children and parents. Parents need to consider several important realities:

1. Grades will always be used to evaluate performance, and thus will open and close opportunity doors.

2. Children will always be able to control their own grades to some extent, but never completely. The vicissitudes of teachers and evaluators will always be part of the outcome.

3. Children should be expected to earn the best grades they are able to earn. However, if the outcome is not satisfactory after trying their best, children should look first at their own work habits to determine if they are indeed studying as efficiently as possible. At the same time, it also is fair for them to examine teacher grading styles and possible teacher biases.

4. Children should not be urged to close doors on some types of schoolwork (for example, math or science) because of less-than-outstanding grades. This point will be addressed further when we discuss the "Winning Is Everything" message.

5. If low or mediocre grades do close one door for children, they need to learn to be resilient enough to search out other opportunities and to recognize that they need not view themselves as "failures" in schoolwork. Other "open doors" can be other subjects, other years, other teachers, and other eventual careers.

6. For gifted and talented students, high grades in core academic areas are important, even if the course content is seen as "boring;" however, high grades in all courses are not equally important. Thus gifted children should be expected to get good grades in math and reading, even though they may dislike math facts or reading and language-arts workbooks.

It is certainly all right for children to receive *A*'s in physical education, but unless they plan to direct their careers toward the sports world, *B*'s and *C*'s are acceptable, and enjoyable physical activity should be a more important goal than the grade. Gifted and talented children also should be relieved of strong pressure to earn straight *A*'s in home economics, manual arts, and perhaps even art, drama, and orchestra unless these represent a central college or career direction.

It seems important to give gifted children a message of what is *central* to their education versus what is *peripheral* (that is, primarily valuable for one's general education, cultural enrichment, or even enjoyment). This message must come from parents, since teachers of "peripheral" subjects will have different opinions.

The "Winning Is Everything" Message

Competition in school presents multiple messages that can confuse both adults and children. For gifted children, competition provides special difficulties. Gifted children usually enter school as "winners" and if they are high achievers, they may continue as winners with little effort. Because of their effortless successes, there is little early challenge, and they may not easily see the relationship between competitive effort and achievement. However, at some point in their school career—for some gifted children by the second grade, but for others not until college—they discover that they are effortless winners no longer.

If they do not also discover that, with effort, they can again become winners, they may adopt maladaptive coping strategies. For example, they may write themselves off as school "losers" and *mentally* drop out. That is, they may choose sports, the drama club, or mischief as their area of winning, thus competing in nonacademic, non-career areas. They might also stop competing completely and view themselves as "average kids" who do not need to compete, who do not need to work very hard to "get by." None of these self-messages encourages the gifted child to use his or her superior abilities.

In many cases, students' self-messages are a reflection of their parent's misleading messages. One such message is to "be a winner—and if not at academics, then at sports or something else." This message encourages the gifted child to redirect the efforts from the academic classroom to the gymnasium or athletic field, where the delighted parents can cheer their child's victories. A related and equally misleading message sent by parents is, "If you can't win, you're a loser." This message causes the gifted child to accept his or her losing status as evidence of lack of ability.

Neither message helps children see that there are

many levels of winning other than being "Number 1." Also, children and adolescents should learn that using their superior abilities to succeed in school will sooner or later extend their options for important lifetime winning.

Of course, achievement involves excellence, and excellence certainly can be translated by children as "winning." However, if excellence and winning are viewed by parents only as achieving "first place," their children obviously run a high risk of failure. As a consequence, they will come to view their performances that are actually successful as less than adequate, and will continue to search in frustration for areas where they may compete to win "first place." Alternatively, they may give up the competition entirely. Gifted teenagers, we might note, are overrepresented in the ranks of high school dropouts.

A shocking statistic, which should certainly give parents and teachers of the gifted good reason to clarify the "first place" competitive message, is that a full 40 percent of the top 5 percent of our high school graduates do not graduate from college. While the reasons for some of those nongraduations may be related to cultural or financial problems, from the second author's clinical experience it appears that many gifted, high-achieving students are not prepared for the competitive environments they find in college. Here is a true case:

Amanda was given a leave of absence from Harvard College after the first semester of her sophomore year. Her grades were poor, and some course requirements were not completed. Lack of self-confidence and related health problems were issues that persuaded her to take some time off in the hope that she might eventually return to school. Amanda had been an outstanding student in a challenging high school environment and had graduated third in her class. "She was not first," she explained, "only because she was involved in so many extracurricular activities." She perceived her high

school years as socially and academically successful. She indicated that she did not really recall any serious challenge. She had always felt certain that there would be no academic challenge that would be too difficult.

At Harvard, she found that even dedicated study brought her no As. She tried her favorite extracurricular activity, drama, but continued to feel inadequate by comparison to her peers. She continually compared herself to others. Her confidence dissipated, and her excuses for skipping classes multiplied. She soon felt so inadequate that she was unable to continue. Only after therapy was Amanda able to return to cope with the competition that had made her feel so inadequate.

Amanda is just one of many students who accept the "winning is everything" message as a child and adolescent. Gifted college students who feel strong pressure from parents or have internalized their own pressure to be "Number 1" must learn to function in competition with students who are equally or more capable. Or else learn to cope with strong feelings of inadequacy.

The "Mom (or Dad) Is An Ogre" Message: Parent Rivalry

Even in good marriage relationships there is often subtle competition between parents for the favor and control of children. The result, frequently, is "ogre games" (described earlier in Chapter 13) in which one parent takes for him or herself the role of "good, kind parent," leaving the spouse the role of disciplinarian—the *ogre* ("It's fine with me if you stay over at Susan's—but your mother doesn't want you to"). Gifted kids easily learn to manipulate this relationship very effectively ("Dad says it's okay, but you won't let me do anything!"). Ackerman (1980), in his recommendations for family therapy, emphasized that a coalition formed between one parent and an adolescent leads to family disequilibrium and heightened stress between the child and the other parent.

What seems like a healthy parent-child alliance easily transforms the other parent into the "ogre."

Of course, parents cannot ignore each other's opinions related to child rearing. However, as in all other components of a marriage, parents must make compromises in what they believe is good parenting, and they must support each other in their decisions. There is no one correct way for bringing up gifted children. However, if there is just one message from educational and clinical research that seems critically important to effective parenting, it is that two parents who show overt mutual respect for each other's opinions and each other's accomplishments provide ideal models for gifted children of both sexes.

How Clear is Too Clear?: Parenting for Creativity and Conformity

Kegley and Siggers (1989) addressed a traditional problem in the field of creativity from the point of view of parenting: How can we teach children to both "think creatively and freely," yet conform to necessary social rules and "do what they are told?" They pointed out that if parents are too dogmatic, rigid, singular, restrictive, and lack playfulness and free thinking, their child's creativity will suffer. They recommended that parents "extend to the child permission to become creative" (p. 3), and offer a safe setting in which the child is free to experiment, take risks, and be exuberant, expansive, and open to new and divergent possibilities. The child should be able to operate from a basis of security, yet be free to be different.

What Can Parents Do?

Perhaps we first should accept the inevitable. As parents, we will not do and say what is "right" all of the time, nor do we need such absolute consistency. However, we do need to avoid a pattern of double messages and creativity squelchers that cause problems for our children.

If the gifted child (or children) in the family are performing well, enjoying the expression of their talents, and growing positively in other ways, it is reasonable to assume that parents are doing their parenting job very well. Again, there is no one right way, but many. However, if the children (1) appear to be under stress, (2) are not achieving well and responsibly, (3) have serious social problems, and/or (4) have unusually difficult family relationships, one should look for a possible family pattern causing the problem. Our list of double messages and half-truths includes some common sources of such problems. When parents can clarify these messages, the results may profoundly help gifted children both in their family relationships and in the classroom.

Parents can certainly be effective mentors for their children (Meador, 1992; McCollim, 1992; Roberts, 1992). A comment by one gifted person bears this out (Krueger, 1978):

> My family has valued education and has strong interests in art, literature, and music. Because we are close, I've tried to emulate my parents. It is by imitating them, rather than from their telling me what to do, that I've developed a passion for learning and a compulsion to work in an organized manner. But I strongly believe that because of their love and affection, my parents gave me the self-esteem which is an essential element in constructive thinking.

In studies of giftedness and eminence (Bloom, 1985; MacKinnon, 1965; Walberg and Herbig, 1991; Rimm and Lowe, 1988), there were always themes of family organization and consistent and predictable expectations for conduct. High energy and an achievement orientation were also characteristic of almost all parents (Albert, 1980; Bloom, 1985; Goertzel and Goertzel, 1962).

COMPETITION AND PRESSURE

Competition encourages and motivates gifted children to perform to the best of their high ability, and the recognition they receive for their successes provides the motivation for continued competition. However, there are some negative side effects of extreme competitiveness. Several of these will be discussed separately.

Stress

The very competitive child may feel under continuous *stress*. Such children may exhibit symptoms of tension such as nail biting, enuresis (bed wetting), extreme sibling rivalry, loss of appetite, irritability, stomach pains, headaches, or nightmares. These problems can complicate children's lives; they also can be informative to parents who are aware of the potential meaning of such symptoms. Of course, every normal child exhibits these symptoms occasionally. However, continued or increased symptoms very often can be attributed to competitive stress; they are physical reactions to frustrations and anxieties.

Parents and teachers should try to help the child identify specific stressors, and then restructure tasks and goals to diminish the stress. For example, the parents or teachers of a high school student can help the student decide upon a sensible academic load that challenges his or her abilities but is not overwhelming. Extracurricular activities must be made manageable. Younger children also can find themselves under too much pressure, with plenty of homework, music lessons, Little League, soccer, and trying hard to excel in all subjects and interests while simultaneously burdened with too many friends who have plenty of ideas of their own.

A subtle source of competitive stress comes from repeated adult praise which comments on being "perfect" or the "best" or the "smartest" or the "most beautiful." Such superlatives may have the impact of creating unreasonable pressure to be perfect or the best or the smartest or the most beautiful. Adults do not intend to create pressure for children by such comments. To the contrary, their intent is to build confidence. However, if children receive too much attention based on "being first," it takes on a value which they may feel pressured to maintain.

Comments from adults which address effort, improvement, perseverance, good thinking, creative problem solving, kindness, sensitivity, talent, and intelligence—and which do not emphasize "best" and "first"—will encourage motivation without pressure. Exaggerated praise which uses such terms as *brilliance, genius, smartest, most creative,* or *most talented* leads to pressure. Although well intended, such extreme praise may do serious harm.

Cornell and Grossberg (1989) found that all of the 83 families of children who were involved in gifted programs thought of their children as gifted. There were no significant differences between children in either achievement or adjustment regardless of how parents defined *giftedness* or whether they thought of their children as "usually" or "sometimes" gifted. However, among the 25 percent of the children who were verbally referred to as "gifted" by their parents, there were more likely to be adjustment problems which included discipline and/or poor self-control plus anxiety and guilt. The authors suggest that direct reference to the child as "gifted" places excessive pressure on the child. Perhaps telling the child he or she is "gifted" operates in precisely the same way as does extreme praise.

In some cases children who appear to "not get anything done" also may be feeling stress. The tension may stem more from worries about inadequacy and from work undone than by the actual hard work. Here is an example:

> Bobby, a gifted fourth-grader, complained of stomachaches which he related to worrying about the difficulty of his mathematics. He said that even while he watched TV and tried not to think about his math, he felt sick to his stomach. It was recommended that Bobby change his study habits and do his math right after school, before watching TV and worrying. The stomachaches "miraculously" disappeared and Bobby found math to be much simpler than he thought.

Rimm's Law (Rimm, 1986b) that covers this case states:

Children feel more tension when they are worrying about their work than when they are doing that work.

If parents or teachers cannot identify the source of the stress, professional help from a guidance counselor or a school or clinical psychologist may be required. It is much easier to identify and treat a stress problem early than after it leads to habitual maladaptive coping patterns for the child.

A helpful way to understand the relationship between stress and efficient performance is illustrated by the classic *Yerkes-Dodson law* (Hebb, 1972; Figure 16.1). This principle holds that under very low stress (or motivation, or "psychological arousal") people perform inefficiently. As the stress or arousal level increases, efficiency also increases. Performance and efficiency peak at an intermediate level, which will vary somewhat for different persons and for different tasks. As stress continues to increase after that, efficiency decreases until, at extreme tension levels, performance is disorganized.

Any reader can relate to this experience. At some time, probably, you studied hard for an important and difficult examination, one which caused a great deal of stress. On examination day, you anxiously entered the classroom, stared at the examination on your desk, and for at least the first few minutes felt as if you could not recall any but the most simple ideas. Your stomach may have felt tight, and you probably felt hot or cold all over and slightly nauseous. Sometimes, the inability to perform will increase the anxiety and stress still further. Other times, one is able to calm down to a more optimal level of arousal and then perform very well.

Competitive children—and most gifted children are competitive—are more vulnerable to stress. Parents and teachers cannot deliver them from stress, but they can model and teach stress reduction measures. Involvement in many different competitive activities may help children learn to cope with competition in a more routine way. Suggesting that they concentrate on the activity itself instead of their place in the competition encourages less stress and better quality performance.

Some other simple approaches to dealing with stress include regular physical exercise, recreational and "fun" activities, and especially the availability of a safe and empathic environment where children can talk openly about their pressures and anxieties. A caution, however, is that in providing that safe environment it is important that parents not counteridentify so much with the stress that their own felt anxiety actually increases the anxiety level of their child.

Webb, Meckstroth, and Tolan (1982) recommend using humor to help reduce stress. For example, parents can be melodramatic about their own "intolerable" stresses and problems—making it clear that they are laughing at themselves. Parents can also encourage the child to "think out loud" about stress by gently raising questions such as, "What is the worst thing that could happen in that situation?" and "How big a catastrophe would that be?"

In sum, parents and teachers can best help children deal with stress from competition by (1) identifying the source of the stress and then helping the

FIGURE 16.1.   The Yerkes-Dodson Law Relating Stress (or Arousal) to Level of Effectiveness.
From *Textbook of Psychology*, 3rd. ed. (1972), by D.O. Hebb. Copyright © 1972 by Saunders College Publishing, a division of Holt, Rinehart and Winston Inc., reprinted by permission of the publisher.

student redefine priorities to reduce the stress, (2) recognizing that a moderate and manageable amount of stress is necessary for peak performance, (3) helping provide outlets or "therapy" in the form of physical and other enjoyable activities, and (4) lending an understanding, empathic, and perhaps humorous ear. These techniques can be very useful in preventing deterioration of performance due to high stress.

Failure

Gail Sheehy (1982) in her book *Pathfinders* discussed differences among adults in handling their own development crises. In comparing adults who viewed themselves as successful and who led reasonably fullfilled lives versus those who saw their lives as filled with frustration and failure, she concluded that the main difference was the way in which they dealt with their *failures*. "Pathfinders," the term she used for the more satisfied persons, experienced just as many failure experiences as did the others; however, they were able to use those failures to grow and move forward. The less fulfilled persons, on the other hand, came to identify themselves as failures and remained in their less-than-satisfactory life positions.

It appears that gifted children, and perhaps all children, establish similar patterns. Children who are high achievers, creative, and success oriented, view their failures and losses as learning experiences (Covington and Beery, 1976). When failure occurs, they identify the problems, remedy the deficiencies, reset their goals, and grow from the experience. Failure is only a temporary setback, and they learn to attribute their failure to lack of effort, the unusual difficulty of a task, or perhaps the extraordinary skill of other competitors. As coping strategies, they may laugh at their errors, determine to work harder, and/or redesign their achievement goals. Importantly, they see themselves as falling short of a *goal*, not falling short as *persons*.

Other children, the nonpathfinders, usually take one of two main paths. Some children will persevere in the same direction, disappointed by their performance but determined to achieve that initial goal. If the goal is realistic, the renewed effort and determination may produce a satisfying success and they may feel like "winners" in the competitive game. If the goal is unrealistic, their continued efforts are likely to fail and produce continued frustration and stress.

The other path is even more destructive. With failure, they become *failure oriented* (Covington and Beery, 1976). They come to view school as a competitive game they are incapable of winning, and so they decide that there is little purpose in playing. They learn to give up easily and they "get by" with a minimum of effort. The skill deficits increase, and these gifted children become underachievers who have little or no confidence in their ability to compete successfully in the school game.

To help their gifted child cope with failure, parents should first examine their own competitive style; the child may have learned maladaptive responses to failure from one or both parents. For example, parents may model an attitude of quitting too quickly if a problem gets difficult, of avoiding any type of competition, or of habitually blaming external sources for their own shortcomings or lack of effort. A possible restructuring of parent attitudes and expectancies may be the first item on the agenda for helping the gifted child who is not faring well in academic competition.

As another remedy, children may be taught to identify creative alternatives for their losses or failures. For example, they should recognize that normal people—even very talented ones—cannot be "Number 1" in absolutely everything, and that each has compensating areas in which they are quite outstanding. The child need not feel insecure or threatened by an occasional setback. Note, however, that a discussion of a child's failure may need to wait until after the emotional tension is reduced in order to avoid defensive behaviors. Parents cannot expect rational perception or logical thinking during the immediate stress period following an upsetting defeat.

A questioning approach, rather than a lecture,

may better help the child understand that (1) one cannot always win, (2) disappointment does not mean that he or she is a failure, (3) the particular experience simply was not as successful as he or she had hoped it would be, and especially (4) the central goal is to play the learning game at the student's best performance level, regardless of his or her competitive ranking.

Peripheral Diversion. It is important for parents to send a clear and direct message to their gifted child about the central role that school learning plays in their life. Indeed, if the child is to succeed academically in a way that both capitalizes on all of his or her abilities and optimally prepares the child for higher education, then the "learning game" should be played above all others. As noted earlier, if parent messages stress that winning—regardless of the game—is all important, then winning at tennis, on the swim team, or in popularity contests may become too critical to the gifted child. A sad sight is unfulfilled adults in their twenties or thirties whose peak life achievement was election to junior class president or being star of the basketball team. Their competitive strivings helped them perform at their best, but in areas we might call peripheral. Of course, high school should not be all drudgery. However, with gifted and talented students who should be aiming at higher education and professional careers, academics should not play second fiddle to socializing or athletics.

Noncompetitive Intellectual Activities. Gifted high achievers and gifted underachievers both may be highly competitive and competition conscious. In the case of the high achievers, such competitiveness is functional. For underachievers it is dysfunctional, since they may perceive themselves as "losers" in the school game and therefore stop making an effort to compete.

For both groups, however, involvement in intellectual activities that are noncompetitive can be extremely valuable. Some examples of noncompetitive intellectual activities might include individualized self-paced instruction (for example, at learning centers or with language-learning cassettes), after-school clubs or interest groups, home hobbies or interests such as computers or reading, small-group field trips, independent research projects, or creative arts or writing. For the highly competitive achiever, such activities broaden knowledge and interests, encourage the reflective pause necessary for creativity, and provide a comfortable respite from the more highly competitive efforts. For underachievers, noncompetitive intellectual activities entice them into playing the learning/thinking game without fear of failure. To experience the joy of intellectual discovery is a critical goal for all gifted children, and noncompetitive intellectual activities are a good route to this goal.

Sibling Problems

Sibling rivalry seems inherent in Western civilization family structure. It can be minimized and adjusted for, but it will not disappear. The underlying cause of sibling rivalry is competition for parents' attention and, sometimes, resources. With gifted children, particular sibling combinations seem to cause special complications and therefore require special handling by parents and teachers. Several of these will be described shortly.

First, however, it is important to recognize a vital underlying principal for the care and handling of all children: *Each and every child in a family should be provided the most ideal opportunity for intellectual and creative development for that particular child.* Individual opportunities should not be eliminated because of a misguided democratic commitment to precisely equal treatment for every child. Opportunities for gifted children should not be avoided or ignored simply because less able and less interested siblings cannot participate in the same activity. Other children can be offered comparably attractive—but not necessarily identical—educational or recreational opportunities. For example, if one child strongly wishes to attend a Russian language camp or a Saturday computer class, then an alternative in music, art, swimming or tennis could be offered to a sibling who might feel cheated. Children have different abilities and different needs, and the most productive, and most fair, approach is to accommodate those differences. Treating siblings the same actually exacerbates competition as children vie for recognition of their own individuality (see Inset 16.2).

A subtle source of sibling rivalry may stem from preferential treatment of one child over the other from significant others, for example, grandparents, aunts, uncles, or neighbors. Certainly parents should ask those adults to be cautious and fair to all siblings. Sometimes this does not work and parents must take responsibility for monitoring fair treatment. Grandparents and important adults may continue to provide individual children with special opportunities based on age or particular interests and abilities, but not based on a favored child relationship.

Some typical sibling relationships that cause special problems for gifted children, and some suggestions for dealing with them, are outlined in the following.

INSET 16.2

A Chicken Rivalry Story

A children's book called *The Most Wonderful Egg in the World*, by Helme Heine (1983), provides a delightful vehicle for parents to deal with differences among siblings and their concerns about being best.

Dotty, Stalky, and Plumy are three hens who argue about which is the most beautiful. They visit the king for his judgment. The wise king views all three and announces "What you can do is more important than what you look like" and challenges the three to produce beautiful eggs. To the producer of the most beautiful egg he offers the award of status as princess.

Dotty begins the egg laying contest by producing an egg so white and spotless and perfect that all agree it will not be surpassed. Stalky gains the sympathy of all until she produces the largest egg that any have ever seen. The sympathy is then directed toward Plumy, for surely she will not be able to compete. To everyone's surprise she produces a perfectly square egg which is surely the most unusual. The philosophical king recognizes the merit of the different excellences and awards all three with princess status. They no longer argue and go on producing wonderful eggs forever.

The king's message of the importance of the production (work) rather than appearance is the first critical family communication. Equally valuable, however, is the message that family members can excel in different ways and can all be valued for their talents without one being the "best." That makes it possible for children to understand that they can all be smart without pressure to outdo each other. They can have a "whole smart family" without putting their brother or sister down so that they can feel smarter. Of course, the concept of many excellences without any one superlative can be generalized to their friends and classmates as well.

From *The Most Wonderful Egg in the World* by Helme Heine. Copyright © 1983 by Gertrude Middelhauve Verlag, Koln. English translation copyright © 1983 J.M. Dent & Sons, Ltd. Reprinted with permission of Margaret K. McElderry Books, an imprint of Macmillan Publishing Company.

The Gifted Child with Less Talented Siblings.
The gifted child with very high intelligence or an extraordinary special talent provides impossible competition in his or her area of giftedness for other children. The unique ability often requires an investment of an inordinate amount of time and resources to provide the special educational opportunities necessary to develop the talent and meet this child's unconventional needs. In the process, the gifted child naturally receives a large amount of attention and recognition. His or her brothers and sisters need to be able to admire the gifted sibling's success, but also recognize that a similar level of success probably is not attainable for them. They must use a different measuring stick to evaluate their own abilities, or they may fall into the trap of viewing their own real successes (and themselves) as failures. In the words of one successful and gifted "second sibling:"

> Once I realized that there was nothing I could do to achieve as well as my sister, I decided to stop competing with her, to do the best I could, and to realize that what I was doing was really good too.

Although this youngster came to realize that he could be successful despite his being a "second place" student, that realization was not automatic. In addition to rewarding the victories of their most gifted child, parents also must recognize and reward the successes of other siblings—basing those rewards on each child's abilities and efforts.

Research on families where one child is identified as gifted and others are not confirms that problems arise for the nonlabeled child. In one study, parents reported a negative and disruptive effect on the nongifted siblings, which disturbed the status quo of the family (Fisher, 1981). Cornell (1983) also found "nongifted" siblings of gifted children to be less well-adjusted than a control group of other nongifted children. In a study by Cornell and Grossberg (1986), children who had been rated as "less gifted" than their siblings had higher anxiety and lower self-esteem than their sisters and brothers in gifted programs. Grenier

(1985) also reported higher self-esteem for children labeled "gifted," compared with their siblings. Furthermore, there was increased friction when the age difference between siblings was less than three years. Pfouts (1980) similarly found that the closer the age spacing the more the siblings were affected negatively in family relationships and personal adjustment, and also that younger siblings were also affected negatively in academic performance. Strangely, Ballering and Koch (1984) found that the gifted children perceived the sibling relationships as more negative than did their nongifted brothers and sisters.

Although all the above studies included gifted children and their nonlabeled siblings, the Pfouts (1980) study was based on siblings at all intelligence levels—suggesting that the results of gifted/nongifted comparing may be less related to the labeling than to sibling rivalry in general. Furthermore, Colangelo and Brower (1987) concluded that there were no long-term effects (five years or more) from the differential labeling within the family, and that nongifted siblings eventually "came to terms" with the gifted label of their siblings.

The Gifted Child in a Family of Other Achieving Gifted Children.   It is not unusual to find that all of the children in a family are gifted; this could be due to genetics, a favorable environment, positive parent and teacher expectations, or most likely "all of the above." It is important to recognize that each child in the family will feel increased pressure to fulfill the expectations set by preceding siblings. The first day of school for "child two," "child three," or "child four" inevitably begins with, "Oh yes, I know your sister. She was such a good student!" If the child is gifted and confident, this identification may be pleasing because he or she recognizes that the teacher has expectations that can be fulfilled. Moreover, this early recognition may quickly produce privileges and trust that otherwise would take longer to earn.

On the other hand, a less confident child may see the early identification by the teacher as a threat, since the child may worry that his or her performance will be less impressive than that of the older sibling. A sensitive teacher will quickly learn to recognize differences between siblings. Nonetheless, parents still may need to explain that "Mrs. Jones had Carlos too, but she'll soon get to know that you're also a good worker, even though you're different than your brother."

Perhaps most important, parents of several gifted children may need to make a specific effort to ease the grade pressure for younger children. Parents should let them know that the parents understand the special pressures the children feel due to the inevitable comparisons with their siblings. The parent's "expectation message" should be that each child is expected to do the very best he or she can, and that the child's performance will be individually evaluated, not compared with the record of the older brother or sister.

The Gifted Child with a Close-Age Older Sibling of Lesser Ability.

One of the most difficult relationships exists when a younger gifted child has a brother or sister of average ability (or less) who is older by just one or two years. The most typical tendency is for parents to refrain from providing appropriate enriched opportunities for the gifted child in fear of embarrassing the inevitably insecure older child. For the gifted child, this strategy produces both frustration, from the reduced opportunities for skill development, plus pressure to underarchive and hide the high ability. The older child, of course, feels the sibling pressure anyway. In many cases, the older child also acquires lower achievement motivation due to the continual assurances that he or she is not really expected to achieve at a high level.

A better approach is to reinforce the gifted child's achievements, even if it means acceleration to the same grade as the older child. (Needless to say, it will be best if the siblings are *not* in the same classroom.) Also, parents absolutely must reinforce the older child's achievements according to that child's efforts and abilities. As the children become mature enough to discuss their differing abilities and the sense of competition

they feel, such open discussions will help them deal with their sense of personal worth despite obvious differences in talent, school grades, and academic recognition.

Some parents will feel an altruistic commitment to "root for the underdog." While it's very American, this attitude can put unpleasant pressure on all children. Especially, the younger high achiever will not receive recognition at home for his or her superior achievements. In extreme cases, he or she may exhibit some of the symptoms of pressure described earlier (nail biting, nightmares, and so on), although he or she will continue to achieve. The less talented older child may become even less motivated to achieve, since he or she can earn more parent attention by not achieving. The child thus may learn to use nonachievement to manipulate and control the parents' attention.

Regardless of differences in sibling ability, it usually is better to acknowledge achievements and to reward them, relative, as we noted before, to each child's capabilities. Democratically pretending that differences do not exist, withholding important opportunities from the gifted child, or else accepting less than the best efforts from less capable children are common but unproductive responses of parents of gifted children.

Generally, helping parents to deal with their children's competitive feelings—stress, failure, sibling rivalry—is a difficult problem. However, the patterns described in this section are common and recurrent ones, and the recommended solutions have proven effective again and again. The teacher should be aware of the patterns, set to recognize them, and prepared to make good recommendations to parents.

PEER PRESSURE

During early childhood, virtually all children are motivated by a desire to please parents and teachers and to be "good" children. Kohlberg (1974, 1976; Kuhmerker, 1991), in fact, titled this period the "good boy, good girl" stage in children's moral development. During these years, there is little peer pressure to distract the child from parental and school goals. Beginning usually in the preadolescent period, grades 4 or 5, however, the normal tendency to conform to peer norms and expectancies begins to exert its influence. The peer pressures become strongest and most influential in the adolescent years.

Adolescence marks the beginning of a crucial development phenomenon, the formation of a perhaps permanent *identity*—a personal knowledge of who and what one is and where one is going in life (Erikson, 1968). The youth, who is changing rapidly both physically and mentally, may have a difficult time during this "identity crisis" period. It is the structured standards of adolescent peers that often provide the needed direction, support, and strength. Close family relationships and good parent models will help to diffuse some of the ambiguity, but the necessary chore of establishing an identity separate from family ties reduces parental influence during this period—and strengthens peer influence.

While positive relationships with parents typically are not harmful to peer relationships (Montemayor, 1984), reliance on peers for advice and acceptance can be negatively associated with closeness to parents (Kandel and Lesser, 1972). Continuous bickering with parents seems to propel adolescents to more dependence on and acceptance of peer norms, with rejection of parent norms (e.g., Hill, 1980). The gifted child who previously had taken pride in earning high grades now faces a difficult personal contradiction. The greatest tragedy occurs when the gifted young person mentally drops out of school, accepting literally the peer mandate that "studying is not cool." Maintaining a positive family environment helps gifted children deal with the anti-gifted peer pressure they may feel during adolescence. A case study:

Jon came to the psychological clinic of his own volition. He felt desperately in need of help. As a junior in a highly academic high school he had little confidence that he could do anything about his problem. Although Jon's IQ score was 147, his grades were mainly C's with the exception of one D. He was no longer in accelerated courses. He wanted to go to the University of Wisconsin-Madison but no longer ranked in the top third of his class, an absolute requirement for entrance. He had been a straight A student until sixth grade. When he entered junior high school he decided that he no longer wanted to be known as a "nerd." He looked at his older brothers who were underachievers and decided that they were much more "casual." His two sisters were excellent students but they were known as nerds. He embarked on his new "casual" approach to school. His grades went down to B's at first, and then to C's. He never failed a course and was not worried until he heard about the new college entrance requirements. He then felt it might be too late to again open opportunities for the college of his choice.

Uncomfortable peer pressures will be reduced for scholarly adolescent boys if they can dissipate their brainy image with excellence in sports, and for girls if they have the good fortune to be pretty (Coleman, 1961). Another important qualification for peer acceptance is skill in playing down one's academic ability and excellence, for example, by not using a sophisticated vocabulary, not showing high enthusiasm for high achievement, not carrying too many books at one time, and not mentioning one's large quantity of reading and studying or one's enjoyment of intellectual matters. A gifted student may continue to achieve, however.

A survey conducted by Brown and Steinberg (1990) of 8,000 high school students in California and Wisconsin found that less than 10 percent of the high achievers were willing to be identified as part of the "brain" crowd, and students often withdrew from debate, computer clubs, and honors classes to avoid being labeled a "geek" or "nerd." The percentage was lower for females than for males, higher for Asians (14%), and lower for African-American students. *None* of the high-achieving African-Americans were willing to be considered part of the brain crowd. Luftig and Nichols (1989) also found evidence that gifted boys hide or mask their giftedness, for example, by being funny. In contrast, Luftig and Nichols (1990) found that gifted boys ranked as most popular, nongifted boys and nongifted girls as second most popular, and finally, gifted girls as least popular of the four groups. Rachel Seligman (1990) described the peer pressure she experienced at the beginning of 9th grade:

"The most foolish thing I have done this year is to compromise my intelligence. You may ask why, and the answer is simple: Love. I was dating a sophomore who has also been identified as gifted. At the beginning of the relationship I let him do all the talking. It finally got to the point where I would say nothing even though I knew I was right or I knew I was comprehending something a lot better than he was. He grew so accustomed to my saying inane things that I continued to act silly around him. Once in a while I would pop out with something intelligent, but he'd just look at me as if I were crazy. Isn't it awful what love can do to a person?"

Overall, these studies show peer pressures on gifted students to which parents should be alerted. Brown and Steinberg (1990) ask a critical question: "Are we supporting a peer system that trains students to harbor diminished aspirations so that, as adults, gifted individuals continue to underachieve in order to be socially acceptable?"

Many studies that have compared peer pressures of moderately gifted students to students with extremely high IQs have concluded that popularity is a much greater problem for students with unusually high intelligence (e.g., Austin and Draper, 1981; Feldman, 1986; Gallagher, 1958; Hollingworth, 1942; Ross and Parker, 1980).

As we have mentioned several times, probably the best way to stimulate gifted and talented students, particularly adolescents, is to help assemble a gifted cohort group. Such a group will encourage high achievement and reinforce the full use of one's talents. For example, youth symphony orchestras, high-level Saturday and summer programs, special classes, and gifted-peer discussion groups help young people to value their talent and build constructive self-concepts and identities.

It also is important for parents to value and support their children's talent during this precarious period in their development, and to not add to the pressures the child already is feeling, for example, by sending messages stressing high popularity and social success. Parents will actually have to counter peer messages of popularity by pointing out that the emphasis on popularity, as a competitive form of friendship, ends at high school graduation (Rimm, 1988b). They will need to point out, subtly if possible, that students who are conscientious about their studies will carry away the best scholarships and will be accepted to first-rate colleges, and that once college begins the stress on popularity is viewed as irrelevant and immature.

Finally, consider two thoughts pertaining to peer pressures and the stresses of adolescence: First, if the gifted child has been accelerated, there is a tendency to blame difficulties of the adolescent period on the acceleration practice—"Well, skipping sixth grade just didn't work!" Maybe the acceleration was working fine, and the child might have been worse off without it. Second, if a gifted child is not achieving up to capacity—due entirely to an unchallenging curriculum—it is not unusual to blame anti-academic peer pressures rather than educational deficiencies.

PARENT SUPPORT GROUPS

Since gifted children by definition are a minority, in many cases adequate educational opportunities will be provided for them only if there is a vocal and visible support group in the community. If adequate G/T programs are not available, joining or organizing a parent support group should be a top priority for concerned parents of gifted children and for teachers interested in gifted education. A fringe benefit of such visible membership is that parents make a clear statement to their children that education, cultural growth, and challenge are top priorities in family values.

Gina Ginsberg Riggs (1984), Executive Director of the Gifted Child Society of New Jersey, recommends that if parents "want to earn partner status [in education], they should leave negative attitudes at home and concentrate on making their education partners [schools] look good at every opportunity." Riggs also reminds parents that "standing still really means going backwards," and that there must be continuous efforts to involve more parents of the gifted and to grow and change with the times. The results of a survey of 1,039 parents of gifted students (Gogel *et al.*, 1985) showed that "parental persistence was the key factor in success in working with schools." Perhaps positive persistence and school advocacy are the best ways to describe appropriate parents' roles.

Incidentally, the Fresno (California) Parents for the Gifted organization had to ignore the positive "lukewarm" approaches advocated by most parent gifted organizations. They succeeded in getting a gifted specialty school by using an adversarial approach (Rowe, 1990). However, this "negative" strategy was adopted only after more positive approaches failed. Fortunately, most parent groups need not resort to antagonism, which risks alienating persons whose help is needed.

Names and addresses of two national organizations are listed at the end of this chapter. These organizations can direct parents and teachers to state and local groups. They are also a source of information and have publications on giftedness and gifted education.

As a teacher of gifted children, it is critical to recognize the important role of parent groups and parent support. Teachers must not view these parents as threatening, even though they are certain to make their desires known. Parent groups can help educate individual parents regarding the problems and needs of gifted children and the educational opportunities that are—or should be—provided to them. Parent groups can also help organize enrichment activities for gifted children, such as Saturday, summer, or mentor programs. Individual parents

themselves may teach special art, music, math, or computer mini-courses (for example, Tkach, 1986, 1987). Parents also can serve as the important volunteer staff—tutoring, transporting, chaperoning—which will extend the opportunities that schools can provide to gifted and talented children.

Parenting gifted and talented children is an important job, and one that teachers can help make more effective.

SOME SPECIAL FAMILY CONCERNS

Apart from our discussion thus far, some other issues related to gifted children in the family must be addressed. Teachers can also be helpful in advising parents in these areas.

Preschool Learning

Parents of very young gifted children frequently ask teachers how they can best help their children before they enter school. It is an important matter, because research evidence clearly demonstrates the strong impact of early environment on language and cognitive development.

For example, White, Kaban, and Attanucci (1979) found in their Harvard Preschool Project that "live language" directed at the child during his or her first three years was the single most critical factor in the child's later competence in cognitive, linguistic, and social areas. Morrow (1983) compared the home environments of 58 kindergarten children showing high interest in reading with the homes of 58 children showing low interest. The high-interest children came from homes with supportive literary environments. That is, the family used the public library, parents did a great deal of reading, and parents read to children frequently; there were more books in the home and, specifically, in the children's bedroom. In a study of the parenting differences between a gifted and nongifted group of middle-class children (Karnes *et al.*, 1984), the clearest difference was in the amount of time spent reading and engaging in academically related activities with the child.

The evidence provides a clear directive to parents regarding the need for early concentrated involvement with their child for the full development of both the child's language and nonlinguistic abilities.

Language experience is probably the most critical kind of involvement. Talking to children, reading and telling stories, rhyming and imitation, word games, children's records, and even simply listening to children all increase the children's opportunities to learn communication and attention skills. Being read to at home continues to be the best indicator of advanced reading ability in the preschool years (Teale, 1984). Puzzles, blocks, and construction toys help them develop small-muscle coordination, spatial abilities, and concentration skill. Large toys (tricycles, wagons, riding horses) help the development of large-muscle coordination. Many games help children learn to follow directions and cooperate. Questioning, curiosity, and independence also should be encouraged.

Moss (1983) compared the teaching strategies of 14 mothers with gifted preschoolers against those of 14 mothers with nongifted children of the same age. The first group of mothers tended to structure problems and then permit their children to derive their own solutions, learning to relate parts of the task to the goal. In the second group, mothers were more directive and actually tended to provide solutions to their children rather than permitting them to arrive at their own solutions. It seems important for gifted children to gain early experience in independent thinking and problem solving.

The following are a few more preschool precautions, some *do*'s and *don't*'s in helping gifted children. First, television watching, which is basically a passive-receptive activity, should be monitored and limited. In the Morrow (1983) study mentioned earlier, the high-interest kindergarten readers came from homes in which there were rules regarding television, and in which mothers watched less television than mothers in the homes of low-interest readers. Educational programs should obviously be included within the limited watching.

Second, overstimulation, for example, from too many peers or too much adult talk, can confuse children and detract from active involvement, concentration, and learning. While parent communication to the child is desirable, continuous talk and long abstract lectures are virtually meaningless, certainly boring, and exceed children's limited attention span. For some children, endless chatter will cause them to become restless and "hyperactive;" they know they should pay attention, but they cannot. For other children, overwhelming talking by a parent has the opposite effect, preventing the child's contributions and encouraging him or her to slow down and become very quiet. They give up trying to communicate with this parent.

Third, if your child is reading spontaneously, teach the child some basic writing skills. A simple workbook purchased from a local department store can be used for teaching the child to copy printing. Exercising that fine motor coordination will help a gifted child feel more evenly skilled in the classroom. Teachers often suggest leaving writing until school, but this unevenness in abilities often causes children anxiety related to their writing skills. Be sure not to pressure the child. Five minutes a day will provide sufficient practice and will help the child feel more comfortable with pencils.

Fourth, some daily "alone time" for a preschool child also is helpful. Interaction with peers and siblings is important to preschoolers, but some small amount of time each day for a child to play alone will encourage independent behavior and imagination. Creative persons of all ages seem to thrive on some amount of time alone.

Fifth, parents of the gifted require flexibility and tolerance of ambiguity. Orth (1988) found that parents who displayed flexible characteristics related to their child's questions, expressions of fear and anxieties, needs for attention, play behavior, getting dirty at play, and making noise, had preschool children who scored higher on the Torrance (1982) creativity test for preschoolers, *Thinking Creatively in Action and Movement.*

These precautions can help children be active participants in their environments, take initiative very early, and think more creatively.

Early Identification and Testing

There is good evidence that parents can recognize their children's giftedness quite early. Table 16.1 (Gogel *et al.*, 1985) summarizes the identification results of a national survey of 1039 parents of gifted children. Note that 70 percent of these children were identified accurately by parents by age three, most of those between ages one and three. Of the characteristics which caused parents to suspect giftedness, "early verbal expressions" was mentioned most frequently. Other observed characteristics included an unusually long attention span, a good memory, high level of curiosity and an early demonstration of original and creative behavior.

The reliability of parents' recognition of preschool giftedness was also supported by a program at Towson State University in Baltimore, Maryland (Hanson, 1984). Parents were encouraged to enroll their children in a program for four, five, and six-year-old gifted children based on their own perceptions of the children's verbal giftedness. After enrollment these children were given a battery of tests. Ninety percent of the children tested at least one year above grade level in reading and all of the five- and six-year-olds had high scores in the *Fund of Knowledge* subtests. Mathematics scores were not as consistently high, but parents had not been asked to consider math skill in their decision making. Louis and Lewis (1922) also found that parents' beliefs about their preschool children's giftedness squared well with the children's actual abilities.

Research certainly does confirm parents' ability to recognize giftedness in their children. Although we have no way of knowing the percentage of children who are missed by a parent identification procedure, the evidence suggests that parents do not overidentify to the extent that teachers often believe. Some studies indicate that parents usually underestimate rather than overestimate their children's giftedness (Chitwood, 1986).

In Inset 16.3 Silverman and Kearney (1989) summarize some of the impact and challenges that accompany the evaluation and identification of highly gifted children. Many parental and family adjustments clearly will be in order.

If parents believe their preschool children are gifted, they should ask to have them evaluated. Tests of preschool children are appropriate with the caution that such early tests are somewhat unreliable. Scores can be adversely affected by many factors, including fatigue, stress, and diet (Perino and Perino, 1981). The scores should not be taken as an absolute measure of the child's ability and certainly not viewed as a limit to that ability. Tests of young children are likely to be conservative estimates of their ability since "test construction makes it virtually impossible to score at a level higher than his or her potential" (Chitwood, 1986). But they can score at a lower level. If parents are considering early entrance to school or entrance to a particular school, preschool testing can help them to make a more informed decision.

If parents have doubts about early entrance, then start the child at the regular age, with subject acceleration in the child's areas of greatest strength. Observation by the teacher in the accelerated subject will provide the required evidence for the next decision. Teachers will be good ob-

TABLE 16.1 Percentage of Children Identified as Gifted at Various Ages by Parents

Percentage	Age
7	0–6 months
15	6–12 months
23	1–2 years
25	2–3 years
17	4–5 years
13	Later
100	

From Gogel *et al.*, 1985, reprinted by permission of the first author and *The Gifted Child Today* magazine.

INSET 16.3 _____

Impact of Extraordinarily Gifted Children On Parents

The discovery of one or more exceptionally gifted children in a family brings with it some extraordinary challenges. Some of these challenges are unique to families of very highly gifted children, and some are intensified issues that all families of the gifted face. Among these issues are:

- Gaining an accurate assessment of the child's abilities.
- Coming to terms with the results of testing.
- Determining appropriate educational provisions for their children.
- Handling financial stress—even in upper-middle class families.
- Dealing with society's lack of understanding of and responsiveness toward this group.
- Coping with the heightened sensitivity, intensity, and perfectionism of these children.
- Facing the possibility of an early empty nest because of the extreme acceleration of the children.
- Discovering and coming to terms with one's own giftedness.
- Developing one's own aspirations versus devoting oneself to nurturing the child's development.

From Silverman and Kearney (1989). Reprinted by permission of the first author and *Advanced Development Journal.*

servers provided they, too, have knowledge about gifted children and acceleration research (Rimm and Lovance, 1992a; 1992b).

Recently there has been a trend to delay entrance to kindergarten in the belief that an older, more mature child will have an educational and confidence advantage. However, research consistently confirms that average children who are delayed entrants do not achieve better academically or socially than typical age entrants (e.g., Davis, Trimble, and Vincent, 1980; Gredler, 1980; Laidig, 1991; Langer, Kalk, and Searls, 1984; Shepard and Smith, 1985).

Day Care and Nursery Schools

Day care and nursery schools for preschool gifted children have become increasingly common as more women seek to combine careers with child rearing. The findings of previously discussed stud-

ies of the importance of language stimulation during early childhood seem to recommend a close parent-child relationship during this critical period. A day care center on a full-time basis cannot substitute for that unique attentional experience, although part-time care may be satisfactory. A high-quality babysitter, who will talk to and interact with the child on a one-to-one basis, is a good alternative for a full-time working mother.

Attending nursery school for two or three half-days per week for a year or two before kindergarten can provide excellent language training and other forms of skill development and educational enrichment for any three- to five-year-old child. Note, however, that (1) the quality of the nursery school, (2) its sensitivity to the needs of very bright children, and (3) its encouragement of language and creative expression would be important considerations in making a selection.

Creel and Karnes (1988) found that parents of

gifted preschool children were eager to have educational services for their young children. Forty-nine of 51 such parents surveyed indicated that they would support having a specialized gifted preschool program on at least a half-day basis. Strom *et al.* (1992) designed a curriculum for *parents* of 68 gifted minority and low-income preschool and primary children which was very helpful to them in developing a family/school partnership.

The decision as to whether to place the gifted child in day care or a nursery school is not an easy "yes" or "no" one. It must be a careful decision based on an examination of the particular needs of the child and the alternatives available for that child.

Nontraditional Parenting

Many gifted children are raised in single-parent families or families with other than the two traditional parents. These nontraditional families can cause extra stress for parents and children. However, there are some precautions that can be followed to lessen that stress and enhance the child's adjustment.

Single-Parent Families.   One estimate is that as of 1990, a full 50 percent of today's children will have spent part of their childhood in a single-parent setting (Schreeve *et al.*, 1986). More anxiety and emotional disturbance exist for children in single-parent homes compared to children in homes that have two parents (Henderson, 1981; Hetherington, Cox, and Cox, 1982). However, there also are some positive effects.

In research reported by Cornelius and Yawkey (1985), children in single-parent families tended to have higher imaginativeness scores, had more imaginary companions, used more imaginative talk with their fantasy friends, played more imaginative games alone, and engaged in more imaginative out-of-doors games than those in two-parent families. These results were based on a group of 50 preschoolers aged four and five who were administered a 28-item *Imaginative Predisposition Interview Scale* (Yawkey, 1983). Manosevitz,

Prentice, and Wilson (1973) suggested that individual imaginativeness and single-parent families reciprocally nurture each other by reason of the amounts of "empty space" preschoolers have within single-parent families.

An example of the impact of increased attention and stimulation stemming from single parenting comes from a clinical case study.

Elizabeth was born to a teenage mother of average ability. Her father left the area immediately after he discovered the pregnancy. There was no indication of his having above average ability. Elizabeth's mother felt a great deal of guilt about the out-of-wedlock pregnancy and promised herself she would compensate Elizabeth by almost total attention. Elizabeth received extraordinary amounts of time, attention, talk, and reading to during her preschool years. In third grade her measured IQ score was 155.

Increased stimulation and attention, as well as valued time alone for the child in a single-parent family, can provide some advantages for giftedness and imagination. However, there also are risks for these children. Schreeve *et al.* (1986) found in a sample of normal ability children that those from single-parent homes ranked lower in achievement than peers from two-parent families. Gelbrich and Hare (1989) found that gifted male and female students in single-parent families achieved at lower levels than students from traditional families; the underachievement problem was greater for males than for females. In Inset 16.4, Rimm (1986b) summarizes some precautions for single parents.

Multiple-Parent Families.   When children have multiple parents living in different homes by reason of divorce or remarriage, the challenge of appropriate parenting is certainly extended. There are many books written specifically on the topic, so this brief summary will emphasize only some key risks related to giftedness. Since gifted children by reason of vocabulary and advanced rea-

INSET 16.4 _____

Suggestions for Single Parents

As a single parent are you destined to have a problem underachieving child? Of course not, but your job is more difficult. Here are some simple rules to guide you— simple only in that they are few and straightforward. In reality they are terribly difficult for single parents to negotiate. Pat yourself on the back for each successful day. You deserve it. Now the rules:

1. Find a career direction for your life to give you a sense of purpose and to build your self-confidence. Making your children your only purpose gives them power and pressure that will be too stressful for them to manage.
2. Find some adult social outlets for yourself. Don't feel guilty about enjoying yourself as an adult.
3. Find a reliable babysitter or day care center facility for your children. Consistency in care givers and surroundings is very important for young children.
4. Treat your child as a child—not a toy to be played with or an adult to be depended on. Do not share your bed with your child (except during thunderstorms).
5. Take time (I know you have little) to enjoy your children's achievements and encourage them to take responsibilities.

Now two special rules for single mothers parenting boys.

1. Boys should have an older male to serve them as a model. Find effective role models for your boys—uncles, grandfathers, teachers, Boy Scout leaders may all be helpful to your son in learning to be comfortable with his masculinity.
2. If you do not view your children's natural father as an effective role model, absolutely do not tell your boys how much they look like and remind you of him. Also, avoid power struggles with him. If he mistreats you and shows open disrespect, your son is likely to imitate this powerful but disrespectful behavior.

These rules will sound simplistic to some and impossible to others. They may be difficult for a single parent to live by, but they are effective for parenting your children. Tape them up on your refrigerator.

From Rimm, 1986b.

soning appear so adultlike, the biggest problem is that during a divorce one or both parents will assign them adult roles. That is, they are often treated as confidant, partner, and counselor. Initially they may enjoy this new adult status because they feel empowered by it. However, the risks are great. These children feel torn by their loyalty to both parents who no longer seem to like each other. They feel insecure because of the adult responsibility given too early. They easily fall victims to manipulations and learn a manipulative style of relating to both parents. Actually, the mother who confides in her adolescent gifted child in an adult manner during the immediate pre- and post-divorce period is likely to find herself with an unmanageable adolescent. It is as if the teenager who has been given adult status refuses to acknowledge the parent's right to parent him or her thereafter. Even during the trauma of divorce, gifted children must reserve the right to remain children, or their social-emotional health will suffer. Parents going through divorce should get professional counseling for support rather than depending on their children at this vulnerable time. Children also should have the opportunity to talk things through with a "safe" person who is not an involved member of the family strife.

SUMMARY

Some parents will deny their child's giftedness; others may exaggerate it.

With the "Who's in Charge" problem, children are given too much adultlike decision-making power, leading to later conflicts.

Parenting by positive expectations includes expectations of high achievement, good attitudes and constructive behavior, and the minimizing of punishments, double messages, and half-truths.

Counteridentification involves parents who vicariously experience their child's successes and failures. They may criticize, correct, and take over the child's homework and projects, leading to feelings of doubt, ambiguity, and low confidence. Children may become perfectionistic and defensive.

There are also many double, inconsistent messages related to grades. Children should be expected to earn the best grades they can. Even with their best efforts, however, teacher biases and other circumstances put grades beyond children's complete control. When low grades occur, G/T children should learn (1) not to close doors entirely on the subject, and/or (2) to look for alternatives: new subjects, new school years that will be better, new teachers, or other career interests.

Gifted children usually have to learn that winning at academics sooner or later will require effort. Some parents send a "Winning Is Everything" message, which may redirect efforts from academics to athletics. Children need to learn that success need not include being "Number 1."

"Ogre games" occur when one parent competes for the child's favor by being the "kind and benevolent" parent and making the other parent the disciplinarian; children then learn to play one parent against the other. Parents should support each other's decisions.

If children show symptoms of stress, underachievement, and/or have social problems, a family pattern of double messages may be the problem. Clarifying the messages for parents will help.

Parental rigidity and restrictiveness squelch creativity; an atmosphere of freedom to take risks, be exuberant, and be open to new possibilities enhances creative development.

Competitiveness motivates high achievement. However, feelings of competitiveness that are too strong cause stress, perhaps leading to loss of appetite, enuresis, nightmares, irritability, and so forth. Parents should help gifted children and adolescents to identify sources of stress and guide them in making the burdens more manageable. A subtle source of stress may come from exaggerated and too-frequent adult praise which emphasizes superlatives and perfection.

As demonstrated in the Yerkes-Dodson law, an intermediate level of stress (arousal) produces optimal performances; stress beyond that level becomes counterproductive. Recreation, exercise, an empathic environment, and humor can help reduce stress.

Failure may be used as a learning and growing experience (by "pathfinders"), or it may lead to feelings of inadequacy ("nonpathfinders"). Failure will lead some children to persevere in the same direction, which may or may not produce success. Other children become "failure oriented;" they give up easily or get by with minimal effort. This attitude may be learned from parents.

Noncompetitive intellectual activities, such as individualized learning, clubs, hobbies, field trips, or independent research projects, lead to enjoyable experiences of intellectual discovery without fear of failure.

Sibling rivalry usually is due to competition for parents' attention or resources. One basic recommendation is that each child should receive individualized opportunities for creative and intellectual development; a democratic attitude of treating all children alike is counterproductive. Each child should be evaluated and reinforced for accomplishments relative to his or her own abilities and efforts. Preferential treatment by significant others such as grandparents, aunts, and uncles may exacerbate sibling rivalry.

Peer pressure, combined with adolescent identity formation, severely reduces parental influence. A disdain for academic accomplishment is a common form of peer influence that can lead to underachievement, that is, mentally dropping out. Popularity should be deemphasized by parents and explained as a competitive form of friendship which ends at high school graduation.

The gifted student can learn to downplay his or her "brainy image" but still be a high achiever. The best solution is to help assemble interest groups of gifted peers who will support the gifted student's achievement orientation.

Parent support groups can lead to the creation of G/T programs, teach children that parents value education, help educate individual parents, organize enrichment activities, teach mini-courses, and assist with the G/T program.

Preschool learning is critically important for language and cognitive development. Research indicates that habits of reading and skills of independent problem solving also are acquired in the early home environment. Early identification and testing are recommended with the caution that although scores may not be reliable, they may provide guidance for decisions about early school entrance.

Excessive TV watching and parent chattering should be moderated, and some daily time alone is recommended.

A babysitter who talks and interacts with a small child may be preferable to a day care center. A good nursery school for two or three half-days per week can be immensely valuable.

Nontraditional parenting and multiple parent families provide special problems for gifted children.

NATIONAL GIFTED AND TALENTED EDUCATIONAL ORGANIZATIONS

Council for Exceptional Children—Talented and
    Gifted (CEC-TAG)
1920 Association Drive
Reston, VA 22091

National Association for Gifted Children (NAGC)
1155 15th Street N.W., Suite 1002
Washington, DC 20005.

CHAPTER 17

UNDERSTANDING AND COUNSELING GIFTED STUDENTS

Counselors of the gifted should be attuned to differences in the emotional as well as the intellectual systems of gifted students and work with students based on these differences.
Joyce Van Tassel-Baska (1983a, p. 3)

Counseling gifted students is a misunderstood and too-often ignored component of programs for the gifted. Indeed, when we hear the phase "counseling the gifted" we may think only of the common educational and career counseling needed by all high school youth as they approach graduation. In this chapter we will see that gifted students from the lowest elementary grades through high school—and sometimes into college—need help with a variety of self-definitional, social, and family issues along with career-related problems. We will examine some of these unique problems and present counseling strategies for coping with them.

Many thoughtful specialists in gifted education continue to argue strongly that counseling and guidance are essential for the full development of gifted children, and that counseling should be an integral component of every gifted program (e.g., Bireley and Genshaft, 1991; Colangelo, 1991; Delisle, 1987, 1992; Gallagher, 1990, 1991a; Landrum, 1987; Perrone, 1990, 1991; Roeper, 1982; Silverman, 1983a, 1991; Van Tassel-Baska, 1983a, 1983b; Webb, Meckstroth, and Tolan, 1982).

As a general rule, the greater the gift, the greater the counseling need.

As a preliminary sample of counseling needs, the common problem of feeling different and not

fitting in with family and friends is a virtual given with highly gifted children and adolescents. Many are confused about the meaning of "giftedness" because it is admired yet sometimes criticized and ridiculed. Bright students usually become idealistic thinkers many years ahead of their peers. The average child's narrow personal concerns contrast sharply with the gifted child's deep concerns for moral issues and justice, such as world hunger, high divorce rates, and the unequal distribution of wealth that creates prisons jammed with the minority poor. Personal and home problems range from temporary conflicts with parents, siblings, and peers to alcoholism, drug addiction, and delinquency. Some gifted students lack motivation to complete high school or pursue college. Many express boredom with school learning. Still others find themselves overinvolved in school and outside activities and need help coping with the pressures.

Non-gifted peers and family members may not understand giftedness, leading in some cases to unrealistic expectations and in others to jealousy, resentment, or outright hostility about the high ability (Clasen and Clasen, 1992; Silverman, 1983b; Webb, Meckstroth, and Tolan, 1982). As noted in Chapter 16, research by Brown and Steinberg (1990) showed that many teenagers express their resentment of high achievers by relating the label *brain*, meaning high-achiever, to the label *nerd*, meaning loser in the peer social system. Underachievement and its seeming reverse, an irrational compulsion for perfectionism, both are common. Their high intelligence, self-analytic ability, perfectionism, and creative uniqueness lead many highly gifted youth to evaluate themselves critically, often harshly. As described by Piechowski (1991), highly gifted and creative students will feel different; they will experience self-judgment, self-doubt, self-criticism, and sometimes even self-loathing; they may desperately search for a deeper meaning in their lives and their place in the world; they may feel weak, unbalanced, and irrational; and as we will explain later, many are intricately sensitive yet relentlessly intense. Because of their obvious uniqueness, many ask themselves "What's wrong with me?" and some look for themselves in descriptions of mental disorders (Piechowski, 1991; Tolan, 1987).

Some of the most frequently occurring problems are these (Delisle, 1992; Landrum, 1987; Silverman, 1983):

- Difficulty with social relationships; isolation from peers
- Conformity pressures; hiding talents in order to be accepted by peers
- Anxiety; depression
- Difficulty in accepting criticism
- Nonconformity and resistance to authority
- Lack of sufficient challenge in schoolwork
- Refusal to do routine, repetitive assignments
- Excessive competitiveness
- Poor study habits
- Understanding the nature and significance of intellectual differences
- Intellectual frustration in day-to-day and life situations
- Difficulty in selecting a satisfying vocation from among a diversity of interests [multipotentiality]
- Developing a satisfying philosophy of life

Drawing from many sources, Landrum (1987) itemized goals of counseling programs in the categories of personal-social, career-vocational, and academic needs (Inset 17.1).

Counseling should be done by those who are sensitive to the unique emotional and cognitive characteristics of the gifted. Usually, persons in the best position to council are the gifted program teacher/coordinators as well as other teachers, counselors, and school psychologists who work with gifted children. There sometimes are important roles for gifted peers, mentors, and as we will see later, parents and school administrators.

A main goal of this chapter is *understanding* the unique personal and educational problems of gifted students. When teachers, counselors, parents, or gifted peers comprehend the problems, then they can aid and support the troubled gifted, helping them realize they are not abnormal, they are not weird, and they are not alone. Many counseling activities are designed to assist gifted students in self-discovery—understanding themselves and their abilities, motives, interests, and values. A second goal is to suggest counseling functions, activities, and strategies that can be carried out by teachers, counselors, parents, and others.

As a further introduction to the topic of counseling the gifted, see the principles formulated by Joyce Van Tassel-Baska in Inset 17.2.

The remainder of this chapter will review the topics of:

Historical background
Personal and social issues
Perfectionism
Emotional sensitivity and overexcitability: The emotionally gifted
Parents and counseling
Career guidance and counseling
Personal essay writing and bibliotherapy
Stress management
Developing a counseling program for gifted students
Counseling functions of administrators, teachers, counselors, and parents

HISTORICAL BACKGROUND

In Chapters 1 and 2 we commented briefly on Terman's landmark longitudinal studies of high IQ gifted persons (Burks, Jensen, and Terman, 1930);

INSET 17.1 _____

Goals of Counseling Programs

Landrum (1987) collated information from several sources related to goals of counseling programs in personal-social, career-vocational, and academic areas. These suggest foci and activities for teachers and counselors of the gifted at the elementary school (E), middle school (M), and secondary (middle/high) school levels(S).

In the *personal-social* area, teachers and counselors can help students:

- Develop an appreciation for similarities and differences between themselves and others (E)
- Develop skills in social adaptation (E)
- Recognize and accept their abilities and limitations, and learn that superiority may not permeate all activities (E)
- Participate with and get along with others (E)
- Develop and understand positive attitudes toward school and learning, community, and society (E)
- Clarify their values and resolve moral conflicts (E)
- Understand and learn to cope with intellectual, social-emotional, and physical changes occurring during adolescence (M)
- Explore interests (M)
- Analyze personal problems (S)
- Become self-directive and responsible for their behavior (S)

In the *career/vocational* area, students can be helped to:

- Develop a sense of career opportunity based on their strengths and weaknesses (S)
- Explore implications of various careers through independent study and first-hand experience (S)
- Examine colleges and universities that are consistent with career and academic needs and interests (S)
- Develop an understanding of the world of work and one's competence as a future worker (S)

In the *academic* area students will:

- Experience educational and extracurricular activities that provide balance and satisfaction (E)
- Experience academic programs that are intellectually stimulating (E)
- Acquire effective problem-solving skills (E)
- Resolve problems that interrupt learning (E)
- Establish attainable and realistic goals (M)
- Locate resources that will help satisfy needs (S)
- Analyze academic problems (S)
- Develop study skills and test-taking skills (S)
- Enroll in classes that pursue identified interests (S)

Adapted from Landrum (1987). By permission of *Roeper Review.*

INSET 17.2 _____

Guiding Principles for Counseling the Gifted

In the introduction to her small-but-excellent book of readings entitled *A Practical Guide to Counseling the Gifted in a School Setting*, Joyce Van Tassel-Baska (1983) summarized some of the most important counseling principles as follows:

1. Persons who counsel the gifted should be conscious of differences in emotional as well as intellectual characteristics.

2. To prevent feelings of differentness, inferiority, or social alienation, counselors must help gifted students understand their special characteristics.

3. Academic, career, and psychosocial counseling programs should focus on both cognitive and affective (emotional) needs of gifted students.

4. Counselors should act as advocates for the gifted, assisting with their individual progress through appropriate school experiences.

5. Counselors should provide an information clearinghouse for valuable outside resources, not only mentors and role models but material resources as well, such as libraries, universities, museums, and the like.

6. Because gifted students will have more educational and career choices than other students, and may make them earlier, counselors should aid them in decision-making and planning skills.

7. Counselors should encourage and help students value self-initiated and independent learning.

8. Counselors should develop procedures for evaluating the strengths and weaknesses of gifted students, and help students develop plans around them.

9. Counselors should encourage students to read about their particular problems or situations (bibliotherapy), and provide relevant reading lists and arrange follow-up discussions.

10. Counselors should be sensitive to value conflicts of low socioeconomic gifted students. These students require help clarifying and actualizing their own goals.

11. Counselors should establish a special network of female gifted students to promote high-level academic aspirations and taking more courses in math and science.

12. Counselors must communicate with other school staff regarding problems and needs of individual gifted students.

13. Counselors should initiate processes for identifying gifted students for G/T programs and for individual attention from other staff.

14. Counselors should work with parents, psychologists, and others to arrange in-service staff training related to severe problems such as underachievement, social adjustment, or personal crises. Outside specialists likely would be used.

___

Adaptation of counseling principles from the Introduction to *A Practical Guide to Counseling the Gifted in a School Setting*, by Joyce Van Tassel-Baska, pp. 1–5. Copyright 1983 by The Council for Exceptional Children. Reprinted with permission.

Terman, 1925; Terman and Oden, 1947, 1959), One of the best-known findings of that research flew in the face of the folklore assumption that intellectually gifted people are physically and mentally inferior. In 1895, for example, Cesare Lombroso tied genius to insanity and feebleness. The philosophy of the nineteenth century seemed to be that the "average man" is nature's ideal, and deviations toward better or worse are nature's mistakes (Boring, 1950; Silverman, 1983). Kretschmer (1931) claimed that genius children were born of ill-matched parents, a type of bastardization. Silverman (1983b) noted that in the past many parents were ashamed of and frightened by their child's "abnormal" precocity, and sought to hide the gifts and teach the child to conform and be "normal."

Terman and company found that, in fact, his 135+ IQ people were physically, psychologically, and socially superior. Colangelo (1991, p. 273) emphasized that Terman's conclusions "erased some myths but created others, most notably the myth that gifted children are well adjusted and therefore do not need counseling services." While it was a relief to learn that, as a group, intellectually gifted people are not physically inferior nor psychologically disturbed, the backlash was to ignore real personal and social problems that are both common and damaging.

To continue our history, Leta Hollingworth (1926, 1942) made some early contributions to counseling the gifted. For example, she noted that because regular schooling fails to meet the needs of the gifted, many become apathetic. She also identified problems stemming from gaps between intellectual, emotional, and physical development. "To have the intellect of an adult and the emotions of a child combined in a childish body is to encounter certain difficulties" (Hollingworth, 1942, p. 282).

In the early 1930s, John Rothney and John Gowan studied at Harvard University under the direction of John Brewer and Truman Kelly. Brewer and Kelly were pioneers in educational guidance: Brewer wrote the first book on educa-

tional guidance; Kelly produced the first doctoral dissertation (Silverman, 1983a). Gowan, founder of the National Association for Gifted Children, argued the case for counseling services for the gifted throughout his career (see, e.g., Gowan, 1960, 1967, 1977; Gowan and Demos, 1964). He developed a summer program entitled the San Fernando State College Workshops for Gifted Children, which included a large counseling component. Some counseling was psychological and therapeutic, using individual and group counseling to help youngsters relieve tensions, gain self-understanding and self-confidence, and value their creative potential (Gowan, 1977). Counseling also focused on career information and decision-making. The workshops also provided training in guidance for the participating teachers and counselors.

In the 1950s, John Rothney, the other Harvard student, founded the Guidance Laboratory for Superior Students at the University of Wisconsin in Madison. Later renamed the Guidance Institute for Talented Students (GIFTS), the lab then as today conducted inservice training and workshops on counseling the gifted, helped establish guidance programs in schools, and provided direct counseling services to gifted high school students.

SENG—Supporting the Emotional Needs of the Gifted—was founded by James T. Webb at Wright State University following the 1980 suicide of Dallas Egbert, a highly precocious 17-year-old. SENG continues to focus on the counseling and psychological needs of the gifted. In 1982, Barbara Kerr at the University of Nebraska established the Guidance Laboratory for Gifted and Talented, extending the work of both GIFTS and SENG (Colangelo, 1991). 1988 saw the birth of the Connie Belin National Center for Gifted Education at the University of Iowa, created by Nicholas Colangelo and Barbara Kerr. The Center retains a strong focus on personal counseling, career guidance, and family counseling (Colangelo, 1991).

Silverman (1983a) noted that in the first half-century of interest in counseling the gifted, the greatest strides have been made in understanding underachievement, describing characteristics of the creative, recognizing the special problems of culturally diverse, the plight of gifted women, and developing career counseling programs. While these topics require much more exploration, other issues and problems remain less studied and understood. For example, the effects of acceleration upon personal and social adjustment have been ambiguously tangled with individual differences in prior self-concept and adjustment, family relationships, participating in a residential versus live-at-home program, intelligence level, missing data for presumably unsuccessful students who drop out, and even perceptions of one's physical appearance (Cornell, Callahan, and Lloyd, 1991a, 1991b; Stanley, 1991).

PERSONAL AND SOCIAL ISSUES

Self-Concept, Self-Esteem, Social Adjustment, and Identity

Problems and challenges associated with giftedness begin early. Silverman (1991) related that beginning at birth gifted children are active babies who may sleep less than their parents, respond intensely to their environment, and may exhaust their parents with their need for stimulation. "Two gifted children in a family may be highly competitive . . . More than two and the parents are outnumbered," said Silverman (1991, p. 307).

Development may be uneven, for example, precocious verbal skills may accompany average small muscle coordination (Rimm, 1986b). They may prefer to play with older children, sometimes "mother" younger children, and often relate well to adults. They sometimes have problems playing with average agemates.

Because regular classes group students according to chronological age, not mental age, gifted students find themselves in situations that meet neither their intellectual nor their social needs. Many experience feelings of isolation and social frustration. They may develop poor social skills from their inability to find "true peers"—other gifted students with similar abilities, interests,

problems, and needs. They may become social outcasts among agemates who do not appreciate peers who are more adult in their abilities and interests, who are labeled *gifted*, and who learn and excel with little apparent effort (Sanborn, 1979a). Said one high-IQ child, "I feel too smart for them to like me" (Janos, Fung, and Robinson, 1985). See the response of one 12-year old girl to the question "What does it mean to be gifted?" in Inset 17.3.

Now the self-esteem of all school children is affected by their level of academic achievement. It follows logically that—in general—gifted children will have higher self-esteem and self-confidence than regular students—at least regarding academic matters (Colangelo, 1991; Janos, Fung, and Robinson, 1985). Indeed, while *academic* self-concepts are strong, *social* self-concepts often are poor (e.g., Ross and Parker, 1980; Winne, Woodlands, and Wong, 1982). Two studies confirmed that gifted young people generally were pleased about their giftedness in regard to personal growth and academics, but did not like the effects of "being gifted" on social/peer relations; for example, they believed that nongifted peers and teachers held negative views of them (Colangelo and Kelly, 1983; Kerr, Colangelo, and Gaeth, 1988). They may hide their giftedness in fear of being judged a "nerd" or "geek."

It seems that the higher the IQ, the greater the chances of poor peer relations. Silverman, Chitwood, and Waters (1986; Silverman, 1991), for example, found no discrepancy between intellectual and social self-concepts for non-gifted students, small but insignificant differences with "mildly gifted" students (IQ = 120–131), but intellectual self-concepts were much stronger than social self-concepts with a more highly gifted group. A half-century ago Hollingworth (1942) noted that children with IQ scores between 120 and 145 are in an ideal range—able to achieve virtually whatever they wish, yet capable of normal social relations. Above that IQ level, however, the child may be too different, too alone, too impatient with slow-witted friends and teachers, too aware of so many irrationalities and hypocrisies in the world.

INSET 17.3

What Does It Mean To Be Gifted?

James R. Delisle (1987) compiled a small volume of delightful and insightful remarks from gifted children entitled *Gifted Kids Speak Out.* For example, when asked "What does it mean to be gifted?", a 12-year-old girl from Germany replied, "Being gifted means having to stay in for kindergarten recess to do first-grade math." (Chances are good that not many Deutsch kinder wanted to be "gifted" with this school policy.)

A thoughtful 12-year-old Pennsylvania girl responded in writing to "What does it mean to be gifted?" with this thoughtful reaction:

A   Afraid, that at some point in time I'll slip and do something wrong and everyone will notice.

G   Guilty, when pressured into *not* doing my best.

I   Isolated, when others make me feel left out of "the group."

F   Frustrated, when I do something great and everyone laughs.

T   Terrified, when I don't know the answer and everyone stares at me.

E   Excited, when I create something that everyone appreciates.

D   Disgusted, that my special needs are neglected.

P   Privileged, when I get extra time during school to do something for myself.

E   Embarrassed, when the teacher announces my grades.

R   Relieved, when people don't laugh at me for getting less than 100 percent.

S   Satisfied, when I am able to help someone else with something they don't understand.

O   On top of the world, when somebody says they enjoyed my work.

N   Nervous, when pressured to always be the best.

Due to their social isolation, uniqueness, feelings of not being normal, and self-analytic ability, many gifted youth experience severe identity problems regarding who they are and what they wish to become. Colangelo (1991) recommended that counselors help gifted students clarify and understand self-perceptions and relationships with others. He recommended, for example, exploring these discussion questions with individuals or groups:

What does it mean to be gifted?
What do I like about being gifted?
What do I not like about being gifted?
If I were not gifted, what would be better for me?

If I were not gifted, what would be worse for me?

It also is true that when students are placed in schools, classes, and programs for the gifted—which includes that critical component of interacting with mental peers—both intellectual and social needs can be met; and both academic and social self-concepts become strong (Higham and Buescher, 1987; Silverman, 1991). "Where all students are gifted and where intelligence and ability are highly valued, social relationships flourish" (Higham and Buescher, 1987, p. 30).

The downside of special schools and special classes is that highly gifted students also profit from interacting with regular students, and regular students profit from high-achieving models.

Some gifted students are less popular even among gifted peers. Cornell (1990) studied unpopular, average, and popular gifted students in grades 5 through 11 who attended a residential university-based summer enrichment program. There were no average differences between the three groups in academic achievement or ability. What did differ was self-concept and father's occupation. Unpopular gifted students had lower social self-concepts, but not lower academic, athletic, or physical appearance self-concepts. Fathers of popular students held more prestigious occupations, perhaps leading to a difference in clothing, speech, confidence, or other behavior associated with family social status. Teacher ratings suggested problematic patterns that may alienate peers: Unpopular gifted students lacked initiative in working independently, making decisions, and undertaking new challenges; had excessive needs for attention, making them less quiet and less cooperative; and did not tolerate failure well, often overreacting to criticism.

In a study of 44 adolescent girls, ages 13 to 17, who were accelerated into a residential college program, Cornell, Callahan, and Lloyd (1991b) found that individual social and personal maladjustment—for example, depression, suicide threats, lack of friends, need for counseling, behavior problems such as rule-breaking, or dropping out due to stress—was related to prior adjustment and family relationships. Specifically, these adolescents were more likely to have adjustment problems if they entered the program with a poor self-concept (social, academic, or physical) or weak sense of responsibility, or had disharmonious family relationships, particularly a poor quality relationship with their *mothers*.

Adjustment Problems of Rural, Poor, and Culturally Different Students

In rural, economically disadvantaged, and many minority communities the absence of adult models—successful, gifted adults who understand and empathize with gifted students—adds to problems of isolation and identity. For gifted African-American students, Exum (1983) recommended family counseling that addresses such parental concerns as loss of authority over the gifted child, worries about the student's loss of respect for family and culture, the student's emotional stability, and the student's ability to interact normally with other people. Exum warned that a gifted student might deliberately underachieve to preserve the integrity of a family that is threatened by the giftedness. There also may be strong peer pressures on gifted minority students *not* to achieve.

The choice between personal development and growth versus group acceptance is a deplorable dilemma for the youngster, and a true challenge for counselors.

Labeling

Labeling has always been a dilemma in gifted education as well as special education designed for retarded, emotionally disturbed, and learning disabled children. The classification and labeling is necessary for obtaining funding and for the process of providing appropriate programs. Nonetheless, when students are labeled "gifted" or as having "retardation, "emotional disturbance," or "a learning disability," these labels cause adults to make stereotyped and often false assumptions about individual children. The labels also cause the children to perceive themselves differently (Colangelo, 1991; Rist and Harrell, 1982).

Although the *gifted* label strikes most of us as strongly positive, Colangelo (1991), Colangelo and Davis (1991), and Weiss and Gallagher (1980) pointed out that *giftedness* and *gifted programs* run counter to the idea of a democratic, egalitarian society. The ambivalence has produced a "love-hate" relationship between society and the concept of giftedness: We value and admire talent and drive, especially in someone who rises from a humble beginning, but we also are deeply committed to the egalitarian concept that "All people are created equal" (Colangelo and Davis, 1991; Gardner, 1961). As we noted in Chapter 1, the love-hate relationship seems to have peaked in the early 1990s, due largely to trends toward abolishing ability grouping and promoting cooperative learning, leading Joseph Renzulli (1992) to tell an American Educational Research Association audience that "the word *gifted* has become the worst ethnic, gender slur word."

Most elementary school children are willing to be labeled "gifted" and to participate in school G/T programs; but when they become conformity-conscious adolescents, many do not want such a label and they drop out of secondary gifted programs.

There is little research into the effects of labeling itself on family dynamics. However, there is evidence that having a gifted child in the family increases sibling jealousy and competition (Peterson, 1977). Further, siblings of gifted children may be less well-adjusted socially and emotionally than siblings of nongifted children (Cornell,

1983). Colangelo and Brower (1987a, 1987b) found that sibling difficulties appear to be most intense when the sib is first labeled *gifted*; within five years the negative effects seem to wear off.

Inset 17.4 shows some responses Delisle (1987) elicited to the question of how students came to label themselves as "gifted."

As we noted in Chapter 8, Renzulli and Reis (1991b) avoid some labeling problems by referring to students' *behavior* as gifted, not the students themselves. "Giftedness" is thus not a label bestowed on students in the identification process, but a behavior to be developed and displayed. The strategy circumvents at least some classroom social problems due to labeling a few students "gifted" and the rest, by inference, "not gifted."

Subtypes of Giftedness

Betts and Neihart (1986) suggested labels that can help us understand six categories of gifted students that are based on both cognitive and personality/

INSET 17.4 _____

How Did You Find Out You Were Gifted?

In Delisle's (1987) *Gifted Kids Speak Out* the question "How did you find out you were gifted?" provoked a variety of informative and entertaining responses:

"In second grade; it was announced over the intercom" (girl, age 12).
"When I was first born. My doctor told my mother and my mother told me" (girl, 13).
"I learned I was gifted on September 12, 1982. I found out when I got a letter from my teacher" (boy, 10).
"I learned I was gifted from my mother. (Intelligence is hereditary in our family)" (girl, 12).
"In grade four, although I had the suspicion since grade two" (boy, 10).
"In first grade in a first/second mixed class. I would use big words and even the second graders didn't know what I meant" (girl, 10).
"When I passed the gifted test, my mommy told me" (girl, 7).
"I found out in third grade. I always finished my work early and would disturb others because I had nothing to do" (girl, 12).
"In third grade. I was in school on a Tuesday afternoon and my teacher called me into the hall and broke it to me easy" (boy, 11).

motivational dimensions. Their profiles include what each type needs for better functioning.

1. The *successful* gifted are conforming, achieving, and perfectionistic. While admired and liked by peers and adults, they need to develop risk-taking, assertiveness, and intrinsic motivation.

2. The *challenging* gifted are creative, but frustrated, bored, rebellious, and lean toward power struggles. They need greater self-awareness, self-control, flexibility, and sense of group belonging, as well as support for their creativeness.

3. The *underground* gifted are insecure, shy and quiet, and have poor self-concepts. They may be unrecognized as gifted, or else viewed as conformers and poor risk-takers. They need more self-awareness, self-acceptance, interaction with gifted peers, and independence in making choices.

4. Gifted *dropouts* are resentful, angry, explosive, and burned out because the system has not met their needs for many years. Adults may see them as rebellious loners; their high school peers may see them as "airheads" or even "dopers." Self-esteem is low. They need a close working relationship with an adult they can trust, supplemented with individual and family counseling.

5. The *double-labeled* gifted may have a learning disability, physical handicap, or emotional disturbance. They have low self-esteem and feel frustrated, powerless, and angry. Adults and peers alike may see them as of average ability or weird; they may see only the handicap. Such gifted students require coping skills, emphases on strengths, skill development, and a support group of adults and peers who reinforce their giftedness.

6. Finally, the *autonomous* gifted have a good sense of self and accept both their strengths and weaknesses. They are enthusiastic, intrinsically motivated, and psychologically healthy. They are admired and viewed as responsible by adults and peers. They require support, advocacy, and facilitation and opportunities for developing their gifts and talents.

It is noteworthy that four of eight stated goals of Betts's (1991) Autonomous Learner Model (Chapter 7) were counseling-related ones of helping students (1) develop more positive self-concepts, (2) comprehend their own giftedness in relation to self and society, (3) interact more effectively with peers, siblings, parents, and other adults, and (4) integrate their cognitive, emotional, and social development.

PERFECTIONISM

According to one estimate, half the population of America has perfectionist tendencies (Adderholdt-Elliot, 1987). While perfectionism is not a huge problem for most, it creates great difficulties for gifted students.

Perfectionism in the gifted stems from their long history of "A's" and "A+'s" and the continual glowing feedback from parents and teachers. For example, because of their advanced vocabulary and adult-sounding reasoning parents may call them "genius," "Einstein," or "perfect." The children internalize this extreme praise, become dependent on continued praise for their self-definition, and feel strong pressure to accomplish at a level that matches the praise (Rimm, 1990a, 1990b). There also may be other family pressures, peer pressures, and self-pressures for "perfect" work. First-born children especially are victimized by insecure parents who sometimes overdo the baby gymnastics, Suzuki violin for tots, French for toddlers, early math and reading, and so on. Role models also may be unrealistic, including those on TV who appear perfectly thin, good looking, rich, and successful. All of these cause the gifted child unrealistically to expect perfection is all arenas; and if they do less than perfect work, they feel like failures. Some spend their lives worrying, feeling guilty, and working too hard. Their identity is at stake, and they work desperately to protect it (Adderholdt-Elliot, 1987).

Because no one is perfect, and no one can be perfect in all things, perfectionism is a heavy burden.

TABLE 17.1   Characteristics of Perfectionism

People with perfectionist tendencies:

- Stay up all night (or two nights) working on a paper and then turn it in late, because it had to be absolutely perfect.
- Make themselves sick trying to maintain straight *A* grades. They might even cheat.
- Argue about test scores, even then they don't affect final grades.
- Have sweaty palms and accelerated heart rate the morning of tests—because there is a chance of missing a couple of questions.
- Compulsively compare test scores with those of other good students.
- Procrastinate—they study and write papers at the last minute. While procrastination sounds inconsistent with perfectionism, it is not. Each new project contains the threat of failure, and so starting is put off. Procrastination also presents an ego-saving insurance policy—"If I don't have enough time, I can't do perfect work."
- Work alone, because no one is as good as they are.
- Are resentful of editorial changes to their work.
- Are critical of and refuse to associate with non-straight *A* students.
- Avoid new experiences, because they pose a threat of making mistakes or failing.
- Get upset if something started cannot be finished.
- Are overly precise.
- Often feel dissatisfied with or even guilty about good work.

Adapted from Adderholdt-Elliot (1987), by permission of Free Spirit Publishing Co.

Are you a perfectionist? See traits and behavior patterns of perfectionism in Table 17.1.

Perfectionist students need to understand the impossibility of perfection in everything. They need to understand the difference between "doing your best" and "overdoing it;" the difference between reasonable pursuit of excellence and compulsive perfectionism. They must set reasonable standards. They must learn to balance three main life areas—work and school, play and hobbies, and family and social relationships. They must learn to consider alternative paths in case one leads nowhere or they get bogged down. They need to give themselves permission to make mistakes. They should try to be comfortable with uncertainty and ambiguity. They need to be able to laugh at themselves. Many famous, successful people were not perfect in every respect: Charles Dickens, Claude Monet, Isadora Duncan, and

Mark Twain never finished grade school; George Gershwin, Will Rogers, both Wright Brothers, and newscaster Peter Jennings were high school dropouts (Adderholdt-Elliot, 1987). (What do you call the person who finishes at the bottom of the medical school class?[1])

It is a counselor's challenge to help distraught perfectionists achieve these understandings.

EMOTIONAL SENSITIVITY AND OVEREXCITABILITY: THE EMOTIONALLY GIFTED

Many highly intellectually or creatively gifted young people possess a level of emotional sensitivity and "overexcitability" that is quite foreign to other children and adolescents, parents, teachers,

[1]Doctor.

and others.[2] As an example of "emotional gifted-ness" Silverman (1983a, p. 6) reproduced this essay, written for her by a high school valedictorian whose "cry of outrage against the emotionally barren school environment went unanswered. No one heard. . . . no one responded to her despair. While other students were busy trying to master the course material, she was trying to grasp the purpose of her existence:"

What can I say about school? It was a way of life for twelve years, a lesson in accommodation and retreat, a pervasive and debilitating servility which the circumstances thrust upon all of us, even the very strongest. It was a few ephemeral brilliances—here a teacher deeply loved, and here another, years later. It was lessons in one's capacity to comfort and to care, the cries of a once-friend or a friend-to-be which went unanswered. But most of all it was silence, an illimitable silence which pressed me ever deeper into myself, so that I felt myself growing weaker day by day, growing less human because I was treated as a student, as a thing, not as "she who," but as "it that." To teach is to love, to learn as well. And we loved each other so little, these others and I. We were creatures of the system; I bowed to the grade, they to the bells and a harsh word from above. We treated each other as functions, Teacher and Student: far easier than to attempt the terrifying leap of the I-Thou, the leap of humanity over void, over sullen gray mornings—over silence.

I was a good student. I learned my lessons thoroughly . . . and well. A good student; indeed, a superb student. But not, after all, a model student, because there were too many questions, too many rude hopes piercing the lost, desolate hours, too much rage in the face of fatuity and lies and cruel indifference, too wild a desperation in the attempt to discover

what being human in this world could possible mean for me . . .

The essay reveals not only the young woman's intellect and creativity, but her perceptiveness of the nature of social institutions, sensitivity to an emotional void, and idealistic vision of the way the world ought to be (Silverman, 1983a). Note this dilemma: *It is precisely this high level of sensitivity and excitability that energizes the highly gifted to great accomplishments and interesting lives.* Yet the sensitivity and emotionality may be ignored or even repressed by others, not only peers but teachers and counselors. A predicament indeed.

Drawing from Dabrowski (1967, 1972), Piechowski described the effects of heightened emotional sensitivity and overexcitability in five areas: psychomotor, intellectual, imaginational, sensual, and emotional.

In the *psychomotor* area such students show a surplus of energy, drive, enthusiasm, and restlessness, marked by compulsive talking and rapid speech. They feel pressure for action and often act impulsively. They may have nervous habits such as nail biting. They may be workaholics, like fast games and sports, and may get caught up in delinquent behavior. Note that these characteristics also typify Attention Deficit-Hyperactivity Disorder (ADHD), creating a high risk of ADHD diagnosis (Rimm, 1991a). As noted earlier, one teacher of the gifted advised Rimm that—incredibly—*half* of her students were receiving Ritalin, the calming drug prescribed for ADHD children.

In the *intellectual* area these students enjoy questioning, discovery, the search for truth, and they love ideas and theoretical analysis. They are curious. Their learning is characterized by extensive reading, sustained concentration and effort, probing questions, problem solving, conceptual integration, metathinking (thinking about thinking), and a preoccupation with certain problems. A concern for values and moral thinking leads to the development of strong universal values, values that are right and good based on effects upon oth-

[2]Two good summary descriptions of this syndrome appear in Piechowski (1991) and Silverman (1983a).

ers, independent of authority (Davis and Warren, 1994).

The *imaginational* area includes typical characteristics and activities of highly creative people, and more. Sensitive, overexcitable students enjoy free play of their imaginations, with vivid imagery, fantasy, dreams, animistic thinking, magical (e.g., paranormal) thinking, metaphorical thought, inventions, and poetic and dramatic perceptions. There may be a mixing of truth and fiction, high visual recall, and despite their liking of the unusual, there may be fears of the unknown.

In the *sensual* area there is an aliveness of sensual experience. These students take pleasure in seeing, smelling, tasting, touching, and hearing. According to Piechowski (1979, 1991), sensual expression may include overeating, buying sprees, and masturbation and other sexual activity.

Finally, the *emotional* area includes intensely positive and negative feelings, with soaring highs and dark lows. The "highs" include waves of joy, feeling fantastically alive and stimulated, and feeling incredibly energetic. Integrated with their strong sense of right and wrong, emotionally gifted students identify with others' feelings, show concern for others, and are sensitive to injustice. Roeper (1982) proposed that emotionally gifted children are "particularly sensitive toward their own and other people's feelings and dare to act upon this awareness . . . (they) show enormous empathy with others, surpassing at times the compassion of adults" (p. 24). Silverman (1983a) reported emotional sensitivity and compassion in 2½- and 3-year-old highly gifted children. The emotionally gifted may become attached to animals and build other strong relationships and emotional ties. They tend to have good "affective memory," able to remember emotions easily. They may experience needs for protection.

The emotional area also includes these troublesome "lows:" The emotionally gifted may be shy, fearful, and anxious. They may show symptoms of a tense stomach, sinking heart, flushing, concern with death, feelings of guilt, depressive and suicidal moods, scrupulous self-evaluation and self-

judgment, and feelings of inadequacy and inferiority (Piechowski, 1979, 1991). They examine themselves and their lives, sensing the discrepancy between the real and the ideal—the way one *is* versus the way one *should be*.

Children and adolescents characterized by the above traits—and who realize that others are not—feel different, embarrassed, and even guilty for their differentness. Others may tease or criticize. Because they cannot help their extraordinary level of sensitivity and excitability, they feel isolated, doubtful about themselves, and may come to believe there is something wrong with them. To resolve the conflict they might disguise their tendencies, try to be more "normal," or emotionally withdraw, sometimes taking refuge in the fantasy worlds they so ably create. Such solutions are an "inner shield," exacting a severe cost in lost vitality, reduced enjoyment of achievements, and confusion about one's own identity (Piechowski, 1991).

What can counselors do? In the words of Piechowski (1991, p. 287):

> When gifted people, and those who live and work with them, are introduced to these concepts, there is often an instant recognition and a sense of relief. It helps to find out that there is a theoretical model that makes sense out of a manner of feeling and acting that is so often at odds with normal behavior and expectations of happy—or grim, as the case may be—adjustment. It helps for once to feel legitimate in one's "abnormal" reactions and what one cannot help experiencing and wanting to express.

As we mentioned earlier, emotional giftedness, with its components of high energy and thirst for knowledge, powers the achievements and accomplishments of the gifted. Further, their sense of justice, sensitivity to others' feelings, and compassion present strong potential for moral leadership and inspiration to others. Indeed, these are the traits that motivated Eleanor Roosevelt, Mahatma Gandhi, and Socrates (Gardner, 1983; Piechowski, 1991). Unfortunately, it may be difficult for an emotionally gifted student to find a teacher or counselor who understands this syndrome. It is indeed a loss when teachers, counselors, and parents who do not grasp the value of emotional sensitivity and excitability ignore it or even try to squelch it.

As a final comment, or case study, regarding this significant but subtle topic of emotional giftedness—heightened sensitivity, overexcitability—we present a brief statement by a gifted male, age 16, from Piechowski (1991, p. 301):

> *I am a very misunderstood person. . . . People think that my life is easy because I am talented, but I have a lot of problems of my own just because of these talents. I often even get cut down for something good that I do. This is very hard to cope with. I am a very sensitive and emotional person. I get angered or saddened very easily. I can also get happy easily. I think I like this part of me. All these emotions somehow make me feel good about myself. . . . I am not a very confident person, though people think I am.*

CAREER GUIDANCE AND COUNSELING

Career selection is significant for everyone, and it is rightly perceived by gifted students as crucial. Their future career in, for example, the arts, medical research, law, business, or military leadership, will be their identity and means of self-expression. Their career will reflect their philosophy of life and values.

Career Decision Making

Career selection is a source of conflicts, pressures, and dilemmas. For example, gifted female students may need to be convinced that a professional career and a family are compatible. All gifted students must understand the commitment in time and finances and the necessity for deferred rewards, which are required for high levels of professional development. Some gifted students need to realize that responsibility, effort, and following social rules are closely tied to career and life success. Many will need help locating financial resources for an extended education.

Despite lip-service to affirmative action and gender equality, parents, teachers, and even counselors will steer students into gender-appropriate career paths. Noted Bireley and Genshaft (1991, p. 14), "Young men are often pushed into math and science with the same fervor that young women are discouraged from those fields. . . . Adolescents are often discouraged . . . when they attempt to make atypical choices. . . . Young men who wish to choose 'women's work' need support and guidance."

Gifted students need help in relating their personalities, interests, and abilities to specific career alternatives, and in understanding the personal requirements, training, lifestyles, advantages, and disadvantages of various careers. Field trips, mentor programs, and work-study programs can be helpful.

Tests and evaluations can help teachers, counselors, and other school staff understand particular gifted students and their abilities, interests, problems, and educational and career needs. For example, there are intelligence tests, achievement tests, interest inventories, personality tests, cognitive styles tests, creativity tests, work samples, and observations by teachers, parents, community leaders, or others (Pulvino, Colangelo, and Zaffrann, 1976).

Perrone (1991) pointed out that *social class, intelligence,* and *gender* are three main determiners of self-concepts and career ambitions. That is, career-planning decisions and compromises are based on self-expectations and others' expectations, which are rooted in social class, perceptions of one's own ability, and on one's self-definition relative to sex roles. Perrone also observed that when adolescents begin to make career decisions, actual job activities are less important in career decision-making than the lifestyle that accompanies an occupation and the personalities of people they know who are in a given occupation. Because of these influences, counselors sometimes must help students modify their confused or shortsighted career perceptions, values, and aspirations.

Perrone summarized Gottfredson's (1981) four "stages of occupational aspirations," plus a fifth stage of Perrone's own, that describe the evolution of career decision-making and the roles of social class, intelligence, and gender in that process. Briefly:

In Stage 1 (age 3 to 5 years), the child values adulthood because of the *size and power* of adults, which allow control over activities, resources, and gratifications. Career aspirations are based in fantasy, with an emphasis on controlling gratifications. The common aspiration to own a candy or toy store fits this stage.

Stage 2 (age 6 to 8) includes a heightened orientation to *sex roles*, and so occupational preferences reflect the child's concern with gender appropriateness. At this age not many girls want to be a soldier or mailman; not many boys want to be a secretary or nurse.

In Stage 3 (ages 9 to 13) the orientation is to *social valuation*. The parallel factors of social class and job prestige affect aspirations and expectations. Students also recognize that ability is a determining factor, and students with higher intelligence generally aspire to higher-level careers. Peer influence on behavior and aspirations is strong. Higher social class students have higher career aspirations, even within ability levels. Students of high ability and high social class see most occupations as accessible, and attending college is assumed.

Beginning about age 14, in Stage 4, the so-called "adolescent identity crisis" begins and the focus is on one's *internal unique self*. Here, additional criteria help evaluate the attractiveness and compatibility of various careers. Careers perceived as sex-inappropriate are eliminated first. Next to go are occupations above or below one's "social class comfort range." The amount of effort required to reach a career also is considered, and those that appear to demand too much effort are discarded—although as Perrone (1991, p. 323) noted, "this thought may not enter the minds of many gifted students."

Perrone added Stage 5, late adolescence and early adulthood, which he described as a value-based stage of *conceptual wisdom* related to one's *integrated world view*. Building on rich and diverse life experiences, gifted students come to understand and accept their relationship to society and their conflicts with society. They acquire a world view that supersedes self-interest. Gifted persons develop and trust their intuitions; means become equally valuable as ends; and the career and life emphases are on *becoming*. Noted Perrone (1991, p. 323), such high-level thinking probably constitutes a "second series of career decisions that follow the completion of a college degree and possibly working for a few years."

Career decision-making by gifted persons differs in many ways from such decision-making by others. See Inset 17.5.

Logically, one's personality should match one's life career. With a view toward vocational guidance, Holland (1973) described six personality types and their relationships to career decisions. See Inset 17.6.

Multipotentiality

The dilemma of *multipotentiality* is described as an "embarrassment of riches," the ability to excel in virtually any area of interest (Colangelo, 1991; Delisle, 1992; Sanborn, 1979). While some gifted students show abilities and interests in one concentrated area, the majority possess capabilities in many areas. While such talent is invigorating, the gifted student can find it confusing and difficult to make one or two choices from among the many possibilities.

In a case known to the authors, a gifted student who took the *Differential Aptitude Career Test* scored above the 95th percentile in eight of the nine possible career areas. Such feedback hardly provides clear future direction.

Sanborn (1979) reproduced the following written concerns of a gifted 12th-grade male: "Nothing is so simple for me that I can do a perfect job without effort, but nothing is so hard that I cannot do it. This is why it is so difficult to decide my

INSET 17.5 _____

Features of Career Decision-Making by Gifted Students

Based on his lengthy leadership at the Guidance Institute for Talented Students at the University of Wisconsin, Philip Perrone (1991) described unique features of career decision-making by gifted persons which he placed in the categories of psychological, psychocreative, and social factors:

In the category of *psychological* factors:

- Sex-role stereotypes are less a factor for gifted students.
- Gifted persons are more likely to work at one job for life.
- The career is central to the identity of gifted persons; ego involvement in the career is high.
- Their achievement and mastery needs are strong.
- Gifted students have a strong urge to make an impact on society.
- They frequently feel exhilarated when pursuing a goal, which makes both means and ends satisfying.

Psychocreative factors include:

- Gifted persons habitually test personal and environmental limits, challenge the status quo, question themselves and others, and have less need for closure on a project.
- They are capable of creating their own futures.
- They are risk takers.
- Gifted persons are likely to create and maintain dissonance in their lives as evidence to themselves that they are fully immersed in life.

In the category of *social* factors:

- Gifted persons have higher "future awareness," reflecting their greater emphasis on becoming than being.
- They take a wider world view.
- They possess a larger and more developed sense of social responsibility.

Adapted from Perrone (1991).

place in the future." From a female: "There are so many things I'd like to do and be, and I'd like to try them all; where to start is the problem . . . I'd like to be a physical therapist, a foreign correspondent, a psychiatrist, an anthropologist, a linguist, a folk singer, an espionage agent, and a social worker."

The following are two examples of the multi-potentiality problem known to the authors. One extraordinary student took college courses in philosophy and computer science while in high school; both professors were rightly impressed and invited her to major in their subjects. When in college, professors in literature and science areas similarly encouraged her to major in their fields. Another college sophomore shared this confusion

INSET 17.6 _____

Matching Personality Types with Career Decisions

Holland (1973) described six personality types that a counselor might consider when discussion career choices with students. An assumption is that there are six corresponding types of work environments, creating optimum compatibility between the person and the career.

Few individuals will fall exclusively into just one category. Rather, a counselor can help a person identify and explore occupations related to both primary and secondary personality types (Holland, 1973; Perrone, 1991).

1. _Investigative._ The investigative or researcher type enjoys the opportunity to creatively design research, observe the outcomes, and interpret and communicate the information. The person may study social, biological, or physical phenomena, for example, in a university or commercial research setting.

2. _Artistic._ The aitistic person prefers the freedom to design, manipulate, express, and create in one or more modes of art.

3. _Social._ The social personality type enjoys teaching, training, supporting, and working with others. They prefer to avoid routine, systematic, and fully predictable activities.

4. _Enterprising._ The enterprising person shows entrepreneurial and leadership traits in manipulating others to achieve goals. Again, there is an aversion to explicit, systematic routine.

5. _Conventional._ This and the next personality type do not fit most descriptions of gifted and creative individuals. The conventional type enjoys explicit and well-organized manipulation of data, with low tolerance for ambiguity or lack of order; bookkeeping, for example.

6. _Realistic._ The realistic type resembles the conventional type in enjoying explicit, ordered manipulations, but this time with tools, machines, or animals. Again, there is little tolerance for ambiguity or lack of structure.

---

about college majors: He had earned a 3.9 grade-point average in engineering, political science, chemistry, math, history, and psychology and liked them all. How could he make a firm career decision?

It is critical that gifted students consider vocations that have potential for extensive professional _growth_. Too often students are attracted to careers that whet their immediate interests but do not promise long-term challenge and absorption.

Simply telling bright students that "Gee whiz, with your brains you can do whatever you want" does not solve the problem. Counselors should acquaint students with the kinds of careers that are sufficiently open-ended to permit them to be continually challenged and to grow. Research, of course, perhaps tied to college teaching, permits limitless creativity and opportunity. In recent years many talented students have pursued "mixed" college degrees that create unique career challenges and opportunities. For example, they might combine a law degree with training in business, medicine, or geology; combine history with photography; or create some combination of a technical field (e.g., engineering, biochemistry) with an art area.

Expectations

The problem of *expectations* has many facets. For example, some parents, keenly aware of their child's high ability, may expect great things—the highest test scores and grades, academic awards, enrollment in a prestigious university, and a high status profession (Zaffrann and Colangelo, 1979). Other parents may ignore their children's special abilities and talents and expect them to enter the family business or work on the farm, with little or no support for the essential college education. Parents without a college education may have little knowledge, experience, or confidence related to setting expectations for their gifted children.

While parents and relatives, and even gifted students themselves, may expect high academic and career accomplishments, the students actually may prefer to live in a totally different way. From a high school girl's essay:

> I'd like to move to England and live in the fog with a house by the sea ... I'd like to write books ... [but] my future probably will be much different. I'll go to college for four years and major in something like math. Then I'll teach high school for a while and get married and have a bunch of kids. ... I'm saying to myself that this is what you should do with your life, and if I keep saying it maybe I'll start believing it.

Delisle (1992, p. 40) reported these quotes: "I'd love to be an artist, but my mom says I should get a *real* job." "When I told my dad I wanted to be a teacher, he said I was too smart for that—besides, there's no money in it. Oh yeah, he also added, 'Boys aren't teachers.'"

The gifted student's career expectations may be limited by socioeconomic status. It is especially important that counselors help gifted students from economically deprived homes to aspire beyond the lifestyle familiar to them. In guiding these students, counselors must be innovative in searching out scholarship assistance that can make high career aspirations possible. In a case known to the authors, a guidance counselor helped a high school student from a financially squeezed family discover enough scholarship aid to support her entire college education. This guidance counselor changed the girl's life, opening doors to a professional career. The girl's name is Sylvia Rimm.

PERSONAL ESSAY WRITING AND BIBLIOTHERAPY

Personal Essay Writing

Many gifted high school students may be uncomfortable talking with a counselor, yet are good at writing. *Personal essay writing* helps gifted students clarify their problems, feelings, perceptions, and aspirations without an anxious student-to-counselor speech (Pulvino, Colangelo, and Zaffrann, 1976; Sanborn, 1979). Students may be asked to write about important personal, social, educational, or career problems and their impressions and emotions regarding those problems. One productive topic is "My Place in the Future." The essays provide unique information for counselors to use in personal interviews and guidance.

Kenny (1987b) used a variety of creative writing strategies to clarify—for the counselor and student—areas of tension, stress, and anxiety related to self-concepts and peer-group relations. Creative writing of this type also assists in building a helping relationship between the student and the teacher/counselor.

The creative writing may take the form of essays; poetry; short stories; letters of the "Dear Abby" type addressed to "Dear Sigmund;" fictitious resumés based on personal, educational, and professional qualities the student hopes to possess; character self-sketches from the point of view of another person; autobiographies; takeoffs on "This is Your Life;" and others. The writing focuses on such title-topics as "My Hidden Self," "Secret Dreams," "The Inside Story," "Let Me Out of Here!", "Who Am I?", "I Can't, But I Can,"

"I Am Mary's Angry Feelings," "What I Do and Don't Like About Myself," "Me, Myself, and I," "My Secret Hopes," and "My Future Plans."

Bibliotherapy

Bibliotherapy is "the use of reading material to help solve emotional problems and to promote mental health" (Delisle, 1992). With gifted students, bibliotherapy is reading about the predicaments and benefits of being gifted as a route to self-understanding and reassurance. *The Bookfinder: When Kids Need Books* (Spredmann-Dryer, 1989) is a primary source for bibliotherapeutic literature.[3] The volume provides synopses of books that address a seemingly exhaustive list of social problems encountered by children ages 5 to 18, for example, sibling rivalry, friendship, obesity—and having intellectual talents. For busy educators, Delisle (1992) called the book "an inexpensive gold mine."

The value of bibliotherapy is reflected in this 12-year-old girl's response to the question, "How did you find out you were gifted?" (Delisle, 1987, p. 11): "I've been in a gifted program since fourth grade but I didn't know I was 'gifted' until sixth grade when we were given these pamphlets on what being gifted really meant."

Rimm (1990a) recently published *Gifted Kids Have Feelings Too: And Other Not-So-Fictitious Stories For And About Teenagers* for the express purpose of helping gifted teenagers grapple with such problems and topics as being a "nerd," hiding one's giftedness, popularity and social life, underachievement, emotional sensitivity, boredom and intolerance with school, drugs, abusive family relationships, teachers who do not support smart kids, sibling problems, peer pressures, competition, and being overweight. The stories are based on lives of gifted adolescents Rimm has known or treated in her underachievement clinic.

[3]The politically aware author of *The Bookfinder* took the precaution of indicating which books contain language or scenarios that some school districts or parents might find offensive.

As a sample of the stories, "The Boy Who Wouldn't Go To School" begins:

"Brad, why won't you go to school?" Dr. Ann Ryan, the psychologist, queried pleasantly.

Brad hesitated, eyed the floor and responded briefly, "I can't. I'm just too bored. I can't learn like that."

"Like what, Brad?" she continued, puzzled. "Do you mean that there aren't any classes in your high school that you find appropriately interesting and challenging?"

"Not really. I absolutely hate Shakespeare and that boredom I won't ever tolerate. But I'd like the math, science and computers if only they'd let me learn it my way."

Rimm reproduced a poem entitled "The GIFT" written by an 11 year-old girl:

She was a wild flower
  refusing to be bred
Into a hybrid
  just like the others.
Didn't they know
  she was perfect already?
She may have been revolting
  to others' eyes
But to her the
  shelves she saw
With identical plants
  were the most revolting sight.
Zombie slaves to human monsters,
  that she will not become.
She will not be one of many,
  but will keep her individuality.
She refuses to bloom,
  except on the wild forest floor
Or will wait until the pressure builds
  and crushes her velvety petals.

A companion book, *Exploring Feelings: Discussion Book for Gifted Kids Have Feelings Too* (Rimm and Priest, 1990), includes discussion questions and projects and activities aimed at helping gifted students understand their feelings and problems. For example, some discussion questions to accompany *The Boy Who Wouldn't Go To School* include:

1. Have you ever felt so bored in a class that you believed you couldn't sit through it? If so, What did you do?

2. If Brad couldn't have left his school and you were Dr. Ryan, can you think of ways you might have helped him at his old school?

3. Are there students you know who seem "socially awkward," for example, just don't know how to talk to friends? If you had a friend who didn't know how to fit in with friends socially, what advice would you give him or her?

4. When Brad refused to go to school and did nothing but sit and watch TV, he was feeling depressed. What are the characteristics of depression? Have you ever felt depressed? What seems to help you get out of your depression?

For "The GIFT" three discussion questions were:

1. Do you think that Lisa felt lonely or good about her individuality? Have you had similar feelings? Describe feelings of pressure which you may feel to be either similar or different from others.

2. How do you feel about Lisa's use of the word "perfect"? What are the advantages and disadvantages of feeling "perfect" or never feeling "perfect" enough?

3. What are some of the difficulties associated with being an individual or being different? Begin with some of the ideas that Lisa reveals in the lines of her poem. Add other ideas that you have seen in your observations of others or that you may have experienced yourself.

As an example of a creative writing project that accompanied the poem: "Write a personal letter to Lisa to explain how you feel about the issues she has presented to you in her poem. Then share your letters with your class. Did you interpret Lisa's poem differently? Did you respond to her with different advice or explanations? What accounts for the differences and similarities in the responses?"

Overall, the stories in Rimm's books, and bibliotherapy generally, help gifted students understand their problems and realize that they and their feelings are not unique nor "wrong."

STRESS MANAGEMENT

Everyone experiences stress. In part, it is biological, related to innate differences in temperament and anxiety levels (e.g., Eysenck, 1967). Some people, gifted or not, therefore easily become more distraught and upset than others. It also is true that people function best at an optimum, medium level of stress—enough challenge to raise interest and energy, but not so much as to devitalize or paralyze from anxiety and frustration.

Throughout this chapter we have noted that gifted children are subject to unique forms of stress that do not afflict other young people. Particularly, problems of feeling "different" or "out of step" are common sources of stress, which can be amplified by their emotional sensitivity and overexcitability. As Webb, Meckstroth, and Tolan (1982, p. 107) point out, "For the exceptionally gifted child, a certain amount of stress is virtually an absolute. The child with an IQ above 160 is likely to have difficulty fitting in anywhere—and must endure the stresses that accompany this."

Webb, Meckstroth, and Tolan itemized a number of stress-management strategies that counselors can help gifted students understand and use. All aim at raising students' awareness of personal values, priorities, and beliefs, and strengthening confidence in their worth as people.

Managing Yourself.   Gifted students can be upset—stressed—by jealous, resentful, or other insensitive behavior of peers. They can learn that they cannot control others' thoughtless behavior, but they can control their own reactions. They can be polite without accepting the stressors from others; they can tolerate and cope with stressful behavior from others. Because "giving up" is an easy way to resolve conflict, gifted students can learn to conform when necessary, but without necessarily giving up their probably better ideas or attitudes.

Self-talk.   We all engage in self-talk—"Boy, did I do lousy that time" or "Hey, I was really good!" Gifted children may evaluate themselves in self-talk at the age of two or three (Webb, Meckstroth, and Tolan, 1982). *Negative* self-talk—self-criticisms and put-downs—happen when one's behavior falls short of personal goals, which for perfectionistic gifted children can be quite often.

Of course, the negative self-talk is stressful. Gifted students can learn to recognize the negative self-talk that occurs when they think they are not meeting their high standards, or when there are conflicts about what others think they should be doing or thinking. They also can recognize *positive* self-talk, and verbally reward themselves for doing a good job or just for being proud of their capabilities and values.

Awareness of Irrational Beliefs.   Some negative self-talk is rooted in irrational belief systems about what we "should" do, think, or believe about ourselves. Gifted students can be made aware of these traps, and probably will laugh about some. The following list of irrational beliefs is adapted from Webb, Meckstroth, and Tolan (1982), Ellis and Harper (1975), Adderholdt-Elliot (1987), and Delisle, (1992):

- I must be perfect in all things.
- Everyone must like me.
- I must like everyone.
- I must not disappoint anyone.
- The majority is always right
- The majority is always wrong.
- If I'm not popular, then I'm a social outcast.
- Boys are supposed to be smart, girls are supposed to be popular.
- I always have to finish what I start.
- Everything must be done precisely correct, right down to the last detail.
- When things do not go the way I want them to, it is horrible, terrible, dreadful, beastly, shocking, and awful.
- If something unpleasant occurs, it is essential that I become preoccupied and upset about it.

- It is important for me to worry continually about "all-important" things in the past, in order to limit my future possibilities.
- People and things should be better, and it is a terrible catastrophe if perfect solutions are not found immediately.
- If I happen to behave badly, I therefore am a bad person.
- My happiness is caused only by other people and events, not by how I think about myself.

Other Suggestions for Reducing Stress.   Webb, Meckstroth, and Tolan (1982) itemized other strategies for helping gifted students control their stress levels. For example, students can be helped to understand that covering up problems and denying difficulties usually increase stress, while talking about them reduces stress—even if that confrontation temporarily intensifies the discomfort.

As noted in Chapter 16, if a student shares a stress source with a G/T teacher or other counselor, the adult can ask "What is the worst thing that could happen?" and then "And how disastrous would that be?" Such questions help the student gain a better, less stressful perspective.

Students also can be helped to understand that *"failures" provide feedback*—stepping stones toward success. When you fail, you know more than you did before. Failures should not just trigger depression or blame. One story describes how Edison failed over 1,500 times in creating a successful filament for his light bulb; he announced with pleasure that he now knows 1,500 solutions that won't work.[4]

Students also can come to understand that blaming someone else for their failure ("I can't get anything done because you won't do your part!") will only immobilize them. It puts them in the position of being a passive and helpless victim because the other person is perceived as having control. It is better to accept at least part responsibility for failure, and view themselves as active, competent, and creative problem solvers.

[4]Other versions of this story put the number of failures at 2,000 or 3,000. Whatever the truth, he failed a lot and learned a lot.

Students can learn to *compartmentalize*. If one life area is stressful, for example, a theater production or trouble with one teacher, all other areas need not be affected.

Calming techniques can help students who overreact or who suffer acute stresses such as anger, fear, or excessive tension. Physical exercise such as jogging or aerobics is known to be therapeutic. One also can learn to deliberately relax muscles, concentrate on breathing (thus clearing the mind), and to count slowly to 10. Sleep also is known to be a stress reducer.

Counselors can raise students' awareness of the HALT phenomenon (Webb, Meckstroth, and Tolan, 1982). When we are *H*ungry, *A*ngry, *L*onely, or *T*ired, we tend to experience greater stress and to overreact irrationally. Some families use "HALT" as a code word to alert an upset child to these sources of exaggerated feelings, and to self-talk about how the stress may be due to magnified feelings of hunger, anger, loneliness, or being tired.

Humor typically is quite keen among gifted students, and it can be used therapeutically to reduce stress. Absurdities in situations can be pointed out. A counselor also can be humorously melodramatic about a problem. However, the counselor must be careful that the humor does not appear cynical or derisive; the counselor must not appear to be laughing at the student. Some students will be able to use humor to handle stressful situations. Said one child, "When being smart is handy is when others try to put you down. You can turn it around and make it a joke" (Webb, Meckstroth, and Tolan, 1982, p. 119).

Active ignoring is another coping strategy. Students can deliberately think about something else, and reduce the stewing by putting the stress source out of mind.

DEVELOPING A COUNSELING PROGRAM FOR GIFTED STUDENTS

Colangelo (1991) described two possible approaches to developing counseling programs for the gifted, *remedial* and *developmental*. The remedial approach essentially is a therapeutic model based on the assumptions that gifted students have serious problems and are at risk (which are true). With this approach a counselor is "on call" to help solve problems or minimize difficulties as they occur.

The developmental approach is preferred. While a counselor is available for therapy, the primary goal is to create a school environment and home circumstances that support the educational growth of gifted students.

A developmental counseling plan would include the following components:

- An articulated and coherent rationale.
- Activities based on affective/emotional and cognitive/intellectual needs.
- Counselors who are knowledgeable about giftedness and attendant problems.
- A strong component of individual, family, and teacher consultations, along with rehabilitative/therapy services.
- Input and participation from teachers, parents, administrators, and students who are served.
- Continual professional development for counselors to keep them abreast of research and practice related to counseling needs of gifted young people.

Counseling Roles for Administrators, Teachers, Counselors, and Parents

The following are some specific counseling-related roles and responsibilities for administrators, teachers, counselors, and parents (adapted from Landrum, 1987):

Administrators will:
- Learn what *gifted* is and what it means.
- Recognize that the needs and problems of gifted students might be best met if specialized individuals are given responsibility and time to coordinate the process.
- Coordinate cooperative working between the teacher, counseling personnel, and other pupil personnel workers.
- Ensure that the teachers and other personnel receive proper training.

- Provide school and district inservices on gifted education, including counseling-related concerns.
- Allow for regular meetings for G/T staff members.
- Know the educational options.
- Listen and respond to concerned staff.
- Ensure that adequate monies are earmarked to finance the program.
- Provide suitable facilities for the program.

Teachers will:

- Listen to gifted and talented students.
- Know the children's talents and limits and not expect them to be gifted all the time in every subject.
- Make an effort to understand test data and other information on cumulative records.
- Intellectually challenge the students.
- Support and stimulate students' personal interests.
- Acquaint students with occupational information.
- Share information about students with other members of the counseling/guidance staff.
- Establish a list of resource personnel and community mentors.

Counselors will:

- Listen to students.
- Orient young students to counseling.
- Help children with values clarification.
- Arrange for students to make self-referrals to the guidance office.
- Provide individual and group conferences.
- Assist students in finding appropriate resources, for example, bibliotherapy, educational, or career information.
- Locate special services when necessary.
- Conduct classroom guidance activities and assist teachers in doing the same.
- Explore students' interests in relation to educational and work pursuits.
- Collect information about individual students as "unique persons."
- Work with teachers, principals, and other staff to foster a better school climate for gifted and talented students.
- Consult with parents.
- Coordinate the total guidance/counseling program.
- Evaluate strengths and weaknesses of the guidance program.

Parents will:

- Listen to the student.
- Keep open communications with the school.
- Get involved in the educational process.
- Form parent advocacy groups.
- Give children quality time.
- Help the child to learn time management.
- Guide their child in wise decision making.
- Allow creative thinking time.
- Promote reading.
- Model appropriate risk-taking and leisure activities.
- Expect age-related behavior.
- Support the child's interests.
- Not expect the child to fill the parent's unfilled aspirations.

Counseling Activities for Teachers and Counselors

The following are samples of intervention strategies and activities that can be conducted by teachers and counselors in the personal-social, academic, and career-vocational areas (adapted from Landrum, 1987):

These strategies meet *personal-social* goals of raising self-awareness, developing strong self-concepts, and working toward self-discovery, self-improvement, and self-actualization:

- Use group counseling to create a peer community and to provide gifted students with a context to discuss problems and issues.
- Use simulations and role-playing activities to aid understanding of problems.
- Use bibliotherapy and personal writing to raise self-awareness.
- Encourage girls to take courses in math, science, and computers.

These strategies are directed toward *academic* goals such as improving studying, problem solving, and self-directed learning:

- Conduct units on note-taking, summarizing, reviewing, memorizing, test-taking, and reading for fun.
- Create activities in which problem-solving skills are practiced and developed, for example, analyzing and clarifying problems, clarifying solution needs, formulating solution strategies, and planning courses of action.
- Foster the development of independent learning and research skills, such as the use of library resources and information-retrieval systems.
- Use questioning to promote higher-level thinking—applying, analyzing, synthesizing, and evaluating—for example, related to social issues.
- Expose children to art, music, science, and reading, particularly those with deprived backgrounds.
- Be alert to and support students' spontaneous areas of interest.
- Hold Saturday seminars taught by community resource persons.

These strategies can help meet *career-vocational* goals:

- Have students collect newspaper and magazine pictures for individual career portfolios.
- Take pictures of career people; create collages.
- Have students interview and prepare class reports about people in various careers.
- Accompany PTO members on a "day the job."
- On birthdays of famous people, discuss their careers.
- Create one or more class businesses.
- Use parents and members of the community as mentors.
- Visit universities.
- Review college application procedures with students (you may need to contact college admissions staff for information).
- Have graduates return to the classroom to discuss their education, careers, and related problems and challenges.

COMMENT

Many students who are highly intelligent, creative, or artistic will have special kinds of problems and conflicts. These require special—and individual—understanding and guidance by regular teachers, G/T teacher-coordinators, counselors, parents, and sometimes specialty teachers (e.g., artists, researchers, business persons). An overriding strategy noted throughout this text is to bring gifted students together; they need friends and peers with whom they can share feelings, problems, and aspirations.

While gifted students may indeed "make it on their own," knowledgeable counseling and guidance will make the task less painful and more sensible. It also will help those gifted and talented youth who will not "make it on their own."

SUMMARY

Gifted students need help with personal problems, social and family problems, and educational/career guidance problems. Aiding students' self-understanding is a major counseling goal.

Historically, Terman's conclusions about the superior physical and mental health of his gifted subjects created the illusion that gifted children do not need counseling. Hollingworth noted early that gifted children's mental, emotional, and physical development is uneven, and some become apathetic about school. Rothney founded the Guidance Laboratory for Superior Students at Wisconsin in the 1950s; Gowan directed summer workshops for the gifted. Webb created SENG following the 1980 suicide of Dallas Egbert. Kerr in 1982 created a guidance laboratory at the University of Nebraska; Kerr and Colangelo in 1988 founded the guidance-oriented Connie Belin National Center for Gifted Education at the University of Iowa.

The high activity levels of gifted children may appear at birth.

Regular school programs meet neither academic nor social needs. Gifted students may be rejected due to differentness.

High achievement leads to good academic self-concepts; but poor peer relations lead to poor social self-concepts. Hollingworth noted that IQs between 120 and 145 are ideal for both success and social adjustment. Both academic and social self-concepts are good when students are placed in programs for the gifted.

Research on unpopular, average, and popular gifted students showed no differences in academic achievement or ability, but differences in self-concept and father's occupation. Success in an acceleration program depended upon prior adjustment and harmonious family relationships, especially with mother.

Counseling problems with minority students include the absence of role models, strained family relationships, and peer pressures.

Labeling leads adults to make stereotyped assumptions about individual students, causes students to perceive themselves differently, and may increase sibling jealousy. The label *gifted* elicits a "love-hate" reaction. Renzulli and Reis solve the labeling problem by referring to gifted behaviors, not gifted students.

Betts and Neihart identified six categories of gifted students, successful (conforming), challenging (creative), underground (poor self-concepts), dropouts, double-labeled (e.g., handicapped), and autonomous learners (psychologically healthy).

Perfectionism stems from continual success, feedback from parents and teachers, and even "perfect" TV role models. The syndrome includes, for example, compulsive work to produce "perfect" papers, compulsively studying for exams and worrying about grades, anxiety symptoms on test days, procrastination, avoiding new experiences, being overly precise, and being dissatisfied with good work.

Heightened emotional sensitivity and "overexcitability" are common among highly intellectually gifted children and adolescents. The syndrome includes high energy, curiosity, compassion, idealism, an active imagination, high sensuality, and intensely positive and negative feelings, as well as anxiety, feelings of inadequacy, and other negatives. An awareness of their (normal) heightened sensitivity is therapeutic, according to Piechowski.

Career guidance aims at clarifying personal and educational requirements for various careers. Perrone summarized five age-related stages of occupational aspirations that evolve around social class, intelligence, and gender. Perrone also itemized characteristics of the gifted that influence career decision-making in the areas of psychological, psychocreative, and social factors.

Assuming that one's personality should match one's career, Holland described six personality-career types: investigative, artistic, social, enterprising, conventional, and realistic.

Multipotentiality is the dilemma of having too many abilities and interests to make easy educational and career choices. Counselors should encourage open-ended careers that offer continual creative challenge.

The problem of expectations includes both family and self-expectations. Parents may expect high or low career achievement. Students may prefer a life other than what the family expects. Socioeconomic level lowers self-expectations.

Personal essay writing and other creative writing projects help counselors and students clarify areas of stress related to self-concepts and peer relations.

Bibliotherapy promotes self-understanding by having students read about other gifted students with similar problems.

Stress management strategies include helping gifted students manage their reactions to stress, recognize negative self-talk, become aware of irrational beliefs, accept failures as feedback, compartmentalize different life areas, learn calming techniques, use humor, and put the stress source out of mind.

Counseling programs can be remedial or developmental. With the remedial approach, the counselor is "on call" when needed. The preferred developmental approach provides a coherent service directed toward emotional and intellectual needs.

Administrators oversee and coordinate counseling and other services for gifted students. Teachers listen to and challenge students, and supply occupational and community resource information.

Counselors have many functions, for example, orienting students to counseling, holding individual and group conferences, assisting students with bibliotherapy and career resources, and consulting with parents. Parents can get involved with schooling and promote decision making, creativity, reading, and time management.

Intervention strategies, like all of counseling, focus on personal-social, academic, and career-vocational interests and problems.

Gifted students have special kinds of problems and conflicts that require special understanding and guidance by G/T teachers, counselors, and parents.

RECOMMENDED READING

Adderholdt-Elliott, M. (1987). *Perfectionism: What's bad about being too good?* Minneapolis, MN: Free Spirit Publishing.

Bireley, M., and Genshaft, J. (Eds.). (1991). *Understanding the gifted adolescent: Educational, developmental, and multicultural issues.* New York: Teachers College Press.

Colangelo, N. (1991). Counseling gifted students. In N. Colangelo and G. A. Davis (Eds.), *Handbook of gifted education* (pp. 273–284). Needham Heights, MA: Allyn & Bacon.

Delisle, J. R. (1992). *Guiding the social and emotional development of gifted youth.* New York: Longman.

Perrone, P. (1991). Career development. In N. Colangelo and G. A. Davis (Eds.), *Handbook of gifted education* (pp. 321–327). Needham Heights, MA: Allyn & Bacon.

Piechowski, M. M. (1991). Emotional development and emotional giftedness. In N. Colangelo and G. A. Davis (Eds.), *Handbook of gifted education* (pp. 285–306). Needham Heights, MA: Allyn & Bacon.

Van Tassel-Baska, J. (Ed.). (1983). *A practical guide to counseling the gifted in a school setting.* Reston, VA: Council for Exceptional Children.

Webb, J. T., Meckstroth, E. A., and Tolan, S. S. (1982). *Guiding the gifted child.* Dayton, OH: Ohio Psychology Press.

CHAPTER 18

PROGRAM EVALUATION

Many of the objectives in programs for the gifted are very complex and not easily defined.

Carolyn Callahan (1986)

WHY MUST PROGRAMS BE EVALUATED?

As a general trend, developers of programs for the gifted tend not to evaluate the success of their programs or the effectiveness of program components. There seem to be several reasons for this reluctance. First, they typically feel that because they created their program in good faith it necessarily is "successful." Second, they prefer to invest their time in planning and teaching. "The primacy must be the intervention, not the evaluation," according to Cook (1986). A third reason is that "success" in teaching gifted and talented students is difficult to assess, compared with using achievement test data to evaluate remedial or basic skills programs. A fourth reason for hesitancy is that the evaluation results could threaten the program itself. For example, if the creativity tests, thinking skills tests, self-concept inventories, or other measures of complex constructs fail to show an improvement—perhaps because the instruments were unreliable or unrelated to what was taught—the data might be taken as evidence of program failure.

Traxler (1987) surveyed 192 school districts having gifted programs. She found that half of the programs were not evaluated at all, and of those evaluated most did not employ trained evaluators. Observations by teachers and evaluations of student products were the most common types of assessments.

Although gifted programs are more difficult to evaluate than other programs, this evaluation is vital. Gifted programs come and go; the record of continuity is dismal. Therefore, if teachers and program directors hope to maintain or expand their programs, they must be able to demonstrate the success of the program to their administration, to school board members, to parents, and to state or federal funding sources. This is *accountability*. These publics will want to know who is being served by the program, how they are being served, and the beneficial effects of the program. They also will want to know if the program is cost-effective—if the costs in time, personnel, and resources are producing optimal results. Equally important, teachers and program directors need information that will allow them to revise and improve the program. Beyond creating classroom quizzes or evaluating student papers and projects, teachers and coordinators usually have little training or experience in educational evaluation. This chapter is intended to simplify and clarify the evaluation of G/T programs and guide the teacher or coordinator in the evaluation process.

EVALUATION DESIGN: BEGIN AT THE BEGINNING

Although evaluation is the topic of the last chapter in this book, evaluation of a gifted program belongs at the *beginning* of program planning. At the outset, when setting goals and objectives for a G/T program one should design a methodology for measuring whether or not those objectives are reached.

"Difficult" and "Easy" Evaluations

Callahan (1986) set forth some of the difficulties which are unique to evaluations of gifted programs. She pointed out that (1) "no agreed upon standards of good programming exist within the field of gifted education and (2) many of the objectives in programs for the gifted are very complex and not easily defined."

Some examples of *difficult* objectives for evaluation are improvements in leadership, self-awareness, self-concept, decision making, reasoning, analyzing, synthesizing, evaluating, social responsibility, intrinsic motivation, critical thinking, and creative thinking. Other objectives are comparatively *easy* to evaluate. Acceleration programs, for example, provide almost self-evident evaluation data. Did students succeed in the advanced classes, the college courses, or the correspondence courses? Did the grade-skipping or the early admission to kindergarten work well for the students involved? Enrichment plans that result in a bona fide product—a school newspaper, a report of a research project, a poetry book, a dramatic production, artwork, a movie—also provide relatively easy evaluation data. Such products reflect a clear change in student skills and performances that, most likely, would not have occurred without the G/T program (Renzulli and Smith, 1979). Smith, LeRose, and Clasen (1991) used easily-obtained statistics to show a profound effect of the Racine, Wisconsin, Lighthouse Project (LeRose, 1977, 1978): *None* of the minority students who participated in the program dropped out of high school and 76 percent planned to attend college. Among comparably talented minority students in the Racine district, 45 percent dropped out.

Whether objectives are difficult or easy to evaluate, we nonetheless must try to evaluate every planned objective.

EVALUATION MODELS

There are many models for structuring the evaluation of education programs. Several will be summarized here in an admittedly oversimplified fashion. In all cases, the intrigued reader will need to explore the more complete, original statements.

Provus's (1972) *discrepancy* model assumes five stages in the creation of a program. At each stage the reality of the program is compared with a standard, and any discrepancy is fed back in order to improve the program by, naturally, correcting the discrepancy. In Stage 1, *Design*, the initial program plan is compared with a set of theory-based design criteria, perhaps as defined by an outside consultant. If there is a discrepancy, the program plan is modified accordingly. In Stage 2, *Installation*, the actual reality of the program as it is implemented is compared with the design adopted in Stage 1. Again, any discrepancies between program design and installation would be used to guide changes. These changes could be in the actual installation or in the Stage 1 design criteria. In Stage 3, *Process*, the actual program activities are compared with the proposed program activities, and any discrepancies will result in corrective alternatives. Stage 3 is especially important for creating an effective, successful program. In Stage 4, *Product*, actual student products are compared with the planned ones. This may be the main evaluation of program objectives. Stage 5, *Product Comparison*, involves a comparison of students' products and learning outcomes with those of other programs to determine program efficiency in the cost-benefit sense.

Part of Eash's (1972; see also Renzulli, 1975) *differential evaluation* model involves three considerations in the evaluation process: (1) *Effort*—how time is spent (that is, the program activities); (2) *Effect*—products and outcomes; and (3) *Efficiency*—the relationship of effort and resources to the quality of effects realized. As the program evolves from a newly planned, innovative program (initiatory stage), through the implementation and field testing of the program (developmental stage), to the established and stable level (integrated stage), more emphasis is placed on evaluating effects and efficiency (2 and 3).

The Renzulli and Ward (1969) DESDEG (*Diagnostic and Evaluative Scales for Differential Education for the Gifted*) model was designed specifically for evaluating programs for gifted and talented students. It also may be used for program planning and development (Renzulli, 1975). DESDEG includes a set of five published documents corresponding to the five parts of the model. Part I is the Manual, which explains everything you ever wanted to know about DESDEG. Part II, Evaluative Scales, includes scales for evaluating each of 15 "ideally conceived educational practices" or Program Requirements, which subdivide into the five Key Features (general areas) in Table 18.1. Part III consists of Basic In-

formation Forms, ". . . a comprehensive inventory of factual information about all aspects of a program . . . organized and keyed . . . to each of the five Key Features. . . ." These aid in the objective collection of data. Part IV is the Evaluator's Workbook, designed to aid the evaluator in handling the information derived from the Basic Information Forms and from observations. Part V is the Summary Report which (1) permits the evaluator to transfer numerical data to statistical and graphic summary sheets, and (2) aids in the creation of a summary narrative related to each Program Requirement.

It can be seen even in these sketchy outlines that the evaluation of education programs, including G/T programs, can be approached from many different viewpoints, use different strategies, and focus on a variety of dimensions and considerations.

TABLE 18.1   The DESDEG Model

Key Feature A: Philosophy and Objectives	
Program Requirement 1:	Existence and Adequacy of a Document
Program Requirement 2:	Application of the Document
Key Feature B: Student Identification and Placement	
Program Requirement 3:	Validity of Conception and Adequacy of Procedures
Program Requirement 4:	Appropriateness of Relationship Between Capacity and Curriculum
Key Feature C: The Curriculum	
Program Requirement 5:	Relevance of Conception
Program Requirement 6:	Comprehensiveness
Program Requirement 7:	Articulation
Program Requirement 8:	Adequacy of Instructional Facilities
Key Feature D: The Teacher	
Program Requirement 9:	Selection
Program Requirement 10:	Training
Key Feature E: Program Organization and Operation	
Program Requirement 11:	General Staff Orientation
Program Requirement 12:	Administrative Responsibility and Leadership
Program Requirement 13:	Functional Adequacy of the Organization
Program Requirement 14:	Financial Allocation
Program Requirement 15:	Provision for Evaluation

Joseph S. Renzulli, DESDEG Model. Reprinted by permission.

THE RIMM MODEL

Rimm's (1977) model both (1) structures program evaluation in a relatively easy-to-follow fashion and (2) ties it to the initial program plan. To begin, summarizing a program in one picture is very helpful for conceptualizing program components and, therefore, for relating evaluation needs to those components (see Figure 18.1). The diagram demonstrates how the different parts of a program fit together and, importantly, how evaluation can help one monitor all educational *Inputs (resources)*, all *Processes (activities)*, and all *Outcomes (goals and objectives)*. Using the model has many advantages. First, it helps us understand the relationships among educational resources, processes, and outcomes. Second, using the model helps prevent the implementation of any activity without considering its eventual *evaluation*. Third, the model helps us become more sensitive to the close relationship of program decisions to the many student outcomes. Finally, and most importantly, the model itemizes on one page the program components that should be evaluated in regard to both (1) how well the component was implemented, and/or (2) how successfully that component helped achieve program goals.

The components within each of the three steps

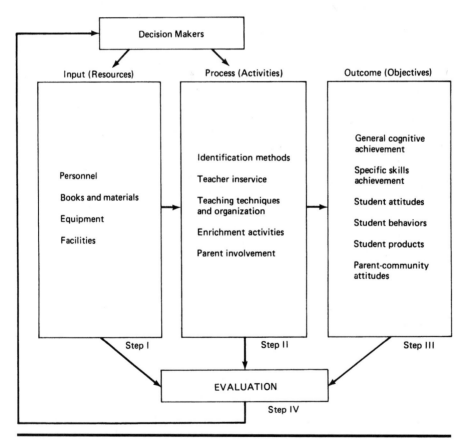

FIGURE 18.1. Framework for the Evaluation and Monitoring of a Gifted Program.

of the model reflect specific areas that should be evaluated. That is, each of the various types of input/resources (Step I), processes/activities (Step II), and outcomes/objectives (Step III) should be evaluated. Evaluation data (Step IV) from the components will present a comprehensive picture of the success and impact of a gifted program. This information is brought together and fed back to the decision makers who will use it for further planning—for modifying the input and process steps, which may include program expansion. Without the crucial evaluation step, there would be little clear basis for good decisions. The success of this approach depends heavily on the relevance and the clarity of the evaluation information obtained in Step IV.

The reader may wish to draw a blank framework to outline his or her own program and evaluation model and complete the diagram as this chapter is read.

Step I: *Input* represents resources. Resources typically include such program ingredients as teaching and support personnel, books, materials, equipment, and facilities. Resources may also include more specific categories such as community resource persons, specific student populations, or funding sources. Resources are the investments in the program and they usually are relatively easy to identify and list.

Step II: *Process* includes the activities of the program—everything that is planned to make the program effective. Typical categories of activities include identification procedures, teaching techniques, educational groupings, enrichment experiences, acceleration plans, teacher in-service training, and parent involvement activities. One may wish to itemize more specific curriculum activity components of the program, for example, creative-thinking instruction, creative writing, a computer mini-course, accelerated mathematics, Renzulli's (1977) Enrichment Triad model, and so on. The list of categories of activities should be exhaustive, which means that each and every specific program activity would fit into a process category.

Step III: *Outcome* represents the goals and objectives of the gifted program. It actually may be easier to complete the list for Step III *before* completing Steps I and II. What do you expect to accomplish? What are the purposes of the program? Ideas for program goals were listed in Chapter 3.

Note that increased academic achievement is not necessarily a central outcome of a gifted program, although it may be an objective for gifted underachievers or, for example, for an accelerated math, biology, or reading program. More frequently, increases in specific *skills* are the intended outcomes of a program, for example, creative, critical, or evaluative thinking and independent study and research skills. Positive student *attitudes*, including self-concepts, attitudes toward education, and high career aspirations, are also frequently stated goals. In addition, scientific, literary, and artistic *products* are important and potentially measurable objectives. Parent and community attitudes toward the program and toward the needs of gifted children are further important outcomes to monitor.

Completing the model by inserting program components into each of the four steps should provide the reader with an overview of the entire program and assist with planning the necessary evaluations.

EVALUATING THE WRITTEN PLAN VERSUS ACTUAL ACTIVITIES

Outside persons (for example, the principal, members of the school board, the district superintendent, parents) may evaluate the results of a program strictly according to the written program plan, including the statement of philosophy, rationale, and goals. This type of evaluation is relatively easy for outsiders to conduct and requires no particular measurement skills; the written plans and goals are simply compared with the actual apparent activities and outcomes. The Provus (1972) *discrepancy evaluation* concept mentioned earlier is a similar approach. The outsiders may ask such questions as: Were the identification procedures sensible, effective, and fair? Were the inservice workshops held as scheduled? Were the instructional strategies (grouping, acceleration, enrichment) carried out as planned? Did the planned field trips materialize? Were mentors/ professionals in the community used as planned? Did students really become independent learners, thinkers, creators, and problem solvers? Were skills of analysis, synthesis, evaluation, critical thinking, and divergent thinking really strengthened? Were the evaluation and modification procedures carried out as planned?

Such questions clearly serve as a means of "checking up" on the program and its leaders, and may easily be perceived as threatening. However, the intent typically is constructive.

COMPLEXITY OF EVALUATION AND AUDIENCE: A HIERARCHY

The sophistication of an evaluation will be related to the intended audience—the persons who are the decision makers for a particular program. These decision makers can be placed in a *hierarchy* in terms of the quantity and the quality (statistical complexity) of the information they must have to carry out their own responsibilities. The goal should be to provide the appropriate information to match the information needs of these decision makers.

Briefly, (1) students and parents will need less

information than (2) teachers and program directors, who in turn need less information than (3) administrators and school board members. (4) The state department of education will require still more technical information; and (5) the federal government, with its highly experienced grant reviewers, will require the greatest amount and the highest technical level of information.

Table 18.2 summarizes the relationship between levels of the decision-making hierarchy, components of the program emphasized, and the persons primarily responsible for the evaluation.

The hierarchy of decision makers is based on the different purposes or uses of the program evaluation information. A student or his or her parents may need to know only if the activity is generally interesting, challenging, motivating, and beneficial in very personal terms in order to decide if the student should continue in the program. A relatively small amount of information is needed for a decision that may have an important impact upon just one student, but no particular impact on the program as a whole. The student and his or her parents, with the help of the program teacher and/or coordinator, can assess the value of the program for that student.

The teacher or program director requires quite a bit more information than students and parents in

TABLE 18.2   Summary of the Relationship Between Hierarchy of Decision Making and Evaluation Plan

Hierarchy of Decision Making	Model Component Emphasized	Staff Responsibility
Individual Student or Parent	Individual Process and Outcome	Pupil, Teacher, and/or Parent
Teacher or Program Director	Process and Outcomes	Teacher, Program Director, or Administrator with some background in evaluation or Independent Evaluator
State or Federal Government	Input, Process, and Outcomes	Independent Evaluator with support of Program Staff

order to modify, improve, and perhaps expand the program. This function of evaluation is called *formative evaluation*. Conducted throughout the school year, it is intended to provide immediate and continuous feedback to the staff regarding program strengths and weaknesses. The main focus of formative evaluation will be on *process* (Figure 18.1); that is, on the value of various activities and experiences. Formative evaluation usually is conducted quite effectively by program staff, although observations of an independent (outside) evaluator usually add objectivity, insights, and ideas to the evaluation.

The school principal, district administrators, and members of the elected school board must decide whether to continue, change, or expand the gifted program, and hopefully not to fold it up. To make these kinds of decisions a *summative evaluation* must be conducted. The emphasis is on *outcomes*, and so a summative evaluation is conducted at the end of a unit, project, or most often, the school year. It "sums up" program success. Administrators and school board members may expect the staff to relate program *input* and *process* to outcomes in order to estimate some kind of cost-effectiveness. A teacher or program director with training in evaluation and statistics sometimes can successfully conduct such an evaluation. Board of education members primarily will want to know if a program has been "effective," and so the *hows* and *whys* of its effectiveness must be clearly and simply communicated.

Generally, local school people will feel their accountability obligation is met if one can prove that (1) the program was conducted as planned, (2) the students learned what was taught, and (3) the process of learning was a positive one.

However, if a program is state or federally funded, a professional summative evaluation conducted by an experienced outside evaluator probably will be necessary. This evaluation typically includes a more technical, experimentally oriented evaluation. The teacher's role then becomes one of *cooperator*. The teacher need only inform the evaluator of the resources, activities, and objectives, and provide him or her with the needed data. Some test administration may be involved. Clear communication with the evaluator and full cooperation in gathering the necessary data will facilitate an accurate evaluation of the program. The outside evaluator should not be considered an adversary who is anxious to pounce on weaknesses. His or her role is to provide constructive feedback to the staff for program improvement, and to objectively report the reasonableness and effectiveness of the program plans, methods, activities, and so forth. Although the objectivity of outside evaluators may appear threatening during early program development, that same objectivity will be extraordinarily reinforcing when a program is stabilized and functioning well.

The outside evaluation may require the use of a *control group* of subjects (for example, students of similar ability in another school district where there is no program). Test scores from such a control group, when compared with scores of students in the program, would help determine if any improvements (for instance, in creativity scores, self-concept development, achievement) are actually due to the program and not due simply to maturation, the passage of time, or other educational experiences. Teacher-coordinators likely will drown in a sea of statistics if they attempt this type of evaluation on their own.

As emphasized earlier, an important first consideration for effective evaluation is outlining the evaluation design at the same time the rest of the program is planned, namely, before the program begins. Even an expert evaluator will be less able to do his or her job if the program begins without coordinating the program objectives with their eventual evaluation. Beginning a G/T program without an evaluation design is comparable to beginning one's classroom teaching without a curriculum plan. In both cases, the preplanning helps outline where you are going, how to get there, and what to do when you arrive.

In summary, no program for the gifted should be conducted without some evaluation. Whether the decision makers are students, parents, teachers, administrators, school board members, or state or federal agencies, they will want to know about the success and the particular effects of the program.

INSTRUMENT SELECTION

Some form of measurement is almost always necessary to determine the degree to which program objectives have been achieved (for example, those in the *outcome* rectangle of Figure 18.1). Ideally, in order to reach sound conclusions one should try to obtain *two* measurements of each objective, particularly the most important ones. Also, whenever possible one should use instruments—tests, questionnaires, rating forms—already available. To do a proper job of developing one's own instruments requires a considerable amount of time, and usually requires training and experience in test construction.

Besides, with a little digging a teacher-coordinator most likely will discover that the test-building work already has been done. Many instruments for assessing innumerable aspects of G/T programs are available, for example, in Renzulli (1975), Renzulli, Reis, and Smith (1981), Renzulli and Reis (1985a), Feldhusen (1991), Sjogren, Hopkins, and Gooler (1975), and the Association for the Gifted Evaluation Committee (1979). If the same or similar program plans are used in several schools or districts, evaluation questionnaires may be shared.

A parent questionnaire for an Enrichment Triad, Revolving Door Model, or Schoolwide Enrichment Model program appears in Appendix 18.1 (Renzulli and Reis, 1985a). Teacher, student, and parent questionnaires are available for the evaluation of many components of the Renzulli program models, for example, a *Student Product Assessment Form, Type I Enrichment Evaluation Form, Scale for Evaluating Creativity Teaching Materials*, and others (see Renzulli and Reis, 1985a).

For new evaluation ideas, check current journals on gifted education and creativity; they frequently describe instruments that have been recently developed and validated. Some sample instruments appear at the end of this chapter.

Tests with *norms* for different grades are desirable. Such information allows one more easily to interpret and communicate the performance of gifted students compared with students in the norm group.

Although there are indeed many different tests for review, it can happen that an instrument exactly right for a specific purpose will not be found. Do not make the mistake of using an instrument—no matter how carefully designed—that measures something other than what the program plans to teach. It is essential that the *objectives* of the program activities, on one hand, be matched with the *purposes* and the *contents* of the tests and inventories, on the other. If test purposes or contents do not match program objectives and activities, one is not very likely to find a measurable effect of the program. This simple point may seem self-evident to the sensible reader. However, it is a common error for G/T teachers and coordinators to teach one set of contents and skills (for example, creativity), yet evaluate others (for example, advanced reading)—and then be surprised and disappointed to find "no effects" or "no transfer" of the training experience. As mentioned earlier, negative evaluation findings can easily be misused; they can readily and logically be interpreted as evidence that the program was ineffective.

Pilot Testing

A program evaluator may need to *pilot* a test, that is, try it out with a few children to help decide if it is appropriate for the desired purpose. For example, suppose a program included accelerated reading or math and the evaluator wanted to determine if a particular norm-referenced test could be used to evaluate student achievement.[1] If the test is administered to two or three students and they "top out" near the maximum possible score, this would immediately signal that the test is not satis-

---

[1]A *norm-referenced* test is one of moderate difficulty that is designed to produce a normal, bell-curve distribution of scores, for example, a standardized achievement test.

factory. It would not assess the high achievement level of the gifted students. It may be necessary to pilot three or four tests to find an appropriate one. One strategy is to pilot several tests simultaneously with several small groups of students. This quickly provides plenty of information for test comparison and selection.

Topping Out, Regression Toward the Mean, and Reliability

As discussed earlier in this book, the topping-out phenomenon is a frequent occurrence when gifted students take standardized, norm-referenced achievement tests. The tests often are not difficult enough to discriminate among or evaluate the learning of high-achieving gifted children. If we measure improvements from pretests to post-tests but students have already achieved ceiling scores on the pretests, it will appear that the students showed no measurable improvement. In fact, there simply was no place for the scores to go. Actual progress could not be measured.

A potentially more serious problem related to using too-easy achievement tests comes from the *regression toward the mean* effect. This simply means that given a first score that is extreme (either very high or very low), by chance alone the next score is likely to "regress" toward the mean. Now if some gifted students score near the very top of a pretest, their scores on the post-test by chance alone are likely to be lower—incorrectly suggesting that participation in the special G/T activities damaged their learning. For example, with regressed scores on a basic skills test, an audience could conclude that the gifted program is having a negative effect on the basic skills of students. They probably would attribute this damage to students missing instructional time in the regular classroom. Because pulling students out of the regular classroom often is a controversial issue in the first place, such an interpretation could be devastating to an excellent program.

Tests should be precise enough to measure changes from pretest to post-test. Therefore, tests should have good test-retest and/or alternate forms reliability. Rating scales must have a sufficiently wide scoring range to detect pre- to post-test differences (Beggs, Mouw, and Barton, 1989).

Divergent thinking tests can produce different results depending on variations in instructions, differences in motivational levels, or other reasons. In one evaluation by the second author, post-test scores on the *Torrance Tests of Creative Thinking* (TTCT) were significantly *lower* than pretest scores, despite an excellent creative thinking program. Perhaps the lower scores were due to a less motivating classroom climate toward the end of the year, compared with the more stimulating new opportunity at the beginning of the program. It also was possible that the two TTCT test forms are not equivalent (i.e., the more difficult form was given as a post-test); or that these divergent thinking tests simply did not measure the kinds of changes in creative dispositions and abilities that were learned (Davis, 1992a). Whatever the reason(s), such findings can be damaging to a good program.

TEST CONSTRUCTION

There are times when a state or federal agency will require evidence for the effectiveness of a program, but the exactly appropriate tests and measures simply do not exist. It therefore may be necessary to construct original tests or questionnaires in order to evaluate specific student skills, information, attitudes, or abilities, the effectiveness of specific program components, or even the overall quality of the total program. Technical help from an evaluation expert at a university or private consulting firm, someone experienced in evaluating G/T programs and in constructing tests, probably will be needed.

To select a consultant, contact directors of other G/T programs and state or even national leaders in gifted education to find who in the area is available and qualified. When a consultant is recommended, one can elicit opinions of his or her work from teachers and program directors for whom the consultant has provided services. One also can ask to review tests and reports the consultant has prepared for other clients.

Competitive bidding can be misleading, since there is a considerable range of quality that fixed evaluation dollars can buy. Also, a poor instrument or evaluation is worse than none at all, even if the cost is low. Test construction may be expensive, so be prepared. The high cost of test construction is one very good reason to use established tests, as recommended earlier.

Rating Students' Products

Artistic, literary, scientific, or other types of student products may be outcomes of a program, and although they are difficult to evaluate reliably, their quality is measurable. Product evaluation usually involves either of two approaches. With the first *gain score* approach, samples of students' work obtained at the outset of the program (pretest products) are compared with students' products at the end of the educational experience (post-test products). Gain scores may be used to evaluate products that reflect the development of such skills and abilities as art, creative writing, divergent thinking, technical skills, and others.

With the second *absolute* approach, individual students' products are evaluated according to their excellence without an objective comparison with earlier products. The absolute approach would be used if science or other major projects (for example, of the Renzulli Type III variety) are evaluated for which earlier comparison products are not available.

With either the gain score or the absolute method, rating scales may be used to quantify the judgments. As two examples, Renzulli (1975) recommended the scale in Appendix 18.2, developed by the Warwick, Rhode Island, Public Schools for evaluating the quality of visual arts products. This art scale includes a "growth" rating, which would make no sense in a pretest. Therefore, if this scale were used to assess gain scores the "growth" item would be omitted from both the pretest and the post-test. The scale in Appendix 4.4, developed by

the state of Michigan Department of Education, may be used to evaluate the excellence of virtually any type of student product.

The rating scales in Appendixes 18.2 and 4.4 could serve as models for creating one's own product-rating scales. Alternatively, the following steps could be used to develop and apply original rating scales:

Step 1. Determine the evaluation criteria (for example, creativeness, technical skill) and the specific scales for rating those criteria. The criteria should come from the teaching objectives. Note the objectives reflected in each scale in Appendixes 18.2 and 4.4. As for the rating scales themselves, while Appendix 18.2 uses six-point scales, a five-point scale as in Appendix 4.4 usually is most comfortable. It is best to describe the meaning of each point on the scale. The "low," "moderate," and "high" descriptions of Appendix 18.2 and the "To a great extent," "Somewhat," and "To a limited extent" of Appendix 4.4 are very minimal descriptions. For example, a scale for evaluating the use of *humor* in creative writing might be based on the following descriptors:

"1": No use of humor.
"2": One humorous comment, which does not appear original.
"3": Two or three humorous statements or paragraphs, which do not appear original.
"4": Two or three statements or paragraphs that do appear original.
"5": Original humorous themes are skillfully integrated into the entire story.

Such scale-point descriptions will improve the accuracy (reliability) of the ratings.

Step 2. Collect pretest creative products from each child in the program. All products should be identified with code numbers so that the students' names and the date of collection will not be obvious to the raters.

Step 3. Select at least two raters. They may be teachers or community members. Train them to use the particular scales with extra products that will not be used as evaluation data. After rating several products together, use a few more extra products for individual raters each to rate separately.

Step 4. Calculate the percentage of rater agreement. With five-point scales, two raters should agree on at least 80 percent of the practice ratings before they begin rating the pretest and post-test products. If the raters do not agree at an 80 percent level, they need more training, including a discussion of the reasons for their disagreements.

Step 5. After interrater reliability is established, to minimize bias each rater should rate all products. This should be done without knowing the names of the children and without knowing which are pretest products and which are post-test products.

Step 6. Calculate the average pretest ratings for the group and compare them with the average post-test ratings. If a program is effective, the average post-test rating should be higher, indicating that skill development increased since the pretest products were created. Statistics may be necessary in order to conclude that the overall increase is not due to chance. Also, as noted earlier, a control group may be necessary to prove that the improvement of the trained students was not due to the passage of time or to other educational experiences.

For information regarding the gains (or losses) of individual students, one would examine the differences between pretest and post-test ratings for each student.

Step 7. In reporting the findings, the means (and other statistics, if any) must be meaningful, reliable, and valid. If possible, include a few sample products (for example, samples of creative writing, scientific reports, photos of artwork) to illustrate the student gains. These sample products will help any audience understand the meaning of the ratings.

Hennessey and Amabile (1988) used a much more informal system for rating the creativeness of children's stories given orally in response to pictures. Three teachers, experienced in children's creative writing, were simply asked to rate the cre-

ativeness of each story "using your own subjective definition of creativity." They were given no training, and made their assessments independently. Despite the lack of training and simplicity of the rating task, the interjudge reliability was a high .91. These results are sufficiently impressive and surprising that your authors would recommend a replication before using teacher ratings of creative stories, for example, as a prudent measure of the success of a creative writing program.

Classroom Observation Data

Parents, administrators, school board members, and government agencies usually like to know what happens in a gifted program, and so classroom observation data are good data to collect. A structured observation form can be developed for a program and used to describe "who is doing what with whom and when" in a very specific way. As one example, Appendix 18.3 (from Rimm, 1981a) shows a structured observation form used for monitoring a reading program. The letters at the top of each column represent each of the ten students observed. Filling in a circle indicates that a student is involved in one of the activities listed in the rows. An objective observer would enter the classroom at random times of the day and observe ten randomly selected students, recording their activities on the checklist. Descriptive comment may be added to each observation to provide a richer description of the class environment.

A form such as the one in Appendix 18.3 could be adapted for use with any particular G/T program. Category headings could be modified or new ones created; each would have specific subcategories. For example, one might wish to record pupil's interest level, pupil's behavior, pupil's interactions, teacher's instructional activities, materials and equipment in use, or activities of other adults. Additional headings, each with specific subcategories, could be included depending upon the special activities of the program.

If desirable, at the end of the year summary forms can be tabulated and percentages calculated to describe the specific *type* and *extent* of the activities engaged in during that year. This summary provides objective documentation of the year's program activities. Thus if a school board member wanted to know how much time microcomputers were in use, how many students participated in the *Great Books* discussions, or what proportion of the G/T program time was spent in independent projects, numbers and percentages would be available to support personal observations and impressions. There is nothing quite so convincing as hard data.

Questionnaires

Activities in both the *process* and *outcomes* components of Rimm's model may be evaluated with questionnaires. While students, teachers, parents, board members, and administrators all find paperwork burdensome, the best way to find answers is to ask questions. Decision makers at all levels will want to know (and have a right to know) the effectiveness and special strengths of a program as well as its weaknesses as perceived by others. They also are interested in others' constructive suggestions for improving the program. If questionnaires are brief and require only that a few numbers be circled and/or a few questions be answered, most persons will respond. You can bet that those who are strongly enthusiastic and those who are most disappointed or critical will be certain to respond.

Questionnaires use various types of items. Objective items include *checklists, rating scales, rankings*, and *multiple-choice* statements. The advantages of objective items include ease of development, efficiency of administration, clear response options, easy and objective scoring, and ready quantifiability for statistical purposes. Some disadvantages include the limited nature of the response options, along with little or no information about the *reasons* for the judgments.

Because of these disadvantages, many objective questionnaires also include open-ended items. Open-ended items provide an opportunity for students, teachers, parents, principals, and/or school board members to voice reasons for their opinions, as well as to contribute suggestions and potential solutions to problems. Information can indeed be rich and valuable. For formative evaluation purposes, open-ended items usually are more valuable than objective items. In the negative column, open-ended items are more time-consuming for both respondents and scorers, interpretations may be ambiguous, and the answers are not readily quantifiable.

As examples of combining objective with open-ended questionnaires, Appendix 18.4 presents an example of a brief questionnaire that could be used by teacher participants in an in-service program. Appendix 18.5 shows a questionnaire that allows school board members to evaluate G/T services of a high school. Appendix 18.6 presents a nonobjective open-ended form that students could use to evaluate a learning center.

Generally, it is wise to set aside a few minutes in every program for teachers and students to complete the evaluation forms. If you create the time, persons will fill out the questionnaires on the spot; questionnaires taken home or mailed often are not returned.

DAILY LOGS

As a general principle, *log everything*. Each staff member should keep a notebook handy in which to make brief notes on daily activities. The value of the entries will far outweigh the few minutes invested each day. The kinds of information that could be logged include:

A description of activities
Preparation for the activities
Number of participants
Perceived effectiveness of the activities
Modifications for the future
Any data collected
Any anecdotal material

A personal log kept by each staff member can provide important program documentation serving at least three purposes. First and foremost, it can provide a description of the activities and accomplishments of the students, and therefore of the value of the specific learning activities and projects. Second, it can assure administration and board members that the staff member has indeed made critical contributions to the program. Third, it will serve to remind the teacher of the quantity and quality of his or her own contributions and accomplishments.

STUDENT SELF-EVALUATIONS

Student self-evaluations are important in G/T programs. Primarily, they provide individual students with a clear measure of accomplishment relative to their own goals and objectives. Positive feedback reinforces student motivation and commitment, while objectively documenting their personal progress. For program evaluators, when individual self-evaluations are combined they become important measures of student outcomes, some of which could not be obtained in any other way.

Independent self-monitoring usually can be conducted quite handily by students in junior and senior high school. Younger children also can take responsibility for self-evaluation, with a little help from their teachers. One example of a summative, end-of-the-year student self-evaluation form appears in Appendix 18.7.

PERFORMANCE CONTRACTING

Student *performance contracting* is another vehicle for individual student evaluation. Within the student contract the teacher and the student spell out:

1. Specific *objectives*, including skills to be learned and final projects and papers to be completed.

2. The *activities* in which the student plans to engage to achieve the objectives.

3. The *deadline* by which the objectives will be completed.

4. The *materials* the student will produce (or collect) in support of his or her attainment of the objectives.

5. The *methods* and *criteria* by which the attainment of the objectives will be evaluated.

The student contract is a "study guide" for both the student and the teacher, as well as the basis for an evaluation and documentation of the student's personal performance. The emphasis of the contract should be on student responsibility, with the teacher as a facilitator. Performance contracts are a type of learning activity that encourages the independence and creativity that most gifted students thrive on. Thus individual student needs are served while providing program evaluation and accountability data.

COMMITMENT TO EVALUATION

Teachers and coordinators in gifted programs are likely to view evaluation as burdensome. Their time always is scarce, and time used for evaluation will be at the expense of time for students. It thus is very tempting simply to avoid evaluation altogether. However, skipping the evaluation process is a short-sighted decision for gifted programs— which, we repeat, have a history of being quickly cut from district, state, and federal budgets. Good evaluation is the only way to determine the most effective way to enhance the education of gifted learners. It also is the only way to prove to sponsors and decision makers that the program has indeed accomplished its objectives.

SUMMARY

Evaluation in gifted education has been minimal. However, it is important both for demonstrating success to outsiders and for improving the program. Evaluation plans should be made at the outset of program planning.

Some objectives are difficult to evaluate, such as improvements in self-awareness, creativity, analyzing, and social responsibility. Other outcomes are comparatively easy to assess, such as the success of acceleration or the improved quality of student products.

Provus's discrepancy model includes five steps: Design, Installation, Process (activities), Product, and Product Comparison. At each step one compares the program reality with a standard and then corrects the discrepancy. Eash's differential evaluation model focuses on three considerations, Effort (activities), Effect (products and outcomes), and Efficiency (the relationships of effort and resources to the quality of the Effects).

Renzulli's DESDEG model included five steps corresponding to five documents: the Manual, Evaluation Scales, Basic Information Forms, Evaluator's Workbook, and the Summary Report.

Rimm's model structures the program evaluation and ties it to the initial program plan. The three steps of Input (resources), Process (activities), and Outcome (objectives), each with specific subcategories, all may be evaluated.

Increased academic achievement may or may not be a central outcome. Rather, improvements in process skills and attitudes are usual goals of G/T programs.

Outside persons may evaluate a program by comparing the written plans and goals with the actual activities and outcomes.

Audiences form a hierarchy in the quality and quantity of needed evaluation information. Students and parents need relatively little information to decide whether to continue in the program. Teachers and program directors require more information, particularly continuous, formative evaluation for program improvement. Administrators and school board members will require summative information to decide whether to continue or expand the program. State or federal funding sources will need considerable detailed information, including, for example, test scores and statistical comparisons with control groups.

One should try to obtain two measurements of each important objective. It is usually easier and cheaper to locate already validated tests than to construct your own. It is important to be certain that the test measures the objectives that were the basis of the teaching. Using the wrong tests will produce negative results, creating a bad impression.

Pilot testing is advisable, for example, to cope with the topping-out problem common with gifted students. On a second testing, very high scores may regress toward the mean, creating the appearance that the program damaged, for example, basic skill development. Tests should be sufficiently precise (reliable, wide scoring range) to measure pre- to post-test changes.

With a gain-score approach, ratings of preprogram projects are compared with ratings of postprogram projects. With the absolute approach, complex projects are evaluated without comparison to earlier projects.

In creating original rating scales, one would determine the evaluation criteria, collect pretest products, select and train at least two raters, determine rater agreement, use "blind" ratings, and compare average pretest ratings with average post-test ratings. It is desirable to include sample projects in final reports.

Classroom observation data present objective information regarding what happens in a gifted program.

The process (activities) and outcome (objectives) sections of Rimm's model may be evaluated with questionnaires.

Objective questionnaire items (for example, checklists, rating scales, multiple-choice questions) are easily administered and scored. They may be combined with less objective and more time-consuming—but highly informative—open-ended questions.

Daily logs provide valuable records of activities, preparation, participants, perceived effectiveness, ideas for modifications, and anecdotal information.

Self-evaluations provide positive, motivating feedback to students as well as unique program evaluation data.

Performance contracting can be used to individualize instruction and to document student accomplishments.

Good evaluation is absolutely essential for program continuity and program improvement.

APPENDIX 18.1 SAMPLE PAGE FROM A PARENT QUESTIONNAIRE

Revolving Door TAG Program Parent Questionnaire

Directions:

Please do not sign your name to this questionnaire. No attempt will be made to identify persons completing these forms. Please return the questionnaire in the enclosed envelope within the next two or three days.

You can help to make our program better by giving careful thought to each of the questions that follow. Because of the relatively small number of persons involved in the project, each person's opinion will weigh heavily in analyzing the results. We appreciate your cooperation and assistance in helping us to evaluate this program. We suggest that you read through the entire questionnaire before you begin to answer the questions.

	YES	NO
1. Did you attend the meeting held earlier this year at which we explained the Revolving Door TAG Program?	___	___
2. Do you feel that you have been provided with enough information about the Revolving Door Identification Model in general?	___	___
3. Are you familiar with the procedures for revolving a student into the resource room?	___	___
4. Has your child been revolved into the resource room this year?	___	___
5. If the answer to Question No. 4 is yes, are you familiar with the project or topic that your child worked on while in the resource room?	___	___
6. Are you familiar with the procedures for revolving a student out of the resource room?	___	___
7. Are you familiar with a procedure we use in the TAG Program called "Curriculum Compacting?"	___	___
8. Have you been invited to visit the resource room?	___	___
9. Do you feel that you have been offered sufficient opportunity to contact the school or make an appointment to discuss your child's work in the TAG Program?	___	___
10. Has your child encountered any problems with his/her friends as a result of being involved in the TAG Program? If yes, please explain.	___	___
11. Has your child encountered any problems as a result of leaving the regular classroom to participate in the TAG resource room? If yes, please explain.	___	___
12. Has your child expressed a concern about missing work in the regular classroom or making up assignments because he or she is out of the classroom to attend the TAG resource room?	___	___
13. Have you had any communication with your child's classroom teacher about his/her participation in the TAG Program? If yes, please describe.	___	___

From Renzulli and Reis (1985), reprinted by permission.

APPENDIX 18.2 PROJECT GIFTED: EVALUATION SCALE FOR VISUAL ARTS

Code No. _____ Age _____ Boy/Girl _____ TOTAL SCORE _____

Evaluator _____ Position _____ Date _____

Elements	Low		Moderate		High	
	1	2	3	4	5	6
1. Creative Expression, Imagination, Uniqueness						
2. Flexibility, Appreciation, and Adaptability to Various Media						
3. Fluency, Variety or Number of Ideas						
4. Sensitivity-Composition-Design						
5. Manipulative Skills: Construction, Weaving, etc.						
6. Growth						
Column Total						
Weight	1	2	3	4	5	6
Weighted Column Total						
TOTAL SCORE						

J.S. Renzulli, *An Evaluation of Project Gifted.* Storrs, University of Connecticut, 1973.
Reprinted by permission

APPENDIX 18.3 EXAMPLE OF A STRUCTURED OBSERVATION FORM

Date _____ a.m. _____ p.m. _____ Observer _____

	a.m. abc	def	ghij	p.m. abc	def	ghij
1. Pupil's Location						
Desk or table	000	000	0000			
Carrel	000	000	0000			
Open area	000	000	0000			
Materials center	000	000	0000			
Other (specify):	000	000	0000			
2. Instructional Content						
Readiness	000	000	0000			
Decoding skills	000	000	0000			
Comprehension	000	000	0000			
Enjoyment or appreciation	000	000	0000			
Vocabulary	000	000	0000			
Spelling	000	000	0000			
Grammar	000	000	0000			
Composition	000	000	0000			
Oral expression	000	000	0000			
School library usage	000	000	0000			
Speed reading	000	000	0000			
Dictionary skills	000	000	0000			
Other (specify):	000	000	0000			

	abc	def	ghij
3. Pupil's Instructional Grouping			
Whole-class group instruction	000	000	0000
Partial-class group instruction	000	000	0000
Tutorial (one to one) instruction	000	000	0000
Independent work on individually-assigned activity	000	000	0000
Independent work on a group-assigned activity	000	000	0000
Shared work on group-assigned activity	000	000	0000
Shifting group patterns	000	000	0000
4. Instructional and Audiovisual Materials and Equipment in Use			
5. Pupil's Behavior			
6. Person Relating to Pupil			
7. Person's Instructional Role			

S. Rimm, "Evaluation of gifted programs—as easy as ABC." In R.E. Clasen et al. (eds.), *Programming for the Gifted, Talented, and Creative* (Madison: Universtiy of Wisconsin, 1981).

APPENDIX 18.4 EVALUATION FORM FOR INSERVICE WORKSHOPS

```
Workshop Title:        CREATIVITY IN THE CLASSROOM


Circle the appropriate numbers below.

1.  I found this program to be . . .

    1              2              3              4              5
    Dull                    Of average                    Very
                            Interest                    Interesting

2.  I think that what I learned today will be . . .

    1              2              3              4              5
    Useless                 Somewhat                      Very
                            Useful                        Useful

3.  I would like to have more inservice programs on this topic.

    1                    2              3                    4
    No, not         Yes, but       Yes, more         Other
    at all          not for        this year         (Explain
                    a while                          Below):

    Explanation:   _____

    _____

    _____


4.  The things I liked most about this inservice were:   _____

    _____

    _____

    _____


5.  The things I liked least about this inservice were:   _____

    _____

    _____

    _____
```

APPENDIX 18.5 SCHOOL BOARD QUESTIONNAIRE

We suggest you read the questionnaire before you start to answer.

Please indicate the extent to which you agree or disagree with each of the following statements by circling the appropriate letter. The letters mean the following:

SA — Strongly agree
A — Generally agree
U — Undecided
D — Generally disagree
SD — Strongly disagree

Please use the comment line if you want to explain your answer. Answer question 9 only if you have children in the high school.

1. School E High School provides a well-balanced educational program.   SA   A   U   D   SD

   Comment_____

2. This school has a good program for able students.   SA   A   U   D   SD

   Comment_____

3. Most parents feel School E is a good school.   SA   A   U   D   SD

   Comment_____

4. The School E program is mainly for the college-bound student.   SA   A   U   D   SD

   Comment_____

5. Students at School E are receiving a good education in the basics like math, English, history, science.   SA   A   U   D   SD

   Comment_____

6. There are too many frills in the School E program.   SA   A   U   D   SD

   Comment_____

7. School E has a good extracurricular program, i.e., athletics, music, school paper, drama, clubs, etc.   SA   A   U   D   SD

   Comment_____

8. School E should have more vocational courses.   SA   A   U   D   SD

   Comment_____

9. Most of the teachers our child has had at School E have done a good job.   SA   A   U   D   SD

   Comment_____

D. Sjogren, T. Hopkins, and D. Gooler, *Evaluation Plans and Instruments: Illustrative Cases of Gifted Program Evaluation Techniques.* Center for Instructional Research and Curriculum Evaluation, Urbana-Champaign:University of Illinois. Reprinted by permission.

APPENDIX 18.6 STUDENT EVALUATION: LEARNING CENTER PROGRAM

STUDENT EVALUATION
LEARNING CENTER PROGRAM

For the past sixteen weeks you have been attending sessions at the _____ County Learning Center. We would like to know some of your feelings about the program. By answering questions and completing the following sentences, you can help us in improving the program.

1. Which class did you like best? _____

2. Why? _____

3. Of the classes I was not in, I wish I could have taken _____

   _____

4. Why? _____

5. I wish my classes at the Learning Center were longer _____,

   shorter _____, the same _____ (check one).

6. The Learning Center needs more _____

7. The class in which I learned or accomplished most was _____

   _____

8. If I could change three things about the Learning Center, I would

   a. _____

   b. _____

   c. _____

9. Has the Learning Center helped you in any way with things you do

   at school? _____

10. How? _____

11. Has the Learning Center helped you in any way with things you do

    at home? _____

12. How? _____

13. Has the Learning Center helped in any way with the way you get

    along with or feel about people? _____. If so, how? ___

    _____

From Florida's *State Resource Manual for Gifted Child Education*. State of Florida Department of Education, 1973. Reprinted by permission.

APPENDIX 18.7 PUPIL SELF-EVALUATION

PUPIL SELF-EVALUATION

Pupil's Name _____

Think of yourself at the present time in comparison to last year. As a result of <u>this year's</u> work, please rate yourself on the following items. Place the letters <u>a</u>, <u>b</u>, <u>c</u>, <u>d</u>, and <u>e</u> on the line following each item according to the scale below.

(a) Much less   (d) More
(b) Less   (e) Much more
(c) About the same

1. Ability to think things through for yourself   _____

2. Knowledge of subject matter areas (science, social
    studies, and others I have taken)   _____

3. Interest in school   _____

4. Ability to see how things go together in a situation
    (see relationships)   _____

5. Ability to find information   _____

6. Ability to work well by myself   _____

7. The liking and respect of other pupils for me   _____

8. Ability to judge the usefulness of facts   _____

9. Ability to get along with my teacher(s)   _____

10. Enjoyment of learning   _____

11. Knowledge of arithmetic, spelling, and other basic
    skills   _____

12. Curiosity about learning new things   _____

13. Ability to accept responsibility   _____

14. Opportunity to make things, experiment, and use ideas _____

15. Knowledge of my strengths and weaknesses   _____

16. Willingness to do work as a leader   _____

Please answer the following questions:

17. Has the school year been helpful to you? Yes _____   No _____
    Please explain.

    _____

    _____

18. Has any part of the school work this year created any problems for
    you?   Yes _____   No _____
    Please explain.

    _____

    _____

R.E. Simpson and R.A. Martinson, *Educational Program for Gifted Pupils*. Sacramento, Calif.: California State Department of Education, 1961. Reprinted by permission.

Abraham, W. (1976). The early years: Prologue to tomorrow. *Exceptional Child, 42,* 330–335.

Ackerman, N. J. (1980). The family with adolescents. In E. A. Carter and M. McGildrich (Eds.). *The family life cycle: A framework for family therapy.* New York: Gardner.

Adams, A. A. (1989). Prospective minority scientists. *Gifted Child Today, 12*(4), 40.

Adams, M. (1981). *Attribution theory and gifted females.* Presented at the CEC-TAG National Topical Conference on the Gifted and Talented Child, Orlando, FL.

Adderholdt-Elliott, M. (1987). *Perfectionism: What's bad about being too good?* Minneapolis, MN: Free Spirit Publishing.

Adderholdt-Elliott, M. (1989). Perfectionism and underachievement. *Gifted Child Today, 12*(1), 19-21.

Addison, L. (1981, December). Attribution theory and gifted females. Presented at the CEC-TAG National Topical Conference on the Gifted and Talented Child, Orlando, FL.

Adler, T. (1991, September). Support and challenge: Both key for smart kids. *Science Monitor,* 10.

Alamprese, J. A. and Erlanger (1988). *No gift wasted: Effective strategies for educating highly able, disadvantaged students in mathematics and science. Vol. I: Findings.* Washington, DC: COSMOS Corporation.

Albert, R. S. (1975). Toward a behavioral definition of genius. *American Psychologist, 30,* 140-151.

Albert, R. S. (1980). Family positions and the attainment of eminence: A study of special family positions and special family experiences. *Gifted Child Quarterly, 24,* 87-95.

Allen, R. R., Kauffeld, F. J., and O'Brien, W. R. A. (1968). *Semiprogrammed introduction to verbal argument,* Parts 1-4. Madison, WI: Wisconsin Research and Development Center for Cognitive Learning.

Allen, R. R. and Rott, R. K. (1969). *The nature of critical thinking* (Theoretical Paper No. 20). Madison, WI: University of Wisconsin, Wisconsin Research and Development Center for Cognitive Learning.

Almquist, E. M. and Angrist, S. (1971). Role model influences in college women's career aspirations. *Merrill-Palmer Quarterly, 17,* 263-279.

Alper, T. G. (1974). Achievement motivation in college women: A now-you-see-it-now-you-don't phenomenon. *American Psychologist, 29,* 194-203.

Alschuler, A. S. (1973). *Developing achievement motivation in adolescents.* Englewood Cliffs, NJ: Educational Technology Publications.

Altman, S. L. and Grossman, F. K. (1977). Women's career plans and maternal employment. *Psychology of Women Quarterly, 1,* 365-376.

Alvino, J. (1990, February). Building better thinkers. *Learning90,* 40-41.

Amabile, T. (1986). The personality of creativity. *Creative Living, 15*(3), 12-16.

Anastopoulos, A. D. and Barkley, R. A. (1991). Biological factors in attention deficit-hyperactivity disorder. *CH.A.D.D.ER, 5*(1), 15-16 and 27-28.

Anderson, R. S. (1975). *Education in Japan: A century of modern development.* Washington, DC: U.S. Government Printing Office.

Archambault, F. X. and Hallmark, B. W. (1992). Regular classroom practices: Results of a national survey. In J. S. Renzulli (Chair), *Regular classroom practices with gifted students: Findings from the National Research Center on the Gifted and Talented.* Symposium conducted at the annual meeting of the American Educational Research Association, San Francisco.

Armstrong, J. M. (1979). *A national assessment of achievement and participation of women in mathematics.* (Final Report to the National Institute of Education on Grant No. NIE-G-77-0061.) Denver, CO: Education Commission of the States.

Armstrong, J. M. (1980). *Achievement and participation of women in mathematics: An overview.* Denver, CO: Education Commission of the States. (ERIC Document Reproduction Service No. Ed 184878).

Arnold, K. and Denny, T. (1985). *The lives of academic achievers: The career aspirations of male and female valedictorians and salutatorians.* Paper presented at the meeting of the American Educational Research Association, Chicago, IL.

Aronson, E., Blaney, N., Sikes, J., Stephan, C., and Snapp, M. (1975). Busing and racial tension: The jigsaw route to learning and liking. *Psychology Today, 8*(9), 43-50.

Arthur, G. (1950). *The Arthur adaptation of the Leiter International Performance Scale.* Chicago, IL: Stoelting.

Asimov, I. (1978). *Asimov's Guide to Shakespeare.* New York: Avenel Books.

Association for the Gifted Evaluation Committee. (1979). *Sample instruments for the evaluation of programs for the gifted and talented.* Storrs, CT: University of Connecticut.

Association for Supervision and Curriculum Development. (1987). *Dimensions of thinking.* Reston, VA: Association for Supervision and Curriculum Development.

Atkinson, J. W. (1974). The mainsprings of achievement-oriented activity. In G. A. Davis and T. F. Warren (Eds.), *Psychology of education: New looks.* Lexington, MA: D. C. Heath.

Austin, A. B. and Draper, D. C. (1981). Peer relationships of the academically gifted: A review. *Gifted Child Quarterly, 25,* 129-133.

Augustine, D. K., Gruber, K. D., and Hanson, L. R. (1990). Cooperation works! *Educational Leadership, 47*(4), 4-6.

Baldwin, A. Y. (1977). *Baldwin identification matrix inservice kit for the identification of gifted and talented students.* East Aurora, NY: DOK Publishers.

Baldwin, A. Y. (1978). The Baldwin identification matrix. In A. Y. Baldwin, G. H. Gear, and L. J. Lucito (Eds.), *Educational planning for the gifted: Overcoming cultural, geographic, and socioeconomic barriers.* Reston, VA: Council for Exceptional Children.

Baldwin, A. Y. (1984). *The Baldwin identification matrix 2 for identification of the gifted and talented: A handbook for its use.* New York: Trillium Press.

Baldwin, A. Y. (1987a). I'm black, but look at me, I am also gifted. *Gifted Child Quarterly, 31,* 180-185.

Baldwin, A. Y. (1987b). Undiscovered diamonds: The minority gifted child. *Journal for the Education of the Gifted, 10*(4), 271-285.

Baldwin, A. Y. (1991a). Ethnic and cultural issues. In N. Colangelo and G. A. Davis (Eds.), *Handbook of gifted education* (416-427). Needham Heights, MA: Allyn and Bacon.

Baldwin, A. Y. (1991b). Gifted black adolescents: Beyond racism to pride. In M. Bireley and J. Genshaft (Eds.). *Understanding the gifted adolescent: Educational, developmental, and multicultural issues* (231-239). New York: Teachers College Press.

Baldwin, B. A. (1988). *Beyond the cornucopia kids: How to raise healthy achieving children.* Wilmington, NC: Directions Dynamics.

Ballering, L. D. and Koch, A. (1984). Family relations when a child is gifted. *Gifted Child Quarterly, 28,* 140-143.

Banbury, M. M. and Wellington, B. (1989). Designing and using peer nomination forms. *Gifted Child Quarterly, 33,* 161-164.

Bandura, A. (1986). *Social learning theory.* Englewood Cliffs, NJ: Prentice-Hall.

Banks, W. (1979). *Teaching strategies for ethnic studies* (2nd Ed.). Boston: Allyn and Bacon.

Baratz, J. C. (1974). Teaching reading in an urban negro school system. In G. A. Davis and T. F. Warren (Eds.), *Psychology of education: New looks.* Lexington, MA: D. C. Heath.

Barbie's remarks don't quite add up. (1992, October 21). *New York Times,* 142.

Bardwick, J. M. (1971). *Psychology of women.* New York: Harper and Row.

Barell, J. (1984). Reflective thinking and education for the gifted. *Roeper Review, 6,* 194-196.

Barell, J. (1991a). Creating our own pathways: Teaching students to think and become self-directed. In N. Colangelo and G. A. Davis (Eds.), *Handbook of gifted education* (256-272). Needham Heights, MA: Allyn and Bacon.

Barell, J. (1991b). *Teaching for thoughtfulness.* White Plains, NY: Longman.

Barkan, J. H. and Bernal, E. M. (1991). Gifted education for bilingual and limited English proficient students. *Gifted Child Quarterly, 35,* 144-147.

Barron, F. (1969). *Creative person and creative process.* New York: Holt.

Barron, F. (1978). An eye more fantastical. In G. A. Davis and J. A. Scott (Eds.), *Training creative thinking.* Huntington, NY: Krieger.

Barron, F. (1988). Putting creativity to work. In R. J. Sternberg (Ed.), *The nature of creativity* (76-98). New York: Cambridge University Press.

Bartkovich, K. G. and Mezynski, K. (1981). Fast-paced precalculus mathematics for talented junior high students: Two recent SMPY programs. *Gifted Child Quarterly, 25,* 73-80.

Baum, S. (1984). Meeting the needs of learning disabled gifted students. *Roeper Review, 7,* 16-19.

Baum, S. (1988). An enrichment program for gifted learning disabled students. *Gifted Child Quarterly, 32,* 226-230.

Baum, S. and Owen, S. V. (1988). High ability/learning disabled students: How are they different? *Gifted Child Quarterly, 32,* 321-326.

Bauman, M. K. and Kropf, C. A. (1979). Psychological tests used with blind and visually handicapped persons. *School Psychology Digest, 8,* 257-270.

Becker, D. and Forsyth, R. (1990, April). *Gender differences in grades 3 through 12: A longitudinal analysis.* Paper presented at the meeting of the American Educational Research Association, Boston, MA.

Beggs, D. L., Mouw, J. T., and Barton, J. A. (1989). Evaluating gifted programs: Documenting individual and programmatic outcomes. *Roeper Review, 12,* 73-76.

Bem, S. L. (1974). The measurement of psychological androgyny. *Journal of Consulting and Clinical Psychology, 42,* 155-162.

Benbow, C. P. (1986). SMPY's model for teaching mathematically precocious students. In J. S. Renzulli (Ed.), *Systems and models for developing programs for the gifted and talented* (2-25). Mansfield Center, CT: Creative Learning Press.

Benbow, C. P. (1991). Mathematically talented children: Can acceleration meet their educational needs? In N. Colangelo and G. A. Davis (Eds.), *Handbook of gifted education* (154-165). Needham Heights, MA: Allyn and Bacon.

Benbow, C. P. (1992a). Mathematical talent: Its origins and consequences. In N. Colangelo, S. G. Assouline, and D. L. Ambroson (Eds.), *Talent development: Proceedings from the 1991 Henry B. and Jocelyn Wallace national research symposium on talent development* (95-123). Unionville, NY: Trillium Press.

Benbow, C. P. (1992b). Progress in gifted education—everywhere but here. *Gifted Child Today, 15*(2), 2-8.

Benbow, C. P. (1993). Meeting the needs of gifted students through use of acceleration. In M. C. Wang, M. Reynolds, and H. Walberg (Eds.)., *Handbook of special education: Research and practice,* Vol. 4. Elmsford, NY: Pergamon.

Benbow, C. P., Argo, T. A., and Glass, L. W. (1992). Meeting the needs of the gifted in rural areas through acceleration. *Gifted Child Today, 15*(2), 15–19.

Benbow, C. P. and Arjmand, O. (1990). Predictors of high academic achievement in mathematics and science by mathematically talented students: A longitudinal study. *Journal of Educational Psychology, 82,* 430-441.

Benbow, C. P. and Minor, L. L. (1990). Cognitive profiles of verbally and mathematically precocious students: Implications for identification of the gifted. *Gifted Child Quarterly, 34,* 21–26.

Bernal, E. M. (1978, February). *Alternative avenues of assessment of culturally different gifted.* Speech presented to the Department of Educational Psychology, University of Georgia.

Bernal, E. M. (1979). The education of the culturally different gifted. In A. H. Passow (Ed.), *The gifted and the talented.* Chicago: National Society for the Study of Education.

Bernard, J. (1972). *The future of marriage.* New York: Bantam.

Bestor, A. E. (1953). *Educational wastelands.* Urbana, IL: University of Illinois Press.

Betts, G. T. (1985). *Autonomous learner model: For the gifted and talented.* Greeley, CO: Autonomous Learning Publications and Specialists.

Betts, G. T. (1991). The autonomous learner for the gifted and talented. In N. Colangelo and G. A. Davis (Eds.), *Handbook of gifted education* (142-153). Needham Heights, MA: Allyn and Bacon.

Betts, G. T. and Knapp, J. (1981). Autonomous learning and the gifted: A secondary model. In A. Arnold (Ed.), *Secondary programs for the gifted.* Ventura, CA: Office of the Ventura Superintendent of Schools.

Betts, G. T. and Neihart, M. (1988). Profiles of the gifted and talented. *Gifted Child Quarterly, 32,* 248-253.

Beyer, B. K. (1987). *Practical strategies for the teaching of thinking*. Needham Heights, MA: Allyn and Bacon.

Beyer, B. K. (1988). *Developing a thinking skills program*. Needham Heights, MA: Allyn and Bacon.

Binet, A. and Simon, T. (1905a). Methodes nouvelles pour le diagnostic du niveau intellectuel des anormaux. *L'Année Psychologique, 11*, 191-244.

Binet, A. and Simon, T. (1905b). Sur la necessité d'établir un diagnostic scientific des états inférieurs de l'intelligence. *L'Année Psychologique, 11*, 163-90.

Birch, J. W. (1954). Early school admission for mentally advanced children. *Exceptional Children, 21*(3), 84-87.

Bireley, M. (1991). The paradoxical needs of the disabled gifted. In M. Bireley and J. Genshaft (Eds.). *Understanding the gifted adolescent: Educational, developmental, and multicultural issues* (163-175). New York: Teachers College Press.

Bireley, M. and Genshaft, J. (1991). Adolescence and giftedness: A look at the issues. In M. Bireley and J. Genshaft (Eds.), *Understanding the gifted adolescent: Educational, developmental, and multicultural issues*. New York: Teachers College Press.

Birnbaum, J. A. (1975). Life patterns and self-esteem in gifted family-oriented and career-committed women. In M. T. Mednick, S. S. Tangri, and L. W. Hoffman (Eds.), *Women and achievement: Social and motivational analyses*. New York: Halsted Press.

Black, H. and Black, S. (1985). *Building thinking skills, book 3—verbal*. Pacific Grove, CA: Midwest Publications/Critical Thinking Press and Software.

Black, H. and Black, S. (1986). *Lesson plans and teacher's manual: Building thinking skills, book 1*. Pacific Grove, CA: Midwest Publications/Critical Thinking Press and Software.

Black, H. and Black, S. (1987). *Lesson plans and teacher's manual: Building thinking skills, book 2*. Pacific Grove, CA: Midwest Publications/Critical Thinking Press and Software.

Black, H. and Black, S. (1988). *Lesson plans and teacher's manual: Building thinking skills, book 3— verbal*. Pacific Grove, CA: Midwest Publications/ Critical Thinking Press and Software.

Blanton, M. (1982, September/October). Bloom's taxonomy revisited. *G/C/T*, 22.

Bloom, B. S. (1964). *Stability and change in human characteristics*. New York: Wiley.

Bloom, B. S. (Ed.). (1974). *Taxonomy of educational objectives*. New York: McKay.

Bloom, B. S. (Ed.). (1985). *Developing talent in young people*. New York: Ballantine Books.

Bloom, B. S., Englehart, M. D., Furst, E. J., Hill, W. H., and Krathwohl, D. R. (1956). *Taxonomy of educational objectives, handbook 1: Cognitive domain*. New York: Longmans Green.

Bloom, B. S. and Sosniak, L A. (1981). Talent development vs. schooling. *Educational Leadership, 39*, 86-94.

Boodoo, G. M., Bradley, C. L., Frontera, R. L., Pitts, J. R., and Wright, L. B. (1989). A survey of procedures used for identifying gifted learning disabled children. *Gifted Child Quarterly, 33*, 110-114.

Boring, E. G. (1950). *History of psychology*. New York: Appleton-Century-Crofts.

Bower, B. (1990). Doubt cast on biology of giftedness. *Science News, 138*, 124.

Brandon, P. R., Newton, B. J., and Hammond, O. W. (1987). Children's mathematics achievement in Hawaii: Sex differences favoring girls. *American Educational Research Journal, 24*, 437-461.

Breggin, P. R. (1991). *Toxic psychiatry*. New York: St. Martin's Press.

Bridgeman, B. and Burbach, H. (1976). Effects of black and white peer models on academic expectations and actual performance of fifth-grade students. *Journal of Experimental Education, 45*, 9-12.

Brody, L. E. (1989, November). *Characteristics of extremely mathematically talented females*. Paper presented at The National Association for Gifted Children, Cincinnati, OH.

Brody, L. E., Assouline, S. G., and Stanley, J. C. (1990). Five years of early entrants: Predicting successful achievement in college. *Gifted Child Quarterly, 34*, 138-142.

Brody, L. E. and Benbow, C. P. (1987). Accelerative strategies: How effective are they for the gifted? *Gifted Child Quarterly, 31*, 105-110.

Brody, L. E. and Fox, L. H. An accelerative intervention program for mathematically gifted girls. In L. H. Fox, L. Brody, and D. Tobin (Eds.), *Women and the mathematical mystique*. Baltimore, MD: Johns Hopkins University Press.

Brody, L. E. and Stanley, J. C. (1991). Young college students: Assessing factors that contribute to success. In W. T. Southern and E. D. Jones (Eds.), *The academic acceleration of gifted children* (102-132). New York: Teachers College Press.

Bronson, F. H. and Desjardins, C. (1968). Aggression in adult mice: Modification by neonatal injection of gonadal hormones. *Science, 161,* 705-706.

Brophy, J. E. (1982, April). *Research on the self-fulfilling prophecy and teacher expectations.* Presented at the American Educational Research Association, New York.

Brown, B. B. and Steinberg, L. (1990). Academic achievement and social acceptance: Skirting the "brain-nerd" connection. *Education Digest, 55*(7), 55-60.

Brown, S. W. (1984). The use of WISC-R subtest scatter in the identification of intellectually gifted handicapped children: An inappropriate task? *Roeper Review, 7*(1).

Brown, S. W., Emmons, C. L., and Zhang, W. (1992). The survey sample and district and school policies concerning the gifted. In J. S. Renzulli (Chair), *Regular classroom practices with gifted students: Findings from the National Research Center on the Gifted and Talented.* Symposium conducted at the annual meeting of the American Educational Research Association, San Francisco.

Browne, M. W. (1991, November 22). 57% of U.S. math doctorates going to foreigners. *New York Times,* A14.

Bruch, C. B. and Curry, J. A. (1978). Personal learnings: A current synthesis on the culturally different gifted. *Gifted Child Quarterly, 22,* 313-321.

Brush, S. G. (1991). Women in science and engineering. *American Scientist, 79,* 406.

Bryant, M. S. (1989). Challenging gifted learners through children's literature. *Gifted Child Today, 12*(4), 45-48.

Budmen, K. O. (1967). What do you think, teacher? Critical thinking, a partnership in learning. *Peabody Journal of Education, 45,* 2-5.

Buffery, A. W. H. and Gray, J. A. (1972). Sex differences in the development of spatial and linguistic skills. In C. Ounsted and D. C. Taylor (Eds.), *General differences: Their ontogeny and significance.* Baltimore, MD: Williams and Wilkins.

Burk, E. A. (1980). *Relationship of temperamental traits to achievement and adjustment in gifted children.* Ann Arbor, MI: University Microfilms International.

Burks, B. S., Jensen, D. W., and Terman, L. M. (1930). *Genetic studies of genius: Vol. 3. The promise of youth: Follow-up studies of a thousand gifted children.* Stanford, CA: Stanford University Press.

Burns, J. M., Mathews, F. N., and Mason. (1990). Essential steps in screening and identifying preschool gifted children. *Gifted Child Quarterly, 34,* 102-107.

Bushman, J. H. and Jones, S. K. (1977). *Effective communication: A handbook of discussion skills.* Buffalo, NY: DOK Publishers.

Butler, O. (1988). *Kindred.* Boston: Beacon.

Callahan, C. M. (1986). Asking the right questions: The central issue in evaluating programs for the gifted and talented. *Gifted Child Quarterly, 30,* 38-42.

Callahan, C. M. (1991). An update on gifted females. *Journal for the Education of the Gifted, 14*(3), 284-311.

Callahan, C. M., Cornell, D. G., and Loyd, B. (1990). Perceived competence and parent-adolescent communication in high ability adolescent females. *Journal for the Education of the Gifted, 13*(3), 256-269.

Carelli, A. O. (1981). Creative dramatics for the gifted: A multi-disciplinary approach. *Roeper Review, 5*(2), 29-31.

Carelli, A. O. (1982, Nov./Dec.) Sex equity and the gifted. *G/C/T,* 2-7.

Carlsmith, L. (1964). Effect of early father absence on scholastic aptitude. *Harvard Educational Review, 34,* 3-21.

Carnine, D. (1989). Teaching complex content to learning disabled students: The role of technology. *Exceptional Children, 55*(6), 524-533.

Carter, K. R. (1986). Evaluation design: Issues confronting evaluators of gifted programs. *Gifted Child Quarterly, 30,* 88-92.

Carter, K. R. and Hamilton, W. (1985). Formative evaluation of gifted programs: A process and model. *Gifted Child Quarterly, 29,* 5-11.

Casserly, P. L. (1979). Helping able young women take math and science seriously in school. In N. Colangelo and R. T. Zaffrann (Eds.), *New voices in counseling the gifted.* Dubuque, IA: Kendall/Hunt.

Cassidy, J. and Hossler, A. (1992). State and federal definitions of the gifted: An update. *Gifted Child Today, 15*(1), 46-53.

Cassidy, J. and Johnson, N. (1986). Federal and state definitions of giftedness: Then and now. *Gifted Child Today, 9*(6), 15-21.

Chambers, J. A., Barron, F., and Sprecher, J. W. (1980). Identifying gifted Mexican-American students. *Gifted Child Quarterly, 24,* 123-128.

Chapman, J. W. and McAlpine, D. (1988). Students' perceptions of ability. *Gifted Child Quarterly, 32,* 222-225.

Chapman, S. M. (1991). Introducing young children to real problems of today and tomorrow. *Gifted Child Today, 14*(2), 14-18.

Chisholm, S. (1978, November/December). Address at the National Forum on the Culturally Disadvantaged Gifted Youth. *G/C/T, 2-4,* 40-41.

Chitwood, D. G. (1986). Guiding parents seeking testing. *Roeper Review, 8,* 177-179.

Clance, P.R. and Imes, S. A. (1978). The imposter phenomenon in high achieving women: Dynamics and therapeutic intervention. *Psychotherapy: Theory, research and practice, 15*(3), 241-245.

Clarizio, H. F. and Mehrens, W. A. (1985). Psychometric limitations of Guilford's structure-of-intellect model for identification and programming of the gifted. *Gifted Child Quarterly, 29,* 113-120.

Clark, B. (1983). *Growing up gifted* (2nd Ed.). Columbus, OH: Merrill.

Clark, G. A. and Wilson, T. (1991). Screening and identifying gifted/talented students in the visual arts with Clark's Drawing Abilities Test. *Roeper Review, 13,* 92-97.

Clasen, D. R. (1982). *Meeting the rage to know: College for kids, an innovative enrichment program for gifted elementary children.* (Unpublished report), Madison, WI: University of Wisconsin, Department of Educational Psychology.

Clasen, D. R. and Clasen, R. E. (1989). Using telecommunications to meet the staff development and networking needs of educators of the gifted in small or rural school districts. *Roeper Review, 11,* 202-205.

Clasen, D. R. and Clasen, R. E. (1992). The acceptance-rejection model (ARM): Adolescent responses to the gift vs. group conflict. In N. Colangelo, S. G. Assouline, and D. L. Ambroson (Eds.), *Talent development: Proceedings from the 1991 Henry B. and Jocelyn Wallace national research symposium on talent development* (353-356). Unionville, NY: Trillium Press.

Clasen, D. R. and Hansen, M. (1987). Double mentoring: A process for facilitating mentorships for gifted students. *Roeper Review, 10,* 107-110.

Clasen, R. E. and Clasen, D. R. (1989). *Identification revisited.* Occasional Paper No. 8, University Outreach to the Talented and Gifted, School of Education, University of Wisconsin-Madison.

Clasen, R. E. and Robinson, B. (Eds.). (1979). *Simple gifts.* Madison, WI: University of Wisconsin-Extension.

Clasen, R. E., Robinson, B., Clasen, D. R., and Libster, G. (Eds.). (1981). *Programming for the gifted, talented and creative: Models and methods.* Madison, WI: University of Wisconsin-Extension.

Clinkenbeard, P. R. (1989). The motivation to win—Negative aspects of success at competition. *Journal for the Education of the Gifted, 12*(4), 293-305.

Cohn, R. J. (1980, March/April). Thoughts on acceleration. *G/C/T,* 6-7.

Cohn, S. J. (1981). What is giftedness? A multidimensional approach. In A. H. Kramer (Ed.), *Gifted children: Challenging their potential.* New York: Trillium Press.

Cohn, S. J. (1983a). Talent searches: A national and international effort. *Chronical of Academic and Artistic Precocity, 2,* 1-3.

Cohn, S. J. (1983b). *Summer classes sponsored by the Project for the Study of Academic Precocity.* Tempe, AZ: Arizona State University, Department of Special Education.

Cohn, S. J. (1991). Talent searches. In N. Colangelo and G. A. Davis (Eds.), *Handbook of gifted education* (166-177). Needham Heights, MA: Allyn and Bacon.

Colangelo, N. (1991). Counseling gifted students. In N. Colangelo and G. A. Davis (Eds.), *Handbook of gifted education* (273-284). Needham Heights, MA: Allyn and Bacon.

Colangelo, N. and Brower, P. (1987a). Gifted youngsters and their siblings: Long-term impact of labeling on their academic and social self-concepts. *Roeper Review, 10,* 101-103.

Colangelo, N. and Brower, P. (1987b). Labeling gifted youngsters: Long-term impact on families. *Gifted Child Quarterly, 31,* 75-78.

Colangelo, N. and Davis, G. A. (1991). Introduction and historical overview. In N. Colangelo and G. A. Davis (Eds.), *Handbook of gifted education* (3-13). Needham Heights, MA: Allyn and Bacon.

Colangelo, N. and Kelly, K. R. (1983). A study of student, parent, and teacher attitudes toward gifted programs and gifted students. *Gifted Child Quarterly, 27,* 107-110.

Cole, J. R. and Zuckerman, H. (1987, June). Motherhood and science do mix. *Psychology Today, 57.*

Coleman, J. S. (1961). *The adolescent society.* New York: The Free Press.

Coleman, J. S. (1981, April). *Public and private schools.* Invited address to the American Educational Research Association, Los Angeles, CA.

Coleman, M. R. (1992). A comparison of how gifted/ld and average/ld boys cope with school frustration. *Journal for the Education of the Gifted, 15*(3), 239-265.

Conner, R. S., Levine, S., and Wertheim, G. S. (1969). Hormonal determinants of aggressive behavior. *Annals of the New York Academy of Science, 159,* 760-776.

Connor, E. W. (1991). Gifted all the time. *Gifted Child Today, 14*(5), 14-17.

Cook, T. D. (1986). Using evaluation and research theory to improve programs in applied settings: An interview with Thomas D. Cook by Thomas M. Buescher. *Journal for the Education of the Gifted, 9*(3), 169-179.

Cooley, M. R., Cornell, D. G., and Lee, C. (1991). Peer acceptance and self-concept of Black students in a summer gifted program. *Journal for the Education of the Gifted, 14*(2), 166-177.

Coren, S. and Halpern, D. (1991). Left-handedness: A marker for decreased survival fitness? *Psychological Bulletin, 109,* 90-106.

Cornelius, G. M. and Yawkey, T. D. (1985). Imaginativeness in preschoolers and single parent families. *Journal of Creative Behavior, 19,* 56-66.

Cornell, D. G. (1983). Gifted children: The impact of positive labeling on the family system. *American Journal of Orthopsychiatry, 53*(2), 322-355.

Cornell, D. G. (1990). High ability students who are unpopular with their peers. *Gifted Child Quarterly, 34,* 155-160.

Cornell, D. G., Callahan, C. M., Bassin, L. E., and Ramsay, S. G. (1991). Affective development in accelerated students. In W. T. Southern and E. D. Jones (Eds.), *The academic acceleration of gifted children* (74-101). New York: Teachers College Press.

Cornell, D. G., Callahan, C. M., and Lloyd, B. H. (1991a). Personality growth of female early college entrants: A controlled, prospective study. *Gifted Child Quarterly, 35,* 135-143.

Cornell, D. G., Callahan, C. M., and Lloyd, B. H. (1991b). Socioemotional adjustment of adolescent girls enrolled in a residential acceleration program. *Gifted Child Quarterly, 35,* 58-66.

Cornell, D. G. and Grossberg, I. N. (1986). Siblings of

children in gifted programs. *Journal for the Education of the Gifted, 9*(4), 253-264.

Cornell, D. G. and Grossberg, I. N. (1989). Parent use of the term "gifted": Correlates with family environment and child adjustment. *Journal for the Education of the Gifted, 12*(3), 218-230.

Costa, A. L. (1986). Teaching for, of, and about thinking. In A. L. Costa (Ed.), *Developing minds: A resource book for teaching thinking.* Washington, DC: National Assessment of Educational Progress.

Costa, A. L. and Lowery, L. E. (1989). *Techniques for teaching thinking.* Pacific Grove, CA: Critical Thinking Press and Software.

Covington, M. V. and Beery, R. G. (1976). *Self-worth and school learning.* New York: Holt.

Covington, M. V. and Omelich, C. L. (1979). It's best to be able and virtuous too: Student and teacher evaluative responses to successful effort. *Journal of Educational Psychology, 71,* 688-700.

Cox, C. M. (1926). *The early mental traits of three hundred geniuses. Volume II: Genetic studies of genius.* Stanford, CA: Stanford University Press.

Cox, J. (1986). The Richardson Study: Results and recommendations. In J. Van Tassel-Baska (Ed.), *The Richardson Study: A catalyst for policy change in gifted education.* Evanston, IL: Northwestern University.

Cox, J. and Daniel, N. (1983a, November/December). Identification: Special problems and special populations. *G/C/T,* 54-61.

Cox, J. and Daniel, N. (1983b, September/October) The role of the mentor. *G/C/T,* 54-61.

Cox, J. and Daniel, N. (1985, March/April). The Richardson survey concludes. *G/C/T,* 33-36.

Cox, J. and Daniel, N. (1988). The Richardson study concludes. *Gifted Child Today, 11*(1), 45-47.

Cox, J. and Daniel, N. (1991). The International Baccalaureate. In R. E. Clasen (Ed.), *Educating able learners* (157-166). Madison, WI: Madison Education Extension Programs, University of Wisconsin-Madison.

Cox, J., Daniel, N., and Boston, B. A. (1985). *Educating able learners: Programs and promising practices.* Austin, TX: University of Texas Press.

Crabbe, A. B. (1982). Creating a brighter future: An update on the future problem solving program. *Journal for the Education of the Gifted, 5,* 2-9.

Crabbe, A. B. (1991). Preparing today's students to solve tomorrow's problems. *Gifted Child Today, 14*(2), 2-5.

Cramer, R. H. (1991). The education of gifted children in the United States: A Delphi study. *Gifted Child Quarterly, 35*, 84–91.

Crawford, R. P. (1978). The techniques of creative thinking. In G. A. Davis and J. A. Scott (Eds.), *Training creative thinking.* Huntington, NY: Krieger.

Creel, C. S. and Karnes, F. A. (1988). Parental expectancies and young gifted children. *Roeper Review, 11*, 48-50.

Cresci, M. M. (1989). *Creative dramatics for children.* Glenview, IL: Scott, Foresman.

Cross, T. L., Hernandez, N. R., and Coleman, L. (1991). Governor's schools: An idea whose time has come. *Gifted Child Today, 14*(3), 29-30.

Culross, R. (1989). Measurement issues in the screening and selection of the gifted. *Roeper Review, 12*, 76-78.

Dabney, M. (1983, July). *Perspectives and directive in assessment of the black child.* Paper presented at the meeting of the Council for Exceptional Children, Atlanta, GA.

Dabrowski, K. (1967). *Personality shaping through positive disintegration.* Boston: Little, Brown.

Dabrowski, K. (1972). *Psychoneurosis is not all an illness.* London: Gryf.

Dacey, J. S. (1989). *Fundamentals of creative thinking.* Lexington, MA: Lexington Books.

Daniels, P. R. (1983). *Teaching the gifted/learning disabled child.* Rockville, MD: Aspen.

Dauber, S. L. (1988). International mathematical olympiad. *Gifted Child Today, 11*(5), 8-11.

Dauber, S. L. and Benbow, C. P. (1990). Aspects of personality and peer relations of extremely talented adolescents. *Gifted Child Quarterly, 34*, 10-15.

Daurio, S. P. (1979). Educational enrichment vs. acceleration: A review of the literature. In W. C. George, S. J. Cohen, and J. C. Stanley (Eds.), *Acceleration and enrichment: Strategies for educating the gifted.* Baltimore, MD: Study of Mathematically Precocious Youth, Johns Hopkins University.

Davidson, J. E. (1986). The role of insight in giftedness. In R. J. Sternberg and J. E. Davidson (Eds.), *Conceptions of giftedness.* Cambridge, MA: Cambridge University Press.

Davidson, J. E. and Sternberg, R. J. (1984). The role of insight in intellectual giftedness. *Gifted Child Quarterly, 28*, 58-64.

Davidson, K. (1986). The case against formal identification. *Gifted Child Today, 9*(6), 7–11.

Davis, B. G., Trimble, C. S., and Vincent, D. R. (1980). Does age of entrance affect school achievement? *The Elementary School Journal, 80*(3), 133-143.

Davis, G. A. (1973). *Psychology of problem solving: Theory and practice.* New York: Basic Books.

Davis, G. A. (1975). In frumious pursuit of the creative person. *Journal of Creative Behavior, 9*, 75-87.

Davis, G. A. (1981a). Personal creative thinking techniques. *Gifted Child Quarterly, 25*, 99-101.

Davis, G. A. (1981b). Review of the Revolving Door Identification Model. *Gifted Child Quarterly, 25*, 185-186.

Davis, G. A. (1985). *Creative thinking and problem solving.* (Apple computer disk and manual). Buffalo, NY: Bearly Limited.

Davis, G. A. (1987). How to get a hippo out of the bathtub: What to teach when you teach creativity. *Gifted Child Today, 10*(1), 7-19.

Davis, G. A. (1989a). Gary Davis speaks to teachers: Objectives and activities for teaching creative thinking. *Gifted Child Quarterly, 33*, 81-84.

Davis, G. A. (1989b). Testing for creative potential. *Contemporary Educational Psychology, 14*, 157-174.

Davis, G. A. (1991). Teaching creative thinking. In N. Colangelo and G. A. Davis (Eds.), *Handbook of gifted education* (236-244). Needham Heights, MA: Allyn and Bacon.

Davis, G. A. (1992a). *Creativity is forever* (3rd Ed.). Dubuque, IA: Kendall/Hunt.

Davis, G. A. (1992b). *Good person book: Creative teaching of values and moral thinking.* Buffalo, NY: DOK. (Prepublication edition available from the author.)

Davis, G. A. (1993). Identifying the creatively gifted. In J. Genshaft, M. Bireley, and C. L. Hollinger (Eds.), *A guidebook for serving the gifted and talented.* Washington, DC: National Association of School Psychologists.

Davis, G. A. and Bull, K. S. (1978). Strengthening affective components of creativity in a college course. *Journal of Educational Psychology, 70*, 833-836.

Davis, G. A. and DiPego, G. (1973). *Imagination express: Saturday subway ride.* Buffalo, NY: DOK Publishers.

Davis, G. A., Helfert, C. J., and Shapiro, G. R. (1992).

Let's be an ice cream machine! Creative Dramatics. In S. J. Parnes (Ed.), *Source book for creative problem solving* (384-392). Buffalo, NY: Creative Education Foundation Press.

Davis, G. A., Peterson, J. M., and Farley, F. H. (1974). Attitudes, motivation, sensation seeking, and belief in ESP as predictors of real creative behavior. *Journal of Creative Behavior, 8,* 31-39.

Davis, G. A. and Rimm, S. B. (1980). *GIFFI II: Group inventory for finding interests.* Watertown, WI: Educational Assessment Service.

Davis, G. A. and Rimm, S. B. (1982). Group inventory for finding interests (GIFFI) I and II: Instruments for identifying creative potential in the junior and senior high school. *Journal of Creative Behavior, 16,* 50-57.

Davis, G. A. and Rimm, S. B. (1985). *Education of the gifted and talented.* Englewood Cliffs, NJ: Prentice-Hall.

Davis, G. A. and Thomas, M. A. (1989). *Effective schools and effective teachers.* Needham Heights, MA: Allyn and Bacon.

Davis, G. A. and Warren, T. F. (1994, in preparation). *Educational psychology and effective teaching* (2nd Ed.).

Davis, S. J. and Johns, J. (1989). Students as authors: Helping gifted students get published. *Gifted Child Today, 12*(6), 20-22.

Deaux, K. (1976). Ahhh, she was just lucky. *Psychology Today, 10,* 70.

DeBono, E. (1973). *CoRT Thinking.* Elmsford, NY: Pergamon.

DeBono, E. (1983). The direct teaching of thinking as a skill. *Phi Delta Kappan, 64,* 703-708.

DeBono, E. (1985, September). Partnerships of the mind: Teaching society to think. *ProEducation,* 56-58.

DeLeon, P. H. (1989, February). *Why we must attend to minority gifted: A national perspective.* Presented at the Johnson Foundation Wingspread Conference, Racine, WI.

Delisle, J. R. (1982). Reaching towards tomorrow: Career education and guidance for the gifted and talented. *Roeper Review, 5*(2), 8-11.

Delisle, J. R. (1987). *Gifted kids speak out.* Minneapolis, MN: Free Spirit Publishing.

Delisle, J. R. (1992). *Guiding the social and emotional development of gifted youth.* New York: Longman.

DeMille, R. (1973). *Put your mother on the ceiling.* New York: Viking/Compass.

DeMott, B. (1981). Mind-expanding teachers. *Psychology Today, 4,* 110-119.

Department of Educational Research and Program Development. (1979). *ESEA Title VII bilingual/bicultural educational program, 1978-1979.* Milwaukee, WI: Milwaukee Public Schools.

DeVries, R. and Kohlberg, L. (1990). *Constructivist early education: Overview and comparison with other programs.* Washington, DC: National Association for the Education of Young Children.

Dickens, M. (1990). *Parental influences on the mathematics self-concept of high achieving adolescent girls.* Unpublished doctoral dissertation. University of Virginia, Charlottesville, VA.

Diessner, R. (1983, May/June) The relationship between cognitive abilities and moral development. *G/C/T,* 15-17.

Donahue, T. J. and Costar, J. W. (1977). Counselor discrimination against young women in career selection. *Journal of Counseling Psychology, 24,* 481-486.

Dooley, D., Chauvin, J. C., and Karnes, F. A. (1984). Gifted females: A comparison of attitudes by male and female teachers. *Roeper Review, 6,* 164-167.

Dressel, P. L. and Mayhew, L. B. (1954). *General education: Explorations in evaluation.* Washington, DC: American Council on Education.

Drews, E. and Teahan, J. (1957). Parental attitudes and academic achievement. *Journal of Clinical Psychology, 13,* 328-332.

Dunn, R., Bruno, A., and Gardiner, B. (1984). Put a cap on your gifted program. *Gifted Child Quarterly, 28,* 70-72.

Dunn, R. and Dunn, K. (1978). *Teaching students through their individual learning styles.* Reston, VA: Reston.

Dunn, R. and Dunn, K. (1987). Dispelling outmoded beliefs about student learning. *Educational Leadership, 44*(6), 55-62.

Dunn, R., Dunn, K., and Price, G. E. (1981). *Learning style inventory.* Lawrence, KS: Price Systems.

Dunn, R. and Griggs, S. A. (1985, November/December). Teaching and counseling gifted students with their learning styles preferences: Two case studies. *G/C/T,* 40-43.

Dunn, R. and Griggs, S. A. (1988). *Learning styles:*

Quiet revolution in American secondary schools. Reston, VA: National Association of Secondary Principals.

Durden-Smith, J. and DeSimone, D. (1982, November). Is there is superior sex? *Readers Digest,* 263-270.

Dweck, C. S. and Bush, E. S. (1976). Sex differences in learned helplessness: I. Differential debilitation with peer and adult evaluators. *Developmental Psychology, 12,* 147-156.

Eash, M. (1972). *Issues in evaluation and accountability in special programs for gifted and talented children.* Chicago: University of Illinois-Chicago Circle.

Eberle, B. (1971). *Scamper.* Buffalo, NY: DOK.

Eberle, B. and Hall, R. (1975). *Affective education guidebook: Classroom activities in the realm of feelings.* Buffalo, NY: DOK.

Eberle, B. and Hall, R. (1979). *Affective direction: Planning and teaching for thinking and feeling.* Buffalo, NY: DOK.

Eberle, B. and Stanish, B. (1985). *CPS for kids.* Carthage, IL: Good Apple.

Edlind, E. P. and Haensly, P. A. (1985). Gifts of mentorships. *Gifted Child Quarterly, 29,* 55-60.

Educational Testing Service (1989a). *1989 profile of SAT and achievement test takers.* Princeton, NJ: Educational Testing Service.

Educational Testing Service (1989b). *What Americans study.* Princeton, NJ: Educational Testing Service.

Edwards, D. A. (1969). Early androgen stimulation and aggressive behavior in male and female mice. *Physiological Behavior, 4,* 333-338.

Eilber, C. R. (1987). The North Carolina School of Science and Mathematics. *Phi Delta Kappan, 68,* 773-777.

Eisenberg, D. and Epstein, E. (1981, December). *The discovery and development of giftedness in handicapped children.* Paper presented at the CEC-TAG National Topical Conference on the Gifted and Talented Child, Orlando, FL.

Elkind, D. (1981). *The hurried child: Growing up too fast too soon.* Reading, MA: Addison-Wesley.

Ellingson, M., Haeger, W., and Feldhusen, J. F. (1986, March/April). The Purdue mentor program. *G/C/T,* 2-53.

Ellis, A. and Harper, R. A. (1975). *A new guide to rational living.* New York: Institute for Rational Living.

Emerick, L. J. (1989). *The gifted underachiever: Classroom strategies for reversing the pattern.* Paper presented at The National Association for Gifted Children, Cincinnati, OH.

Emerick, L. J. (1992). Academic underachievement among the gifted: Students' perception of factors that reverse the pattern. *Gifted Child Quarterly, 36,* 140-146.

Ennis, R. H. (1962). A concept of critical thinking: A proposed basis for research in the teaching and evaluation of critical thinking ability. *Harvard Educational Review, 32,* 83.

Ennis, R. H. (1964). *Critical thinking readiness in grades 1-12: Phase I. Deductive reasoning in adolescence.* Project No. 1680, School of Education, Cornell University.

Epstein, J. (1981). *Portraits of great teachers.* New York: Basic Books.

Erickson, D. P. and Ellett, F. S. (1990). Taking student responsibility seriously. *Educational Researcher, 19*(9), 3-9.

Erikson, E. H. (1959). *Identity and the life cycle: Selected papers by Erik H. Erikson.* New York: International Universities Press.

Erikson, E. H. (1968). *Identity: Youth and crisis.* New York: Norton.

Ernest, J. (1976). Mathematics and sex. *American Mathematical Monthly, 83,* 595-614.

Exum, H. (1983). Key issues in family counseling with gifted and talented black students. *Roeper Review, 5*(3), 28-31.

Eysenck, H. J. (1967). *The biological bases of personality.* Springfield, IL: Charles C. Thomas.

Fabun, D. (1968). *You and creativity.* New York: Macmillan.

Fantini, M. D. (1981). A caring curriculum for gifted children. *Roeper Review, 3*(4), 3-4.

Farley, F. H. (1986. May). The big T in personality. *Psychology Today,* 47-52.

Farnham, P. (1988, February). Women in science: Numbers have improved, but problems remain. *Federation Journal Public Affairs,* Federation of American Societies for Experimental Biology, 171.

Fedler, F. (1973). The mass media and minority groups. *Journalism Quarterly, 50,* 109-117.

Feingold, A. (1988). Cognitive gender differences are disappearing. *American Psychologist, 43,* 95-103.

Feldhusen, H. J. (1981). Teaching gifted, creative, and talented students in an individualized classroom. *Gifted Child Quarterly, 25,* 108-111.

Feldhusen, H. J. (1987). *Individualized teaching of*

gifted children in regular classrooms. Buffalo, NY: DOK.

Feldhusen, J. F. (1986). A new conception of giftedness and programming for the gifted. *Illinois Council for the Gifted Journal, 5,* 2-6.

Feldhusen, J. F. (1989a). Synthesis of research on gifted youth. *Educational Leadership, 46*(6), 6-11.

Feldhusen, J. F. (1989b). Why the public schools will continue to neglect the gifted. *Gifted Child Today, 12*(2), 55-59.

Feldhusen, J. F. (1991a). From the editor. *Gifted Child Quarterly, 35,* 3.

Feldhusen, J. F. (1991b). Saturday and summer programs. In N. Colangelo and G. A. Davis (Eds.), *Handbook of gifted education* (197-208). Needham Heights, MA: Allyn and Bacon.

Feldhusen, J. F. (1992). Talent identification and development in education. *Gifted Child Quarterly, 36,* 123.

Feldhusen, J. F. and Clinkenbeard, P. R. (1982). Summer programs for the gifted: Purdue's residential programs for high achievers. *Journal for the Education of the Gifted, 5,* 178-184.

Feldhusen, J. F., Enersen, D. L., and Sayler, M. F. (1992). Challenging the gifted through problem solving experiences—design and evaluation of the COMET program. *Gifted Child Today, 15*(4), 49-54.

Feldhusen, J. F., Hansen, J. B., and Kennedy, D. M. (1989). Curriculum development for GCT teachers. *Gifted Child Today, 12*(6), 12-19.

Feldhusen, J. F., Hoover, S. M., and Sayler, M. F. (1990). *Identifying and educating gifted students at the secondary level.* New York: Trillium Press.

Feldhusen, J. F. and Kolloff, P. B. (1978, January/February). A three-stage model of gifted education. *G/C/T,* 3-5, 53-57.

Feldhusen, J. F. and Kolloff, P. B. (1981a). A self-concept scale for gifted students. *Perceptual and Motor Skills, 53,* 319-323.

Feldhusen, J. F. and Kolloff, P. B. (1981b). A three-stage model for gifted education. In R. E. Clasen, B. Robinson, D. R. Clasen, and G. Libster (Eds.), *Programming for the gifted, talented and creative: Models and methods.* Madison, WI: University of Wisconsin-Extension.

Feldhusen, J. F. and Kolloff, P. B. (1986). The Purdue three-stage enrichment model for gifted education at the elementary level. In J. S. Renzulli (Ed.), *Systems and models for developing programs for the gifted*

and talented (126-152). Mansfield Center, CT: Creative Learning Press.

Feldhusen, J. F., Proctor, T. B., and Black, K. N. (1986). Guidelines for grade advancement of precocious children. *Roeper Review, 9,* 25-27.

Feldhusen, J. F., Rebhorn, L. S., and Sayler, M. F. (1988). Appropriate design for summer gifted programs. *Gifted Child Today, 11*(4), 2-5.

Feldhusen, J. F. and Ruckman, D. R. (1988). A guide to the development of Saturday programs for gifted and talented youths. *Gifted Child Today, 11*(5), 56-61.

Feldhusen, J. F. and Sayler, M. F. (1990). Special classes for academically gifted youth. *Roeper Review, 12,* 244-249.

Feldhusen, J. F. and Wyman, A. R. (1980). Super Saturday: Design and implementation of Purdue's special program for gifted children. *Gifted Child Quarterly, 24.* 15-21.

Feldman, D. H. (1986a). Giftedness as a developmentalist sees it. In R. J. Sternberg and J. E. Davidson (Eds.), *Conceptions of giftedness.* Cambridge, MA: Cambridge University Press.

Feldman, D. H. (1986b). *Nature's gambit: Child prodigies and the development of human potential.* New York: Basic Books.

Feldman, D. H. and Goldsmith, L. T. (1986). Transgenerational influences on the development of early prodigious behavior: A case study approach. In W. Fowler (Ed.), *Early experience and the development of competence: New directions for child development* (67-85). San Francisco: Jossey-Bass.

Feldman, R. D. (1982). *Whatever happened to the Quiz Kids?* Chicago: Chicago Review Press.

Feldman, R. D. (1985, October). The pyramid project: Do we have the answer for the gifted? *Instructor,* 62-65.

Felton, G. S. and Biggs, B. E. (1977). *Up from underachievement.* Springfield, IL: Thomas.

Fennema, E. (1980). Sex-related differences in mathematics achievement: Where and why. In L. H. Fox, L. Brody, and D. Tobin (Eds.), *Women and the mathematical mystique.* Baltimore, MD: Johns Hopkins University Press.

Fennema, E. and Sherman, J. A. (1978). Sex-related differences in mathematics achievement and related factors: A further study. *Journal for Research in Mathematics Education, 9,* 189-203.

Feuerstein, R. (1980a). *Instrumental enrichment: An intervention program for cognitive modifiability.* Baltimore, MD: University Park Press.

Feuerstein, R. (1980b). *Instrumental Enrichment* (thinking skills materials). Washington, DC: Curriculum Development Associates.

Fiedler-Brand, E., Lange, R. E., and Winebrenner, S. (1990). *Tracking, ability grouping, and the gifted: Myths and realities.* Glenview, IL: Illinois Association for Gifted Children.

Fine, M. J. and Pitts, R. (1980). Intervention with underachieving gifted children: Rationale and strategies. *Gifted Child Quarterly, 24,* 51-55.

First Official U.S. Education Mission to the USSR. (1959). *Soviet commitment to education, Bulletin 1959, No. 16.* Washington, DC: Office of Education, Department of Health, Education, and Welfare.

Fisher, E. (1981). The effect of labeling on gifted children and their families. *Roeper Review, 3*(2), 49-51.

Fox, C. L. (1989). Peer acceptance of learning disabled children in the regular classroom. *Exceptional Children, 56*(1), 50-59.

Fox, L. H. (1974). *Facilitating the development of mathematical talent in young women.* Unpublished Ph.D. thesis, Johns Hopkins University.

Fox, L. H. (1977). Sex differences: Implications for program planning for the academically gifted. In J. C. Stanley, W. C. George, and C. H. Solano (Eds.), *The gifted and the creative: A fifty-year perspective.* Baltimore, MD: Johns Hopkins University Press.

Fox, L. H. (1979). Programs for the gifted and talented: An overview. In A. H. Passow (Ed.), *The gifted and talented.* Chicago: National Society for the Study of Education.

Fox, L. H. (1981a, February). Mathematically able girls: A special challenge. *Arithmetic Teacher,* 22-23.

Fox, L. H. (1981b, March/April). Preparing gifted girls for future leadership roles. *G/C/T,* 7-11.

Fox, L. H. and Brody, L. (1983). Models for identifying giftedness: Issues related to the learning-disabled child. In L. H. Fox, L. Brody, and D. Tobin (Eds.), *Learning disabled gifted children* (101-116). Boston: University Park Press.

Franks, B. and Dolan, L. (1982). Affective characteristics of gifted children: Educational implications. *Gifted Child Quarterly, 26,* 172-178.

Frasier, M. M. (1989). Poor and minority students can be gifted too. *Educational Leadership, 46*(6), 16-18.

Frasier, M. M. (1990, April). *The equitable identification of the gifted and talented children.* Paper presented at the annual meeting of the American Educational Research Association, Boston, MA.

Frasier, M. M. (1991a). Disadvantaged and culturally diverse gifted students. *Journal for the Education of the Gifted, 14*(3), 234-245.

Frasier, M. M. (1991b). Response to Kitano: The sharing of giftedness between culturally diverse and non-diverse gifted students. *Journal for the Education of the Gifted, 15*(1), 20-30.

Frazier, A., Passow, A. H., and Goldberg, M. L. (1958). Curriculum research; Study of underachieving gifted. *Educational Leadership, 16,* 121-125.

Freedman, D. G. (1974). *Human infancy: An evolutionary perspective.* Hillsdale, NJ: Erlbaum.

French, J. I. (1964). *Pictorial test of intelligence.* Boston: Houghton Mifflin.

French, J. L. (1959). *Educating the gifted: A book of readings.* New York: Holt.

Freud, S. (1949). *An outline of psychoanalysis.* New York: Norton.

Frey, C. (1980, May/June). The resource room. *G/C/T,* 26–27.

Friedman, J. M. and Master, D. (1980). School and museum: A partnership for learning. *Gifted Child Quarterly, 25,* 42-48.

Frierson, H. T., Jr. (1990). The situation of black educational researchers: Continuation of a crisis. *Educational Researcher, 19*(2), 12-17.

Frieze, I. H. (1975). Women's expectations for and causal attributions of success and failure. In M. T. Mednick, S. S. Tangri, and L. W. Hoffman (Eds.), *Women and achievement: Social and motivational analyses.* New York: Halsted.

Frost, D. (1981, December). *The great debates: For enrichment.* Presented at the CEC-TAG National Topical Conference on the Gifted and Talented Child, Orlando, FL.

Fuchs, D. and Fuchs, L. S. (1989). Effects of examiner familiarity on black, caucasian, and hispanic children: A meta-analysis. *Exceptional Children, 55*(4), 303-308.

Gage, N. L., and Berliner, D. C. (1988). *Educational psychology* (4th ed.). Boston: Houghton Mifflin.

Gagné, F. (1985). Giftedness and talent: Reexamining a reexamination of the definitions. *Gifted Child Quarterly, 29,* 103-112.

Gagné, F. (1989). Peer nominations as a psychometric instrument: Many questions asked but few answered. *Gifted Child Quarterly, 33,* 53-58.

Gagné, F. (1991). Toward a differentiated model of giftedness and talent. In N. Colangelo and G. A. Davis

(Eds.), *Handbook of gifted education* (65-80). Needham Heights, MA: Allyn and Bacon.

Gallagher, J. J. (1958). Peer acceptance of highly gifted children in elementary school. *Elementary School Journal*, 465-470.

Gallagher, J. J. (1959). *The gifted child in the elementary school.* Washington, DC: National Education Association.

Gallagher, J. J. (1990). Editorial: The public and professional perception of the emotional status of gifted children. *Journal for the Education of the Gifted, 13*(3), 202-211.

Gallagher, J. J. (1991a). Educational reform, values, and gifted students. *Gifted Child Quarterly, 35,* 12-19.

Gallagher, J. J. (1991b). Issues in the education of gifted students. In N. Colangelo and G. A. Davis (Eds.), *Handbook of gifted education* (14-23). Needham Heights, MA: Allyn and Bacon.

Gallagher, J. J. (1991c). Personal patterns of underachievement. *Journal for the Education of the Gifted, 14*(3), 221-233.

Gallagher, J. J., Weiss, P., Oglesby, K., and Thomas, T. (1983). *The status of gifted/talented education: United States surveys of needs, practices, and policies.* Los Angeles: Leadership Training Institute.

Gallagher, R. M. (1991). Programs for gifted students in Chicago public schools: Yesterday, today, and tomorrow. *Gifted Child Today, 14*(6), 4-8.

Gallagher, S., Barr, D., Barron, M., Marshall, S. P., and Smith, L. (1991). The Illinois mathematics and science academy. *Gifted Child Today, 14*(6), 16-21.

Gallucci, N. T. (1988). Emotional adjustment of gifted children. *Gifted Child Quarterly, 32,* 273-276.

Galton, F. (1869). *Hereditary genius.* London: Macmillan.

Ganapole, S. J. (1989). Designing an integrated curriculum for gifted learners: An organizational framework. *Roeper Review, 12,* 81-86.

Gangi, J. M. (1990). Higher level thinking skills through drama. *Gifted Child Today, 13*(1), 16-19.

Gardner, H. (1983). *Frames of mind: The theory of multiple intelligences.* New York: Basic Books.

Gardner, H. (1986, November/December). Comments. *G/C/T,* 11.

Gardner, J. W. (1961). *Can we be equal and excellent too?* New York: Harper & Row.

Gartner, A., Kohler, M., and Reissman, F. (1971). *Children teach children.* New York: Harper and Row.

Gartner, A., and Lipsky, D. K. (1987). *The transition from school to post-secondary education and training: A resource guide for students with a disability.* New York: Center for Advanced Study in Education, Graduate School and University Center, City University of New York.

Gay, J. E. (1978). A proposed plan for identifying black gifted children. *Gifted Child Quarterly, 22,* 353-357.

Gaynor, C. (1990, February). Good thinking. *Learning90,* 2.

Gelbrich, J. A. and Hare, E. K. (1989). The effects of single parenthood on school achievement in a gifted population. *Gifted Child Quarterly, 33,* 115-117.

Getzels, J. W. (1977). General discussion immediately after the Terman memorial symposium. In J. C. Stanley, W. C. George, and C. H. Solano (Eds.), *The gifted and the creative: A fifty-year perspective.* Baltimore, MD: Johns Hopkins University Press.

Getzels, J. W. and Jackson, P. W. (1962). *Creativity and intelligence.* New York: Wiley.

Giele, J. Z. (1978). *Women and the future: Changing sex roles in modern America.* New York: Free Press.

Gifted Child Society. (1990). *The Saturday workshop: Activities for gifted children and their parents.* Glen Rock, NJ: Gifted Child Society, Inc.

Ginsberg, G. and Harrison, C. H. (1977). *How to help your gifted child.* New York: Monarch Press.

Gleason, M., Carnine, D., and Boriero, D. (in press). A comparison of CAI with teacher instruction in teaching math story problems to mildly handicapped students. *Journal of Special Education Technology.*

Goertzel, M. G., Goertzel, V., and Goertzel, T. G. (1978). *300 eminent personalities.* San Francisco: Jossey-Bass.

Goertzel, V. and Goertzel, M. G. (1962). *Cradles of eminence.* Boston: Little, Brown.

Gogul, E. M., McCumsey, J., and Hewett, G. (1985, November/December). What parents are saying. *G/C/T,* 7-9.

Goldstein, D., Stocking, V. B., and Sawyer, R. N. (1992). The talented adolescent: Data from TIP's first decade. In N. Colangelo, S. G. Assouline, and D. L. Ambroson, (Eds.), *Talent Development: Proceedings from the 1991 Henry B. and Jocelyn Wallace National Research Symposium on Talent Development.* Unionville, NY: Trillium Press.

Gonsalves, W. C., Grimm, J., and Welsh, J. M. (1981). Leadership training: A lesson in living. *Roeper Review, 3*(3), 16-19.

454   REFERENCES

Good, H. G. (1960). *A history of western education* (2nd Ed.). New York: Macmillan.

Good, T. L. and Weinstein, R. S. (1986). Teacher expectations: A framework for exploring classrooms. In K. Zumwalt (Ed.), *Improving teaching: 1986 ASCD yearbook*. Alexandria, VA: Association for Supervision and Curriculum Development.

Goodlad, J. and Oakes, J. (1988). We must offer equal access to knowledge. *Educational Leadership, 45,* 16-22.

Gordon, W. J. J. (1961). *Synectics.* New York: Harper & Row.

Gordon, W. J. J. (1974). *Making it strange.* Books 1-4. New York: Harper & Row.

Gordon, W. J. J. and Poze, T. (1972a). *Teaching is listening.* Cambridge, MA: SES Associates.

Gordon, W. J. J. and Poze, T. (1972b). *Strange and familiar.* Cambridge, MA: SES Associates.

Gottfredson, L. S. (1981). Circumspection and compromise: A developmental theory of occupation aspirations. *Journal of Counseling Psychology Monograph, 28,* 545-579.

Gourley, T. J. (1981). Adapting the varsity sports model to nonpsychomotor gifted students. *Gifted Child Quarterly, 25,* 164-166.

Gowan, J. C. (1960). The organization of guidance for the able. *Personnel and Guidance Journal, 39,* 275-279.

Gowan, J. C. (1967). Issues in the guidance of gifted and creative children. *Gifted Child Quarterly, 11,* 140-143.

Gowan, J. C. (1979). Differentiated guidance for the gifted: A developmental view. In J. C. Gowan, J. Khatena, and E. Paul Torrance (Eds.), *Educating the ablest: A book of readings* (190-199). Itasca, IL: Peacock.

Gowan, J. C. and Demos, G. (1964). *Education and guidance of the ablest.* Springfield, IL: Thomas.

Goy, R. W. and Resko, J. A. (1972). Gonadal hormones and behavior of normal and pseudohermaphroditic nonhuman female primates. *Recent Progress in Hormone Research, 28,* 707-733.

Granzin, K. L. and Granzin, W. J. (1969). Peer group choice as a device for screening intellectually gifated children. *Gifted Child Quarterly, 13,* 189-194.

Gredler, G. R. (1980). The birthdate effect: Fact or artifact? *Journal of Learning Disabilities, 13*(5), 9-12.

Green, M. H. (1992). Remanent monasticism. *Science, 258,* 829-830.

Greenlaw, M. J., and McIntosh, M. E. (1988). *Educating the gifted: A source book.* Chicago: American Library Association.

Gregory, A. (1982, January/February). Super Saturday: A description of Purdue University's special program for gifted children with special emphasis on the studio arts areas. *G/C/T,* 13-16.

Gregory, E. H. (1984). Search for exceptional academic achievement at California State University, Los Angeles. *Gifted Child Quarterly, 28,* 21-24.

Gregory, E. H. and March, E. (1985). Early entrance program at California State University, Los Angeles. *Gifted Child Quarterly, 29,* 83-86.

Grenier, M. E. (1985). Gifted children and other siblings. *Gifted Child Quarterly, 29,* 164-167.

Gresham, F. M. and Reschly, D. J. (1988). Issues in the conceptualization, classification, and assessment of social skills in the mildly handicapped. In T. R. Kratochwill (Ed.), *Advances in School Psychology, 6.* Hillsdale, NJ: Lawrence Erlbaum.

Gross, M. U. M. (1992). The use of radical acceleration in cases of extreme intellectual precocity. *Gifted Child Quarterly, 36,* 91–99.

Gubbins, E. J. (1991, April). Research needs of the gifted and talented through the year 2000. In J. S. Renzulli (Chair), *The National Research Center on the Gifted and Talented: Present activities, future plans, and an invitation for input and involvement.* Symposium conducted at the annual meeting of the American Educational Research Association, Chicago.

Guilford, J. P. (1967). *The nature of human intelligence.* New York: McGraw-Hill.

Guilford, J. P. (1977). *Way beyond the IQ.* Buffalo, NY: Creative Education Foundation.

Guilford, J. P. (1979). Some incubated thoughts on incubation. *Journal of Creative Behavior, 13,* 1–8.

Guilford, J. P. (1986). *Creative talents: Their nature, uses and development.* Buffalo, NY: Bearly Limited.

Guilford, J. P. (1988). Some changes in the structure of intellect model. *Educational and Psychological Measurement, 48,* 1–4.

Gurin, P., and Epps, E. (1966). Some characteristics of students from poverty backgrounds attending predominantly Negro colleges in the deep south. *Social Forces, 45,* 27–39.

Hackney, P. W. (1986). Education of the visually handicapped-gifted: A program description. *Education of the Visually Handicapped, 18*(2), 85-95.

Hadary, D., Cohen, S., and Haushalter, R. (1979). Out of darkness and silence. *Social Forces, 45,* 27–39.

Hall, E. G. (1980). Sex differences in IQ development for intellectual gifted students. *Roeper Review, 2*(3), 25-28.

Hall, E. G. (1982, November/December). Accelerating gifted girls. *G/C/T,* 49-50.

Hallinan, M. and Sorensen, A. (1987). Ability grouping and sex differences in mathematics achievement. *Sociology of Education, 60,* 63-72.

Hallowell, K. (1991). Recruitment and selection procedures of governors' schools: A national survey. *Gifted Child Today, 14*(3), 24-27.

Halpern, D. (1989). The disappearance of cognitive gender differences: What you see depends on where you look. *American Psychologist, 44,* 1156-1158.

Halverson, C. and Victor, J. (1976). Minor physical anomalies and problem behavior in elementary school children. *Child Development, 47,* 281-285.

Hannigan, M. R. (1990). Cooperative learning in elementary school science. *Educational Leadership, 47*(4), 25.

Hanson, I. (1984). A comparison between parent identification of young bright children and subsequent testing. *Roeper Review, 7*(1), 44-45.

Harnadek, A. (1976). *Reasoning by analogy: Inductive reasoning series.* Pacific Grove, CA: Midwest Publications.

Harnadek, A. (1977). *Basic thinking skills: Analogies-B.* Pacific Grove, CA: Midwest Publications.

Harnadek, A. (1978). *Mind benders B1: Deductive thinking skills.* Pacific Grove, CA: Midwest Publications.

Harnadek, A. (1979). *Inference-B: Inductive thinking skills.* Pacific Grove, CA: Midwest Publications.

Harris, C. R. (1991, Summer). Identifying and serving the gifted new immigrant. *Teaching Exceptional Children,* 26-30.

Healy, B. (1992). Women in science: From panes to ceilings. *Science, 255,* 1333.

Hebb, D. O. (1972). *Textbook of psychology,* (3rd Ed.). Philadelphia, PA: W. B. Saunders.

Heck, A. O. (1953). *The education of exceptional children* (2nd ed.). New York: McGraw-Hill.

Heilbrun, A. B. (1973). *Aversive maternal control.* New York: Wiley.

Heilbrun, A. B., Harrell, S. N., and Gillard, B. J. (1967). Perceived childrearing attitudes of fathers and cognitive control in daughters. *Journal of Genetic Psychology, 111,* 29-40.

Helms, J. E. (1992). Why is there no study of cultural equivalence in standardized cognitive ability testing? *American Psychologist, 47,* 1083-1101.

Helson, R. (1971). Women mathematicians and the creative personality. *Journal of Consulting and Clinical Psychology, 36,* 210-211, 217-220.

Henderson, R. W. (1981). *Parent-child interaction: Theory, research and prospects.* New York: Academic Press.

Hengen, T. (1983, November). *Identification and enhancement of giftedness in Canadian Indians.* Paper presented at the annual meeting of the National Association for Gifted Children, New Orleans.

Hennessey, B. A. and Amabile, T. M. (1988). Storytelling: A method for assessing children's creativity. *Journal of Creative Behavior, 22,* 235-246.

Hermann, K. E. and Stanley, J. C. (1983, November/December). An exchange: Thoughts on nonrational precocity. *G/C/T,* 30-36.

Hershey, M. and Crowe, B. (1989). When independent study doesn't work. *Gifted Child Today, 12*(1), 31-33.

Hess, R. J. (1975). *Hess school readiness scale.* Johnstown, PA: Mafex.

Hetherington, E. M. (1972). Effects of father-absence on personality development in adolescent daughters. *Developmental Psychology, 7,* 313-326.

Hetherington, E. M., Cox, J., and Cox R. (1982). Effects of divorce on parents and children. In M. E. Lamb (Ed.), *Nontraditional families: Parenting and child development* (233-288). Hillsdale, NJ: Lawrence Erlbaum.

Hetherington, E. M. and Frankie, G. (1967). Effects of parental dominance, warmth and conflict on imitation in children. *Journal of Personality and Social Psychology, 6,* 119–125.

Heward, W. L. and Orlansky, M. D. (1992). *Exceptional children* (4th Ed.). Columbus, OH: Merrill.

Hickey, M. G. (1990). Classroom teachers' concerns and recommendations for improvement of gifted programs. *Roeper Review, 12,* 265-267.

Higham, S. J. and Buescher, T. M. (1987). What young gifted adolescents understand about feeling different. In T. M. Buescher (Ed.), *Understanding gifted and talented adolescents: A resource guide for counselors, educators, and parents* (26-30). Evanston, IL: Center for Talent Development, Northwestern University.

Hill, J. P. (1980). The family. In M. Johnson (Ed.), *Toward adolescence: The middle school years.* (Seventy-ninth Yearbook of the National Society for the Study of Education.) Chicago: University of Chicago Press.

Hiskey, M. (1966). *Hiskey-Nebraska test of learning aptitude*. Lincoln, NE: Union College Press.

Hobbs, N. (1980). Feuerstein's instrumental enrichment. Teaching intelligence to adolescents. *Educational Leadership, 38,* 566-568.

Hobson, J. R. (1948). Mental age as a workable criterion for school admission. *Elementary School Journal, 48,* 312-321.

Hoepfner, R. and Hemenway, J. (1973). *Test of creative potential*. Hollywood, CA: Monitor.

Hoffman, B. (1964). *The tyranny of testing*. New York: Collier Books.

Hoffman, J. L, Wasson, F. R., and Christianson, B. P. (1985, May/June). Personal development for the gifted underachiever. *G/C/T,* 12-14.

Hofstadter, R. (1963). *Anti-intellectualism in American life*. New York: Knopf.

Holahan, C. K. (1981). Lifetime achievement patterns, retirement and life satisfaction of gifted aged women. *Journal of Gerontology, 36,* 741-749.

Holland, J. L. (1973). *Making vocational choices: A theory of careers*. Englewood Cliffs, NJ: Prentice-Hall.

Holland, S. H. (1991). Positive role models for primary-grade black inner-city males. *Equity & Excellence*, The University of Massachusetts School of Education Journal, *25*(1), 40-44.

Hollinger, C. L. (1985). The stability of self perceptions of instrumental and expressive traits and social self esteem among gifted and talented female adolescents. *Journal for the Education of the Gifted, 8*(1), 107-126.

Hollinger, C. L. and Kosek, S. (1986). Beyond the use of full scale IQ scores. *Gifted Child Quarterly, 30,* 74–77.

Hollingworth, L. S. (1926). *Gifted children: Their nature and nurture*. New York: Macmillan.

Hollingworth, L. S. (1942). *Children above 180 IQ Stanford-Binet: Origin and development*. New York: World Book Co.

Hollingworth, L. S. and Kaunitz, R. M. (1934). The centile status of gifted children at maturity. *Journal of Genetic Psychology, 45,* 106-120.

Hollingsworth, P. L. (1990). Making it through parenting. *Gifted Child Today, 13*(3), 2-7.

Hollingsworth, P. L. (1991). Parts of the whole: Private schools, public schools, and the community. *Gifted Child Today, 14*(5), 54-56.

Horner, M. S. (1972). Toward an understanding of achievement related conflicts in women. *Journal of Social Issues, 28,* 155-175.

Hostettler, S. (1989). *Honors for underachievers: The class that never was*. Chico, CA: Chico Unified School District.

Howard, R. E. and Block, S. (1991). A university-based private school science program. *Gifted Child Today, 14*(5), 21-22.

Hunkins, F. P. (1976). *Involving students in questioning*. Needham Heights, MA: Allyn and Bacon.

Hunt, E. B. (1991). Reform: The plight of the gifted. *Illinois Council for the Gifted Journal, 10,* 44-48.

Huntley, L. B. (1990). Setting up shop: A program for gifted learning disabled students. *Gifted Child Today, 13*(4), 52-56.

Hyde, J. and Fennema, E. (1990, April). *Gender differences in mathematics performance and affect: Results of two meta-analyses*. Paper presented at the meeting of the American Educational Research Association, Boston, MA.

Hymowitz, C. and Schellhardt, T. (1986, March 24). The glass ceiling, why women can't seem to break the invisible barrier that blocks them from top jobs. *Wall Street Journal*, 1.

Jackson, N. E. (1988). Precocious reading ability: What does it mean? *Gifted Child Quarterly, 32,* 196-199.

Jackson, R. M., Cleveland, J. C., and Mirenda, P. F. (1975). The longitudinal effects of early identification and counseling of underachievers. *Journal of School Psychology, 13,* 119-128.

Jacobs, J. E. and Eccles, J. S. (1985, March). Gender differences in math ability: The impact of media reports on parents. *Educational Researcher*, 20-25.

Janos, P. M. *et al.* (1988). A cross-sectional developmental study of the social relations of students who enter college early. *Gifted Child Quarterly, 32,* 210-215.

Janos, P. M., Fung, H. C., and Robinson, N. M. (1985).

Self-concepts, self-esteem, and peer relations among gifted children who feel "different." *Gifted Child Quarterly, 29,* 78-82.

Jenkins, R. C. (1979). The identification of gifted and talented students through peer nomination. Unpublished doctoral dissertation, University of Connecticut. *Dissertation Abstracts International, 40,* 167A. (University Microfilms No. 7914161)

Jensen, A. R. (1980). *Bias in mental testing.* New York: Free Press.

Jensen, A. R. (1982, April). *Changing conceptions of intelligence.* Presented at the American Educational Research Association, New York.

Johnson, D. W. and Johnson, R. T. (1987). *Learning together and alone: Cooperative, competitive, and individualistic learning* (2nd Ed.). Englewood Cliffs, NJ: Prentice-Hall.

Johnson, D. W. and Johnson, R. T. (1989). *Cooperation and competition: Theory and research.* Edina, MN: Interaction Book Co.

Johnson, D. W. and Johnson, R. T. (1990a). *Circles of learning: Cooperation in the classroom* (3rd Ed.). Edina, MN: Interaction Book Co.

Johnson, D. W. and Johnson, R. T. (1990b). Social skills for successful group work. *Educational Leadership, 47*(4), 30-34.

Johnson, D. W., Johnson, R. T., and Holubec, E. (1988). *Cooperation in the classroom.* Edina, MN: Interaction Book Co.

Johnson, S., Starnes, W., Gregory, D., and Blaylock, A. (1985). Program of assessment, diagnosis, and instruction (PADA): Identifying and nurturing potentially gifted and talented minority students. *The Journal of Negro Education, 54*(3), 416-430.

Johnson, T. D. (1986). *The development of children's concepts of peers' attributes.* Paper presented at the bicentennial meeting of the Southwestern Society for Research in Human Development. (ERIC Document Reproduction Service No. ED 269 140)

Jordon, T. J. (1981). Self-concepts, motivation, and academic achievement of black adolescents. *Journal of Educational Psychology, 73,* 509-517.

Juntune, J. E. (1981). *Successful programs for the gifted and talented.* Washington, DC: National Association for the Gifted and Talented.

Juntune, J. E. (1986). *Summer opportunities for the gifted.* Washington, DC: National Association for Gifted Children.

Kagan, J. (1965). Impulsive and reflective children: Significance of conceptual tempo. In J. D. Krumboltz (Ed.), *Learning and the educational process.* Chicago: Rand McNally.

Kammer, P. P. (1984). Conceptual level of development as it relates to student participation in gifted programs. *Gifted Child Quarterly, 28,* 89-91.

Kandel, D. B. and Lesser, G. S. (1972). *Youth in two worlds.* San Francisco: Jossey-Bass.

Kaplan, S. N. (1974). *Providing programs for the gifted and talented.* Ventura, CA: Office of the Ventura County Superintendent of Schools.

Kaplan, S. N. (1990, February). Where to begin. *Learning90,* 42-43.

Karnes, F. A. and Brown, K. E. (1981). Moral development and the gifted: An initial investigation. *Roeper Review, 3*(4), 8-10.

Karnes, F. A. and Chauvin, J. C. (1982a, September/October). Almost everything that parents and teachers of gifted secondary school students should know about early college enrollment and college credit by examination. *G/C/T,* 39-42.

Karnes, F. A. and Chauvin, J. C. (1982b). A survey of early admission policies for younger than average students: Implications for gifted youth. *Gifted Child Quarterly, 26,* 68-73.

Karnes, F. A. and Chauvin, J. C. (1987). *Leadership skills development program: Leadership skills inventory and leadership skills activities handbook.* Buffalo, NY: DOK.

Karnes, F. A. and D'Ilio, V. R. (1989). Leadership positions and sex role stereotyping among gifted children. *Gifted Child Quarterly, 33,* 76-78.

Karnes, M. B. (1979). Young handicapped children can be gifted and talented. *Journal for the Education of the Gifted, 2,* 157-172.

Karnes, M. B. (1984). A demonstration/outreach model for young gifted/talented handicapped. *Roeper Review, 7*(1), 23-26.

Karnes, M. B., and Johnson, L. J. (1991). Gifted handicapped. In N. Colangelo and G. A. Davis (Eds.), *Handbook of gifted education* (428–437). Needham Heights, MA: Allyn and Bacon.

Karnes, M. B. and Shwedel, A. M. (1981). *RAPYHT Project: Activities for talent identification.* Urbana, IL: University of Illinois, Institute for Child Behavior and Development.

Karnes, M. B., Shwedel, A. M., and Lewis, G. F.

(1983). Long-term effects of early programming for the gifted/talented handicapped. *Journal for the Education of the Gifted, 6,* 266-276.

Karnes, M. B., Shwedel, A. M., and Steenberg, D. (1984). Styles of parenting among parents of young gifted children. *Roeper Review, 6,* 232-235.

Katt, T. (1988). Gifted students develop handicap awareness. *Gifted Child Today, 11*(5), 26-27.

Katz, M. L. (1973). *Female motive to avoid success: A psychological barrier or a response to deviancy.* Princeton, NJ: Educational Testing Service.

Kaufman, A. S. (1976a). A new approach to the interpretation of test scatter on the WISC-R. *Journal of Learning Disabilities, 9,* 160-168.

Kaufman, A. S. (1976b). Verbal-performance IQ discrepancies on the WISC-R. *Journal of Consulting and Clinical Psychology, 44,* 739-744.

Kaufman, A. S. (1979a). WISC-R research: Implications for interpretation. *School Psychology Digest, 15,* 176-179.

Kaufman, A. S. (1979b). *Intelligence testing with the WISC-R.* New York: Wiley-Interscience.

Kaufmann, F. (1986). *Helping the muskrat guard his musk: A new look at underachievement.* Bossier City, LA: Bossier Parish School Board.

Kaufmann, F. A., Harnel, G., Milam, C. P., Woolverton, N., and Miller, J. (1986). The nature, role, and influence of mentors in the lives of gifted adults. *Journal of Counseling and Development, 64,* 576-578.

Keating, D. P. (1980). Four faces of creativity: The continuing plight of the intellectually underserved. *Gifted Child Quarterly, 24,* 56-61.

Kegley, J. F. and Siggers, W. W. (1989). The creative child in an orderly environment: The parents' challenge. *Gifted Child Today, 14*(4), 2-5.

Kelble, E. S. (1991). Overview of private schools for the gifted. *Gifted Child Today, 14*(5), 2-4.

Kelly, D. A. (1991). Cooperative learning—Mastering the bundle of sticks. *Childhood Education, 67,* 179.

Kelly, K. R. and Colangelo, N. (1984). Academic and social self-concepts of gifted, general, and special students. *Exceptional Children, 50,* 551-554.

Kelly-Benjamin, K. (1990, April). *Performance differences on SAT math questions.* Paper presented at the meeting of the American Educational Research Association, Boston, MA.

Keneal, P. (1991). Teacher expectations as predictors of academic success. *Journal of Social Psychology, 31,* 305-306.

Kenny, A. (1987). Counseling the gifted, creative, and talented: Creative writing and poetry therapy. *Gifted Child Today, 49*(2), 33-37.

Kerr, B. A. (1985). *Smart girls, gifted women.* Dayton, OH: Ohio Psychology Press.

Kerr, B. A. (1991). Educating gifted girls. In N. Colangelo and G. A. Davis (Eds.), *Handbook of gifted education* (402-415). Needham Heights, MA: Allyn and Bacon.

Kerr, B. A., Colangelo, N., and Gaeth, J. (1988). Gifted adolescents' attitudes toward their giftedness. *Gifted Child Quarterly, 32,* 245-247.

Kimura, D. (1985, November). Male brain, female brain: The hidden difference. *Psychology Today,* 50-58.

Kitano, M. K. (1991). A multicultural educational perspective on serving the culturally diverse gifted. *Journal for the Education of the Gifted, 15*(1), 4-19.

Kitano, M. K. (1986, July/August). Counseling gifted preschoolers. *G/C/T,* 20-25.

Kluever, R. C. and Green, K. E. (1990). Identification of gifted children: A comparison of the scores on Stanford-Binet 4th Edition and Form LM. *Roeper Review, 13,* 16-20.

Kohlberg, L. (1974). The child as moral philosopher. In G. A. Davis and T. F. Warren (Eds.), *Psychology of Education: New looks.* Lexington, MA: D. C. Heath.

Kohlberg, L. (1976). Moral states and moralization: The cognitive developmental approach. In T. Lockona (Ed.), *Moral development and behavior.* New York: Holt, Rinehart, and Winston.

Kolata, G. B. (1980). Math and sex: Are girls born with less ability? *Science, 210,* 1234-1235.

Kolata, G. B. (1983). Math genius may have hormonal basis. *Science, 222,* 1312.

Kolloff, P. B. (1991). Special residential high schools. In N. Colangelo and G. A. Davis (Eds.), *Handbook of gifted education* (209-218). Needham Heights, MA: Allyn and Bacon.

Kolloff, P. B. and Feldhusen, J. F. (1984). The effects of enrichment on self-concept and creative thinking. *Gifted Child Quarterly, 28,* 53-57.

Kolloff, P. B. and Feldhusen, J. F. (1986). Seminar: An instructional approach for gifted students. *Gifted Child Today, 9*(5), 2-7.

Kranz, B. (1981). *Kranz talent identification instrument*. Moorhead, MN: Moorhead State College.

Kranz, B. (1991). Promising practices in identification: The KTII. *Equity in Gifted Education* (College of Education, Northeastern Illinois University Newsletter), *2*(1), 11.

Kranz, B. (1993). *Curriculum by design: Challenging gifted learners*. New York: Longman.

Krauss, M. W. (1990). New precedent in family policy: Individualized family service plan. *Exceptional Children, 56*(5), 388-395.

Kretschmer, E. (1931). *The psychology of men of genius* (R. B. Cattell, Trans.). New York: Harcourt, Brace.

Krueger, M. L. (1978). *On being gifted*. New York: Walker.

Kryaniuk, L. W. and Das, J. P. (1976). Cognitive strategies in native children: Analysis and intervention. *Alberta Journal of Educational Research, 22*, 271-280.

Kuhmerker, L. (1991). *The Kohlberg legacy for the helping professions*. Birmingham, AL: R.E.P. Books.

Kulik, J. A. (1991, May). *Ability grouping and gifted students*. Invited address presented at the National Research Symposium on Talent Development, University of Iowa, Iowa City, IA.

Kulik, J. A. (1992). *An analysis of the research on ability grouping: Historical and contemporary perspectives*. Storrs, CT: National Research Center on the Gifted and Talented, University of Connecticut.

Kulik, J. A. and Kulik, C.-L. (1984). Effects of accelerated instruction on students. *Review of Educational Research, 54*, 409-425.

Kulik, J. A. and Kulik, C.-L. (1991). Ability grouping and gifted students. In N. Colangelo and G. A. Davis (Eds.), *Handbook of gifted education* (178-106). Needham Heights, MA: Allyn and Bacon.

Kulik, J. A. and Kulik, C.-L. (1992). Meta-analytic findings on grouping programs. *Gifted Child Quarterly, 36*, 73-77.

Kutner, L. (1991). The new family. *Newsweek*, November 18, 18-19.

Labov, W. (1974). Academic ignorance and black intelligence. In G. A. Davis and T. F. Warren (Eds.), *Psychology of education: New looks*. Lexington, MA: D. C. Heath.

Laffoon, K. S., Jenkins-Friedman, R., and Tollefson, N. (1989). Causal attributions of underachieving gifted, achieving gifted, and nongifted students. *Journal for the Education of the Gifted, 13*(1), 4-21.

Laidig, P. (1991, Summer). The summer birthday dilemma: Outcomes of delayed school entry. *The Wisconsin School Psychologist*, 1, 3.

Lajoie, S. P. and Shore, B. M. (1981). Three myths? The over-representation of the gifted among dropouts, delinquents, and suicides. *Gifted Child Quarterly, 25*, 138-141.

Lamb, M. E. (1976). *The role of the father in child development*. New York: Wiley.

Lamb, R. A. and Busse, C. A. (1983). Leadership beyond lip service. *Roeper Review, 5*(3), 21-23.

Landrum, M. S. (1987). Guidelines for implementing a guidance/counseling program for gifted and talented students. *Roeper Review, 10*, 103-107.

Langer, P., Kalk, J. V., and Searls, D. T. (1984). Age of admission and trends in achievement: A comparison of Blacks and Caucasians. *American Educational Research Journal, 21*, 61-78.

Larsen, R. J. and Diener, E. (1987). Affective intensity as an individual difference characteristic: A review. *Journal of Research in Personality, 21*, 1-39.

Lazear, D. (1991). *Seven ways of teaching: The artistry of teaching with multiple intelligences*. Palatine, IL: Skylight.

Lefkowitz, W. (1975). Communication grows in a "Magic Circle." In D. A. Read and S. B. Simon (Eds.), *Humanistic education sourcebook*. Englewood Cliffs, NJ: Prentice-Hall.

Lehman, E. B. and Erdwins, C. J. (1981). The social and emotional adjustment of young intellectually gifted children. *Gifted Child Quarterly, 25*, 134-137.

Leifer, A., Neal, G., and Graves, S. (1974). Children's television: More than more entertainment. *Harvard Educational Revue, 44*, 1213-1245.

LeRose, B. (1977). *The lighthouse design: A model for educating children*. Racine, WI: Racine Unified School District.

LeRose, B. (1978). A quota system for gifted minority children: A viable solution. *Gifted Child Quarterly, 22*, 394-403.

LeTendre, J. J. (1991). Improving Chapter 1 programs: We can do better. *Phi Delta Kappan, 72*, 576-580.

Levy-Agresti, J. and Sperry, R. W. (1968). Differential perceptual capacities in major and minor hemispheres. *Proceedings of the National Academy of Sciences,* 61.

Lewis, A. (1982). *Ensuring excellence in rural education*. Proceedings of the rural education seminar. Washington D.C.: American Association of School Administrators.

Lewis, G. (1989). Telelearning: Making maximum use of the medium. *Roeper Review, 11*, 195-198.

Li, A. K. F. and Adamson, G. (1992). Gifted secondary students' preferred learning style: Cooperative, competitive, or individualistic. *Journal for the Education of the Gifted, 16*, 46-54.

Lindsey, M. (1980). *Training teachers of the gifted and talented*. New York: Teachers College Press.

Linn, M. and Hyde, J. (1989). Gender, mathematics, and science. *Educational Researcher, 14*, 51-71.

Lipman, M. (1980). *Social inquiry: Instructional manual to accompany Mark*. Upper Montclair, NJ: Institute for the Advancement of Philosophy for Children.

Lipman, M. (1981). What is different about the education of the gifted? *Roeper Review, 4*(1), 19-20.

Lipman, M. (1988a, April). Critical thinking: What can it be? *Educational Leadership*, 38-43.

Lipman, M. (1988b). *Philosophy goes to school*. Philadelphia: Temple University Press.

Lipman, M. (1991). *Thinking in education*. New York: Cambridge University Press.

Lipman, M. and Sharp, A. M. (1986). *Wondering at the world: Instructional manual to accompany Kio and Gus*. Upper Montclair, NJ: Institute for the Advancement of Philosophy for Children.

Lipman, M., Sharp, A. M., and Oscanyan, F. S. (1977). *Ethical inquiry: Instructional manual to accompany Lisa*. Upper Montclair, NJ: Institute for the Advancement of Philosophy for Children.

Lipman, M., Sharp, A. M., and Oscanyan, F. S. (1980). *Philosophy in the classroom* (2nd Ed.). Phildelphia: Temple University Press.

Loeb, R. C. and Jay, G. (1987). Self-concept in gifted children: Differential impact in boys and girls. *Gifted Child Quarterly, 31*, 9-14.

Lombroso, C. (1895). *The man of genius*. London: Scribner's.

Long, R. (1981, April). *An approach to a defensible non-discriminatory identification model for the gifted*. Paper presented at the meeting of the Council for Exceptional Children, New York.

Louis, B. and Lewis, M. (1992). Parental beliefs about giftedness in young children and their relationship to actual ability level. *Gifted Child Quarterly, 36*, 27-31.

Ludwig, G. and Cullinan, D. (1984). Behavior problems of gifted and nongifted elementary girls and boys. *Gifted Child Quarterly, 28*, 37-39.

Lupkowski, A. E., Assouline, S. G., and Vestal, J. (1992). Mentors in math. *Gifted Child Today, 15*(3), 26-32.

Luftig, R. L. and Nichols, M. L. (1989). *Assessing the perceived loneliness and self-concept functioning of gifted students in self-contained and integrated settings*. Unpublished manuscript.

Luftig, R. L. and Nichols, M. L. (1990). Assessing the social status of gifted students by their age peers. *Gifted Child Quarterly, 34*, 111-115.

Lupkowski, A. E. (1984). Gifted students in small rural schools do not have to move to the city. *Roeper Review, 7*, 13-16.

Lutey, C. (1977). *Individual intelligence testing: A manual and sourcebook* (2nd Ed.). Greeley, CO: Carol I. Lutey Publishing.

Lynch, S. and Mills, C. J. (1990). The skills reinforcement project (SRP): An academic program for high potential minority youth. *Journal for the Education of the Gifted, 13*(4), 364-379.

Lynn, D. B. (1974). *The father: His role in child development*. Monterey, CA: Brooks/Cole.

Lytle, W. G. and Campbell, N. J. (1979). Do special programs affect the social status of the gifted? *Elementary School Journal, 80*, 93-97.

Maccoby, E. E. and Jacklin, C. (1974). *Psychology of sex differences*. Stanford, CA: Stanford University Press.

MacKinnon, D. W. (1962). The nature and nurture of creative talent. *American Psychologist, 17*, 484-495.

MacKinnon, D. W. (1965). Personality and the realization of creative potential. *American Psychologist, 20*, 273-281.

MacKinnon, D. W. (1975). IPAR's contribution to the conceptualization and study of creativity. In I. A. Taylor and J. W. Getzels (Eds.), *Perspectives in creativity* (60-89). Chicago: Aldine.

MacKinnon, D. W. (1978). Educating for creativity: A modern myth? In G. A. Davis and J. A. Scott (Eds.), *Training creative thinking*. Huntington, NY: Krieger.

Magoon, R. A. (1980, March/April). Developing leadership skills in the gifted, creative, and talented. *G/C/T*, 40-43.

Magoon, R. A. (1981). A proposed model for leadership development. *Roeper Review, 3*(3), 7-9.

Maker, C. J. (1977). *Providing programs for the handicapped gifted*. Reston, VA: Council for Exceptional Children.

Maker, C. J. (1982). *Curriculum development for the gifted*. Rockville, MD: Aspen.

Maker, C. J. and Udall, A. (1983). A pilot program for elementary-age learning disabled/gifted students. In L. Fox, L. Brody, and D. Tobin (Eds.), *Learning disabled gifted children* (141-152). Baltimore: University Park Press.

Makler, S. J. (1980). On instrumental enrichment: A conversation with Frances Link. *Educational Leadership*, 569-571, 582.

Malcomson, B. and Laurence, M. (1986, November/December). Quicksand and healthy minds. *G/C/T*, 2-6.

Manosevitz, M., Prentice, N. M., and Wilson, F. (1973). Individual and family correlates of imaginary play companions in preschool children. *Developmental Psychology, 8*(1), 72-79.

Marini, M. M. (1978). Sex differences in the determination of adolescent aspirations: A review of research. *Sex Roles: A Journal of Research, 4*, 723-754.

Marland, S. P., Jr. (1972). *Education of the gifted and talented, Volume 1. Report to the Congress of the United States by the U. S. Commissioner of Education*. Washington, DC: U.S. Government Printing Office.

Marone, N. (1988). *How to father a successful daughter*. New York: Ballantine Books.

Marshall, S. P. (1988). The Illinois Mathematics and Science Academy. *Gifted Child Today, 11*(2), 8-9.

Martin, S. C., Parker, R. M., and Arnold, R. M. (1988). Careers of women physicians: Choices and constraints. In Women and Medicine [Special Issue]. *Western Journal of Medicine, 149*, 758-760.

Martindale, C. (1975). What makes a person different? *Psychology Today, 9*(7), 44-50.

Martinson, R. A. (1974). *The identification of the gifted and talented*. Ventura, CA: Office of the Ventura County Superintendent of Schools.

Marx, J. L. (1982). Autoimmunity in left-handers. *Science, 217*, 141-142, 144.

Mathematicians talk tough to new Barbie. (1992). *Science, 258*, 396.

Mathew, S. T. (1984). A creative problem-solving (CPS) program for emotionally handicapped children to reduce aggression. *Journal of Creative Behavior, 18*(4), 278.

Matthew, J. L., Golin, A. K., Moore, M. W., and Baker, C. (1992). Use of SOMPA in identification of gifted African-American children. *Journal for the Education of the Gifted, 15*(4), 344-356.

Mattson, B. D. (1983, March/April). Mentors for the gifted and talented: Whom to seek and where to look. *G/C/T*, 10-11.

McBeath, M., Blackshear, P., and Smart, L. (1981, August). *Identifying low income, minority gifted and talented youngsters*. Paper presented at the annual meeting of the American Psychological Association, Los Angeles, CA.

McCaslin, N. (1974). *Creative dramatics in the classroom*. New York: McKay.

McClelland, D. C. (1976). *The achieving society*. New York: Irvington.

McCollim, L. (1992). Mentors at home: Empowering parents. *Gifted Child Today, 15*(3), 15-17.

McKenzie, J. (1986). The influence of identification practices, race, and SES on the identification of gifted students. *Gifted Child Quarterly, 30*, 93-95.

Mead, M. (1935). Sex and achievement. *Forum, 94*, 302.

Meador, K. (1992). My teacher, my mentor, my friend. *Gifted Child Today, 14*(3), 14.

Meckstroth, E. (1989, November). Parenting. *Understanding Our Gifted*, 4.

Meeker, M. N. (1969). *The structure of intellect: Its interpretation and uses*. Columbus, OH: Merrill.

Meeker, M. N. (1978). Nondiscriminatory testing procedures to assess giftedness in Black, Chicano, Navajo and Anglo children. In A. Baldwin, G. Gear, and L. Lucito (Eds.), *Educational planning for the gifted*. Reston, VA: Council for Exceptional children.

Meeker, M. N. (1981). *Using SOI test results: A teacher's guide*. El Segundo, CA: SOI Institute.

Meeker, M. N. and Meeker, R. (1986). The SOI system for gifted education. In J. S. Renzulli (Ed.), *Systems and models for developing programs for the gifted and talented* (194-215). Mansfield Center, CT: Creative Learning Press.

Meeker, M. N., Meeker, R., and Roid, G. (1985). *Structure-of-intellect learning abilities test (SOI-LA)*. Los Angeles: Western Psychological Services.

Meichenbaum, D. H. (1977). *Cognitive-behavior modification*. New York: Plenum.

Mercer, J. (1973). *Labeling the mentally retarded: Clinical and social system perspectives on mental retardation*. Berkeley: University of California Press.

Mercer, J. and Lewis, J. (1978). Using the system of multicultural pluralistic assessment (SOMPA) to identify the gifted minority child. In A. Baldwin, G. Gear, and L. Lucito (Eds.). *Educational planning for the gifted*. Reston, VA: Council for Exceptional Children.

Metfessel, N. S., Michael, W. B., and Kirsner, D. A. (1969). Instrumentation of Bloom's and Krathwohl's taxonomies for the writing of educational objectives. *Psychology in the Schools, 6,* 227–231.

Meyer, A. E. (1965). *An educational history of the western world.* New York: McGraw-Hill.

Michael, R. T. (1976). *Factors affecting divorce: A study of the Terman sample.* Working Paper No. 147. Stanford, CA: National Bureau of Economic Research.

Micklus, S. (1982). *Odyssey of the mind handbook.* Glassboro, NJ: OM Association.

Micklus, S. (1986). *OMAha!* Glassboro, NJ: OM Association.

Micklus, S. and Gourley, T. (1982). *Problems, problems, problems.* Glassboro, NJ: OM Association.

Milam, C. P. and Schwartz, B. (1992). The mentorship connection. *Gifted Child Today, 15*(3), 9-13.

Milgram, R. M. (1989). Teaching gifted and talented children in regular classrooms: An impossible dream or a full-time solution for a full-time problem. In R. M. Milgram (Ed.), *Teaching gifted and talented learners in regular classrooms.* Springfield, IL: Thomas.

Milgram, R. M. and Milgram, N. A. (1976). Personality characteristics of gifted Israeli children. *Journal of Genetic Psychology, 125,* 185-192.

Miller, M. (1991). Self-assessment as a specific strategy for teaching the gifted learning disabled. *Journal for the Education of the Gifted, 14*(2), 178-188.

Miller, W. D. and Norris, R. C. (1967). Entrance age and school success. *Journal of School Psychology, 6*(1), 47-60.

Mills, C. (1980). Sex-role-related personality correlates of intellectual abilities in adolescents. *Roeper Review, 2*(3), 29-31.

Mills, C. J. and Durden, W. G. (1992). Cooperative learning and ability grouping: An issue of choice. *Gifted Child Quarterly, 36,* 11-16.

Milton, G. A. (1957). The effects of sex-role identification upon problem-solving skill. *Journal of Abnormal and Social Psychology, 55,* 208-212.

Minner, S. (1990). Teacher evaluations of case descriptions of LD gifted children. *Gifted Child Quarterly, 34,* 37-39.

Mitchell, P. (Ed.). (1981). *An advocate's guide to building support for gifted and talented education.* Washington, DC: National Association of State Boards of Education.

Money, J. (1987). Sin, sickness, or status? Homosexual gender identity and psychoneuroendocrinology. *American Psychologist, 42,* 384–399.

Montagu, A. (1980, February/March). My idea of education. *Today's Education,* 49.

Montague, M. (1991). Gifted and learning-disabled gifted students' knowledge and use of mathematical problem-solving strategies. *Journal for the Education of the Gifted, 14*(4), 393-411.

Montemayer, R. (1984). Changes in parent and peer relationships between childhood and adolescence: A research agenda for gifted adolescents. *Journal for the Education of the Gifted, 8*(1), 9-23.

Moore, B. A. (1979). A model career education program for gifted disadvantaged students. *Roeper Review, 2*(2), 20-22.

Morelock, M. J. and Feldman, D. H. (1990). Extreme precocity. In N. Colangelo and G. A. Davis (Eds.), *Handbook of gifted education* (347-364). Needham Heights, MA: Allyn and Bacon.

Morrow, L. (1983, April). *Home and school correlates of early interest in literature.* Paper presented at the American Educational Research Association, Montreal.

Moses, S. (1991, July). Ties that bind can limit minority valedictorians. *Education Monitor,* 47.

Mosley, J. H. (1982, November/December). Ten suggestions to insure the brevity of your gifted program. *G/C/T,* 46.

Moss, E. (1990). Social interaction and metacognitive development in gifted preschoolers. *Gifted Child Quarterly, 34,* 16-20.

Moss, E. S. (1983, April). *Mothers and gifted preschoolers—teaching and learning strategies.* Paper presented at the American Educational Research Association, Montreal.

Moyer, K. E. (1974). Sex differences in aggression. In R. C. Friedman, R. M. Richart, and R. L. Vande Weile (Eds.), *Sex difference in behavior.* New York: Wiley.

Mullis, I. and Jenkins, L. (1988). *The science report card: Elements of risk and recovery*. Princeton, New Jersey: Educational Testing Service.

Munger, A. (1983). The parent's role in counseling the gifted: The balance between home and school. In J. Van Tassel-Baska (Ed.), *A pratical guide to counseling the gifted in a school setting* (31-39). Reston, VA: Council for Exceptional Children.

Mussen, P. H. and Rutherford, E. (1963). Parent-child relations and parental personality in relation to young children's sex-role preferences. *Child Development, 34*, 589-607.

Nadelson, T. and Eisenberg, L. (1977). On being married to a professional woman. *American Journal of Psychiatry, 134*, 1071-1076.

National Assessment of Educational Progress. (1982). *Reading, thinking, and writing*. Denver: National Assessment of Educational Progress.

National Association of School Psychologists. (1991). *Position statement on students with attention deficits*. Washington, DC: National Association of School Psychologists.

National Commission on Excellence in Education. (1984). *A nation at risk: The imperative for educational reform*. Washington, DC: U.S. Government Printing Office.

National Science Foundation (1990). *Women and minorities in science and engineering*. Washington, DC.

Navarre, J. (1980). Is what is good for the gander, good for the goose: Should gifted girls receive differential treatment? *Roeper Review, 3*(2), 21-25.

Neinstein, L. S. (1984). *Adolescent health care: A practical guide*. Baltimore: Urban and Schwartzberg.

Nelson-Jones, R. (1990). *Managing and preventing personal problems*. Pacific Grove, CA: Brooks-Cole.

Nevo, D. (1983). The conceptualization of educational evaluation. *Review of Educational Research, 53*, 117-128.

Newburg, N. A. (1977). *Affective education in Philadelphia*. Bloomington, IN: Phi Delta Kappa Educational Foundation.

Newland, T. E. (1960). *Manual for the blind learning aptitude test: Experimental edition*. Urbana, IL: Newland.

Newland, T. E. (1976). *The gifted in socioeducational perspective*. Englewood Cliffs, NJ: Prentice-Hall.

Nichols, J. G. (1979). Development of perception of own attainment and causal attribution for success and failure in reading. *Journal of Educational Psychology, 71*, 94-99.

Nichols, T. M. (1992). The Junior Great Books program. *Gifted Child Today, 15*(5), 50-51.

Nickerson, K. G., Bennett, N. M., Estes, D., and Shea, S. (1990). The status of women at one academic medical center: Breaking through the glass ceiling. *Journal of the American Medical Association, 264*, 1813-1817.

Nielsen, M. E. and Mortorff-Albert, S. (1989). The effects of special education service on the self-concept and school attitude of learning disabled/gifted students. *Roeper Review, 12*, 29-36.

Noble, D. F. (1992). *A world without women*. Knopf, NY: The Christian Clerical Culture of Western Science.

Noble, K. D. (1989). Counseling gifted women: Becoming the heroes of our own stories. *Journal for the Education of the Gifted, 12*(2), 131-141.

Nochlin, L. (1988). *Women, art, and power and other essays*. New York: Harper and Row.

Norman, C. (1988). Math education: A mixed picture. *Science, 241*, 408-409.

Nyquist, E., (1973). *The gifted: The invisibly handicapped, or there is no heavier burden than a great potential*. Paper presented at the National Conference on the Gifted, Albany, NY.

Oakes, J. (1985). *Keeping track*. New Haven: Yale University Press.

Oakes, J. (1991a, April). *Can tracking research influence school practice?* Invited address to the Annual Meeting of the American Educational Research Association, Chicago.

Oakes, J. (1991b, April). *Alternatives to tracking: Critical commonplaces*. Presented in a symposium entitled "Ability grouping in the middle grades" at the Annual Meeting of the American Educational Research Association, Chicago.

O'Connell, B. (1982). *Arts for the handicapped, ESEA Title IV-C Model Sites Project*. Sheboygan, WI: Wisconsin Department of Public Instruction.

Ogbu, J. U. (1992). Understanding cultural diversity and learning. *Educational Researcher, 21*(8), 5-14.

Olenchak, F. R. and Renzulli, J. S. (1989). The effectiveness of the Schoolwide Enrichment Model on selected aspects of elementary school change. *Gifted Child Quarterly, 33*, 36-46.

Olsen, H. (1970). A comparison of academic self-concept, significant others of black and black pre-college students. *Child Study Journal, 1*, 28-32.

Olshen, S. R. (1987). The disappearance of giftedness in girls: An intervention strategy. *Roeper Review, 9*, 251-254.

Olszewski-Kubilius, P., Kulieke, M. J., and Krasney, N. (1988). Personality dimensions of gifted adolescents: A review of the empirical literature. *Gifted Child Quarterly, 32*, 347-352.

Olszewski-Kubilius, P., Shaw, B., Kulieke, M. J., and Willis, G. B. (1990). Predictors of achievement in mathematics for gifted males and females. *Gifted Child Quarterly, 34*, 64-71.

OM Association. (1983). *What is Odyssey of the Mind?* Glassboro, NJ: OM Association.

OM Association. (1992). *Synopses of the 1992-93 long-term problems.* Glassboro, NJ: OM Association.

Omond, J. (1985, July/August). Extracurricular centres for the gifted in South Africa. *G/C/T*, 36-37.

Ondo, E. and Session, E. (1989). Update: The pyramid project. *Gifted Child Today, 12*(3), 46-49.

Orange County Department of Education. (1984). *Project IMPACT.* Costa Mesa, CA: Orange County Department of Education.

Orth, L. C. (1988). Abstract: The relationship of parental child-rearing attitudes to creativity in gifted pre-school children. *Journal of Creative Behavior, 22*, 70.

Ortiz, V. Z. and Gonzalez, A. (1989). A validation study of a WISC-R short form with accelerated and gifted Hispanic students. *Gifted Child Quarterly, 33*, 152-155.

Ortiz, V. Z. and Gonzalez, A. (1991). Gifted Hispanic adolescents. In M. Bireley and J. Genshaft (Eds.). *Understanding the gifted adolescent: Educational, developmental, and multicultural issues* (240-247). New York: Teachers College Press.

Osborn, A. F. (1963). *Applied imagination* (3rd Ed.). New York: Scribner's.

Pallas, A. M. and Alexander, K. L. (1983). Sex differences in quantitative SAT performance: New evidence on the differential coursework hypothesis. *American Educational Research Journal, 20,* 165-182.

Pallone, N., Richard, F., and Hurley, R. (1973). Further data on key influencers of occupational expectations of minority youth. *Journal of Counselling Psychology, 20,* 484-486.

Parish, T. S. and Nunn, G. D. (1983, April). *Locus of control as a function of family type and age at onset of father absence.* Paper presented at the American Educational Research Association, Montreal, Canada.

Parke, B. N. and Buescher, T. M. (1982). Evaluating programs through student self-documentation. *Roeper Review, 5*(1), 15-17.

Parker, J. (1983, September/October). The leadership training model. *G/C/T*, 8-13.

Parker, M. (1979, September/October). Bright kids in trouble with the law. *G/C/T*, 62-63.

Parnes, S. J. (1981). *The magic of your mind.* Buffalo, NY: Creative Education Foundation.

Parsons, J. E. (1982, April). *Women and mathematics: Synthesis of recent research.* Paper presented at the American Educational Research Association, New York.

Parsons, J. E., Adler, T., and Kaczala, C. (1982). Socialization of achievement attitudes and beliefs: Parental influences. *Child Development, 53*, 310-321.

Parsons, J. E., Frieze, I. H., and Ruble, D. M. (1978). Intrapsychic factors influencing career aspirations in college women. *Sex Roles: A Journal of Research, 4*, 337-348.

Passow, A. H. (1958). Enrichment of education for the gifted. In N. B. Henry (Ed.), *Education for the gifted,* Part II. Chicago: National Society for the Study of Education.

Passow, A. H. (1981). The nature of giftedness and talent. *Gifted Child Quarterly, 25*, 5-10.

Passow, A. H. (1989). Designing a global curriculum. *Gifted Child Today, 62*(3), 24-26.

Patton, J. M. (1992). Assessment and identification of African-American learners with gifts and talents. *Exceptional Children, 59*(2), 150-159.

Patton, J. M., Prillaman, D., and Van Tassel-Baska, J. (1990). The nature and extent of programs for the disadvantaged gifted in the United States and territories. *Gifted Child Quarterly, 34*, 94-96.

Paul, R., Binker, A. J. A., Martin, D., Vetrano, C., and Kreklau, H. (1989). *Critical thinking handbook: 6th-9th grades: A guide for remodelling lesson plans in language arts, social studies, and science.* Rohnert Park, CA: Center for Critical Thinking and Moral Critique, Sonoma State University.

Perino, S. C. and Perino, J. (1981). *Parenting the gifted—developing the promise.* New York: R. R. Bowker Company.

Perkins, D. N. (1988). The possibility of invention. In

R. J. Sternberg (Ed.), *The nature of creativity* (362-385). New York: Cambridge University Press.

Perkins, E. (1975). *Home is a dirty street: The social oppression of black children*. Chicago: Third World Press.

Perlmutter, B. F. and Bryan, J. H. (1984). First impressions, ingratiation, and the learning disabled child. *Journal of Learning Disabilities, 17*, 157-162.

Perrone, P. (1990). Social and psychological concerns of gifted persons. In R. Blocksom and J. Smutney (Eds.), *Educating the gifted person*. Buffalo, NY: DOK Publishers.

Perrone, P. (1991). Career development. In N. Colangelo and G. A. Davis (Eds.), *Handbook of gifted education* (321-327). Needham Heights, MA: Allyn and Bacon.

Perrone, P. A., Karshner, W. W., and Male, R. A. (1979). Identification of talented students. In N. Colangelo and R. T. Zaffrann (Eds.), *New voices in counseling the gifted*. Dubuque, IA: Kendall/Hunt.

Perrone, P. A. and Pulvino, C. J. (1979). New directions in the guidance of the gifted and talented. In J. C. Gowan, J. Khatena, and E. P. Torrance (Eds.), *Educating the ablest* (2nd Ed.). Chicago: Peacock.

Peterson, D. (1977). The heterogeneously gifted child. *Gifted Child Quarterly, 21*, 396-408.

Petro, C. S. and Putnam, B. A. (1979). Sex-role stereotypes: Issues of attitudinal changes. *Signs, 5*, 1-4.

Pfeil, M. P. (1978, March). Fourth Street School's new claim to fame. *American Education*, 10-13.

Pfouts, J. H. (1980). Birth order, age spacing, IQ differences and family relations. *Journal of Marriage and the Family, 42*, 517-521.

Piaget, J. and Inhelder, B. (1969). *The psychology of the child* (H. Weaver, Trans.). New York: Basic Books.

Piechowski, M. M. (1979). Developmental potential. In N. Colangelo and R. T. Zaffrann (Eds.), *New voices in counseling the gifted* (25-57). Dubuque, IA: Kendall/Hunt.

Piechowski, M. M. (1991). Emotional development and emotional giftedness. In N. Colangelo and G. A. Davis (Eds.), *Handbook of gifted education* (285-306). Needham Heights, MA: Allyn and Bacon.

Piechowski, M. M. and Colangelo, N. (1984). Developing potential of the gifted. *Gifted Child Quarterly, 28*, 80-88.

Pierce, J. W. and Bowman, P. (1960). Motivation patterns of superior high school students. *Cooperative Research Monograph No. 2*, 33-36.

Pigott, I. (1990). Drama in the classroom. *Gifted Child Today, 13*(1), 3-5.

Piirto, J. (1991). Why are there so few? (Creative women, visual artists, mathematicians, musicians). *Roeper Review, 13*, 142-147.

Pine, G. J. and Boy, A. V. (1977). *Learner-centered teaching: A humanistic view*. Denver, CO: Love Publishing Co.

Pinegree, S. (1978). The effects of nonsexist television commercials and perceptions of reality on children's attitudes about women. *Psychology of Women Quarterly, 2*, 262-277.

Plowman, P. D. (1981). Training extraordinary leaders. *Roeper Review, 3*(3), 13-16.

Poloma, M. M. (1972). Role conflict and the married professional woman. In C. Safilios-Rothchild (Ed.), *Toward a sociology of women*. Lexington, MA: Xerox College Publishing.

Pool, R. (1990). A lost generation? *Science, 248*, 435.

Post, R. D. (1981). Causal explanations of male and female academic performance as a function of sex-role biases. *Sex Roles, 7*, 691-698.

Postman, N. (1976). *Crazy talk, stupid talk*. New York: Dell.

Power, F. C., Higgins, A., and Kohlberg, L. (1989). *Lawrence Kohlberg's approach to moral education*. New York: Columbia University Press.

Presseisen, B. A. (1986). *Thinking skills: Research and practice*. Washington, DC: National Education Association.

Prillaman, D. and Richardson, R. (1989). The William and Mary mentorship model: College students as a resource for the gifted. *Roeper Review, 12*, 114-118.

Proctor, T. B., Black, K. N., and Feldhusen, J. F. (1986). Early admission of selected children to elementary school: A review of the research literature. *Journal of Educational Research, 80*(2), 70-76.

Proctor, T. B., Black, K. N., and Feldhusen, J. F. (1988). Early admission to elementary school: Barriers versus benefits. *Roeper Review, 11*, 85-87.

Proctor, T. B., Feldhusen, J. F., and Black, K. N. (1988). Guidelines for early admission to elementary school. *Psychology in the Schools, 25*, 41-43.

Provus, M. M. (1972). *Discrepancy evaluation*. Berkeley, CA: McCutchan.

Pulvino, C. J., Colangelo, N., and Zaffrann, R. T. (1976). *Laboratory counseling programs*. Madison, WI: Department of Counseling and Guidance, University of Wisconsin.

Radin, N. (1974). Observed maternal behavior with four-year-old boys and girls in lower-class families. *Child Development, 45,* 1126–1131

Radin, N. (1976). The role of the father in cognitive, affective and intellectual development. In M. E. Lamb (Ed.), *The role of the father in child development.* New York: Wiley.

Ramos-Ford, V. and Gardner, H. (1991). Giftedness from a multiple intelligence perspective. In N. Colangelo and G. A. Davis (Eds.), *Handbook of gifted education* (55-64). Needham Heights, MA: Allyn and Bacon.

Raymond, C. L. and Benbow, C. P. (1989). Educational encouragement by parents: Its relationship to precocity and gender. *Gifted Child Quarterly, 33,* 144-151.

Rebbeck, B. J. (1985, May/June). Chats with GATs. *G/C/T, 37-40.*

Redding, R. E. (1990). Learning preferences and skills patterns among underachieving gifted adolescents. *Gifted Child Quarterly, 34,* 72-75.

Reilly, J. (1992). When does a student really need a professional mentor? *Gifted Child Today, 15*(3), 2-7.

Reis, S. M. (1987). We can't change what we don't recognize: Understanding the special needs of gifted females. *Gifted Child Quarterly, 31,* 83-89.

Reis, S. M. (1990a, February). Teaching techniques. *Learning90,* 46-47.

Reis, S. M. (1990b, February). What to teach, when to teach it. *Learning90,* 44-45.

Reis, S. M. (1991). The need for clarification in research designed to examine gender differences in achievement and accomplishment. *Roeper Review, 13,* 193-198.

Reis, S. M., Atamian, G. C., and Renzulli, J. S. (1985). The effectiveness of a self-instructional curricular unit in the development of advanced level concepts in astronomy. *Gifted Child Quarterly, 29,* 151-154.

Reis, S. M. and Burns, D. E. (1987). A schoolwide enrichment team invites you to read about methods for promoting community and faculty involvement in a gifted education program. *Gifted Child Today, 49*(2), 27-32.

Reis, S. M. and Callahan, C. M. (1989). Gifted females: They've come a long way—or have they? *Journal for the Education of the Gifted, 12*(2), 99-117.

Reis, S. M. and Dobyns, S. M. (1991). An annotated bibliography of non-fictional books and curricular materials to encourage gifted females. *Roeper Review, 13,* 129-130.

Reis, S. M. and Renzulli, J. S. (1986). The secondary triad model. In J. S. Renzulli (Ed.), *Systems and models for developing programs for the gifted and talented.* Mansfield Center, CT: Creative Learning Press.

Reis, S. M., Westberg, K., Kulikowich, J., Caillard, F., Hebert, T., Purcell, J., Rogers, J., and Smist, J. (1992, April). Modifying regular classroom instruction with curriculum compacting. In J. S. Renzulli (Chair), *Regular classroom practices with gifted students: Findings from the National Research Center on the Gifted and Talented.* Symposium conducted at the annual meeting of the American Educational Research Association, San Francisco.

Renzulli, J. S. (1975). *A guidebook for evaluating programs for the gifted and talented.* Ventura, CA: Office of the Ventura County Superintendent of Schools.

Renzulli, J. S. (1977). *The enrichment triad model: A guide for developing defensible programs for the gifted and talented.* Mansfield, CT: Creative Learning Press.

Renzulli, J. S. (1978). What makes giftedness? Reexamining a definition. *Phi Delta Kappan, 60,* 180-184.

Renzulli, J. S. (1983, September/October). Rating the behavioral characteristics of superior students *G/C/T, 30-35.*

Renzulli, J. S. (1984). The triad-revolving door system: A research-based approach to identification and programming for the gifted and talented. *Gifted Child Quarterly, 28,* 163-171.

Renzulli, J. S. (1986). The three-ring conception of giftedness: A developmental model for creative productivity. In R. J. Sternberg and J. E. Davidson (Eds.), *Conceptions of Giftedness.* Cambridge, MA: Cambridge University Press.

Renzulli, J. S. (1987, April). *The triad/revolving door model.* Workshop presented in Madison, Wisconsin.

Renzulli, J. S. (1988). *The multiple menu model for developing differentiated curriculum for the gifted and talented.* Unpublished manuscript, Bureau of Educational Research, University of Connecticut, Storrs, CT.

Renzulli, J. S. (1991a). The National Research Center on the Gifted and Talented: The dream, the design, and the destination. *Gifted Child Quarterly, 35,* 73-80.

Renzulli, J. S. (1991b, April). Chair/discussant comments. In J. S. Renzulli (Chair), *The National Research Center on the Gifted and Talented: Present activities, future plans, and an invitation for input and involvement.* Symposium conducted at the annual meeting of the American Educational Research Association, Chicago.

Renzulli, J. S. (1992, April). Chair/discussant comments. In J. S. Renzulli (Chair), *Regular classroom practices with gifted students: Findings from the National Research Center on the Gifted and Talented.* Symposium conducted at the annual meeting of the American Educational Research Association, San Francisco.

Renzulli, J. S. and Reis, S. M. (1985a). *The schoolwide enrichment model: A comprehensive plan for educational excellence.* Mansfield Center, CT: Creative Learning Press.

Renzulli, J. S. and Reis, S. M. (1985b, March/April). Scope and sequence approach to process development. *G/C/T,* 2-6.

Renzulli, J. S. and Reis, S. M. (1986). The enrichment triad/revolving door model: A schoolwide plan for the development of creative productivity. In J. S. Renzulli (Ed.), *Systems and models for developing programs for the gifted and talented* (216-266). Mansfield Center, CT: Creative Learning Press.

Renzulli, J. S. and Reis, S. M. (1991a). The reform movement and the quiet crisis in gifted education. *Gifted Child Quarterly, 35,* 26-35.

Renzulli, J. S. and Reis, S. M. (1991b). The Schoolwide Enrichment Model: A comprehensive plan for the development of creative productivity. In N. Colangelo and G. A. Davis (Eds.), *Handbook of gifted education* (111-141). Needham Heights, MA: Allyn and Bacon.

Renzulli, J. S., Reis, S. M., and Smith, L. H. (1981). *The revolving door identification model.* Mansfield, CT: Creative Learning Press.

Renzulli, J. S. and Smith, L. H. (1978a). Developing defensible programs for the gifted and talented. *Journal of Creative Behavior, 12,* 21-29, 51.

Renzulli, J. S. and Smith, L. H. (1978b). *Learning styles inventory.* Mansfield Center, CT: Creative Learning Press.

Renzulli, J. S. and Smith, L. H. (1979). Issues and procedures in evaluating gifted programs. In A. H. Passow (Ed.), *The gifted and the talented.* Chicago: National Society for the Study of Education.

Renzulli, J. S. and Ward, V. S. (1969). *Diagnostic and evaluative scales for differential education for the gifted.* Storrs, CT: University of Connecticut.

Resnick, L. B. (1985). *Education and learning to think.* Pittsburgh, PA: Learning Research and Development Center, University of Pittsburgh.

Restak, R. (1979). *The brain: The last frontier.* New York: Doubleday.

Ricca, J. (1984). Learning styles and preferred instructional strategies of gifted students. *Gifted Child Quarterly, 28,* 121-126.

Richardson, T. M. and Benbow, C. P. (1990). Long-term effects of acceleration on the social-emotional adjustment of mathematically precocious youths. *Journal of Educational Psychology, 82,* 464-470.

Richardson, W. B. and Feldhusen, J. F. (1986). *Leadership education: Developing skills for youth.* New York: Trillium Press.

Richert, E. S. (1985). Identification of gifted students: An update. *Roeper Review, 8,* 68-72.

Richert, E. S. (1987). Rampant problems and promising practices in the identification of disadvantaged gifted students. *Gifted Child Quarterly, 31,* 149-154.

Richert, E. S. (1991a). Patterns of underachievement among gifted students. In M. Bireley and J. Genshaft (Eds.), *Understanding the gifted adolescent: Educational, developmental, and multicultural issues* (139-162). New York: Teachers College Press.

Richert, E. S. (1991b). Rampant problems and promising practices in identification. In N. Colangelo and G. A. Davis (Eds.), *Handbook of gifted education* (81-96). Needham Heights, MA: Allyn and Bacon.

Richert, E. S., Alvino, J. J., and McDonnel, R. C. (1982). *National report on identification: Assessment and recommendations for comprehensive identification of gifted and talented youth.* Washington, DC: Educational Information Resource Center, U.S. Department of Education.

Riggs, G. G. (1984). Parent power: Wanted for organization. *Gifted Child Quarterly, 28,* 111-114.

Rimm, S. B. (1976). *GIFT: Group inventory for finding creative talent.* Watertown, WI: Educational Assessment Service.

Rimm, S. B. (1977, Fall). A comprehensive framework for total educational evaluation. Foreword, *Journal* of the Wisconsin Association for Supervision and Curriculum Development, 9-18.

Rimm, S. B. (1981). Evaluation of gifted programs—as easy as ABC. In R. E. Clasen, B. Robinson, D. R. Clasen, and G. Libster (Eds.), *Programming for the gifted, talented and creative: Models and methods.* Madison, WI: University of Wisconsin-Extension.

Rimm, S. B. (1982). *PRIDE: Preschool interest descriptor.* Watertown, WI: Educational Assessment Service.

Rimm, S. B. (1983, March/April). Identifying creativity, Part 1. *G/C/T,* 34-37.

Rimm, S. B. (1984, January/February). If God had meant gifted children to run our homes, she would have created them bigger. *G/C/T,* 26-29.

Rimm, S. B. (1986a). *AIM: Achievement identification measure.* Watertown, WI: Educational Assessment Service.

Rimm, S. B. (1986b). *Underachievement syndrome: Causes and cures.* Watertown, WI: Apple Publishing Company.

Rimm, S. B. (1987a). *GAIM: Group achievement identification measure.* Watertown, WI: Educational Assessment Service.

Rimm, S. B. (1987b). Marching to the beat of a different drummer. *Gifted Child Today, 10*(1), 2-6.

Rimm, S. B. (1987c). Why do bright children underachieve? The pressures they feel. *Gifted Child Today, 10*(6), 30-36.

Rimm, S. B. (1988). AIM-TO: *Achievement identification measure—Teacher observation.*Watertown, WI: Apple Publishing Co.

Rimm, S. B. (1990a). A theory of relativity. *Gifted Child Today, 13*(3), 32-36.

Rimm, S. B. (1990b). *Gifted kids have feelings too.* Watertown, WI: Apple Publishing Co.

Rimm, S. B. (1990c). *How to parent so children will learn.* Watertown, WI: Apple Publishing Co.

Rimm, S. B. (1991a). Underachievement and superachievement: Flip sides of the same psychological coin. In N. Colangelo and G. A. Davis (Eds.), *Handbook of gifted education.* Needham Heights, MA: Allyn and Bacon.

Rimm, S. B. (1991b). What's the hurry. *How to Stop Underachievement* Newsletter, *1*(4), 1-3. Educational Assessment Service, Inc., Watertown, Wisconsin.

Rimm, S. B. (1991c). Teaching competition to prevent and cure underachievement. *How to Stop Under-achievement* Newsletter, *2*(2), 1-2. Educational Assessment Service, Inc., Watertown, Wisconsin.

Rimm, S. B. (1992a). A response on competition from Kansas. *How to Stop Underachievement* Newsletter, *2*(4), 6-7. Educational Assessment Service, Watertown, Wisconsin.

Rimm, S. B. (1992b). *On raising kids.* Watertown, WI: Apple Publishing Co.

Rimm, S. B. (1992c). A bicycle ride: Why we need grouping. *How to Stop Underachievement* Newsletter, *1*(3), 1-3. Educational Assessment Service, Inc., Watertown, Wisconsin.

Rimm, S. B. (In press a). Creativity and underachievement. In J. F. Smutney, and C. A. Siewers (Eds.), *From toddlers to taxonomies: A collection of readings on gifted pre-primary and primary.* Buffalo, NY: DOK Publishers.

Rimm, S. B. (In press b). Will we now drug those troublesome gifted children? *Gifted Child Today.*

Rimm, S. B., Cornale, M., Manos, R., and Behrend, J. (1989). *Guidebook for implementing the trifocal underachievement program in schools.* Watertown, WI: Apple Publishing Co.

Rimm, S. B. and Davis, G. A. (1976). GIFT: An instrument for the identification of creativity. *Journal of Creative Behavior, 10,* 178-182.

Rimm, S. B. and Davis, G. A. (1980). Five years of international research with GIFT: An instrument for the identification of creativity. *Journal of Creative Behavior, 14,* 35-36.

Rimm, S. B. and Davis, G. A. (1982). Identifying creativity: A characteristics approach. *Gifted Child Quarterly, 26,* 165-171.

Rimm, S. B. and Davis, G. A. (1983, September/October). Identifying creativity, Part II. *G/C/T,* 19-23.

Rimm, S. B., Davis, G. A., and Bien, Y. (1982). Identifying creativity: A characteristics approach. *Gifted Child Quarterly, 26,* 165–171.

Rimm, S. B., and Lovance, K. J. (1992a). How acceleration may prevent underachievement syndrome. *Gifted Child Today, 15*(2), 9-14.

Rimm, S. B. and Lovance, K. J. (1992b). The use of subject and grade skipping for the prevention and reversal of underachievement. *Gifted Child Quarterly, 36,* 100-105.

Rimm, S. B. and Lowe, B. (1988). Family environments of underachieving gifted students. *Gifted Child Quarterly, 32,* 353-359.

Rimm, S. B. and Olenchak, F. R. (1991). How FPS helps underachieving gifted students. *Gifted Child Today, 14*(2), 19-22.

Rimm, S. B. and Priest, C. (1990). *Exploring feelings.* Watertown, WI: Apple Publishing Co.

Rimmerman, H. (1991). Response to Dr. Sylvia Rimm on the article "Teaching Competition to Prevent and Cure Underachievement." *How to Stop Underachievement* Newsletter, *2*(2), 6-7.

Riordan, C. (1990). *Girls and boys in school: Together or separate?* New York: Teachers College Press.

Rist, R. and Harrell, J. (1982). Labeling the learning disabled child: The social ecology of educational practice. *American Journal of Orthopsychiatry, 52,* 146-160.

Robbins, B. W. (1988). *Creative dramatics in the language arts classroom.* Bloomington, IN: Clearinghouse on Reading and Communication Skills.

Roberts, J. L. (1992). Parents can be mentors, too. *Gifted Child Today, 15*(3), 36-38.

Roberts, J. L. and Roberts, R. (1986). Differentiating inservice through teacher concerns about education for the gifted. *Gifted Child Quarterly, 30,* 107-109.

Robinson, A. (1991). *Cooperative learning and the academically talented student.* Storrs, CT: National Research Center on the Gifted and Talented, University of Connecticut.

Robinson, N. M. and Noble, K. D. (1992a). A radical leap from middle school to college: Can it work? In N. Colangelo, S. G. Assouline, and D. L. Ambroson (Eds.), *Talent development: Proceedings from the 1991 Henry B. and Jocelyn Wallace national research symposium on talent development* (267-277). Unionville, NY: Trillium Press

Robinson, N. M. and Noble, K. D. (1992b). Acceleration: Valuable high school to college options. *Gifted Child Today, 15*(2), 20-23.

Rodenstein, J. M. and Glickauf-Hughes, C. (1979). Career and lifestyle determinants of gifted women. In N. Colangelo and R. T. Zaffrann (Eds.), *New voices in counseling the gifted.* Dubuque, IA: Kendall/Hunt.

Rodenstein, J., Pfleger, L., and Colangelo, N. (1977). Career development needs of the gifted: Special considerations for gifted women. *Gifted Child Quarterly, 20,* 340-347.

Roeper, A. (1982, November). How the gifted cope with their emotions. *Roeper Review, 5*(2), 21-24.

Rogers, C. R. (1949). A coordinated research in psychotherapy: A non-objective introduction. *Journal of Consulting Psychology, 13,* 49-51.

Rogers, C. R. (1962). Toward a theory of creativity. In S. J. Parnes and H. F. Harding (Eds.), *A source book for creative thinking.* New York: Scribner's.

Rogers, K. B. (1990, November). *Using effect size to make good decisions about acceleration.* Paper presented at the annual meeting of the National Association for Gifted Children, Little Rock, Arkansas.

Rogers, K. B. (1991). *The relationship of grouping practices to the education of the gifted and talented learner.* Storrs, CT: National Research Center on the Gifted and Talented, University of Connecticut.

Rosenthal, R. J. and Jacobson, L. (1968). *Pygmalion in the classroom.* New York: Holt.

Rosner, S. (1985, May/June). Guidelines for developing effective programs for gifted children with special learning disabilities. *G/C/T,* 55-58.

Rosner, S. and Seymour, J. (1983). The gifted child with a learning disability: Clinical evidence. In L. Fox, L. Brody, and D. Tobin (Eds.), *Learning disabled/gifted children* (77-97). Baltimore: University Park Press.

Ross, A. and Parker, H. (1980). Academic and social self-concepts of the academically gifted. *Exceptional Children, 47,* 6-10.

Rowe, I. H. (1990). The power of parent persuasion. In S. Baily, E. Braggett, and M. Robinson (Eds.), *The challenge of excellence: A vision splendid* (358-361). Australia: The Australian Association for the Education of the Gifted and Talented.

Ruckman, D. R. and Feldhusen, J. F. (1988). Evaluation of a university/school district consortium for gifted education. *Roeper Review, 11,* 79-85.

Sabornie, E. J. and Kauffman, J. M. (1985). Regular classroom sociometric status of behaviorally disordered adolescents. *Behavioral Disorders, 10,* 268-274.

Sadker, M. P., Sadker, D. M., and Hicks, T. The one-percent solution? Sexism in teacher education texts. *Phi Delta Kappan, 61,* 550-553.

Safer, D. J. and Krager, J. M. (1988). A survey of medication treatments for hyperactive/inattentive students. *Journal of the American Medical Association, 260,* 2256–2258.

Sainato, D. M., Strain, P. S., Lefebvre, D., and Rapp, N. (1990). Effects of self-evaluation on the independent work skills of preschool children with disabilities. *Exceptional Children, 56*(6), 540-549.

Salter, J. and Tozier, L. (1971). A review of intelligence test modifications used with the cerebral palsied and other handicapped groups. *Journal of Special Education, 4,* 391-398.

Sanborn, M. (1979). Career development: Problems of gifted and talented students. In N. Colangelo and R. T. Zaffrann (Eds.), *New voices in counseling the gifted.* Dubuque, IA: Kendall/Hunt.

Satler, M. (1982). *Assessment of children's intelligence and special abilities* (2nd Ed.). Needham Heights, MA: Allyn and Bacon, Inc.

Sato, I. S., Birnbaum, M., and LoCicero, J. E. (1974). *Developing a written plan for the education of gifted and talented students.* Ventura, CA: Office of the Ventura County Superintendent of Schools.

Sato, I. S. and Johnson, B. (1978). Multifaceted training meets multidimensionally gifted. *Journal of Creative Behavior, 12,* 63-71.

Schaefer, C. E. (1969). Imaginary companions and creative adolescents. *Developmental Psychology, 1,* 747-749.

Schaefer, C. E. (1971). *Creativity attitude survey.* Jacksonville, IL: Psychologists and Educators, Inc.

Schafer, M. (1974). *Die sprache des pferdes.* Munich: Nymfenburger Verlagshandlung.

Schatz, E. (1990, May/June). Ability grouping for gifted learners. *Educating Able Learners,* 3-5, 15.

Schenck, C. and Schenck, S. (1990). 1990 directory of summer opportunities for the gifted. *Gifted Child Today, 13*(2), 50-59.

Schenck, C. and Schenck, S. (1991). 1991 directory of summer opportunities for the gifted. *Gifted Child Today, 14*(2), 44-59.

Schiever, S. W. and Maker, C. J. (1991). Enrichment and acceleration: An overview and new directions. In N. Colangelo and G. A. Davis (Eds.), *Handbook of gifted education* (99-110). Needham Heights, MA: Allyn and Bacon.

Schiff, M. M., Kaufman, A. S., and Kaufman, N. L. (1981). Scatter analysis of WISC-R profiles for learning disabled children with superior intelligence. *Journal of Learning Disabilities, 14,* 400-404.

Schlichter, C. L. (1986a). Talents unlimited: An inservice education model for teaching thinking skills. *Gifted Child Quarterly, 30,* 119-123.

Schlichter, C. L. (1986b). Talents unlimited: Applying the multiple-talent approach in mainstream and gifted programs. In J. S. Renzulli (Ed.), *Systems and models for developing programs for the gifted and talented.* Mansfield Center, CT: Creative Learning Press.

Schlichter, C. L. (1987). Thinking skills instruction for classrooms. *Gifted Child Today, 10*(2), 2-7.

Schlichter, C. L. and Palmer, W. R. (1993). *Thinking smart: A primer of the Talents Unlimited model.* Mansfield Center, CT: Creative Learning Press.

Schnur, J. O. and Stefanich, G. P. (1979). Science for the handicapped gifted child. *Roeper Review, 2*(2), 26-28.

Schreeve, W., Goetter, W. G. J., Bunn, A., Norby, J. R., Stueckle, A. F., Midgley, T. K., and de Michele, B. (1986). Single parents and students' achievements—a national tragedy. *Early Child Development and Care, 23,* 175-184.

Sciara, R. and Jantz, R. (1974). Father absence and its apparent effect on the reading achievement of black children from low income families. *Journal of Negro Education, 43,* 221-227.

Scruggs, T. E. and Cohn, S. J. (1983). A university-based summer program for a highly able but poorly achieving Indian child. *Gifted Child Quarterly, 27,* 90-93.

Sears, P. S. (1979). The Terman genetic studies of genius, 1922-1972. In A. H. Passow (Ed.), *The gifted and the talented.* Chicago: National Society for the Study of Education.

Sears, P. S. and Barbee, A. H. (1977). Career and life satisfactions among Terman's gifted women. In J. C. Stanley, W. C. George, and C. H. Solano (Eds.), *The gifted and the creative: A fifty-year perspective.* Baltimore, MD: Johns Hopkins University Press.

Sears, R. R. (1977). Sources of life satisfactions of the Terman gifted men. *American Psychologist, 32,* 119-128.

Sebrechts, J. S. (1992). The cultivation of scientists at women's colleges. *The Journal of NIH Research, 4,* 22-26.

Sebring, A. D. (1983). Parental factors on the social and emotional adjustment of the gifted. *Roeper Review, 6*(2), 97-99.

Segoe, M. V. (1975). *Terman and the gifted.* Los Altos, CA: Kaufman.

Seligman, R. (1990). A gifted ninth grader tells it like it is. *Gifted Child Today, 13*(4), 9-11.

Serbin, L. and O'Leary, D. K. (1975). How nursery schools teach girls to shut up. *Psychology Today, 9*(12), 56-58.

Shade, B. J. (1978, April). Social-psychological characteristics of achieving black children. *The Negro Educational Review, 29*(2), 80-86.

Shade, B. J. (1983, December). The social success of black youth. The impact of significant others. *Journal of Black Studies, 14*(2), 137-150.

Shallcross, D. J. (1981). *Teaching creative behavior.* Englewood Cliffs, NJ: Prentice-Hall.

Shaller, J. G. (1990). Commentary: The advancement of women in academic medicine. *Journal of the American Medical Association, 264,* 1854-1855.

Sharan, Y. and Sharan, S. (1990). Group investigation expands cooperative learning. *Educational Leadership, 47*(4), 17-21.

Sharan, Y. and Sharan, S. (1992). *Expanding cooperative learning through group investigation.* New York: Teachers College Press.

Sharp, A. M. and Reed, R. F. (1992). *Studies in philosophy for children: Harry Stottlemeier's discovery.* Philadelphia: Temple University Press.

Shaw, M. C. and McCuen, J. T. (1960). The onset of academic underachievement in bright children. *Journal of Educational Psychology, 51,* 103-108.

Shaw, M. C. and White, D. L. (1965). The relationship between child-parent identification and academic underachievement. *Journal of Clinical Psychology, 21,* 10-13.

Sheehy, G. (1982). *Pathfinders.* New York: Bantam Books.

Shepard, L. A. and Smith, M. L. (1985). *Boulder Valley kindergarten study: Retention practices and retention effects.* Boulder, CO: Boulder Valley Public Schools.

Shore, B. M. (1986, November/December). Reactions. *G/C/T,* 11.

Silrum, L. (1986, July/August). The mentor connection. *G/C/T,* 55-56.

Silverman, L. K. (1983a). Issues in affective development of the gifted. In J. Van Tassel-Baska (Ed.), *A practical guide to counseling the gifted in a school setting.* Reston, VA: Council for Exceptional Children.

Silverman, L. K. (1983b). Personality development: The pursuit of excellence. *Journal for the Education of the Gifted, 6,* 5-19.

Silverman, L. K. (1986). An interview with Elizabeth Hagen: Giftedness, intelligence and the new Stanford-Binet. *Roeper Review, 8,* 168-171.

Silverman, L. K. (1989). Invisible gifts, invisible handicaps. *Roeper Review, 12,* 37-42.

Silverman, L. K. (1991a). Family counseling. In N. Colangelo and G. A. Davis (Eds.), *Handbook of gifted education* (307-320). Needham Heights, MA: Allyn and Bacon.

Silverman, L. K. (1991b). Helping gifted girls reach their potential. *Roeper Review, 13,* 122-123.

Silverman, L. K., Chitwood, D. G., and Water, J. L. (1986). Young gifted children: Can parents identify giftedness? *Topics in Early Childhood Special Education, 6,* 23-38.

Silverman, L. K. and Kearney, K. (1989). Parents of the extraordinarily gifted. *Advanced Development Journal, 1,* 41-56.

Simberg, A. L. (1964). *Creativity at work.* Boston: Industrial Education Institute.

Simon, S. B., Howe, L., and Kirschenbaum, H. (1972). *Value clarification: A handbook of practical strategies for teachers and students.* New York: Hart.

Simon, S. B., Howe, L., and Kirschenbaum, H. (1978). *Value clarification: A handbook of practical strategies for teachers and students* (rev. ed.). New York: Hart.

Simon, S. B. and Massey, S. (1973). Value clarification. *Educational Leadership, 5,* 738-739.

Simonton, D. K. (1988). Creativity, leadership, and chance. In R. J. Sternberg (Ed.), *The nature of creativity* (386-426). New York: Cambridge University Press.

Sisk, D. A. (1980). Issues and future directions in gifted education. *Gifted Child Quarterly, 24,* 29-36.

Sisk, D. A. (1990). Expanding worldwide awareness of gifted and talented children and youth. *Gifted Child Today, 13*(5), 19-25.

Sisk, D. A., Gilbert, P., and Gosch, R. (1991). Developing leadership in a multi-cultural society. *Gifted Child Today, 14*(4), 60-61.

Sjogren, D., Hopkins, T., and Gooler, D. (1975). *Evaluation plans and instruments: Illustrative cases of gifted program evaluation techniques.* Champaign, IL: Center for Instructional Research and Curriculum Evaluation, University of Illinois.

Skuy, M., Gaydon, V., Hoffenberg, S., and Fridjhon, P. (1990). Predictors of performance of disadvantaged adolescents in a gifted program. *Gifted Child Quarterly, 34*, 97-101.

Slavin, R. E. (1987a). Ability grouping and student achievement in elementary schools: A best-evidence synthesis. *Review of Educational Research, 57*, 293-336.

Slavin, R. E. (1987b). Grouping for instruction in the elementary school. *Educational Leadership, 22*, 109-127.

Slavin, R. E. (1990a). Ability grouping, cooperative learning and the gifted. *Journal for the Education of the Gifted, 14*(1), 3-8.

Slavin, R. E. (1990b). *Cooperative learning: Theory, research, and practice.* Englewood Cliffs, NJ: Prentice-Hall.

Slavin, R. E. (1990c). Research on cooperative learning: Consensus and controversy. *Educational Leadership, 47*(4), 52-54.

Slavin, R. E. (1991a). Are cooperative learning and "untracking" harmful to the gifted? *Educational Leadership, 48*(6), 68-71.

Slavin, R. E. (1991b). Group rewards make groupwork work. *Educational Leadership, 48*(5), 83-88.

Slavin, R. E., Madden, N. A., and Stevens, R. J. (1990). Cooperative learning models for the 3 R's. *Educational Leadership, 47*(4), 22-28.

Smith, C. B. (1991). Literature for gifted and talented. *The Reading Teacher, 44*, 608-609.

Smith, J., LeRose, B., and Clasen, R. E. (1991). Underrepresentation of minority students in gifted programs: Yes! It matters. *Gifted Child Quarterly, 35*, 81-83.

Smith, J. M. (1966). *Setting conditions for creative teaching in the elementary school.* Boston: Allyn and Bacon.

Smith, L. G. (1981). Centuries of educational inequities. *Educational Horizons, 60*, 4-10.

Smith, S. J. (1990). What are you counting as service to gifted and talented students? *Gifted Child Today, 13*(4), 23-24.

Solomon, A. O. (1974). Analysis of creative thinking of disadvantaged children. *Journal of Creative Behavior, 8*, 293-295.

Somers, J. V. and Yawkey, T. D. (1984). Imaginary play companions: Contributions to creativity and intellectual abilities of young children. *Journal of Creative Behavior, 18*, 77-89.

Southern, W. T. and Jones, E. D. (1991). Objections to early entrance and grade skipping. In W. T. Southern

and E. D. Jones (Eds.), *The academic acceleration of gifted children* (51-73). New York: Teachers College Press.

Southern, W. T. and Jones, E. D. (1992). The real problems with academic acceleration. *Gifted Child Today, 15*(2), 34-38.

Southern, W. T., Jones, E. D., and Fiscus, E. D. (1989). Practitioner objections to the academic acceleration of gifted students. *Gifted Child Quarterly, 33*, 29-35.

Southern, W. T., and Spicker, H. H. (1989). The rural gifted on line: Bulletin boards and electronic curriculum. *Roeper Review, 11*, 199-202.

Spicker, H. H., Southern, W. T., and Davis, B. I. (1987). The rural gifted child. *Gifted Child Quarterly, 31*, 155-157.

Spredemann-Dryer, S. (1989). *The bookfinder: When kids need books.* Circle Pines, MN: American Guidance Services.

Springer, S. P., and Deutsch, G. (1985). *Left brain, right brain* (rev. ed.). New York: Freeman.

Stacey, J. (1990, November 26). USA snapshots: Pay inequity. *USA Today.*

Staines, G., Tavris, C., and Jayaratne, C. (1974). The Queen Bee syndrome. *Psychology Today, 7*(8), 55-60.

Stake, J. E. (1981). The educator's role in fostering female career aspirations. *Journal of NAWDAC*, 3-10.

Stanish, B. (1977). *Sunflowering.* Carthage, IL: Good Apple.

Stanish, B. (1979). *I believe in unicorns.* Carthage, IL: Good Apple.

Stanish, B. (1981). *Hippogriff feathers.* Carthage, IL: Good Apple.

Stanish, B. (1986). *Mindglow.* Carthage, IL: Good Apple.

Stanish, B. (1988). *Lessons from the hearthstone traveler: An instructional guide to the creative thinking process.* Carthage, IL: Good Apple.

Stankowski, W. M. (1978). Definition. In R. E. Clasen and B. Robinson (Eds.), *Simple gifts.* Madison, WI: University of Wisconsin-Extension.

Stanley, J. C. (1976). *American Psychologist, 31*, 313-314.

Stanley, J. C. (1978a). Concern for intellectually talented youths: How it originated and fluctuated. In R. E. Clasen and B. Robinson (Eds.), *Simple gifts.* Madison, WI: University of Wisconsin-Extension.

Stanley, J. C. (1978b). Identifying and nurturing the intellectually gifted. In R. E. Clasen and B. Robinson

(Eds.), *Simple gifts*. Madison, WI: University of Wisconsin-Extension.

Stanley, J. C. (1979). The study and facilitation of talent for mathematics. In A. H. Passow (Ed.), *The gifted and the talented*. Chicago: National Society for the Study of Education.

Stanley, J. C. (1982, October). *Finding intellectually talented youths and helping them greatly via educational acceleration*. Speech to the Wisconsin Council on Gifted and Talented, Madison, WI.

Stanley, J. C. (1985a, August). *Fostering use of mathematical talent in the USA: SMPY's rationale*. Keynote address at the Sixth World Conference on Gifted and Talented Children, Hamburg, Germany.

Stanley, J. C. (1985b). How did six highly accelerated gifted students fare in graduate school? *Gifted Child Quarterly, 29*, 180.

Stanley, J. C. (1987). State residential high schools for mathematically talented youth. *Phi Delta Kappan, 68*, 770-772.

Stanley, J. C. (1989). A look back at educational non-acceleration: An international tragedy. *Gifted Child Today, 12*(4), 60-61.

Stanley, J. C. (1991a). An academic model for educating the mathematically talented. *Gifted Child Quarterly, 35*, 36-42.

Stanley, J. C. (1991b). Critique of "Socioemotional adjustment of adolescent girls enrolled in a residential acceleration program." *Gifted Child Quarterly, 35*, 67-70.

Stanley, J. C. and Benbow, C. P. (1983). Educating mathematically precocious youths: Twelve policy recommendations. *Educational Researcher, 11*(5), 4-9.

Stanley, J. C. and Benbow, C. P. (1986a). Extremely young college graduates: Evidence of their success. *College and University, 58*, 361-371.

Stanley, J. C. and Benbow, C. P. (1986b). Youths who reason exceptionally well mathematically. In R. J. Sternberg and J. E. Davidson (Eds.), *Conceptions of giftedness* (361-387). New York: Cambridge University Press.

Stanley, J. C. and George, W. C. (1980). SMPY's ever-increasing D4. *Gifted Child Quarterly, 24*, 41-48.

Stanley, J. C., Lupkowski, A. E., and Assouline, S. G. (1990). Applying a mentor model for young mathematically talented students. *Gifted Child Today, 13*(2), 15-19.

Stanley, J. C. and McGill, A. M. (1986). More about

"young entrants to college: How did they fare?" *Gifted Child Quarterly, 30*, 70-73.

Starko, A. J. (1990). Life and death of a gifted program: Lessons not yet learned. *Roeper Review, 13*, 33-38.

Steele, K. J. (1991). Improving the quality of elementary education through full time gifted classes. *Gifted Child Today, 14*(6), 52-55.

Steinberg, L., Dornbusch, S. M., and Brown, B. B. (1992). Ethnic differences in adolescent achievement—An ecological perspective. *American Psychologist, 47*, 723-729.

Sternberg, R. J. (1982). Lies we live by: Misapplication of tests in identifying the gifted. *Gifted Child Quarterly, 26*, 157.

Sternberg, R. J. (1983). Criteria for intellectual skills training. *Educational Research, 12*, 6-13.

Sternberg, R. J. (1984). How can we teach intelligence? *Educational Leadership, 42*, 38-48.

Sternberg, R. J. (1988). Three-facet model of creativity. In R. J. Sternberg (Ed.), *The nature of creativity* (125-147). New York: Cambridge University Press.

Sternberg, R. J. (1990). *Robert Sternberg's ten tips to enhance creativity* (poster). Minneapolis, MN: Free Spirit Publishing.

Sternglanz, S. H. and Serbin, L. A. (1974). Sex-role stereotyping in children's television programs. *Developmental Psychology, 10*, 710-715.

Stockard, J. and Wood, J. W. (1984). The myth of female underachievement: A reexamination of sex differences in academic underachievement. *American Educational Research Journal, 21*, 825-838.

Strom, R., Johnson, A., Strom, S., and Strom, P. (1992). Designing curriculum for parents of gifted children. *Journal for the Education of the Gifted, 15*(2), 182-200.

Stryker, F. (undated). *Creative writing workbook and the morphological approach to plotting*. Unpublished manuscript, University of Buffalo.

Strykowski, B. and Walberg, H. J. (1983). Psychological traits and childhood environments of eminent writers. *Roeper Review, 6*(2), 102-105.

Subotnik, R. and Strauss, S. (1990, April). *Gender differences in achievement and classroom participation: An experiment involving advanced placement calculus classes*. Paper presented at the annual meeting of the American Educational Research Association, Boston, MA.

Sullivan, P. M. and Vernon, M. (1979). Psychological

assessment of hearing impaired children. *School Psychology Digest, 8,* 271-290.

Suter, D. P. and Wolf, J. S. (1987). Issues in the identification and programming of the gifted/learning disabled child. *Journal for the Education of the Gifted, 10*(3), 227-237.

Sutherland, S. L. (1978). The unambitious female: Women's low professional aspirations. *Signs: Journal of Women in Culture and Society, 3,* 774-794.

Sutton-Smith, B., Rosenberg, B. G., and Landy, F. (1968). Father-absence effects in families of different sibling compositions. *Child Development, 39,* 1213-1221.

Swartz, R. J. and Perkins, D. N. (1990). *Teaching thinking: Issues and approaches.* Pacific Grove, CA: Critical Thinking Press and Software.

Swenson, E. V. (1978). Teacher assessment of creative behavior in disadvantaged children. *Gifted Child Quarterly, 22,* 338-343.

Swiatek, M. A. and Benbow, C. P. (1992). *A ten-year longitudinal followup of participants in a fast-paced mathematics course.* Unpublished report, Department of Psychology, Iowa State University.

Tan-Willman, C. and Gutteridge, D. (1981). Creative thinking and moral reasoning of academically gifted secondary school adolescents. *Gifted Child Quarterly, 25,* 149-153.

Tannen, D. (1990). *You just don't understand: Women and men in conversation.* New York: Ballantine Books.

Tannenbaum, A. J. (1979). Pre-Sputnik to post-Watergate concern about the gifted. In A. H. Passow (Ed.), *The gifted and the talented.* Chicago: National Society for the Study of Education.

Tardif, T. Z. and Sternberg, R. J. (1988). What do we know about creativity? In R. J. Sternberg (Ed.), *The nature of creativity* (429-440). New York: Cambridge University Press.

Taylor, C. W. (1978). How many types of giftedness can your program tolerate? *Journal of Creative Behavior, 12,* 39-51.

Taylor, C. W. (1986). Cultivating simultaneous student growth in both multiple creative talents and knowledge. In J. S. Renzulli (Ed.), *Systems and models for developing programs for the gifted and talented.* Mansfield Center, CT: Creative Learning Press.

Taylor, C. W. (1988). Various approaches to and definitions of creativity. In R. J. Sternberg (Ed.), *The nature of creativity* (99-121). New York: Cambridge University Press.

Teale, W. (1984). Reading to young children: Its significance for literacy development. In H. Goelman, A. Oberg, and T. Smith (Eds.), *Awakening to literacy* (110-121). Portsmouth, NH: Heinemann.

Terman, L. M. (1925). *Genetic studies of genius: Vol. 1. Mental and physical traits of a thousand gifted children.* Stanford, CA: Stanford University Press.

Terman, L. M. (1954). The discovery and encouragement of exceptional talent. *American Psychologist, 9,* 221-230.

Terman, L. M. (1981). The discovery and encouragement of exceptional talent. In W. B. Barbe and J. S., Renzulli (Eds.), *Psychology and education of the gifted,* (3rd Ed.). New York: Irvington.

Terman, L. M., Burks, B. S., and Jensen, D. W. (1930). *Genetic studies of genius: Vol. 3. The promise of youth: Follow-up studies of a thousand gifted children.* Stanford, CA: Stanford University Press.

Terman, L. M. and Oden, M. H. (1947). *Genetic studies of genius: Vol. 4. The gifted child grows up.* Stanford, CA: Stanford University Press.

Terman, L. M. and Oden, M. H. (1951). The Stanford studies of the gifted. In P. A. Witty (Ed.), *The gifted child.* Lexington, MA: D. C. Heath.

Terman, L. M. and Oden, M. H. (1959). *Genetic studies of genius: Vol. 5. The gifted group at midlife: Thirty-five years' follow-up of a superior group.* Stanford, CA: Stanford University Press.

Thomas, A. (1989). Ability and achievement expectations: Implications of research for classroom practice. *Childhood Education, 65,* 235-241.

Thomson, R. A. (1989). Operation adventure in Wisconsin. *Gifted Child Today, 12*(5), 58-59.

Thorndike, R. S. and Hagen, E. P. (1977). *Management and evaluation in psychology and education.* New York: Wiley.

Tidball, E. (1986). Baccalaureate origins of recent natural science doctorates. *Journal of Higher Education, 57,* 606-620.

Tidball, M. E. (1973). Perspective on academic women and affirmative action. *Educational Records, 54,* 130-135.

Tidwell, R. (1980). Gifted students' self-image as a function of identification procedure, race, and sex. *Journal of Pediatric Psychology, 5*(1), 57-69.

Tkach, J. R. (1986, March/April). What to do with a gifted kid this summer. *G/C/T,* 24-25.

Tobin, D. (1979, September/October). Accelerated mathematics for the gifted. *G/C/T,* 48-50.

Tolan, S. S. (1987). Parents and professionals, a question of priorities. *Roeper Review, 9,* 184-187.

Toll, M. F. (1991). Full-time gifted programs: Where do I begin. *Gifted Child Today, 14*(6), 12-13.

Tomlinson, S. (1986). A survey of participant expectations for inservice in education of the gifted. *Gifted Child Quarterly, 30,* 110-113.

Tongue, C. and Sperling, C. (1976). *Parent nomination form.* Raleigh, NC: North Carolina Department of Public Instruction.

Torrance, E. P. (1962). *Guiding creative talent.* Englewood Cliffs, NJ: Prentice-Hall.

Torrance, E. P. (1966). *Torrance tests of creative thinking.* Bensenville, IL: Scholastic Testing Service.

Torrance, E. P. (1971). Are the Torrance tests of creative thinking biased against or in favor of disadvantaged groups? *Gifted Child Quarterly, 15,* 75-81.

Torrance, E. P. (1977). *Creativity in the classroom.* Washington, DC: National Educational Association.

Torrance, E. P. (1979). *The search for satori and creativity.* Buffalo, NY: Creative Education Foundation.

Torrance, E. P. (1980). Assessing the further reaches of creative potential. *Journal of Creative Behavior, 14,* 1-19.

Torrance, E. P. (1981a). Creative teaching makes a difference. In J. C. Gowan, J. Khatena, and E. P. Torrance (Eds.), *Creativity: Its educational implications* (2nd Ed.). Dubuque, IA: Kendall/Hunt.

Torrance, E. P. (1981b). Non-test ways of identifying the creatively gifted. In J. C. Gowan, J. Khatena, and E. P. Torrance (Eds.), *Creativity: Its educational implications* (2nd Ed.). Dubuque, IA: Kendall/Hunt.

Torrance, E. P. (1981c). Sociodrama as a creative problem-solving approach to studying the future. In J. C. Gowan, J. Khatena, and E. P. Torrance (Eds.), *Creativity: Its educational implications* (2nd Ed.). Dubuque, IA: Kendall/Hunt.

Torrance, E. P. (1982). *Thinking creatively in action and movement.* Bensenville, IL: Scholastic Testing Service.

Torrance, E. P. (1984). Teaching gifted and creative learners. In M. Wittrock (Ed.), *Handbook of research on teaching* (3rd Ed.). Chicago: Rand-McNally.

Torrance, E. P. (1987). *The blazing drive: The creative personality.* Buffalo, NY: Bearly Limited.

Torrance, E. P. (1988). The nature of creativity as manifest in its testing. In R. J. Sternberg (Ed.), *The nature of creativity* (43-75). New York: Cambridge University Press.

Torrance, E. P. and Ball, O. E. (1984). *Torrance tests of creative thinking: Streamlined (revised) manual, figural A and B.* Bensenville, IL: Scholastic Testing Service.

Torrance, E. P., Khatena, J., and Cunnington, B. F. (1973). *Thinking creatively with sounds and words.* Bensenville, IL: Scholastic Testing Service.

Torrance, E. P. and Myers, R. E. (1970). *Creative learning and teaching.* New York: Dodd, Mead.

Torrance, E. P. and Torrance, J. P. (1978). The 1977-78 future problem-solving program: Interscholastic competition and curriculum project. *Journal of Creative Behavior, 12,* 87-89.

Torrance, E. P., Williams, S. E., Torrance, J. P., and Horng, R. (1978). *Handbook for training future problem-solving teams.* Athens, GA: Georgia Studies of Creative Behavior, University of Georgia.

Traxler, M. A. (1987). Gifted education program evaluation: A national review. *Journal for the Education of the Gifted, 10*(2), 107-113.

Treffert, D. A. (1989). *Extraordinary people: Understanding "idiot savants."* New York: Harper and Row.

Treffinger, D. J. (1975). Teaching for self-directed learning: A priority of the gifted and talented. *Gifted Child Quarterly, 19,* 46-59.

Treffinger, D. J. (1978). Guidelines for encouraging independence and self-direction among gifted students. *Journal of Creative Behavior, 12,* 14-20.

Treffinger, D. J. (1981). *Blending gifted education with the total school program.* Sarasota, FL: Center for Creative Learning.

Treffinger, D. J. (1982a). Demythologizing gifted education: An editorial essay. *Gifted Child Quarterly, 26,* 3-8.

Treffinger, D. J. (1982b). Gifted students, regular students: Sixty ingredients for a better blend. *Elementary School Journal, 82,* 267-273.

Treffinger, D. J. (1983, April). *Creativity: Celebrating the vision.* Speech presented at the Third Annual Midwest Conference on Gifted and Talented Children, Milwaukee, WI.

Treffinger, D. J. (1986a). *Blending gifted education*

with the total school program (2nd Ed.). Buffalo, NY: DOK.

Treffinger, D. J. (1986b). Fostering effective, independent learning through individualized programming. In J. S. Renzulli (Ed.), *Systems and models for developing programs for the gifted and talented.* Mansfield Center, CT: Creative Learning Press.

Treffinger, D. J. (1992, May). *Rethinking gifted education.* Keynote address presented to the Wisconsin Association of Educators of the Gifted and Talented, Madison.

Treffinger, D. J. and Barton, B. L. (1988). Fostering independent learning. *Gifted Child Today, 11*(1), 28-30.

Treffinger, D. J. and Firestien, R. L. (1989). Update: Guidelines for effective facilitation of creative problem solving. *Gifted Child Today, 12*(4), 35-39.

Treffinger, D. J., Isaksen, S. G., and Firestien, R. L. (1982). *Handbook of creative learning* (Vol. 1). Sarasota, FL: Center for Creative Learning.

Treffinger, D. J., Isaksen, S. G., and McEwen, P. (1987). *Checklist for preparing for evaluating thinking skills instructional programs.* Sarasota, FL: Center for Creative Learning.

Treffinger, D. J. and Perez, G. S. (1980). Self-description of instructional style for encouraging self-directed learning. In H. W. Singleton (Ed.), *Gifted/talented education: Perspectives on curriculum and instruction.* Toledo, OH: University of Toledo, College of Education.

Treffinger, D. J. and Renzulli, J. S. (1986). Giftedness as potential for creative productivity: Transcending IQ scores. *Roeper Review, 8,* 150-154.

Trigg, L. J. and Perlman, D. (1976). Social influences on women's pursuit of a nontraditional career. *Psychology of Women Quarterly, 1*(2), 138-150.

Tsuin-chen, O. (1961). Some facts and ideas about talent and genius in Chinese history. In G. Z. F. Bereday and J. A. Lauwerys (Eds.), *Concepts of excellence in education: The yearbook of education.* New York: Harcourt, Brace and World.

Tucker, B. F. (1982). Providing for the mathematically gifted child in the regular classroom. *Roeper Review, 4*(4), 11-12.

Turner, S. E. and Bowen, W. G. (1990, October). The flight from the arts and sciences: Trends in degrees conferred, *Science,* 517-520.

Tyler-Wood, T. and Carri, L. (1991). Identification of gifted children: The effectiveness of various measures of cognitive ability. *Roeper Review, 14,* 63-64.

U.S. Department of Education (1988). Tenth annual report to Congress on the implementation of the education of the handicapped. In *Exceptional Children, 56*(1), 7-9.

U.S. Department of Labor, Census Bureau (1991). National Center for Research in Vocational Education.

University of Wisconsin-Eau Claire. (1992). *The distance learning pilot project for gifted and talented students.* Eau Claire, WI: University of Wisconsin-Eau Claire Education Outreach and CESA 11.

Vail, P. L. (1990, February). Obstacles to thinking. *Learning90,* 48-50.

Van Tassel-Baska, J. (1981, December). *The great debates: For acceleration.* CEC/TAG National Topical Conference on the Gifted and Talented Child, Orlando, FL.

Van Tassel-Baska, J. (1983a). Introduction. In J. Van Tassel-Baska (Ed.), *A practical guide to counseling the gifted in a school setting* (1-5). Reston, VA: Council for Exceptional Children.

Van Tassel-Baska, J. (1983b). Purdue offers summer programs. *Midwest Talent Search Quarterly, 1*(1), 11.

Van Tassel-Baska, J. (1983c). School counseling needs and successful strategies to meet them. In J. Van Tassel-Baska (Ed.), *A practical guide to counseling the gifted in a school setting* (40-46). Reston, VA: Council for Exceptional Children.

Van Tassel-Baska, J. (1986). Acceleration. In C. J. Maker (Ed.), *Critical issues in gifted education* (179-196). Rockville, MD: Aspen Publishers.

Van Tassel-Baska, J. (1988a). *Comprehensive curricula for gifted learners.* Boston, MA: Allyn and Bacon.

Van Tassel-Baska, J. (1988b). Developing scope and sequence in curriculum for the gifted learner: A comprehensive approach. Part 1. *Gifted Child Today, 11*(2), 2-7.

Van Tassel-Baska, J. (1988c, September/October). Developing scope and sequence in curriculum for the gifted learner: A comprehensive approach. Part 4. *Gifted Child Today, 11*(5), 42-45.

Van Tassel-Baska, J. (1989). The role of the family in the success of disadvantaged gifted learners. *Journal for the Education of the Gifted, 13*(1), 22-36.

Van Tassel-Baska, J. (1991a). Counseling. In R. E. Clasen (Ed.), *Educating able learners* (videotape series, No. 10). Madison, WI: University of Wisconsin-Extension.

Van Tassel-Baska, J. (1991b). Serving the disabled gifted through educational collaboration. *Journal for the Education of the Gifted, 14*(3), 246-266.

Van Tassel-Baska, J., Patton, J., and Prillaman, D. (1989). Disadvantaged gifted learners: At risk for educational attention. *Focus on Exceptional Children, 22*(3), 1-15.

Vaughn, V. L, Feldhusen, J. F., and Asher, J. W. (1991). Meta-analysis and review of research on pullout programs in gifted education. *Gifted Child Quarterly, 35,* 92-98.

Velle, W. (1982). Sex hormones and behavior in animals and man. *Perspectives in Biology and Medicine, 25,* 295-315.

Vespi, L. and Yewchuk, C. (1992). A phenomenological study of the social/emotional characteristics of gifted learning disabled children. *Journal for the Education of the Gifted, 16*(1), 55-72.

Walberg, H. J. (1982). Child traits and environmental conditions of highly eminent adults. *Gifted Child Quarterly, 25,* 103-107.

Walberg, H. J. (1988). Creativity and talent as learning. In R. J. Sternberg (Ed.), *The nature of creativity* (340-361). New York: Cambridge University Press.

Walberg, H. J. and Herbig, M. P. (1991). Developing talent, creativity, and eminence. In N. Colangelo and G. A. Davis (Eds.), *Handbook of gifted education* (245-255). Needham Heights, MA: Allyn and Bacon.

Walberg, H. J., Tsai, S., Weinstein, T., Gabriel, C. L., Rasher, S. P., Rosecrans, T., Rovai, E., Ide, J., Truijillo, M., and Vukosavich, P. (1981). Childhood traits and environmental conditions of highly eminent adults. *Gifted Child Quarterly, 25,* 103-107.

Wallach, M. A. and Kogan, N. (1965). *Modes of thinking in young children.* New York: Holt.

Wallas, G. (1925). *The art of thought.* New York: Harcourt, Brace, & World.

Warmington, E. H. (1961). Ability and genius in ancient Greece and Rome. In G. Z. G. Bereday and J. A. Lauwerys (Eds.), *Concepts of excellence in education: The yearbook of education.* New York: Harcourt, Brace, and World.

Warren, T. F. (1974). How to squelch ideas. In G. A. Davis and T. F. Warren (Eds.), *Psychology of education: New looks.* Lexington, MA: D. C. Heath.

Wasserman, S. (1985). *Thinking and learning.* New York: Coronado Publications.

Waters, M. L. and Bostwick, A. (1989). Gifted kids create a large scale museum exhibit in Indianapolis. *Gifted Child Today, 12*(5), 24-25.

Way, B. (1967). *Development through drama.* London: Longman.

Webb, J. (1993, August). *Gifted intensity or attention deficit-hyperactivity disorder.* Paper presented at the Seventh National Rimm Underachievement Institute, Milwaukee, WI.

Webb, J. T., Meckstroth, E. A., and Tolan, S. S. (1982). *Guiding the gifted child.* Dayton, OH: Ohio Psychology Press.

Weber, J. (1981). Moral dilemmas in the classroom. *Roeper Review, 3*(4), 11-13.

Wechsler, D. (1991). *WISC-III: Wechsler intelligence Scale for children—third edition.* New York: The Psychological Corporation.

Weiner, B. (1985). *Human motivation* (2nd Ed.). New York: Holt.

Weiner, N. C. and Robinson, S. E. (1986). Cognitive abilities, personality and gender differences in math achievement of gifted adolescents. *Gifted Child Quarterly, 30,* 83-87.

Weinstein, J. and Laufman, L. (1981). The fourth R: Reasoning. *Roeper Review, 4*(1), 20-22.

Weiss, P. and Gallagher, J. J. (1980). The effects of personal experience on attitudes toward gifted children. *Journal for the Education of the Gifted, 3,* 194-206.

Weiss, P. and Gallagher, J. J. (1983, November/December). Parental expectations for the gifted children. *G/C/T, 2-6.*

Weitzman, L. J. and Rizzo, D. (1974). Images of males and females in elementary school textbooks in five subject areas. In *Biased textbooks.* Washington, DC: National Foundation for the Improvement of Education.

Welsh, G. S. and Barron, F. (1963). *Barron-Welsh art scale.* Palo Alto, CA: Consulting Psychologists Press.

Werner, E. (1989). Children of the garden island. *Scientific American, 234*(1), 106-111.

Westberg, K. L., Dobyns, S., and Salvin, T. (1992). Regular classroom practices observation results. In J. S. Renzulli (Chair), *Regular classroom practices with gifted students: Findings from the National Research Center on the Gifted and Talented.* Symposium conducted at the annual meeting of the American Educational Research Association, San Francisco.

White, B. L. (1975). *The first three years of life.* Englewood Cliffs, NJ: Prentice-Hall.

White, B. L., Kaban, B. T., and Attanucci, J. S. (1979). *The origins of human competence: Final report of the Harvard Preschool Project.* Lexington, MA: D. C. Heath.

Whitmore, J. R. (1980). *Giftedness, conflict, and underachievement.* Needham Heights, MA: Allyn and Bacon.

Whitmore, J. R. (1986). Understanding a lack of motivation to excel. *Gifted Child Quarterly, 30,* 66-69.

Wiley, J. and Goldstein, D. (1991). Sex, handedness, and allergy: Are they related to academic giftedness? *Journal for the Education of the Gifted, 14,* 412-422.

Wilkie, V. (1985, January/February). Richardson Study Q's and A's. *G/C/T,* 2-9.

Will, H. (1986, January/February). Junior great books. *G/C/T,* 6-7.

Williams, A. T. (1980, March/April). Academic game bowls: Competition for the gifted and talented. *G/C/T,* 10-12.

Williams, A. T. (1986, January/February). Academic game bowls as a teaching/learning tool. *G/C/T,* 2-5.

Williams, F. E. (1970). *Classroom ideas for encouraging thinking and feeling.* Buffalo, NY: DOK Publishers.

Williams, F. E. (1972). *A total creativity program for individualizing and humanizing the learning process.* Englewood Cliffs, NJ: Educational Technology Publications.

Williams, F. E. (1979, September/October). Williams' strategies to orchestrate Renzulli's triad. *G/C/T,* 2-6, 10.

Williams, F. E. (1980). *Creativity assessment packet.* Buffalo, NY: DOK Publishers.

Williams, F. E. (1982). *Classroom ideas for encouraging thinking and feeling* (Vol. 2). Buffalo, NY: DOK Publishers.

Williams, F. E. (1986). The cognitive-affective interaction model for enriching gifted programs. In J. S. Renzulli (Ed.), *Systems and models for developing programs for the gifted and talented.* Mansfield Center, CT: Creative Learning Press.

Winne, P., Woodlands, M., and Wong, B. (1982). Comparability of self-concept among learning disabled,

normal, and gifted students. *Journal of Learning Disabilities, 15,* 470-475.

Witham, J. (1991). A full-time solution to part-time problems. *Gifted Child Today, 14*(6), 10-12.

Witters, L. A. and Vasa, S. F. (1981). Programming alternatives for educating the gifted in rural schools. *Roeper Review, 3*(4), 22-24.

Witty, P. A. (1967). Twenty years in education of the gifted. *Education, 88*(1), 4–10.

Witty, P. A. (1971). The education of the gifted and the creative in the U.S.A. *Gifted Child Quarterly, 15,* 109–116.

Witty, P. A. (1978). Equal educational opportunity for gifted minority group children: Promise or possibility? *Gifted Child Quarterly, 22,* 344-351.

Wolf, J. and Gygi, J. (1981). Learning disabled and gifted: Success or failure? *Journal for the Education of the Gifted, 4,* 199-206.

Wolfe, D. M., Mondschein, S., and Eicher, B. K. (1991). Governor's schools: Spinning webs for educational change. *Gifted Child Today, 14*(3), 28-30.

Woliver, R. and Woliver, G. M. (1991). Gifted adolescents in the emerging minorities: Asians and Pacific Islanders. In M. Bireley and J. Genshaft (Eds.). *Understanding the gifted adolescent: Educational, developmental, and multicultural issues* (248-257). New York: Teachers College Press.

Wolleat, P. L. (1979). Guiding the career development of gifted females. In N. Colangelo and R. T. Zaffrann (Eds.), *New voices in counseling the gifted.* Dubuque, IA: Kendall/Hunt.

Woods, S. B. and Achey, V. H. (1990). Successful identification of gifted racial/ethnic group students without changing classification requirements. *Roeper Review, 13,* 21-26.

Yalom, I. D., Green, R., and Fisk, N. (1973). Prenatal exposure to female hormones: Effect on psychosexual development in boys. *Archives of General Psychiatry, 28,* 554-561.

Yawkey, T. D. (1983). *Imaginative predisposition interview scale: Test and administration manual.* Unpublished Report. University Park, PA: Pennsylvania State University.

Yell, M. L. and Espin, C. A. (1990). The handicapped children's protection act of 1986: Time to pay the piper? *Exceptional Children, 56*(5), 396-407.

Yoder, J. (1985, September). Gifted education is for rural students too. *NASSP Bulletin,* 68-74.

Zacharias, J. R. (1977). The trouble with IQ tests. In P. L. Houts (Ed.), *The myth of measurability*. New York: Hart.

Zaffrann, R. T. and Colangelo, N. (1979). Counseling with gifted and talented students. In N. Colangelo and R. T. Zaffrann (Eds.), *New voices in counseling the gifted*. Dubuque, IA: Kendall/Hunt.

Zametkin, A. J. (1989). The neurobiology of attention deficit-hyperactivity disorder. *Psychiatric Annals, 19,* 584–586.

Zigler, E. and Muenchow, S. (1970). Mainstreaming: The proof is in the implementation. *American Psychologist, 34,* 993-996.

Zilli, M. G. (1971). Reasons why the gifted adolescent underachieves and some of the implications of guid-ance and counseling to this problem. *Gifted Child Quarterly, 15,* 279-292.

Zimmerman, W. E. and Brody, L. E. (1986, March/April). Part-time college for gifted high school students. *G/C/T,* 32-33.

Zinberg, D. (1974). College: When the future becomes the present. In R. B. Kundsin (Ed.), *Women and success: The anatomy of achievement*. New York: William Morrow.

Zinner, J. (1985, June). Thinking makes an IMPACT. *Thrust,* 30-32.

Zurmuehlen, M. (1991). A summer art workshop for high school students with special interest in art. *Roeper Review, 13,* 64-68.

Author Index

Abraham, W., 4
Achey, V. H., 266, 268
Ackerman, N. J., 373
Adams, A. A., 278
Adams, M., 318
Adamson, G., 13, 15
Adderholdt-Elliott, M., 286–287, 402–403, 413
Addison, L., 332, 337
Adler, T., 329, 368
Alamprese, J. A., 257, 266, 273–274, 277
Albert, R. S., 374
Alexander, K. L., 324
Allen, R. R., 239
Almquist, E. M., 294
Alper, T. G., 334
Alschuler, A. S.,
Altman, S. L., 329
Alvarez, L., 27
Alvino, J., 73–74, 87, 225–226, 228
Amabile, T. M., 35, 429
Anastopoulos, A. D., 356
Anderson, R. S., 3
Angrist, S., 294
Archambault, F. X., 9–10, 298
Argo, T. A., 112
Arjmand, O., 119, 325
Armstrong, J. M., 324
Arnold, K., 259, 337
Arnold, R. M., 315, 321
Aronson, E., 360
Arthur, G., 352
Asher, J. W., 86, 142
Association for Supervision and Curriculum Development, 233
Association for the Gifted Evaluation Committee, 426
Assouline, S. G., 114–115, 131
Atkinson, J. W., 333

Attanucci, J. S., 384
Augustine, D. K., 15–16
Austin, A. B., 383

Baker, C., 260
Bagley, M. T., 209
Baillie, R., 136
Baldwin, A. Y., 70, 72, 84–86, 258, 263, 269
Baldwin, B. A., 368
Ball, O. E., 79
Ballering, L. D., 380
Banbury, M. M., 81–82
Bandura, A., 292
Banks, W., 269–270
Baratz, J. C., 260
Barbee, A. H., 6
Bardwick, J. M., 330
Barell, J., 229
Barkan, J. H., 269
Barkley, R. A., 356
Barron, F., 35–36, 187, 265
Barton, B. L., 161
Barton, J. A., 427
Baum, S., 350, 362–364
Bauman, M. K., 352
Becker, D., 326
Beery, R. G., 172–173, 286, 300, 371, 377
Beggs, D. L., 427
Bem, S. L., 324
Benbow, C. P., 25, 28, 31, 69, 76, 103, 110, 112, 118–120, 323–330
Bennett, N. M., 314
Berliner, D. C., 5
Bernal, E. M., 265, 269
Bernard, J. 319
Bestor, A. E., 7
Betts, G. T., 147, 161–163, 204, 401–402

Beyer, B. K., 226–227, 229
Bien, Y., 265
Biggs, B. E., 300
Binet, A., 4–5, 6, 28
Birch, J. W., 106
Bireley, M., 350, 393, 406
Birnbaum, J. A., 319–320
Birnbaum, M., 50
Black, H., 158, 247–251
Black, K. N., 106–107, 110–111
Black, S., 158, 247–251
Blackshear, P., 263
Blaney, N., 360
Blanton, M., 234
Blaylock, A., 266
Block, S., 138
Bloom, B. S., 25, 38–39, 86, 140, 210, 230, 233–237, 295, 307, 368, 374
Boodoo, G. M., 351
Boriero, D., 358
Boring, E. G., 397
Boston, B. A., 17, 81, 142, 147, 156
Bostwick, A., 125
Bowen, W. G., 314, 330
Bowman, P., 330
Boy, A. V., 178–179
Bradley, C. L., 351
Brandon, P. R., 325
Breggin, P. R., 356
Brewer, J., 397
Bridgeman, B., 274
Brody, L. E., 110, 113–115, 314, 329, 354
Bronson, F. H., 322
Brophy, J. E., 329
Brower, P., 380, 401
Brown, B. B., 272, 295, 382–383, 393–394
Brown, K. E., 174

481